Person-Centered Politics

Person-Centered Politics

A Personalist Approach to Political Philosophy

Eamonn Gerard O'Higgins, L.C.

Foreword by Dr. Rocco Buttiglione

HAMILTON BOOKS
Lanham • Boulder • New York • London

Published by Hamilton Books
An imprint of The Rowman & Littlefield Publishing Group, Inc.
4501 Forbes Boulevard, Suite 200, Lanham, Maryland 20706
www.rowman.com

86-90 Paul Street, London EC2A 4NE

British Library Cataloguing in Publication Information Available

Library of Congress Cataloging-in-Publication Data

Names: O'Higgins, P. Eamonn Gerard, 1962- author. | Buttiglione, Rocco, 1948- author of foreword.
Title: Person-centered politics : a personalist approach to political philosophy / P. Eamonn Gerard O'Higgins ; foreword by Rocco Buttiglione.
Description: Lanham, Maryland : Hamilton Books, [2024] | Includes bibliographical references and index. | Summary: "Person-centered Politics, in dialogue with some of major contemporary philosophers and thinkers, proposes a renewed vision of politics by presenting a renewal of the real social and transcendent dimensions of personal existence"—Provided by publisher.
Identifiers: LCCN 2024004890 (print) | LCCN 2024004891 (ebook) |
  ISBN 9780761874423 (cloth) | ISBN 9780761874430 (epub) |
  ISBN 978-0-7618-7476-8 (pbk)
Subjects: LCSH: Political science. | Democracy—Religious aspects—Catholic Church. | Philosophical anthropology. | Political psychology. | Truth.
Classification: LCC JA71 .O35 2024 (print) | LCC JA71 (ebook) | DDC 320.01—dc23/eng/20240301
LC record available at https://lccn.loc.gov/2024004890
LC ebook record available at https://lccn.loc.gov/2024004891

Go naofar d'ainm
Go dtaga do ríocht

Contents

Foreword   ix
    Dr. Rocco Buttiglione

Acknowledgments   xvii

Abbreviations   xix

Introduction   1

Chapter 1: A Philosophical Approach to Politics   5

Chapter 2: Person and Politics   35

Chapter 3: Truth and Politics   65

Chapter 4: Living Publicly in the Truth   101

Chapter 5: The Person's Transcendent Social Destiny   135

Chapter 6: Political Authority and Its Justifications   167

Chapter 7: Forms of Political Government   199

Chapter 8: Law and Society   235

Chapter 9: Human Rights   267

Chapter 10: The Unity of the Nations   297

Chapter 11: Political Ideologies and Their Justifications   329

Chapter 12: Politics and Religion   361

Contents

Bibliography   395

Index   417

About the Author   437

Foreword

Dr. Rocco Buttiglione

Father Eamonn O'Higgins L.C. presents us with a book of astonishing erudition and profound philosophical depth. There is a text of Scripture that delineates the intellectual horizon of this magnificent investigation, Psalm 127: "Unless the Lord builds the house / Those who build it labour in vain."[1]

The book is on politics and the main question is: what does a politics centered on the person look like? Today's politics, and especially Western democratic politics, presupposes to have the human person at its center. Is this presupposition justified? O'Higgins' answer raises serious doubts. The modern state is an abstract juridical order whose foundation lies in the monopoly of power over a certain territory. The state considers the people dwelling in that territory as isolated individuals standing each one in direct relation to the state. Considering them as isolated individuals, the state becomes their collective identity, and the individual citizens are conformed to assume this collective identity.

One of the texts most often quoted by O'Higgins is Václav Havel's essay *The Power of the Powerless*.[2] In this essay, Havel describes the post-totalitarian society in which there are no real bonds between citizens. The only significant relation each one has is to the state and this relation is only a relation of power, in which the state, of course, is much more powerful than the individual. In relation to this isolated being we cannot speak of "person" but only of "individual." The individual is required to act *as if* he or she had accepted as true whatever the state presents as such. The individual is not really required to believe the propaganda; it is enough that he or she does not challenge the official "truth." By accepting this code of behavior, the individual implicitly recognizes that there is no truth or that, even if truth exists, it is not worthwhile challenging power in the name of truth. In this case, we can say that power makes truth. Havel is describing the post-totalitarian societies of the Communist system, but his description fits almost equally well our own societies.

In the 1980s, however, something happened. I can say this because I was there. A small number of young (and not so young) women and men began to enter in relation with one another based on an honest search for truth. Many were religious, some were not. They made the truth the rule of their community. This brought them to investigate the roots of their culture, going back to the Christian and philosophical roots of Europe. In particular, the seminar on *Plato and Europe*, led by Jan Patocka,[3] attracted as visitors some of the best minds of Western philosophy, such as Emmanuel Levinas and Paul Ricoeur. The Communist powers felt threatened and intensified their persecution. Something similar was, however, taking place in a neighboring country, in Poland. A Polish Pope was elected, and he made a pilgrimage to his native country. He spoke to the people of Poland not as to a mass of isolated individuals, but as to a nation of people, unified by a common language, a common culture, a common history, and on a common path to the truth of the human person. Unexpectedly, these words resounded in the soul of the people: the mass of isolated individuals started thinking and acting as a community of persons that were united by the bond of truth. St. John Paul II pointed to the Baptism of Poland (966) and the celebration of the sacrifice of Jesus Christ as the one fundamental root of their being as a nation. The people of Poland felt that, as a community, they had a responsibility for their country and a right to take into their own hands their common future. In the end, the post-totalitarian regime collapsed before the eyes of a people that had recovered the reasons for their unity in solidarity and in truth.

I am telling this story because it seems to me that it exemplifies the main tenets of O'Higgins' book. You cannot have a democracy if you do not have a *demos*, and a *demos* is a community of persons united in truth, in the possession of a truth that has become manifest in their history, and in recognition of a greater truth they do not possess and that is the object both of their striving and of their desire. Truth is always greater than us, greater also than our nations. O'Higgins tells us that we cannot be a people without God. God is the greater truth within which the smaller truths of our everyday life can find their place and thus be saved from the danger of their being lost in insignificance, on the one hand, and of being absolutized and becoming idols, on the other hand. In order to have a democracy, you need a *demos* and a *demos* is something more than a mass of isolated individuals.

I remember once having a clash with Lord Ralf Dahrendorf[4] at a congress in Vienna, immediately after the fall of the Berlin Wall. Dahrendorf contended that the project of a United Europe did not have any chance because there was not a European *demos*. He thought the project could not be realized and, if it could, only in an utterly bureaucratic and undemocratic form. I answered that the word *demos*, in Greek, has not an ethnic but a political and religious meaning. This is the essential difference between *demos* and *etne*. The *etne* is an ethnic kinship based on common blood; the *demos* is based on common worship. One day, the Athenians decided to dwell together (συνοικέω) and they built a common home. The common home was the temple of the divinity under whose protection the city was placed. The Athenians built a temple and established a mythical kinship that was religious before being political.

The problem was, then, the following: were Europeans willing to constitute themselves as a people? The events in Europe that led from the rejection of Christian values in the proposed *European Constitution* (2004)[5] to the rejection of the *European Constitution* itself and to the accepted *Treaty of Lisbon* (2007), a minimalistic compromise under whose rules the European Union cannot thrive but, at most, barely survive, have shown that there was no such will. The experience of the multiple crises we have been going through (the financial crisis, the COVID crisis, the Ukrainian War crisis) has made it apparent that our material interests demand us to be united. Whether we still have the capacity to find out and to accept what is needed to be a people remains doubtful. This example enlightens the meaning of O'Higgins' tenet: to put the person at the center of politics, we need to be formed as a people, and to be a people we need to accept God as the transcendental horizon of our dwelling together. O'Higgins explains abundantly that this is not a demand for a confessional state. It is a demand for a politics in which the pursuit of the truth of the human person stands in the center.

Protagoras of Abdera once said: "Of all things the measure is man,"[6] and that is true. But what is the measure of man? Man does not possess his own measure. Only the Divine in man is this measure and this is the reason why the search for the truth of man never ends. We must defend the truth of man that we have seen and experienced and, at the same time, we must be open to listening to other dimensions of this truth, what others have seen and discovered, and we must try to find out the way in which different experiences of truth can be reconciled in a broader vision. This seems to coincide with the vision of Pope Francis of truth having the form of a polyhedron, and also with the grandiose idea of Maximus the Confessor of a Cosmic Liturgy, in which all things are progressively attracted to the ultimate truth that is Jesus Christ.

O'Higgins comes back more than once to the issue of the *method* of the search for truth in a democratic and pluralistic society. It cannot be a deductive method that presupposes a certain pregiven set of truths. In a pluralistic society, you cannot take for granted that any set of values are universally accepted. You must then start from the beginning, from the way in which values manifest themselves in common human experience. This is what, broadly speaking, O'Higgins calls the phenomenological method, and in his text, you can find numerous references to two masters of this method, Karol Wojtyla (Pope John Paul II) and Robert Sokolowski. This is a middle ground between a metaphysical/deductive method and the liberal pretension that there is no common truth, that every person has a particular truth and one should therefore be free to do whatever one pleases until those actions impinge upon the equal sphere of liberty of another individual.

This liberal pretension is absurd because we all live on the same earth and whatever we do has consequences (both intended and unintended) for all human beings. On this truth dwells the recent encyclical of Pope Francis, *Laudato sì'* (2015).[7] This is the first reason we need a common truth and a non-dogmatical method to seek and establish that truth. A second reason is that the most fascinating and interesting object toward whom our action can be directed is another human being. When I am in love, my freedom does not consist in being left alone, in being master of myself. Quite on the contrary: I am free if the other person corresponds to my love, if the other accepts the free gift of my person. My freedom consists in the overcoming of the narrow borders of my ego and in the formation, with my beloved, of a "we," a couple, and later a family. This can only happen through the discovery of a common truth greater than either of us that we never cease exploring until the last day of our lives. Liberty is like a dance, a dance you cannot dance alone.

I remember being one day in the Hall of the Catholic University of Milan with Don Giussani[8] while a procession of pro-abortion feminists passed by shouting: "I am mine. I belong to myself." Don Giussani commented: "Poor girls! Thank God it is not true. They belong to their mothers and fathers, to their boyfriends, to their social and political groups. . . . The life of a human being who belongs only to himself or herself would be desperately alienated and poor. The richness of our lives is found in the relations we are engaged in." He knew very well, of course, that St. Thomas Aquinas has written: "Persona est sui juris et altero incommunicabilis" ("a person is a being which belongs to itself and does not share its being with another").[9] It is unworthy of man to be the slave of another. There is, however, another kind of belonging, the belonging in truth and in love. For this reason, Don Giussani, after a while, referring to Charles Péguy, said: "What is the use of freedom, if not to be given?" O'Higgins explores the delicate balance that exists (and which must be preserved) between the "belonging to oneself" and the "free gift of oneself."

O'Higgins has given us a teratology of our modern democracies, that is, an accurate description of their sickness unto death. I see an important parallel between this accurate description of the ills of our democracy and the diagnosis of Plato at the deathbed of Greek democracy. We have been accustomed to thinking (on the basis of a rather superficial reading of Karl Popper's philosophy) that the cultural allies of democracy are relativistic philosophies, because those who hold strong convictions of truth with regard to certain issues may easily succumb to the temptation of imposing their convictions on others. I do not want to belittle this preoccupation or to deny its legitimacy. It applies, however, in different ways to different kinds of convictions.

The firm conviction of Christians is that Truth is to become the form of life of each individual human person, and this can only take place through the free assent of each person. I do not need to doubt my faith in order to respect the freedom of the other. Quite the contrary is true: my faith commands me to respect the freedom of the other.

Plato held a strongly divergent opinion. He thought that when the sophists (in modern language the moral relativists) take over government, no moral restraint will forbid them to appropriate public money for private purposes, to make use of violence to favor their particular interests, to lie to the public, and to corrupt the whole political life of the city, thus dissolving the bond that keeps the city together. Then the people will be disposed to follow a demagogue or a tyrant who promises to restore a minimum of honesty and public probity. Not an excess of truth, but rather corruption, originating in the lack of truth, is the enemy of democracy. This is the reason why the dawn of an era of post-truth may easily coincide with the doom of democracies.

After this diagnosis of impending doom, we now want to ask ourselves: what is the cure, if a cure does in fact exist? We call two illustrious doctors to our patient's hospital. The first one is Zygmunt Bauman.[10] We owe to him the descriptive diagnostic of our democracies as "liquid societies." Does he envisage a therapy? You will not find in his writings any elaborate proposal to heal the ills of our society. Once, however, he was asked if there was any counteracting force to the dissolving tendency of all social bonds and the end of society itself. He answered that whenever two people fall in love with each other a new social bond comes into existence. Not by chance, O'Higgins is one of the very few philosophers who speaks of love and who attributes to love its fundamental role as constitutive of society. There is, however, a significant difference that needs to be pointed out between Bauman and O'Higgins. Bauman speaks of falling in love; O'Higgins speaks of love. This is not exactly the same thing. To fall in love is an emotional experience; something that just happens in us quite independently of our will and of our decision. It is an undeserved and unexpected gift, wholly gratuitous. It has also, however, another less pleasing side. One may fall in love with the wrong person, the sentiment may be disordered, and may not necessarily last for long. In the beginning of Shakespeare's *Romeo and Juliet*, we meet Romeo who is desperately in love, not with Juliet, but with Rosalind. Love is something more than just being in love. Love is an act of the person. The person engages his or her intellect and will in this act of accepting and confirming the intuition contained in the process of "falling in love," and it is in this way that the family is born, the first and most fundamental social bond.

Our second doctor is Pope Francis. He moves along the same path of Bauman but in a highly differentiated way. First of all, the Pope warns us not to waste our energies in defending residual spaces of power that we may have inherited from a more or less distant past or in attempting to restore social forms that do not correspond any more to the changed sensibilities of our time. He invites us to initiate processes that allow the eternal values to become a new and fascinating proposal for the people of our time. This is the meaning of the formula, contained in *Evangelii Gaudium* (2013),[11] "Time is greater than space."[12] How can we reconstitute a people out of a mass of individuals? Shall we first conquer the power of the state, to impose from above on a mass of individuals, the consciousness of being a people united through worship and truth? This will hardly work. The methodology that Pope Francis proposes is strikingly similar to that we have already encountered in discussing the message of Havel and St. John Paul II. The starting point is the *missionary disciple.* The missionary disciple is the person who has a consciousness of communion. The encounter with Christ creates in the disciple a capacity to build bonds among people based on truth, a group of people who decide to live in truth and propose a new way of life to the greater society in which they are immersed. This community convinces because the life they live is more human and corresponds to the deepest longings that dwell in the depth of each human person. What is important is to start processes that convoke and reconstitute people. There will be no political renewal if, first of all, a *demos* is not reconstituted through a new evangelization. The community created by the missionary disciples reactivates a profound interest in the life of others and the will to take care of each other and to exercise a new political responsibility. This is the way in which the European nations were originally constituted through evangelization and baptism, and this is the way in which they may be reconstituted and a *politeia* may again be reborn. By building up the holy people of God, the Church makes a fundamental contribution to the reconstitution of the peoples of this earth.

O'Higgins leads us with competence and passion through several centuries of social and intellectual development of our societies to confront us with the great questions of the meaning and destiny of the human person, the love of man, and the love of God. What shall we do if the Temple has been destroyed? The answer is simple: we must rebuild the Temple.

NOTES

1. Bible quotes will be from The Holy Bible, *Revised Standard Version, Second Catholic Edition* (San Francisco: Ignatius Press, 2006) (hereafter RSV), unless otherwise noted.

2. Václav Havel et al., *The Power of the Powerless: Citizens Against the State in Central Eastern Europe*, ed. John Keane (London: Routledge Classics, 1985).

3. Jan Patocka (1907–1977), a Czech philosopher who studied under Edmund Husserl and Martin Heidegger, and one of the founding members of Charter 77. The Charter 77 Declaration was a demand for human rights in Czechoslovakia.

4. Lord Ralf Gustav Dahrendorf (1929–2009) was a German-British sociologist and philosopher, and class-conflict theorist.

5. The *European Constitution* (2004) was an unratified treaty intended to codify and consolidate all European Union treaties. *The Treaty of Lisbon* (2007) was the more modest attempt to merge with preexisting European legislation.

6. Protagoras of Abdera (485–415BC): "Of all things the measure is man: of those that are, that they are; and of those that are not, that they are not" (DK 80B1). DK represents the Diels-Kranz reference numbering, *Die Fragmente der Vorsokratiker* (*The Fragments of the Pre-Socratics*), by Hermann Alexander Diels.

7. Pope Francis, "Laudato sì,'" *Acta Apostolicae Sedis (AAS)* 107 (2015), 937–38, https://www.vatican.va/content/francesco/en/encyclicals/documents/papa-francesco _20150524_enciclica-laudato-si.html (accessed October 16, 2023).

8. Mons. Luigi Giovanni Giussani (1922–2005) was a priest, theologian, teacher, and founder of the *Communio e Liberazione* Movement.

9. The phrase has its origin in Roman law and this idea of the person as an incommunicable and unique individual within a common rational nature can be found, for example, in Aquinas' *Summa Theologiae* I, q.30, a.4, particularly in the response to the second objection.

10. Zygmunt Bauman (1925–2017) was a Polish philosopher and sociologist, perhaps best known for his *Liquid Modernity* (Cambridge: Polity Press, 2000).

11. Pope Francis, "Evangelii Gaudium," *Acta Apostolicae Sedis (AAS)* 105 (2013): 1–224. https://www.vatican.va/content/francesco/en/apost_exhortations /documents/papa-francesco_esortazione-ap_20131124_evangelii-gaudium.html (accessed October 16, 2023).

12. Francis, "Evangelii Gaudium," n222.

Acknowledgments

It is an impossible and yet necessary task to thank all the persons who have instructed, enlightened, and edified me in so many ways over the years, and who, by doing so, have contributed to and enriched this text. To each I offer a heartfelt prayer of gratitude.

I am very grateful to Professor Rocco Buttiglione for agreeing to write the foreword to these essays. I have read and heard Dr. Buttiglione speak many times over these years and have been privileged to learn from a wonderfully philosophical mind and an experienced stateman of politics. He is also a generous and kind person.

I thank Professor Davd Walsh of The Catholic University of America for his helpful comments and critique, and the gift of his time to do so.

I thank all who have contributed in many other ways to this endeavour, in particular to my Legionary confreres Devin Roza, Michael Ryan, and Rodrigo Ramírez, LLCC, who have facilitated the process and production of this text. I also thank the Rector of the *Pontifical Athenaeum Regina Apostolorum,* Fr. José Oyarzún, L.C., for his personal encouragement, as well as the former Dean of the Faculty of Philosophy, Fr. Alex Yeung, L.C., for his trust and patience. Also, to MEBM, with great gratitude.

Abbreviations

AAS   *Acta Apostolicae Sedis*, official gazette of the Holy See.
DK   Diels-Kranz reference numbering, *Die Fragmente der Vorsokratiker*
      (*The Fragments of the Pre-Socratics*), by Hermann Alexander Diels
ITC   International Theological Commission
RSV   Bible (The Holy Bible). *Revised Standard Version. Second Catholic
      Edition*. San Francisco: Ignatius Press, 2006.

Introduction

As I write, the war on Ukrainian soil enters its 593rd day of conflict. The coverage of the war fits into photos, news segments, and video clips that can reduce and relativise what is really happening to the lives of millions of men, women, and children. What becomes apparent is that there are no banal solutions to this tragic conflict. To try to reconcile the real need to oppose evil aggression, the horrors of war, and the consequent suffering of millions of people is something very difficult to do. Perhaps we in Europe had thought that we had, by the end of the twentieth century, finally overcome such barbarous international conflicts. This war reminds us of the real circumstances of actual human existence and the burden we are required to carry if truth and goodness are to prevail, eventually. Ultimately, the necessary response required of each of us is not technological or economic, nor governmental or institutional, but personal, moral, and religious, because only the *hope* in a transcendent destiny and the *trust* in redemptive suffering can make sense of the burden of human existence and make it meaningful, and therefore bearable. This is the hope we live by, that above and beyond the difficult and often painful circumstances of human existence, there is the hope of all things being made right and good and of our being led beyond this precarious existence to the joyful peace and fulfilment that we know awaits us but that we have not yet experienced.

These twelve essays are on fundamental themes of political philosophy and have as their purpose a renewal of how politics can and should be understood and practiced.

A philosophical approach requires above and before all else an openness to the experience of reality in all its varying modes of disclosure, the willingness to see and to perceive all of what we experience, to try to grasp its significance and appeal, and to respond to such experience as *agents of the truth* of that experience. Philosophising is thus our basic and limited capacity to apprehend the reality in which we are immersed, in all its varying modes of disclosure, and to respond adequately to that experience.

The fundamental truth of disclosure of all things political is that politics is to serve the person in all dimensions of personal existence. This seems to be a truth that has been forgotten or ignored, and it is a fundamental theme of these essays to recover a more complete perception of personal human existence and the dynamism of love that is essential to human communion. Political structures and processes are of course necessary, but today these structures and processes seem to presuppose and impose on persons an emaciated caricature of their being. In this way, the call to personal communion remains stultified and the real ambition of political life remains frustrated. The liberation of the potential of the person is a vital requirement of the common good of politics.

To rediscover the real dimensions of human existence requires reference to the transcendence of this mundane existence as a fact of human experience that needs to be recognised philosophically. For various reasons, we seem today to live within a confined perception of human existence, in which the dynamic call to transcend our present existence is suppressed or explained away. So too, the reality of the Supreme Being, as experienced and as the postulate of all that exists, is largely denied or excluded from public reason and we are required to construct meaning and purpose *etsi Deus non daretur*, as if God did not exist. I suggest that this assumption of the irrelevance of religious experience and of the Being of God are obstacles to a genuine and truthful approach to politics.

I engage in the themes of these essays in dialogue with some contemporary authors who, in my opinion, elucidate very well the truths that should shape our politics. Some of these authors are not primarily dedicated to the field of politics. I consider this to be an advantage; at times a necessary light that can perhaps only come from outside a particular area of inquiry.

The authors with whom I am principally in dialogue are Joseph Ratzinger (Pope Benedict XVI), Eric Voegelin, Václav Havel, Professor Robert A. Nisbet, Professor Pierre Manent, Professor David Walsh, Rev. Professor Robert Sokolowski, and Professor Peter L. P. Simpson. I have tried to bring their wisdom and vision to bear on the themes I present, and I willingly acknowledge a great intellectual debt to each.

I have chosen this method of dialogue because my intention is to enlighten the truth of each theme and not just to present my theory or model. In fact, my aim is to make evident at the level of principle how we should understand each theme, and not to attempt to propose particular models or theories. Politics is so varied, diverse, and transient that it is illusionary to hold up one model or theory as the answer to all situations. Instead, I try to suggest fundamental and essential truths that can and should enlighten diverse political situations.

I have sporadically made reference to particular and personal examples of the themes presented. I do this not for the possible entertainment value, but because I believe profoundly that it is in personal experience that our grasp of truth begins and ends. Philosophising at times remains at the level of abstraction and thus can become remote from its origin in personal experience and from its ultimate purpose, to enlighten and to move to adequate action. The personal experience of living in the truth is the source and the maximum expression of philosophising.

Each theme attempts to understand both *how we do in fact* think about and value politics today and *how we should* think about and value each particular theme. I make no apologies for appealing to what we can know to be better. I do think that there is much to transform in our way perceiving and judging political realities; we seem to be locked into certain ways of thinking and living that do not do justice to the full potential of the person. At the same time, this is no call to revert to previous ages and epochs; we are called to repropose a renewed vision of political society according to our present and future times. The truths of the great philosophers of history are still, of course, valid—I make obvious reference to them in these essays—and yet a new synthesis of their wisdom, together with the valid insights of our age, needs to be proposed.

It is never enough merely to diagnose problems and difficulties. Lamentation serves no real purpose. Although I am critical of much of what passes as politics today (and this critical view seems to be a general perception), my intention is to repropose what can really inspire and motivate our social communion, of which politics is an expression. Yes, there is much to criticise, especially the spurious notions that discredit and stifle the common search for the truth of the person. These essays do identify what impedes true political expression, but also propose tentatively the truth of reality on which human and personal society can be built, however provisionally and imperfectly.

Each chapter begins with an overview of the presentation of the theme and its relation to previous themes.

The endnotes to these essays generally serve the purpose of offering further references to the points in question and expanding avenues of further exploration.

Chapter 1

A Philosophical
Approach to Politics

In this overview of this chapter, I summarize a particular philosophical approach to politics, one that gave rise to the origins of politics as a philosophy.

While the language and terms of politics are more or less common, their meaning—the phenomena they refer to—differs considerably in different political historical contexts. This requires of our attention to discover what is implicitly assumed each time we refer to politics, the state, the common good, and so on. Another curious phenomenon is the widespread disillusionment with politics today, especially in the light of the political hopes raised by the events of 1989, the fall of the Berlin Wall, and the subsequent disintegration of the states of the Soviet bloc. At the same time, the political disenchantment seems to indicate deeper roots than the imperfections of our daily politics.

Our epoch has been described as post-modern, which politically is interpreted as the loss of trust in human progress that the various Enlightenment movements seemed to inspire in human reason and intentions. Relativism, as a skeptical attitude to constructive and shared human values, is the predominant political condition of these post-modern times. At the same time, and precisely because of the evident rupture of modern certainties, there is the opportunity to establish real foundations of social and political life.

To do this, to perceive, understand, and act on real foundations for political life, requires a philosophizing approach to reality. I take a definition of this philosophizing approach of the American philosopher W. Norris Clarke as a descriptive account of the essential elements of this approach. I also suggest that our method of appreciating and responding to our perceptions of reality needs to adapt to these times, as we are required to live in times that demand a new approach to confronting reality.

Is politics a science or a philosophy? Today a particular understanding of political science seems to eliminate a normative philosophical approach. This is to rely on a very reduced notion of what science (true knowledge) is and I revert to Plato and Aristotle to show that politics is indeed a philosophical science that has the human person at its center. In Eric Voegelin's words, "the right order of the soul through philosophy furnishes the standard for the right order of society."[1]

This accounts for a personalist approach to politics, a normative understanding of politics that is to reflect and to promote the real dimensions of personal existence in their necessarily social and transcendent context. This truth of the person provides the source of renewal for the various political themes of each chapter.

The conclusion is that fundamentally it is the person who shapes politics, and not politics that determines what type of subject is required of political power. This also requires of each person the free and responsible commitment to a greater social communion—of which politics is a part—as the only way to personal self-fulfillment.

WHAT POLITICS SPONTANEOUSLY IMPLIES

Politics today spontaneously brings to mind a fairly common set of images, structures, issues, and vocabulary, such as the state, assemblies of government, legislature, elections, representative democracy, and so on. And most discussions, however divergent, of politics, presuppose this common background of images and nomenclature as the assumed setting for debate.

While all these phenomena of politics are real, in the sense that these institutions and structures exist in similar forms, the question arises as to whether the assumptions and suppositions on which they are based and by which they are publicly justified, are the same. A cursory glance at the history of political theory and practice shows that the institutions and practices change according to the many circumstances of social life, as do the justifications for their existence. For example, it is common to compare and to contrast the city (*polis*) of Aristotle with the state with which we are familiar today. Nevertheless, the political philosopher Peter L. P. Simpson, in his own compilation and translation of Aristotle's *Politics*, considers it a mistake to do so, reasoning that, even given the expansion of the term to cover the size of the modern state, it is a corruption rather than an extension of meaning:

> Aristotle talks not of individuals but of men and not of structures but of communities (or only of structures in view of communities). Aristotle talks of the city and man, but we talk of institutions and individuals. For Aristotle, what matters are not individuals but men, or only individuals insofar as they can become men. The city exists for man because, as an education in virtue, it exists for the

perfection of man. The modern institution or state, by contrast, exists for the individual, because it exists for the satisfaction of the individual.[2]

Philosopher Robert Sokolowski further clarifies the conceptual difference between the ancient *polis* (republic) and the modern state:

> The republic is the political form in which laws, not partial, one-sided, self-interested men, rule; it is Aristotle's *politeia*, the constitution that is generally the best that can be attained by most people in most places. The modern state, on the other hand, is something that arose through modern political philosophy. It claims to be something radically new and radically different from earlier forms of government. It is meant to be a definitive solution to the human political problem, not a solution for this time and place. It was initially visualized by Machiavelli and baptized by Jean Bodin with the name sovereignty. It was comprehensively described by Hobbes and worked out and adjusted by subsequent thinkers like Locke, Rousseau, Kant, and Hegel.[3]

What, then, do we all mean by such common political terms as law, rights, the state, and what varying presuppositions does each term assume? This fundamental difficulty is found not only in the historical comparison of political terms, but also between and among contemporary cultures of thought. One need only think of the fundamental difference of meaning to the common political terms of liberalism, socialism, or conservatism as, indeed, the moving multi-dimensional scale of left- and right-wing politics, to recognize the fundamental ambiguities of meaning of apparently similar terms.

Eric Voegelin noticed this ambiguity of language, especially language used in an ideological context, "language symbols that pretend to be concepts but in fact are unanalysed *topoi* or topics":

> Moreover, anyone who is exposed to this dominant climate of opinion has to cope with the problem that language is a social phenomenon. He cannot deal with users of ideological language as partners in a discussion, but he has to make them the object of investigation. There is no community of language with the representatives of the dominant ideologies. Hence, the community of language that he himself wants to use to criticize the users of ideological language must first be discovered and, if necessary, established.[4]

THE DISILLUSIONMENT OF RECENT TIMES

Whatever politics actually means, there is also today a fairly general disillusionment with its activity, its processes, and its protagonists. Perhaps there is much to be discouraged about at the day-to-day working of a political system, with the usual list of misuse and corruption of political processes. Even the brightly optimistic Francis Fukuyama,[5] in his survey of the condition of democracy in the different states of the world, found grave cause for concern with already established democratic systems of government. Having traced the growth in numbers of free, democratic systems of government in the period from 1970 to 2010, from 47 states to 117, according to Freedom House,[6] Fukuyama goes on to describe the outright reversal of democratic gains in countries such as Russia, Venezuela, and Iran, as well as the grey zone of transitional democracies that stall in the process of transformation. He then points to signs in established democracies of political decay, caused, as he claims, when political systems fail to adjust to changing circumstances. He mentions as signs of democratic decay the lack of social consensus, economic mismanagement, the growth of entrenched interest groups, the disproportionate political power of the economically wealthy, and so on.

Even if liberal democracy is the favored term of political government today, the signs of decay, as mentioned by Fukuyama, are evident. This may indeed be inevitable in any human process, with its inherent limitations and less than perfect ministers of government. The resulting disillusionment is exacerbated by information and communication technology that instantaneously and ubiquitously diffuses and interprets everything of political life.

In an article titled "How Liberalism Became 'the God That Failed' in Eastern Europe," written in 2019, the authors try to understand both the failure and the rejection of democratic liberalism in Eastern European countries and elsewhere:

> No single factor can explain the simultaneous emergence of authoritarian anti-liberalisms in so many differently situated countries in the second decade of the 21st century. Yet resentment at liberal democracy's canonical status and the politics of imitation in general has played a decisive role. This lack of alternatives, rather than the gravitational pull of an authoritarian past or historically ingrained hostility to liberalism, is what best explains the anti-western ethos dominating post-communist societies today. The very conceit that "there is no other way" provided an independent motive for the wave of populist xenophobia and reactionary nativism that began in central and eastern Europe and is now washing across much of the world.[7]

At the same time, there seems to me to be a deeper cause and effect of the political disenchantment today. It seems that the political project in established democracies no longer attracts the vast majority of people. While in Hong Kong and Belarus today, students and working men and women are prepared to protest against unjust laws or governments, at times with great personal sacrifice, the general involvement in what is political in established democracies is marked by passivity, resentment, and disenchantment.

The perspective here is of the ordinary person, not the political leader. The contention here is that the vision of politics, that is, the goals that inspire political activity and the established processes of political activity are perceived in ways that promote the sense of personal remoteness from political involvement and participation. Whatever politics has become in established democracies, it no longer inspires the vast majority of people to purpose or to action.

The French political philosopher Pierre Manent writes of the current political repression of the soul. In Manent's *Metamorphoses of the City: On the Western Dynamic*,[8] he states that the particular construction of the modern state causes the frustration of two fundamental human aspirations. Firstly, the modern state greatly curbs the public expression of religious values and beliefs by reducing religion to something merely of private practice and irrelevant to the public domain and the common public good. Secondly, Manent also recognizes that the fundamental human aspiration to personal participation in public matters is also curtailed and indeed made impossible; public actions may only be done through others, that is, by public representatives. Manent sees that the modern state thus excludes these two fundamental aspirations of active involvement in what is the common political good and the desire to express belief in the transcendence of human existence and the common bonds of religious belief. This is so much the case that Manent concludes that we are alienated from the political dimension of our existence and, as others have also observed, we live not only in a post-Christian order, but also a post-civic one as well.[9]

The contention, therefore, is not fundamentally what is wrong with our system of government, as if the difficulty were simply something mechanical, but what it is that inspires political interest and involvement, such as we have occasionally seen in those men and women who rose against oppression and dedicated themselves to the public good, in the name of all. How is this spark of political dedication to be ignited in societies that seem to require so little of their peoples?

Václav Havel has written of a demoralization and disenchantment of people within a consumer value system:

> A person who has been seduced by the consumer value system, whose identity is dissolved in an amalgam of the accoutrements of mass civilization, and who has no roots in the order of being, no sense of responsibility for anything higher than his or her own personal survival, is a demoralized person. The system depends on this demoralization, deepens it, is in fact a projection of it into society.[10]

In his third Reith Lecture in 1948, Bertrand Russell pointed to the deadening effect on the individual of a massive and yet bottle-necked democratic government:

> In national politics, where you are one of some twenty million voters, your influence is infinitesimal unless you are exceptional or occupy an exceptional position. You have, it is true, a twenty-millionth share in the government of others, but only a twenty-millionth share in the government of yourself. You are therefore much more conscious of being governed than of governing. The government becomes in your thoughts a remote and largely malevolent "they," not a set of men whom you, in concert with others who share your opinions, have chosen to carry out your wishes. Your individual feeling about politics, in these circumstances, is not that intended to be brought about by democracy, but much more nearly what it would be under a dictatorship.[11]

My search is along these lines. The very disillusionment with politics as it is given to us today is a sign that we—each one of us—desire something greater and better than what is on offer. We are also capable of wanting to commit to something greater than ourselves and our legitimate individual interests. The flags of national unity, the symbolic torches of a common humanity, the appeal of unity, and the call to greater purpose are essential parts of our humanity. To flourish, we need to express, not stifle, these desires in adequate ways. Whatever the causes, politics today does not draw from people this sense of greater purpose, of participation, and of commitment. The renewal of politics requires the renewal of this inner sense of participation by the many.

This obviously requires much more than completing one's civic duties of voting, jury service, and paying legitimate taxes. These are activities that are legally required of us, not actions that originate in our desire to participate in social communion.

Neither am I claiming that politics, commonly understood as civil public authority, is the only area of this expression of communion or the most important. What I do affirm is that this essential dimension of human existence is only sustained by the spark of personal interest and participation. Politics today, as we see it, does not produce any spark of participation.

Ultimately, political participation does not depend on the type of government, economic resources, party systems, or propaganda, although all these elements, and others, influence public participation. In the last analysis, the decision is personal. Neither is it the case of having to do something as an obligation, but rather to discover the desire within oneself to want to go beyond oneself in communion with others. The political arena is one area of expression of this social communion with others.

IS A POLITICAL VISION POSSIBLE IN
OUR POSTMODERN TIMES?

At the same time, the diffidence toward politics is only symptomatic of a greater cultural context of thought and perception. We are historical beings, in the sense that we find ourselves in a cultural context into which we are born and which, to a great extent, influences our perceptions and values. It is important to recognize, as far as possible, our historical context and perspective, in order to adjust, counterbalance, and, if necessary, correct a particular way of perceiving and valuing reality that we can too easily take to be the only possible perspective.

The American political philosopher David Walsh at the beginning of his *After Ideology: Recovering the Spiritual Foundations of Freedom*,[12] describes the contemporary political context in the following way. He notes that the spiritual crisis we face today is in reality the outcome of the modern age that began with the Age of Reason and the stimulating potential of scientific discoveries and their practical applications, as well as the political revolutions that transformed the ideas and practices of social living. Walsh sees a profound relation between the modern belief and confidence in inevitable progress produced by human ingenuity with its newfound scientific and technical capabilities, and the abysmal tragedies and political aberrations of power of the twentieth century. Is it that the modern conceit of thinking that we can construct a new world of our own making has been responsible for the evident and humiliating failures of humanity of this last century? Walsh thinks so and recognizes that we are now living precisely at a time when this grandiose error has become most evident and therefore opens the possibility of a new and better beginning.[13]

Here we find the description of a fundamental rupture in human society and the identification of a breakdown of assumptions and confidence about human progress from the high point of the various European Enlightenments to the dismal failures of two world wars and innumerable acts of inhumanity in the last century, and this new one. Certainly, it is difficult to categorize human history, although the terms of modernity and postmodernity indicate the recognition, as Walsh writes, of a decisive turning point in our forms of perception. Modernity has much longer roots than the Enlightenment and is more a combination of diverse historical currents than any one feature.[14] What Walsh identifies as particularly relevant for the understanding of the contemporary political context is the exaggerated trust and confidence in human science, power, and technology to bring about a better and more peaceful world. It seems that the opposite has happened, with the resultant skepticism and reticence toward such political ideals. This profound skepticism seems to pervade our political vision today, as if to eliminate *a priori* the possibility of dimensions of reality and of aspirations that transcend the immediate and the material. This pervasive skepticism has a contemporary name, relativism, which is the cultural and philosophical inheritance of the break-up of modern certainties. Philosophers Maria Baghramian and Annalisa Coliva describe this contemporary relativism in this way:

> The disappearance of old certainties in the religious, political, and scientific arenas has been instrumental in the popularity of relativism in recent times. The collapse of a religiously motivated cosmology, which fixed the position of individual human beings within a larger and immutable framework and provided firm foundations for their ethical outlook, helped to create a climate that was conducive to relativistic views. In science, the discovery of the possibility of non-Euclidean geometries, followed by developments of the early twentieth century, particularly Einstein's theory of relativity and the discoveries in quantum physics, eroded the confidence once placed in what was considered unassailable. The disillusionment with utopian political ideologies that espoused global aspirations, and the dismay experienced at the intractability of ethical and political problems also added to the attraction of relativism. As there seems to be neither a decision procedure for solving ideological conflicts nor a neutral ground to adjudicate between incompatible moral viewpoints, the only alternatives appear to be Relativism either to impose our worldview on others or to grant each person or culture full and incorrigible authority over the truth and justification of her beliefs and convictions.[15]

This oscillation between the hope in misplaced means to ideals, on the one hand, and the inevitable experience of disillusion at their failure, on the other hand, has also been recognized by the German philosopher Josef Pieper. Writing on the same Enlightenment confidence in perpetual peace, in his *The End of Time: A Meditation on the Philosophy of History*,[16] Pieper also notes the pendulum swing from the enlightened modern confidence in assuring inevitable human progress and peace to the experience of disillusion and despair at the equally inevitable failure of such beliefs:

> This simplification, whose inaptness is ever more remorselessly laid bare by the course of history itself, this optimistic abridgment, arose (and arises) out of an attitude which finds the road to an extra-temporal and post-historical "New Earth," leading through a catastrophic End and a divine transposition, insufficiently "evident" in theory and, above all, too arduous of "political realization." It has, inevitably, been answered by a retaliatory pessimism which, having lost its illusions regarding real history, is preparing for a catastrophic End; in equal, indeed, even greater contradiction to the traditional notion of history.[17]

There seems, therefore, to be a deeper cause of our residual disillusion with politics. From the optimism in scientific discoveries and the power of human reason to solve our difficulties and to guarantee a necessarily better future, we have swung to the despair of experienced failure in this last century and in the beginning of this millennium.

It is important to note that neither Walsh nor Pieper resign themselves to the *fait accompli* of human failure. Walsh sees in the break-up of modernity's illusions an opportunity, precisely in the experience of failure, to glimpse the real foundations of human existence and, on those real foundations, the authentic aspirations of politics. He emphasizes that these real foundations are not just theoretical hypotheses but can be personally experienced in the depths of our common failures.

Pieper, also, intends to explain that facile optimism in shallow notions of human progress, and their consequent pessimism, are due primarily to a truncated understanding of history, one that confines the fulfilment of human existence to the conditions of this actual world. According to Pieper, hope in perpetual peace and a future definitive resolution of human life is not in vain; it is fulfilled in an understanding of history that is infinitely broader than the confines of a narrowly construed human reason. Here, too, the breaking up of this mental "prison of finitude" can lead to the opening of the real horizons of human existence and the fulfilment of human hopes and aspirations.[18]

The task, then, is to discover anew our existence as it really is, to see things, persons, and all of reality as they disclose themselves to us, what they really promise to us, and then, only then, to see how we can respond adequately to our task. The renewal of politics begins, therefore, not with what "they should do," but with a profound personal renewal of how I see and perceive existence, in all its depth and breath. From the vision of what is, what is real, surges the adequate response in action.

THE PHILOSOPHICAL APPROACH

Whatever philosophy may mean, there seems to be little confidence in or use for philosophy in the world of political activity. In political reality things just happen. The power of coercion determines the context of political decisions, advantages are exploited, agreements are based on compromises, and the impermanence of people and structures all indicate that political activity is entirely remote from the abstract and the ideal. The democratic form of politics itself seems to imply the necessary competition of goals, methods, and values subject to the prevailing opinions of the day. There is the further concern today as to whether the prevailing opinions are, indeed, constituted by a majority of informed and free-thinking people, or rather conditioned and induced responses imposed by powerful groups with any and all means at their disposal. In any case, what prevail are interests rather than truths.[19]

The philosophical approach is also often understood today to mean the assertion of one's freedom with respect to political authority. This seems to be more and more the case, the assertion of individual freedom of expression in reference to a political government seen not as a freely chosen expression of popular will, but rather as an imposition and threat to the freedom of its people. The claim, therefore, that political activity and institutions can and may express the genuine and profound aspirations of a people seems grossly and naively misplaced and is seen as an unwarranted encroachment on people's freedom by a so-called liberal society.

Coupled with this mistrust is the utter remoteness of political determination from the lives of the many whom, supposedly, politics is to favor.

Clearly, there is much to sort out here. To start with, one needs to clarify what philosophizing is, and its surrogates and its deniers. This is not easy in a cultural context of the predomination of particular ways of thinking that limit or preclude the genuine and essential task of philosophizing. What does it mean to philosophize? The best descriptive definition I have found is from the American philosopher W. Norris Clarke:

> It is our destiny, written into us by the very structure of our nature, to be the ones to listen to being, as it reveals itself to us through the mute message of its action, interpret its significance, gather into unity its multifarious voices, speak out the *logos* of Being (as mediated by the many beings which are its bearers), and respond accordingly by our own action.[20]

There are several key elements in this description of the philosophizing perspective. In the first place, we encounter the given reality of everything, including ourselves, and *we are destined to listen to the given reality of all things.* Even the discovery of ourselves is only ever a response to an *a priori* encounter with reality; we slowly begin to realize that we, I, am distinct from other things and other persons, and, in the process, I discover that I am and have a certain way of being, in distinction to the way other things and persons are. This is the first and most fundamental disposition of our perception and what underlies any form of knowing and science.[21]

In similar terms, Voegelin describes this basic existential circumstance in which we discover ourselves to be immersed:

> Reason and spirit are the two modes of constitution of man, which were generalized as the idea of man. We have not gone beyond these contents of the idea of man, that is, his constitution by reason and spirit. That seems to be the definitive discovery. What does it mean to exist as constituted by reason and spirit? The experiences of reason and spirit agree on the point that man experiences himself

as a being who does not exist from himself. He exists in an already given world. This world itself exists by reason of a mystery, and the name for the mystery, for the cause of this being of the world, of which man is a component, is referred to as "God." So, dependence of existence (*Dasein*) on the divine causation of existence (*Existenz*) has remained the basic question of philosophy up to today.[22]

This listening to being is not some specialized operation of a particular science, but the fundamental conscious act of all our perceiving.[23]

Our listening to reality comes to us in an *experience of being, of reality*. We are often accustomed to certain ways of abstracting information and data from our experience of reality. The more complete disposition is to open ourselves to the full disclosure of what we experience, in ways that describe what we experience that may not be quantifiable or statistical but are equally real manifestations of being. It is a case of discovering equally valid and distinct modes of disclosure of reality, what Clarke refers to as the multifarious voices of being. Again, this is not a specialized task, only the basic, fully human, apprehension of reality.

There is also the need *to gather into unity all the distinct elements of experience*. What this means is that we bring into some type of harmony all of what we experience according to the value of what we experience. This is perhaps hard to do today, as we have lost the theoretical confidence in what Simpson calls "a comprehensive vision" of reality.[24] This effort to comprehend and to bring into synthesis all our diverse experiences of reality does not result in some closed and truncated perspective, but, quite the opposite, expands our perception beyond the confines of our present material existence. As Simpson claims, "we have urges and longings that transcend our own best efforts to attain them."[25] In political terms, this may explain the passions that politics arouse, the desire to explain and to justify, beyond the immediate phenomena of experience, an understanding of the totality of social existence, a comprehensive vision.

This is not to say that a comprehensive vision, a gathering into unity, is fully attainable. In classical times, the sophists were the ones who claimed to have the answers; the philosophers, the lovers of wisdom, knew that a comprehensive vision of reality was beyond human capacity, but not less worth striving for.[26] This is admittedly an unsatisfactory condition of our human experience, that we need and seek more than we can know. The temptation to both skepticism and to presumption are easy options to which we humans are all too gullible. The third option is the more realistic, to rely on what we can know comprehensively, while recognizing what is beyond our comprehension.

And it is the "*logos* of Being [capital 'B'] that we can recognise and speak out," according to Clarke.[27] What Clarke is implying here is that the comprehensive vision, to the degree that we are able to comprehend the unity of the multifarious voices, necessarily refers to the Being of all beings, who is called God. The *logos* is the evident expression of "the Mind that expresses itself." As Joseph Ratzinger explains this *Logos* of Being in a Christian context:

> But what is it, this "*Logos*"? The word "*Logos*" means, first of all, the same thing as "mind" (Sinn). To say that the world comes from the Logos, accordingly, means: the word is intelligible (sinnvoll); it is the creature of the Mind that expresses itself. Even before we make sense (*Sinn machen*) of anything, meaning (*Sinn*) is there. It embraces us. We stand upon it. The intelligibility (*Sinn*) does not depend on our creative effort but, rather, precedes and enables it. This means that the question about our Wherefore (our reason for being) is answered in our Whence (our origin). The Whence itself is the Wherefore. Creation is not just information about something that once happened; rather, it is an expression of the way the world is, here and now, and a statement about what its future will be like. The Whence of the world is at the same time the basis for its hope.[28]

Here a particular difficulty arises. For historical reasons, we tend to consider our human experience of reality as of a particular kind, what is subject to and explained by sense perception. What we have come to discard are real experiences that are, according to our senses, in some way defective. In other words, experiences that have their source and origin in something or someone not perceptible to our senses. It is not reasonable to suppose that there can be nothing beyond what we see and hear (we have already remarked that we experience the limitation of our comprehensive vision). Also, the vast history of religious experience, invariably of this humanly defective type (consistently so, if the object of experience is of a greater being than ours), suggests evidently that our experience includes the experience of the *Logos* of Being, whom we humans can know only defectively.

If this is the case, then a comprehensive vision of reality, based on the multifarious voices of being, reasonably must include the acknowledged experience of the *Logos* of Being, of God. It is an integral part of our human experience. It is in this sense that Pieper comments that: "At the beginning of human history, as well as at the beginning of each individual biography, philosophy and theology are undivided, one."[29]

As Pieper remarks,[30] this theological awareness was the original habitat of the philosophic mind, one that was evident in Plato and also in the "scientific ontology" of Aristotle. Pieper refers to German classicist Werner Jaeger's text on Aristotle:

> Metaphysics arose in his (Aristotle's) mind, and it arose out of the conflict of the religious and cosmological visions that he owed to Plato with his own

scientific and analytical mode of thinking. This inner disunion was unknown to Plato. It was a consequence of the collapse of the procedure on which Plato had based the knowledge of his new supersensible reality, and in which for one instant exact science and the most ecstatic enjoyment of the inexperienceable had seemed to coincide without remainder. When this concrete unity of myth and logic fell to pieces Aristotle carried away as a *depositum fidei* the unshakable confidence that in the Platonic creed of his youth the inmost kernel must somehow or other be true. The Metaphysics is his grand attempt to make this Something that transcends the limits of human experience accessible to the critical understanding. . . . The history of his development shows that behind his metaphysics, too, there lies the credo *ut intelligam.*[31]

Clarke finishes his description of the fundamental disposition for all knowledge by referring to the need to "respond accordingly by our own action." Knowledge is often understood as something impartial, objective, and detached from the subject (person) who knows. In fact, the degree of objectivity, in this sense of detachment from subjective involvement, is considered as what validates the truth of knowledge. While this is true, to the extent that the experience of reality is the experience of something and someone really distinct from me, as an object is to a subject, it is a mistake, I suggest, to take this distinction as what validates our experience of the truth of reality.[32] Our human experience is (or should be) greatly more compelling than the neutral bystander's observation of impervious "fact," and our re-action, evoked by the compelling nature of our experience, should be inspired by the rightness and goodness of the being we encounter.[33]

In a real way, our adequate response is the authentic test of our experience of reality. Only if our experience of reality has been integral, in the sense of experiencing the many diverse ways and modes that reality reveals itself to us, will we experience the call of being to respond actively and adequately. Our active response then leads us to a fuller experience of reality, to which an ever-greater response is given.[34]

Voegelin reminds us that the postmodern pessimism that seems to be the underlying current of our political vision today is not something inevitable or unchangeable, and that our reaction is determined by our free response:

The spiritual disorder of our time, the civilizational crisis of which everyone so readily speaks, does not by any means have to be borne as an inevitable fate; that, on the contrary, everyone possesses the means of overcoming it in his own life. And our effort should not only indicate the means, but also show how to employ them. No one is obliged to take part in the spiritual crisis of a society; on the contrary, everyone is obliged to avoid this folly and live his life in order.[35]

   This, then, is the *philosophizing* approach, and which needs to be present, even if implicitly, in our experience, understanding, and response to what we call politics.

   There are different ways of philosophizing, different emphases, according to the varying historical and cultural conditions. We need to find the most suitable philosophical approach to what we call politics, according to our present outlook and perspective on reality, especially in light of what Walsh has identified as a decisive turning point in the modern age. Particularly in the area of politics, as with epistemology, modern philosophy has consciously taken a new approach, often understood as a rejection of classical and medieval forms.[36] This requires of us a sensibility to modern and postmodern forms of perception and comprehension, and a way of philosophizing that is in dialogue with these times. Yale historian Louis Dupré warns us of the difficulty of returning *simpliciter* to pre-modern thought. While recognizing, for example, that "Plato and Aristotle still have more to say to us than any of our contemporaries," Dupré comments that:

> Past thought cannot solve modern problems. Though eternal in its own way, it does not address conditions that are exclusively ours—such as the fragmentation of our world picture. It may assist us in sorting out modern issues, but it does not provide ready answers. Modern culture has introduced us into a totally new way of confronting the real.[37]

   In his own comment on the new premises of modern thinking, Ratzinger contrasts the Ulysses of Dante's *Divine Comedy* with Columbus, the factual Ulysses, who discovers America:

> According to Dante, Ulysses is shipwrecked on the mountain of Purgatory, at the western limit of the earth; there is a direct transition from the earthly to the metaphysical. The factual Ulysses, though, Columbus, discovers, not Purgatory, but America. The sudden change from medieval thinking that the discoveries of the modern era brought about could not be depicted more graphically than was done by history itself in this event. The world loses its metaphysical borders; wherever man may advance, it appears to be merely the world. What until now had been the heavens is unmasked now as the world, which has the same consistency all around, in which there is no Above and no Below but only the same construct of matter on all sides with the same laws in effect everywhere. The earth is neither a centre nor a foundation, nor is the sky a heaven—everything is just "world."[38]

   It is not scientific discovery *per se*, or mechanics, or the experimental method that obfuscate a philosophical vision, but the predominance of these premises and methods as determining all of what reality is:

The situation becomes critical only when what is accessible to this method with its necessary methodological limitation turns into a positivistic world view which accepts as reality only what is accessible to this method and thus converts the methodological limitation into a fundamental one. The temptation to do so, however, becomes ever greater in the modern era and today appears almost insuperable.[39]

There are also, of course, ways *not* to see what is real and to deny, stunt, or stifle, our experience of reality. Our human experience of the multifarious voices of reality is unevenly distributed and therefore requires dependence on others for what we do not see for ourselves. Neither do we approach reality as neutral and indifferent bystanders; our needs, emotions, and fears often predispose us not to see and experience what is before us, or to project onto reality what are only our desires or imagination. Also, as Pieper reminds us: "there is an infinitude of hidden, often barely discernible modes of shutting the doors of the mind and the heart."[40] There is also, of course, the temptation to reverse the philosophical approach, to begin to fashion reality according to our own preconceived "reasonable premises," making absolute our own particular experiences.[41]

All of this implies an effort that is not always easy or convenient, to want to see, to try to discern, to decide, and to do. Sokolowski notices this personal task of truth and thus prefers to describe the human person as "an agent of truth," because agency supposes a personal activity and responsibility toward the truth, more so than the usual description of man as a rational animal: "the term [agent of truth] shows that attaining truth is an accomplishment and not merely passive reception. It speaks not just about reasoning but about success in reasoning, and so designates human being in terms of its highest achievement: the human person is defined by being engaged in truth, and human action is based on truth."[42]

A PHILOSOPHICAL APPROACH TO POLITICS

How does one approach the phenomenon of politics from a philosophical perspective? The enormity and complexity of contemporary political activity seems to impede the possibility of any personally assumed comprehensive vision. At the same time, many of the terms of classical political philosophy, as we have mentioned, seem to have changed their meaning in history, so that while we can continue to speak of society, the common good, government, laws, and so on, the meaning of these terms is quite distinct from pre-modern usage. Indeed, it seems that the philosophical approach, as I have described it, has been abandoned in favor of political *science*, understood as a descriptive awareness of political phenomena in a way analogous to the physical sciences.[43]

American political philosopher Harvey C. Mansfield explains the essential difference between political philosophy and political science (in the modern sense of science) in this way:

> Political philosophy reaches for the best regime, a regime so good that it can hardly exist. Political science advances a theory—in fact, a number of theories—that promises to bring agreement and put an end to partisan dispute. The one rises above partisanship, the other, as we shall see, undercuts it. . . . Today political science is often said to be "descriptive" or "empirical," concerned with facts; political philosophy is called "normative" because it expresses values. But these terms merely repeat in more abstract form the difference between political science, which seeks agreement, and political philosophy, which seeks the best. Political science likes facts because it is thought possible to agree on facts as opposed to values, and political philosophy provides values or norms because it seeks what is best. When we contrast political science and political philosophy we are really speaking of two kinds of political philosophy, modern and ancient.[44]

In classical philosophical terms, politics as much as ethics was a science because politics elaborated:

> Empirically and critically, the problems of order which derive from philosophical anthropology as part of a general ontology. Only when ontology as a science was lost, and when consequently ethics and politics could no longer be understood as sciences of the order in which human nature reaches its maximal actualization, was it possible for this realm of knowledge to become suspect as a field of subjective, uncritical opinion.[45]

What I am proposing here is the perspective of the person at the center of all political activity, and the renewal of political activity through the renewal of the personal philosophical vision. The human person is not primarily an organizational part of some vast and remote system and procedures, but is, should be, the measure of all systems and procedures. It is by only appreciating man's freedom to flourish, and everything implied in human freedom and human flourishing, that political activity can become meaningful. This was Havel's insight into the renewal of politics:

> More than ever before, such a change will have to derive from human existence, from the fundamental reconstitution of the position of people in the world, their relationships to themselves and to each other, and to the universe. If a better economic and political model is to be created, then perhaps more than ever before it must derive from profound existential and moral changes in society. This is

are its self-transcending source and are, in turn, embraced as the transcending purpose of the political. Persons are the origin and end of politics.[53]

At the same time, it is remarkable how remote from our present-day mentality is the idea of the right to and the responsibility for a personal appropriation of a true and comprehensive vision of society.

A PERSONALIST PHILOSOPHICAL
APPROACH TO POLITICS

The proposal, therefore, is to examine political phenomena in the light of and from the perspective of the individual person, any person in human society, and to evaluate to what degree the political processes and structures contribute to the personal flourishing of persons, if at all, or to their detriment, and the outlines of possible better ways these structures and processes may do so.

There is no one best way of politics. Political phenomena are part of a people's culture and way of being and this necessarily reflects the differences of history, religion, culture, language, and even traits of character of different peoples. By respecting and affirming this legitimate divergence of expression, there is a consciousness today of a common dignity and worth that must indicate something shared in our humanity. As Ratzinger points out: "there is a common truth of a single humanity present in every man. The tradition has called this truth 'man's nature.'"[54] It is this commonness, expressed in many unique ways, that forms the common basis and measure of the variant political structures and processes.

Each chapter pursues a particular theme of politics centered on the person. The theme in chapter 2, *Person and Politics*, looks to clarify, beyond the present caricatures of isolated individuals, who and what we are in common, as persons. This includes not only our common structure as persons but also the hopes and aspirations that are also part of our common dynamism. A key dimension here is to clarify in what way and to what extent we are social and transcendent beings, while retaining the unique identity of each personal self.

Chapter 3, *Truth and Politics*, examines the role of a consensus of truth as the basis for political society. Claims to truth are problematic today and politics seems to be based on maximizing freedoms, or pragmatic, short-term considerations of what works in matters of material and economic relevance. What is in fact fundamental, and constitutive of politics, is the truth about the human person. All political endeavor depends on a truthful vision of the person in society, as challenging as the path to a public consensus of truth is—or have we given up on this conviction and papered over the reconciliating of differences, as the phrase "democracy before philosophy" indicates?

The theme in chapter 4, called *Living Publicly in the Truth*, refers to what it means to live publicly according to the way of being human. It may be obvious from political history that this is no easy task, that often this task requires facing conflict and powerful resistance, and paying the price of one's personal or common truthful coherence. Is paying the price ultimately worth it, is it ultimately effective, or is it only a useless sacrifice on the altar of prevailing power?

The Person's Transcendent Social Destiny, examined in chapter 5, tries to clarify the real dimensions of human existence. Given our actual existence, is there evidence of an original existence, in the sense of how we were meant to be, distinct from our actual existence? The other fundamental question is whether there is a final state of existence to which we aspire or are destined. Although we are habituated to our actual state of existence, answers to these two questions would clarify the real context of this actual existence and its activities, including politics.

A second set of themes deal with particular fundamental political phenomena. Chapter 6, *Political Authority and Its Justification*, asks about the legitimacy of public political authority. In an age of highly sensitive individual freedom and autonomy, what justifies a public call to a task or responsibility beyond our own self-determination? Is authority characterized only by power ("holding the legitimate means of coercion," as Max Weber described government[55]) or are there personal reasons for wanting and for being required to serve a social need or interest?

The next theme in chapter 7, *Forms of Political Government*, is on the traditional category of the forms of government and the varying types of political structures and processes. What is of particular importance here is the form of the modern political state and the suppositions of its historical origin. Modern democracy has become, at least in name, the acceptable form of government today, and yet the word democracy both promises and conceals much that needs to be clarified and examined. What really is a democratic government and what sustains the true good of each one, and the collective good, in the face of systems and processes that can be steered in opposing ways? Does the present democratic form have structural and well as practical weaknesses and what are democracy's "pre-political foundations"?[56]

In chapter 8, *Law and Society* deals with the role of law as the legitimate instrument for the exercise of political government. Even so, the contemporary understanding of law is much different to pre-modern conceptions, and therefore we need to know what we assume laws to be and do. The rule of law and due process are essential elements of social cohesion, but, of themselves, an insufficient basis for man's life in society. "To play by the rules" is a minimum, but not sufficient, social requirement. Also, what makes law right?

As discussed in chapter 9, *Human Rights* are today often seen as a juridical theme as legal courts search to uphold and enforce human rights according to the Roman Law maxim *ubi ius, ibi remedium* (where there is a right, there is a remedy). The legal vindication of human rights is a notable phenomenon of the latter part of the twentieth century.[57] At the same time, questions are now raised as to the content of so-called human rights and whether human rights can and should be seen in a greater context of social responsibility rather than only in terms of individual freedoms. This discrepancy calls into question who the person is, someone defined ultimately and only by freedom, or by a social context that requires a concomitant responsibility.

International politics spontaneously seems to be circumscribed by the notion of the modern state. This notion is also at the basis of both public and private international law.[58] There are a vast number of political issues between states, both public and private, and the increasing number of international organizations of different types has spurred a growth of international law and practice, if in a necessarily fragmented way. Giving due importance to the practical relations between states, it is also important, I suggest, to reframe the context of international politics; there is more to the international context than what state representatives declare and do, however visible and eloquently staged. That is why the title of chapter 10's theme is *The Unity of the Nations*, because this title suggests a form of unity deeper than inter-state agreements, and because the title suggests other, and perhaps more meaningful, protagonists of unity than state representatives.

The need for a comprehensive meaning of politics and the historical attempts to implement a political vision for society has been responsible for the descriptive terms used today and the systems of ideas (ideologies) they represent. The theme of chapter 11, *Political Ideologies and Their Justifications*, is an attempt to get to the heart of the various visions of political society, what they really mean, the truths they attempt to give effect to, and their limitations and errors. While attempts to justify a totalizing vision today are few, we do confront partial ideological visions that, on particular themes, claim to be true and aim to implement their vision. In the light of the totalitarian dictatorships of this last century, do we advocate an open, ideologically free society on the lines of Karl Popper's *The Open Society and Its Enemies*, with his belief in "piecemeal social engineering"?[59] How does this fragmented approach tally with the need for a comprehensive vision of politics, understood as "the drive for a complete life, for the fullest attainable happiness"?[60]

Although the religious dimension of man's existence is referred to in the theme of chapter 2's *Person and Politics* and chapter 5's *The Person's Transcendent Social Destiny*, the fact that politics and religion seem to be framed in terms of necessary conflict and exclusion requires, I suggest, another look at their real relation and at the present unsatisfactory forms of inclusion and exclusion of what is termed religion. It may seem obvious to some that religious belief and practice are to be entirely private and individual matters, of no public relevance; in fact, religion is viewed as a common source of conflict and war that is best downgraded to the private conscience of each person. My suggestion is that when we legislate for this removal of religion, we create a vacuum into which rush less benign absolutes.[61] It is easy to think of caricatures of the relation between religion and politics; it is much harder and very necessary to know their real relation. It is intimated in this chapter that the recognition of the Absolute Being, of God, however perceived, is essential for a comprehensive vision of a fundamental personal and social order. The real relation of politics to religion is the fundamental question of the final theme, chapter 12, *Politics and Religion.*

CONCLUSION

The general theme running through these meditations is that it is the person who shapes politics. Fundamentally, the complex phenomenon of politics, with its institutions, processes, structures, and ministers reflects an accepted type of vision of the person—the question is what type of person we envisage. The effort in these essays is to renew the real dimensions of human existence and the aspirations to a truly human society as the only worthy response to the given circumstances of our social and political existence. To aspire socially to what is truly best is, in the end, the only practical way to live politically as persons in society.

This is primarily a personal commitment. Each person is required and able to live the truth in politics. The primary and ultimate government is of oneself and the greatest contribution to political life in society is the personal commitment to living publicly the truth of one's personal being. This means to experience freedom by rejecting imposed models of passive, consumerist citizens; to choose freedom by assuming responsibility for oneself and for others, and not to abdicate this responsible freedom by citing the misdeeds or injustices of others, however real they are. In freedom, to choose not just what is good, but also what is best, and, in freedom, to know that serving a greater cause is the only way to personal fulfillment. This, I suggest, is the primary impulse that our politics requires.

NOTES

1. Eric Voegelin, *Order and History*, vol. 2, 227, as cited in Dante Germino, "Eric Voegelin's Contribution to Contemporary Political Theory," *Review of Politics* 26, no. 3 (1964): 390, https://doi.org/10.1017/S003467050000509X.

2. Peter L. P. Simpson, *Political Illiberalism: A Defence of Freedom* (London: Routledge, 2015), 131. Simpson writes that the modern state "is not at all the sort of community that Aristotle has in mind by the *polis*. The *polis* is that community which responds to the natural desire of human beings to perfect themselves in happy and noble living and which exists by nature in order to realize that goal (Aristotle, *Politics* 1.2, 3.9)." Simpson argues that the modern state is commonly understood in Weberian terms of the centrality of legitimate coercion. Simpson, *A Philosophical Commentary on the Politics of Aristotle* (Chapel Hill: University of North Carolina Press, 1998), xxv–xxvi. Simpson also queries, although finally accepts, the use of the term city for Aristotle's social community. Cf. Simpson, "Making the Citizens Good: Aristotle's City and Its Contemporary Relevance," *Philosophical Forum* 22, no. 2 (1990): 149–66.

3. Robert Sokolowski, "The Human Person and Political Life," in *Christian Faith and Human Understanding: Studies on the Eucharist, Trinity, and the Human Person* (Washington DC: Catholic University of America Press, 2006), 188–89.

4. Eric Voegelin, "Why Philosophize? To Recapture Reality!" *Communio* 28, no. 4 (2001): 875.

5. Francis Fukuyama wrote the optimistic *The End of History and the Last Man* (New York: Free Press, 2006), based on his essay "The End of History?" *National Interest*, no. 16 (Summer 1989), https://www.jstor.org/stable/24027184, claiming Western liberal democracy as the final evolutionary form of human government (3–4). This was followed by two related books, Fukuyama, *The Origins of Political Order: From Prehuman Times to the French Revolution* (New York: Farrar, Straus, and Giroux, 2011); and Fukuyama, *Political Order and Political Decay: From the Industrial Revolution to the Globalization of Democracy* (New York: Farrar, Straus, and Giroux, 2015), in which Fukuyama details the historical development of and the necessary conditions for the liberal democratic tradition. The facts and views above are taken from *Origins of Political Order*, 9–32.

6. As cited in Fukuyama, *Origins of Political Order*, 3. Freedom House is a non-governmental organization based in Washington, DC, founded in 1941, and dedicated to research and lobbying on themes of democracy, human rights, and political freedoms. Fukuyama's theses continue to be discussed, as in Graham McAleer, "Not the End of Politics," *Law and Liberty*, May 31, 2022, https://lawliberty.org/forum/not-the-end-of-politics (accessed October 16, 2023).

7. This article is an edited extract from Ivan Krastev and Stephen Holmes, *The Light that Failed: A Reckoning* (London: Allen Lane, 2019).

8. Pierre Manent, *Metamorphoses of the City: On the Western Dynamic*, trans. Marc LePain (Cambridge, MA: Harvard University Press, 2013).

9. Manent, *Metamorphoses of the City*, 217. Manent refers to the absence of "a great political existence" (220).

10. Václav Havel et al., *The Power of the Powerless: Citizens Against the State in Central-Eastern Europe*, ed. John Keane (London: Routledge Classics, 2015), 45.

11. Bertrand Russell, *Authority and the Individual* (London: Routledge Classics, 2010), 1141. American sociologist Robert A. Nisbet opens his *Twilight of Authority*, first published in 1975, with the observation: "I believe the single most remarkable fact at the present time in the West is neither technological not economic, but political: the waning of the historic political community, the widening sense of the obsolescence of politics as a civilized pursuit, even as a habit of mind. I have in mind the whole fabric of rights, liberties, participations, and protections that has been, even above industrialism, I think, the dominant element of modernity in the West" Nisbet, *Twilight of Authority* (Indianapolis: Liberty Fund, 2000), 1.

12. David Walsh, *After Ideology: Recovering the Spiritual Foundations of Freedom* (San Francisco: HarperCollins, 1990).

13. Walsh, *After Ideology*, 9. This volume represents the first of a trilogy by David Walsh. The second volume is *The Growth of the Liberal Soul* (Columbia: University of Missouri Press, 1997), and the third is *The Modern Philosophical Revolution: The Luminosity of Existence* (Cambridge: Cambridge University Press, 2008). For a summary of this trilogy see John von Heyking, "David Walsh's Anamnesis of Modernity: A Preface to a Preface," *Political Science Reviewer* 39 (Spring 2010): 140–69. For an historical tracing of the modern notion of progress see Glenn W. Olsen, *The Turn to Transcendence; The Role of Religion in the Twenty-First Century* (Washington DC: Catholic University of America Press, 2010), 55–87.

14. Yale historian Louis Dupré considers the modern perspective to have come in three stages: Humanism and the Renaissance, the Enlightenment, and the period following the French Revolution. Dupré sees these stages as connected but independently caused: "Each expressed a different innovative impulse, yet together they constituted a single cultural epoch" Dupré, *Religion and the Rise of Modern Culture* (Notre Dame, IN: University of Notre Dame Press, 2008), 5. Dupré has written extensively on the modern period, especially in *Passage to Modernity: An Essay in the Hermeneutics of Nature and Culture* (New Haven, CT: Yale University Press, 1993). For the historical roots of modernity, see Peter Henrici, "Modernity and Christianity," *Communio* 17, no. 2 (1990): 141–51. For the possible links between modernity and postmodernity, see Kenneth L. Schmitz, "Post-Modernity or Modern-Plus?" *Communio* 17, no. 2 (1990): 152–66.

15. Maria Baghramian and Annalisa Coliva, *Relativism* (London: Routledge, 2004), 311.

16. Josef Pieper, *The End of Time: A Meditation on the Philosophy of History* (San Francisco: Ignatius Press, 1999), especially chap. 2. In this short text, Pieper comments particularly on Immanuel Kant's belief in the progress of human history in his works on history, begun by Kant when in his sixties. Kant's titles themselves are significant: *Ideal of a Universal History on the Principle of World Citizenship* (1784); *Conjectural Beginning of Human History* (1786); *The Victory of the Good Principle over the Evil and the Establishment of the Kingdom of God on Earth* (1792); and "Whether the Human Race Is Continually Advancing toward the Better," written in 1792 (published in 1798); *The End of All Things* (1794); and *Toward Perpetual*

Peace (1795). The titles themselves sound so remote from our own expectations of the future.

17. Pieper, *End of Time*, 91.

18. On this theme of the real grounds for hope and progress see Richard John Neuhaus, "The Idea of Moral Progress," *First Things* (August 1999), https://www.firstthings.com/article/1999/08/the-idea-of-moral-progress (accessed October 16, 2023).

19. Richard Rorty has written to justify this approach of the contingency of all convictions and the danger of searching for or proposing foundational truths. A summary of Rorty's views may be found in chap. 11, "The Priority of Democracy to Philosophy," in *Prospects for a Common Morality*, ed. Gene Outka and John P. Reeder (Princeton, NJ: Princeton University Press, 1993), 254–78. Walsh comments on Rorty's views, and other non-foundational approaches "Enduring Moral Authority," in *Growth of the Liberal Soul*, chap. 2, 46–76.

20. W. Norris Clarke, *Explorations in Metaphysics: Being-God-Person* (Notre Dame, IN: University of Notre Dame Press, 1994), 54. In a similar way, Clarke defines the philosophical approach as: "the critically reflective, systematically articulated attempt to illumine our human experience in depth and set it in a vision of the whole" Clarke, *The One and the Many: A Contemporary Thomistic Metaphysics* (Notre Dame, IN: University of Notre Dame Press, 2001), 5. Eric Voegelin's description of philosophy is "the love of being through the love of divine Being as the source of its order," from his *Order and History*, cited by Ellis Sandoz in his introduction to Eric Voegelin, *Science, Politics, and Gnosticism: Two Essays* (Washington, DC: Gateway Editions, 2012), 48.

21. What we are describing here is reality as it is disclosed to us, as the first, spontaneous reaction of our perceptive capacity of experiencing reality, what in modern terms is called the *truth of disclosure*, or, in classical terms the *truth of predication*, what Aristotle called *apophansis*. The truth of disclosure is a term coined by the American philosopher and theologian R. Sokolowski to translate better the philosophical method of phenomenology. Cf. Robert Sokolowski, *Introduction to Phenomenology* (Cambridge: Cambridge University Press, 2000), 158; and *Phenomenology of the Human Person*, chap. 4 and his chapter on Aristotle, (Cambridge: Cambridge University Press, 2000), 273–85.

22. Eric Voegelin, *Hitler and the Germans*, in *Collected Works of Eric Voegelin*, vol. 1. Trans. and ed. Detlev Clemens and Brendan Purcell (Columbia, MI: University of Missouri Press, 1999), 1580.

23. Josef Pieper has written extensively on this theme of the *intus-leggere* of our experience of reality, especially in *Leisure: The Basis of Culture* (South Bend, IN: St. Augustine's Press, 1998); *For the Love of Wisdom: Essays on the Nature of Philosophy* (San Francisco: Ignatius Press, 2007); *Only the Lover Sings: Art and Contemplation* (San Francisco: Ignatius Press, 1990); *In Tune with the World: A Theory of Festivity* (South Bend, IN: St. Augustine's Press, 1999); and *Happiness and Contemplation* (South Bend, IN: St. Augustine's Press, 1998).

24. Simpson, *Political Illiberalism*, chap. 4.

25. Simpson, *Political Illiberalism*, 68.

26. Josef Pieper points out that Hegel, in the preface to his *Phenomenology of Spirit*, claims that philosophy can "come closer to the goal of being able to set aside the epithet 'love of wisdom,' and become real knowledge—that is the task that I have set myself." Goethe responds dismissively to "these men who believe themselves capable of mastering God, the soul, and the world (and whatever other names might exist for what no one comprehends" Pieper, *For the Love of Wisdom*, 65–66. The reference from G. W. F. [George Wilhelm Friedrich] Hegel is from *The Phenomenology of Spirt*, ed. and trans. Terry Pinkard and Michael Baur (Cambridge: Cambridge University Press, 2018).

27. Clarke, *Explorations in Metaphysics*, 54.

28. Joseph Ratzinger [Pope Benedict XVI], *Dogma and Preaching: Applying Christian Doctrine to Daily Life* (San Francisco: Ignatius Press, 2011), 93.

29. Pieper, *For the Love of Wisdom*, 313. In another essay in the same volume, "The Dilemma Posed by a Non-Christian Philosophy," Pieper claims that classical philosophy (the love of wisdom), such as understood by Pythagoras, Plato, and Aristotle, necessarily includes "a methodological openness to theology" (299).

30. Pieper, *For the Love of Wisdom*, 299.

31. Werner Jaeger, *Aristotle: Fundamentals of the History of his Development*, 2nd ed., trans. Richard Robinson (Oxford: Oxford University Press, 1968), 378. On the personal response to the *Logos*, see Hans Urs von Balthasar, "Truth and Sanctity," in *Explorations in Theology* (San Francisco: Ignatius Press, 1989), 181–209; and David L. Schindler, "Sanctity and the Intellectual Life," *Communio* 20, no. 4 (1993): 652–72.

32. Michael J. Buckley points out that in metaphysical language *objectum* did not denote a thing but was a term in reference to human consciousness. "Metaphysically, things were not *objecta*; they were *res* as they were indeed beings. One could classically list six terms for things, terms that are mutually convertible, what were later called transcendentals: *ens, res, unum, bonum, verum, aliquid*. But *objectum* is not among them. To make that term convertible with 'thing' demanded a very different intellectual world" Buckley, *Denying and Disclosing God: The Ambiguous Progress of Modern Atheism* (New Haven, CT: Yale University Press, 2004), 94.

33. John H. Newman makes clear the difference between mere notional knowledge and real knowledge: "After all, man is not a reasoning animal; he is a seeing, feeling, contemplating, acting animal . . . . The heart is commonly reached, not through the reason, but through imagination, by means of direct impressions, by the testimony of facts and events, by history, by description. Persons influence us, voices melt us, looks subdue us, deeds inflame us" Newman, *An Essay in Aid of a Grammar of Ascent*, ed. Ian Ker (Oxford: Clarendon Press, 1985), 67, 65–66. Here Newman emphasises the wide range of human, especially inter-personal, experience that impels us to respond.

34. One of the modern philosophers who has emphasized this necessary role of active response as an integral part of cognitive experience is the French philosopher M. Blondel: "Being is never in the idea separated from action; and metaphysics itself, considered first under its speculative aspect, is true then only inasmuch as, like a rung in the system of phenomena, it enters into the general dynamism of life. Action grounds the reality of the ideal and moral order; it contains the real presence of what,

without it, knowledge can simply represent, but of what, with it and through it, is vivifying truth" Maurice Blondel, *Action (1893): Essay on a Critique of Life and a Science of Practice*, trans. Oliva Blanchette (Notre Dame, IN: University of Notre Dame Press, 1984), 434.

35. Voegelin, *Science, Politics, and Gnosticism*, 358.

36. Sokolowski has interesting comments on the differences of philosophical approach in modernity and postmodernity in "Phenomenology in the Present Historical Context," in *Introduction to Phenomenology*, 198–209.

37. Dupré, *Passage to Modernity*, 7.

38. Ratzinger, *Dogma and Preaching*,78–79.

39. Ratzinger, *Dogma and Preaching*, 79.

40. Josef Pieper, *Faith, Hope, Love* (San Francisco: Ignatius Press, 1977), 64. Pieper quotes on the same page Pascal's dictum: "If you do not take the trouble to know the truth, there is enough truth at hand so that you can live in peace. But if you crave it with all your heart, then it is not enough to know it."

41. "Reason, the faculty that directs human action, operates by drawing its conclusions from the premises that it posits, in this way fashioning its own system. By its very nature, reason wants always to be right. It is argumentative and loath to let itself be convinced. Jealous of its autonomy, reason upholds the independence of man, a rational animal, who derives his dignity from it—not to mention his pride. Thus, whether it is established on the altars, or whether it sets itself up as a mean-spirited purveyor of excuses, 'vain-glorious reason' is *par excellence* the instrument of human pride, an instrument by the aid of which 'God is dispensed with in an atmosphere of haughty disdain'" Peter Henrici, "The Spiritual Dimension and Its Form of Reason," *Communio* 20, no. 4 (1993): 638.

42. Sokolowski, *Phenomenology of the Human Person*, 1.

43. Robert Sokolowski notes that "In the departmental structure and the philosophical curricula that prevailed in many Catholic colleges and universities during the first two thirds of the twentieth century, political philosophy would usually be located not in philosophy departments but in political science" Sokolowski, *Christian Faith and Human Understanding*, 179.

44. Harvey C. Mansfield, *A Student's Guide to Political Philosophy* (Wilmington, DE: ISI Books, 2014), 80, 93.

45. Eric Voegelin, *The New Science of Politics: An Introduction* (Chicago: University of Chicago Press, 1987), 12. In this sense political philosophy is a science because "science is a search for truth concerning the nature of the various realms of being" (4).

46. Havel et al., *Power of the Powerless*, 51–52.

47. Germino, "Eric Voegelin's Contribution," 384,

48. Joseph Ratzinger, *A Turning Point for Europe? The Church in the Modern World: Assessment and Forecast* (San Francisco: Ignatius Press, 2010), 1218. As American philosopher Michael Novak comments: "Societies are not like the weather, merely given, since human beings are responsible for their form. Social forms are constructs of the human spirit" Novak, *The Spirit of Democratic Capitalism* (Lanham, MD: Madison Books, 1992), 20.

49. Ratzinger, *Turning Point for Europe?*, 1224. On the Greek meaning of *nous*, Professor Andrew Louth writes: "*Nous* is usually translated as 'mind' or 'intellect.' Part of the problem is that neither of these words is as rich in derived forms as the Greek *nous* (they have, most significantly, no verb). But beyond that, the words 'mind' and 'intellect' and their derivatives (intellection, intellectual, etc.) have quite different overtones from the Greek *nous* . . . . This means that *nous* and its derivatives have a quite different feel from our words, mind, mental, intellect, intellection, etc. Our words suggest our reasoning, our thinking; *nous, noesis*, etc. suggest an almost intuitive grasp of reality. To quote Festugière: It is one thing to approach truths by reason, it is quite another to attain to them by that intuitive faculty called *nous* by the ancients, the 'fine point of the soul' by St Francis de Sales, and the 'heart' by Pascal." Cf. Louth, *The Origins of the Christian Mystical Tradition from Plato to Denys*, 2nd ed. (Oxford: Oxford University Press, 2007), 145. For a contemporary explanation of this more encompassing grasp of reality, see Andrew Tallon, *Head and Heart: Affection, Cognition, Volition as Triune Consciousness* (New York: Fordham University Press, 1997).

50. Eric Voegelin, *Order and History*, vol. 2, 227, as cited in Germino, "Eric Voegelin's Contribution," 390.

51. Simpson, *Political Illiberalism*.

52. Simpson, *Political Illiberalism*, 139.

53. David Walsh *The Priority of the Person: Political, Philosophical, and Historical Discoveries* (Notre Dame, IN: University of Notre Dame Press, 2020), 96, 4087.

54. Joseph Ratzinger, "Truth and Freedom," *Communio* 23, no. 1 (1996): 32.

55. "It is rather the case that in the final analysis the modern state can be defined only sociologically by the specific means that are peculiar to it, as to every political organisation, namely, physical violence. 'Every state is based on force,' Trotsky remarked at Brest-Litovsk. That is indeed the case" Max Weber, *The Vocation Lectures: "Science as a Vocation" and "Politics as a Vocation,"* ed. David Owen and Tracy B. Strong, trans. Rodney (Livingstone. Indianapolis: Hackett, 2004), 2103

56. This phrase is, I think, coined by Joseph Ratzinger, who develops this theme in an essay titled "That Which Holds the World Together: The Pre-Political Moral Foundations of a Free State," in *Europe: Today and Tomorrow* (San Francisco: Ignatius Press, 2007), 67–80. Interestingly, Ratzinger claims that the moral foundations of the state necessarily include resource to the light of religious traditions. "reason must learn a willingness to listen to the great religious traditions of mankind. If it cuts itself completely adrift and rejects this willingness to learn this relatedness, reason becomes destructive" (79–80).

57. This is noted, for example, by the Irish jurist J. M. [John Maurice] Kelly in his *A Short History of Western Legal Theory* (Oxford: Oxford University Press, 1992), 425–30, while recognising the divergent legal and philosophical justifications for such rights to be found in authors such as Ronald Myles Dworkin, *Taking Rights Seriously* (1978) and John Finnis, *Natural Law and Natural Rights* (1980), as well as the jurisprudence of Western supreme court judges.

58. For example, James Crawford's *Brownlie's Principles of Public International Law* declares the usual subjects of international law to be "sovereign political states," cf. 9th ed., (Oxford: Oxford University Press, 2019), 124.

59. Karl Popper, *The Open Society and Its Enemies* (London: Routledge Classics, 2011), 513.

60. Simpson, *Political Illiberalism*, 67. Simpson holds that, in line with what he says is the political theory inherited from the past, "We want a political life, or even at the limit a politically transcendent life, that fully answers our deepest longings" (67).

61. This was the idea behind Richard James Neuhaus' metaphor of the naked public square. Neuhaus writes that when religion is radically privatized and individualized, when religion is just individual conscience and conviction, then the public square is naked and "will be filled by *ersatz* religion, by religion bootlegged into public space under other names" Neuhaus, *The Naked Public Square: Religion and Democracy in America*, 2nd ed. (Grand Rapids, MI: Eerdmans Publishing Company, 1997), 80.

Chapter 2

Person and Politics

The overview of this chapter begins with examples of the unique perspective of personal experience as the primary reality of political philosophy—a journalist covering war-torn countries and the observation of Václav Havel that the political reforms of the Prague Spring of 1968 were only the final result of "a long drama originally played out chiefly in the theatre of the spirit and the conscience of society."[1]

To understand how the person is understood in politics today, I explain briefly the fundamental ideas that gave rise to the form of the modern political state and its assumed role as the dominating center of all social authority and power. The modern state effectively redefines all social relations in terms of the sovereign state and the individual subject.

This new form of government recreates the human person as an individual and isolated subject of the state who (supposedly) has delegated his political participation in exchange for individual rights and freedom. This new separated individual has also been shaped by scientific empiricism and a subjectivism that isolates the human person's inner experience from its source in reality, such that "the subject lends to things its own shape and takes their utility for itself to be their significance."[2] The primary political goal becomes the liberty of the undifferentiated individual. This—undifferentiated individuals living within their own interior space of undetermined freedom—is what each person has become in politics.

The challenge is to rediscover the real depth and dimensions of the human person to overcome the emaciated individual as the subject of politics. To do this, I suggest what Paul C. Vitz has termed a trans-modern approach, that accepts the valid insights of modernity and at the same time transforms and transcends their limitations. In this approach, contemporary personalist philosophy is rediscovering the many dimensions of the specific and uniquely human existence of the person that have been lost from view and that, taken together, sketch the real being and dynamism of personhood.

The descriptive analysis of personal experience—known as a philosophy of disclosure (or "phenomenology")—is a particularly apt method of discovering the truth of personal being from within human experience and therefore as something that attracts and convinces. This is important today as the truth of personhood needs to be experienced if it is to be known and accepted.

One of the most important dimensions of personhood is the fundamental relational structure of the person; we do not just have, but we are, relational beings, a personal unity of identity and relationality, in which our own flourishing and the flourishing of others are mutually dependent. While historian Larry Siedentop traces the political primacy of the person to its Christian foundations, Siedentop's account of this Christian discovery of the worth of the individual may need to be developed in its constitutive relational dimension, something that was also present in early Christian thought.

As a conclusion, it is the reality of the person, personal being, that should define everything that politics is, and not, as we have it today, that politics determines who and what its subjects are. The reality of personal being, our transcendent personal and social aspirations, the essential relational character of personal being, and what W. Norris Clarke has expressed as the metaphysics of love as the path of personal fulfilment, are what constitute real human society, politics included. There are inevitable risks involved in promoting a comprehensive vision of political society, but the greater danger is in ignoring the capabilities, the vital potential, and the truth of the human person. The urgent task is to reconsider and refashion our politics in terms of the person of politics.

PERSONS IN POLITICS

In the last chapter, I suggested an approach to politics primarily from the perspective of the reality of the person rather than from the structures and processes that often seem to define politics today. This personal approach serves both to broaden and deepen the purposes of politics and also to reignite the response of persons to appreciate and to participate in the political dimension of their society.

Marie Colvin was an American journalist working for the British newspaper the *Sunday Times*. She was a journalist who had to see for herself the war-torn parts of Europe, Africa, and Asia that she was assigned to cover, or that she herself offered to report on. She lost an eye reporting first-hand during the Tamil civil war in Sri Lanka and she suffered from post-traumatic stress disorder. She was killed in February 2012, in the rubble of the Syrian city of Homs just after she had managed to send a report on the suffering civilians to her press office in London.

What moved her to put her life at risk was the need to see the situation for herself, the real individual people being bombed in Syria or the suffering of women and children in Saddam Hussain's Iraq. This was the political truth, not in terms of abstract commentary, but the real lives of those who were suffering at the hands of others:

> In truth, Colvin identified with her subjects and found her own emotions in their plights. Her particular talent was giving voice to the voiceless—widows holding their mangled husbands in Kosovo, Tamil Tigers rebelling against the government in Sri Lanka. . . . For four days straight, she broadcast the plight of 1,000 victims, mostly women and children, trapped in a siege that had killed thousands of Timorese.[3]

Colvin shows the difference between politics understood in terms of abstract structures and processes, and politics from the perspective of real individual persons in their real circumstances. There is need for general terms, concepts, and principles, but they all need to find their source and their purpose in the reality of persons and their actual circumstances. This theme aims to uncover the worth and the wealth of each person, whom politics is to serve.

This change in perspective from a detached and often remote analysis of politics to a person-centered understanding of political phenomena as the real measure of reality and the source and purpose of politics is also seen in Václav Havel's account of the Prague Spring of 1968, when the people of Czechoslovakia protested against their Soviet controlled government. Havel, who had participated in the protest, observed:

> The Prague Spring is usually understood as a clash between two groups on the level of real power: those who wanted to maintain the system as it was and those who wanted to reform it. It is frequently forgotten, however, that this encounter was merely the final act and the inevitable consequence of a long drama originally played out chiefly in the theatre of the spirit and the conscience of society. And that somewhere at the beginning of this drama, there were individuals who were willing to live within the truth, even when things were at their worst.[4]

These individuals were not primarily politicians in positions of power, but ordinary people from varied backgrounds who chose to live in the truth, even at personal cost, and release the contagious presence of truth into the tissue of lies of the political system:

> These people had no access to real power, nor did they aspire to it. The sphere in which they were living the truth was not necessarily even that of political thought. They could equally have been poets, painters, musicians, or simply

ordinary citizens who were able to maintain their human dignity. Today it is naturally difficult to pinpoint when and through which hidden, winding channel a certain action or attitude influenced a given milieu, and to trace the virus of truth as it slowly spread through the tissue of the life of lies, gradually causing it to disintegrate. One thing, however, seems clear: the attempt at political reform was not the cause of society's reawakening, but rather the final outcome of that reawakening.[5]

Havel points out that the individual personal response of living in the truth was at the origin of political protest and reform and that the real center of politics lies precisely here, in the expression of true meaning that ordinary people give to their lives. For this reason, the real concern of politics, its original power, and its final purposes, is living in the truth of the response to reality of each person; the flourishing of politics depends on this personal living in the truth.

In his twisted way, Screwtape makes a similar point, exhorting his nephew Wormword to foster in human minds:

The delusion that the fate of nations is in itself more important than that of individual souls. The overthrow of free peoples and the multiplication of slave-states are for us a means (besides, of course, being fun); but the real end is the destruction of individuals. For only individuals can be saved or damned, can be become sons of the Enemy or food for us. The ultimate value, for us, of any revolution, war, or famine lies in the individual anguish, treachery, hated, rage, and despair which it may produce.[6]

It is not difficult to observe today the almost total detachment of what politics has come to mean from its real center of individual persons and their true human and social capabilities and aspirations.

THE MODERN STATE AND THE INDIVIDUAL SUBJECT

The contemporary relationship between persons and the modern political state is marked by two fundamental concepts; the formation of the modern state, characterized by its concentration of power, and the role of individual freedom within that state sovereignty of power.

It is important to remember that the modern state was formed in times of fundamental religious division in Europe and the need, at least in theory, to guarantee public order at a time the unified Christian political foundation was shattered. As David Walsh explains, we should not underestimate the profound and traumatic divisions that the Reformation of Christianity had on European society. What had once been a shared cultural and religious heritage which had formed Christian European culture now was itself the source of hostile division between and among the newly formed and emerging political states. This split went to the heart of European society and seemed to jeopardize its very foundations:

> We are perhaps inclined to give too much emphasis to the crisis of pluralism that afflicts our own society and not enough weight to the gulf opened up by the religious conflicts of the early modern era. After all, they did not have the example of several centuries of the liberal solution of tolerance to demonstrate how a public order can be maintained in the absence of agreement on fundamental questions. It seemed unthinkable that people who disagreed so radically could trust one another in anything. The whole basis on which a res publica, or common order, was based seemed to have been shattered.[7]

The modern conception of the sovereign state has taken various historical forms, from the age of absolute monarchs, to constitutional monarchies and later republics, to the contemporary notion of state as defined, for example, by international law and assumed to be the universal notion of government.[8] The modern state today usually takes on the form of constitutional government, a system of division of powers, the rule of law, due process, representative government, and so on, all of which we are familiar with.

The relationship between the modern state and the individual subject has been imagined and described since the seventeenth century in terms of contract law, but a very particular type of contract, a social contract between the necessary absolute secular power and individuals who subject themselves to this secular power in order to secure their basic rights to peace and security. Based on a new theology of power rather than of order, the initial form of the modern state establishes itself in quasi-theological terms as a realm of absolute secular power to which persons were related as individual subjects. The aim of these individual subjects was freedom and the secular power determined and provided this freedom for individuals by its absolute dominion over all institutions, summed up in the word "sovereign." What is important to appreciate here is the radically changed social context in which political purposes and relations are redefined:

> As John Milbank has argued, modern politics is founded on the voluntarist replacement of a theology of participation with a theology of will, such that the assumption of humanity into the Trinity by the divine *logos* is supplanted by an undifferentiated God who commands the lesser discrete wills of individual humans by sheer power. . . . The loss of a theology of participation is a loss of teleology, the intrinsic ends of human life.[9]

The new social and political arrangement of the central sovereign power is represented in quasi-Christian terms of a body:

> The metaphor of the body is most obvious in Hobbes' figure of the great Leviathan, the artificial man, the commonwealth or state, in which sovereignty is the soul, the magistrates the joints, reward or punishment the nerves, and "lastly, the pacts and covenants, by which the parts of the body politic were at first made, set together, and united, resemble that *fiat*, or the let us make man, pronounced by God in the creation." Leviathan, then, is the new Adam, now of human creation, which saves us from each other.[10]

Within this new modern context, the central power that was to become the state redefines human society such that political power becomes the absolute and determining context for all individuals and groups:

> When Hobbes and Rousseau theorized the emergent state in the seventeenth and eighteenth centuries, they understood quite clearly the imperative to defeat the lesser associations within the state body in order to vanquish multiplicity. Locke was less clear on this point, but in practice the modern sovereign state has been defined by its usurping of power from lesser communal bodies. The view that the state is a natural outgrowth of family and community is false. As Robert Nisbet points out, the modern state arose from opposition to kinship and other local groupings: "the history of the Western State has been characterized by the gradual absorption of powers and responsibilities formerly resident in other associations and by an increasing directness between the sovereign authority of the State and the individual citizen."[11]

Within this context of the sovereign power of the modern state, the gains of the diverse liberal forms of government are obvious and represent a history of hard-won battles of franchise, representation, due process, political accountability, the limitation of public office, and so on. At the same time, the modern state, and the dependent relation of the individual subject to the state, presupposes a particular context and premises of thought that need to be recognized and examined.

American sociologist Robert A. Nisbet sees the particular model of the modern political state as at the root of the dislocation of community. In his *The Quest for Community: A Study in the Ethics of Order and Freedom,*[12] Nisbet identifies the source of our contemporary breakdown of the bonds of community in the modern and contemporary conflict between the concentrated political power of the State and all the other forms of real social bonds and functions. This political dominance of the state is at the root of the loss of social status and social structures, the sense of social placement and social belonging, that we experience today.[13]

The modern state has as its primary purpose to be the prevailing instrument of public power, and the devices of government are internal checks and balances of the sovereign power of the state. The state is an abstract that justifies the use of public power over all its subjects. The modern state defines politics in terms of power, absolute determining power that resides, not in persons, but in the abstract state. Nisbet recognizes the gradual centralization of sovereign power in the state and its increasing pervasiveness in all areas of society. He describes an absolute state as one that has all power over the use of force within the jurisdiction, as well as a description of what we would consider normal state powers, that is, to determine war and peace, to tax, powers of compulsory acquisition, a controlling influence over the educational process, increasing encroachment on areas of family and personal life (perhaps even in terms of rights and freedoms), and so on. When we consider the present arrangement, Nisbet says, it is obvious that all states do in reality exercise these manifestations of absolute power and, in this sense, there is no real difference between democratic and totalitarian forms of government.[14]

The state's power is also absolute, in the sense of determining the legitimacy of all other groups and institutions within its jurisdiction. Even if these groups and institutions are free to act, they do so with the explicit or implicit permission of the state power. The concentration of power in the state has meant in practice the increasing involvement of the state in more and more sectors of society and, thereby, the gradual disappearance of other associations that find their purposes and their means absorbed by and into the state. Effectively, the state takes the common public task from the hands of persons and associations and substitutes the abstract state responsibility for the response of personal initiative and involvement. On this Nisbet comments that the underlying political struggle in history has not been marked by the attempt to emancipate the individual from the dominance of the state, but rather the rivalry of the state to the other social forms of authority. It has been this conflict that has had the greatest political and social consequences. The gradual absorption by the state of all these other forms of social authority has, in Nisbet's view, brought about the breakup of medieval communities and the predominance of the centralized power of the state in its relation to the individual citizen.[15]

The theoretical justification of the use of this power is the freedom of the subjects. As the public instrument for the use and control of power for the sake of freedom, the state, as the center of civil power, officially does not propose aims and purposes beyond the guarantee of personal freedoms. The state remains supposedly neutral toward visions of a common good or a common purpose of a society. Gone is the idea of the polis as a social expression of human flourishing, as is found, for example, in Plato and Aristotle, with the ideas of what is collectively to be achieved in society; the political state now serves to preserve and to control the individual frontiers of freedom. In the context of the modern state, itself a reflection of a voluntarist notion of freedom and of the use of power, the real good of persons is reduced to an equality of freedoms which entails a denial of common purpose and the truth of the person.[16]

This gives us today a very particular political context within which political themes are already shaped and made to fit into this setting. As William T. Cavanaugh points out:

> In fact, civil society is not the natural source of the state, but both society and state are enacted artificially "from above." The spontaneous life of traditional social groups from below tends to be delegitimated because such groups tend not to be representative, that is, based in consensus. . . . The state is the source of social life. In the absence of a common good or *telos*, the state can only expand its reach, precisely in order to keep the welter of individuals pursuing their own goods from interfering with each other. Where there is a unitary simple space, pluralism of ends will always be a threat. To solve this threat, the demand will always be to absorb the many into the one. In the absence of shared ends, devotion to the state itself as the end in itself becomes ever more urgent. The result is not true pluralism but an ever-increasing directness of relationship between the individual and the state as foundation of social interaction.[17]

This is not to condemn the modern liberal state in its various forms of structures and of processes, nor is it to deny the benefits of this enduring liberal political structure.[18] What is necessary to recognize is that the political state is not the end-product of human society, although it is often considered to be; it is *a* way of expressing and preserving political freedom; it is not *the* expression of social and political society. As its historical origins show, the liberal political state assumes a whole series of political premises that gives a very distinct interpretation of political authority, human society, the political role of the person, the common good, social roles and purposes, and the public expression of dimensions and aspirations of social life.

THE SUBJECT OF THE MODERN STATE

What becomes evident in the features of the modern state is the type of subject (rather than citizen) that the modern state supposes and requires. The hypothetical contractual basis between the person and the state assumes a limited binding agreement about certain mutually acceptable conditions. The principal contributors and exponents of this new civic accord were Richard Hooker, Thomas Hobbes, John Locke, Baron de Montesquieu, Jean Jacques Rousseau, and John Stuart Mill. In varying but similar ways, these architects

of the modern state emphasize above all the purpose of the contract as preserving individual freedom and therefore the necessary requirement of the
agreed sovereign power as the condition for this preservation of individual
freedom. This is the primary political meaning of the term liberal:

> At the same time, one should recognise that the term liberal is not simply
> equivocal. Its various meanings can be more or less intelligibly related on a
> spectrum of interpretations. These meanings coalesce around the core emphasis
> on individual liberty as the beginning and the end of political order and vary in
> their assessments of the impediments to the full exercise of that liberty and the
> correlative means of removing or ameliorating such obstacles.[19]

Little else is required, apart from paying usually relatively expensive
taxes. There are the representative structures of the use of political power,
the legislative process, the opportunity to elect representatives, and so on, but
effectively little else is required or wanted of the subject in political participation. The understanding, ever more so today, is that all the major concerns of
social living will be dealt with by the state, given as benefits to the subjects
who have paid for them.

At the same time, this shifting political role of the person can be seen in the
difference between the person as citizen and the person as subject:

> In the Middle Ages the essence of citizenship was urban man's freedom from
> the exactions of obedience which existed in the more feudal countryside. One
> was a citizen by virtue of free association in the town, and although individual
> identity certainly existed in the towns and cities, there were nevertheless sub-
> stantial contexts of kinship, occupation, religion, and other associations which
> in effect put the individual at the centre of a series of concentric circles. There
> was a great difference between the status of citizen and that of subject. The
> medieval expression "the city makes free" was apt description of the status, for
> the most part, of the citizen.
>
> Over the centuries, however, the concept of citizen tended to become increas-
> ingly merged with that of political subject. In Hobbes' Leviathan and also his
> Behemoth one can see vividly the transition that takes place. . . . In Rousseau's
> Social Contract the whole matter is resolved by the absolute destruction of any
> individual or associative right whatever and the assimilation of both into the
> monolithic General Will. . . . The [French] Revolution achieved what absolute
> monarchy had never been able to achieve; it swept with "gigantic broom," in
> Marx's words, all the smaller patriotisms away, leaving individual and national
> state as the two ascendent realities. The new citizenship, far from being based
> upon, rooted in, the social groups in which human beings actually lived, was
> now the exclusive property of the unitary state. In substantial degree it has been
> this way ever since.[20]

The modern political understanding of "citizen" is thus very different to pre-modern political societies and comprises the notion of equal and undifferentiated individuals as subjects of the state who have delegated their political participation to representatives, and whose imposed political purpose is each one's own individual welfare. While this arrangement brings benefits at a cost, it is not difficult to see that sovereign political power has created a type of political subject that bears little resemblance to the dynamism of the person oriented freely toward a transcendent social destiny.

This identity and role of the political subject is also a product of the variant currents that comprise the historical modern era. The Canadian philosopher Kenneth L. Schmitz identifies two such currents that have influenced and shaped the modern notion of the person that is reflected in this modern political contract. First, the Enlightenment science of mechanics, as a specific expression of the broader philosophical nominalism and empiricism, which, as Schmitz claims, indirectly influenced the way social relations were to be understood by Hobbes, Locke, Gottfried Wilhelm Leibniz, David Hume, and Immanuel Kant, among others. It is not difficult to relate the subject of the political contract in the following terms of mechanical science:

> The status of an ultimate and elementary particle in mechanism is that it possesses a self-sufficiency which it retains even after it has entered into relations with other elementary particles. For that reason, its relations must remain external to it. In sum, then, the ultimate nature of the differential unity proposed by nominalism and pursued by mechanism consists in its *incomplexity*. For the ultimate nature of such differential units resides in their lack of parts. The ultimate units were ultimate precisely because they were simple in the sense of being the last possible point of analysis. To be one was to be simple, and to be ultimate was to be absolutely one—indivisible and irreducible. All relationships had to fall "outside" of them, therefore, taking the form of attachments to and detachments from a distinct and separate elemental unit.[21]

The mechanistic perspective also viewed reality in terms of motion, not purpose (or final cause, in classical metaphysics). Schmitz points out that this changed the notion of liberty:

> The nature of choice itself has changed. Or rather, the character of liberal liberty is not simply the power to choose: it is equally, even primarily, the power to *unchoose*. For what has primacy in this general view of the self is not that it is free to complete itself by choosing a good already somehow prescribed for it or inscribed in it, but rather that it achieves its own highest good by retaining the power not only to choose but also to relinquish that choice and to take up another. . . . The foundation and force of liberalism lies in the simplicity of the individual's power to move—the impulse to change one's mind and one's place

and, where possible, the world. In this motility lies its exaltation of the freedom of the individual.[22]

The second major contributory factor to the modern individual expressed in the relation between the political state and the subject is precisely what Schmitz calls "the primacy of the subject," an epistemological shift that bases our knowledge not on our experience of what is real, but on the subjectivity of what we experience, whether it be in empirical or rational form. What this means now is that, instead of our common experience of reality and our adequate response to it, "[the subject] lends to things its own shape and takes their utility for itself to be their significance."[23]

What we end with is a very distinct view of the person and society, which is in the background of so much political philosophy today:

> This strategy recognizes the indifferent equality of a plurality of dominant selves, and—out of a prudential fear—negotiates rival claims by contract, by appeal to the maximization of happiness, or more recently by procedural rules. The liberal strategy has as its primary aim to safeguard and promote—not happiness or virtue so much—as the liberty of the differential individual.[24]

The point here is not to condemn political liberalism or the modern state, or the historical era of modernity, the last being understood as a complex concurrence of perspectives, scientific advances, and philosophical understanding. It is, rather, to draw attention to the suppositions of these notions and their contemporary political expressions. It is also to argue a fundamental point: given the advances and enrichment of this modern form of politics, both in its theoretical and practical expressions, even so, *the central purposes of social and political living and the central personal response of social participation are not being addressed by these modern forms of politics.* The principal reason for this absence of purpose and response, and the content itself of that purpose and response, is to be found in the vital need for a renewed vision of the human person. It is the truth of the communion of persons that provides the real measure and context for all the institutions, purposes, procedures, structures, and processes that we call politics.

MAN AS PERSON

It seems that there is, locked into the political relation of subject and state, a conception of persons as isolated selves, living within subjectivity, at odds with anything or anyone that may encroach on them. This existential isolation and fear may account for the perceived need of individuals and groups for public affirmation and recognition.

In *Quest for Community*, Nisbet describes the existential consequences of the freedom from social and religious bonds that were supposed to liberate humans from the chains of slavery. Nisbet notes that the contemporary social phenomena of secularism and individualism have caused new contemporary problems. While it is observable that the breaking of bonds of religious and social association have enhanced the sense of individual freedom today, at the same time Nisbet recognizes that this sense of individual freedom has not brought about new forms of association and belief, but rather the opposite experience of being alienated and disillusioned. Nisbet perceives that the alienation of the person from others is a consequence of the loss of shared moral truth that had been a traditional source of social bonds.[25]

Nisbet sees this present general condition of human existence in contrast with the confident assumptions of the modern rationalist age. He recognizes that the image of the human person has changed in contemporary perception. Whereas previously rationalist confidence inspired self-reliance and self-assurance, this has now changed. Today persons are perceived in their insecurity, insufficiency, and instability. Evidence of this is to be found in modern existential literature. Nisbet points out that this contemporary ephemeral notion of the human person is derived from precisely the rupture of the social bonds of shared culture and belief. In place of the free, open, and outward-looking person, we find contemporary expressions of loneliness, doubt, and inhibition.[26]

We are thus faced with overcoming this truncated notion of the isolated and disoriented individual that politics, as well as other economic, social, intellectual, and humanist influences and forces have shaped, and to reconstruct a more authentic vision of the human individual, both personal and social.

We are faced with two basic philosophical approaches to understanding the human person that are generally independent of each other. We have on the one hand a scientific view of the person that will express the truth of the person in terms of the numbers, data, and laws of the physical sciences and claiming to present the factual reality of man. On the other hand, we have those who do seem to address the fundamental issues of human existence in language that is often imprecise and vague and does not seem verifiable as reality:

> It is one of the saddest features of our age that we are faced with an entirely unnecessary dichotomy: on the one hand there are those whose devotion to intellectual cleanliness and rigor is exemplary but who refuse to deal with anything but small, and often downright trivial questions; in the other camp are men like Toynbee and some of the existentialists who deal with the big and interesting

questions, but in such a manner that the positivists point to them as living proofs that any such effort of this kind is doomed to failure.[27]

In order to rediscover and renew the real person of politics, I propose five avenues of approach that can help make evident the depths and dimensions of personal existence. In this way, from a greater appreciation of the person, political activity can express the real meaning and purpose of persons in political society.

A TRANSMODERN APPROACH

In an effort to gather together the dismembered dimensions of the human person and to provide for the person a new unity of science and philosophy, some philosophers, scientists, and psychologists have forged what they call a transmodern approach to the human person:

> As an answer to the modern and postmodern problem, we should consider an alternative understanding of the person, one that has been emerging since the 1990s. I use the term "transmodern" to describe this new vision of the person and perhaps the new historical mentality that will follow the postmodern period. Transmodern means a new understanding that transforms the modern and also transcends it. This new approach does not reject most modern contributions but transforms their meaning. Moreover, the new meaning is often of a higher, transcendent nature—sometimes explicitly theological or spiritual, but always with an emphasis on higher meaning.[28]

This approach aims to take all the valid insights of modernity—as, for example, the sciences, the role of subjectivity—and link and relate them to a more complete understanding of what it means to be a person. The aim is to reconstruct a more complete understanding of the person from various perspectives—theological, philosophical, psychological, neurological, cultural—and integrate the evidence and reflections of these dimensions of existence into the full meaning of human personhood. This requires overcoming the emaciated isolated self that has been produced over the previous centuries and developing an enriched—and more real—notion of the person. Psychologist Paul C. Vitz explains the positive nature of this renewal of the person:

> I have proposed the term transmodern to describe a new era or historical period which I believe is dawning. The transmodern culture would take the best of modernity and transform, transcend, and transfigure it. Transforming modernity means taking the developments of modernism and contextualizing them within a

larger framework. Rather than rejecting modernity, the transmodern removes the antireligious bias, but retains the core objective findings. . . . Transmodernism contrasts sharply with fundamentalism. Fundamentalists of whatever stripe— Protestant, Catholic, Islam, Hindu—seek to reset the world to where it was 150, 200, or 500 years ago. Transforming modernity does not return to the past, but lives in the present without discarding the past. Transcending modernity incorporates a religious or spiritual view and an idealistic moral system. Transmodern culture recognizes that the human person is not a mere machine, but called to go beyond the self. As a result of this transforming and transcending, modernism will be transfigured, such that the actual shape or physical environment in which we live will be changed.[29]

Personalist Philosophy

This approach is complemented by the rise of a new anthropological current of personalism that begins to rediscover the many dimensions of the specific and unique existence of the human person. What characterizes this general current is the emphasis on what is specifically unique to the human person as distinct (but not separate) from a more general metaphysical approach. Categories of experience such as love, communion, the body-soul unity, friendship, the man-woman relationship, and so on, are recognized and given a place in the description of who the human person is.

The fundamental insight here is that the human person cannot adequately be reduced to terms and measurements of quantity, space, and matter, and that personhood introduces real categories of being that are unique to human beings among other material beings. These categories of being are not recognized in physical, mechanical, or biological analysis, but pertain to a spiritual reality that is perceived in the interior experience of persons, in the reality of their subjectivity.

This openness to the manifestation of personal being that is experienced interiorly through the experience of the person as subject, makes evident the specific reality of the human person in terms and categories, as mentioned above, that are unique among material reality. Among other consequences, this personalist approach rejects:

> both liberal individualism and collectivism. In other words, all the personalist thinkers resist turning persons into autonomous selves and then detaching them from all bonds of solidarity, and they resist no less the opposite error of absorbing the individual person into the social whole, as if the individual were nothing but a part of the community to which it belongs.[30]

More than this, the personalistic approach rediscovers the diverse dimensions of human existence that have been lost sight of and, on the basis of this rediscovery, the personalistic approach aims to contribute to the reconstruction of an adequate understanding of the person, which then becomes the real measure and standard of all social relations, politics included.

The Phenomenological Description of Human Experience

Related to this current, and often used as its philosophical approach, is the phenomenological method as applied to personal experience. In essence, this is the description of human experience as related to the person and the approach aims to discern what that experience implies in terms of the reality it discloses. It is the appropriation of subjective human experience according to its own unique terms (not subject to the categories of other particular sciences or other modes of disclosure) as manifesting the presence of spiritual reality as evidenced subjectively in human experience.

In the first place, this method emphasizes the importance of personal experience of reality, not just a clarity of notional concepts, as important as such stages of the apprehension of reality are. Phenomenology, or, as Robert Sokolowski describes it, a philosophy or theology of disclosure, starts with the recognition of modes of experience. This is particularly apt as a transmodern approach.

A similar emphasis on personal experience is to be found in David Walsh's *After Ideology*. Commenting on Eric Voegelin's approach to the history of politics, Walsh asserts that an encounter with the truth of reality is not to be had by the mere expression of abstract forms of truth, but rather is to be found within an experience of being drawn to the transcendent Source of truth. Walsh notes that this is what Voegelin concentrated on, the identification of lived experience rather than the abstract form or idea. For this reason, Voegelin did not advocate a mere restitution of a form of natural and universal law because this abstract form does not reveal the lived experience from which it is derived. Voegelin searched for the experience that gave rise to the conceptual form. As Walsh points out, Voegelin noted that the ancient Greek philosophy of ethics and politics was not founded on the statement of logical propositions but was an expression of the soul's experience of being drawn to the transcendent source of the Good, a source that was beyond any other experience of being.[31]

What the phenomenological method makes evident is a greater role for reason than what reason is usually considered to be and how it is supposed to function. As Sokolowski explains, we normally think of reason as the instrument of the truth of correctness, "the activity of moving from one statement or proposition to another, from premises to conclusions or from effects to causes."[32] Even so, there is another, and anterior role of reason:

> There is a more elementary form of truth that can occur even apart from the confirmation of a claim. This second sense of truth, the truth of disclosure, is simply the display of a state of affairs. It is the simple presencing to us of an intelligible object, the manifestation of what is real or actual. . . . The truth of correctness depends on the truth of disclosure; the latter can serve as the intelligibility that confirms or disconfirms a claim. . . . The truth of disclosure, therefore, flanks the truth of correctness. It comes before and after.[33]

The importance of this truth of disclosure when applied to disclosure of the personal experience of interiority, is the manifestation of what is specifically human, personal, and necessarily relational. This provides us with the evidence, the facts, of the real dimensions of the person and of personal existence. Commenting on Karol Wojtyla's use of the descriptive disclosure of personal experience, Peter L. P. Simpson writes:

> To objectify the problem of human subjectivity is to give an explicit place in our science of man to that experience of man which everyone has always had but which few, until recently, have brought to fully philosophic reflection. It is not easy to do this correctly. It is not easy to express the subjective: what we all readily experience we cannot all readily describe. Thus, phenomenological personalism is an ongoing and unfinished task. But it is a peculiarly modern task, a task for the thinkers of our time, and Wojtyla is a striking exemplar of what the task is and what can be achieved when one devotes oneself to it.[34]

All of this is to rediscover in a modern way the depth and the dynamism of the reality of the human person and the meaning and value the person brings to reality, including politics. These approaches are ways to go beyond emaciated descriptions of the autonomous selves, living within their subjectively constructed inner and isolated world of meaning.

The Relational Structure of the Human Person

One of the most important rediscoveries is the fundamental relational structure of personal being. For Aristotle, relation was an accident of being, something that may or may not be present and that was therefore non-essential to man, as relation was unessential to the metaphysical figure of the Unmoved Mover. The theological experience of Judeo-Christian experience exploded this isolationist notion of the perfection of the autonomous substance. God, in Judeo-Christian revelation, is relational being. The Christian consequence, in many ways corroborated now by dialogical personalism, is that the human persons are not only "ends in themselves," but find that fulfilment of purpose in, with and from others (and the Other). What this means is that persons are both affirmed in their own being and at the same time only achieve the plenitude of that being in active relation with others and with the Other. W. Norris Clarke expresses this dynamic notion of being a person in this way:

> A person, like every other real being, is a living synthesis of substantiality and relationality, and the relational side is equally important as the substantial side, because it is only through the former that the self as substance can actualize its potentiality and fulfil its destiny. . . . This is especially true of the human person. For human consciousness does not start off in full, luminous self-presence like the angels. It begins rather in a kind of darkness, somewhat like a dark theatre, in a state of potency toward knowing all things, in act toward none. To actualise itself, make it luminously present to itself in act, it must first open itself to the world of others, be waked up by their action on it and its own response. . . . Only then, through the mediation of the other, can it return to itself, to discover itself as self-conscious "I," as this unique human person. . . . I discover positively what and who I am by engaging actively—and receptively—in interpersonal relations with other human beings like me who treat me as a "Thou" in an inter-personal social matrix of "I-Thou-We."[35]

This understanding of the being-as-relation of the person is a lot different to the various notions of a person in the state of nature that were assumed to be at the foundation of the political contract with the sovereign power. Again, we know that these several social projects were built in a time of great social upheaval, civil war in some cases, or in times of oppressive monarchs or empires in other cases. One can perhaps understand the necessary reticence and caution. Even so, it is a mistake to confuse the actual condition (as bad as it may sometimes be) of existence with the real and necessary ideal of human fulfilment.

Clarke continues to explain what is at the root of human social flourishing, politics included:

> But the outgoing, self-expressive, self-communicating, relational aspect must be an equally intrinsic and primordial aspect of every person as its interiority and self-possession . . . This intrinsic expansiveness of the person towards action and the relationality flowing from it, not just for self-fulfilment but for com-municating one's own richness to others—both rooted in the expansiveness of existence as intensive act—open up a new perspective for viewing the meaning of the person, in the universe. We are moving towards a metaphysics of love.[36]

Joseph Ratzinger also insists on the primordial mode of persons as beings of relation, and that the constitutive development of personal being and iden-tity only occurs in the dynamic movement toward others (and the Other):

The essence of mind or spirit in general is being-in-relation, the capability of seeing oneself and the other . . . openness, relatedness to the whole, is an essential element of spirit. And it comes to itself precisely by the fact that it not only is but also reaches beyond itself. In going beyond itself, it possesses itself; only by being with the other does it become itself and come into its own. Or, to put it yet another way: being with another is its form of being with itself.[37]

The Person as Unique Self and Relational Being

Much of the history of Western political development has been marked by the progressive identification of the free and equal individual as the point of reference in political society. This is a distinct and important achievement of European thought and certainly not a spontaneous political occurrence. American-born British political philosopher Larry Siedentop has traced the long path of the recognition of the individual person as a focal point of political development: "So I tell a story about how the 'individual' became the organizing social role in the West—that is, how the 'civil society' which we take for granted emerged, with its characteristic distinction between public and private spheres and its emphasis on the role of conscience and choice."[38]

He claims that Christianity was at the source of this unique development, the emphasis on the individual persons, and their rights, conscience, and freedom:

> If we want to understand the distinctive constitution of Europe, we must go back
> to its religious foundations. For the moral beliefs which Christianity fostered
> still underpin civil society in Europe, the institutions that surround us . . . It was
> the arrival of Christianity which accomplished that moral revolution. In that way
> Christianity provided the moral foundations of modern democracy, by creating a
> moral status for individuals—as children of God—which was eventually trans-
> lated into a social status or role.[39]

This view of history is specifically unmodern, as the Enlightenment view that sought to illumine the "dark" Middle Ages, characterized by Christian and Church hierarchical oppression, and sought to rediscover, as Siedentop describes it, "the freer, secular spirit of antiquity."[40] Siedentop recounts a different story, one that describes the slow and progressive political recognition of the individual due to gradual assimilation of Christian categories of thought into the public and political arenas.[41] As important and interesting as this historical account is, there is also the constitutive relational dimension of "the individual" present in Christian theology from the earliest centuries that today needs to be given equal expression in liberal political thought.[42] The notion of person can serve to describe this relational being better than the term "individual."[43]

These political ideas of the equal dignity of all persons combined with relations of solidarity is seen, for example, in the writings and action of an early archbishop of Constantinople, John Chrysostom (349–407):

> Chrysostom upheld the primacy of the individual Christian, of the person as such, even of the slave and the poor person. His project thus corrected the traditional Greek vision of the *"polis,"* the city in which large sectors of the population had no access to the rights of citizenship while in the Christian city all are brothers and sisters with equal rights. The primacy of the person is also a consequence of the fact that it is truly by starting with the person that the city is built, whereas in the Greek *"polis"* the homeland took precedence over the individual, who was totally subordinated to the city as a whole. So it was that a society built on the Christian conscience came into being with Chrysostom. And he tells us that our *"polis"* (city) is another, "our commonwealth is in heaven" (Phil 3:20), and our homeland, even on this earth, makes us all equal, brothers and sisters, and binds us to solidarity.[44]

The subject of politics, therefore, is a person, not merely an enclosed individual with property rights and a no-trespassing sign. Persons have a deep experience and involvement with the spiritual-material reality that surrounds them and are both called by that reality and inspired from within to shape and contribute to life in communion with others and with the Other. The American personalist philosopher John F. Crosby describes in these terms who the person is: "unrepeatably and incommunicably himself or herself, that each is not only an objective but also a subjective being, that each lives out of his interiority, that each is a being of surpassing, indeed infinite worth and dignity, that each can live and thrive only by existing with and for other persons."[45]

A POLITICS OF THE PERSON

These rich, eloquent descriptive terms serve to indicate the depth and relationality of the human person and may seem remote from political reality. I suggest, rather, that they are the real foundation for all human activity, especially politics.

In the first place, we see that the human person has a vast interiority of needs and aspirations, that include and go beyond physical essentials, all equally real and necessary for flourishing, and that these aspirations become the source of political strife and unrest when they are denied or ignored. To reduce the common political good to the provision of material goods, to economics, or to consider that all other human needs will be answered in this way is a dangerous, though popular, political premise.

Ratzinger, commenting on the political collapses of 1989 and 1990 and about the needs and the power of the human spirit for truth, love, freedom, and aspiration, writes that the dramatic events of those years showed precisely the power of the human spirit, the power of human hope, to overcome the suffocating pressures of material barriers and obstacles and eventually the power of the spirit to break through them. This is evidence of the reality of spirit over material and economic structures and systems, and over all explanations that try to reduce the human spirit to merely material causes. But it is here that Ratzinger reminds us that the materialism at the heart of Marxism is also to be found in our non-Marxist societies. Materialism, the obsession with the merely material dimension of our lives, is a mentality that pervades our politics, our economics, and our social culture.[46]

This human need and aspiration for more than material satisfaction was recognized in the ancient political worlds of Greece and Rome. In *Metamorphoses of the City,* Pierre Manent recognizes the pursuit of glory as the political passion *par excellence*, and as something inherent in human nature. Manent recognizes that this ambition for glory in the classical world that we may misinterpret as mere hyperbolic fantasy, reveals something essential to the dynamism of our human nature, something that is an instinctive response to who we are and what we aspire to, as also a response to the contingency of our existential circumstances. In reality, this aspiration for glory is provoked by the consciousness of our own finitude and mortality.[47]

It is interesting that Augustine's critique of the pagan expressions of the political aspiration for glory is not a critique of the aspiration itself, but the way glory is really to be obtained. As Manent explains, the Christian rejection of pagan glory did not imply an outright rejection of the aspiration for glory, but rather invoked the belief in real immortality as the real answer to the human desire for glory. In this way, Christianity recognizes the legitimacy of the pagan aspiration for glory as the human search for the immortality of the divine, and it is Christianity that claimed to bring that noble human aspiration to its real fulfilment.[48]

It is apparent that the expectations of politics today are considerably more mundane and do not cater for the greater human aspirations that are the essential dynamic thrust of our human existence toward ultimate fulfilment.

In the second place, we can recognize that relation is constitutive of the person, in the sense that the selfhood of the person only grows and flourishes in participation—giving and receiving—with others, what Clarke called a metaphysics of love, to the point of discovering one's own self through the free and conscious gift of self, and in receiving the gift of others' selves. This is what constitutes real human society, politics included. At the heart of the criticism of political liberalism is the substitution of this social bond for a political agreement that takes the fundamental participatory role out of the hands of individuals and places it in the processes and structures of the abstract political state. The state absorbs the social bond, becomes the social bond, and individuals remain with perfunctory and nominal tasks, and dependent on the state for their society. Nisbet noticed this unhealthy relationship between the person treated as individual and concentrated political power:

> It is impossible to understand the massive concentrations of political power in the twentieth century, appearing so paradoxically, as it has seemed, right after a century and a half of individualism in economics and morals, unless we see clearly the close relationship that prevailed all through the nineteenth century between individualism and State power and between both of these together and the general weakening of the area of association that lies intermediate to man and the State.[49]

The notion of human individuals that is implied in the modern political state and their relation to the modern state is, evidently, much different to the classical political nature and role of the human person as found in Plato and Aristotle. As we saw, for Plato, the ideal republic *was* the just the human person written in large letters and was a reflection of the ideal person, who is formed in the political virtues to contribute to the ideal, just republic. The shortcoming of this Platonic relation of the virtuous person and the virtuous republic is that the uniqueness of the person seems to disappear into the overriding purposes of the republic.

For Aristotle, too, society is, or should be, an expression of virtue where justice gives way to friendship as the basis for social living. Social living meant living in authentic friendship and this was the natural purpose of people living in society. These social relations were essential for people to achieve their purpose, to be virtuous. Now although Aristotle affirms, in contrast to Plato, the distinctness of the individual person, Aristotle's notion of individuality is different to the modern notion of separateness. Commenting on Aristotle's term for the individual, *tode ti* (*hoc aliquid*, "this something of a certain kind"), Schmitz points out that the word "this" captures the singularity of each real and individual thing, while the "of a certain kind" indicates what it shares in common. Schmitz concludes that:

> It is upon this formal nature with its inherent sociality that Aristotle rests his *polis*. The principle of human form resident in Aristotelean individuals is, then, the very ground of community according to Aristotle. Such a nature is not, however, a mere mental abstraction for classifying or defining individual men, rather, it is the real principle for the non-restriction of the individual to his individuality. It is the real ground for the very actuality of the ontological sharing that is the root and traffic of community.[50]

This individual identity and the sense of belonging to a communion is also found in Thomas Aquinas' commentary on Aristotle's *Politics*:

> Aquinas mentions that one of the natural goods to which human beings are inclined is "to live in society." This remark presents the ideal point of departure for one of the most important teachings of Thomistic political philosophy, namely, the political nature of man. This doctrine is taken primarily from the first book of Aristotle's Politics upon which Aquinas wrote an extensive commentary (although the commentary is only completed through book 3, chapter 8 of Aristotle's Politics, Aquinas seems to have commented upon what he considered to be the Politics' theoretical core). Following "the Philosopher" Aquinas believes that political society (*civitas*) emerges from the needs and aspirations of human nature itself. Thus understood, it is not an invention of human ingenuity (as in the political teachings of modern social contract theorists) nor an artificial construction designed to make up for human nature's shortcomings. It is, rather, a prompting of nature itself that sets humans apart from all other natural creatures. To be sure, political society is not simply given by nature. It is rather something to which human beings naturally aspire and which is necessary for the full perfection of their existence.[51]

My point here is to highlight the reduced, emaciated notion of the human person that is implied in modern political liberalism. The references to Plato and Aristotle are to indicate the greater possibilities for political philosophy to broaden and deepen its vision to contribute to human flourishing in a real social bond, to contribute to authentic human society. This is not to say that the Platonic and Aristotelean forms are adequate today; philosophical personalism makes many advances on both models. Neither do I want to dismiss the value of individual freedom that modern political liberalism aims to protect. What is required is to hold in a greater unity these diverse dimensions of personhood. Michael J. Sandel, in his critique of political liberalism, refers to the relational nature of the person as one that has constitutive attachments. In reference to the relations of family, community, and nation, Sandel writes:

> Allegiances such as these are more than values I happen to have or aims I "espouse at any given time." They go beyond the obligations I voluntarily incur and the "natural duties" I owe to human beings as such. They allow that to some I owe more than justice requires or even permits, not by reason of agreements I have made but instead in virtue of those more or less enduring attachments and commitments which taken together partly define the person I am.[52]

Is the modern political form of the contractual relation of the subject with the state compatible or reconcilable with the more expansive purposes and flourishing of the person in society? Some would argue affirmatively.[53] I am less sure, precisely because the understanding of the person is so different in each case. The danger of the contractual understanding of the relation between human persons and their political society is that we depend more and more on the structures and processes of themselves to produce our human society, ignoring the fact that these structures and processes are themselves determined by the intentions, good or bad, of those who use them.

Of course, proposing the greater purposes of politics also presupposes inherent dangers. Historian Paul Johnson has noted the twentieth-century political zeal for "the engineering of society for lofty purposes" with the inevitable misery and suffering inflicted on millions of people.

> By the year 1900 politics was already replacing religion as the chief form of zealotry. To archetypes of the new class, such as Lenin, Hitler and Mao Tse-tung, politics—by which they meant the engineering of society for lofty purposes—was the one legitimate form of moral activity, the only one sure means of improving humanity. This view, which would have struck an earlier age as fantastic, even insane, became to some extent the orthodoxy everywhere: diluted in the West, in virulent form in Communist countries and much of the Third Word. At the democratic end of the spectrum, the political zealot offered New Deals, Great Societies and welfare states; at the totalitarian end, cultural revolutions; always and everywhere, Plans. These zealots marched across the decades and hemispheres: mountebanks, charismatics, *exaltés*, secular saints, mass murderers, all united by their belief that politics was the cure for human ills.[54]

Even so, as a thesis of political philosophy, politics and political activity are, I suggest, a necessary and fundamental part of personal flourishing and is not, therefore, neutral or indifferent to that flourishing, nor can the real political aspirations of persons be reduced to minimalist accounts of "the relief of man's estate."[55] Recognizing the risks and the ever-imperfect nature of our efforts, we either strive to form a political society of persons who aspire to the full range of human social expression, or we fail to live as humans—and we have enough recent historical evidence of what is less than human.

The French political philosopher Yves R. Simon adverted to the danger of separating the good of human persons from the good of the state, "two ethical systems, one of which expresses the necessary law of man and the other the no less necessary law of the state."[56] There is a misconception today of ethics as an abstract set of rules, understood as limits beyond which one may not go, and within which one can do as one pleases, something similar to the modern political self. Ethics are considered primarily as preserving freedom rather than establishing or promoting what is good. If it is true that human flourishing is the source and the purpose of all human activity, politics included, then the minimalist notion of ethics is inadequate. Simon explains it this way: "Politics would never have been construed as foreign to morality, or as conflicting with human morality, if we had not first misconceived virtue as a purely private affair. The best way to perceive the ethical character politics is to realise fully the political character of ethics."[57]

What this means is that the true flourishing of the person is to be reflected in political activity, with its processes and structures, in the measure that politics is at the service of the social destiny of man. Walsh makes the profound assertion that the central question of political organization and structure is whom we understand the human person to be:

> Our politics is inescapably politics of the person. . . . In living up to what is demanded of it, the political discloses that by which it is constituted. It shows that it answers to that which is more than the political, that which comes before it as that which it must serve. The political is led forth by what is before it exists. That is its intimation. Politics of the person is the politics of being.[58]

This is our justification for reflecting on politics with the person in mind. While politics today drives us to the reverse operation—to shape the person according to the political system and priorities—the renewal of the political vocation has its origin where politics also has its origin, the authentic personal aspirations of transcendent social destiny.

As Simpson indicates in *Political Illiberalism*, the vital impulse that should animate political thought is what Simpson terms "the drive for comprehensive truth" that forms and inspires a community. He notes that this search for comprehensive truth is only ever an attempt to reach an ideal of understanding and expression, it is never complete and conclusive. It is, Simpson proposes, probably something revealed to the human person rather than the discovery of person's own capabilities. Simpson points out that the complete vision and its accomplishment are not to be achieved in this present existence, as the great religions indicate, but are to be searched for and attempted now, to the extent possible. Even with this limitation, it is this vision of authentic community as it should be that gives the vital form to politics, and to its structures and processes.[59]

Admittedly, as Simpson writes, we do not come to the full grasp of the comprehensive vision of reality. Even so, what is essential is to strive for a unified vision of what we can know and to strive to live by that truth of reality. In politics, that means the rediscovery of the real depth and extension of human existence as the bedrock for living in political society. We need to rediscover the person of politics.

NOTES

1. Václav Havel et al., *The Power of the Powerless: Citizens Against the State in Central-Eastern Europe* (London: Routledge, 1985), 42.
2. Kenneth L. Schmitz, "Is Liberalism Good Enough?" in *The Texture of Being: Essays in First Philosophy*, ed. Paul O'Herron (Washington, DC: Catholic University of America Press, 2007), 230.
3. Marie Brenner, "Marie Colvin's Private War," *Vanity Fair*, July 18, 2012, https://www.vanityfair.com/news/politics/2012/08/marie-colvin-private-war (accessed October 12, 2023). A similar perspective is found in Richard Gunderman's article "The Cries of the Children," *Law & Liberty*, April 14, 2022, https://lawliberty.org/the-cries-of-the-children/ (accessed October 17, 2023).
4. Havel et al., *Power of the Powerless*, 42.
5. Havel et al., *Power of the Powerless*, 43. Mahatma Gandhi, speaking of his doctrine of *Satyagraha* ("The Power of Love" or "The Power of Truth"), places the intimate family relations between persons at the centre of politics. He says that *Satyagraha* "is merely an extension of the rule of domestic life to the political . . . . I feel that nations cannot be one in reality, nor can their activities be conducive to the common good of the whole humanity, unless there is this definite recognition and acceptance of the law of the family in national and international affairs, in other words, on the political platform. Nations can be called civilised, only to the extent that they obey this law" Cf. "The Doctrine of *Satyagraha* as set forth by M. K. Gandhi," in *The Collected Works of Jacques Maritain*, ed. John Hittinger and Richard Lemp (Notre Dame, IN: University of Notre Dame Press, 1996), vol. 2, 113. Gandhi's concise explanation of *Satyagraha* is found in vol. 2, 112–15.
6. [Clive Staples] C. S. Lewis, *The Screwtape Letters* (New York: HarperCollins, 2002), 207.
7. David Walsh, *The Growth of the Liberal Soul* (Columbia: University of Missouri, 1997), 107–8. In what follows of my account of the rise of state sovereignty I emphasize the growth and dominance of state power and do not refer to the growing constitutional resistance, beginning in the seventeenth century, to monarchical sovereignty. I thank Professor Walsh for this observation. At the same time, I suggest that the emerging constitutional form of sovereignty did (and does not) always avoid the dangers of absolute power.
8. Statehood, in traditional terms of international law, is described in article 1 of the Montevideo Convention on Rights and Duties of States of 1933: "(a) a permanent population; (b) a defined territory: (c) government; and (d) capacity to enter into relations with other states," as cited in Malcom N. Shaw, *International Law*, 7th ed. (Cambridge: Cambridge University Press, 2014), 144.
9. William T. Cavanaugh, "The City: Beyond Secular Parodies," in *Radical Orthodoxy: A New Theology*, ed. John Milbank, Catherine Pickstock, and Graham Ward (London: Routledge, 1999), 187. The reference is to John Milbank, *Theology and Social Theory: Beyond Secular Reason*, 2nd ed. (Malden, MA: Blackwell Publishing, 1990), 12–15. Milbank's chapter ("Political Theology and the New Science of Politics," 9–25) describes the historical appropriation of sovereign power by secular

forces, and the refashioning of societies in terms of contractual relations with the state, as well as the theological justifications for this new and radically different social construction.

10. Cavanaugh, "City," 188. The quotation is from Thomas Hobbes, *Leviathan*, ed. J. C. A. Gaskin (Oxford: Oxford University Press, 1998), the author's Introduction. As Milbank points out: "by abandoning participation in divine Being and Unity for a 'covenantal bond' between God and man, it provided a model for human interrelationships as 'contractual' ones." Milbank, *Theology and Social Theory*, 16.

11. Cavanaugh, "City," 191–92. The quotation is from Robert A. Nisbet's *The Quest for Community: A Study in the Ethics of Order and Freedom* (Washington, DC: ISI Books, 2010). Cavanaugh concludes his article by stating that the political state, far from being a neutral forum for resolving conflicts, is historically based on an "alternative soteriology."

12. Nisbet, *Quest for Community*. The book was first published in 1953 and the 2010 ISI edition is evidence of its perduring relevance.

13. Nisbet, *Quest for Community*, 1897. Nisbet regards the historical role of the state as "a process of permanent revolution," a phrase that the German jurist Otto von Gierke (1841–1921) used to describe Jean Jacques Rousseau's General Will.

14. Nisbet, *Quest for Community*, 1953.

15. Nisbet, *Quest for Community*, 2061.

16. In reference to notions of the person and the family, for example, David S. Crawford writes that the modern voluntarist notion of political freedom as the purpose of society: "remakes the person and the 'family' in the image of its voluntarist and procedural concept of justice and the basic anthropology this entails" Crawford, "Recognising the Roots of Society in the Family, Foundation of Justice," *Communio* 34, no. 3 (2007): 400.

17. William T. Cavanaugh, *Migrations of the Holy: God, State, and the Political Meaning of the Church* (Grand Rapids, MI: Eerdmans, 2011), 365.

18. Walsh points to the enduring nature of political liberalism as a sign of its true value: "The primary evidence for the continuing viability of liberal order is that, despite its deficiencies, it continues to function as the authoritative public symbolism. Politically this is evident in the remarkable stability of the liberal democracies. It is the one modern form that has endured through the vicissitudes of history and the conflicts of competition" Walsh, *Growth of the Liberal Soul*, 47. Whether, as Walsh goes on to say, "we have now reached the point where liberalism is the undisputed exemplar of political order throughout the world" is debatable.

19. Walsh, *Growth of the Liberal Soul*, 4. Walsh notes that while the political use of the term liberal is from the Spanish Liberal party of 1812, its core meaning goes back to the British Whig party at the time of the 1688 Revolution and constitutional (limited) monarchism and parliamentary system. Walsh also suggests that these seventeenth-century forms reach back to medieval constitutional and classical republican forms. (4). For a description of modern political liberalism and its historical background, see Michael J. Sandel, "Liberalism and the Primacy of Justice," introduction to *Liberalism and the Limits of Justice* (Cambridge: Cambridge University Press, 1998), 1–14.

20. Robert A. Nisbet, *Twilight of Authority* (Indianapolis: Liberty Fund, 2000), 260. In *Quest for Community*, Nisbet comments: "It was with a kind of unwonted historical wisdom that leaders of the Revolution in Paris in 1790 made the term citizen the highest of address. It connoted freedom from old authorities and absolute subjection to France *une et indivisible*" (5510).

21. Schmitz, "Is Liberalism Good Enough?" 226; emphasis in the original. There is another essay of Kenneth L. Schmitz that describes the various historical notions of political individuality: "Community: The Elusive Unity," *Review of Metaphysics* 37, no. 2 (1983): 245–64, https://www.jstor.org/stable/20128006.

22. Schmitz, "Is Liberalism Good Enough?" 228.

23. Schmitz, "Is Liberalism Good Enough?" 230.

24. Schmitz, "Is Liberalism Good Enough?" 232. The reference to procedural rules is in John Rawls's *A Theory of Justice* (Cambridge, MA: Belknap Press, 1971). Rawls says that "a legal system is a coercive order of public rules addressed to rational persons for the purpose of regulating their conduct and providing the framework for social cooperation" (235).

25. Nisbet, *Quest for Community*, 546.

26. Nisbet, *Quest for Community*, 667, 575.

27. Walter Kaufmann, ed., *Existentialism from Dostoevsky to Sartre*, rev. and expanded ed. (Harmondsworth, UK: Penguin Books, 1975), 51.

28. Paul C. Vitz and Susan M. Felch, eds., *The Self: Beyond the Postmodern Crisis* (Wilmington, DE: ISI Books, 2006), xviii.

29. E. Christian Brugger, "Interview with Paul C. Vitz: A Catholic Looks at the Past, Present and Future of Christian Psychology," *Edification: Journal of the Society for Christian Psychology* 3, no. 1 (2009): 5–19.

30. Brugger, "Interview with Paul C. Vitz," x.

31. David Walsh, *After Ideology: Recovering the Spiritual Foundations of Freedom* (San Francisco: HarperCollins, 1990),194. Walsh quotes Plato's *Republic* in this attraction of the soul toward the Good, which is "beyond being, exceeding it in dignity and power." The reference is given to Plato's *The Republic*, in *The Complete Works of Plato*, trans. Benjamin Jowett (Kirkland, WA: Latus e-Publishing, 2012. Kindle), 509b.

32. Robert Sokolowski, *Christian Faith and Human Understanding: Studies on the Eucharist, Trinity, and the Human Person* (Washington, DC: Catholic University Press, 2006), 9.

33. Robert Sokolowski, *Introduction to Phenomenology* (Cambridge: Cambridge University Press, 2000), 158–59.

34. Peter L. P. Simpson, "What's It Like To Be a Christian," *First Things*, June 1, 2004, 29, https://www.firstthings.com/article/2004/06/what-its-like-to-be-a-christian (accessed October 15, 2023). This is Simpson's comment on a quotation from Karol Wojtyla's [Pope John Paul II] *Person and Community*, in the same article: "Today more than ever before we feel the need—and also see a greater possibility—of objectifying the problem of the subjectivity of the human being . . . . we can no longer go on treating the human being exclusively as an objective being, but we must also

somehow treat the human being as a subject in the dimension in which the specifically human subjectivity of the human being is determined by consciousness" (28).

35. W. Norris Clarke, *Person and Being. The Aquinas Lecture 1993* (Milwaukee,
WI: Marquette University Press, 1993), 64–65. Clarke takes the phenomenon of
human language as evidence of the real relationality of persons in his article "Interpersonal Dialogue: Key to Realism," in *Person and Community: A Philosophical
Exploration*, ed. Robert J. Roth (Fordham University Press, 1975), 141–53.

36. Clarke, *Person and Being*, 71, 72. From the point of view of metaphysical
reflection, there have been various attempts to describe this concept of substance-as-
relation. See John S. Grabowski, "Person: Substance and Relation," *Communio* 22,
no. 1 (1995): 139–63; and W. Norris Clarke, "Person, Being, and St. Thomas," *Communio* 19, no. 4 (1992): 601–18.

37. Joseph Ratzinger [Pope Bendedict XVI], "On the Understanding of 'Person' in
Theology," in *Dogma and Preaching: Applying Christian Doctrine to Daily Life* (San
Francisco: Ignatius Press, 2012), 192, 193. Interestingly, from a Christian theological
perspective, Ratzinger sees in the total relation of the Son to the Father the origin and
expression of freedom: "The human will of Jesus enters into the will of the Son. By
doing so, it receives the identity of the Son, which consists in entire subordination of
the I to the Thou, in the giving and transferring of the I to the Thou. This is the mode
of being of the one who is pure relation and pure act. When the 'I' gives itself to the
'Thou,' freedom originates, because the 'form of God' has been assumed" Ratzinger,
Journey to Easter, Spiritual Reflections for the Lenten Season (New York: Crossroad,
1987), 103.

38. Larry Siedentop, *Inventing the Individual: The Origins of Western Liberalism*
(Cambridge, MA: Belknap Press, 2014), 8.

39. Larry Siedentop, *Democracy in Europe* (London: Penguin Books, 2011), 3346,
3403. Siedentop admits that the recognition of this historical fact has become problematic: "The pieces of our past lie scattered around us. But we seem afraid to pick
them up and assemble them. Why is that? There are at least two reasons. One is the
survival, beyond its time, of anti-clericalism in Europe. The other is a more recent
phenomenon, the development of the outlook described as 'multiculturalism' . . . In
Europe, where residual anti-clericalism and multiculturalism sometimes enter into a
marriage of convenience, matters are worse. As a result, the moral identity of Europe
has become problematic" (3346)."

40. Siedentop, *Inventing the Individual*, 13.

41. Siedentop obviously qualifies a simplified or one-dimensional or linear view of
historical development: "This book, by contrast, will take moral beliefs as seriously as
possible, by looking at a series of 'moments' when changed beliefs began to impact
on social relations over a period of nearly two millennia. That is not to say that beliefs
have been the only cause at work. The story of Western development is not simple
or unilinear. No cause has been uniquely powerful at all times. Nonetheless, it seems
to me that moral beliefs have given a clear overall 'direction' to Western history"
Siedentop, *Inventing the Individual*, 110.

42. For examples of Christian theologians' understanding of the original unity of mankind, see Henri de Lubac, *Catholicism: Christ and the Common Destiny of Man,* trans. Lancelot Sheppard (San Francisco: Ignatius Press, 1988), 25–47.

43. The enhancement of the term "person" over "individual" has been commented on by the Swiss theologian Hans Urs von Balthasar: "Jacques Maritain, and not he alone, always held to the principle, 'The individual exists for the society, but the society exists for the person.' Herein lies implicit a first decision: if one distinguishes between individual and person (and we should for the sake of clarity), then a special dignity is ascribed to the person, which the individual as such does not possess . . . . We will speak of a 'person,' however, when considering the uniqueness, the incomparability and therefore irreplaceability of the individual" Balthasar, *On the Concept of Person,* as cited in John F. Crosby, *Personalist Papers* (Washington, DC: Catholic University of America Press, 2004), 12–13.

44. Benedict XVI, *Church Fathers: From Clement of Rome to Augustine* (San Francisco: Ignatius Press, 2017), 105. The reference is to John Chrysostom's *Commentary on the Acts of the Apostles.*

45. Crosby, *Personalist Papers,* ix. Interestingly, Crosby points out that while the Greek philosophers did indeed see reason as the divine element in man, Aristotle ascribes a passive role for man in man's following of reason: "Of course, Plato and Aristotle saw reason at work in nature and in the cosmos, but here creatures only passively undergo reason, being ordered according to a rational plan; man by contrast has an essentially more intimate relation to reason. Reason is internalised in man as it is in no subhuman being, so that he is not just governed by reason but governs himself with his own reason" (6). Is "with his own appropriation of reason." more accurate?

46. Joseph Ratzinger, *A Turning Point for Europe? The Church in the Modern World: Assessment and Forecast* (San Francisco: Ignatius Press, 1991), 772. Ratzinger goes on to explain the subtle center of materialism as he sees it: "The essence of modern materialism is more subtle: it consists in the way in which the relationship between matter and spirit is conceived. Here, matter is the first and original element; it is matter, not the *Logos,* that stands at the beginning . . . . Spirit is never more than the product of matter. If one knows the laws of matter and can manipulate them, then one can also direct the course of the spirit. One changes the spirit by rearranging its material conditions. Thus one can enlarge and remodel history in a mechanical way by enlarging and remodelling structures"(786).

47. Pierre Manent, *Metamorphoses of the City: On the Western Dynamic,* trans. Marc LePain (Cambridge, MA: Harvard University Press, 2013),261.

48. Manent, *Metamorphoses of the City,* 265.

49. Nisbet, *Quest for Community,* 2796.

50. Schmitz, "Community, 250. This articles complements Schmitz's article "Is Liberalism Good Enough?" to which I have referred earlier.

51. Peter Karl Koritansky, "Thomas Aquinas: Political Philosophy." *Internet Encyclopaedia of Philosophy,* 2007, 4. https://iep.utm.edu/thomas-aquinas-political-philosophy/ (accessed October 14, 2023).

52. Sandel, *Liberalism,* 3529.

53. Political philosopher Martin Rhonheimer suggests that contractualism can be seen, not as a rejection of man's natural political being, but as a transformation of this doctrine and precisely as evidence of man's social nature: "In this sense, therefore, the doctrine of contractualism can be understood as an attempt to rearticulate and rationally justify man's political nature." Rhonheimer concludes that contractualism, while expressing a part of the truth of man, is insufficient of itself to be the basis of social and political life, and that "everything depends on the concept of individual (or human person) and freedom one uses. To think of social bonds contractualistically can mean many different things, according to the concept we have of the parties to the contract. Ultimately, an anthropological question is implicit in the question we have addressed, on which the existence or conception of a 'common good' essentially depends" Rhonheimer, *The Common Good of Constitutional Democracy*, trans. William F. Murphy Jr. (Washington, DC: Catholic University of America Press, 2013), 92, 102.

54. Paul Johnson, *Modern Times. The World from The Twenties to the Nineties* (New York: Harper Perennial, 1992), 784, within the relevant chap. 20 "The Recovery of Freedom." Johnson refers to Jean Jacques Rousseau's belief that each human beings could and would be transformed into a' new man' by the state and its power (783).

55. Francis Bacon, *The Advancement of Learning (English Edition)*, (Classics, Literature, Politics & Social Sciences), Annotated ed., KTHTK 2021, Kindle, 60.

56. Yves R. Simon, *A General Theory of Authority* (Notre Dame, IN: University of Notre Dame Press, 1980), 141.

57. Simon, *General Theory of Authority*, 141.

58. David Walsh, *Politics of the Person as the Politics of Being* (Notre Dame, IN: University of Notre Dame Press, 2016), 91, 103.

59. Peter L. P. Simpson, *Political Illiberalism: A Defence of Freedom* (London: Routledge, 2015), 83.

Chapter 3

Truth and Politics

In this overview to chapter 3, I refer to the notion of truth in politics, something problematic today. Claims to the truth seem to imply an imposition on personal freedom, which is the hallmark of the democratic form of government. For this reason, claims to truth are seen as a threat to political coexistence, where, as Richard Rorty suggests, democracy must take precedence over philosophy.

What, then, are the bases for political unity? The substitutes for a truthful comprehensive vision for society often take the form of procedural measures based on claims of equality and of fairness, and the notion of "public reason," understood as a common minimal content of agreement that precludes truth as a universal category of public application.

Another substitute for a truthful common vision is the limitation of the aspirations of human society to what is immediate, material, and can be technically produced. This pragmatic view rejects political ideals and greater human horizons, and deals with what needs to be done now, with what works and responds to our immediate and generally material needs—hence our political obsession with the economy as the measure and purpose of human society.

British political theorist Michael Oakeshott contrasts a politics of faith, understood as a politics directed by a comprehensive vision, with what he advocates as a politics of skepticism, which renounces any greater purposes and adapts at each moment to the ever-changing circumstances as best one can.

The combination of procedures and pragmatism, justified by the notion of public reason, seems to constitute the core of what we call democracy today, which, in reality, has become a form of obtaining and maintaining power rather than the attempt to construct a society that truly reflects the human person's social aspirations and destiny.

The experience of the truth of reality needs to be rediscovered as the necessary response to Being in which we are immersed. There is no detached perspective from which we can pick and choose; we are constrained to respond to the experience of reality and our common capacity to do so provides the consensus of truth essential for social living. As David Walsh states, "The very existence of the political community is dependent on the attainment of truth for only then is the public realm properly constituted."[1] Truth is brought to fullness in action, living and participating in the truth.

Our experience of truth recognizes varying modes of experience, which disclose varying dimensions and depths of existence. While today we seem to be dominated by certain narrow measurements of experience, we need to rediscover the reality of moral and religious experience of Personal Being as equally valid modes of perception. It is the real experience of Personal Being that provides the content of the consensus of truth.

And yet, the path to truth is a difficult one and requires dispositions of intellect and of action to grow in the truth, to become agents of the truth. Many social conflicts occur due, as Josef Pieper states, to the "infinitude of hidden, often barely discernible modes of shutting the doors of the mind and heart."[2] Politics is the battlefield of truth, in particular for the real affective-cognitive interpersonal experience of Personal Being that is at the center and constitutive of the social and political bond, and the common basis for political dialogue.

NEXUS

We have seen that the philosophizing disposition, as an innate human capacity that opens one to the full range of experience of reality (Being), discerns reality in the different modes of disclosure that reality has, and evokes in us a personal experience that leads us to an adequate response to reality. There is, therefore, in human experience both the perception of what is real and the personal response to that reality.

At the same time, we are, or should be, aware of the limitations of our perceptions and the conscious insufficiency of what we can know compared to what we need to know. This is important to remember as we tend to have the idea of truth as a vision that is perfect, clear in all its details, and spontaneously evident. This is not the human experience of the truth of reality, which is necessarily much more modest. Consider the experience of the Christian apologist C. S. Lewis on the death of his wife to cancer:

> Five senses; an incurably abstract intellect; a haphazardly selective memory; a set of preconceptions and assumptions so numerous that I can never examine more than a minority of them—never become even conscious of them all. How much of total reality can such an apparatus let through?[3]

It is with this reminder and warning that we approach the theme of truth and politics. The political dimension of the human person's existence implies that there is a common reality to which we are to respond collectively, not just individually. This implies that we can share, to some basic and essential degree, a common vision of what is real and what we strive for together. The purpose of this chapter is to ask whether this conviction of a common truthful vision is valid, to recognize and to understand the challenges to this common political vision, to propose how these challenges may be answered, and the importance of doing so.

TRUTH AS WE PERCEIVE IT TODAY

In my description of the relationship between the individual and the modern state, I pointed to the understanding of the human person that the modern state presupposes. Without denying the fundamental historical importance of the political recognition of the individual's freedom and rights, even so, persons are determined politically in their relation to the modern sovereign state fundamentally by their individuality and by their freedom. We have seen the main contributions to this vision of the human person as an individual in philosophical nominalism and scientific mechanism, and the primacy of the subjectivity of our experience over our experience of what is real, which leads to freedom being considered exclusively in terms of unconstrained subjective determination, where "[the subject] lends to things its own shape and takes their utility for itself to be their significance."[4] The fundamental purpose of modern politics, therefore, is "the liberty of the differential individual."[5]

Again, both individuality and freedom are essential aspects of the human person's political determination. At the same time *how* these two aspects are understood and justified is critical.

Today reference to truth in politics is problematic. This is very understandable when the relation of the huma person to political society is defined in terms of individuality and of unfettered freedom. Speaking of the popularity of the notion of freedom today, Joseph Ratzinger notes that today freedom is viewed as nothing more than freedom from all constraints, and freedom from anything that represents constraint, such as laws and obligations toward others, to society in general, or to God. What is sought for are the free and unfettered actions of individuals who have everything and do what they want. Anything that impedes this individual freedom is considered a burden and the desired goal today is for ever greater freedom from any and all constraints. Ratzinger observes that this entirely uninhibited freedom has become such an obsession that all social bonds are perceived as mere constraints and burdens, whether these are family bonds, the Church, moral requirements toward others, or even to God. As Ratzinger points out, all are considered enemies of individual freedom because they demand a response from the individual. God makes demands on human freedom, as is seen clearly in the moral demands of the Commandments. The Church and the family are the necessary contexts within which the individual is required to respond to God and to others. Ratzinger notes that even the political state is seen as repressive of individual freedom because it invokes laws to regulate human society.[6]

To speak of truth in politics, therefore, seems to be something of a lost cause, certainly not as a claim to convince others. Understanding the political context of the human person as self-enclosed and self-determining anarchical freedom—"the freedom to choose and to unchoose"[7]—claims to truth appear as the negation of man and his possibilities. Ratzinger also refers to the political and scientific abuse of the term truth as causes of current skepticism:

> In contrast [to the notion of freedom], we are inclined to react with suspicion to the concept of truth: we recall that the term truth has already been claimed for many opinions and systems, and that the assertion of truth has often been a means of suppressing freedom. In addition, natural science has nourished a scepticism with regard to everything which cannot be explained or proved by its exact methods: all such things seem in the end to be a mere subjective assignment of value which cannot pretend to be universally binding. The modern attitude toward truth is summed up most succinctly in Pilate's question, "What is truth?." Anyone who maintains that he is serving the truth by his life, speech and action must prepare himself to be classified as a dreamer or as a fanatic. For "the world beyond is closed to our gaze"; this sentence from Goethe's Faust characterizes our common sensibility today.[8]

So much so, that invoking the authority of truth is perceived today as being subject to an unreasonable passion, something similar to the wild illusion of the fanatic. Italian philosopher Flores d'Arcais claimed that John Paul II's encyclical letter *Fides et Ratio* [Faith and Reason], with its dogmatic tone, "had murderous consequences for democracy."[9]

It seems that the person who lives in the truth is considered a fanatic, the person whom Umberto Eco refers to as one suffering from "insane passion for the truth."[10]

American philosopher Richard Rorty sees no need for complex questions of truth in social or political discourse. In his comment on John Rawls' *A Theory of Justice*,[11] Rorty interprets Rawls as advocating a society of tolerated opinions according to a principle of fairness, in other words, a society where "democracy takes precedence over philosophy":

> Rawls puts democratic politics first, and philosophy second. He retains the Socratic commitment to free exchange of views without the Platonic

commitment to the possibility of universal agreement—a possibility underwritten by epistemological doctrines like Plato's Theory of Recollection or Kant's theory of the relation between pure and empirical concepts. He disengages the question of whether we ought to be tolerant and Socratic from the question of whether this strategy will lead to truth. He is content that it should lead to whatever intersubjective reflective equilibrium may be obtainable, given the contingent make-up of the subjects in question. Truth, viewed in the Platonic way, as the grasp of what Rawls calls "an order antecedent to and given to us," is simply not relevant to democratic politics. So philosophy, as the explanation of the relation between such an order and human nature, is not relevant either. When the two come into conflict, democracy takes precedence over philosophy.[12]

POLITICAL FORMS THAT DENY TRUTH

Today, therefore, a common philosophical vision of persons in society seems to find no place in politics. There is an *a priori* exclusion of the possibility of a common political truth. American political theorist Sheldon S. Wolin, in a critique of Plato's understanding of political philosophy, writes the following:

> For these reasons it is fatuous to assert, as one recent writer has, that "agreement may produce peace but it cannot produce truth." The agreement that issues from participation is not intended as a symbol of truth but as a tangible expression of that sense of belonging which forms a vital dike against the forces of anomie. In its political aspect, a community is held together not by truth but by consensus.[13]

In what way is consensus achieved if not by a fundamental appeal to truth? There are two common ways of justifying the absence of truth in politics, one which accepts that the social task is to build the greatest consensus not through the possibility of arriving at the shared experience of what may be right or good, but through procedural rules of fairness, equality, and numerical majority, that will give the greatest expression to individual freedom and opportunity for all. This understanding leaves intact and undetermined any specific notion of what may be right or good and shifts the political focus to procedural laws and regulations. In reference to what may be right or good, this way considers such notions only as relative to each individual and therefore insufficient for common agreement.

Social Consensus Based on Procedure

The Austrian jurist and political philosopher Hans Kelsen drew an association between philosophical absolutism, "the metaphysical view that there is an absolute reality, that is, a reality that exists independently of human knowledge,"[14] and political absolutism, "synonymous with despotism, dictatorship, autocracy."[15] At the same time, Kelsen sees a similar connection between philosophical relativism, described as:

> Antimetaphysical empiricism, [which] emphasizes the unintelligibility of the absolute as a sphere beyond experience. It insists upon a clear separation of reality and value, and distinguishes between propositions about reality and genuine value judgments which, in the last analysis, are not based on rational cognition of reality but on the emotional forces of human consciousness, on man's wishes and fears.[16]
>
> And democracy as the counterpart of philosophical relativism, characterised by "the state seen as a specific relation among individuals, established by a legal order—as a community of human beings constituted by this order, the national legal order."[17]

Kelsen's association of democracy and relativism seems to be generally accepted in political theories today. Given the impossibility of knowing the truth of value judgments, whether based on emotional wishes and fears, or simply because they belong to the subjective experience of the individual, or because of the supposedly contradictory nature of diverse moral and religious claims to truth, the democratic process necessarily needs to depend on procedural criteria in building a consensus.[18]

And yet Kelsen ends this essay with the representation of the conflict between absolutism and relativism as given in the Gospel of Saint John, which he calls, "one of the sublimest pieces of world literature"[19] The perspective is from Pilate's role as judge in a case of criminal law. In answer to the accused's mention of truth, Pilate responds with his "What is truth?" Kelsen proceeds: "And because he, the sceptical relativist, did not know what the truth was, the absolute truth in which this man believed, Pilate—consistently—proceeded in a democratic way by putting the decision of the case to a popular vote."[20] Kelsen concludes with the following:

> For those who believe in the son of God and king of the Jews as witness of the absolute truth, this plebiscite is certainly a strong argument against democracy. And this argument we political scientists must accept. But only under one condition: that we are as sure of our political truth, to be enforced, if necessary, with blood and tears—that we are as sure of our truth as was, of his truth, the son of God.[21]

What Kelsen is saying is that, given our inherent incapacity to ascertain truth, the democratic plebiscite, the majority vote, is the best we can do, however wrong a result the process may occasionally give. As much as we might want, we have no greater sources of certainty. This view may express well the unease we have with claims to truth, both personal and collective, and the apparent safety of not having to decide such issues ("above our pay grade"). At the same time, the case of Pilate reveals the possibility of horrendous results by democratic process.[22]

It may be obvious that Kelsen's straightforward association of philosophical absolutism with absolute forms of political power, and philosophical relativism with democracy, is too simplistic, as also his contrast of truth and uncertainty. One of the more subtle impositions of democratic relativism is what is referred to as public reason, the content and type of arguments that may be invoked in public debate. Given the assumed premise that any and all claims to truth are necessarily unknowable, all arguments must be presented only as relative values, nothing that could be true or good for all. If there were absolute truths (God, the structure of the person, the respect for human life at all stages of existence, etc.) these truths could only ever be legitimated as a relative opinion never to be imposed on all. This democratic relativism excludes *a priori* any possibility of recognizing claims of truth. This may be the origin of the phenomenon of political correctness, the imposed criterion that all truth claims, necessarily wrong, are harmful to the consensus on which the political accord depends.

In *Political Illiberalism*, Peter L. P. Simpson explains that there is in the accepted form of public reason today an *a priori* exclusion of the possibility of claims to universal truths, especially in matters of religion. What is expected today in dialogue and debate about public policy and laws is, from the outset, the necessary rejection of a view or vision of society that claims to be true or good for all. Precisely because such a view or vision may not be accepted by all, or even by a majority, therefore all such views become controversial, and they are required to abandon their claim to truth and to take their place among all other possible views and opinions and find there some sort of common ground.[23]

The major difficulty with this reasonably sounding posture is that it presupposes that truthful consensus is an *a priori* impossibility and that public human reason is necessarily contradictory, that is, that different groups can think in contradictory ways and yet are equally right and equally reasonable. What this view of public reason in fact acknowledges is the fundamental impossibility of a common good. Simpson points out that a community is formed precisely on a common vision of meaning and purpose. This essential vision will always be at the heart of the community's discernment and will determine its actions and programs in particular issues. To remove the possibility of clarifying this common vision and purpose, which public reason today requires, is to nullify the possibility of forming a genuine political community.[24]

One of the consequences of this pre-emptive denial of claims to truth is political liberalism's "neutrality" toward all visions of the human person's structure, purpose, and flourishing. What rules definitively is the freedom to choose, which thus eliminates the possibility of one claim being true, or better than another. Here the respect for freedom precludes the discussion of the possibility of the real social value of one form of living over another. For example, the *possibility* of considering the family (man and woman in a stable union) as the better social atmosphere for raising children, with public consequences for society, is reduced to the recognition of the equal respect for individual choice of lifestyle.

Such individual freedom is a fundamental good for society, but it is hard to see why its recognition should preclude the recognition of forms of social lifestyle that may benefit society better. American theologian David S. Crawford puts it this way, "Liberalism's rejection of comprehensive views of the good as a legitimate part of political discourse precludes any positive or definite statement about who the person is or what his nature is."[25]

It is not difficult to understand, therefore, why formal and procedural criteria are taken as the only possible grounds of social and political union among people who hold diverse and often contradictory comprehensive visions and values, and which are considered equally reasonable and rational. At the same time, it may also be clear that the admission of irreconcilable social visions is, as Simpson pointed out, to deny the very idea of community—and of politics.

Social Consensus Based on Practical and Material Concerns

The other way to build political consensus is by considering all political considerations to be about what is immediate, practical, on hand, and material, and reacting in the best practical way to immediate concerns and goals, leaving ideological considerations aside for the sake of what is clear and immediate and practical.

Francis Bacon's *Novum Organum* (1620) was to replace Aristotle's logical tools of philosophy with a new instrument of controlled experiment that would yield nature's laws to human uses and purposes. For Bacon, the power to transform the world lay in mechanical technology, as seen in such inventions as gunpowder, the printing press, and the magnetic compass.[26] As a professional legal inquisitor in witch trials, Bacon's imagery in describing the interrogation of nature for her secrets takes on a dramatic tone. He speaks of approaching nature "under constraint and vexed; that is to say, when by art and the hand of man she is forced out of her natural state, and squeezed and moulded" and that man must "follow and as it were hound nature in her wanderings, and you will be able, when you like, to lead and drive her after-wards to the same place again."[27]

This technical and pragmatic dominion of the powers, resources, and laws of nature gives rise to a new optimism of faith in progress and a new future kingdom of humankind. As Benedict XVI writes:

> Thus hope too, in Bacon, acquires a new form. Now it is called: faith in prog-ress. For Bacon, it is clear that the recent spate of discoveries and inventions is just the beginning; through the interplay of science and praxis, totally new discoveries will follow, a totally new world will emerge, the kingdom of man. He even put forward a vision of foreseeable inventions including the aeroplane and the submarine. As the ideology of progress developed further, joy at visible advances in human potential remained a continuing confirmation of faith in progress as such.[28]

At the core of this technological shift of mentality is the use of nature and its resources for particular purposes. Nature now becomes a type of raw material that can be used and shaped according to defined purposes. The approach is not now the apprehension of the world as given to us, but the technical transformation of nature's capacities according to human needs and desires.[29] This is what the pragmatic approach to existence means, the practi-cal fashioning of the powers and potentials of the world (and, increasingly, of personal being as well[30]) according to one's own or collective purposes and desires. Augusto Del Noce, quotes Karl Marx's second of the *Theses on Feuerbach* to explain that:

> "The question whether objective truth can be attributed to human thinking is not a question of theory but is a practical question. In practice man must prove the truth, i.e., the reality and power, the 'this-sidedness' of his thinking. The dispute over the reality or non-reality of thinking which is isolated from practice is a purely scholastic question." In other words, the truth of a philosophy is verified by the historical reality it is able to produce. Modern philosophy breaks away from scholasticism, and from whatever scholastic elements it still includes, only inasmuch as it becomes philosophy of praxis. Since the characteristic of Marxism that distinguishes it from Hegelianism is that of being a philosophy *ante factum* rather than a philosophy *post factum*—i.e., aimed at realizing a totality instead of understanding an already-realized totality—we could go as far as to regard the history of the twentieth century as a philosophical experiment, and ask ourselves whether that experiment failed or not.[31]

This pragmatic approach fits in well with anti-ideological and post-modern times as it seems to discard preconceived ideas as to how reality is and or should be and presents us with the apparent freedom of using and fashioning a world without limits or constraints.

Political pragmatism combines several elements in its outlook. The fundamental starting point is from the individual or collective freedom to make and fashion our world according to how we want and suppose it to be; the basis of collective agreement is consensus, a consensus not on what is or should be, but on the basis of common agreement as to what we want according to the freedom of each, to be decided by appeal to a formal procedure of approval, which, in a democracy, means the numerical majority of views.

Jointly with this perspective is the rejection of higher purposes or ideals as either unknowable or dependent on variant opinions that have no universal application. What is of immediate relevance is what is material, functional, and economically useful, and it is assumed that these practical issues are what matter most in forming and sustaining human society. What is also assumed is that what is really useful, what we really need, is within our power to produce or manufacture. Here we have a "technocratic society . . . a society that replaces, as its own foundation, the philosophy of being with the philosophy of doing."[32]

American professor Alex Worsnip understands pragmatism in this sense: "concern for ordinary people's well-being and an efficient socioeconomic system ('what works') ahead of highfaluting moral ideals."[33] Worsnip goes on to state that when politicians speak about being pragmatic, emphasizing that their only concern is to "make things work," they are in fact making implicit assumptions of value as to what should be done. Even so, the veneer of practicality does not permit these tacit assumptions to be recognized publicly. Worsnip concludes that ideological premises and values are surreptitiously sold to the public with the label of just making things work, doing what is obviously necessary, mere common-sense policies. Far from being a merely technical solution to immediate problems, pragmatism imports a very distinctive view of what is of value to pragmatists, what pragmatists think should be done, and what pragmatists choose to reject or ignore.[34]

In other words, the pragmatic political perspective has already predetermined for all a comprehensive truth, that the material, functional, and economically useful is all that really matters to the common good, and that these practical goods can be technically produced and made to function mechanically. This surreptitious comprehensive "truth" is what Italian philosopher Del Noce calls "the latent metaphysics within contemporary politics."[35] This is so much the case today, according to Del Noce, that the justification of political programs and policies is precisely in their denial of ideological elements and their belief in the practical construction of a better material world with the raw materials at our disposal. This resulting denial of any possible claims to comprehensive truth is identified by Del Noce as nihilism and is the consequence of the experience of the proponents of failed revolution, "it is the result of the revolution: of its success in demolishing the old values and of its failure to build new values."[36] What has remained is the belief in the human person's ability to change and fashion matter, disconnected from the idealistic dreams of a classless equal society and universal brotherhood. This pragmatic sense of post-revolutionary nihilism is similar to exaggerated Western forms of belief in material production and profit as the horizon of the good and happy society, something that Ratzinger has noted that is:

> The real essence of materialism, which does not just consist of the denial of one sphere of reality but is at bottom an anthropological program that is necessarily connected with a certain idea about the interrelations among the individual spheres of reality. The claim that mind or spirit is not the origin of matter but only a product of material developments corresponds to the notion that morality is produced by the economy (instead of the economy being shaped, ultimately, by fundamental human decisions).[37]

Del Noce asks a question of this pragmatic approach to politics, that trusts that "the truth of a philosophy is verified by the historical reality it is able to produce." He suggests: "we could go so far as to regard the history of the twentieth century as a philosophical_experiment and ask ourselves whether that experiment failed or not."[38]

Political pragmatism, therefore, is based on the notion of a nihilistic view of all claims to comprehensive truth; what is left is the capacity to harness matter to our needs and wants and the belief that our means of production, including our political society's produced structures, are sufficient to answer the aspirations of human persons in society. American political philosopher Charles N. R. McCoy draws this conclusion:

> Speaking broadly, but nonetheless accurately, totalitarianism, modern liberalism, and modern conservatism all have their roots in the reversal of the relation between man and nature; all of them, if in quite different ways, attribute to social processes the kind of intelligence that lurks in the kind of stupidity that defines nature in its pure autonomy as a substitute intelligence.[39]

The basic ingredients of our political landscape are a combination of this nihilistic rejection of the possibility of an accessible comprehensive truth of human persons and their social destiny that is disguised in the appearance of humble pragmatism, together with a gloss of equality and fairness produced by procedural and functional rules that purport to legitimize and justify the absence of any substantive and real common good.

A MODEST MODERN PROPOSAL

The English philosopher and political theorist Michael Oakeshott, in his attempt to understand the politics of the modern state, identified an historical polarity between, on the one hand, all political attempts to make or change society by ideological or technical means, what he would term "a politics of faith," and, on the other hand, a minimalist approach to political power that would allow for only the minimum use of government power, what he called a "politics of scepticism."[40] This perspective is based on the view that:

> The radical belief that human perfection is an illusion, or in the less radical belief that we know too little about the conditions of human perfection for it to be wise to concentrate our energies in a single direction by associating its pursuit with the activity of governing . . . to pursue perfection in one direction only (and particularly to pursue it as the crow flies, regardless of what there may be to do in the interval before we embrace it) is to invite disappointment and (what might be worse than the mortification of non-arrival) misery on the way.[41]

Oakeshott judged the development of politics over the last five centuries in terms of the tension between these two poles, with the pole of overreaching ideology predominating over the pole of skeptical limitation, and the present need of the trimmer's role to reassert a healthy politics of skepticism to keep in check the politics of faith:

> In political activity, then, men sail a boundless and bottomless sea; there is neither harbour for shelter nor floor for anchorage, neither starting-place nor appointed destination. The enterprise is to keep afloat on an even keel; the sea is both friend and enemy; and the seamanship consists in using the resources of a traditional manner of behaviour in order to make a friend of every hostile occasion.[42]

What, then, for Oakeshott, is the role of political authority? The modern state, what Oakeshott identifies as a *societas*, has a minimal, procedural role, it does not have a *telos*. Government is to keep the rules in place, and not to determine ends and purposes: "His office is to keep the conversation going, not to determine what is said."[43]

There is much wisdom in Oakeshott's political view, particularly in his distinction between the voluntary associations with freely chosen substantive purposes, and the type of public organism that the state should be. Interestingly, Walsh points out that Oakeshott observed this confusion of roles in the modern nation-state. Walsh observes that Oakeshott recognized this confusion in the development of the modern state that instead of maintaining for itself a minimal role of government, an arrangement that provides a basic framework of coexistence, made itself the primary and paramount purpose of human society.[44]

Thus, admitting the practical wisdom in Oakeshott's view, one can also ask if indeed the path of politics is to be determined between ideological exaggeration and reactionary skepticism, and if truth in politics is only a question of keeping a balance between these two extremes of presumptuous knowledge and accepted skepticism. Is it possible to accept a vision of truth that does not require one pole or the other? One can also ask if this minimalist role of political government is sufficient to support man's fundamental social and political aspirations. It is clear that political government is not nearly the fulness of human society, and it is also true that, in the modern era, the politics of faith in the form of vastly destructive political ideologies has been all too evident. At the same time, it may be possible to realign in a more proper way political authority and substantive human purposes. Political structures and processes themselves may also depend on a more substantive conviction than procedural observance.

The modern approaches to politics that seem to solve conflictive issues by simplifying the approach and eliminating more difficult, substantive issues, may in fact not solve our social issues, but just evade what precisely our political institutions and structures are for; the resolution of what are precisely the difficult, substantive issues of what constitutes social and political life.

The overriding emphasis today on political structures seen in terms of procedures and pragmatism as to means and goals reveals a fundamental shift in understanding of political life. The common truth and good of social reality to which varying political forms aspire to has given way to projects of political power and the means to obtain and perpetuate such power. As American political philosopher Francis Slade states:

The modern version of political philosophy abandons the perspective of actual political life, the contention about who should rule in the city, which is implicitly the question of the best city (Prince 15). It steps back from that, it steps back toward possibility, toward what takes its origin from within our minds, that is, toward potential (power), toward what I can bring about, that is, toward effectivity. This is the movement from end to ideal, or projected possibility, for the ideal is a projection of a form whose origin is within our own power to effect. The state is such an ideal. Detached from ends, ideal forms, forms that take their origin from thought, lack the end's "gravitational pull." Ideal forms "push," they do not "pull." Ideal forms, because they exist only as posited by thought, manifest thought's power to realize itself. From contemplation philosophy turns to action.[45]

It is not surprising that today truth and politics seem so foreign to each other, and we are at risk of substituting one form of dominant power with another, as John Paul II proposes:

> Today, when many countries have seen the fall of ideologies which bound politics to a totalitarian conception of the world—Marxism being the foremost of these—there is no less grave a danger that the fundamental rights of the human person will be denied and that the religious yearnings which arise in the heart of every human being will be absorbed once again into politics. This is the risk of an alliance between democracy and ethical relativism, which would remove any sure moral reference point from political and social life, and on a deeper level make the acknowledgement of truth impossible. Indeed, "if there is no ultimate truth to guide and direct political activity, then ideas and convictions can easily be manipulated for reasons of power. As history demonstrates, a democracy without values easily turns into open or thinly disguised totalitarianism."[46]

It is interesting to note that the benign appearance of the democratic form of government can be equally totalitarian in its abuse of power, if there is no ultimate truth to guide and direct political activity. Dictatorial power is the consequence of the suffocation of truth in politics, as Eric Voegelin declares: "This repression of the authoritative source of order in the soul is the cause of the bleak atrocity of totalitarian governments in their dealings with individual human beings."[47]

Hanna Arendt writes in a similar vein, "The ideal subject of totalitarian rule is not the convinced Nazi or the convinced Communist, but people for whom the distinction between fact and fiction (i.e., the reality of experience) and the distinction between true and false (i.e., the standards of thought) no longer exist."[48]

In this critique of political forms and structures, I do not mean to take lightly the deeper political concern for toleration, or not to value the need for sound and sufficient political structures, but rather to maintain that the exclusive emphasis on procedures, as often occurs today, is inadequate as a basis or foundation of political society.

LIVING IN THE TRUTH OF REALITY

The predominant mentalities that reign in politics today may well have little or nothing to do with truth. We have seen how claims to comprehensive visions of truth are met with skepticism, with denial of their possibility, and with the belief that it is the power of praxis that produces desired effects. In summary, it seems that what we base our social calculations on is the visible certainty of material facts and the untrammeled use of subjective freedom.

These seem to be ways of avoiding the question of the truth of reality. The facts of science can be viewed in a detached and remote way and unfettered freedom makes no claim on citizens of responsibility or correspondence. And yet, in something like the atmosphere of a phony war—that time between the declaration of war and the reality of combat—we find ourselves living on assumptions that are hardly adequate for human existence and that do not correspond to the real circumstances of our existence. Let us try to describe better the pre-conditions of our social and political life.

We Are Immersed in Being

The illusion that we look from within some protected space, in a detached way, out onto a remote reality, is one that may have its origin in historical empirical, scientific methods. We have already commented on the supposed criterion of the separation of the object from the subject as the hallmark of what is real. This contains a false notion that we are detached from our circumstances and from what is outside our consciousness, living within an impervious freedom to choose and to *unchoose* from what is remote and detached from us. Robert Sokolowski describes this illusion of detachment in this way:

> In the Cartesian, Hobbesian, and Lockean traditions, which dominate our culture, we are told that when we are conscious, we are primarily aware of ourselves or our own ideas. Consciousness is taken to be like a bubble or an enclosed cabinet; the mind comes in a box. . . . We get to things only by reasoning from our mental impressions, not by having them presented to us. Our consciousness, first and foremost, is not "of" anything at all. Rather, we are caught in what has been called an "egocentric predicament"; all we can really be sure of at the start is our own conscious existence and the states of that consciousness.[49]

The difficulty with this widespread view, as with the political expressions of the equality of all opinions and the so-called neutral stance toward any partial or comprehensive vision of truth, is that real social bonds, on which politics depends, are made impossible due to the mutual incomprehension of "subjective ideas." The language of real relation, truth, understood as the common apprehension of reality, is formally excluded from politics. In its place come the subterfuges of consensus, dialogue, and tolerance of all opinions, all of which take on a gloss of high-sounding meaning and value that, in the context in which the words are used, they do not contain. Consensus, dialogue, and the tolerance of opinions un-sustained by a common conviction of the possibility of common truth, are merely coverings for the power struggle of conflicting interests.

Men are capable of reciprocal comprehension because, far from being wholly separate islands of being, they communicate in the same truth. The greater their inner contact with the one reality which unites them, namely, the truth, the greater their capacity to meet on common ground. Dialogue without this interior obedient listening to the truth would be nothing more than a discussion among the deaf.[50]

The political charade can only go on for so long; sooner or later all these words translate into tyranny.[51]

Walsh claims that politics is the battlefield of truth, so much so that if there is not common truth there is no real political society:

The very existence of the political community is dependent on the attainment of truth for only then is the public realm properly constituted. Not only is consent evoked in the arrival at truth, but also there is nothing to which consent can be given if it is not the common acknowledgment of truth. The public and truth are synonymous when the alternative is the assertion of the private under the guise of the public. Only truth can constitute a public realm. But it cannot impose itself upon the community, for it must arise through the dialogic process by which truth ever emerges. The city in speech is none other than the city in truth. Just as there can be no dialogue unless it centers on the emergence of truth so there can be no city unless the event of truth is the ground of authority. Mere assertion of private perspectives does not frame a dialogue, just as the exercise of power without authority does not make a city.[52]

In *The Growth of the Liberal Soul*,[53] Walsh makes the case that there are fundamental issues in society about which we cannot agree to disagree—that possibility is excluded. He takes the case of abortion. Here the issue is either the acceptance or the refusal to take innocent human life. One cannot really hold the view that for me this may be wrong but for others it may be right or acceptable. Any public provision to legislate for abortion requires everyone at least to accept that this practice is tolerable in certain circumstances, for others, etc. This means excluding the view that abortion is a moral wrong, and this public provision imposes on all one view over another. What this makes clear is that, on a basic issue of social bonding such as the respect for life, we are obliged to choose between opposite and contrary positions—there is no middle ground where the clash of views can be avoided, ignored, or tolerated. The discernment of the truth of the matter is the only valid and possible answer.[54]

Common human experience points to a different relation between human persons and their circumstances and in society with others. The consciousness of self is not the original experience of anyone; rather, it is a consequence of our pre-existing experience of reality, of being immersed in a world to which we are drawn, and which serves to help us discover our own being and identity in, for, and from the world of which we are part. It is in this experience of all Being that surrounds us, including other persons, that we can discover the common ground of existence of all there is and of ourselves as well. It is this experience of the relatedness of our common being as persons that is the source of our social existence and aspirations, and our starting point as persons immersed in reality. W. Norris Clarke explains in this way the origin of our interpersonal experience:

> The self-consciousness of a human person, then, does not start off in full, luminous self-presence. It begins rather in a kind of darkness, a state of being in potency toward knowing all beings, in act toward none. To actualize itself it must first open itself to the world of others, be waked up by their action on it and its own active response. Only then, through the mediation of the other, can it return fully to itself . . . to discover itself as this unique person. And this process can come to fruition only by actively engaging in interpersonal relations with other human persons like me, who treat me as a Thou in an interpersonalist social matrix of I-Thou-We that constitutes the human community. Animals are incapable of this total return to self to become self-conscious. Hence they cannot be persons; they cannot say "I."[55]

What is fundamental here is our original experience of being immersed in Being, including, most importantly, the reality of other human persons. It is this common experience of Being, of reality, that forms and shapes us and that gives us social understanding and recognition of ourselves and others, and what that social relation is and should be. We respond to reality; when we do this rightly, when we respond to how reality is, then we respond truthfully. This language of truth is the precondition of politics. Whatever our culture, our personal education, our conditions of life contribute—and they can and should contribute much—they are not what constitute the bedrock of our original experience of reality. This foundational experience is of reality, as Being structured or ordered in ways that we can discover. This is what is given and to what (and to whom) we respond:

> The only knowledge of order available to us is through our participation within it. . . . No starting point exists outside of an awareness of order, however inchoate or inarticulate. When we first become conscious of questions of right and wrong, our awareness is already structured by some sense of the differences between them and of the direction in which our obligations lie.[56]

This is why no bystander attitude to truth is ever sufficient; it is only by the living openness to Being that we can experience the compelling reality and goodness of Being, which is the experiential foundation of conceptual moral and religious formulations of truth:

> It is not enough to assert the rightness of one's principles. Their rightness must be grasped as an overwhelming truth within the experiential movement toward transcendent reality. . . . The criterion of right order and the formation of the will that enables us to carry it out, is not the result of a train of discursive reasoning. Rather it is the concrete movement of the soul toward the ineffable divine reality that sheds light over the whole of our existence. Aristotle refers to it in the Nicomachean Ethics as the process of "immortalizing," athanatizein (1177b33). Voegelin stresses the centrality of this "ontological" conception of ethics, if we wish to understand the classic understanding of "right by nature." For classical ethics is never about general propositions or formulas. Whenever there is a question of the rightness or wrongness of action, the appeal is always made to the experience of the *spoudaios*, the mature man, who contains the authoritative measure within his divinely informed soul. . . . It is the experience of touching or participating in divine reality that is the self-justifying end of all existence.[57]

To repropose the truth of politics is to assert that the experiential movement toward transcendent reality is a universal and vital human experience and one that, at the same time, requires the innate desire for such experience and its free acceptance. This *originary* experience, as David L. Schindler calls it, "implies engagement of the whole of our being with the whole of reality, with God at its center," and therefore in discovering "the ontological implications of the givenness of things as originally experienced."[58]

This bedrock of experience of reality also provides the context for the freedom of our response. Given this experience of order, our adequate response to reality is required of us freely; it is a freedom for an adequate response, not just a freedom from constraint. The illusion of *unchoosing* reality is not ours and never was; neither are we free *not* to choose; we are destined, required to respond—freely. Not to choose is to choose an alternative.

Truth, as the adequate response to Being, is therefore a life-sustaining disposition, both for each person's own identity and for the life of society. As existing persons, we are either only for or against the truth of Being. The social and political life of persons either reflects truly human forms of existence, and thus causes human life to flourish, or militates against human life and contributes to inhuman forms of oppression and tyranny. The love of this truth of social Being is the fundamental disposition for political life, and forms part of "the love of being through love of divine Being as the source of its order."[59]

The Modes of the Truth of Being

I have already made reference to the multifarious voices of the being of reality.[60] What this refers to is the complex and varied ways reality reveals itself to us, which requires of us multiple modes of perception of reality. I have also drawn attention to contemporary personalism, understood as the specific and unique mode of the revelation of personal being, distinct among a more cosmological metaphysis of being. This attention to the experience of the unique being of the person opens up the recognition of categories of being and order that are real and unique to the category of personal being. The descriptive experience of interpersonal relation reveals categories of love, friendship, dignity, and communion that are the personal bedrock of society and politics. These experiences reveal the quality of being of the person, each person, not only what and who each person is, but also what is owed to each as personal beings. This is both active, in the sense of eliciting from us persons the adequate response of affirmative love, and passive, in the sense of requiring for ourselves the same dispositions as we experience toward others. What is important to note here is that this fundamental interpersonal experience is much more than the notion of equality or even justice but involves the desired affirming of each person in each person's totality and uniqueness. We are not expressing here some condition of celestial harmony, but the fundamental social need and condition of growth of persons.

In various ways, this original experience of personal being does not seem to find recognition as a practical point of departure for modern politics. On the one hand, the contractual relation of the individual with the state frames the relation with society in terms of a legal contract entered into for one's own purposes and interests. Relations with others become to be seen more and more from a contractual perspective, as the form of individual protection of one's rights and concerns.

On the other hand, the domination of scientific forms of knowledge, and the industrial and technological revolutions of human society, with their exactness, their predictability, and the power they yield, have privileged one mode of perception of reality over other equally valid and perhaps more vital experiences. The distinction and separation of "facts" and "values" is based on a perspective of reality that privileges a material perception and domination of reality while dismissing as "subjective," incommensurate, and therefore unreliable, other factual perceptions that depend on other modes of perception. This predominant one-dimensional view of reality also contributes to the *a priori* rejection of a political comprehensive vision of social and political life, reducing the perception of social communion to merely material and inanimate concerns.

I have spoken of social and political nihilism, in the sense of this denial of the possibility of greater social and political meaning for our lives. Certainly, claims to comprehensive truth can be dangerously wrong, and there are many ways of being mistaken, of associating one's own experience with the totality of reality, of ignoring the condition of freedom as the basis of human decisions and actions. There is also the difficult recognition of the inherent limitation of our human experience, of what we want to know but which goes beyond the limited human capacity to know. One tendency can be either to take as total a necessarily partial experience of reality, and to explain all social and political phenomena in terms of one, perhaps valid, insight. Most ideologies seem to take this path; right in what they affirm, wrong in omitting what they do not recognize.

The other tendency is the skepticism that refuses to accept any claim to truth because of the very partial and deficient condition of our knowing.[61] This difficulty is real and can be in the form of judging one experience of reality in terms of another mode of experience, of demanding a degree of precision, measurement and clarity that is not given to us to have, and therefore disqualifying other modes of experience. Alfred North Whitehead, the American mathematician, who co-wrote *Principia Mathematica* with Bertrand Russell, gave his last lecture in 1941 on the theme of immortality. The final words of the lecture were the following: "My point is that the final outlook of Philosophic thought cannot be based upon the exact statements which form the basis of special sciences. The exactness is a fake."[62]

Our experience of reality is, then, perceived by us in different ways or modes of disclosure and also, therefore, to differing measures and degrees of certainty. When we move beyond the subterfuges of denying our experience of the truth of reality by "relativism" or "subjectivity," there is much to be done to come to recognize these various modes of disclosure of our experience. Instrumental reason also does not emphasize this apprehension of experience but imposes itself on reality as if the being of reality were nothing more than raw material to be reconfigured for whatever use we have for it. Yale philosopher John E. Smith has noticed this impoverished and instrumental sense of human experience:

> More often than not, experience has not been consulted for what it actually does disclose; instead, it has been used merely to illustrate foregone conclusions about what it must reveal if it is to meet the requirements of some rationalist program. Experience has suffered not only from the stigma of being subjective in the sense of being unreliable as a guide or standard, but it has been hedged in by various types of *a priori* demands. Concentration upon language, upon the forms of expression, upon experience only after it has been well formed and articulated has frequently had the effect of filtering out of the rich

content of primary experience only what can be expressed in some conventional language.[63]

The exclusive insistence and reliance on only certain types of experience, usually the mathematical and the empirical, for certain purposes, has thus deformed human reason by defining truth and knowledge primarily in terms of these sciences and thereby excluding other experiences that do not conform to the same criteria of observation and exactitude. Everything else is "relative to the subject" and therefore of no common foundation.

Ratzinger, in words spoken at the German Bundestag in Berlin, referred to the insufficiency of this positivist perspective as a foundation of human culture, and consequently, of political activity. The speech is significantly titled *The Listening Heart—Reflections on the Foundations of Law* and he says:

> In its self-proclaimed exclusivity, the positivist reason which recognizes nothing beyond mere functionality resembles a concrete bunker with no windows, in which we ourselves provide lighting and atmospheric conditions, being no longer willing to obtain either from God's wide world. And yet we cannot hide from ourselves the fact that even in this artificial world, we are still covertly drawing upon God's raw materials, which we refashion into our own products. The windows must be flung open again, we must see the wide world, the sky and the earth once more and learn to make proper use of all this.[64]

At the center of our politics of skepticism is the basic need to recognize again the full depth and extension of our human experience and to rediscover dimensions of reality that are fundamental for human political society, categories of truth such as friendship, love, communion, and religious experience, as constitutive of personal political reality.[65]

This rediscovery of experience holds also for the unique religious experience of God as ultimate and foundational reality. The impoverishment of experience today makes the truth of religious experience entirely irrelevant to the social bond, if not a threat to its existence. This, of course, generates a great social problem as the possibility of a comprehensive religious truth is denied in a society that proclaims and imposes the equality of all views and opinions. It is understandable that religious truth should be seen as an undue imposition when religious experience is no longer recognized or valued for what it is:

> God is absent, not because he has absconded, but because we can no longer conceive of how he might make himself known. The way to the transcendent seems irrevocably blocked when the inward has shrunk to the subjective. Even while yielding to the abundance of experience we have become incapable of

perceiving its reality. God continues to be heard in a secular age; the difficulty is that he can no longer be recognised.[66]

The mention of the Absolute Being, of God, and the many names and experiences by which God may be perceived, strikes us today as something foreign to reason—and yet vast numbers of people claim that the experience of God is something real in their lives. We may ask why this is so, why a particular mode of human experience has been excluded or disqualified from our categories of experience of reality. As Yale historian Louis Dupré remarked: "Only its origin in experience makes the idea of God worthy of being logically explored."[67]

The Difficult Path to Truth

One of our misconceptions today is that the experience of truth should be something facile and obvious, similar to reading a label on a bottle. This is due to the narrow categories of what we think the experience of truth to be, which, in turn, ignores the necessary subjective condition and response to the experience of truth for us to know the truth, "to hope to be in the truth."[68] There are, of course, natural human limitations inherent in our perspective of truth; we glimpse truth from one perspective, we can experience what we do not or cannot know, and our expression of truth in language contains its own limitations and boundaries.[69] Truth needs to be enhanced in dialogue; we depend on the varying human capacities to perceive and interpret varying human experiences—we do not all have equal powers of perception and interpretation. For these reasons, our experience of truth is one of entering into what goes infinitely beyond us because "'To be in the truth,' however, also means that the truth is always unattainably greater and more comprehensive, that it lies beyond me and that I can never hope to exhaust it. I am in the truth, the truth is not (simply) in me."[70]

Apart from these inherent limitations to our knowledge of truth, there are the subjective obstacles and difficulties, impediments within ourselves, as we recognize that we are immersed in reality and as we open ourselves to the full range of our human experience. The Aristotelean principle "*qualis unusquisque est, talis finis videtur ei*" (as each one is, so the end—purpose—seems to him) requires us to examine our own dispositions toward the openness and acceptance of what we experience.[71]

The 1997 remake of the film *Twelve Angry Men* portrays the struggle of a jury to agree on a verdict for a young Latino on trial for his life, accused of murdering his father. What becomes quickly evident is that none of the twelve jurors approach the case as a neutral, objective bystander. Each of the jurors, in different ways, is predisposed by his own outlook, past experiences, other concerns or priorities, the opinion of others, religious fanaticism, or by mistaken or unseen empirical facts. Ironically, the juror whose view finally prevails is the one who is uncertain and raises (in dialogue with the other jurors) a case for reasonable doubt. One by one the jurors recognize their own predispositions that did not let them see and judge correctly what, at first, appeared clear and obvious ("the boy's guilty"). Ironically, too, the juror who finally raises sufficient doubt is the oldest and weakest of the group, who has difficulty making his voice heard.

American philosopher James V. Schall suggests that the conflicting confusion of facts, theories, and views on even very basic issues has more to do with how we are than with the complexities of issues:

> I am concerned with something that I found in Aristotle, among other places. It is not directly a problem of epistemology or even metaphysics, but rather of morals, of choice. Indeed, I often think that, for most people, thinkers included, the epistemological and metaphysical theory comes from the morals, not vice versa. I think that most of such intellectual aberrations are consequences of an effort to defend what one does or chooses to do. They are not directly from perplexity about objectivity understanding what is.[72]

What becomes clear is that the capacity to experience and enter into truth is a much more difficult process than we assume and that our openness and acceptance of experience involves much more than the simple apprehension of apparently obvious facts. Even the apprehension of empirical facts can be easily mistaken by our own preconceived notions of what should be there or what we would want to be there.[73]

Small actions of living in the truth also have the effect of broadening our intellectual horizon to seeing and recognizing the values of truth and goodness that before were not seen or appreciated or were even denied. Truthful actions that are the adequate response to the experience of reality cause us to comprehend in a greater way—and the knowledge of truth is only completed in the action of truth.

> Being is never in the idea separated from action; and metaphysics itself, considered first under its speculative aspect, is true then only inasmuch as, like a rung in the system of phenomena, it enters into the general dynamism of life. Action grounds the reality of the ideal and moral order; it contains the real presence of what, without it, knowledge can simply represent, but of what, with it and through it, is vivifying truth.[74]

For this reason, our moral and religious perceptions are not merely spontaneous reactions to experience but depend on and increase to the degree in which we live in truth. In *The Growth of the Liberal Soul*, Walsh insists that

it is only be attempting to live rightly that we can grow in our judgment of
what right living entails. He makes an eloquent reference to the resources of
moral strength that were shown by those who opposed the holocaust and the
tyranny of oppressive government. It is impressive to recognize the depths of
our moral values in those persons who, in circumstances beyond their choosing, displayed heroic virtue and wanted to respond freely and nobly to the
extreme demands of moral goodness. This shows us that, as Walsh notes, it is
by commitment to action that we discover our growth in the moral experience
of what is right and good.[75]

A cursory glance at recent social history shows just how partial and
weak our perception of some great moral truths can be, truths unanimously
accepted today that, a hundred years ago, were largely unseen and tranquilly
ignored. Today, there are issues that are fundamental to the social bond and
on which there is profound disagreement. Differences on some of these issues
can no doubt be explained by unresolved rational or scientific investigation;
other differences can only be explained, not on rational grounds, but by morally inadequate dispositions, motives of power, economic advantage, perverse
motives that may prevail from time to time, even in subconscious ways.

Clearly, there is much more to human perception than the facts and data
we are accustomed. There is also much more that needs to be cultivated in
the person so that a truly moral and religious human response can be given
to interpersonal experience. There is much more to the human person's
receptivity and response to reality than the remote and detached registra-
tion of facts. The ultimate source of human receptivity and response is the
heart and the receiving and giving of the experience of personal being.
Unconditional affirmation, human and divine, of one's personal being is the
foundational experience on which one's response relies. It is only through this
received experience of unconditioned love that one receives the security of
self-affirmation that releases in freedom the powers of the heart to apprehend
experience and respond in a personal way to reality.[76]

It is this affective-cognitive experience of personal being, both (firstly)
received and (consequently) given, that provides the essential background
for the human apprehension and response to reality. What is important to
realize is that the affective experience of personal being, both as received
and as given, is also a cognitive experience of the intellect, an experience of
real being (and of the Real Being, God), an essential aspect of personal cognition.[77] Its cognitive absence jeopardizes the adequate moral and religious
response to personal being. French theologian Jean Mouroux recognizes that:

> The knowledge of a spiritual person is not discursive; consciousness cannot
> be constructed from the outside; a person does not come upon himself at the
> end of a series of abstract relations. The discursive function of the intellect can

certainly prepare for, but cannot accomplish this grasping of a concrete existence. It cannot bring about this phenomenon of interpretation *en bloc* which is the discovery of a person similar to the "self," still less can it enter into the privacy of this spiritual person who is both unique and "social."[78]

Clearly, in this view, our common understanding of intellect means much more than the assimilation of data and facts, or even rational discourse, as important as are these capacities. The capacity for the affective apprehension and response to personal being is at the center of the human person's *intellectus* and corresponds more to the notion of heart than our modern terms such as mind or brain.[79]

Sokolowski, in *Christian Faith and Human Understanding: Studies on the Eucharist, Trinity, and the Human Person*,[80] commenting on German philosopher Robert Spaemann's account of the heart as the "unfounded foundation" of the human person, writes that the "unfounded foundation" of the human heart is not merely some vital urge or instinct, such as appears in the writings of Friedrich Nietzsche, but includes our instinctive acceptance or rejection of the truth of things and persons, which is what determines whether or not we become the persons we are. In this sense, there is a free and responsible choice that we need to make, to be open to and to accept the reality of things and persons as they disclose themselves to us, or not to do so. This is so because the heart chooses what it wants to perceive and accept or what it wants to refuse and deny. Whether we are truthful persons depends on our free and responsible decision for or against the light of the truth of reality. Clearly, this is a fundamental and free moral act that determines the use of our reason and will: "It underlies both reason and will; it is not one act of the will among many. It establishes us as agents of truth."[81]

This may be seen in the great moral conflicts of our time, and of anytime. The fundamental problem may indeed have a logical expression and a reasoned answer; on a practical level, the difficulty is one of perception, not "seeing the form" (as Hans Urs von Balthasar calls it), not perceiving the attraction of the real adequacy of one way over another. Some of the great moral issues such as slavery, apartheid, racial discrimination, the trafficking of human persons, are not, I suggest, problems of rationality (although they have consequences for the proper functioning of our rationality); the fundamental problem is the collective "not seeing" (experiencing), consciously or subconsciously, the real goodness of the other, for whatever innate or cultural, historical, or economic justifications. As Pieper reminds us: "there is an infinitude of hidden, often barely discernible modes of shutting the doors of the mind and heart."[82]

American Aristotelean philosopher Kurt Pritzl noticed this personal affective-cognitive apprehension of truth in his own experience of helping in a pro-life pregnancy center. The welcoming and caring atmosphere toward women who were many times frightened and alone was conducive to the openness to truth:

> Most conversations began with justifications for abortion in the circumstances, justifications that included downplaying the human status of what was growing within them, and ended with acknowledgements of what these women knew deep inside, that they were proposing to take the lives of their babies. The dynamic of partial and obscure truths giving way to some clarity of truth was, to my mind, indisputable. It is a dynamic different from asserting propositions, however clearly true.[83]

To claim to be in the truth is a daring affirmation, one that requires, at least, the inner central experience of the love of personal being. Truth has many caricatures that are a disservice to the true depths of human cognition, as they misrepresent, often in miserly terms, the splendor that the experience of real interpersonal being.[84] At the same time, the real affective-cognitive interpersonal experience is at the center of our social and political bond and is the common basis for political dialogue.

St. Augustine wrote: "It seems to me that the hope of finding the truth must be restored to mankind."[85] Finding truth is not a luxury pastime but a vital political capacity and necessity that is required to replace the false compromises and empty agreements of those who would deny the possibility of a true and comprehensive vision of political society. What Ratzinger writes about the need for meaning—the truth of reality—applies, of course, not only to each person's striving for personal meaning as an agent of truth, but also to the collective need for meaning, without which social and political life become inoperable:

> For in fact man does not live on the bread of practicability alone; he lives as man and, precisely in the intrinsically human part of his being, on the word, on love, on meaning. Meaning is the bread on which man, in the intrinsically human part of his being, subsists. Without the word, without meaning, without love he falls into the situation of no longer being able to live, even when earthly comfort is present in abundance. Everyone knows how sharply this situation of "not being able to go on any more" can arise in the midst of outward abundance. But meaning is not derived from knowledge. To try to manufacture it in this way, that is, out of the provable knowledge of what can be made, would resemble Baron Munchhausen's absurd attempt to pull himself up out of the bog by his own hair. I believe that the absurdity of this story mirrors very accurately the basic situation of man. No one can pull himself up out of the bog of uncertainty, of not being able to live, by his own exertions; nor can we pull ourselves up, as Descartes still thought we could, by a *cogito ergo sum*, by a series of intellectual deductions. Meaning that is self-made is in the last analysis no meaning.

Meaning, that is, the ground on which our existence as a totality can stand and live, cannot be made but only received.[86]

NOTES

1. David Walsh, *Politics of the Person as the Politics of Being* (Notre Dame, IN: University of Notre Dame Press, 2016), 4201.
2. Josef Pieper, *Faith, Hope, Love* (San Francisco: Ignatius Press, 1977), 64. Pieper on the same page quotes Pascal's dictum: "If you do not take the trouble to know the truth, there is enough truth at hand so that you can live in peace. But if you crave it with all your heart, then it is not enough to know it." Pieper mentions a spiritual root of this turning away from reality, *acedia*, a deliberate denial of the true capacity and calling of human nature (117).
3. C. S. [Clive Staples] Lewis, *A Grief Observed* (New York: HarperCollins, 2001), 64.
4. Kenneth L. Schmitz, *The Texture of Being: Essays in First Philosophy*, ed. Paul O'Herron (Washington, DC: Catholic University of America Press, 2007), 230.
5. Schmitz, *Texture of Being*, 232.
6. Joseph Ratzinger [Pope Benedict XVI], "Freedom and Liberation," in *Church, Ecumenism, and Politics. New Endeavours in Ecclesiology* (San Francisco: Ignatius Press, 2008), 242–43. In another essay on the notion of freedom, Ratzinger notes that there is a curious phenomenon in this desire for totally unfettered freedom. The desire for freedom that we recognise in the world comes from the exhilarating experience of such freedom, and yet there is, at the same time, the perception of a fear that this freedom is somehow threatened and insecure. Ratzinger notices that this fear of losing ever greater freedom is also to be found in Western societies, where perhaps the expressions of uninhibited freedom have maximum expression. This indicates to Ratzinger something enigmatic about the nature of freedom that cannot be reduced to a mere freedom from constraint. Ratzinger also observes ironically about the multiple new constraints of our society: "the determination of the slope of the roof to rules about gravestones, from traffic regulations to an establishment for universal education that harnesses teachers and students to a network of legal prescriptions resulting from—what else?—efforts to safeguard the citizens' rights to freedom" Ratzinger, "Freedom and Constraint in the Church," in *Church*, 175.
7. Schmitz, *Texture of Being*, 228.
8. Joseph Ratzinger, "Truth and Freedom," *Communio* 23, no. 1 (1996): 16–17.
9. As cited in Gediminas T. Jankunas, *The Dictatorship of Relativism: Pope Benedict XVI's Response* (New York: Alba House, 2011), 517. Ratzinger responded: "When man is shut out from the truth, he can only be dominated by what is accidental and arbitrary. That is why it is not 'fundamentalism' but a duty of humanity to protect man from the dictatorship of what is accidental and to restore to him his dignity, which consists precisely in the fact that no human institution can ultimately dominate him, because he is open to the truth" (534).

10. Umberto Eco, *The Name of the Rose*, trans. William Weaver (New York: Random House, 2006), 7892. It seems that the author is not dismissing truth, but what, in his view, is an exaggerated zeal for truth. In the novel, as William and Adso watch the Benedictine abbey, and its vast library, burn to the ground, William says: "the Antichrist is truly at hand, because no learning will hinder him any more . . . . In that face, deformed by hatred of philosophy, I saw for the first time the portrait of the Antichrist, who does not come from the tribe of Judas, as his heralds have it, or from a far country. The Antichrist can be born from piety itself, from excessive love of God or of the truth, as the heretic is born from the saint and the possessed from the seer. Fear prophets, Adso, and those prepared to die for the truth, for as a rule they make many others die with them, often before them, at times instead of them . . . . Perhaps the mission of those who love mankind is to make people laugh at the truth, to make truth laugh, because the only truth lies in learning to free ourselves from insane passion for the truth" (7892). Ratzinger titles a section of his *A New Song for the Lord*, "Passion for the Truth," Cf. Joseph Ratzinger, *A New Song for the Lord* (New York: Crossroad, 1996), 212–15.

11. John Rawls, *A Theory of Justice* (Cambridge, MA: Belknap Press, 1971).

12. Richard Rorty, "The Priority of Democracy to Philosophy," in *The Pragmatism Reader: From Peirce through the Present*, ed. Robert B. Talisse and Scott F. Aikin (Princeton, NJ: Princeton University Press, 2011), 392. David Walsh comments that Rorty "is convinced, with Foucault, that the quest for truth has been at the source of the cruelty that human beings have inflicted on each other" Walsh, *The Growth of the Liberal Soul* (Columbia: University of Missouri, 1997),43.

13. Sheldon S. Wolin, *Politics and Vision. Continuity and Innovation in Western Political Thought*, expanded ed. (Princeton, NJ: Princeton University Press, 2016), 53. Wolin's reference to the recent writer is to Leo Strauss, *Natural Rights and History*, 11. For Wolin's views on theory, practice, and method in political science, see Sheldon S. Wolin, *Fugitive Democracy: And Other Essays* (Princeton, NJ: Princeton University Press, 2018).

14. Hans Kelsen, "Philosophy and Politics," in *What Is Justice? Justice, Law, and Politics in the Mirror of Science* (Clark, NJ: Lawbook Exchange, 2013), 3575.

15. Kelsen, "Philosophy and Politics," in *What Is Justice?* 3634.

16. Kelsen, "Philosophy and Politics," in *What Is Justice?* 3596.

17. Kelsen, "Philosophy and Politics," in *What Is Justice?* 3658.

18. Although Kelsen mentions the need to respect the views of minorities, "because what is right today may be wrong tomorrow" ("Philosophy and Politics," in *What Is Justice?* 3720), it is hard to imagine this respect in practice, in a politics of winners and losers.

19. Kelsen, "Philosophy and Politics," in *What Is Justice?* 3720.

20. Kelsen, "Philosophy and Politics," in *What Is Justice?* 3732.

21. Kelsen, "Philosophy and Politics," in *What Is Justice?* 3732. As a relevant point, the exegesis of this passage of St. John's Gospel reveals that the account of the trial follows exactly the structure of a Roman Criminal Law case, with the Indictment, the Examination, the Defence, and the Judgment. Pontius Pilate was a Praetor with plenipotentiary powers, and therefore represented the maximum legal authority

within his jurisdiction of the province of Judea. His finding of the accused innocent ("I find no guilt in this man"), should have been the final verdict. Everything that happened afterward was illegal according to Roman Law and an abdication of Pilate's legal authority. Cf. Walter M. Chandler, *The Trial of Jesus from a Lawyer's Standpoint* (New York: Empire Publishing, 1908), esp. vol. 2, *The Roman Trial*, chap. 11, "Legal Analysis and Summary of the Roman Trial of Jesus."

22. Hans Kelsen's use of this Christian text has been taken up by Vittorio Possenti in his *Le società liberali al bivio. Lineamenti di filosofia della società* [*Liberal Societies at a Crossroads: An Outline of Social Philosophy*] (Città Castello: Marietti, 1992), 334–36, and by Joseph Ratzinger in his essay "What is Truth," in *Values in a Time of Upheaval* (New York: Crossroad, 2006), 57–58.

23. Peter L. P. Simpson, *Political Illiberalism: A Defence of Freedom* (London: Routledge, 2015),125. On this exclusionary role of public reason, see 125–29. Simpson refers to the *Stanford Encyclopaedia of Philosophy* discussion on Public Reason and to Robert B. Talisse, *Pluralism and Liberal Politics* (London: Routledge, 2012). For the classic contemporary exposition of public reason, see John Rawls' essays published in *Political Liberalism* (New York: Columbia University Press, 2005): Lecture VI "What is Public Reason?," 212–54; and "The Idea of Public Reason Revisited (1977)," 435–90.

24. Simpson, *Political Illiberalism*, 127.

25. David S. Crawford, "Recognising the Roots of Society in the Family, Foundation of Justice," *Communio* 34, no. 3 (2007): 383, https://www.communio-icr.com/files/crawford34-3.pdf.

26. As David Fideler explains: "Bacon complained that when 'contemplation' and the 'doctrinal science' of the Aristotelians began, 'the discovery of useful works ceased.' Among the writings of the ancients, he wrote, 'There is hardly one single experiment that has a tendency to assist mankind.' By contrast, nothing in human history has 'changed the appearance and state of the whole world' more than the printing press, gunpowder, and the magnetic compass. The key to transforming the world for human benefit lay in a similar application of mechanical technology." Fideler, *Restoring the Soul of the World: Our Living Bond with Nature's Intelligence* (Rochester, VT: Inner Traditions, 2014), 140–41. The references are to Bacon's *Novum Organum.*

27. Francis Bacon, "The Great Instauration," in *The Works of Francis Bacon*, 4:29 and "The Dignity and Advancement of learning," in *The Works of Francis Bacon*, 4:296, both quotations from Fideler, *Restoring the Soul*, 143.

28. Benedict XVI, *Spe salvi* (Vatican City: Libreria editrice vaticana, 2007), sec.17. The reference to the kingdom of man is to Bacon's unfinished novel *New Atlantis*, published posthumously as part of a work on natural history, *Sylva Sylvarum* (1626).

29. Josef Pieper describes this historical shift in thought from the perception of the truth of all real things to the modern apprehension of truth in the subjective mind in such thinkers as Hobbes, Spinoza, Leibnitz and Kant, to whom (Kant) is attributed "the conquest of the metaphysics of being, the transfer of the centre of gravity from the object to the subject." Pieper, *Living the Truth: The Truth of All Things: An*

Inquiry into the Anthropology of the High Middle Ages, chap. 1, and (quoting historian R. Kroner), *Reality and the Good* (San Francisco: Ignatius Press 1989), 1540.

30. Technological transhumanism is described and evaluated in Paschal Corby, *The Hope and Despair of Human Bioenchantment: A Virtual Dialogue between the Oxford Transhumanists and Joseph Ratzinger* (Eugene, OR: Pickwick Publications, 2019). On the twentieth century influence and domination of "fabrication of appearances," see Robert Sokolowski, *Eucharistic Presence: A Study in the Theology of Disclosure* (Washington, DC: Catholic University Press, 1993), esp. 186–90.

31. Augusto Del Noce, *The Crisis of Modernity*, ed. and trans. Carlo Lancellotti (Montreal: McGill Queens University Press, 2015), 60. The reference is to Friedrich Engels, *Ludwig Feuerbach and the Outcome of Classical German Philosophy* (New York: International, 1941), 82.

32. Del Noce, *Crisis of Modernity*, 71.

33. Alex Worsnip, "Against Pragmatism: The Vapid Philosophy of Modern Politics," *Prospect Magazine*, December 29, 2012, https://www.prospectmagazine.co.uk/politics/50637/against-pragmatism (accessed October 15, 2023).

34. Worsnip, "Vapid Philosophy of Modern Politics." Michael J. Sandel has noted the surreptitious nature of what he calls a "public philosophy": "A public philosophy is an elusive thing, for it is constantly before our eyes. It forms the often unreflective background to our political discourse and pursuits. In ordinary times, the public philosophy can easily escape the notice of those who live by it. But anxious times compel a certain clarity. They force first principles to the surface and offer an occasion for critical reflection" Sandel, *Democracy's Discontent: America in Search of a Public Philosophy* (Cambridge, MA: Harvard University Press, 1998), 4.

35. Del Noce, *Crisis of Modernity*, chap. 4 "The Latent Metaphysics within Contemporary Politics," 64–78.

36. Del Noce, *Crisis of Modernity*, 62.

37. Joseph Ratzinger, "A Christian Orientation in a Pluralistic Democracy," in *Church*, 3023.

38. Ratzinger, "Christian Orientation," in *Church*, 66.

39. Charles N. R. McCoy, ed., *The Structure of Political Thought: A Study in the History of ideas* (London: Routledge, 2017), 519. McCoy explains the Aristotelean notion of substitute intelligence: "Nature was thought of, in the tradition of Aristotle, as a 'substitute intelligence' because it acts always or for the most part in the same way and without knowledge of the end, because it does not intend the individual as such but only for the sake of the species, and lastly because it does not extend to the diversity of the species of things—all these characteristics are found once again, on the human level, in modern political movements—in liberalism, in conservatism, and in totalitarianism"(533).

40. As Timothy Fuller explains, the phrase "politics of faith," as Michael Oakeshott uses it, means a type of rationalism which "corresponds to Eric Voegelin's use of the term 'gnosticism' in describing a misplaced claim of the autonomy of human reason, when armed with 'appropriate methods,' to remake the world according to our independently premeditated goals." Timothy Fuller, "On the Modern State," in

Reassessing the Liberal State: Reading Maritain's Man and the State, ed. Timothy Fuller and John P. Hittinger (Washington, DC: Catholic University of America Press, 2001), 30.

41. Michael Oakeshott, *The Politics of Faith and the Politics of Scepticism* (New Haven, CT: Yale University Press, 1996), 31.

42. Michael Oakeshott, *Rationalism in Politics and Other Essays*, new and expanded ed. (Indianapolis: Liberty Fund, 1991), 60.

43. Michael Oakeshott, *On Human Conduct* (Oxford: Oxford Clarendon Press, 1975), 202–3. Oakeshott's rejection of a greater meaningful context as expressed in the politics of faith is similar to Karl Popper's rejection of ideologies based on what he terms "metaphysics of history and destiny, such as are fashionable nowadays. [The Open Society and its Enemies] rather tries to show that this prophetic wisdom is harmful, that the metaphysics of history impedes the application of the piecemeal methods of science to the problems of social reform. And it further tries to show that we may become the makers of our fate when we have ceased to pose as its prophets" Cf. Popper, *The Open Society and Its Enemies* (London: Routledge Classics, 2011), 550.

44. Walsh, *Growth of the Liberal Soul*, 64.

45. Francis Slade, "Two Versions of Political Philosophy: Teleology and the Conceptual Genesis of the Modern State," in *Natural Moral Law in Contemporary Society*, ed. Holger Zaborowski (Washington, DC: Catholic University of America Press, 2010), 241–242. The reference is to Niccolò Machiavelli's *The Prince*, 2nd ed., trans. Harvey C. Mansfield (Chicago: University of Chicago Press, 1998), chap. 15.

46. John Paul II, *Veritatis splendor* [The Splendor of Truth], *Acta Apostolicae Sedis (AAS)* 85 (1993): 1225–28, n101. The reference is to John Paul II's *Centesimus annus* [The Hundredth Year], *Acta Apostolicae Sedis (AAS)* 83 (1991): 793–867, n46. Similar arguments are presented in John Paul's *Evangelium vitae* [The Gospel of Life], *Acta Apostolicae Sedis (AAS)* 87(1995): 401–522, esp. nn68–74. "Democracy cannot be idolized to the point of making it a substitute for morality or a panacea for immorality. Fundamentally, democracy is a 'system' and as such is a means and not an end. Its 'moral' value is not automatic, but depends on conformity to the moral law to which it, like every other form of human behaviour, must be subject: in other words, its morality depends on the morality of the ends which it pursues and of the means which it employs" John Paul, *Evangelium vitae*, n70.

47. Eric Voegelin, *The New Science of Politics: An Introduction* (Chicago: University of Chicago Press, 1987), 164.

48. Hanna Arendt, *The Origins of Totalitarianism* (New York: Mariner Books, 1976), 474.

49. Robert Sokolowski, *Introduction to Phenomenology* (Cambridge: Cambridge University Press, 2000), 9.

50. Joseph Ratzinger, *The Nature and Mission of Theology: Approaches to Understanding Its Role in the Light of Present Controversy* (San Francisco: Ignatius Press, 2010), 34. Pope Francis lays down descriptively the conditions for real dialogue in his encyclical letter *Fratelli tutti* (Vatican City: Libreria Editrice Vaticana, 2020), chap. 6, sec.198–214.

51. One of the fundamental intellectual concerns of Eric Voegelin was to overcome "the idol" of language symbols that have lost their contact with reality. Voegelin, "Why Philosophise? To Recapture Reality!" *Communio* 28, no. 4 (2001): 876.

52. Walsh, *Politics of the Person as the Politics of Being*, 4201. Walsh's reflection on politics as the realm of truth is from 4104–4251.

53. Walsh, *Growth of the Liberal Soul*.

54. Walsh, *Growth of the Liberal Soul*, 303.

55. W. Norris Clarke, *Person and Being: The Aquinas Lecture 1993* (Milwaukee, WI: Marquette University Press, 1993), 74.

56. Walsh, *Growth of the Liberal Soul*, 254, 255. Walsh notes that Eric Voegelin also stresses that human consciousness is a consciousness of the reality of being; "consciousness has a structural dimension by which it belongs, not to man in his bodily existence, but to the reality in which man, the other partners to the community of being, and the participatory relations among them occur." Eric Voegelin, *Order and History*, vol. 5 "In Search of Order," 30, in Walsh, *Growth of the Liberal Soul*, 353.

57. David Walsh, *After Ideology: Recovering the Spiritual Foundations of Freedom* (San Francisco: HarperCollins, 1990), 195. The reference to Aristotle is from the following: "Such a life as this however will be higher than the human level: not in virtue of his humanity will a man achieve it, but in virtue of something within him that is divine; and by as much as this something is superior to his composite nature, by so much is its activity superior to the exercise of the other forms of virtue. If then the intellect is something divine in comparison with man, so is the life of the intellect divine in comparison with human life. Nor ought we to obey those who enjoin that a man should have man's thoughts and a mortal the thoughts of mortality, but we ought so far as possible to achieve immortality, and do all that man may to live in accordance with the highest thing in him; for though this be small in bulk, in power and value it far surpasses all the rest" Aristotle, *Nicomachean Ethics*, ed. Harris Rackham (Cambridge, MA: Harvard University Press, 1934), 1177b.

58. David L. Schindler, *Ordering Love: Liberal Societies and the Memory of God* (Grand Rapids, MI: Eerdmans, 2011), 3659, 3688. The reference to "things" means to reality, to being, and to personal being.

59. Voegelin, *Order and History*, vol. 1, as cited by Ellis Sandoz in Eric Voegelin, *Science, Politics and Gnosticism: Two Essays*, ed. Ellis Sandoz (Washington, DC: Gateway Editions, 2012), 48.

60. W. Norris Clarke, *Explorations in Metaphysics: Being-God-Person* (Notre Dame, IN: University of Notre Dame Press, 1994), 54.

61. W. Norris Clarke suggests that this was a difficulty that Immanuel Kant may have faced. "We might speculate that one consideration that blocks Kant's acceptance of action as an information-bearing medium, revelatory of the thing-in-itself, is an impossibly high ideal, inspired by the rationalists before him, of what such objective knowledge would have to be. He seems to be convinced that if we do not know the thing-in-itself directly and intuitively, without mediation of any kind, precisely as it is in itself apart from, prior to, and independently of any action emerging from it, then we do not know it at all" Clarke, *Explorations in Metaphysics*, 59.

62. Alfred North Whitehead, "Immortality, 1941," in *Essays in Science and Philosophy* (New York: Philosophical Library, 1947), 77–96. The dramatic tone in which these words were pronounced is related by Josef Pieper in *For the Love of Wisdom: Essays on the Nature of Philosophy* (San Francisco: Ignatius Press, 2007),132–33.

63. John E. Smith, *Experience and God* (New York: Fordham University Press, 1995), 12.

64. Benedict XVI, *Address of His Holiness Benedict XVI*, Reichstag Building, Berlin, September 22, 2011, https://www.vatican.va/content/benedict-xvi/en/speeches/2011/september/documents/hf_ben-xvi_spe_20110922_reichstag-berlin.html (accessed October 18, 2023).

65. As quaint as these categories of interpersonal experience may sound to us today, friendship was a central notion of political philosophy until modern times: "Western political speculation finds its origin in a system of thought in which the idea of friendship is the major principle in terms of which political theory and practice are described, explained, and analysed" Horst Hutter, *Politics as Friendship: The Origins of Classical Notions of Politics in the Theory and Practice of Friendship* (Waterloo, ON: Wilfred Laurier University Press, 1978), 2, cited in John Von Heyking, and Richard Avramenko, eds., *Friendship and Politics: Essays in Political Thought* (Notre Dame, IN: University of Notre Dame Press, 2008), 1.

66. Walsh, *Politics of the Person*, 232. Ratzinger notes that "to think through the essence of truth is to arrive at the notion of God" *The Nature and Mission of Theology*, 40.

67. Louis Dupré, *A Dubious Heritage* (New York: Paulist Press, 1977), 174. Dupré understands the original meaning of St. Anselm's ontological argument in this way, as the logical unfolding of prior experience of God, and not, as others have done, as a rational argument for the existence of God. Cf. 171–75. John E. Smith is of the same conviction: "Rational dialectic in religion cannot perform the task it is supposed to perform unless it begins with ideas which themselves have been derived from the direct experience of the individual. Only in this way can the thinking self find itself possessed of genuine conviction for the conclusions attained by thought" Cf. Smith, *Experience and God*, 114.

68. An expression of Paul Ricoeur, cited in Peter Henrici, "Sophistry and Philosophy," *Communio* 15, no. 3 (1988): 393.

69. Limitations and boundaries that are real but should not be exaggerated. For the evidence of interpersonal dialogue for our being immersed in reality, see W. Norris Clarke, "Interpersonal Dialogue: Key to Realism," in *Person and Community: A Philosophical Exploration,* ed. Robert J. Roth (New York: Fordham University Press, 1975), 141–53.

70. Henrici, "Sophistry and Philosophy," 393. It is instructive to recall the care with which St. Thomas Aquinas expresses what and how we humans are capable of knowing: "The substantial forms of things, which, according as they are in themselves, are unknown to us, shine forth to us (*innotescunt*) through their accidental properties" *Sum. Theol.* I, q.77, art. 1, ad 7, and "Sometimes a created intellect does not arrive at the essence of what it knows directly through itself (as do the angels),

---

but only through the mediation of what surrounds the essence, as though through doors placed around it; and this is the mode of apprehending in man, who proceeds to the knowledge of the essence of a thing from its effects and properties. Hence in this knowledge there must be certain discursive character" *Expositio in Libros Sentent.*, III, d.35, q.2, art. 2, sol.1. St. Thomas concludes that "Our knowledge is so weak that no philosopher was ever able to investigate perfectly the nature of a single fly" *Expositio in Symbolum Apostolorum*, all cited in Clarke, *Explorations in Metaphysics*, 56. On the human knowability of being and the human experience of what is humanly unknowable and yet real, see Josef Pieper, *The Silence of St. Thomas* (South Bend, IN: St. Augustine's Press, 1999).

71. Aristotle, *Nicomachean Ethics*, III, 5:982b, cited over twenty times in the writings of St. Thomas Aquinas.

72. James V. Schall, "On Choosing not to See," in *The Mind that is Catholic: Philosophical and Political Essays* (Washington DC: Catholic University of America Press, 2008), 283.

73. Thomas Kuhn's famous *The Structure of Scientific Revolutions*, 4th ed. (Chicago: University of Chicago Press, 2012), describes, *inter alia*, the "subjective" factors involved in scientific perceptions and the influence of patterns of pre-existing scientific theories that can impede the perception of new, disruptive findings.

74. Maurice Blondel, *Action (1893): Essay on a Critique of Life and a Science of Practice,* trans. Oliva Blanchette (Notre Dame, IN: University of Notre Dame Press, 1984), 478, 434.

75. Walsh, *Growth of the Liberal Soul*, 308, 286. Walsh makes this point in another chapter, when he states that we each have an approximate moral compass that gives us a general notion of moral truth, but that it is only by our active response that we come to experience a greater sense of this moral truth. The rightness and goodness of moral truth can be enhanced and developed only when we attempt to live by its light (Cf. 254).

76. American former economics professor Dr. Jennifer Roback Morse explains the essential need of the helpless infant of this unconditioned love and the consequences of detachment disorder when this experience is denied. "After all, we are not born as fully rational adults, capable of grasping our true interests, able to make contracts and other agreements, able to defend our property rights and our legitimate interests. We are born as helpless babies. The fact of infant helplessness is not peripheral; it is a central fact to any coherent social theory" Morse, *Love and Economics: It Takes a Family to Raise a Village* (Lake Charles, LA: Ruth Institute Books, 2008), 11.

77. The Swiss theologian Hans Urs von Balthasar has noted that: "Distinguishing the soul's faculties from one another and from the soul itself should not make us forget their reciprocal compenetration, and the way in which they are themselves penetrated by the soul which acts and suffers through them. Indeed, distinctions of this kind, such as drawn by Thomas Aquinas, should always be ventured only for the sake of the better understanding of the underlying unity. What is termed 'feeling,' in contradistinction to intellect and will, lies neither 'beside' nor 'beneath' the spiritual faculties . . . . It is not by means of one isolated faculty that man is open, in knowledge and in love, to the thou, to things and to God: it is as a whole (through all

of his faculties) that man is attuned to total reality" Von Balthasar, *The Glory of the Lord: A Theological Aesthetics. Volume 1: Seeing the Form* (San Francisco: Ignatius Press, 1989), 243–44.

78. Jean Mouroux, *I Believe: The Personal Structure of Faith* (New York: Sheed and Ward, 1959), 50.

79. For an interesting study on this broader understanding of *intellectus*, see Andrew Tallon, *Head and Heart: Affection, Cognition, Volition as Triune Consciousness* (New York: Fordham University Press, 1997). For a similar expansion of meaning of the Platonic term *nous*, see Andrew Louth, *The Origins of the Christian Mystical Tradition*, 2nd ed. (Oxford: Oxford University Press, 2007), esp. xiv–xv.

80. Robert Sokolowski, *Christian Faith and Human Understanding: Studies on the Eucharist, Trinity, and the Human Person* (Washington DC: Catholic University of America Press, 2006).

81. Sokolowski, *Christian Faith and Human Understanding*, 21. The reference is to Robert Spaemann, *Persons: The Difference Between "Someone" and "Something"* (Oxford: Oxford University Press, 2017), 30.

82. Pieper, *Faith, Hope, Love*, 64. Pieper on the same page quotes Pascal's dictum: "If you do not take the trouble to know the truth, there is enough truth at hand so that you can live in peace. But if you crave it with all your heart, then it is not enough to know it." Pieper mentions a spiritual root of this turning away from reality, *acedia*, a deliberate denial of the true capacity and calling of human nature (117).

83. Kurt Pritzl, "Truth in Fides et Ratio," *Communio* 29, no. 1 (2002): 104.

84. In *The Power and the Glory*, English writer Graham Greene writes of the "pious women, in a state of invincible complacency, full of uncharity." The unnamed priest "watched the pious woman disappear as if for ever through the archway to where her sister waited with the fine: they were both tied up in black shawls like something bought in the market, something hard and dry and second-hand" *The Power and the Glory* (New York: Viking Press, 1968), 1882.

85. Epistulae 1, 1, as cited in Benedict XVI, *Church Fathers: From Clement to Augustine* (San Francisco: Ignatius Press, 2009), 182.

86. Joseph Ratzinger, *Introduction to Christianity* (San Francisco: Ignatius Press, 2004), 42–43.

Chapter 4

Living Publicly in the Truth

In this overview of chapter 4, I suggest that one of consequences of the denial of our common capacity to experience the truth of reality is the split between knowing and acting, or, in Scholastic terms, between the speculative and practical functions of our reason, a split that deforms our notion of knowledge. On the one hand, knowledge is considered as subjectively and interiorly held opinion that has no public legitimacy. On the other hand, our actions are viewed only technically, in function of their capacity to do something, and not in reference to what is true, what responds to our experience of the whole truth of reality.

The political importance of a more complete understanding of truth and of knowledge is in the fact that the response to the truth of reality is only fully expressed in action, which is necessarily public and social. Václav Havel explains the necessity and the political impact of living publicly in the truth and overcoming the acquiescence to public lies.

It is easily recognizable, and yet a curious fact, that living publicly in the truth is not something straightforward but often provokes a hostile reaction and consequent struggle. The difficulty of living in the truth is multiplied in political activity because of many complex considerations and the magnitude of political decisions. This complexity leads to the commonly held approach to politics as tactical, the obtaining and maintaining of political power by means of power, as epitomized in the writings of Niccolò Machiavelli, who observes that "a man who wants to make a profession of good in all regards [that is, live publicly in the truth] must come to ruin among so many who are not good"[1] A counter example, of Abraham Lincoln, seems to refute the false dichotomy between effectual truth and conceptual truth, that is, the capacity to combine tactical awareness with the truth of right purposes and means. This gives a clearer vision of the real meaning and political application of *phronesis*, practical wisdom, prudence.

It is indeed curious that living publicly in the truth provokes such a hostile reaction and consequent struggle for truth to prevail. This observable struggle is much more than just difference of opinion or options, but a spiritual resistance to truth beyond human dimensions of perception. As David Walsh comments, "The truth of order is won only through the struggle with disorder. Conflict and suffering are not to be shunned but accepted as the path apparently fated for human beings to make their way slowly, fitfully and finally toward the order of right that endures."[2]

We then turn to the moral experience of those who have lived publicly in the truth, at great personal risk or cost. What is remarkable in the experience of such people is the almost universal answer that what they did was something normal, the only right thing to do, that "anyone would have done the same." Theirs is evidence of the metaphysics of love, donation as the obvious response to the need of other persons in danger. This may not be what everyone does, but what everyone can know to be the only adequate and right response to reality.

There is also another difficult issue in living publicly in the truth, a question that is not often raised but is often present. Is living publicly in the truth effective—does it achieve anything apart from the example of truthful living? Some would decry the sacrifice for another as weakness and futility, as Friedrich Nietzsche seems to do, as a sign of the lack of the desire to live, or, indeed, of cowardice. Can great personal sacrifice be effective? Examples from Mahatma Gandhi's doctrine of *Satyagraha*, from a Sufi mystic, and from the Judeo-Christian Scriptures indicate that personal sacrifice contributes positively to some real process of manifestation of truth, of conversion and purification of others as well as oneself, to the contribution to real order beyond our human perception. If this is so, the necessary sacrifice, far from being a failure or a lack of the desire to live, is a social and public act of achievement. To die for the people is an effective political act of the highest order and good.

NEXUS

We live immersed in reality and we are completely involved through our human experience in responding to our existential circumstances by the dynamism of our own being. This is where and how we find ourselves, not of our own choosing, but destined to respond freely to where and to how we are. In the measure in which we live by and respond to the light of reality, we live in truth.

As we are destined to live socially, this response in truth has social importance. I contribute to the truth of others' lives and others contribute to the truth of my response to reality. This common basis of truthful agreement is the ultimate foundation of the social bond; attempted consensus without a common truthful agreement is illusory; in this ultimate foundation, to agree to disagree is failure. No abuse of the meaning of words such as democracy, respect, and tolerance can cover over this social and political failure, and all political structures and processes are insufficient to provide or to determine true consensus. Political organization will only make evident and exacerbate the underlying absence of common truth.

At the same time, we have seen that the personal experience of truth is not something that is always spontaneous and easy. Part of our inherited difficulty is to think everything should be clear and obvious. We tend to forget the inherent limitations of our experience of reality; we assume that our subjective experience determines how things and persons are or should be; we speak before we listen, we use before we know what we are using, and we abrogate to ourselves, as if we were magicians, the power to demand and conjure a world to our satisfaction. As Robert Sokolowski points out:

> But now, with our informational and imaging technologies, with artificial viewing and artificial hearing and artificial intelligence, we may like to think that we can master nature on a deeper, more subtle level; we may become exhilarated by the thought that we can change the way the world is simply by changing our words and images. But sooner or later nature will assert itself against our attempt to say and image what it should be, just as it asserts itself from time to time against our engineering and medicine. Nature's way of reasserting itself, moreover, is not always gentle. As a scientist put it in another context, Mother Nature is a mean bastard. She always collects. The only question is who pays and when. She always collects.[3]

We also can recognize that our own dispositions toward reality play a decisive role in what we see, what we want to see, and what we would prefer not to see, and even to deny. We are even capable of projecting what we want to see or to be, so that we see what we want to see and do not see what we prefer not to see. We may also not be interested in what we may need to know and to be indifferent to what does and should involve us.

Our perception of reality and the claims that reality make upon us require a deliberate and positive disposition that is not always morally easy, although we all strangely consider ourselves completely honest. Lying is the ultimate reprehensible moral act today, yet utter truthfulness may demand much more of us than we care to think or want to give.

As we have noted before, we also find ourselves as agents of truth in existential situations that place demands and require answers and commitments of us that, while they do not contradict our understanding, require that we go beyond our reliance on human sources of knowledge. Theological experience is real, and yet appears to us as enlightening our perception from outside of *our* capacity of perception. This source is both vital for what we are required to decide and determine in our lives, and, at the same time, not what we can verify for ourselves. This requires an adaptation to the reliance on our modes of apprehension, less reliance on our more common modes of perception and a dependence on a source of truth which we need but cannot perceive for ourselves. We can only assent to or dissent from a source that enlightens us, that bears on and influences our intellect but does not have its origin in the working of our intellect. To follow this certain and necessary light requires the capacity to recognize the limitation—but not the inconsistency—of our intellect, and to respond adequately with the strength and light of a source that can be experienced *in* our intellect but is not *of* our intellect.[4]

The temptations to skepticism are always present and easy to follow, especially at this last stage of being required to go beyond what we can see for the sake of truth. This ascesis of perception and response to reality has been compared to a sea voyage where one encounters a reef on which our lives can break up or break down or, alternatively, move adequately onward in truth.[5]

This profound and dramatic experience and response to truth has also a social context and drama of its own.

ACTION AS THE CULMINATION
OF LIVING IN THE TRUTH

The rupture between knowing and doing has devalued the importance of both. The real import of believing that our perceptions are only individual subjective ideas does not mean that all such ideas are of equal importance, as a relativist culture seems to imply, but in fact the opposite, that no idea is of real importance. In this sense, precisely because ideas are held to be only our own subjective impressions, these ideas do not have any public consequences. Equally, when what we *do* is all that matters, then all actions are legitimated by their capacity to achieve whatever we may want to achieve. In practice, everything is possible; the only question is how, not why.

We have seen that both views are invalid and obstacles to real, vital political consensus. The social bond is to be found in the common experience of reality and the adequate common response to the demands and opportunities that our experience perceives. What I want to emphasize here is the necessity of responding to our experience of reality, the completion of truth in the adequate re-*action* to our truly perceived experience of reality.[6]

A fully human experience draws from us an adequate response. The necessary conceptual abstraction of our experience is a fundamental part of our cognitive process, our intimation of reality, and yet this capacity to abstract is only a part of our cognitive process. Selective understandings of knowledge as only empirical facts or data will reduce this personal response to a minimum of importance. In this view, detachment is a condition of the validity of knowledge. This detachment is an illusion because human persons are always involved in the process of knowledge, and their decisions, perspectives, and motivations all necessarily influence the perceptions of facts and data. The notion of reading off nature in an empirical way is really only the abstraction and ordering of a small part of nature according to a particular mode of presentation. Valid as a partial mode of understanding, such facts and data, to be comprehended properly, need to be perceived in their greater context of meaning and value, and it is precisely this greater context of meaning and value that elicits my personal response in action. Perhaps no modern philosopher has written more dramatically of the required response to reality than the French philosopher Maurice Blondel (1861–1949). Far from the experience of life being something remote, as at the other end of a microscope, Blondel attempts to show in his thesis the compelling nature of our required reaction to reality:

> No, I must commit myself under pain of losing everything; I must compromise myself. I have no right to wait or else I no longer have the power to choose. If I do not act out of my own movement, there is something in me or outside of me that acts without me; and what acts without me ordinarily acts against me. Peace is a defeat; action leaves no more room for delay than death. Head, heart and hands, I must give them over willingly or else they are taken from me. If I withhold my free dedication, I fall into slavery; no one gets along without idols: neither pious folk nor even the most libertine.[7]

Human perception of social reality makes this evident. The adequate response to the perception of others (and the Other) is love, the affirmation of the value personal being that I experience as the adequate response to that experience. Detachment here would be a sign of deficiency of perception. The response to the experience of the reality of another person requires this involvement as the corresponding adequate action. It is in the experience of the other as person that we see the full import of our involvement with reality and the necessity of responding in action as the authentic sign of perceived experience.

What this means is that truth necessarily has a public expression as an adequate response to reality. One's personal opinions, one's own thoughts and beliefs, one's entire response to others and to the Other all require public expression in action if they are to be truthful. This public expression through action is both a right and a duty of the experience of truth. It is, therefore, a vital element of political life, the public expression of the truth of experience.

This sense of living publicly in the truth, and its opposite, consenting by silence to lies, was clear to the playwright and philosopher Václav Havel. It was not enough to be personally opposed to the wrongful political system that was perpetuated by falsehoods and propaganda; if one wanted to live truthfully, it was necessary to act in the truth by rejecting the public lies and falsehoods, even if only in small matters such as shop signs.

In *The Power of the Powerless: Citizens against the State in Central-Eastern Europe*, Havel writes on the acquiescence in the untruth of a system of lies and he states that it is not essential to believe the falsehoods and propaganda, but that what is necessary is the outward conformity of behavior that suggests compliance and cooperation with those who do believe and promote such falsehoods. Havel notes that this outward conformity is sufficient, which itself is tantamount "to living within a lie." This is what makes the false system work, the conformity of outward behavior that shows that one has accepted the system; this is in fact what the system requires, how it functions, and its desired effect on those living within the system.[8]

Havel goes on to explain the social importance of even small actions that rebuke the system of untruth. Havel notices that the effect of a person who chooses to break with conformity with the system and chooses not to live within the lie has many repercussions. Not only does the person begin to live existentially in a true manner, not only does truth begin to reveal itself with greater clarity, and not only does this act of living in the truth have a luminous quality for others to see, but living in the truth has also a political dimension. Havel notices that a system that depends on compliance with a fundamental lie recognizes that an act of truth puts that system in mortal danger, and, therefore, such acts of truth must be radically quashed.[9]

What is interesting here is Havel's demand that truth be spoken and expressed in action. Only this fulfils the requirement of living the truth. It is not sufficient to be inwardly opposed to falsehood if that opposition is not shown publicly and politically. Living in the truth, therefore, requires the affirmative action of truth in public. Not to do so affirmatively and in public has detrimental consequences for the person himself, for the identity of his own being. Havel recognizes that in each person there is an essential desire and quest for the worth of human dignity, for knowing and wanting to live and express freely the truth of being, and for the sense of transcendence that is the greater context of our existence. Even so, Havel also admits that each person can also yield to the sense of conformity with falsehood and the cheapening of one's existence by doing so. We are capable and at times we want to conform to the crowd and lose ourselves and our authentic identity in the unthinking mass movement of the crowd. Havel judges that what is in play here is not just a mere conflict of interests, but rather the risk of losing oneself and one's own identity in the anonymous crowd.[10]

In *The Growth of the Liberal Soul*, Walsh notes that in fact active participation in living in the truth is essential for the discovery of truth. The detached view of the uncommitted observer is insufficient for growth in the truth. Walsh affirms that our horizon of truth depends on the degree to which we have wanted to be open to that reality, to assimilate the experience, and to response actively to its appeal and its demands. Our sense of freedom denotes the inchoate condition of who we are; at the same time, how we respond to reality determines greatly the growth or the diminution of our experience of reality, which in turn affects how we use our freedom. In whatever way we may intuit or understand the ultimate of source of what transcends us, our openness and response to this transcendent reality brings with it a progressive and necessary understanding and experience of reality and its source.[11]

At the same time, the choice to live and to act publicly in the truth has more than the individual consequences of personal coherence and identity; the public act of truth shatters the public lie and facilitates the capacity of others to live in the truth. This can happen in a common-place way, as when, as Havel comments in *The Power of the Powerless*, by a simple act of a shopkeeper who refuses to place a political propaganda sign among the produce. Havel describes how anyone who wants to can break out of conformity and, even in small and apparently innocuous ways, can disrupt and destroy the web of lies that holds the system of falsehood together. A simple action of correspondence with the truth and disconformity with falsehood makes evident the deceiving nature of such a system. The truthful action itself reveals the deception of the system to which everyone is bound to conform. Havel refers to Hans Christian Anderson's story of *The Emperor's New Clothes*,[12] to show the public and political effect of a single action of truth within the silent conspiracy of a deceitful system. The greengrocer's simple action of non-conformity by not putting a propaganda sign on display with his produce is a public and political action that speaks to everyone. The greengrocer not only exposes the lie that everyone has assumed, but also awakens in others their capacity and their desire to recognize truth and reject falsehood. The deceitful system only works if all acquiesce in the lie; therefore, one single action of truth threatens the very existence of the deceitful system in its totality.[13]

THE PUBLIC STRUGGLE FOR THE
RECOGNITION OF TRUTH

However difficult the essential personal struggle to live in the truth may be, the conflict becomes all the greater in public. This strange struggle is not explained simply by the legitimate differences of ways of seeing and doing things, conflicts of interests, priorities, objectives. While the struggle to live in the truth often manifests itself in these mundane issues, the real opposition to truth seems to have deeper roots. It is not just a case of benign ignorance or innocent miscalculation or innocuous oversight, but a hostile and destructive current that seeks to deny and destroy sources of public and political truth. From whatever ultimate source, there is a willed resistance to what can be recognized as true and a consequent intention to deny and destroy what can be seen to be right and just. In the post-totalitarian situation that Havel describes in *The Power of the Powerless*, this willed resistance to truth can take on the form of suppressing questions and thus imposing a conformity to a systematic lie. Eric Voegelin notices that this insistence on not asking questions can be a characteristic of political ideology, systematic impositions of political organization and values that require of all not to ask questions about the truth:

> There has emerged a phenomenon unknown to antiquity that permeates our modern societies so completely that its ubiquity scarcely leaves us any room to see it at all: the prohibition of questioning. . . . we are confronted here with persons who know that, and why their opinions cannot stand up under critical analysis and who therefore make the prohibition of the examination of their premises part of their dogma. This position of a conscious, deliberate, and painstakingly elaborated obstruction of *ratio* constitutes the new phenomenon.[14]

This was the crime of Socrates, to question a nervous regime about justice and truth, and he was condemned to death for it. The political situation in the city state of Athens in 399 BC was precarious. Sparta had allowed the re-establishment of a certain type of democratic rule after the despotic years of the Thirty Tyrants. At the same time new currents of intellectual thought and the moral and religious disorder created a social climate that was fragile, as the democracy tried to cling onto the religious myths and traditions of the past to preserve its stability. As Romano Guardini explains:

> Socrates' fate is tragic. The true nature of tragedy, however, lies in the fact that good is ruined, not by what is evil and senseless, but by another good which also has its rights; and that this hostile good is too narrow and selfish to see the superior right or the destined hour of the other, but has power enough to trample down the other's claim. The events of the dialogue we are engaged in would be robbed of their peculiar seriousness if we were to see in Socrates only the great and innocent man misunderstood, and in his accusers only the narrow-minded mob clinging to what is old. The truth, which must be emphasised again and again, is that here an epoch—a declining one, it is true, but one still full of values—confronts a man who, great as he is and called to be a bringer of new things, disrupts by his spirit all that has hitherto held sway. In

this incompatibility of these two opposing sets of values and forces lies the real tragedy of the situation.[15]

Socrates is under no illusions as to the personal danger involved in publicly living in the truth and speaking out against what is unjust and, therefore, illegal:

And do not be vexed with me for telling the truth. There is no man who will not preserve his life for long, either in Athens or elsewhere, if he firmly opposes the wishes of the people, and tries to prevent the commission of much injustice and illegality in the State. He who would really fight for justice, must do so as a private man, not in public, if he means to preserve his life, even for a short time.[16]

And yet Socrates, who by now knows the verdict of guilt and the sentence of death, is convinced that, because he has acted rightly, death must not be an evil for him. As he replies to those who had voted for his acquittal, he tells them that the divine prompting he had received had never once opposed him in anything he had said in the trial:

But now, in this matter, it has never once withstood me, either in my words or my actions. I will tell you what I believe to be the reason of that. This thing that has come upon me must be a good: and those of us who think that death is an evil must needs be mistaken. I have a clear proof that that is so; for my accustomed sign would certainly have opposed me, if I had not been going to fare well.[17]

The death of Socrates is indeed a tragedy. That the observant citizen, the loyal soldier, he who fulfilled the public religious duties, should be put to death by a public jury of his peers, following the established legal process of trial, is indeed a clamorous warning of how easily truth and goodness can be determined to be actions treasonable to public welfare and publicly destroyed not necessarily by bad people, but by those who cannot or will not see the greater necessary good.[18]

In classical Greek and Roman literature, there was a specific term for the quality of speaking the truth in public. Though there is a variance of meaning from the fifth century BC to the fifth century AD, the general meaning of *parresia* implies speaking the truth freely and publicly. Etymologically, the word comes from *pan* ("everything") and *rhema* ("the thing you say") and came to imply a number of qualities.[19] In the first place, *parresia* includes saying what one thinks: "But whereas rhetoric provides the speaker with technical devices in order to act upon the audience's mind, whatever his own opinion is, in *parresia*, the speaker acts on other people's minds by showing them as directly as possible what he thinks."[20]

This is what we would call sincerity of expression; but *parresia* means more than this:

> the parrhesiast says what is true because he thinks that it is true, and he thinks that it is true because it is really true. Not only is the parrhesiast sincere, not only does he state his own opinion frankly, but his opinion is also the truth. He says what he knows to be true. In *parresia*, there is a coincidence, an exact coincidence, between belief and truth. And that is the second great characteristic of *parresia*.[21]

Parresia also implies not just any telling or communication of the truth but also doing so when there is a danger to the speaker, when he risks disadvantage, unpopularity, suffering, or even death by speaking the truth, and this threat comes from the person to whom one speaks the truth. *Parresia* thus implies a criticism of one's interlocutor, a challenge to the other's actions or way of being. This means that the speaker of truth faces an opposing power and yet still chooses to communicate the truth. Finally, *parresia* implies the motive of duty, that there is a moral obligation that is freely undertaken. Michel Foucault thus sums up the essential characteristics of this disposition:

> It is a verbal activity in which the subject expresses his personal relation to truth and risks his life because he recognises that telling the truth is his own duty, so as to improve or to help other people. In *parresia*, the speaker uses his freedom and chooses truth instead of lies, death instead of life and security, criticism instead of flattery, and duty instead of interest and selfishness.[22]

Interestingly, the biblical New Testament use of the word *parresia* also maintains this inherent link between speaking publicly and fearlessly about what is true. As Joseph Ratzinger comments in an essay on "Freedom and Constraint in the Church," from the biblical perspective, freedom means much more than mere option, but rather a form of participating in the being of reality, to be a conscious possessor of being. In this biblical sense, Ratzinger understands that free human persons are those who possess their own being and therefore speak and act as persons who are responsible for themselves. Precisely because one knows one's own being, who one is, and is therefore responsible for oneself, that one can rightly act in freedom. Ratzinger points out that to demand free speech requires that one have this conscious self-possession as a condition of freedom. Ratzinger refers to Paul's use of the word παρρησία (*parresia*) to develop a Christian sense of freedom of speech, as opposed to the inhibited speech of the slave, and Paul thus gives a particular Christian sense to the notion of freedom.[23]

Ratzinger thus shows the relation of freedom to truth. Both belong to each other; freedom cannot rightly be exercised except in the context of truth and, conversely, truth can only be made manifest by the valiant exercise of freedom. What this implies is that freedom, to be exercised rightly, requires the prior knowledge of the truth of man's being, so that the free exercise of specific rights has a foundation in reality. Where this is lacking, when freedom is detached from the truth of being, then rights can become not the exercise of freedom, but an oppression of man's freedom.[24]

If the personal effort to live in the truth presents difficulties and resistance, this is magnified in society and in politics. Decisions of moral truth become much harder and more complex when such decisions need to be made for all and not just for one's own moral or religious good. In political circumstances, decisions can be particularly difficult to make, for a variety of reasons; the magnitude of the number of people affected; the need to reconcile differing perspectives (political decisions are collective decisions); the conflicting pressures on public ministers to favor one side or another; the complexity of the data; the convenience of the short-term solutions; the confused public perception of wants and needs; the remoteness of the practical circumstances; the collective nature of these decisions (the party, the government . . .); the volatile nature of public opinion, often dependent on means of communication with their own priorities and interests, and so on.

The imperfect and contingent nature of this existence also means that decisions on solutions will always be partial, contingent, and imperfect. Our technical and controlling mentality can accept only with difficulty the unforeseen and unwanted natural disasters, plagues, and blights, as well as the manmade damage to humans and to natural ecology.

Human error and misjudgment on public affairs also cause multiplied hardship on peoples, economically, educationally, in inefficient and non-existent basic public services.

The abuse of public power and the consequent injustices, invidious discrimination, acts of violence and wars are also many times caused by situations that political powers do not choose but have to respond to in practical and imperfect ways.

All of these considerations require a considerable capacity to combine and weigh conflicting needs and interests, the sense of opportunity, the blend of diverse priorities and the ability to work with imperfect circumstances and with people of differing views to achieve a better society. Here it is easy to contrast the vision of the ideal with the need to resolve in a necessarily imperfect way the practical political situations as they occur, and to be required to choose between the two.

The false contrast between the ideal and the real, between knowledge and practice, between speculative and practical reason, makes Plato's suggestion of the philosopher-king sound quaint and utterly remote from political practice. And yet, the image of the ship, the pilot, and the crew in book 6 of *The Republic* sounds disconcertingly real and actual:

> The sailors are quarrelling with one another about the steering—everyone is of opinion that he has a right to steer, though he has never learned the art of navigation and cannot tell who taught him or when he learned, and will further assert that it cannot be taught, and they are ready to cut in pieces anyone who says the contrary. They throng about the captain, begging and praying him to commit the helm to them; and if at any time they do not prevail, but others are preferred to them, they kill the others or throw them overboard, and having first chained up the noble captain's senses with drink or some narcotic drug, they mutiny and take possession of the ship and make free with the stores; thus, eating and drinking, they proceed on their voyage in such manner as might be expected of them.[25]

In this popular climate, which, would be an abuse of terms to call democratic, while at the same time may appear alarmingly similar to our actual political scene, one can anticipate the type of politician that will become popular:

> Him who is their partisan and cleverly aids them in their plot for getting the ship out of the captain's hands into their own whether by force or persuasion, they compliment with the name of sailor, pilot, able seaman, and abuse the other sort of man, whom they call a good-for-nothing; but that the true pilot must pay attention to the year and seasons and sky and stars and winds, and whatever else belongs to his art, if he intends to be really qualified for the command of a ship, and that he must and will be the steerer, whether other people like or not—the possibility of this union of authority with the steerer's art has never seriously entered into their thoughts or been made part of their calling. Now in vessels which are in a state of mutiny and by sailors who are mutineers, how will the true pilot be regarded? Will he not be called by them a prater, a star-gazer, a good-for-nothing?[26]

This image seems to put into a greater context such notions such as consensus-building, tolerance of values, and the relativist answer to claims to public truth. Our experience of necessary public decisions seems to show that the ideal of truth is an essential element of judgment in our practical decisions, one that only the foolish—those of the unthinking crew or crowd—would discard as irrelevant.

There is much in the writings of Niccolò Machiavelli to claim that the practical claiming and maintaining of political power is the essential element in being able effectively to bring peace and order to society. While in his *Discourses on the First Ten Books of Titus Livius*, Machiavelli favors a free constitutional republic, trusting more in the people's judgment than that of the absolute monarch, where there is division and conflict, as there was in and among the city states of Italy, then the absolute legislator, the prince of power, is the necessary means to impose order and unity.[27] Machiavelli considered that the ruler who tries to live according to the noblest moral vision will fail:

> But since my intent is to write something useful to whoever understands it, it has appeared to me more fitting to go directly to the effectual truth of the thing than to the imagination of it. And many have imagined republics and principalities that have never been seen or known to exist in truth; for it is so far from how one lives to how one should live that he who lets go of what is done for what should be done learns his ruin rather than his preservation. For a man who wants to make a profession of good in all regards must come to ruin among so many who are not good. Hence it is necessary to a prince, if he wants to maintain himself, to learn to be able not to be good, and to use this and not use it according to necessity.[28]

While Machiavelli recognizes the usefulness of civic virtue, the real political virtue for Machiavelli, the effectual truth, is the ability to win and to maintain political power, and through this power to establish peace and unity.

There is no doubt much practical advice in Machiavelli's analysis of political history, and what historical cases show, that works and achieves political purposes, but are we required to eliminate the ideal of truth in order to achieve, maintain, and increase the peace and security of political society? Is this caricature of the good person really valid? Is it a simple choice between noble but unreal ideals and the effective ability to use power for tangible results?

In her preface to *The Forum and the Tower: How Scholars and Politicians Have Imagined the World, from Plato to Eleanor Roosevelt*, Mary A. Glendon raises the multiple practical questions that arise when the truth of the ideal and of the actual political circumstances seem to collide:

> Is politics such a dirty business, or are conditions so unfavorable, that I couldn't make a difference? What kinds of compromises can one make for the sake of getting and keeping a position from which one might be able to have influence on the course of events? What kinds of compromises can one make for the sake of achieving a higher political goal? When does prudent accommodation become pandering? When should one speak truth to power no matter what the risk, and when is it acceptable, as Burke put it, to speak the truth with measure that one may speak it the longer? When does one reach the point at which one concludes, as Plato finally did, that circumstances are so unfavorable that the only reasonable course of action is to "keep quiet and offer up prayers for one's own welfare and for that of one's country"?[29]

Abraham Lincoln, a self-educated Springfield, Illinois lawyer and most untypical politician, came unexpectedly to power as President at a time when the United States union was in great danger of collapse, in the time of the American Civil War and the burning issue of slavery. Lincoln's political achievements brought an end to the Civil War and passed the Thirteenth Amendment to the American Constitution to abolish slavery. He faced innumerable political crises and had to face a panorama of political friends and foes. The historical biography by Doris Kearns Goodwin, *Team of Rivals: The Political Genius of Abraham Lincoln*, describes the personal qualities of Lincoln that were the basis for both the nobility and the astuteness of his presidency:

> His extraordinary array of personal qualities that enabled him to form friendships with men who had previously opposed him; to repair injured feelings that, left untended, might have escalated into permanent hostility; to assume responsibility for the failures of subordinates; to share credit with ease; and to learn from mistakes. He possessed an acute understanding of the sources of power inherent in the presidency, an unparalleled ability to keep his governing coalition intact, a tough-minded appreciation of the need to protect his presidential prerogatives, and a masterful sense of timing. His success in dealing with the strong egos of the men in his cabinet suggests that in the hands of a truly great politician the qualities we generally associate with decency and morality—kindness, sensitivity, compassion, honesty, and empathy—can also be impressive political resources.[30]

In living publicly in the truth, there is nothing that prohibits the astuteness and acumen in the use of political power, provided always that the truth is expressed both in the purposes and in the means to those purposes. The modern caricature of Christian virtue as weakness and unthinking submission does not allow for the real blend of vision with courageous and effective action.[31] Josef Pieper recognizes this perverted meaning of "prudence" which is considered as:

> Timorous, small-minded self-preservation, of a rather selfish concern about oneself. . . . A prudent man is thought to be one who avoids the embarrassing situation of having to be brave. The "prudent" man is the "clever tactician" who contrives to escape personal commitment. Those who shun danger are wont to account for their attitude by appealing to the necessity for "prudence."[32]

It is clear that living publicly in the truth requires and allows for a much more positive, resourceful, and audacious capacity than these caricatures portray. In this way, the false dichotomy between the ideal and the real is overcome; one is not forced to choose between them but, within the contingent and imperfect circumstances of this existence, to shape the real according to the ideal. As Pieper explains: "Now prudence means . . . nothing less than the directing cognition of reality . . . Man's good actions take place in confrontation with reality. The goodness of concrete human actions rests upon the transformation of the truth of real things, of the truth which must be won and perceived by regarding the *ipsa res*, reality itself."[33]

It becomes clear that even (and especially) in the complexity of public government, mere tactics are not enough. What is required, and what is at the basis of the common consent to truth, which is the foundation of the social bond, is "reason perfected in the cognition of truth." As we know, this requires of leaders a particular integrity and fortitude, to transform "knowledge of reality into realization of the good."[34]

In its application to politics, David C. Schindler notes that:

Prudence requires that we recall the whole truth of man, his most basic nature and his ultimate destiny, and that we judge in its light our current conception of politics and the form of existence that conception has established for us as the given context in which we live, even as we continue to work and live within that context . . . prudence seeks, not exactly "the best good possible," but the best possible realization of the true good, given the circumstances.[35]

A GREATER CONTEXT

In a greater context, there also seems to be an inherent antagonism not only within the human person, but also among the human race, as if something of an original unity were broken and a greater cause of antagonism than just human error and oversight runs through human affairs and human history.[36] The unnatural human strife is easy to observe: it is much harder to explain its origin and magnitude. It seems that not only are things and persons not entirely as they should be, but also that there is a disproportionate discordance in the human world. It is as if we experience not only a certain brokenness in a unity and harmony that should be there, but also a virulent tension that exacerbates the actual divisions and disruptions in human and natural society. Ratzinger observes this disturbing social phenomenon:

Man is such that he cannot stand the person who is wholly good, truly upright, truly loving, the person who does evil to no one. It seems that in this world only momentarily is trust met with trust, justice with juice, love with love. The person who exemplifies all these virtues quickly becomes insupportable to others. People will crucify anyone who is really and fully human. Such is man.[37]

On this theme of the visceral conflict and struggle to live publicly in the truth, Ratzinger also comments on Plato's image of the crucified "just man":

> In the Republic the great philosopher asks what is likely to be the position of the completely just man in this world. He comes to the conclusion that a man's righteousness is only complete and guaranteed when he takes on the appearance of unrighteousness, for only then is it clear that he does not follow the opinion of men but pursues justice only for its own sake. So according to Plato the truly just man must be misunderstood and persecuted in this world; indeed, Plato goes so far as to write: "They will say that our just man will be scourged, racked, fettered, will have his eyes burned out, and at last, after all manner of suffering, will be crucified."[38]

This strange but perceptible force intensifies the capacity to misuse power for the purpose of domination and for the destruction of what opposes it: truth and goodness. This context undermines, therefore, merely benign attempts to understand political and social issues as just human limitations that can be put right by good human intentions of togetherness. We see at play greater forces than our own that will not be overcome merely by our own new structures and plans, or by our confidence in technology. We have already seen in this last century the destructive power of people's scientific discoveries.

These real forces are also played out in and through human lives, but their sources are beyond our human capacity to identify. This unsettling phenomenon can be used as an excuse for human evil, as if we were only unthinking actors in some greater dramatic theater. But this is not the case; we know ourselves to be agents of truth, and even from our limited human perspective, we knowingly participate in this dramatic theater by our free decisions that have greater consequences than we can know.

All of this is to try to understand the real context for living publicly in the truth and why this struggle can take on a dramatic and sacrificial nature so foreign to our expectations of easy resolutions and impersonal solutions. Something greater is being played out on our local and public fora, and the intensity and profundity of the human conflict are the signs of a conflict at a much deeper level of being and existence. This also implies that struggle and conflict are necessary conditions for our authentic living, that they are the given actual conditions of our existence to which we are required to respond.

In *The Growth of the Liberal Soul*, Walsh proposes that an existential situation of conflict and struggle is something constant in our history. We should not think (as perhaps we still often do) that strife and forms of conflict are strange aberrations to normal existence, which should be tranquil and passive. Walsh notes that the significant advances in understanding and vision—he refers to the development of classical philosophy and the birth of Christianity—come in times of conflict and even of cultural and social disintegration. These movements forward in human culture in fact only occur in the face of opposition and conflict. Conflict is our constant condition and the price to be paid for learning to live in the truth. This is a condition of our attaining and living in truth, even if today it is far from our consciousness— we expect life to be sedate and pacific. One wonders how such a perception has come to dominate our perspective.[39]

This is not a commodious existential position for human persons and the public and political nature of their existence makes the difficulties all the greater and all the more obvious. Rebellion, in the form of fashioning our own meaning from the circumstances that go beyond us, the merely human comprehension of phenomena and their solutions, the rejection of suffering as something that is unfair and unjust, the clamor for the proximate perfect society, are all symptomatic of a lack of adjustment to a greater context and the inexplicable and imperfect things that happen in our lives for which there is no apparent answer or solution, except the requirement to live through them.

Particular cases stand out in human history, from Socrates to the students of the White Rose Movement of Munich during Nazi Germany, and yet these particular cases are only visible instances of this heightened struggle that is the background to human existence and history and the required commitment to circumstances that may, at times, be freely accepted or rejected, or simply imposed on us, whether we accept them or not. So much of our existence is influenced and determined by the reality of events and circumstances which we do not choose and to which we are obliged to respond. We are not free to *unchoose*.[40]

THE MORAL EXPERIENCE OF PUBLICLY LIVING IN THE TRUTH

What is perhaps remarkable about those who have had to live publicly in the truth in the face of great difficulties and dangers are the accounts, when they exist, of the inner experience of these people. For most of these people the circumstances of their witness to truth, *parresia*, were not chosen by them, but rather thrust upon them without choice. They suddenly found themselves in situations of great danger, to themselves, to their families, or to others, and were required to respond, to confront this danger in a way that required of them an heroic degree of living in the truth.

British historian Martin Gilbert found himself on Mount Zion, in Jerusalem, in February 1974, and noticed a funeral at a Christian cemetery. Many Jews were in attendance, and he discovered that the burial was of Oskar Schindler, the businessman who had saved more than 1,500 Jews during the war. This led Gilbert to investigate the known cases of those non-Jews in Europe who had helped Jews escape. In the afterword to the book of collected stories, Gilbert notes some general conclusions about those who had heroically helped the Jewish people.

In the first place, he recognizes that what these people chose to do was done freely and deliberately:

> Theirs was a deliberate decision to behave in a civilized, humane manner, rather than to do nothing, or to refuse to be involved, or to take the route of barbarism. . . . Yet these were not foolhardy, rash or intemperate people; most of them made their choice calmly, deliberately and with full realisation of the risks—risks that they faced, and took, for months and even years.[41]

The most common answer to the question as to why they chose to do what they did was a simple "We did what we had to do," "Anyone would have done the same," "If I had not done this, that would not have been normal."[42]

These are illuminating examples. They show us that the moral capacity and the desire for *parresia* is inherent in the human person, if only potentially. This was a point made by Mordecai Paldiel, the former director of the *Righteous Among the Nations* at Yad Vashem in Jerusalem. Paldiel observes that modern philosophers have convinced us that human persons are fundamentally corrupted and evil, and that therefore their actions are predominantly determined by selfish and malevolent interests, with little or no evidence of nobler aspirations: "Wittingly or not, together with Hobbes and Freud, we accept the proposition that man is essentially an aggressive being, bent on destruction, involved principally with himself, and only marginally interested in the needs of others."[43]

What these examples also show us is that these responses were *freely* chosen perceptions of what was right and good to do, even at the cost of great personal risk and sacrifice. In the examples described, there was a perceived experience of the goodness and the rightness of the response of *parresia,* its truthfulness, as the only worthy response to a grave situation of life and death, something that spoke clearly above all other considerations as the only adequate response to the dire need of others.

These, and countless other examples of the only adequate heroic and normal reaction to situations of dramatic danger in response to the needs of others, show that human persons, as fallible and ruptured as they are, are capable of perceiving and responding to the needs of others, and in a way that is perceived as entirely normal—what one should expect from a human person—even when the danger to oneself or to one's loved ones is real and immanent. So much so that such responses are considered normal, not heroic.

There is, however, a further question: why is it that the normal or adequate response, which was how practically all of these righteous persons recognized their actions to be, demanded of them such outstanding risks and sacrifices? What is normal and adequate we assume to be easy and straight-forward. Why was what was normal, "what anyone would have done," so demanding of risk and self-sacrifice?

We see here examples of a greater context of struggle and conflict that makes what is normal and adequate something that is great and costly. This exaggeration and distortion of human conflict is the phenomenon that puts ordinary human actions in a greater and extreme context. This implies that social and political decisions may sometimes require a high degree of *parresia* as a normal and adequate response to given circumstances. Not to allow for this is not to see, or want to see, reality and to try to tone down the expectations of what is right and good to what requires little involvement or effort. The difficulty with this is that the circumstances demand of us, as a normal and adequate requirement, what may well require great personal commitment and sacrifice. For the examples of the Righteous, there simply was no easy third way to respond adequately to the plight of others. The demand on these ordinary people was personal and total, and at the same time the only reasonable answer to be given. One can certainly understand those who failed to respond adequately; at the same time, it can only be called failure.

IS LIVING PUBLICLY IN THE TRUTH EFFECTIVE?

There is one final question to consider about the context of living publicly in the truth. In the dramatic situations that *parresia* at times requires, the risks and dangers of the normal and adequate response are often great and require to be taken up. What if all goes wrong? What if what is reasonable and right requires the ultimate sacrifice, no happy ending, the apparent uselessness of the response that is, at the same time, the only adequate one? How does one explain the apparent uselessness and failure to achieve even having made the ultimate sacrifice? Is there a limit to the effectiveness of living publicly in the truth? Can *parresia* lead ultimately to actions that may be right and good, but ultimately useless?

The heroic sacrifice of what may be the normal and only adequate response to others, can be justified by a successful outcome. The struggle, for example, of Martin Luther King Jr., or Nelson Mandela, and of their followers achieved, at least partially or to a significant degree, what they aimed to do and to oppose invidious racial discrimination. It is easy to read back from achievement to the struggle and somehow to imagine these men and women as having the comfort of prescient success. In almost all cases, this was not their experience during the struggle; what maintained them was the rightness of their cause, not the guarantee of its effectiveness or success. Some did achieve what they struggled for, and in a spectacular way, as was the case of Havel, who described his six-month journey from enemy of the state of Czechoslovakia to president as a "miracle."[44] So, too, was the electrician Lech Walesa, who led the Polish Solidarity Union, won the Nobel Prize for Peace, and became the first democratically elected president of Poland in 1990. But what of the cases of apparent total destruction and annihilation, of those who gave the normal and adequate response in exceptional circumstances, who risked everything—and lost, were killed or destroyed?

One can admire the example of *parresia* of Franz Jägerstätter, the Austrian farmer and father of four daughters who refused to take the soldier's oath of allegiance to Hitler, was imprisoned, tried, and guillotined in a Berlin prison in 1943.[45] Jägerstätter's example of living publicly in the truth is, perhaps, exemplary, but what did it achieve, the life of one poor farmer opposing the might of Nazi Austria, and at the cost of leaving his wife as a widow with young children?

As with so many other unsuccessful examples of living in the truth, we can admire their personal courage and truthfulness, we may be moved by their example to try ourselves to live similarly, we may remember their dates and anniversaries, but is there not a certain unexplained enigma to their story? Is there not a dichotomy between what is normal and adequate, and the consequent annihilation of their being? Can it be left hanging unexplained in our reason as a gesture that was ultimately ineffective? The precise question now is not the righteousness of their actions, but the effectiveness of the sacrifice they were called to make. This is a question that is not often raised in ethics—the effectiveness of what is right and good. Speaking of ethical experience, French Jesuit philosopher Joseph de Finance writes:

> He cannot but question himself on how he is actually behaving, and on how he ought to behave so that his life may have meaning. He is confronted, at least in an implicit manner, with the problem of what moral living requires of him. For, as is only too obvious, it is not general and abstract formulas which involve him in this problem: it is in and through extremely particular, extremely concrete, extremely "day-to-day" problems that the question of the meaning of life, of the orientation he is to give to it, presents itself in him and to him.[46]

While this is indeed true, there are times when the experience of what is right to do does not shed any light on the meaning of my personal existence; in fact, what is right and good to do may seem to curtail or even to end my present existence, and yet, as the examples have shown, the only authentic response to the experience necessarily implies such personal sacrifice.

What answer can be given to this disconcerting and apparently incongruous demand of personal sacrifice and in what way may it enlighten the meaning of my life?

Indeed, many times it is the apparent ineffectiveness of what is right and good that seems to be the obstacle to fulfilment and a strong consideration precisely for not doing what is right and good. Is this question of the effectiveness of the adequate response an ethical consideration at all? Are we not entering into pragmatic considerations when we ask if what is right and good works to achieve what is right and good, or in reality are we just assuming the loser mentality of those who hand themselves over to be destroyed?

Some may see in these examples not valor but weakness, a sign of dull acceptance of one's fate and a fundamental lack of the will to live. This was Friedrich Nietzsche's criticism of Socrates:

> Socrates wanted to die: not Athens, but he himself chose the hemlock; he forced Athens to sentence him. "Socrates is no physician," he said softly to himself; "here death alone is the physician. Socrates himself has merely been sick a long time."[47]

Nietzsche's condemnation of this self-deception moral "rationality at any price" is complete. Writing of those who resign themselves to suffering and death, he states:

> Extrication lies beyond their strength: what they choose as a means, as salvation, is itself but another expression of decadence; they change its expression, but they do not get rid of decadence itself. Socrates was a misunderstanding; the whole improvement-morality, including the Christian, was a misunderstanding. . . . To have to fight the instincts, that is the formula of decadence: as long as life is ascending, happiness equals instinct.[48]

Nietzsche's criticism, I suggest, does not correspond to the inner experience of those who have suffered for truth. The response of the righteous was not a denial of the will to live, but the experience of something greater even than this human existence. They did not want to die, but to live in a greater way and not in an inadequate human way. There may well be those who do not really live human lives, or those who adopt a herd mentality, but surely not these people who respond in an unexceptionally human way in exceptional circumstances.

There is, behind Nietzsche's radical criticism, the conflict between the vison of power and the vision of truth. One can understand, given the radical insecurity of the human person's existence and its greater unknown context, the ease with which one can try to assert and shape one's own existence by the power of one's will and to judge those who do not do so as weak and cowardly, not having the will to live and to dominate. On the one hand:

> Inasmuch as at all times, as long as there have been human beings, there have also been herds of men (clans, communities, tribes, peoples, states, churches) and always a great many people who obeyed, compared with the small number of those commanding—considering, then, that nothing has been exercised and cultivated better and longer among men so far than obedience—it may fairly be assumed that the need for it is now innate in the average man, as a kind of formal conscience that commands: "thou shalt unconditionally do something, unconditionally not do something else," in short, "thou shalt." This need seeks to satisfy itself and to fill its form with some content. According to its strength, impatience, and tension, it seizes upon things as a rude appetite, rather indiscriminately, and accepts whatever is shouted into its ears by someone who issues commands—parents, teachers, laws, class prejudices, public opinions.[49]

On the other hand, as Nietzsche sees it, what is vital in personal existence to rediscover one's real self and to become master of all:

> To translate man back into nature; to become master over the many vain and overly enthusiastic interpretations and connotations that have so far been scrawled and painted over that eternal basic text of *homo natura*; to see to it that man henceforth stands before man as even today, hardened in the discipline of science, he stands before the rest of nature with intrepid Oedipus eyes and sealed Odysseus ears, deaf to the siren songs of old metaphysical bird catchers who have been piping at him all too long, "you are more, you are higher, you are of a different origin!"—that may be a strange and insane task, but it is a task—who would deny that? Why did we choose this insane task? Or, putting it differently: "why have knowledge at all?"[50]

Compared to this assertive will to power, the witness to truth seems weak and defenseless. This is the image of truth before power that Reinhold Schneider uses in his novel *Imperial Mission*, which was itself an allegory of the political situation of Nazi Germany.[51] As Ratzinger recounts:

> In his novel about *Las Casas*, Reinhold Schneider impressively portrayed the mystery of conscience in the character of the nameless girl from the Lucayos tribe, who slowly leads the unscrupulous Spanish fortune hunter Bernardino back to an understanding of compassion and the mystery of suffering and in the process reawakens his dead soul within him.[52]

Ratzinger goes on to ask:

Is it not crazy to count on this little-girl conscience, when we see what really matters to the world and the only things that count in it? Faced with today's threats, is it not vain, senseless dreaming to look up to those witnesses to conscience who were able to contribute only their suffering? What are we supposed to do (so runs the retort), conduct politics with poetry and in that way solve the problems of our time?[53]

Quite apart from the influence of these examples, and their capacity to stir the perception and desire for truth in others, is there something manifest in these sacrifices in and beyond the apparent destruction of human life? Here there are things seen and not seen; what is perceived is the rightness and goodness of the response to others. What is not seen may be the ultimate transformation that is achieved in the apparent destruction, something real that is accomplished and therefore effective in and through the act, of which only the destructive part is seen.

The ultimate task then is to grasp in some way the real effectiveness of what is perceived as the normal and adequate response in circumstances that require sacrifice with no apparent achievement in sight, in fact, only the sacrificial requirement being evident. As we have seen with the examples mentioned, and with almost all who have found themselves in such situations, this is not something chosen, but demanded of them, at times freely, as a freely chosen adequate response to the perceived needs, at times demanded of those who are not free to choose but have the consequences of these situations thrust upon them; the only choice is how one chooses to assimilate the sacrifice required, as described, for example, in Viktor E. Frankl's account of concentration camp prisoners.[54] Such cases underline our incapacity to *unchoose* our circumstances.

Is there something to hope for in these situations that seem to demand what is right and good and at the same time necessarily imply the loss or destruction of one's very being or (which may be even harder) the destruction of a loved one? Or do we have only to remember the noble loss, the good sacrifice, the ultimate truthful and useless act?

It seems that we must try to rely on another source of light to answer this existential enigma. In confluent ways the great spiritual traditions, experienced by those who have come to recognize in their intellect another source of truth, shed some light on both the need for and the effectiveness of required suffering by living publicly in the truth.

In a note written by Mahatma Gandhi for the Indian National Congress in 1920, Gandhi explains his doctrine of *Satyagraha*, a word that means "holding on to the truth," the strength of truth and the strength of love.[55] Far from being merely a tactic of social non-cooperation or industrial action, Gandhi perceives in the living of and suffering for the public truth an effectiveness that is able to bring those who oppose truth to an inner change of heart. *Satyagraha* requires strength of soul to live the sacrifice for truth in one's own being and yet it is not a doctrine only for the privileged few:

> Its root meaning is "holding on to the truth" hence, Truth-force. I have also called it Love-force or Soul-force. In the application of *Satyagraha* I discovered in the earliest stages that pursuit of truth did not admit of violence being inflicted on one's opponent, but that he must be weaned from error by patience and sympathy. For what appears to be truth to the one may appear to be error to the other. And patience means self-suffering. So the doctrine came to mean vindication of truth, not by infliction of suffering on the opponent, but one's own self.[56]

The vindication of truth requires and is an expression of, therefore, the law of love. Even the death of the physical body can be welcomed as a means to make the opponent see the truth:

> *Satyagraha* is self-dependent. It does not require the assent of the opponent before it can be brought into play. Indeed it shines out most when the opponent resists. It is therefore irresistible. A *Satyagrahi* does not know what defeat is, for he fights for truth without being exhausted. Death in the fight is a deliverance, and prison a gateway to liberty.[57]

The point here is not to examine the doctrine of *Satyagraha* for its metaphysical completeness or to try to justify non-violence in every situation. Rather, it is to raise the question as to the effectiveness of living publicly in the truth. Above and beyond possible contingent needs of physical strength for self-protection and for the protection of others, the doctrine of *Satyagraha* seems to point to a further need to take on oneself the burden of the conversion of others to the truth, even if this requires the sacrifice of one's physical life. Gandhi's writings even seem to point to a fulfilment or deliverance through such sacrifice. This suggests the effectiveness of an achievement for both the *Satyagrahi* and for the opponent by means of the sacrifice implied in living publicly in the truth.[58]

Noor Inayat Khan was born in 1914, the daughter of a Sufi preacher whose teaching centered on the central role of *mahabbah,* the unconditional love of Allah. Noor grew up in Paris and London and imbibed the particular form of Sufi mysticism taught by her father. She studied child psychology at the Sorbonne. When the war broke out and Paris fell to the Nazis, Noor fled to London and trained as a wireless telegraphist. She was asked to become a radio operator in occupied France and after four months of dangerous work, was captured, tortured, and killed. Her writings reveal why she undertook these great risks:

Noor knew that we pay a price in life: the price we pay to receive life. If paying that price was not, as she said, "the greatest joy, the highest and most inconceivable joy," then it was "not a willing offering." . . . Most sacrifices, she believed, were small, often involving wealth or material possessions. But "the greatest sacrifice," she said, was "the sacrifice of one's self," a sacrifice that "bathes" the world in a "love which purifies and heals the suffering of humanity." This was the "real religion"—faith "conceived through the heart and the mind, not through the mind only." . . . "The heart must be broken in order for the real to come forth."[59]

In the Judeo-Christian tradition, the experience of suffering as a consequence of proclaiming the Word of the Lord God is never far from the lives of the Prophets. The general example of the Scriptures is of the person who is faithful to the Lord God's word, not the hero or the revolutionary.[60] This fidelity often implies suffering and even physical death, as evidenced by the violent death of almost all the prophets. Even so, there is in the figure of the *ebed Yahweh,* found in the prophet Isaiah of the Old Testament, a new dimension to this role of suffering in fidelity to the word of Yahweh.[61] This is the notion of vicarious suffering, suffering in one's own person as atonement for the people, for the many.[62] Exegetical evidence of the New Testament points to Jesus himself as the origin of the association of the role, rather than the title, of the *ebed Yahweh* with himself, that is, the consciousness of his death as atonement for the many. Even though the title of *ebed Yahweh* in reference to Jesus is hardly used in the New Testament writings, the central role of the servant who suffers and dies in atonement for the many is evident in both the Gospels and the other New Testament writings.[63]

Although foreign to an individualistic notion of the human person, this idea of participating in the sufferings of Jesus for the atonement and salvation of the many is a familiar one in the Christian faith. Ultimately, suffering and sacrifice can only be understood in the greater context of God's ultimate power:

First, God is power, the ultimate power. And the ultimate power, which holds the universe in control, is goodness. Power and goodness, in this world so often taken as separate, are identical in the ultimate root of being. If we ask, "Where does being come from?" we can reply with certainly: from an immense power, or also—thinking of the mathematical structure of being—from a powerful and creative reason.[64]

The examples and doctrines mentioned above point to discernible evidence within personal experience of the rationality of power in the goodness of sacrifice.

It may, of course, be confused with a defeatist attitude to human flourishing and the lack of will to live, or the corruption of the goodness of life. This is how it may appear from the outside, from the remote and impersonal perspective of the detached observer.

Each of these explanations of the cost of living publicly in the truth provide, to different degrees and at different levels of reality, a *positive* answer to the given existential situation of particular circumstances that require a great sacrifice by the acceptance of something not wished for but necessary as the normal and adequate personal response. This marks a completely different disposition, and a rebuttal, to the imposition of power as the efficient answer to the opportunities and challenges of life. Power, as the human capacity to dominate and control, experiences its own limit. The temporary imposition by power merely exposes it to the greater transformative process that changes and subdues power into truth, the truth of real order.[65]

In *The Growth of the Liberal Soul*, Walsh comments on Fyodor Dostoyevsky's novels and notices a recurring theme, the emphasis that Dostoyevsky makes in his works of literature on the contrast between the grasp of power as the means for self-assertion and domination and the power of love that in fact transforms and achieves what the power of self-assertion attempts and fails to do. As Walsh observes, Dostoyevsky portrays characters that are driven by the will to power to overcome all moral or religious codes of conduct and to invent and impose themselves, thus showing the superiority of one who can overcome inhibitions and cowardice, along the lines of Nietzsche's Superman. What Dostoyevsky also makes apparent is the fallacy of such attempts at domination; what in fact occurs in this grasping of power is the hermetically sealing off of the individual from any source of truth other than the individual self. The inevitable result of such desire of domination is the emptiness of meaning and the mere defiance of reality that also inevitably imposes itself beyond our desires of self-assertion.[66]

CONCLUSION

Our openness to the various modes of experience of reality manifests dimensions of existence that go beyond the immediate circumstances of our actual existence. What this indicates is that in and through our political activity a greater drama of existence is taking place. This does not trivialize our politics, but enables us, in some real and inchoate way, to put politics in a greater human context of meaning and of purpose.

In this greater context, the necessity to live publicly in the truth often takes the form of a struggle against a destructive opposition to the manifestation of truth, that requires of those who live politically in truth a capacity to confront this resistance. This requires both a vision of practical wisdom and the tactical art of understanding time and place, and the best means to what can be achieved. The real meaning of political prudence thus takes on a much more dynamic, practical, and courageous meaning than is commonly assumed.

This effort to live publicly in the truth is not an option for the virtuous, but the basis of political society, it is what politics is really about. This is, of course, not just a negative task of overcoming the public lie or omission, but the construction of an authentic human society. As Havel writes, the revolt against the lie is one half of living in the truth. Once this has been achieved, if only in part, there occurs the possibility that:

> A more coherent and visible initiative may emerge from this wide and anonymous hinterland, an initiative that transcends "merely" individual revolt and is transformed into more conscious, structured, and purposeful work. The point where living within the truth ceases to be a mere negation of living with a lie and becomes articulate in a particular way, is the point at which something is born that might be called "the independent spiritual, social and political life of society."[67]

It is certainly true that the positive construction of "the independent spiritual, social and political life of society" requires much more than the revolt against political oppression in its many forms, and often can be more politically demanding than the resistance to oppression.

Both necessary tasks, the deconstruction of political lies, and the construction of the political life of society, take place within the greater dimension of the spiritual struggle to establish the order of right that endures, and the necessary personal, spiritual contribution to this order as part of one's political response. This political contribution—often seen only in its manifest appearance of personal sacrifice—is in fact effective in politics' greater dimension of order.

NOTES

1. Niccolò Machiavelli, *The Prince*, 2nd ed., trans. Harvey C. Mansfield. (Chicago: University of Chicago Press, 1998), chap. 15 "Of Those Things for Which Men and Especially Princes are Praised or Blamed" (61).

2. David Walsh, *The Growth of the Liberal Soul* (Missouri: University of Missouri Press, 1997), 320.

3. Robert Sokolowski, *Eucharistic Presence: A Study in the Theology of Disclosure* (Washington DC: Catholic University Press, 1993), 189–90. The reference is to Debra Rosenthal, *At the Heart of the Bomb: The Dangerous Allure of Weapons Work* (Boston: Addison-Wesley, 1990), 215.

4. What this requires of us intellectually is described in Christian terms by Peter Henrici "The Spiritual Dimension and Its Form of Reason," *Communio* 20, no. 4

(1993): 638–51; and David L. Schindler, "Sanctity and the Intellectual Life," *Communio* 20, no. 4 (1993): 652–72. I suggest that, although the articles are both written in explicitly Christian terms, the human experience of what is required of us to live fully in the truth is the same.

5. Cf. John Paul II, *Fides et Ratio*, Saint Peters, Rome, September 14, 1998, https://www.vatican.va/content/john-paul-ii/en/encyclicals/documents/hf_jp-ii_enc _14091998_fides-et-ratio.html (accessed October 19, 2023), see sec.23. Although the reference is explicitly to the crucifixion and resurrection of Christ, I suggest that the human experience of the progressive reliance on the experience of truth is best described as a type of continuous death and resurrection, in greater or lesser dramatic forms.

6. On the importance of action in a metaphysical explanation of reality, W. Norris Clarke's chapter "Action as the Self-Revelation of Being: A Central Theme in the Thought of St. Thomas," in *Explorations in Metaphysics: Being-God-Person* (Notre Dame, IN: University of Notre Dame Press, 1994), 45–64 provides an insight into the importance of action as a metaphysical category of being.

7. Maurice Blondel, *Action (1893): Essay on a Critique of Life and a Science of Practice*, 2nd ed., trans. Olivia Blanchette (Notre Dame, IN: University of Notre Dame Press, 2004), 4.

8. Václav Havel et al., *The Power of the Powerless: Citizens Against the State in Central-Eastern Europe*, ed. John Keane (London: Routledge, 2015), 33.

9. Havel et al., *Power of the Powerless*, 42.

10. Havel et al., *Power of the Powerless*, 38.

11. Walsh, *Growth of the Liberal Soul*, 318–19.

12. Hans Christian Andersen, *The Emperor's New Clothes* (1837) (New York: Random House, 1975).

13. Havel et al., *Power of the Powerless*, 39. D. Walsh also observes that this act of living in the truth is in fact a dynamic process that, when followed, leads us to discover within ourselves capacities, resources, and ever greater actions. Writing of those who suffered in totalitarian regimes, Walsh states: "The testaments of those who resisted the holocausts and purges of the totalitarian terror is a daunting revelation of the reality of good that overcomes evil. No one can read their testimonies without coming away with a profound sense of the depths that lie hidden within a human being, spiritual resources of proportions that remained unknown even to those who possessed them until the day when they were called forth by the circumstances in which they found themselves" Walsh, *Growth of the Liberal Soul*, 286.

14. Eric Voegelin, *Science, Politics and Gnosticism: Two Essays*, ed. Ellis Sandoz (Washington, DC: Gateway Editions, 2012), 358. E. Voegelin detects in Marxism, in Comtean positivism and in National-Socialism the same prohibition of questions as to the truth of their ideological constructs. In their different ideological ways, "The questions of the 'individual man' are cut off by the *ukase* ('decree') of the speculator who will not permit his construct to be disturbed" (392).

15. Romano Guardini, *The Death of Socrates: An Interpretation of the Platonic Dialogues. Euthyphro, Apology, Crito and Phaedo*, trans. Basil Wrighton (London: Sheed and Ward, 1948), 44.

16. Guardini, *Death of Socrates*, 51. As Guardini notes, this theme of sacrifice as the price of living in the truth is developed more in Plato's *Phaedo*.

17. Guardini, *Death of Socrates*, 64.

18. In T .S. [Thomas Stears] Eliot's *Murder in the Cathedral* (London: Faber and Faber, 1968), the four knights who slay the Archbishop Thomas Beckett then address the audience and make speeches justifying the heinous action in terms of disinterested motives of political expediency, public obligation, the preservation of civil law, and by stating that Beckett brought this fate upon himself as a form of suicide while of unsound mind: "It is the only charitable verdict you can give, upon one who was, after all, a great man" (90).

19. I follow here Michel Foucault's series of seminar conferences published in *"Discourse and Truth" and "Parrēsia,"* ed. Henri-Paul Fruchaud and Daniele Lorenzini. (Chicago: University of Chicago Press, 2019), 51 and following.

20. Foucault, *Discourse*, 51.

21. Foucault, *Discourse*, 53.

22. Foucault, *Discourse*, 59. Foucault observes the development of the term *parresia* from the fifth century BC to the Greco-Roman period and then to the first centuries of late antiquity. *Parresia* is applied first in relation to rhetoric, then to politics and then to the care of the self. The term was also used in an early Christian context, as, for example, in Acts 4:13 (RSV) when Peter and John speak courageously before political and religious authorities.

23. Joseph Ratzinger, "Freedom and Constraint in the Church," in *Church, Ecumenism, and Politics: New Endeavours in Ecclesiology*, trans. Michael J. Miller et al. (San Francisco: Ignatius Press, 2008), 188, 189.

24. Ratzinger, "Freedom and Constraint," in *Church, Ecumenism, and Politics*, 190. Ratzinger notes that "The Apostle's frankness consists of speaking the truth into a world ruled by appearances, even though this means that he must face 'great opposition' (1 Thess 2:2). Hence the frankness of the free man presupposes above all a freedom from oneself, 'a detachment from self, because he has begun to proclaim the gospel'" (189). The inserted quotation is from Heinrich Schlier, *Der Apostel*.

25. Plato, *The Republic*, in *The Complete Works of Plato*, ed. Benjamin Jowett (Kirkland, WA: Latus e-Publishing, 2012), 34135. Kindle.

26. Plato, *Republic*, 34135.

27. Niccolò Machiavelli, *Discourses on Livy*, trans. Harvey C. Mansfield and Nathan Tarcov (Chicago: University of Chicago Press, 1996).

28. Machiavelli, *Prince*, 61.

29. Mary A. Glendon, *The Forum and the Tower: How Scholars and Politicians Have Imagined the World, from Plato to Eleanor Roosevelt* (Oxford: Oxford University Press, 2011), xiii. The reference is to Plato's *Seventh Letter.*

30. Doris Kearns Goodwin, *Team of Rivals: The Political Genius of Abraham Lincoln* (New York: Simon & Schuster, 2006), xvii. The political adroitness of President Lincoln to achieve the necessary two-thirds majority in the House (the Senate had already passed the amendment with a two thirds majority the previous spring) is related on pages 686–90. The Amendment passed on January 31, 1865. Goodwin cites Lincoln's old critic William Lloyd Garrison: "And to whom is the country

more immediately indebted for this vital and saving amendment of the Constitution than, perhaps, to any other man? . . . I believe I may confidently answer—to the humble railsplitter of Illinois—to the Presidential chain-breaker for millions of the oppressed—to Abraham Lincoln" (690).

31. Both Niccolò Machiavelli and Friedrich Nietzsche seem to reject Christian morality, especially, according to each's understanding, the value of humility and the ascesis of self-dominion.

32. Josef Pieper, *The Four Cardinal Virtues* (Notre Dame, IN: University of Notre Dame Press, 1966), 4–5.

33. Pieper, *Four Cardinal Virtues*, 25. The reference is to St. Thomas Aquinas' *Summa Theologiae*, I, II, 64, 3, obj.2. As Pieper explains: "This means first of all that the theoretical and the practical reason are not two distinct powers of the soul. Nor are they two separate and independent operations of one and the same 'basic faculty.'" Pieper faults Immanuel Kant for making: "the practical reason entirely independent of the theoretical and of all that can be the object of theoretical activity, that means, independent of all knowledge of reality. Moreover, this is not a harmless unessential speculation for philosophers. In making the practical reason—that is, the power of the soul that determines action—independent of the theoretical reason—that is, the power of the soul that perceives objective being—Kant sees, according to Richard Kroner, nothing less than 'the conquest of the metaphysics of being, the transfer of the centre of gravity from the object to the subject'" Josef Pieper, *Living the Truth: Reality and the Good* and *The Truth of All Things* (San Francisco: Ignatius Press, 1989), 1596. For a different interpretation of Kant's understanding of the relation of practical to theoretical reason, see David Walsh's *The Modern Philosophical Revolution: The Luminosity of Existence* (Cambridge University Press, 2012).

34. Pieper, *Four Cardinal Virtues*, 8, 22. The reference is to St. Thomas Aquinas, *Quaestio disputata de virtutibus in communi*, 9.

35. David C. Schindler, *The Politics of the Real: The Church Between Liberalism and Integralism* (Steubenville, OH: New Polity Press), 299.

36. This is how Judeo-Christian revelation describes the evident phenomenon of rupture in and among men. Cf. Henri de Lubac, *Catholicism: Christ and the Common Destiny of Man*, trans. Lancelot Sheppard (San Francisco: Ignatius Press, 1988), 25–40.

37. Joseph Ratzinger, *Preaching and Dogma: Applying Christian Dogma to Daily Life* (San Francisco: Ignatius Press, 2011), 121. Ratzinger goes on to write that man is also "the creature who is capable of being an expression of God himself. Man is so made that God can enter into union with him. Man, who seems at first sight to be a kind of unfortunate monster produced by evolution, at the same time represents the highest possibility the created order can attain. And this possibility becomes a reality, even if it be amid the saddest kind of failure on the part of the human race" (121).

38. Joseph Ratzinger, *Introduction to Christianity* (San Francisco: Ignatius Press, 2004), 292. The reference is to Plato's *Republic*, book 2, 361e–362a.

39. Walsh, *Growth of the Liberal Soul*, 320. Václav Havel remembered the words of Jan Patocka, a Czech philosopher and disciple of E. Husserl, who had been

harassed by the state police until his death: "There are some things worth dying for," spoken a short time before Patocka's death in 1977 (Cf. 48).

40. Kenneth L. Schmitz, *The Texture of Being: Essays in First Philosophy*, ed. Paul O'Herron (Washington, DC: Catholic University of America Press, 2007), 228.

41. Martin Gilbert, *The Righteous: The Unsung Heroes of the Holocaust* (New York: Henry Holt, 2003), 433.

42. Gilbert, *Righteous*, 433, 439.

43. Mordecai Paldiel, "Is Goodness a Mystery?" *Jerusalem Morning Post*, October 8, 1989.

44. Greeting Pope John Paul II at the airport in Prague, Czechoslovakia, Václav Havel declared: "I do not know if I know what a miracle is. Nevertheless, I dare say that right now I am the witness of one," "On This Day, in 1990: John Paul II Became the First Pope to Visit Prague," *Kafkadesk,* April 21, 2021, https://kafkadesk .org/2021/04/21/on-this-day-in-1990-john-paul-ii-became-the-first-pope-to-visit prague/#:~:text=Greeting%20John%20Paul%20II%20as,am%20the%20witness%20 of%20one%E2%80%9D.

45. Cf. Franz Jägerstätter, *Letters and Writings from Prison*, ed. Erna Putz (Maryknoll, NY: Orbis, 2009).

46. Joseph de Finance, *An Ethical Inquiry* (Rome: Editrice Pontificia Università Gregoriana, 1991), 16. De Finance's definition of ethics is: "the categorically normative science of human actions, pursued in accordance with the natural light which reason casts" (15).

47. Friedrich Nietzsche, *The Portable Nietzsche*, ed. and trans. Walter Kaufmann (Harmondsworth, UK: Penguin Books, 1977), 476.

48. Nietzsche, *Portable Nietzsche*, 475.

49. Friedrich Nietzsche, *Beyond Good and Evil: Prelude to a Philosophy of the Future*, trans. Walter Kaufmann (New York: Vintage Books, 1989), 152.

50. Nietzsche, *Beyond Good and Evil*, 217.

51. Reinhold Schneider, *Imperial Mission*, trans. Walter Oden (New York: Gresham Press, 1948).

52. Ratzinger, "Conscience in Its Time," in *Church, Ecumenism, and Politics*, 162.

53. Ratzinger, "Conscience in its Time," in *Church, Ecumenism, and Politics*, 162.

54. Viktor E. Frankl, *Man's Search for Meaning* (Boston: Beacon Press, 2006).

55. The Report of the Commissioners appointed by the Punjab Sub-Committee of the Indian National Congress, 1920, vol. 1, chap. 4, as published in Jacques Maritain, *The Collected Works of Jacques Maritain* (Notre Dame, IN: University of Notre Dame Press 1996), vol. 2, 112–15.

56. Maritain, *Collected Works*, vol. 2, 112.

57. Maritain, *Collected Works*, vol. 2, 113.

58. While Maritain notes limitations in Gandhi's doctrine of *Satyagraha* and the danger of a non-material approach of angelism to the resolution of human injustice, Maritain retains his appreciation for Gandhi's technique: "The technique of Gandhi if translated to the intellectual climate of a truer and more realist philosophy would retain all its truth and lose all its exclusiveness. One may wonder if with the necessary rectification and readaptation, it could not (as Gandhi has often declared) be applied

in the West as it has been in the East; and give new life to the temporal struggle for freedom and human personality" Maritain, *Collected Works*, vol. 2, 88.

59. Arthur J. Magida, *Code Name Madeleine. A Sufi Spy in Nazi-Occupied Paris* (New York: W. W. Norton, 2020), 133–34. The author's sources for these quotations are from an undated and unpaginated essay on world religions written by Noor in the mid or late 1930s. This essay is in the possession of David Harper, Noor Inayat Khan's nephew.

60. For a comparison and contrast of responses to the Judeo-Christian eschatological promises, see Ratzinger's essay "Eschatology and Utopia" in *Church, Ecumenism, and Politics*, 223–37. "The faith of the New Testament does not know of the revolutionary but is acquainted with the martyr: the martyr recognises the authority of the State but also knows its limits" Joseph Ratzinger, "Political Visions and the Praxis of Politics," in *Europe: Today and Tomorrow* (San Francisco: Ignatius Press, 2007), 56.

61. Oscar Cullmann, the German Biblical scholar, makes the following point: "We have seen that suffering is also of the essence of the Prophet. But he does not consciously suffer vicariously, voluntarily take upon himself the suffering of the people as atonement. He suffers because 'suffering is the inevitable fate of the prophet . . .'" and "We may say in conclusion that official Judaism at the time of Jesus—even in Palestine—did not include atoning suffering as a necessary part of the messianic idea, and that even if one can actually show the existence of the conception of a suffering Messiah, it was at best marginal and weak" Cullmann, *The Christology of the New Testament*, 2nd ed., trans. Shirley C. Guthrie and Charles A. M. Hall (London: SCM Press, 1963), 56, 60.

62. Joseph Ratzinger writes: "The sign of true justice, of perfect justice, is to die voluntarily for the salvation of others. This sign Jesus gave" Ratzinger, *Journey to Easter: Spiritual Reflections for the Lenten Season* (New York: Crossroad, 1987), 42. The acceptance of this comment would require a profound broadening of our assumed notions of justice.

63. Cullmann points out, for example, the deliberate use by all four Evangelists of Jesus' words of giving his life for the many in their accounts of the Last Supper, as St. John's use of the Lamb of God image, and the similarity of Isaiah 42:1 (RSV) with the words of the Lord God spoken at Jesus' baptism, etc. Cf. Cullmann, *Christology of the New Testament*, 60–82. As Pope Benedict explains in his commentary on St. Paul's theology of the cross: "The 'stumbling block' and 'folly' of the Cross lie in the very fact that where there seems to be nothing but failure, sorrow and defeat, there is the full power of God's boundless love, for the Cross is an expression of love, and love is the true power that is revealed precisely in this seeming weakness" Benedict XVI, *Saint Paul* (San Francisco: Ignatius Press, 2009), 63.

64. Ratzinger, *Journey to Easter*, 45.

65. David C. Schindler has made reference to tragic (in the Greek sense) nature of man's history, including his political history. In this classical sense: "tragedy represented the deepest possible affirmation of meaning, the victory of an ultimate saving truth that cannot be overcome by even the most extreme disorder conceivable by man (the '*contra naturam*' par excellence, for example, of feeding sons to their unknowing father), but instead in some unfathomably mysterious way can affirm itself even in

the face of horrors 'than-which-nothing-greater-can-be-thought'" Schindler, *Politics of the Real*, 304.

66. Walsh, *Growth of the Liberal Soul*, 29–30. Walsh also comments on the transformative power of love in David Walsh's *After Ideology: Recovering the Spiritual Foundations of Freedom* (San Francisco: HarperCollins, 1990) esp. from 152–58.

67. Havel et al., *Power of the Powerless*, 65.

Chapter 5

The Person's Transcendent
Social Destiny

In this overview of this chapter, we consider that all politics is an expression of the meaning and purpose of human person's life in society, and it is necessary to clarify what this expression of meaning and purpose is, both what contemporary politics assumes social life to be, and what in reality human society should be. Today, we live with a mentality that seems to have lost the perception of transcendence, that is, the consciousness of a greater dimension of existence beyond the confines of what is immediate and immanent to this physical world. Our political beliefs are shaped by this assumed limit to our existence.

From the perspective of political history, this narrowing of vision is clearly manifest in the political theories of Thomas Hobbes and John Locke who assume a minimum social contract among persons, in contrast to what Aristotle proposes as the *summum bonum* [greatest good] for society. Contemporary political liberal philosophy, such as John Rawls' "Theory of Justice," seems to perpetuate this minimalist approach to the common and greatest good, what we can call a politics of restraint.[1]

The existential experience of hope necessarily moves the human person toward a definitive goal of fulfillment. This experience is what is expressed in all our lesser hopes and is an expression of a structural orientation of our being toward fulfilment. At the same time, we find ourselves within the limits of human history that seem to frustrate what we hope and expect, in some implicit way. In opposition to the politics of restraint, other modern currents of politics have projected the full range of human hope onto political projects of proximate fulfilment. This politics of aspiration, supported by quasi-religious and optimistic beliefs in progress, have been followed by the failure of their promises and, according to Josef Pieper, a "retaliatory pessimism."[2]

A more careful and profound understanding of the person's original unity and actual condition of rupture is required to understand adequately our real existential circumstances. Theological sources shed light on our human experience of original unity, actual rupture, and transcendent aspiration—the real dimensions of personal existence.

The modern political projects of aspiration are of particular relevance because they appeal to the profound hope, both individual and social, of future fulfilment, but assume and propose a human capacity to achieve this fulfilment. These political projects of aspiration take charge of society and enforce the changes to produce personal and social transformation. Augusto del Noce writes, "revolution . . . replaces metaphysics with the ideal of a meta-humanity,"[3] which, in effect, is the attempt to recreate reality in the human person's image and likeness.

The real nature of human hope is for a real, future fulfilment beyond the confines of this actual existence, and beyond the human capacity to achieve. In classical philosophy, hope was a passion to be curtailed within the limits of this actual existence. As Russell Hittinger points out: "The price to be paid for pressing beyond the limits that seem to be intrinsic to human nature, and thus to uncover new scope and content for hope, is the recognition that man is radically dependent on a being other than himself."[4] The real politics of aspiration necessarily depends on and requires a religious answer.

It is clear, therefore, that politics does require a *summum bonum*, that is the inbuilt expectation of hope to which each person is subject. The real answer to the nature and fulfilment of hope requires a comprehension of the human person's original unity, the condition of actual rupture, and trust in the future fulfilment by Another.

This is particularly relevant today as the politics of restraint seems to dominate our political way of thinking. Alexis de Tocqueville reminds us of the political subterfuge we can live in, "a servitude of the regular, quiet, and gentle kind" that frustrates our real political

NEXUS

We have seen that politics is, or should be, an expression of the human person's social flourishing as an adequate response to the reality which surrounds us and in which we are immersed. Within all the varied forms of cultural expression there is a pattern or structure that corresponds to authentic human living. Politics, as a part of human culture, is made possible and sustained by the many expressions of such authentic human culture. This is the meaning we give to Plato's insight of society, the polis, as the *macro-anthropos*, the reflection of authentic human life that is necessarily social.

The human person's insight into authentic human society is through personal experience of reality, including the reality of one's own personhood.

This perception, experience, interpretation, and adequate response to reality is both a capacity to be developed and a necessity for human living. We have seen that while we cannot avoid our being immersed in the experience of all of what is real, the path to authentic interpretation and response to reality is not always spontaneous or easy. These difficulties are magnified in society as we try to communicate and discuss our shared experience of reality that is the essential bedrock of the social bond. To arrive at a shared truthful consensus of what our lives mean and the shared value we give to what is properly human is fundamental, and yet this process of truthful dialogue is often difficult and only partially achieved, sometimes not at all. The pretense of basing our social living on "agreeing to disagree" is both impractical and subversive of society, conducive only to conflict and domination.

Living publicly in the truth is not a straightforward thing. Strangely, there seems to be a greater context of tension and conflict between doing what is right and good and the disproportionate rejection and opposition to what is right and good, as if something greater was at stake than merely our own human actions. The cost of living publicly in the truth can be terrifying and yet still the normal and adequate response to what should be done, what any normal person would do. There are intimations from religious sources of the experience of contributing to a greater purification and transformation of human existence as the reason for the high price of truthful public living.

As unsatisfactory and inchoate as this human condition is, these are our existential circumstances which we have not chosen, but to which we are required, in freedom, to respond adequately. This explains why politics is so difficult and conflictual; we wrongly assume that life in society should be spontaneous and straight-forward, and we therefore avoid conflict, which we consider to be an inherent sign of failure. This facile view of an easy social bond is misleading and may well be one of the sources of a dangerous empty consensus that only yields more conflict and domination, that is, tyranny.

In fact, conflict and struggle are our only way to shared truth. What we do choose are our instruments, difficult dialogue, or military weapons.[5] It helps considerably when we do not underestimate the difficulties of dialogue and when we also include the need for truthful consensus and not just prevailing domination.

All these considerations shape and determine considerably what we mean by politics and how the political good of the social bond may be enhanced. There is also another dimension of existence that bears weightily on the truth of politics; what we may call the historical dimensions of human existence, the reference to an original condition of the human person's social existence, one's actual existence, and the destiny of a final or transcendent social existence.

OUR CONTEMPORARY HISTORICAL PERSPECTIVE

We are engrossed in this actual human existence and this perspective is almost our entire horizon of existence. We think and we are induced to think merely in terms of this material human existence, and all is oriented toward the material conditions of this actual existence. The quality is this existence becomes the benchmark of the motives for living and the recent appeals to the lack of "quality of life" as a justification for terminating one's actual existence seem to have a certain relevance if this existence is the only measure of potential happiness. Canadian philosopher Charles Taylor has noted that: "the main feature of this new context [secular modernity] is that it puts an end to the naïve acknowledgement of the transcendent, or of goals or claims which go beyond human flourishing" [in this actual existence].[6]

Swiss theologian Hans Urs von Balthasar observes the peculiarity of our common and immanent perspective:

> It is something very astonishing and not at all self-evident, nor, surely, an unequivocal sign of historical progress, that all of the ancient peoples reflected in so many diverse ways on the "hereafter," while modern people are scarcely interested in the matter. It is as though modern men and women have had a tendon severed so that walking toward the former goal is no longer possible; as though their wings have been clipped; as though the spiritual organ for the transcendent has atrophied. What might have caused this?[7]

While this immanent perspective is common to us, it is an inheritance of a profound shift of vision from an integrated cosmic perspective of reality to a splintering of self from the cosmos, and the subsequent split of subject and object, and of nature and transcendence.[8] The resulting perception of nature as matter, raw material, and the human person as an individual self that is the source of its own meaning, leave little hope for the perception of a transcendent order within which persons can find their fulfilment. W. Norris Clarke regards as "two insufficiently examined and deeply flawed premises," of many scientists, philosophers, and religious thinkers today:

> (1) The diminishing philosophical recognition of the irreducibly immaterial nature of the human soul . . . and (2) the view that Nature is an all-encompassing, self-contained whole, of which humans are an inseparable part, that contains within itself, with its own immanent resources, all that is needed for the entire evolutionary development of the cosmos, humans included.[9]

What all of this implies is that we live today assuming a narrow and confined horizon of existence that does not correspond to the dynamic impulse of our human structure or to the order and purpose of cosmic proportions that go beyond our self-centered perspectives of meaning and of value. This means that, as human persons, if we are to flourish, we need to open out our existence to experience a greater purpose and fulfilment *as part of something greater than ourselves and the limits of our actual existence*. It is a case of discovering the greater context within which we belong and to which we contribute, rather than attempting to condition reality to a self-centered perspective in a hermetically sealed immanent existence. What is at stake here is how we want to understand the person's political vocation; either we exist for something greater than ourselves that requires the best of ourselves to achieve, or we exist as separated individuals to preserve and to hold on to each one's own precarious human existence.

In *Metamorphoses of the City*, Pierre Manent contrasts the ancient and the modern perception of the human condition. He relates that in the classical world the aspiration to glory represented the sought-for desire for something beyond the boundary of death. This aspiration was itself an instinctive reaction to the consciousness of death. For modern thinkers, this desire for glory was something immoderate, and such an aspiration subjected human existence to demands that were unreasonable and in fact useless.[10]

Manent explains that in Francis Bacon's new order the political aim was to achieve "the relief of man's estate," an easing of the precariousness of human living, nothing more. Hobbes follows this lowering of human ambition and recognizes that all manifestations of human glory and fame were in fact the cause of human problems and needed to be eliminated. This would be done, according to Hobbes, by curtailing all forms of pride and thus free people from the pressure of greater and transcendent goals, that were in any case futile. The only entity capable of achieving this repression of glory was the state. Only the state could oblige people to lower their ambitions, be satisfied with what this existence offers, and forget any transcendent aspirations. In this way, the state could oblige its citizens to be fixed on the here and now instead of living with heaven on their minds.[11]

The aims and purposes of politics today depend fundamentally on the true aspirations and real dimensions of human existence. To release the true aspirations of human existence it is necessary to rediscover the real dimensions of one's existence. In anthropological terms, we need to discover who the human person is originally, by design, who we are, in this existential condition, and what we aspire to ultimately.

To do this is not to add on something extra to our personal existence, though from our atrophied condition it may appear so, some type of unimaginable potential and aspiration that do not really fit into this actual existence. This is precisely the point; we suffer from "a prison of finitude" that denies to the person, individually and socially, the capacity for complete human flourishing. The totalitarian, ideological, and technological attempts to reshape nature and society into some ideal fabricated form seem to indicate that people do not indeed live by bread alone but are required, by their innate structure of being, to achieve fulfilment in a transcendent social destiny.

THE HUMAN PERSON'S ORIGINAL UNITY, ACTUAL BROKENNESS, TRANSCENDENT FULFILMENT

The political emphasis today on structures, processes, economics, technology, and the criteria of comparative equality and distribution tends to reduce the vision of who the human person is to some quantifiable or comparative measure or capability and leaves the reality of the dimensions of human existence unanswered. What is generally presumed is that this actual existence is the extent of the parameters of human existence, where we find ourselves, and what (and whom) we have to deal with, for our survival and coexistence. This actual existence may be interpreted in a pessimistic or optimistic way. For Hobbes, this natural condition or state was not a happy one, but an existence ruled by fear, as were his own times of a deposed and decapitated monarch, civil war, and swaying religious division and persecution. Individuals in society live in an actual natural condition of warfare toward all others.[12]

> Hereby it is manifest, that during the time men live without a common power to keep them all in awe, they are in that condition which is called war; and such a war, as it is of every man, against every man. For WAR, consisteth not in battle only, or the act of fighting; but in a tract of time, wherein the will to contend by battle is sufficiently known . . . so the nature of war, consisteth not in actual fighting; but in the known disposition thereto, during all the time there is no assurance to the contrary. All other time is PEACE.[13]

Hobbes' human-made governing Leviathan is the human force which guarantees a peaceful condition within which all can confront their individual existence. The covenant is made between each one and the Leviathan, a social compact or covenant, that presumes and preserves the actual existence of each one in the state. Each person, motivated by a fearful individual and precarious existence, hands over to Leviathan the right of self-government so that this public authority may protect the peace and rights of each one:

> This done, the multitude so united in one person, is called a COMMONWEALTH, in Latin CIVITAS. This is the generation of that great LEVIATHAN, or rather (to speak more reverently) of that Mortal God, to which we owe under the Immortal God, our peace and deference.[14]

In this way, the governing power, whether by assembly or by one person, is established as the sovereign force that guarantees the conditions of peace for each person, who, by agreement, becomes a subject of this absolute governing power, established by the social compact.

For Locke, the actual (natural) state of the individual is not as violent at that proposed by Hobbes; indeed, more pacific, because, unlike Hobbes, Locke believed in a type of moral law in persons that enlightened their conscience as to their relations with God and with others, recognized as equals. People are naturally free and equal and, therefore, for Locke: "Men living together according to reason, without a common superior on earth, with authority to judge between them, is properly the state of nature."[15]

Even so, Locke's state of nature is an insecure one because people, in their actual condition, do not always follow the moral law. While it is natural for people to form society, it is also a practical necessity to have such things as written laws and judicial systems and government to secure for all what is precarious in nature:

> Thus mankind, notwithstanding all the privileges of the state of nature, being but in an ill condition, while they remain in it, are quickly driven into society. Hence it comes to pass, that we seldom find any number of men live any time in this state. The inconveniences that they are therein exposed to, by the irregular and uncertain exercise of the power every man has of punishing the transgressions of others, make them take sanctuary under the established laws of government, and therein seek the preservation of their property. . . . And in this we have the original right and rise of both the legislative and executive power, as well as of the governments and societies themselves.[16]

For Locke, too, the basis of government is the free consent of all to hand over certain liberties to be exercised by government, a social contract which is justified because it redounds to the benefit of each person.

There is the same need, as Hobbes recognized, for central authority and power, though what Locke develops is a system of a restrained executive and legislature, on trust, and is representative of the people, religious tolerance, and the justification of private property and other individual rights. Even so, while the political institutions proposed by Locke are different to Hobbes' Leviathan, the radical justification of political society is the same as that proposed by Hobbes:

> As for Hobbes, he aims at reaching a result that is not only true but also essentially incontestable, since it is based on something stronger than any discursive reasoning: fear of death. It is important to point out here that Locke's approach is just as "absolutist" as Hobbes's. The original right of each person is essentially above discursive reasoning, above any objection, because it is based on a

solitary and silent activity: labour for consumption. In Locke's eyes, the meaning of justice can only be to guarantee property. It is absurd to doubt the justice
of property rights, since the very idea of justice presupposes ownership.[17]

In both cases of this social contract, the fundamental question of the individual's social fulfilment and flourishing has changed. Now the fundamental
issue is the protection and preservation of individual freedom, and the conditions of freedom such as the private right to property, and not the issue of the
person's true flourishing in society, which presupposes, but is not limited to,
the conditions of individual freedom. This politics of restraint was, however,
the reduced goal of Locke's political project.

As Eric Voegelin points out in *The New Science of Politics*, there is a
fundamental contrast between Aristotle's *Ethics* that examines the virtuous
purposes of human actions toward a highest individual and common good,
a *summum bonum*, and the practical purposes of the lives of individuals of
Hobbes' Leviathan society. Hobbes rejects the higher purposes of individual
and social life of the classical philosophers. For Hobbes, the common higher
or greatest good is not part of his social arrangement, as it was essential to
classical and Christian society. This meant that there was a fundamental
vacuum at the heart of Hobbes' political structure. He conceived society as
comprised of individuals with their passions, not to be brought together by
and for profound common purposes, but to be controlled together for the
individual protection of each.[18]

With this shift in perspective, the question of who the person is and the
real dimensions of personal existence slips from political view and relevance. The modern liberal sense of society becomes paramount. Consider,
for example, the contemporary American political philosopher Rawls and
his fundamental notion of justice as the foundation of political society. In
Political Illiberalism, Peter L. P. Simpson explains that when we consider
today the question of the right form of government, we begin with two basic
themes: the rules of process for the legitimacy of government and the issue
of the protection of individual rights. Simpson notes that these two concerns
have their origin in the doctrine of Hobbes and what he assumes to be the
antagonistic human condition. Simpson recalls that these are the assumptions in the work of the contemporary American political philosopher Rawls
and in particular his *Theory of Justice.* For Rawls, justice, as the primordial
quality of government, means equality, the equal recognition of individual
goods. The individual good is comprised of the values and concerns of each
individual, as each individual sees them. The equal respect for these individual interests thus precludes the question as to whether these interests are
an authentic reflection of a common human nature. The government of the

state has as its concern to respect the freedom of individuals and to avoid and resolve possible clashes of these individual interests.[19]

The resemblance of Rawls' political and social theory to the framing of the political context by Hobbes and Locke is unmistakable, as is the common contrast with the Aristotelean understanding of the aspirations of the political community. Simpson points out that, by contrast, Aristotle's point of departure is not with individuals and structures of power, but rather with people and with communities, with the political community as the highest form of social communion. This contrast of language is telling; Aristotle has in mind the virtuous growth of people into various natural communities, including above all the political community. By contrast, our political language today spontaneously refers to numerical individuals and impersonal structures of power. Simpson explains that the purpose of Aristotle's political community was to form and to perfect people into the necessary communion with others. In our contemporary way of thinking, the state exists to maintain individuals as individuals in the exercise of their individual freedoms and rights.[20]

The conditions of peace and individual freedoms projected by Hobbes and Locke were in general an advance in the respect and worth of the human person and provided an historical path to further structural constraint on political power and personal freedom, recognition, and participation.[21] At the same time something fundamental to human society was shifted to the background and left a political vacuum that could, and was, used by other partisans of political society to justify their ideological visions of a different type of *summum bonum* and their use of unrestrained political power to impose it.

It is by revising the truncated forms of the state of nature doctrine that we can revitalize the dynamic ambition at the heart of political endeavor. The lessons of political liberalism are of vital importance to the role of public civil power in society and, historically, have often been achieved by great struggle and sacrifice. They can also be lost, without struggle or sacrifice. At the same time, political liberalism is fundamentally a doctrine of restraint and not a vision of a greater and stronger social bond. It seems that something essential of the human person's greatness has been compromised in settling for restraint as the public goal of politics.

The *Guardian* newspaper reported an incident that reveals the real and necessary social aspirations that make human society possible. Steve Mallen, whose talented eighteen-year-old son, recently admitted to Cambridge University and inexplicably committed suicide, dedicates his life to organizing institutional awareness and help for persons drawn to the possibility of suicide:

> Mallen was walking in the woods recently when he saw a woman sitting alone, clearly upset. He sat down with her and asked if she was OK. "I just got her to

laugh and smile and made sure she had somewhere safe to go," he says. "Does that make me a good samaritan? No, because it's how we should all behave."[22]

HOPE AND HISTORY

In the context of attempting to understand human history, Pieper finishes his *The End of Time: A Meditation on the Philosophy of History* with this remarkable conclusion:

> Without a return to revealed truth, it is impossible not only to philosophise about history but even to live in the area of real history as a spiritual being: that is to say, as a being who looks with open eyes upon what really happens in the real world, omitting nothing and glossing over nothing, but also abandoning and retracting nothing of that upon which man, by his very nature, cannot cease to set his hopes.[23]

What Pieper has in mind here is the evident tension between the inbuilt, essential hopes of the human person, on the one hand, and the contingent and unsatisfactory unfolding of human history on the other hand. Pieper is one of the great contemporary exponents of the human existential condition as structured toward future fulfilment in hope. This means that persons find themselves already in movement toward an end or purpose, an experience that describes human hope as the inherent dynamism toward an end that will satisfy their aspirations and that obliquely they trust to attain. Death is experienced as an end, an interruption, to this human existence but not its purpose. Pieper uses the Scholastic phrase *status viatoris [being on the way]* to describe this structured movement toward fulfilment, a fulfilment that necessarily is beyond the confines of time. Not to understand this, and to consider personal existence only as a being in time is, for Pieper, to fail to understand both existence in time and existence beyond time.[24] For Pieper, the only adequate response to this given existential condition is hope, an innate spiritual movement that moves me forward in trust, without the presumption of certainty and without the despair of nihilism.

We distinguish here, as Pieper does, between "hopes"—the everyday desires that attract us and that usually find fulfilment in one way or another— and "hope," in the sense of what deep down our entire existence seems to be drawn toward:

> "Fundamental" hope, by contrast, appears to have no object that can be found to exist in the world in this "objectlike" way. There is, then, nothing specific and concrete that can be pointed to; it is directed toward something "indefinite," "nebulous," "formless," "unnameable"—for which reason fundamental hope is

much more difficult to characterize in any way. . . . But of course there is certainly "something hoped for," even if its mode of being is quite different from that of all objective goods and all conceivable changes in the external world. . . . fundamental hope (singular) is not directed toward anything that one could "have" but rather has something to do with what one "is," with one's own being as man; what is hoped for in it he provisionally describes as "self-realization in the future" and as "well-being of the person."[25]

The other phenomenon is the contingency of human history, the deeply unsatisfactory development of human history in the world. There are real reasons for Hobbes' pessimism and Locke's uneasiness with the state of human nature. In classical thought, hope was not considered a virtue, but a passion, because life was precarious and the conditions of human happiness were fragile and temporary.[26] Therefore, as human life was limited and not under the human person's dominion to control, it was unreasonable to trust that everything would result to human satisfaction, even with an understanding of nature and a virtuous response to life.[27] The reasonable response to the unpredictability (and, ultimately, the inadequacy) of human existence was not blind, irrational hope, but courage, magnanimity of soul, to confront what may come, as difficult as it may be. This was particularly true of the Stoic perspective of courageous resignation, a coming to terms with what inevitably happens in life.

This inevitably raises a dilemma. Is the experience of hope a deceiving and irrational passion or is there a particular answer to the personal fundamental hope that justifies its expectation? The answer seems to be affirmative, simply because human existence already includes the experience of the possibility of fulfilment, a fulfilment not just of particular hopes, but the hope of complete existential fulfilment; no one can live with the acceptance of despair.[28] At the same time, it is vital to clarify in what way our fundamental hope is to be realized.

Modern political projects have tended to emphasize the belief and promise of an imminent realization of this experience of the fulfilment of human hope. This requires giving human history an inevitable sense of direction and purpose that unfolds within time. The original traces of this modern belief in fulfilment within history may be found in the Italian monk Joachim of Fiore's identification of the Christian Trinitarian revelation with distinct epochs of time in history, and, at Joachim de Fiore's moment in history, around 1260, the third kingdom of the Holy Spirit.[29] This understanding of the realization of this universal kingdom, the fulfilment of personal fundamental hope, *within* human history was to provide a model of thought for the politically minded that would, in Voegelin's well-known phrase, "immanentize the [Christian]

eschaton."[30] This shift from transcendental to the belief in immanent fulfilment was a gradual one:

> The new age of Joachim would bring an increase of fulfilment within history,
> but the increase would not be due to an immanent eruption; it would come
> through a new transcendental irruption of the spirit. The idea of a radically
> immanent fulfilment grew rather slowly, in a long process that roughly may be
> called "from humanism to enlightenment"; only in the eighteenth century, with
> the idea of progress, had the increase of meaning in history become a completely
> intramundane phenomenon, without transcendental irruptions.[31]

Political projects arose that, while appealing to the hope of the Christian
eschaton, aimed to produce heaven on earth by appealing to the inevitable
march of historical or material determinism, the necessary and inevitable
progress toward human fulfilment at some future point in time. Voegelin finds
in Joachim de Fiore's prophecies four symbols that represent the proximate
"age of fulfilment," which have become characteristic of such political ideologies.[32] As the first of these symbols, de Fiore writes of the Third Realm or
Kingdom, a triad of kingdoms culminating in the third realm of fulfilment.
This threefold development within history was to become evident in the various processes of historical development in Auguste Comte, Georg Wilhelm
Friedrich Hegel, Karl Marx, and Friedrich Engels, and the Nazi's *Dritte Reich*
(Third Kingdom), among others.

The second symbol is the leader who arises at the beginning of the new
kingdom and inspires its realization. In secular translation, this audacious
new leader took the form of the "superman" who goes beyond the static conventions and leads into the new and definitive era. Voegelin recognizes this
type in Nicolas de Condorcet, Comte, in Marx and Engels, and in Friedrich
Nietzsche, a type who would take on himself "the act of taking God back into
man. . . . [and] creating a human type who experiences himself as existing
outside of the institutional bonds and obligations."[33]

The third symbol was the precursor or prophet, which in political terms was
the recognition that "a new type emerges in Western history: the intellectual
who knows the formula for salvation from the misfortunes of the world and
can predict how world history will take its course in the future."[34] De Fiore's
fourth symbol was the community of spiritually autonomous persons.
Voegelin understands this symbol in political terms as "a spiritualised mankind existing in community without the mediation and support of institutions," which he sees represented both in communism and (interestingly) in
the democratic structure as "a community of autonomous men."[35]

Whether of Christian derivation or by appealing to the natural desire and
trust of fulfilment that is the experience of hope, modern political ideologies

that want to offer more than mere political restraint have adopted visions of human fulfilment within time and by human means. We are susceptible to such visions and promises because to hope for final fulfilment is an inbuilt condition of human existence.

Pieper's meditation on *The End of Time* comments on the various Enlightenment views of hope in progress toward a future fulfilment of hope within time in such thinkers as Bacon who trusted the sciences to bring forward an ever more civilized human existence, Giambattista Vico, who believed that successive cultures would necessarily advance to a Republic of Mankind, Johann Gottfried Herder who claimed that "reason and equity must gain ground among men and foster an enduring humanity,"[36] and Immanuel Kant, who in *Ideal of a Universal History Based on the Principle of World-Citizenship*, also proposes "the attainment of a civil society universally governed by justice."[37] Even so, Pieper notices that each and all of these optimistic proposals of fulfilment of human hope for the perfect society within time fails, and causes the pendulum reaction of pessimism as the result of disappointed hope:

> This simplification, whose inaptness is ever more remorselessly laid bare by the course of history itself, this optimistic abridgement arose (and arises) out of an attitude which finds the road to an extra-temporal and post-historical "New Earth," leading through a catastrophic End and a divine transposition, insufficiently "evident" in theory and, above all, too arduous of "political realization." It has, inevitably, been answered by a retaliatory pessimism which, having lost its illusions regarding real history, is preparing for a catastrophic End; in equal, indeed, even greater contradiction to the traditional notion of history, however, this End is construed as final, as a catastrophe beyond which no promise of deliverance is audible, no "City of God" visible, as a catastrophe which is supposed, if that were possible, to possess the character of [annihilation].[38]

Our own prevalent postmodern pessimism toward visions of the future is just another pendulum swing from the naïve optimism of these modern projects to the pessimism of the political and social failures of this last century.

Pieper suggests, in his comment on the constant failure to construct the perfect new world in this temporal existence, how this apparent contradiction of the inbuilt personal hopes destined to temporal failure and frustration may be answered, or at least the recognition of the necessary premises, from which real answers may be given to the enigma of one's ultimate hopes. The individual *state of nature,* as assumed by Hobbes, Locke, Jean Jacques Rousseau, and others, needs to be re-examined more carefully to discern the real condition and extent of the human person's nature and existence. What is proposed here is to try to re-dimension our being and existence and to locate more adequately the realm of politics within the human person's real dimensions of existence.

ORIGINAL UNITY AND ACTUAL RUPTURE

A more careful description of the person's actual state of existence reveals more than a simple unitary existence. Within people we have already observed an existential dynamism toward fulfilment that is not, cannot, be confined to this temporal existence. This is what undermines a politics of restraint, as if the avoidance of danger to oneself or to others were all that were necessary to fulfil the experience of human hope. At the same time, the politics of aspiration always fails, because humans always fail. We aspire to truth, to goodness, to social harmony and integration, to profound communion with others, and with the Other, however obliquely perceived; we are structured in this way to want what makes for the politics of good society. It is this that makes it all the harder to understand why we sometimes, perhaps often, willfully fail to achieve what is within our grasp to hold. This profound dichotomy within and among persons needs to be recognized and described correctly. This fundamental existential ambiguity cannot be simplified; it is internal to the human person and not solved merely by external structures, laws, or conditions. It is the experience of broken order within each one and, concomitantly, the broken order among persons.

In *Metamorphoses of the City*, Manent cites Augustine's remark that the individual is "at once social by nature and quarrelsome by perversion" to explain the ambivalence of social nature that is both oriented toward friendship and at the same time to hostility, given the fundamentally good human nature and its present broken and fallen condition. This accounts for both the noble aspirations and possibilities of people, and also explains the perversion and evil that people are prone to.[39]

This more careful descriptive disclosure of the person's actual condition indicates an original unity, both of personal and social, a subsequent rupture of what was originally harmony in unity, and the remaining aspiration, built into the human person's being, for personal and social fulfilment, beyond this actual existence, something that is both a requirement of the person's being and at the same time, something that is not achieved in this existence.

However unsatisfactory and incomplete this descriptive disclosure of personal existence is, it is, I suggest, more authentically true than the self-justifying and self-enclosed acceptance of this actual existence as the complete explanation of who persons are and what they can and may aspire to. This was the import of Blaise Pascal's presentation of the phenomenon of original sin and his argument against the confident Enlightenment doctrines of the individual's self-justification and self-transcendence, as, indeed, against the politics of restraint, and the belief in a personal destiny as ignoble and uninspiring. Ernst Cassirer describes Pascal's argument against truncated conceptions of the human person's existence in this way:

> His consciousness always places before him a goal he can never reach, and his existence is torn between his incessant striving beyond himself and his constant relapses beneath himself. We cannot escape this conflict which we find in every single phenomenon of human nature, and there is no other way to explain it than to transfer it from the phenomena to their intelligible origin, from the facts to their principle. The irreducible dualism of human nature is resolved only in the mystery of the fall.[40]

To understand further how personal existence was originally, one has to draw on theological sources that can be very illustrative and reinforce what descriptive disclosure can only observe without explaining. At the same time, such sources can provide a real stimulus to appreciating the full extent of the person's political aspirations and provide an adequate context for resolving political conflicts that are, in their origin, conflicts of relation within the human person, socially, and with the Creator God. For example, the early Church Father Origen of Alexandria (184–253) summarized the person's actual condition in the phrase ubi *peccata, ibi multitude*, "where there is sin, there is multiplicity."[41] Maximus the Confessor comments that by human sin "the one nature was shattered into a thousand pieces" and, as Henri de Lubac continues in his explanation of Maximus: "humanity which ought to constitute a harmonious whole, in which 'mine' and 'thine' would be no contradiction, is turned into a multitude of individuals, as numerous as the sands of the seashore, all of whom show violently discordant inclinations."[42]

De Lubac himself notes the actual loss of original unity among people (and not just within the individual person) in this way:

> Instead of trying, as we do almost entirely nowadays to find within each individual nature what is the hidden blemish and, so to speak, of looking for the mechanical source of the trouble which is the cause of the faulty running engine—some exaggerating the trouble, others inclined to minimise it—the fathers preferred to envisage the very constitution of the individuals considered as so many cores of natural opposition.[43]

Many of our social and political problems that present themselves as conflicts—between the individual and the collectively, between private property and what is or should be of common use, the self-determination of peoples and the unity of the nations—can be seen in a greater context not as zero-sum options, as a logic of one or the other, but within a broader compatibility, when we allow for and distinguish the original, the actual, and the final, transcendent conditions of existence of humankind.

TRANSCENDENT FULFILMENT AND
THE POLITICS OF ASPIRATION

If this descriptive setting of the human person's actual existence correctly undermines the expressions of a politics of restraint and its unambitious political horizon, there is also the need to put into its correct context the politics of aspiration, which can thrive on the false hope and mundane optimism of humanly-made solutions for this actual existence. Such an unfounded politics of aspiration can be found in the political and social claims of Rousseau. Rousseau admits with Pascal that the persons find themselves in a corrupt and divided condition, but his explanation is different. As Cassirer writes:

> Rousseau's *Émile* begins with the words: "All is well when it leaves the hands of the Creator of things; all degenerates in the hands of man." Thus God is condoned and guilt for all evil is attributed to man. But since guilt belongs to this world, not to the world beyond; since it does not exist before the empirical, historical existence of mankind, but arises out of this existence, we must therefore seek redemption solely in this world. No help from above can bring us deliverance.[44]

Rousseau thus maintains the original human aspirations but now locates the root of the person's actual ruptured condition not within the person, in an original fall, but in something outside of the person, "society," that corrupts human nature, that introduces private property, that perverts the original love of self into an egotistic self-love that expresses itself in the domination over others. Rousseau proposes in his *Du Contrat Social* [The Social Contract] (1762) a new form of society that will bring to prominence all naturally good aspirations. This will happen when each one follows the *volonté général* [general will], which, supposedly, is to be each one's own will written in large letters. And so:

> No God can bring it about for us; man must rather become his own deliverer and in the ethical sense his own creator. Society heretofore has inflicted the deepest wounds on mankind; yet it is society too which through a transformation and reformation can and should heal these wounds. Such is Rousseau's solution of the problem of theodicy in his philosophy of law. And he has in fact placed this problem on an entirely new footing, removing it from the sphere of metaphysics and making it the focal point of ethics and politics.[45]

In Rousseau, the goals and aspirations of the individual find a reassuring and eloquent expression; the individual is confirmed in his *status viatoris*, as a being of hope. Rousseau also believes that each person needs to be transformed and renewed. At the same time, a new entity was found to be responsible for the evils of life—actual society, the structures, and the conditions, external to the individual, that condition the individual to evil. Rousseau's answer was the project of social engineering to transform people by laws to create a new ethical and political community of naturally happy and good people.

> If it is good to know how to deal with men as they are, it is much better to make them what there is need that they should be. The most absolute authority is that which penetrates into a man's inmost being, and concerns itself no less with his will than with his actions. . . . Make men, therefore, if you would command men: if you would have them obedient to the laws, make them love the laws, and then they will need only to know what is their duty to do it. . . . If you would have the General Will accomplished, bring all the particular wills into conformity with it; in other words, as virtue is nothing more than this conformity of the particular wills with the General Will, establish the reign of virtue.[46]

It is therefore ironic that Rousseau who advocated the goodness of the naturally free individual should propose as a solution the *de facto* subjugation of each free person to the *volonté général* that supposedly manufactures the good society of people. What historically became more mainstream was the idea that the good individual and the good society could be fabricated by human efforts alone. These ideologies appeal to the noble, inbuilt aspirations of the person and therefore collect, among others, many well-intentioned and noble followers. This belief in the possibility of fabricating a new and perfect society is the justification for making concrete plans for the new future society that, if followed, will necessarily produce their results. In this way, the new, better, future society authorizes and justifies all means deemed necessary to achieve its purposes.

The practical difficulty to which this sort of political thinking leads is described by Roger Scruton as the "utopian fallacy" or such thinking's "immunity to refutation":

> The ideal is contradictory and thus unachievable. And for that very reason it can never be refuted! No existing situation will ever qualify as a realization of that longed for and primeval freedom; so nobody will ever be in a position to say that we have achieved it, or to discover its damning faults. The ideal reason remains forever on the horizon of our experience, unsullied and untried, casting judgment on all that is actual, like a sun that cannot be looked at but which creates a dark side to everything on which it shines . . . utopians ae not distinguished by

a few beliefs that the rest of us are unable to share. They see the world differently. They are able to ignore or despise the findings of experience and common
sense, and to place at the centre of every deliberation a project whose absurdity
they regard not as a defect but as a reproach against the one who would point it
out. This frame of mind has for two centuries played a leading role in European
politics and none of the disasters that have stemmed from it has the slightest
weight in deterring its new recruits. The millions dead or enslaved do not refute
utopia, but merely give proof of the evil machinations that have stood in its
way. The "immunity to refutation" is what I mean by the utopian fallacy, and it
is worth exploring it as one of the curious by-ways of optimism, and one that
points the way to a deep explanation of why, in the human spirit, unreason is so
endlessly renewable.[47]

This conflict within the human heart and its bearing on human society is
reformulated by Kant, who seems to return to Pascal's belief of the origin of
evil within the human heart, while at the same time trusting in the providence
of nature to prevail finally over evil. This belief or hope in provident nature
is turned by Hegel into an inexorable law of the progress of history and evil
as part of the necessary dialectic of this historical progress. This historical
framework for the necessary transformation of person and society is taken
up and itself transformed by Marx, all the while "his historical materialism is
also to be read as a travesty of the doctrine of original sin and redemption."[48]

Inherent in Rousseau's transformation of society is the capacity of people
themselves to bring about this future necessary transformation. This theme
of the individual as the protagonist of a future perfect society was radical-
ized and revolutionized by Marx. What humans had attributed to a Creator,
humans must now realize for themselves and it was matter that would be used
to create a new, better world, and better, transformed members of a classless society.[49] Here we see a shift from a metaphysics of being to a praxis of
becoming, which includes the fabrication of a new person and a new society.
As Voegelin comments on Marx's notion of the revolutionary moment of
seizing the power of transformation:

> The transition from the old to the new world will not be achieved by a simple
> change of institutions, but like Bakunin, Marx assumes a *metanoia*, a change
> of heart, as the decisive event that will inaugurate the new epoch. For its pro-
> duction, Marx relies on the experience of the revolution itself. "For the mass
> creation of communist consciousness, as well as for the achievement of the
> object itself, a mass change of man is necessary which can occur only during a
> practical movement, that is during a revolution. Hence, the revolution is neces-
> sary not only because the ruling class cannot be overthrown in any other way,
> but also because only through a revolution can the overthrowing class reach the

point where it gets rid of the old filth (*Dreck*) and becomes capable of a new foundation of society."[50]

Latent within this theory of revolution is a new vision of mankind and mankind's possibilities:

> But it is certain that Marx repudiated the willingness of the ancient and the eagerness of the modern traditions to make peace with, though not to surrender to the weaknesses of human nature, and to be content with society consisting of men as they are. Marx dreamed of that human condition in which good ends would be sought by good men using only good means and responding to (because possessing) only good motives. The basis or presupposition of his dream was the generation of a new man, or the regeneration of man and the instrument of regeneration would be the rational economy rightly understood.[51]

While nominal Marxism, with its particular brand of centrally planned economics, has lost its political and economic credibility, the background belief in the human capacity to refashion and perfect the individual and society perdures, particularly but not exclusively, through the means of political economy. As Italian philosopher del Noce points out:

> Thus, today's mentality is informed historically by the idea of the great break (accepted, by now, as the general framework inside which any legitimate discussion must take place) that supposedly marks the transition to the reign of freedom. In this sense, Revolution means replacing meta-physics with the ideal of a meta-humanity, in which mankind will acquire those powers that it already possesses potentially, but from which it alienated itself during the development of history, projecting them outside of itself in the act of creating God. As Voegelin accurately pointed out, the idea of the "superman" is already present in Marx in connection with the idea of "projection."[52]

The common thread in these theories of transformation is the need to supersede the limitations of this actual existence and the human limitations inherent in this existence, and this is so because persons necessarily experience the call to transcend themselves and the limits of this actual existence. The politics of aspiration is inexorable. Maritain thus terms bourgeois individualism, a self-centered materialist dependence on the state by the individual, as the most irreligious political ideology precisely because it is subhuman in what it offers.[53]

HOPE AS AN ESSENTIAL CONDITION
OF POLITICAL SOCIETY

What is evident in all of this is the relevance of the real conditions and dimensions of human existence for politics. This may not be evident in political
theories that only favor undetermined human freedom as the ultimate good
to be preserved and protected in society; even so, such theories implicitly
recognize an anthropology that expresses various uses and desires as well
as a judgment as to the capacity of people to live with others. We have seen
that these implicit visions can be generally positive or negative and the type
of society one aspires to depends on, and is an expression of, the positive or
negative vision of the person, with the resultant politics of aspiration or politics of restraint, or a combination of both.

What is also evident is that the real aspirations of the human person are not
something originally chosen, but inbuilt into the dynamic of personal being
and therefore essential for human existence. Drawing on Augustine's descriptive analysis of what in Christianity is called eternal life, Jospeh Ratzinger
sketches what each person experiences interiorly of the dynamic pull of
transcendence:

> I think that in this very precise and permanently valid way, Augustine is describ-
> ing man's essential situation, the situation that gives rise to all his contradictions
> and hopes. In some way we want life itself, true life, untouched even by death;
> yet at the same time we do not know the thing toward which we feel driven. We
> cannot stop reaching out for it, and yet we know that all we can experience or
> accomplish is not what we yearn for. This unknown "thing" is the true "hope"
> which drives us, and at the same time the fact that it is unknown is the cause of all
> forms of despair and also of all efforts, whether positive or destructive, directed
> towards worldly authenticity and human authenticity. The term "eternal life" is
> intended to give a name to this known "unknown." Inevitably it is an inadequate
> term that creates confusion. "Eternal," in fact, suggests to us the idea of some-
> thing interminable, and this frightens us; "life" makes us think of the life that we
> know and love and do not want to lose, even though very often it brings more
> toil than satisfaction, so that while on the one hand we desire it, on the other hand
> we do not want it. To imagine ourselves outside the temporality that imprisons
> us and in some way to sense that eternity is not an unending succession of days
> in the calendar, but something more like the supreme moment of satisfaction, in
> which totality embraces us and we embrace totality—this we can only attempt.[54]

We are inexorably drawn forward in hope to future fulfilment and we
depend on reasons for hoping. The loss or negation of those motives signals
sooner or later the condition of despair, which is the destruction of the movement of our free willing toward being. This leaves us in a precarious and

vulnerable position. We are required to hope to continue the dynamism of our existence and yet the adequate object of our hope seems to be beyond our vision. This makes us susceptible to charlatan promises and fake assurances of hope, the appeal that something different is necessarily better, that change is always possible and always for the good. Politics knows how to exploit this vulnerability.

At the same time, this human condition raises a problem. If in politics we do move beyond merely the actual condition of the person, with the possibilities of an optimistic or pessimistic approach to life's contingencies and human moral vagaries and recognize a descriptively more coherent vision of the human person according to an original condition, an actual condition and a final transcendental condition, then we need to answer the vital question how our fundamental hope is to be answered. Are we condemned to aspire to more than we can achieve?

As Hittinger points out, various approaches in classical morality and spirituality have been taken to this existential question.[55] There was the rational spiritual mysticism of some forms of Platonism, and the withdrawal from the passion of hope as evidenced in Stoicism and Epicureanism. There were also occult religious practices to try to foretell future events, and the reliance of Aristotle on the virtue of magnanimity, courage, to face what cannot be known or determined by human action.

It is not difficult to identify the counterparts of these approaches in modern and contemporary morality and politics. Many forms of political liberalism seem to advocate the withdrawal from higher aspirations and the contentment with bettering the here and now. Other technical approaches propose the realization of the human person's aspirations as something within our own present and future technical means, as a fabrication of the future promise. Some of these projects present themselves as scientific and rational; others drape themselves in religious terms and can become all-embracing fanatical ideologies.[56] Certain religious interpretations cast off the present condition as unimportant and live on the promise of future bliss for themselves, withdrawing from human society to live as the enlightened ones whose problems have been solved.[57]

Given this unique and disquieting condition of each human existence, that is not of our choosing but within which we are called to choose and decide, the answer to this quandary needs to come from outside our human condition and capacity. There is a bridge needed to ultimate human fulfilment, we presuppose that bridge, but we do not and cannot build it.

Where this seems to lead us to is an understanding of human existence, in its personal and collective dimensions, similar to the Christian context of human existence and reality, that is, a context that is already given, that is dynamically oriented to fulfilment beyond this existence, and that ultimately

is achieved by Another, beyond human efforts. Human fulfilment is ultimately something that happens to us, that is given to us, rather than what we
can produce for ourselves.[58]

While this may sound as though we have been existentially let off the
hook—the ultimate form of social welfare—in fact the disposition required
of us is not an easy one. Hittinger, in contrasting classical courage with the
novel Christian virtue of hope, says the following:

> The price paid for pressing beyond the limits that seem to be intrinsic to human
> nature, and thus to uncover new scope and content for hoping, is the recognition
> that man is radically dependent on a being other than himself. Once this shift is
> accomplished, hope can be understood as something more than an anticipatory
> passion. It can be seen as a distinctively spiritual perfection that includes trust
> and a number of other attitudes that David Hume mockingly called "the whole
> train of monkish virtues." These "monkish virtues" make sense if man's nature
> is dependent upon a being other than himself.[59]

One can easily understand the difficulties of accepting this radical dependence on Another for our origin, existence, and fulfilment. This type of necessary reliance on Another seems to undermine humankind's sense of their
own security, independence, and all-important freedom. In fact, the belief in
the radical dependence on Another seems to threaten what is most vital to
persons; their self-affirmation through free will. From this perceived threat
arises the project of the individual alone and the implicit or explicit rejection
of all forms of dependence and referral as unworthy and hostile to true human
development. From here come either practical projects of self-made social
reconstruction, as Marx proposed, or the more subtle but equally radical
denial of dependence in forms of political liberalism that presuppose nothing
more than freedom of exploitation.[60]

At the heart of the political project, therefore, is a more complete description
of the extension of human existence and its radical dependence on Another. It
is in this context alone that the human person can place the necessary hope of
fulfilment without the negation or distortion of one's most profound aspirations. This makes a lot of political difference: "A society that takes this virtue
seriously can be expected to gamble on the stakes of life much differently
than a society that regards hope as a fantasy or mere wishing."[61]

THE REAL PREMISES OF POLITICAL ORDER

The theme of this reflection has been to point out both the common and
truncated vision of the human person inherent in our democratic forms of

government today and the real dimensions of human existence, based on the complex but evident human social experience. Instead of confining and condemning the human spirit within the parameters of actual human existence, a more profound discernment of human experience discloses the contours of an original condition of both personal and social unity, an actual condition of personal and social rupture, and, as experienced within the ruptured human spirit, the aspiration for transcendent fulfilment, both personal and social.

This three-act human existence is not merely an abstract conjecture but is written into and experienced in our being as a dynamic and ineluctable movement of hope that is at the source of all our aspirations toward fulfilment and without which we fall back into non-existence. At the same time, the source and fulfilment of this hope comes from outside human resources and reveals the radical dependence of human existence on Another for the origin of its being, its sustenance in existence, and its fulfilment.

Why is this important for politics? The forces and energies for authentic renewal of political society can only come from persons, whether they are creative minorities or majorities. Political mentalities and structures that stifle and suffocate these forces and energies, whether by benign or hostile means, will produce a subservient, passive and ultimately frustrated people.

This last century, in particular, has witnessed totalitarian political ideologies that have justified their doctrines in quasi-religious terms to produce Heaven on earth, thus channeling real transcendent aspirations into illusory plans and projects for earthly perfection. This misplacement of transcendent human aspirations within the actual condition of human society is always a threat to human society:

> I think we must make it clear to ourselves again today, in all earnestness, that neither reason nor faith ever promises that there will be a perfect world someday. It does not exist. Constantly expecting it, playing with the possibility and proximity of it, is the most serious threat to our politics and our society, because anarchical fanaticism necessarily proceeds from it.[62]

The difficulty is that the aspiration for transformation is written into the structure of the human person and therefore appeals to perfection resonate within us. We are susceptible to the claims to bring about the perfect world, without limitations, injustice, and suffering, and the illusion that we can make these permanent and perfect conditions by our own plans and hands.

If the attempt to force our actual existence into some future perfection is destined to failure and disillusion, even more deceptive and disillusioning is the subhuman existence of political programs that negate authentic human aspirations and offer only a passive social existence, inertia, and the increasing claims for more and more from the political authority.

Tocqueville, writing on the theme of "What Sort of Despotism Democratic Nations Have to Fear," describes democratic tyranny in these terms:

> But it would seem that if despotism were to be established amongst the democratic nations of our days, it might assume a different character; it would be more extensive and more mild; it would degrade men without tormenting them. . . . The will of man is not shattered, but softened, bent, and guided: men are seldom forced by it to act, but they are constantly restrained from acting: such a power does not destroy, but it prevents existence; it does not tyrannize, but it compresses, enervates, extinguishes, and stupefies a people, till each nation is reduced to be nothing better than a flock of timid and industrious animals, of which the government is the shepherd. I have always thought that servitude of the regular, quiet, and gentle kind which I have just described, might be combined more easily than is commonly believed with some of the outward forms of freedom; and that it might even establish itself under the wing of the sovereignty of the people.[63]

Tocqueville notes that:

> Our contemporaries are constantly excited by two conflicting passions; they want to be led, and they wish to remain free: as they cannot destroy either one or the other of these contrary propensities, they strive to satisfy them both at once. They devise a sole, tutelary, and all-powerful form of government, but elected by the people.[64]

The stifling of personal authentic aspirations, the fundamental and irreplaceable energies that inform our political society, are due, therefore, to a mutual acquiescence between government and ourselves. We hand over our authentic political role to a state and government that promises to fulfil all responsibilities with ever increasing ambitions and power, and that counts on keeping the people "in perpetual childhood."[65]

The various "states of nature" derived from a narrow and truncated vision of the human person's actual existence, is at the core of this political acquiescence that, on the one hand, accepts as natural the individual, self-interested, and fearful person, and, on the other hand, the necessary exclusive dominance of political power over all individual subjects and social activities. The states of nature also presuppose an officially neutral, effectively negative, vision of the person and social flourishing. What this means is that there is no common vision of the truth of personal existence, but the sole aim of living in—supposedly—peaceful disagreement. This is the modern meaning of equality, quite different from the classical notion:

> For the equality of all men can mean many things. In ancient thinkers, it means that all men are the same in nature and have the same end, which is the

happiness of virtue and wisdom and which is best achieved if the virtuous and wise, and not just anyone, exercise rule. In modern thinkers, influenced as they are by the state of nature doctrine, it means that all men are equal in desire and do not have the same end, because they do not have the same desires. Further, all desires are equal, and none is intrinsically superior or more deserving of satisfaction.[66]

Again, this essentially negative view of personal flourishing is also alluring because it asks nothing of the person in society. It promises individual freedom and abdicates individual responsibility to the state.[67] The system of government based on this modern notion of equality and a subjugated vision of the person and personal capabilities we call representative democracy. Is this stifled political ambition and vocation really representative of our real natural aspirations and collective destiny?

Simpson thinks not. In *Political Illiberalism*, Simpson suggests that Aristotle would claim that what we term representative democracy is neither true representation nor real democracy, but rather a type of subterfuge, oligarchic power in the name of the people, a ruse that is used to deceive the populace into thinking that it is their government. Even if this has become the vastly accepted form of political government today, it is not really any political accomplishment but a deceptive term that conceals the real possessors of political power in the hands of the few who justify their use of power by invoking the name of the people.[68]

The discovery of the more complete vision of personal existence, its original, actual, and transcendent destiny, is a more adequate basis for social and political organization. Not only does it recognize the real aspirations of social unity, but this vision also reflects the personal participation and commitment necessary for political achievement. At the same time, the actual condition of mankind requires realistic expectations as to what can be achieved in this existence. The recognition of a transcendent destiny beyond this existence, one that, ultimately, we are given rather than make ourselves, and the dependence on an order that is not of our making, teaches an openness to sources of truth that are not the product of the capabilities of human reason. The practical decisions of politics can be seen in a greater context that requires an openness of the mind to recognize and accept, sources of light without which our human problems are insoluble. Nothing can be "just politics" but requires to be seen in the light of an order and purpose in which we are immersed and to which, ultimately, we correspond, if we are to fulfil the hope of our most profound aspirations. Nor can the difficult questions of politics be dismissed by the claim that they are "above our pay grade." Precisely then we are obliged to look beyond rational calculations, unwarranted simplifications, to sources of truth that enlighten our minds.

The political path to the transcendent fulfilment of the human person's social destiny is full of risks and dangers. As we have seen, the hope of fulfilled aspirations can be so easily preyed upon and abused. We have also seen that such aspirations can be stifled and suffocated by mutual agreement, so that politics becomes an abdication of freedom in exchange for political irresponsibility, and an ever-increasing governmental control of welfare with its ever-increasing demands and economic invoice.

Embedded in these abusive political forms are visions of the person that are truncated and distorted. The attempt to expand and deepen the real dimensions of people's existence is essential if we are to rediscover the real context of all political endeavor, which is fundamentally ethical and religious, because personal aspirations are fundamentally ethical and religious.

It is also essential to release the energies of participation in the social bond. A person is a being in relation, called to communion, and structured to both give and receive. These potentials need to be awakened to participation.

In the end, the person's necessary social and transcendent fulfilment is not just a theory or a proposition, but the entrance into an experience of this greater context of reality. In *After Ideology*, David Walsh affirms that we are mistaken if we try to uphold a self-contained morality that is self-sufficient and self-sustaining. Walsh points out that modern philosophy has attempted this and failed to produce a rationally self-evident morality. We arrive at authentic moral experience not merely by an effort of detached rational inquiry. What is vital in discerning moral experience is the right orientation of the human will, a right fundamental disposition to want to discover and behold moral truth. The source of moral experience is not something we can summon at our command and have at our control, but rather becomes our experience only when we decide to dispose ourselves, our mind and will, to accept and to submit to the given order of the reality of being and its transcendent Source.[69]

It is only in this greater context of the person's transcendent social destiny that mundane politics can find its real bearings and orientation.

NOTES

1. John Rawls, *A Theory of Justice.* (Cambridge, MA: Belknap Press, 1971).

2. Josef Pieper, *The End of Time: A Meditation on the Philosophy of History*, rev. ed. (San Francisco: Ignatius Press, 1999), 91–92.

3. Augusto del Noce, *The Crisis of Modernity*, ed. and trans. Carlo Lancellotti (Montreal: McGill-Queen's University Press, 2015), 200.

4. Russell Hittinger, *The Virtue of Hope* (New York: World and I Online, 2014. Kindle ed.), Kindle, 186.

5. Scottish moral and political philosopher Alasdair MacIntyre famously said that "Modern politics is civil war carried on by other means." While the intentions in politics may not always be as violent as those who engage in civil war, the necessary conflict of politics is, I suggest, just as real. MacIntyre, *After Virtue: A Study in Moral Theory*, 3rd ed. (Notre Dame, IN: University of Notre Dame Press, 2007), 253.

6. Charles Taylor, *A Secular Age* (Cambridge, MA: Harvard University Press, 2007), 21.

7. Hans Urs Von Balthasar, "Eternal Life and the Human Condition," *Communio* 18, no. 1 (1991): 4. Joseph Ratzinger [Pope Benedict XVI] observes the same phenomenon: "I am convinced that the destruction of transcendence is actually the mutilation of man from which all the other sicknesses spring" Ratzinger, "A Christian Orientation in a Pluralistic Democracy," in *Church, Ecumenism, and Politics: New Endeavours in Ecclesiology* (San Francisco: Ignatius Press, 2008) 3073. Hanna Arendt also notes the modern loss of the sense of human immortality in *The Human Condition* (Chicago: University of Chicago Press, 1998), 320: "The victory of the animal *laborans* would never have been complete had not the process of secularization, the modern loss of faith inevitably arising from the Cartesian doubt, deprived individual life of its immortality, or at least of the certainty of immortality."

8. Glenn W. Olsen, *The Turn to Transcendence: The Role of Religion in the Twenty-First Century* (Washington, DC: Catholic University of America Press, 2010), 236 and chap. 5 "The Loss of Transcendence." For a comprehensive historical account of the currents of the modern philosophical approach, as opposed to classical and medieval approaches, see Louis Dupré, *Passage to Modernity: An Essay in the Hermeneutics of Nature and Culture* (New Haven, CT: Yale University Press, 1993).

9. W. Norris Clarke, *The One and the Many: A Contemporary Thomistic Metaphysics* (Notre Dame, IN: University of Notre dame Press, 2001), 258–59.

10. Pierre Manent, *Metamorphoses of the City: On the Western Dynamic*, trans. Marc LePain (Cambridge, MA: Harvard University Press, 2013), 263.

11. Manent, *Metamorphoses of the City*, 263. Manent goes on to comment that while Christianity rejected pagan glory as ultimately empty and vain, "Christianity invokes and postulates a real immortality. It has a certain sympathy for pagan glory, for it shares with the pagans the sentiment or conviction that the wellspring of human life is a movement toward the divine—a movement that the Christian religion means or claims to lead to its real goal" (265). Manent notes that Augustine shows esteem for the pagan desire for glory while rejecting the pagan religion associated with it (266).

12. Thomas Hobbes viewed philosophy as the knowledge of empirical facts to be used for human benefit. "The end of knowledge is power . . . and the scope of all speculation is the performance of some action or thing to be done" Hobbes, *Concerning Body*, I, I, 6, as cited in Frederic Copleston, *A History of Philosophy* (New York: Doubleday, 1985), vol. 5, 3. Hobbes' understanding of human nature comes, therefore, from his observation of the empirical expression of the passions and instinctual appetites of individuals who seek and serve their own self-preservation. These empirical "laws of nature" are found in part I of *Leviathan*, ed. J. C. A. Gaskin (Oxford: Oxford University Press, 1998), chaps. 14 and 15.

13. Hobbes, *Leviathan*, 2478.

14. Hobbes, *Leviathan*, book 2, chap. 17, 3081.

15. John Locke, *Second Treatise of Government*, ed. C. B. Macpherson (Indianapolis: Hackett,1980), 14. Locke was writing to reject a recently published work (*Patriarcha*, 1680) by Sir John Filmer (1588–1653), which claimed the natural subjection of men and the divine right of kings. As Locke writes in his second *Treatise*: "This equality of men by nature, the judicious Hooker looks upon as so evident in itself, and beyond all question, that he makes it the foundation of that obligation to mutual love amongst men, on which he builds the duties they owe one another, and from whence he derives the great maxims of justice and charity" Locke, *Second Treatise*, 8.

16. Locke, *Second Treatise*, chap. 9, 66.

17. Pierre Manent, *An Intellectual History of Liberalism*, trans. Rebecca Balinski. (Princeton, NJ: Princeton University Press, 1996), 46. Manent points out that, as Hobbes's all-powerful Leviathan imposes the protection of each individual, so "Locke neutralises it [conflict] in a more economic way. Since individual property is the basis of justice, and since property in its origin requires no relationship among men, justice cannot be the object of a genuine uncertainty, and hence of rational debate. Justice is always already realised, as long as property is guaranteed and protected" (46).

18. Eric Voegelin, *The New Science of Politics: An Introduction* (Chicago: University of Chicago Press, 1987), 180. The reference to Hobbes is from part I, "On Man," chap. 11, "On the Difference of Manners": "To which end (on the difference of manners) we are to consider, that the felicity of this life, consisteth not in the repose of a mind satisfied. For there is no such *finis ultimus*, (utmost aim,) nor *summum bonum*, (greatest good,) as is spoken of in the books of the old moral philosophers" Hobbes, *Leviathan*, 2123.

19. Peter L. P. Simpson, *Political Illiberalism: A Defence of Freedom* (London: Routledge, 2015), 131. The references to John Rawls are from his *A Theory of Justice* (Cambridge, MA: Belknap Press, 1971), 1–6, 15, 85.

20. Simpson, *Political Illiberalism*, 132. Simpson refers specifically to Aristotle's *Politics*, trans. Benjamin Jowett, in *Aristotle: The Complete Works* (*English Edition*) (KTHTK 2023, Kindle), 1.1.1252a1–7.

21. For the historical, philosophical, and theological background to the political projects of Hobbes and Locke, see Manent, *Intellectual History of Liberalism*.

22. Simon Usborne, "I Don't Intend to Let My Son Down Twice," *Guardian*, August 11, 2021, https://www.theguardian.com/society/2021/aug/11/i-dont-intend-to -let-my-son-down-twice-the-bereaved-father-trying-to-end-suicide (accessed October 15, 2023).

23. Pieper, *End of Time*, 152–53.

24. Josef Pieper, *Faith, Hope, Love* (San Francisco: Ignatius Press, 1997), 95.

25. Josef Pieper, *Hope and History* (San Francisco: Ignatius Press, 1994), 185. Pieper bases his comments on the clinical studies of German psychiatrist Herbert Plügge, who had analyzed the mental state of persons who were terminally ill or had attempted suicide.

26. Hittinger's informative essay, *Virtue of Hope*, describes the historical difference between hope considered as a blind and unreasonable passion, and the precise understanding of the Christian virtue of hope. Hittinger makes reference to Martha

C. Nussbaum's *Fragility of Goodness: Luck and Ethics in Greek Tragedy and Philosophy*, 2nd ed. (Cambridge: Cambridge University Press, 2001) as a study of the ancient Greek awareness of the contingency and precarity of life, even the virtuous life.

27. As Hittinger reminds us, Aristotle remarks on the precariousness of human existence: "Or we must add, that not only is he to live so, but his death must be in keeping with such life, since the future is dark to us, and Happiness we assume to be in every way an end and complete" Aristotle, *Nicomachean Ethics*, trans. David Ross, book I, chap. X, in *Aristotle: The Complete Works (English Edition)* (KTHTK, 2023), Kindle, 645.

28. States of clinical depression are painful evidence of the incapacity to live even in this existence without sustaining hope.

29. Joachim of Fiore (1135–1202) was an Italian monk and theologian who interpreted the Book of Revelation in terms of three identifiable historical Ages, of the Father, the Son, and, in de Fiore's own time, the Age of the Spirit. This belief of de Fiore's in the present Age of the Spirit practically coincided with the life of St. Francis of Assisi and his new radical way of living the Gospel. Some saw in St. Francis the epitome and exemplar of this new kingdom of the Holy Spirit.

30. Writing of what he termed these Gnostic trends, Eric Voegelin states: "The rise of Gnosticism at this critical juncture now appears in a new light as the incipient formation of a Western civil theology. The immanentization of the Christian eschaton made it possible to endow society in its natural existence with a meaning which Christianity denied to it. And the totalitarianism of our time must be understood as journey's end of the Gnostic search for a civil theology" Voegelin, *New Science of Politics*, 162. Voegelin is so convinced of this reading of secularized modern political ideologies that he recommends reading Irenaeus' *Adversus Haereses* [Against Heretics] (written around 174–189 AD) to understand modern political ideas and movements, Cf. Voegelin, *New Science of Politics*, 126.

31. Voegelin, *New Science of Politics*, 119. For Enlightenment philosophers' undeclared reliance on Christian notions, see Carl Lotus Becker, *The Heavenly City of the Eighteenth-Century Philosophers* (New Haven, CT: Yale University Press, 1932): "I shall attempt to show that the Philosophes demolished the Heavenly City of St. Augustine only to rebuild it with more up-to-date materials" (31). And for the pseudo-religious foundations of contemporary terrorism, see Barry Cooper, *New Political Religions, or An Analysis of Modern Terrorism* (Columbia: University of Missouri Press, 2004).

32. Eric Voegelin, *Science, Politics and Gnosticism: Two Essays*, ed. Ellis Sandoz (Washington DC: Gateway Editions, 1997), 1019.

33. Voegelin, *Science, Politics and Gnosticism*, 1048.

34. Voegelin, *Science, Politics and Gnosticism*, 1048.

35. Voegelin, *Science, Politics and Gnosticism*, 1062. On the general theme of the appropriation of the transcendent religious dimension of the human person's social existence by other political ideologies in the public square, see Richard J. Neuhaus, *The Naked Public Square: Religion and Democracy in America*, 2nd ed. (Grand Rapids, MI: Eerdmans, 1984), esp. chap. 5 "The Vulnerability of the Naked

Square": "When religion in any traditional or recognizable form is excluded from the public square, it does not mean that the public square is in fact naked. This is the other side of the 'naked public square' metaphor. When recognizable religion is excluded, the vacuum will we filled by *ersatz* religion, by religion bootlegged into public pace under other names. Again, to paraphrase Spinoza: transcendence abhors a vacuum" Neuhaus, *Naked Public Square*, 80.

36. *Ideen zur Philosophie der Geschichte* [Reflections on the Philosophy of History] 15 (chap. heading), quoted in Pieper, *End of Time*, 89

37. Immanuel Kant, *Ideal of a Universal History Based on the Principle of World-Citizenship*, quoted in Pieper, *End of Time*, 93.

38. Pieper, *End of Time*, 91–92.

39. Manent, *Metamorphoses of the City*, 278. The reference is to Augustine's *City of God*. Manent's comments are in the context of his analysis of the two cities, the city that is limited to this immanent human existence and the city that is the manifestation of a transcendent existence. Cf. *Metamorphoses of the City*, chap. 8 "The Two Cities," analyzed by Manent in the figures of Romulus and Remus as contrasted with the more profound conflict between Cain and Abel.

40. Ernst Cassirer, *The Philosophy of the Enlightenment* (Princeton, NJ: Princeton University Press, 1951), 143. In this section I am indebted to Peter Henrici's "The Philosophers and Original Sin," *Communio* 18, no. 4 (1991): 489–501.

41. Quoted in Henri de Lubac, *Catholicism: Christ and the Common Destiny of Man*, trans. Lancelot Sheppard (San Francisco: Ignatius Press, 1988), 33.

42. de Lubac, *Catholicism*, 33–34.

43. de Lubac, *Catholicism*, 34.

44. Cassirer, *Philosophy of the Enlightenment*, 156–57.

45. Cassirer, *Philosophy of the Enlightenment*, 158.

46. Jean Jaques Rousseau, *Discourse on Political Economy* (1755), as cited in Robert A. Nisbet's *The Quest for Community: A Study in the Ethics of Order and Freedom* (Washington, DC: ISI Books, 2010), 2739. Rousseau's discourse was first published in the fifth volume of Denis Diderot's *Encyclopédie* (published 1751–1772).

47. Roger Scruton, *The Uses of Pessimism: And the Danger of False Hope* (London: Atlantic Books, 2010), 70–71, 64. Scruton draws on an essay "The Utopian Mind," by Hungarian philosopher Aurel Kolnai.

48. Henrici, "Philosophers and Original Sin," 498. Henrici continues to follow the historical interpretation of this doctrine in Friedrich Schelling, Søren Kierkegaard, and the contemporary Paul Ricoeur.

49. Joseph Ratzinger comments on the Marxist appropriation of the Creator's powers and Ernst Bloch's contemporary intensification of this idea in his affirmation that "truth is now what we take it to be and that the only truth is change. Truth is, accordingly, whatever prevails, and as a result reality is 'a signal to invade and an instruction to attack'" Ratzinger, *"In the Beginning . . .": A Catholic Understanding to the Story of Creation and the Fall* (Grand Rapids, MI: Eerdmans, 1995), 36. The quotations in the text are from Ernst Bloch's *Prinzip Hoffnung* [The Principle of Hope] Russell Hittinger also comments on Bloch's contemporary influence on the theme of man's hope in himself to achieve his final transformation. Cf. Hittinger, *Virtue of Hope*, 266–311.

50. Eric Voegelin, *From Enlightenment to Revolution*, ed. John H. Hallowell (Durham, NC: Duke University Press, 1975), 241. The quote from Karl Marx is from *The German Ideology* (1846; published 1932).

51. Joseph Cropsey, "Karl Marx," in *History of Political Philosophy*, 3rd ed. ed. Leo Strauss and Joseph Cropsey (Chicago: University of Chicago Press, 1987), 16429.

52. Del Noce, *Crisis of Modernity*, 200. The reference is to an Italian translation of an essay titled "Apocalypse and Revolution" by Eric Voegelin. This radical assumption of the human person's supposedly self-possessed powers of transformation, and the rejection of the notion of God as a limiting restraint on human powers and ambitions, is at the heart of much modern political thought and is analyzed and critiqued in Henri de Lubac's *The Drama of Atheist Humanism*, trans. Mark Sebanc (San Francisco: Ignatius Press, 1998).

53. Jaques Maritain, *The Person and the Common Good* (Notre Dame, IN: University of Notre Dame Press, 1966), 97.

54. Benedict XVI [Joseph Ratzinger], *Spe salvi* (Città del Vaticano: Libreria Editrice Vaticana, 2007), sec.12

55. Hittinger, *Virtue of Hope*, 128 and following.

56. British historian Michael Burleigh has written two volumes on the "political religions" from the Enlightenments to the present times. Cf. Burleigh, *Earthly Powers: Religion and Politics in Europe from the Enlightenment to the Great War* (New York: Harper Perennial, 2005); and Burleigh, *Sacred Causes: Religion and Politics from the European Dictators to Al Qaeda* (New York: Harper Press, 2006).

57. De Lubac refers to the historical occurrence of this caricature of Christianity and cites Philippe Régis de Trobriand: "Perhaps Marxism and Leninism would not have arisen and been propagated with such terrible results if the place that belongs to collectivity in the natural as well as in the supernatural order had always been given to it," in De Lubac, *Catholicism*, 309.

58. Joseph Ratzinger describes this human experience to transcendent fulfilment in this way: "Man, to be free, has to be 'like God.' The intention of becoming like God is the central nucleus of so much that is thought out about the liberation of man. Because the desire of liberty belongs to the essence of man, a person necessarily seeks from the start the path to 'being like God.' All other things in fact are not sufficient for man, insatiable where finite things are concerned . . . . Consequently, an anthropology of liberation, if it wants to correspond to the depth of the problem this raises, cannot avoid the query, "How is this end of 'becoming like God,' being divinized, to be achieved?" Ratzinger, *Journey to Easter: Spiritual Reflections for the Lenten Season* (New York: Crossroad, 2005), 97.

59. Hittinger, *Virtue of Hope*, 188.

60. The difficulties in accepting the human person's real and radical dependence on Another are well described in Kenneth L. Schmitz's *The Gift: Creation* (Milwaukee, WI: Marquette University Press, 1982), 63–76. Schmitz refers to the subsequent "humanistic atheisms" of will and action as described in Henri de Lubac, *The Drama of Atheist Humanism*, trans. Mark Sabanc (San Francisco: Ignatius Press, 1998). For a metaphysical analysis of the person's structural dependence on God, there is

W. Norris Clarke's essay "To Be Is to Be Substance-in-Relation," in *Explorations in Metaphysics: Being-God-Person* (Notre Dame, IN: University of Notre Dame Press, 1994),102–22, with a reference to David L. Schindler's complementary remarks about human's existence "from another, in itself, and oriented toward others." Clarke, "To Be Is to Be Substance-in-Relation,"119. Josef Pieper describes and analyses the modern difficulty of accepting a human person's radical need to be loved in Pieper, *Faith, Hope, Love* (San Francisco: Ignatius Press, 1977), 173–86.

61. Hittinger, *Virtue of Hope*, 188.

62. Ratzinger, "A Christian Orientation," 3023. Ratzinger, in a short essay titled *Eschatology and Utopia*, distinguishes among Christian eschatological hope, the final and definitive transformation of all of creation as indicated in the Scriptures, utopian models of thought as legitimate, necessary, and yet always limited, efforts to describe ideal society, and, finally, forms of chiliastic thought, the unwarranted attempts, whether for religious motives or not, to implant Heaven on earth, usually by violent means. Cf. Ratzinger, *Church, Ecumenism, and Politics: New Endeavours in Ecclesiology* (San Francisco: Ignatius Press, 2008), 223–37. Ratzinger also points out that while all attempts to produce earthly paradise are unjustified and dangerous, Christianity does take up and express the dynamism of human hope. It was to express the real hope of a transformed universe that the early Christians refused to call Christ by the imperial title of *Conservator mundi*, but as *Salvator mundi*. Cf. Joseph Ratzinger, "Political Visions and the Praxis of Politics," in *Europe: Today and Tomorrow* (San Francisco: Ignatius Press, 2007) 48.

63. Tocqueville, *Democracy in America*, 13725.

64. Tocqueville, *Democracy in America*, 13739.

65. Tocqueville, *Democracy in America*, 13725.

66. Simpson, *Political Illiberalism*, 41.

67. Simpson draws on the Biblical examples found in the Book of Judges and the Book of Samuel to show the allurement of this abdication of responsibility in handing over to others what depends on each one. From the Book of Judges: "In those days there was no king in Israel: every man did that which was right in his own eyes" (Judges 21:25, RSV). The people's subsequent desire for a king (Samuel 8:6–20, RSV) was their way of not having to live according to the Lord God's Law and at the same time enjoy peace and prosperity, the benefit of following the Lord God's Law. Simpson also refers to book II of Plato's *Republic* and the so-called city of pigs, where all the people, of simple life, "have sufficient knowledge of divine things and of education that they can hymn the gods and rule their families" Simpson, *Political Illiberalism*, 25; in other words, where each one lives responsibly according to wisdom.

68. Simpson, *Political Illiberalism*, 34.

69. David Walsh, *After Ideology: Recovering the Spiritual Foundations of Freedom* (San Francisco: HarperCollins, 1990), 196. See chaps. 5 "The Restoration of Order"; and 6 "Beyond the Crisis of Modernity" which describe the experience of the real foundations of public order.

Chapter 6

Political Authority and Its Justifications

This chapter's overview states that although human persons are structured to flourishing and to attain fulfilment in communion with others, the question of how this communion is established practically, especially in its political dimension, is not easily answered. Public government is spontaneously perceived as an imposition on personal freedom and autonomy, which are rightly valued highly today. This view is reinforced by the historical memory of ideological political programs that intended to transform peoples and societies, and that have been inflicted on peoples with disastrous results.

We look first, therefore, at anarchic attitudes to political authority, to those who in differing ways deny the need for political government, either in immediate form or as a supposed goal of an ideological plan. Francis Fukuyama shows us how political anarchy appears in reality. Even so, it seems that today we still believe that the transformation of the human person and society depends on conditions external to the person and it also seems that a form of moral anarchy is at the heart of what we term as freedom today. And yet, freedom, and its consequent responsibility for oneself and for others, lies at the center of the political common good. How do we differentiate between freedom and anarchy?

Attitudes of political dominance take the opposite view of political government; those who insist that only through enforced public programs can people and society be transformed. While the historical evidence of this abuse of power is apparent, there is also here a kernel of truth—that the human person is called to a collective social destiny. This is why such ideological programs have resonated within the human spirit. There are also today more subtle and equally dominant forms of government imposition and control.

While political authority is a human necessity, the predominant understanding today of authority is in terms of power, a power that is its own justification. As Augusto del Noce summarizes it, "in the philosophy of the primacy of being, authority is the foundation of power, whereas in the philosophy of the primacy of becoming power absorbs authority within itself."[1]

What is the real meaning of political authority? We spontaneously understand authority in different ways, but ultimately, we justify authority in terms of what is true and right, what conforms to reality, and that, therefore, requires to be recognized and enacted. This is also the case politically, as both Plato and Aristotle explained, that the justification of necessary political authority is to be found in its conformity to the true vision of human society.

The modern loss of this sense of political authority is expressed in Niccolò Machiavelli's notion of "effective truth," not indeed truth, but effective power. Subsequent historical architects of the form of the modern political state encased this notion of effective power in the sovereign state and its way of predominating over all other sources of authority. In this political arrangement, the human person is reduced to a numerically equal individual, each one subject to the formalities of state power. Consequently, this leaves "the people" in a very fragile relation of subjection to state dominance.

In conclusion, while public government is a necessary human social condition, today we live generally under forms of political power, not of political authority. This is seen in the pre-emptive systematic public exclusion of questions of truth and rightness, and their replacement in terms of numbers and majorities.

NEXUS

A common thread running through the previous essays is the possibility of, and the vital need for, an authentic vision of people and their society. This vision of the structure of a people and their interpersonal development is something that can be discovered through a person's birth into co-existence with reality and developed through progressive stages of maturity. In philosophical terms, we come to vision by "pondering the ontological implications of the givenness of things (and persons) as originally experienced."[2] Even allowing for the multiple variant forms of human expression of this vision in cultures and in languages, the bedrock of who persons are, their interrelatedness with reality and particularly personal being, and their destiny toward personal and social fulfilment, is constant. This substratum is the necessary and vital basis for social and political communion.

At the same time, this developing discovery is not something automatic or entirely spontaneous. Both the inherent fallibility of the human person's present existential condition and the precarious process of personal development make the shared vision of society something difficult to attain. One of the positive discoveries of recent times is the sensitivity to the early years of

human formation in the proper development of one's response to the givenness of things. Economist Jennifer Roback Morse points out the obvious and
often overlooked reality that:

> We are not born as rational, choosing agents, able to defend ourselves and our
> property, able to negotiate contracts and exchanges. . . . A free society requires
> self-restraining, self-monitoring, self-governing adults. But we are not born as
> adults. Contrary to the romantic view, actual babies are not noble savages: they
> are just cute savages who have the potential to be civilized. They are totally
> self-centered, impulsive, and demanding. It is not a foregone conclusion that
> any particular child will be civilized.[3]

The metaphysics of personal love, love that is received so as to be able to
be given, is fundamental to future interpersonal communion. The deprivation
of this original experience leads to personal attachment disorders and the
possible incapacity to participate in social communion, which can result in:

> The rational, calculating, economic man, the person who considers only his
> own good, who is willing to do anything he deems it in his interest to do, who
> cares for no one. All of his actions are governed by the self-interested calcula-
> tion of costs and benefits. Punishments matter; loss of esteem does not. As for
> his promises, he behaves opportunistically on every possible occasion, breaking
> promises if he deems it in his interest to do so.[4]

Morse's point here is that society and politics cannot depend and will not
survive in a humane way on the mutual interests of autonomous individuals,
but on the essential element of love, the metaphysics of interpersonal love.
This vital formative experience does not just happen spontaneously, but
depends on the deliberate decision of others, primarily parents, to provide.

The adequate conditions for human development, founded on the prerequisite of unconditioned love, provide the freedom to experience reality as it is
given and to respond in an adequate way. When these conditions are fulfilled,
the capacity to experience, value, and respond to reality adequately becomes
possible—and this is what we call living in the truth. This is no philosophical luxury, but the essential basis for any meaningful social and political
communion.

We have seen in law and human rights, both fundamental expressions of
political order, how dependent each is on the right understanding of the human
person and the metaphysics of interpersonal love. Impoverished notions of
the rational, calculating, economic individual distort the nature of law and
human rights, and the bonds of society, which fundamentally depend on the
freely experienced adequate response to interpersonal reality, these bonds
have to be enforced by abstract mechanisms of assertion and control. Given a

metaphysics of love, law and human rights can both express the proper order of human society, a true human society, as variant as its expressions are. An impoverished notion of personal being only exposes the inadequacy of law and rights to form and to maintain a human society.

Liberal political societies put a premium on personal freedom, and rightly so. We are made capable of freely developing with and for others a truly human society. To negate human freedom is to deny the truth of the person in a fundamental dimension. Perhaps it would be so much easier to achieve a mechanical social and political uniformity—the experiment has been tried and continues to be tried—but only achieves the suffocation produced by inhuman conformity, which sooner or later crumbles under the pressure of constrained human freedom:

> It was Jean Jacques Rousseau who had first announced that human beings could be transformed for the better by the political process, and that the agency of change, the creator of what he termed the "new man," would be the state, and the self-appointed benefactors who controlled it for the good of all. In the twentieth century his theory was finally put to the test, on a colossal scale, and tested to destruction. . . . By the year 1900 politics was already replacing religion as the chief form of zealotry. To architypes of the new class, such as Lenin, Hitler and Mao Tse-tung, politics—by which they meant the engineering of society for lofty purposes—was the one legitimate form of moral activity, the only sure means of improving humanity. This view, which would have struck an earlier age as fantastic, even insane, became to some extent the orthodoxy everywhere: diluted in the West, in virulent form in the Communist countries and much of the Third World.[5]

While this is all true, when liberal societies renounce any notion of common truth under the pretense of respecting human freedom, the feigned ignorance of complex and difficult issues (as if choosing to ignore the need to judge these issues resolves the issues), or the fiction of thinking that society is made and maintained simply by freedom, such liberal societies are living beyond their means. These societies promise human society and offer freedom as the only building material. A truthful vision of interpersonal communion, however sketchy and contingent, is as necessary as the architect's blueprint. In the political liberalism of today, a comprehensive notion of a substantive common good is glaringly absent:

In *The Growth of the Liberal Soul*, David Walsh observes that there is little fundamental agreement today as to what political liberalism means, and he also recognizes the growing distance between society and politics in the liberal tradition. Walsh notes that we lack basic shared principles that could guide and discern between the wide variety of political options; it is as if we have competing sets of political practices but no fundamental truths to distinguish one from the other. This is political liberalism's deep malaise, the absence of a compelling vision of human society; the respect for freedoms does not include shared essential purposes of those freedoms. Walsh recognizes that the events of 1989, the fall of the Berlin Wall and the breakup of the Soviet bloc in the following years, brought an end to what may be termed the public enemy of liberalism, but liberalism's lack of fundamental identity and vision points to something more that is missing within political liberalism itself than the lack of public opposition.[6]

This lack of greater and deeper social purpose in a society that has only individual freedom at its center and as its goal accounts in great part for the apathy and resentment toward such a politics. This became clear to T. S. Eliot when Western countries in 1938 were required to oppose a virulent and zealous political ideology:

> It was not, I repeat, a criticism of the government, but a doubt of the validity of a civilisation. We could not match conviction with conviction, we had no ideas with which we could either meet or oppose the ideas opposed to us. Was our society, which had always been so assured of its superiority and rectitude, so confident of its unexamined premises, assembled round anything more permanent than a congeries of banks, insurance companies and industries, and had it any beliefs more essential than a belief in compound interest and the maintenance of dividends?[7]

This absence of a real human society and of what it takes to build social communion raises two questions as to the role of a public government in political society: what, if any, is the necessary role and function of political government? What, if any, is the difference between political authority and political power—or have they in reality become just interchangeable terms?

ANARCHIC ATTITUDES TO POLITICAL AUTHORITY TODAY

In our political societies that promote the notions of freedom and equality, it seems that there is little apparent need for or acceptance of political authority, understood as a moral ascendence over a people that can legitimately be enforced.

In the first place, there have been and are those who claim that individual autonomy is sufficient for the well-being of our societies and that structures and institutions of organization and subsequent control of people is unnecessary. These anarchical claims can be justified in various ways and the various forms of anarchy revolve around general ideas of people's innate goodness and self-sufficiency, the belief in spontaneous cooperation and mutual help, the understanding of institutions and government as instruments of suppression and domination, the removal of structures and controls as the way to inexorable progress, discoverable laws of human development, and so on. Belief in anarchic society can be both in the immediate here and now and, more often, as part of a promissory note toward a society with little or no need for public authority, so that once certain obstacles have been removed, conditions of peace and harmony will then reign spontaneously. In this way, anarchic visions of human society resemble utopian, chiliastic, or, in the terminology of Eric Voegelin, gnostic visions of a future perfect society, the realization of which can be orchestrated by political action.[8] These diverse beliefs in different forms of rule-less social harmony could be brought about by spontaneous action, following discoverable social laws, or by forceful means and by revolution. The Hungarian political philosopher Aurel Kolnai describes such utopian thought in these terms:

> What Utopia purports to be is not the fulfilment of so many tasks but the solution of the puzzle. From the principle of perfection on which it is built everything else derives; and that they so derive makes all these particular achievements valid and inseparable one from the other. The test of their being what they ought to be lies, not in our single, divergent and fallible appraisals, but in the magic key that has opened access to the hidden chambers of perfection whose furniture they compose. The things of Utopia are not right as opposed to wrong things, but manifestations of the right way of being. Every utopia is consummate reality and all-embracing community in relation with those who belong to it, but a solipsistic individual in regard to everything facing it from outside.[9]

One of the modern expressions of utopian anarchism, in the aftermath of the French Revolution and Reign of Terror, was the English political philosopher William Godwin (1756–1836), who published *An Inquiry Concerning Political Justice* (1793), and *Things as They Are: The Adventures of Caleb Williams* (1794), which attacked political institutions and aristocratic privilege. The so-called French Utopians,[10] François Charles Fourier (1772–1837), Henri de Saint-Simon (1760–1825), and Pierre-Joseph. Proudhon (1809–1865), in differing ways, considered that the goals of the French Revolution had only been accomplished in part, and all considered central state control unnecessary for social existence. Fourier believed himself to have discovered laws of social development analogous to Isaac Newton's laws of physics. Saint-Simon also believed in a new science of social evolution which he called social physiology and viewed the rising industrial class as the harbingers of a new solidarity both within national societies and among the nations. The French Revolution itself was but a part of a process that had been developing "for more than six centuries" and was to free the industrial class and industrial society.[11]

Proudhon was also a believer in the natural laws of social development. His solution to "equality-destroying property," on the one hand, and "independence-destroying socialism," on the other hand, was his proposal of "mutualism," anarchy, "a society of producers united by means of free contracts."[12] For Proudhon, "The notion of anarchy in politics is just as rational and positive as any other. It means that once industrial functions have taken over from political functions, then business transactions and exchange alone produce the social order."[13]

The conviction of an imminent future classless society without needs and without coercive means of social control was also at the heart of Karl Marx's future anarchistic society. What was new in Marx was the necessary historical progression toward this future society, where sufficiency will be provided "from each according to his ability, to each according to his need(s)."[14] Progress toward this was historically inexorable and could (and should) be accelerated either by "revolutionary terror" or "a long march through the institutions."[15] Through the change of the economic structure by proletariat ownership, a new and more perfect society would necessarily be produced:

> It seems clear that at least two things are to be expected of the envisioned Marxist future. Human nature will be transformed, or returned to its primitive "unalienated" condition—once the institutions of class oppression have been done away with. Each person will see himself, not as the isolated, right-bearing individual which bourgeois justice focuses upon, but as an integrated member of a community. Its life will be his life. Secondly, modern technology, once released from the shackles of capitalist constraint, will produce abundantly enough to meet all the needs of the transformed humanity; and productive work will become a pleasure. Lenin foretold that people would then spontaneously observe the "elementary rules of social life"—which might be a sort of "law"—and that should there be isolated infractions they would be dealt with by spontaneous reactions, not coercive institutions.[16]

In this view, the political organization of the state will also disappear because there will be no social class to subjugate, as the means of production will be held by all. As Friedrich Engels wrote:

> The first act by virtue of which the state really constitutes itself the representative of the whole of society—the taking possession of the means of production in the name of society—this is, at the same time, its last independent act as a state. State interference in social relations becomes, in one domain after another, superfluous, and then dies out of itself; the government of persons is replaced

by the administration of things, and by the conduct of processes of production. The state is not "abolished." It dies out.[17]

While these notable historical forms of anarchism make explicit the claims to a present or future spontaneous harmony of human society, and appear on the radical wing of politics, there have been and are more subtle beliefs in political anarchism that go by more respectable titles in political liberalisms. For example, the belief in the moral "neutrality" of public reason, or the necessary "privatization" of religious truth from the construction of public society are, understood in a certain real sense, forms of social anarchy that sustain the view that such considerations are irrelevant to the building of human society and therefore anarchic elements of no social importance. Political structures and economic issues do need to be regulated because—it is tacitly assumed—society depends on these to flourish; given these elements, the harmonic society is guaranteed. There is something similar in this belief to the quaint ideas of Fourier and Saint-Simon to have discovered the ascertainable "laws" of human social flourishing, and to the Marxist belief that the economic structures account both for the present injustice and the hope for a future harmonic society.

Jospeh Ratzinger, in his essay "A Christian Orientation in a Pluralistic Democracy?" writes of this belief in a "liberated" society and notes that the good society now no longer depends on the goodness of the people living and contributing to that human society, but rather is seen to depend on the organization and the material structures of such a society. The good and just society depends, in this view, on the material quality of the structures rather than the moral quality of the people. Society can be bettered by improving and changing the structures that, once in place, will guarantee our good society. Ratzinger observes that our confidence is placed in material stability and material well-being, because we have little confidence in the moral goodness of people as a foundation for society. Here Ratzinger recognizes the core of a materialistic perspective on human society, which has great consequences for the understanding of human persons and their social relations. What is being proposed in this materialistic perspective is that matter and material means and structures produce spirit, and that spirit is merely a by-product of material structures. What this means is that we think that it is the economy that produces the good society rather than recognizing that economic decisions are merely manifestations and determinations of the human spirit.[18]

Although utopian anarchy has spontaneously bad connotations, there is a fundamental truth and value that anarchy implies. This is the basic truth of the personal freedom of self-responsibility as the basis of political government, a truth that has often been smothered in the modern relation of political state and individual subject. Often this relation has developed into the commodious abdication of individual political responsibility and the increasing dominance of government control in order to answer the ever-increasing welfare claims of individuals. It is hard otherwise to justify the mutual acquiescence in the running up of national economic debts and the mortgaging of future genera-tions.[19] The same can happen in moral and religious commitments; in this symbiotic relation of individual and state, we the individuals can easily avoid having to ask ourselves about what is *best for all*, and instead we need only decide what is *good for me*. Public reason conveniently justifies morally this abdication of responsibility by precluding, on the grounds of tolerance, any comprehensive moral or religious concern for all. The state has conveniently taken these public considerations out of our hands, and we have thus conve-niently avoided having to confront these questions.

Peter L. P. Simpson finds in the Book of Judges and in the first Book of Samuel a similar situation to the present-day individual acquiescence to what we may call a paternalistic relation of state authority toward its subjects. The clamor of the people of Israel for a king, something displeasing to the Lord God, was so that the people could enjoy peace and prosperity without having to follow the Law of the Lord given to them by Moses. This was because peace and prosperity, and their opposite, war and scarcity, had been shown in the time of the Judges to depend on whether the people followed the wisdom of the God-given Law. The idea of proposing a king was the attempt to secure peace and prosperity through the leadership of the king without having to renounce crime and idolatry. In other words, the deal was to hand over to a chosen government the personal responsibility of each one, the responsibility of each person "to do what was right in his own eyes" (Judges 21:25, RSV), that is, to follow the law of the Lord God in personal conscience.[20] This is an unwarranted abdication of personal commitment, which is, in turn, essential for a peaceful and prosperous society. Simpson draws a parallel with the so-called city of pigs in Plato's Book II of the *Republic*,[21] one without an army or rulers or judges, and according to Socrates "the best city"—why? Because:

> like the children of Israel (or rather like the way God wanted the children of Israel to be), they are ruled by the wisdom present in each of them. . . . Everyone in the healthy city is a self-sufficient philosopher, sharing all in common with all and each. . . . The people, in other words, must, by the nature of the case, all be philosophers (cf. Aristotle, Politics) or philosophers enough to know, indepen-dently of political structures, what justice is and to act on it.[22]

Our point here is that the bad word "anarchy" contains a precious truth of political union. In an extreme way, the anarchist throws off the shackles of external authority and affirms the personal response to living in society, admittedly not always by serene and peaceful means. This sense of personal response is something that our comfortable relation with the state has concealed, even stifled. Our willingness to accept so many norms and regulations without question is a sign of an unhealthy submission of personal responsibility, a happy price we are prepared to pay for not answering our more serious moral, religious, social, and political responsibilities. We are inclined not to want to think of any greater society and our established implicit agreement with state authority assures us that we do not need to. Our structures and processes, our economic policy, and all the many external and impersonal political machinery, as relatively important as they may be, are no valid substitution for the personal conscientious seeing and doing what is right in our own eyes.

This is also the reason that the justification of political authority resides in the collective capacity of persons to know and to choose what truly enhances their society; the varying forms of political government are only representative of, and subject to this collective truthful vision.[23] This presupposes and actively requires the personally formed capacity to know what contributes to human social flourishing and the subsequent agreed collective vision for society. Only on this basis can political forms function. Any political form that denies *a priori*, a comprehensive vision for society, and which treats persons and requires that persons treat themselves only as equal and isolated individuals, is *ipso facto* incapable of representing the real capacities of persons to know their common social good.

In *The Quest for Community*, Robert A Nisbet agrees with Abraham Lincoln's description of democratic government as government of, by, and for the people, but notes that the term "people" is abstract and ambiguous. Nisbet explains that the phrase "the people" can be understood in two very distinct ways. The people can be seen as the sum of all individuals within the jurisdiction of the political state and, in this understanding, the people's identity is determined by and in the terms of the state's constitution and legal determinations. This is one way of describing the people. The other way is to perceive the people as a cultural group or groups, representing all of what constitutes culture; a shared language, traditions, identity, and beliefs, together with the natural and spontaneous institutions and structures that express these various cultural manifestations. Nisbet notes that these alternative interpretations of "the people" determine to a great extent the type or form of political democracy. He notes that when political actions are undertaken in the name "of the people," taken to mean only the numerical sum of individuals, the consequences will be much different than when "the people" represents the sum of social cultural expressions and expressions, which form the context within which political actions are proposed and approved.[24]

While the ideal of a spontaneous, peaceful, and prosperous human society without the compulsive force of external authority and laws is something that inspires us, the present or imminent reality of such an anarchic society is much different. Real anarchy does exist in certain areas and states in the world, but it is not of the idyllic type. Fukuyama points out what spontaneous society can look like:

> Indeed, the kinds of minimal or no-government societies envisioned by dreamers of the Left and Right are not fantasies; they actually exist in the contemporary developing world. Many parts of sub-Sahara Africa are a libertarian's paradise. The region as a whole is a low-tax utopia, with governments often unable to collect more than about 10% of GDP in taxes, compared to more than 30% in the United States and 50% in parts of Europe. Rather than unleashing entrepreneurship, this low rate of taxation means that basic public services like health, education, and pothole filling are starved of funding. The physical infrastructure on which a modern economy rests, like roads, court systems, and police, are missing. In Somalia, where a strong central government has not existed since the late 1980s, ordinary individuals may own not just assault rifles but also rocket-propelled grenades, antiaircraft missiles, and tanks. People are free to protect their own families, and indeed are forced to do so. . . . Political institutions are necessary and cannot be taken for granted. A market economy and high levels of wealth don't magically appear when you "get government out of the way"; they rest on a hidden institutional foundation of property rights, rule of law, and basic political order.[25]

ATTITUDES OF POLITICAL DOMINANCE AND CONTROL

If, therefore, anarchic proposals are grossly unrealistic in their claims to be able to establish human society, so too are the proposals of the opposite extreme of being able to produce a perfect society by the imposition of government programs and structures. As has been mentioned earlier, the promise of the structureless free society was the justifying clause of political programs that claimed to be able to produce this ideal at the cost of present personal freedom and well-being. In this sense, a totalitarian vision of human society claimed to be able to interpret all dimensions of human life and to harness all these dimensions, individual and collective, toward a proximate future ideal society. Often these totalitarian visions were supposed to be manifestations of some necessary historical or material determined process that could be recognized and promoted by political action. These were world visions that included all areas of human existence including moral and religious values; all of reality was reinterpreted in terms of a particular political vision. Although the demise of many, but not all, of such totalitarian visions in the latter half of this last century makes it hard for us to understand the audacious magnitude of such calculating programs and their credibility, this historically new form and methods of total political domination achieved immense proportions. Voegelin describes these political totalitarian approaches in terms of attempts to reinterpret the world "as an alien place into which man has strayed and from which he must find his way back home to the other world of his origin."[26] What characterizes this transformation is an enlightened view held by a few of the new order of the world and how it is to come about, through people's efforts, so that they move from a state of alienation to fulfilment. Voegelin sees in these various political ideological visions something similar to the various currents of historical Gnosticism which, claims Voegelin, can be historically traced from then until the modern political mass movements he describes.[27] What Voegelin sees as characteristic of the modern political forms of Gnosticism are:

> (1) immanentist programs to transform the world; and (2) atheism and the deification of Man as superman, master of nature, and maker of history in the wake of the death of God. Modern Gnosticism is especially distinguished from ancient Gnosticism by its renunciation of "vertical" or otherworldly transcendence and its proclamation of a "horizontal" transcendence or futuristic Parousia of Being (Heidegger)—that is, intramundane or worldly salvific doctrines—as ultimate truth. Modern Gnosticism thus takes the form of speculating on the meaning of history construed as a closed process manipulated by the revolutionary elite—the few who understand the path, process, and goal of history as it moves from stage to stage toward some sort of final perfect realm (Hegel, Marx, Comte, National Socialism).[28]

These political programs thus justify themselves according to what their leaders claim to be implacable laws of movement, whether historical or material. The individuality and freedom of the human person is obliterated in the name of some immanently arriving future better condition. As Hanna Arendt writes:

> Totalitarian lawfulness, defying legality and pretending to establish the direct reign of justice on earth, executes the law of History or of nature without transplanting it into standards of right and wrong for individual behaviour. It applies the law directly to mankind without bothering with the behaviour of men. The law of Nature or the law of History, if properly executed, is expected to produce mankind as its end product; and this expectation lies behind the claim to global rule of all totalitarian governments. Totalitarian policy claims to transform the human species into an active unfailing carrier of a law to which human beings otherwise would only passively and reluctantly be subjected.[29]

Interestingly, in her analysis of the new political form of twentieth-century totalitarianism, Arendt notices that while all tyrannies depend on isolated individuals who are impeded from forming a political collective, totalitarian forms of government go further: "But totalitarian domination as a form of government is new in that it is not content with this isolation and destroys private life as well. It bases itself on loneliness, on the experience of not belonging to the world at all, which is among the most radical and desperate experiences of man."[30]

While the theoretical explanations and justifications of these various totalitarian views have been toned down by the horrors inflicted and the failure of their promises, more apparently benign forms of partial or total political domination continue. In more crude forms, as in China, or in Western ways of withdrawing a necessary and comprehensive vision from public consideration, in the name of respect for freedom, and by presuming that the political processes and structures themselves are all that are publicly necessary. This leaves government with a carte blanche to impose ways of thinking and policies disguised as "freedoms" and "rights." English theologian John Milbank, for example, suggests that there is more to the simple government recognition of diverse forms of marriage. Considering the consequences of the legal recognition homosexual marriage, he writes:

> And this, I argue, reveals what is really at issue here. There was no demand for "gay marriage" and this has nothing to do with gay rights. Instead, it is a strategic move in the modern state's drive to assume direct control over the reproduction of the population, bypassing our interpersonal encounters. This is not about natural justice, but the desire on the part of biopolitical tyranny to destroy marriage and the family as the most fundamental mediating social institution.[31]

The point here is not to discuss the legal status of homosexual unions, but what is in effect being done in the name of individual liberties and freedom, as an example of benign totalitarian control over vital areas of pre-existing structures of freedom.

Even in our skeptical times, there is something in totalitarian ideology that appeals naturally to people. If it is true that the human person is structured to fulfilment in society with others, that is, that only with others (and the Other) can the human person find fulfilment, then the project of something greater than oneself corresponds to fundamental human inclinations and hopes. We are structured toward a transcendent social fulfilment, and we only find fulfilment socially. Therefore, political programs that propose a collective future vision will always resonate within the human heart, even if the promises and the programs are delusional, and even at the cost of individual toil and sacrifice.

George Orwell read and reviewed the first English edition, published in 1939, of Adolf Hitler's *Mein Kampf.* Orwell recognizes the appeal of the person of Hitler in the 1930s, painted as the aggrieved martyr fighting against overwhelming odds and yet who had right on his side. More importantly, Orwell recognizes the appeal on the mind and the emotions of the collective great project to which Hitler convoked the German people. Orwell noticed that Hitler had understood the vacuity of hedonism and the hollowness of the Western preoccupation with well-being and a life that is easy, comfortable, and painless. No heroic qualities are demanded or offered; life in society is supposed to be free of commitments and responsibilities and the basic needs of life are to be offered as cheap or free public services. This is the soporific dream that, in Orwell's view, has predominated in the west since the First World War. Orwell, in his review of *Mein Kampf* [My Struggle], recognizes that Hitler knew that people also want and require a greater purpose and identity in life and are prepared to sacrifice themselves for such a purpose. As Orwell remarks, ideologies such as Fascism and Naziism, in this sense, appeal much better to our desires and aspirations because they supposedly offer something worth living and dying for. As Orwell writes:

> All three of the great dictators have enhanced their power by imposing intolerable burdens on their peoples. Whereas Socialism, and even capitalism in a more grudging way, have said to people "I offer you a good time," Hitler has said to them "I offer you struggle, danger and death," and as a result a whole nation flings itself at his feet.[32]

The extremes of social anarchy, on the one hand, and social domination or engineering, on the other hand, are both inadequate and at the same time both contain a vital element of the truth of the human condition; the necessary free personal responsibility as the only adequate human disposition toward the individual's experience of reality, and the greater social destiny to which each person is convoked, and which depends on the free personal response of each one. I suggest that only on both of these two premises can the *role* and *authority* of political government be justified.

WHAT POLITICAL AUTHORITY IS AND HOW IT IS MISUNDERSTOOD TODAY

It follows from the preceding section that human society is neither spontaneous nor simply mechanically produced. On the one hand, the free personal response of each one is the necessary condition of human flourishing; coercion abuses the self-determining responsibility of each person. On the other hand, there is a collective social destiny to which persons are called, if they are to flourish as persons. As relational beings, authentic social relations are essential for each person and are of such a nature that persons are fulfilled to the degree that they grow in social relations, according to a metaphysics of love. In these conditions, the positive role of political authority becomes clearer, even if only in the broadest of outlines. Given the personal capacity and responsibility for relational self-determination, public civil authority has its role in promoting and protecting this social growth according to the limited areas of public life. Therefore, the social role of political authority is much more than the mere traffic control of a multitude of disparate interests, and presupposes a real social good to be enhanced:

> The common good is central to every theory of authority. It is only in relation to it that authority exercises essential functions, i.e., functions whose necessity does not result from an evil or deficiency, but from the nature and the excellence of things human and social. Accordingly, if a philosophy of society dispenses with the notion of common good and is satisfied with any of the substitutes worked out by the imagination of philosophers and political scientists, there will always be something awkward, to say the least, about the vindication of authority.[33]

We glimpse here an intuitive distinction between political authority and political power, although, as we will see, it seems today that the two realities have collapsed into one. The reality of authority implies spontaneously the element of *justified* power, might that *is* right, and that requires its exercise and its acceptance, independent of, but often including, the physical means of implementation. Italian philosopher Augusto Del Noce notices that the real distinction between the two realities is not always properly recognized, even if the verbal terms are acknowledged. He characterizes power in terms of strength and of force, while, on the contrary, authority "spiritual authority, interior in essence, is affirmed only by itself, independently of any sensible support. . . . If we can speak in this context of strength or force, it is only by analogical transportation."[34]

Del Noce recognizes that the modern use of the term "authority" easily confuses the word with meanings of "power." He refers to Max Weber's description of the forms of authority in his *Economy and Society: An Outline of Interpretive Sociology*, in which Weber depicts authority as a form of domination or power:

> Domination was defined above as the probability that certain specific commands (or all commands) will be obeyed by a given group of persons. It thus does not include every mode of exercising "power" or "influence" over other persons. Domination ("authority") in this sense may be based on the most

diverse motives of compliance: all the way from simple habituation to the most purely rational calculation of advantage. Hence every genuine form of domination implies a minimum of voluntary compliance, that is, an interest (based on ulterior motives or genuine acceptance) in obedience.[35]

In this sense, all authority becomes exclusively a form of power, and the authority of the political state can only be described as referring to legitimate means to an end, and not means to a legitimate end:

> What is a "state"? A state, too, cannot be defined sociologically by enumerating its activities. There is almost no task that a political organization has not undertaken at one time or another; but by the same token there are no tasks of which we could say that they were always, let alone exclusively, proper to the organizations that we call political, and nowadays refer to as states, or that historically were the forerunners of the modern state. It is rather the case that in the final analysis the modern state can be defined only sociologically by the specific means that are peculiar to it, as to every political organization: namely, physical violence. "Every state is based on force," Trotsky remarked at Brest-Litovsk. That is indeed the case.[36]

Here authority is clearly and only a function of power, and Del Noce sees immense consequences of this elision of authority with power. Del Noce recognizes that when the meaning of authority is reduced and distorted into meaning the use of power, however that use of power may be legally acquired, then the sense of reality is lost and changed into ideology. In this sense, ideology masquerades as authority, as an explanation of political facts, while, in fact, such ideology is nothing more than the use of power.[37]

Del Noce summarizes this misappropriation of the real meaning of authority in simple metaphysical terms, "To summarize in a formula, we could say that in the philosophy of the primacy of being, authority is the foundation of power, whereas in the philosophy of the primacy of becoming power absorbs authority within itself, as can be seen in the ultimate outcomes of such a philosophy."[38]

What we have, when the justifying notion of authority is subsumed into external forms of compliance, is a political pragmatism that reshapes reality for its own ideological ends.

It is not difficult to understand why political authority, understood in terms of social truth that legitimizes political power, is hardly recognized today and when referred to, almost always refers to a Weberian sense of agreed compliance with power. While the contemporary libertarian notion of unbounded freedom rejects any and all non-essential limits on its expansion, and an exaggerated individualism curtails any thought of common social good, it seems that the absence of political authority in the terms we have described it, is not just something contemporary. Arendt also recognizes the crisis of authority, which "has vanished from the modern world" and the disappearance of which "has become one of the most spectacular characteristics of the modern world."[39] Arendt also recognizes, as Del Noce did, in this disappearance of authority, a fundamental loss for political and non-political society:

> Its loss is tantamount to the loss of the groundwork of the world, which indeed since then has begun to shift, to change and transform itself with ever-increasing rapidity from one shape into another, as though we were living and struggling with a Protean universe where everything at any moment can become almost anything else.[40]

Arendt recognizes that the loss of authority began with modernity, the modern age, and she asks: "what kind of world came to an end after the modern age not only challenged one or another form of authority in different spheres of life but caused the whole concept of authority to lose its validity altogether?"[41]

THE REAL SENSE OF POLITICAL AUTHORITY

Here some type of preliminary sketch of what we mean by authority and its justification is necessary. The most common understanding of authority is the agreed consent to submit to a particular way of doing something, which usually includes persons or institutions that are to achieve or oversee the particular activity. This is evident in, for example, sports, which have agreed rules and agents of those rules to which those who participate voluntarily submit. This understanding of authority is also what theoretically sustains democratic forms of government and their institutions, although the consent of the people to all aspects of government is more remote, less universal, and therefore more tenuous, to become, perhaps necessarily, at times a fiction. The justification of this understanding of authority is the voluntary exercise of personal freedom. Even the use of the means of force is supposed to originate in each one's agreed consent.

Related to this notion of authority is the authority possessed by persons of ability. In this sense we submit, or at least defer to, persons who are knowledgeable in a certain area or have the capacity to do certain things. Medical doctors will be sought for because we recognize that they knowledgeable in matters of health and therefore have a judgment in medicine that is authoritative, that corresponds to what we search for, good health. Similarly, economists will have an authoritative view of economic matters because we recognize that they will know more than any random opinion. Here authority does not depend primarily on freedom for its justification, but on an inherent or acquired and recognized quality that someone possesses and that therefore has a claim on us; it is not something that is justified primarily by the exercise of my freedom.

In a similar manner, one would suppose that on matters vital to political society, persons of inherent or acquired authority would be recognized as those who draw their authority not from power or popularity, but from the recognized capacity to envisage authentic human society and to know how to progress toward such a human society. Theoretically it is not force that governs, or the legitimacy of the electoral process, or the majority of free votes, but the person's capacity to see and to move society toward a better way of living the social bond. Jacques Maritain writes clearly:

> I shall mean by "authority" the right to direct and to command, to be listened to or obeyed by others. And I shall mean by "power" the force, which one can use, and with the aid of which one can oblige others to listen or to obey. The righteous man, deprived of all power and condemned to hemlock, does not diminish—he increases—in moral authority. The gangster or the tyrant exercises power without authority. . . . All authority, in so far as it concerns social life, demands to be completed (under some mode or other, which need not be juridical) by power, without which it threatens to become useless and inefficacious among men. All power which is not the expression of authority is iniquitous. . . . To separate power and authority is to separate force and justice.[42]

This is the real justification of political authority, the truthfulness of the political vision and the capacity to enhance society, to the degree possible, in the light of that vision.

In this respect, authority based on free consent is a necessary but insufficient political condition. Political liberalism, therefore, requires the criterion of a social vision to rule by authority and not just by processes of numerical majorities. It is not surprising that the political justification by freedom conveniently avoids questions about legitimate ends or purposes, which are the source of real authority that morally evokes free consent. Without the possibility of appealing to the real motives for human consent to authority, it is not surprising that justifying the need for authority merely on electoral processes and structures of power brings little respect for the persons and offices of political authority:

> For to live in a political realm with neither authority nor the concomitant awareness that the source of authority transcends power and those who are in power, means to be confronted anew, without the religious trust in a sacred beginning and without the protection of traditional and therefore self-evident standards of behaviour, by the elementary problems of human living-together.[43]

Both Plato and Aristotle searched for a justification of political authority in the truth of human society that could be known and primordially appealed to. In Plato's *Republic*, the philosopher abandons the cave, where the people are gathered, and begins the search of True Being, and discovers the Ideal Forms that are also the ideal standards by which human society can be measured:

> If the highest idea, in which all other ideas must partake in order to be ideas at all, is that of fitness, then the ideas are applicable by definition, and in the hands of the philosopher, the expert in ideas, they can become rules and standards or, as later in the Laws, they can become laws. (The difference is negligible. What in the Republic is still the philosopher's, the philosopher-king's, direct personal claim to rule has become reason's impersonal claim to dominion in the Laws.).[44]

It was this element, the goodness or rightness of the Ideal Forms, that gave authority to the rule of the philosopher king or, later, as expressed in the *Laws*. The truth of authority is allegorically portrayed in the return of the philosopher to the cave of shadows:

> Wherefore each of you, when his turn comes, must go down to the general underground abode, and get the habit of seeing in the dark. When you have acquired the habit, you will see ten thousand times better than the inhabitants of the den, and you will know what the several images are, and what they represent, because you have seen the beautiful and just and good in their truth. And thus our State, which is also yours, will be a reality, and not a dream only, and will be administered in a spirit unlike that of other States, in which men fight with one another about shadows only and are distracted in the struggle for power, which in their eyes is a great good. Whereas the truth is that the State in which the rulers are most reluctant to govern is always the best and most quietly governed, and the State in which they are most eager, the worst.[45]

The essential point is that the justification of the ruler or the laws is by appeal to the inherent truth of the commands, and not by force or by consensus, which today we understand to mean the unreconciled coexistence of freedoms.

Aristotle also asserts the independent standard of truth or reason as the measure and justification of political authority:

> Aristotle, therefore, without accepting Plato's doctrine of ideas, and even repudiating Plato's ideal state, still followed him in the main not only by separating a "theoretical way of life" (βίος θεωρητικός) from a life devoted to human affairs (βίος πολιτικός)—the first to establish such ways of life in hierarchical order had been Plato in his Phaedrus—but accepted as a matter of course the hierarchical order implied in it.[46]

While for Aristotle, the polis was "a community of equals for the purpose of enjoying the best life possible,"[47] political authority is justified in terms of the contemplative life of reason and the political education within the context of this best life of reason.

THE MODERN POLITICAL TRANSFORMATION
OF AUTHORITY INTO POWER

In glaring contrast to this understanding of authority as an appeal to the rightness and goodness of true social life, stands the modern notion of state power introduced by Niccolò Machiavelli and that is taken up by the principal architects of the modern sovereign state.

The tension between authority and power is perennial and positions of power tend to repress arguments of authority, possession being nine-tenths of the law. *De facto* power does not need to justify itself; it just needs to maintain power. Even so, spurious theoretical justifications are usually offered as a superficial tenth part of their legality, in ideological notions of some utopian vision of future perfection or racial purity or universal equality and abundance. Religious authority can also be invoked to justify the use of public power and is particularly effective as religion appeals to an absolute and self-justifying truth whose source is above human reason. In the early modern period, as Milbank detects, the new understanding of notions such as the right (*ius*) of power, the concept of the political state and the sovereignty of political power were given a religious aura and vocabulary to help justify a radically new visions of man and politics:

> For this reason, it would be inadequate to suppose that late medieval and seventeenth-century voluntarism are "ideological" legitimations of modern absolutism/liberalism regarded as "really" secular and material processes. On the contrary, theology enters into the very construction of the new realities "property" and "sovereignty," helping to create a new space for human manoeuvre. For while it is true that there is a certain recuperation of the Roman patriarchalist notion of possession (though this shows that the *mythos* of the *law* is also constitutively necessary) *dominium* could only have achieved universal sway in the context of a theology of creation *ex nihilo*, reinterpreted in terms of infinite, uninhibited power.[48]

In more recent times, Voegelin has noticed that many political ideologies, while manifestly agnostic or atheist, contain a surreptitious use of religious terms and symbols to enhance their authoritative appeal.[49] Both of historian Michael Burleigh's books on successive periods of nineteenth- and twentieth-century political history focus on "political religions" and "sacred (political) causes."[50]

Historically, the first to justify, not power in terms of authority, but the authority of power itself was Machiavelli. Plato and Aristotle had tried to justify power in terms of the rightness and goodness of the powerful actions of those who ruled. This was in fact what distinguished a philosopher-king from a tyrant, not the form of absolute power which in both cases is the same, but the rightness and goodness expressed in the philosopher-king's ruling actions as opposed to the perverse purposes of the tyrant. In Machiavelli, the justification of political power changes radically:

> The traditional approach was based on the assumption that morality is some-thing substantial. That it is a force in the soul of man, however ineffective it may be especially in the affairs of states and kingdoms. Against this assumption Machiavelli argues as follows: virtue can be practised only within society; man must be habituated to virtue by human means. But to quote that Machiavellian, Karl Marx, the educators themselves must be educated. The original educators, the founders of society, cannot have been educated to virtue: the founder of Rome was a fratricide. Morality is possible only within a context which can-not be created by morality, for morality cannot create itself. The context within which morality is possible is created by immorality. Morality rests on immoral-ity, justice rests on injustice, just as all legitimacy ultimately rests on revolution-ary foundations. Man is not by nature directed toward virtue.[51]

Here political power is its own justification, its own authority; the neces-sary condition of political peace and stability becomes the *de iure* justification for gaining and retaining power by a calculating use of all necessary means, evidenced by the *de facto* history of political kingdoms. For Machiavelli, virtue is now the exercise of "effectual truth," the capacity to gain and to maintain political power, and so the right form of government depends on the person who is capable of gaining and maintaining power. Power itself is the measure of authority.

Machiavelli's authority of power came to be expressed in a new meaning given to the term "sovereignty," a quality that had theological significance in reference to the Lord God as omnipotent, that was transmuted into an adjec-tive of political power by the French political philosopher Jean Bodin.[52] The same new notion of the authority of power and its inherent need to be abso-lute—sovereign—was taken up in varying but substantially similar ways by Thomas Hobbes, John Locke, Jean Jacques Rousseau, Immanuel Kant and is at the core of the modern understanding of political power.[53] Over time the adjective "sovereign" became the noun "state," which does not have at its essential center legitimating purposes or virtuous persons, but power pure and simple, the authority of power.

As political philosopher Francis Slade writes in his essay "Rule as Sovereignty: The Universal and Homogenous State," Machiavelli, Bodin, and Hobbes, in their reference to the sovereignty of civil rule, all refer to the qualities of rule as an abstract concept, rather than the qualities of the ruler. Their political theories all emanate from this abstract concept of sovereign rule. In this sense, the human qualities or virtues of those who rule fall into the background; what prevails is the effective power of the rule to dominate citizens, and what is lost is the human standard by which rules themselves are to be evaluated. What is clear is the shift from the classical standard of virtuous rulers to the abstract and impersonal use of the power of rule to dominate political society. This fundamental shift in perspective begins with Machiavelli and is expressed more formally in the writings of Bodin, who, as Slade mentions, considers sovereignty as applying to the rule and not the ruler.[54]

Overtime, the justification of absolute and concentrated power is to be found in the use of the principle of equality, the equality of all before this abstract and absolute power. What does equality really mean in the political context? The moral justification implied in equality is that the good of each person should be taken into account, according to the particular and different needs and possibilities of each one, because each one is a person. This implies that the particular and different needs of each one be known or represented in political government. What we are really saying is that persons should be treated personally, because of their personal being, not because each one is identically equal. While each one is the bearer of personal being, we are each one manifestly different, with different capabilities, talents, needs, defects, and so on. It seems that the moral justification of "equality" seems to have been extended beyond its proper use to rule out meaningful difference and propose a population of politically identical individuals in which numerical advantage is the only possible fair distinction and justification.

Slade observes that what now becomes paramount in the state is the conferral of rights on citizens, rather than concern for the development of the particular moral qualities or virtues of a people:

> In becoming a citizen everyone exchanges whatever diverse social identities they had possessed for the identity conferred by the common status of State membership. The civil laws emancipate individuals from all forms of social definition and dependence. "Civil liberties" mean that each citizen should be perfectly independent of all his fellow citizens. As a citizen each is an autonomous individual over against society and its institutions . . . But for the State, whose power alone makes the individual, because it makes everyone free vis-à-vis social institutions, all citizens are homogenous. The content of citizenship is universal, egalitarian "human rights." So far as the state is concerned, citizens

might be interchangeable, "the particular features of each individual . . . lost in the common physiognomy."[55]

The other political abuse of the term "equality" is its substitutive function in justifying political authority. "Good" is not the same as "equal"; there is an important subsidiary recognition of equality in political good, as a derivative of the recognition of personal being in each one, but "equality" does not give us a complete answer to what is good and, in fact, can and is used as a smokescreen to obstruct the common perception of what is good. The true moral implications of political equality are used as pre-emptive measures to exclude the common search for what is the common good.

Necessarily, this exaggerated political use of equality eliminates any substantive notion of authority, that is, the possibility of the recognition of what is better or best, or even the distinction between what is right or wrong. The justification of authority becomes the power of numbers.

Arendt observes in her essay on the theme of authority in *Between Past and Future: Eight Exercises in Political Thought*, that it seems that the real significance of authority has been lost in modern political thought and usage. The word remains in use, but the real sense of a basis in reality—the authority of what is right—is not what is being referred to. As Arendt suggests, this may be because we no longer live in a shared culture of what is commonly accepted as right and good. Authority, therefore, has no common foundation and has become a word that no longer means what it originally meant. Historians of politics will note authority's place in previous theories of politics but will find that the notion of authority has disappeared from our conceptual framework. This crisis of authority is not confined to politics but seems to pervade all aspects of social relations to do with the family, educational and religious institutions, as well as the public domain.[56]

What is at the root of this disappearance and subsequent crisis of authority is the political form of sovereign power, the description of the political role in terms of gaining and maintaining absolute power and the reduction of the good of political society to terms of equalities and majorities.

It is not difficult to recognize how susceptible to manipulation such a political apparatus is. The supremacy of political power suppresses all other manifestations of social authority (and indeed personal conscience) to a numerically maneuvered exercise of universal power over persons who are no more than recognized numbers of the state. Even the most sacrosanct provisions of personal or social life, recognized in Constitutional form, are subject to the artful manipulation of political numbers. A case in point is the majority decision in 1983 to amend the Irish *Constitution* to protect the life of unborn children. Article 40 was to include a new subsection which stated that: "The State acknowledges the right to life of the unborn and, with due regard to the equal right to life of the mother, guarantees in its laws to respect, and, as far as practicable, by its laws to defend and vindicate that right (Article 40.3.3.)."

The 2018 referendum saw a majority decide exactly the opposite provision, making way for the most permissive extension of abortion possible, "Provision may be made by law for the regulation of termination of pregnancy (Art. 40.3.3.)."[57]

The process of producing a majority number to reverse such a fundamental cultural value clearly shows a collusion of government power and pressure, managed citizens assemblies, a steered Oireachtas (Parliament) Committee, full-scale media projection of the intended reversal of the protection of life, and massive external funding by non-Irish citizens for the campaign, the tactics of international social media owners, as well as international legal cases to change what Irish people thought and wanted. However one views the outcome, the process can scarcely be called fair and democratic. Instead, concerted power produces a majority number that is then taken to be the will of the people. One can also ask if such majority decisions are the spontaneous expression of the people of Ireland or the use of a political structure to enforce a policy on the people.[58]

Supreme Court decisions on matters on which there is no legislative measure, with unappealable decisions of universal application, are another instance of sovereign state power over a population of individuals. This susceptibility can be seen in virulent forms of totalitarianism that have wanted to shape their subjects to their own ideological image and likeness or in more benign totalitarian forms that quietly domesticate their subjects into passivity with promises of welfare and benefits to be provided by an all-provident state. This can be seen, on the one hand, by the imposition of cultural changes such as the sexual revolution, and on the other hand, by the irresponsibility of national debts run up by the anonymous state.

This vulnerability of our societies is due to the suppression of spontaneous, natural, and diffused forms of social authority, and by an understanding of political power that is justified by its own supremacy of power and its own particular redefinition of man's social being in terms of equal individuals. As Slade points out, commenting on Michael Oakeshott's *On Human Conduct*, this is not a spontaneous social form of government. Slade notes that the very term "state" implies something characterless and generic. The modern state does not represent any natural or spontaneous form of social community that we find ourselves in and with which we identify ourselves. The modern state as a political form is in this sense an artificial construction or project based on specifically selected assumptions about persons and their relationship to society; it is not based on any natural way that human society is found and expressed. Slade suggests that this supplantation of spontaneous communities by the construction of the state model of political society was something deliberate and was promoted to enhance the power of the state over all other spontaneous and natural forms of association.[59]

CONCLUSION

It is clear that, given a social development and destiny of the human person, there is a necessary positive and contributary role of political government in complex human society. The particular historical form of the modern state has assumed that role, but in ways that distort social existence, because essential categories of thought are excluded *a priori* from political consideration. The fundamental substitution of the necessary multiple forms of social authority for the concentrated power of the sovereign state exposes people to anonymous forms of ubiquitous power that is justified by reason of being the greatest power. We have become accustomed to this particular modern shaping of political thought, and it is hard to think outside its assumed premises. It is necessary to do so because the form of the sovereign state exposes persons to forms of political control and manipulation, for two basic reasons; the justification of political power merely in terms of the supremacy of its power, and the concentration of such power in a single anonymous form of the state, by means of which other overbearing forces have unfettered control.

Since the modern justification of political activity in terms of power, the notion of the authority of truth has disappeared from political discourse. In fact, the authority of truth is precisely what is excluded *a priori* from political discussion. What we are left with are self-justifying mechanisms of power, in the hands of those adept in the "effectual truth" of gaining and maintaining power, to be used not for the people, but *on* the people, for interests and purposes that follow no substantial notion of the common good. Arendt observed that the real significance of authority has thus become something foreign and hostile to our social and political perceptions. At the same time, it may not be difficult to realize that without a common source of what we consider to be true and good—and which we commonly refer to by the word "authority"—our basic social bonds become tenuous and problematic.[60]

NOTES

1. Augusto Del Noce, *The Crisis of Modernity* (Montreal: McGill-Queen's University Press, 2015), 197.

2. David L. Schindler, *Ordering Love: Liberal Societies and the Memory of God* (Grand Rapids, MI: Eerdmans, 2011), 3688. For clarity, I have added "persons" in parenthesis.

3. Jennifer Roback Morse, *Love and Economics: It Takes a Family to Raise a Village* (Lake Charles, LA: Ruth Institute Books, 2008), 13, 6–7. Dr. Jennifer Morse is a former economics professor at George Mason University, Virginia.

4. Morse, *Love and Economics*, 16.

5. Paul Johnson, *Modern Times: The World from the Twenties to the Nineties* (New York: Harper Perennial, 1992), 784.

6. David Walsh, *The Growth of the Liberal Soul* (Columbia: University of Missouri, 1997), 1. Walsh later makes a reference to T. S. Eliot's three lectures, given in 1939 and published as *The Idea of a Christian Society* (New York: Harcourt Brace, 1940), in which Eliot contrasts the conviction and zeal of the totalitarian powers of the time with the hollowness of the Western powers as manifested in the "craven capitulation" of the Munich Agreement of March 30, 1938.

7. T. S. Eliot, *The Idea of a Christian Society* (Boston, MA: Houghton Mifflin Harcourt, 2014), 651, as quoted in Walsh, *Growth of the Liberal Soul*, 19–20.

8. For Eric Voegelin's explanation of this term political gnosticism, see his *Science, Politics, and Gnosticism: Two Essays*, ed. Ellis Sandoz (Washington, DC: Gateway Editions, 2012), especially his introduction (18–273). The literary model of utopian literature is a wide one and the presentation of the ideal society can be made with different purposes and intentions in mind. A major study of utopian thought speaks of "seven major utopian constellations and a few minor ones," in Frank E. Manuel and Fritzie P. Manuel, *Utopian Thought on the Western World* (Oxford: Blackwell, 1979). Alternatively, Joseph Ratzinger (Pope Benedict XVI), for example, distinguishes between a necessary utopian presentation of the ideal, and chiliastic notions, usually trusting in an inexorable dynamic of history, that claim to be able to produce the perfect society in the immanent future. Cf. Joseph Ratzinger, "Eschatology and Utopia," in *Church, Ecumenism, and Politics: New Endeavours in Ecclesiology* (San Francisco: Ignatius Press, 2008), 223–37.

9. Aurel Kolnai, "The Utopian Mind," in *Privilege and Liberty and Other Essays in Political Philosophy*, ed. Daniel J. Mahoney (Lanham, MD: Lexington Books, 1999), 154–55.

10. Karl Marx and Friedrich Engels referred to these writers as "utopians" not because they advocated a future, more perfect, society—so did Marx and Engels—but because they, the utopians, thought that this future society would come about by peaceful dialogue and agreement. Marx and Engels believed in revolution as the only practical path to the better society. Cf. Frederic Copleston, *A History of Philosophy* (New York: Doubleday, 1985), vol. 9, 71. See also Karl Marx and Friedrich Engels, *Basic Writings in Politics and Philosophy*, ed. Lewis S. Feuer (New York: Doubleday, 1989).

11. Henri de Saint-Simon, *Oeuvres*, quoted in Copleston, *History of Philosophy*, vol. 9, 60.

12. Copleston, *History of Philosophy*, vol. 9, 65.

13. Pierre-Joseph Proudhon, *On the Federal Principle* (1863), quoted in Copleston, *History of Philosophy*, vol. 9, 69.

14. Karl Marx, *Critique of the Gotha Programme*, in *Marx/Engels Selected Works* (Moscow: Progress Publishers, 1970), vol. 3, 13–30, 1875, https://www.marxists.org/archive/marx/works/1875/gotha/index.htm (accessed October 15, 2023).

15. Marx ended his *The Victory of the Counter-Revolution in Vienna*, trans. Marx-Engels Institute, https://www.marxists.org/archive/marx/works/1848/11/06 .htm (accessed October 15, 2023), with the words: "The purposeless massacres perpetrated since the June and October events, the tedious offering of sacrifices since February and March, the very cannibalism of the counterrevolution will convince the nations that there is only one way in which the murderous death agonies of the old society and the bloody birth throes of the new society can be shortened, simplified and concentrated, and that way is revolutionary terror." Western forms of Communism preferred the "long march through the institutions," a phrase of Rudi Dutschke, a leader of the 1968 German student movement to express the political tactics of Italian Communist Antonio Gramsci (1891–1937) who advocated the infiltration of political and cultural institutions as the most effective way to bring Communist ideas to Western Europe. Polish-born East German Communist Rosa Luxembourg (1871–1919) also repudiated violence and terror. Cf. Richard Huffmann, "The Limits of Violence," *Satya,* March 2004, http://www.satyamag.com.

16. J. W. Harris, *Legal Philosophies*, 2nd ed. (Oxford: Oxford University Press, 2005), 274. For a profound analysis of the thought and consequences of Marx, see Joseph Cropsey, "Karl Marx," in Leo Strauss and Joseph Cropsey, eds., *History of Political Philosophy*, 3rd ed. (Chicago: University of Chicago Press, 1987), 15985–16500.

17. Friedrich Engels, "Socialism: Utopian and Scientific," in Karl Marx and Friedrich Engels, *Basic Writings in Politics and Philosophy*, ed. Lewis S. Feuer (New York: Doubleday, 1989), 106.

18. Joseph Ratzinger, "A Christian Orientation in a Pluralistic Democracy?" in *Church, Ecumenism, and Politics*, 196.

19. For a cursory view of National Debt and the percentage relation of Public Debt to Gross Domestic Product (GDP), and External Debt's percentage relation to GDP, see the US Debt Clock, https://www.usdebtclock.org/world-debt-clock.html

20. Peter L. P. Simpson, *Political Illiberalism: A Defence of Freedom* (London: Routledge, 2015), chap. 2 "Historical Illustrations," 16–46.

21. So called because of the people's rustic diet and simple lifestyle: "But, said Glaucon, interposing, you have not given them a relish to their meal. True, I replied, I had forgotten; of course they must have a relish-salt, and olives, and cheese, and they will boil roots and herbs such as country people prepare; for a dessert we shall give them figs, and peas, and beans; and they will roast myrtle-berries and acorns at the fire, drinking in moderation. And with such a diet they may be expected to live in peace and health to a good old age, and bequeath a similar life to their children after them. Yes, Socrates, he said, and if you were providing for a city of pigs, how else would you feed the beasts?" Plato, *The Republic*, in *The Complete Works of Plato*, trans. Benjamin Jowett (Kirkland, WA: Latus e-Publishing, 2012), book II, 373d, Kindle, 32134.

22. Simpson, *Political Illiberalism*, 27, 26. The reference is to Aristotle's *Politics*, trans. Benjamin Jowett, in *Aristotle: The Complete Works* (*English Edition*) (KTHTK 2023. Kindle),4(7)15.1334a22-34.

23. As Jacques Maritain explains: "the authority which derives from the principle of being, as from its transcendent source, also derives from the people as passing through it in order to reside in its legitimate holders; it not only recognizes that the prince governs as representing in his person the entire people, *ut vices gerens multitudinis* [the vice regent of the whole people]; but it makes of this vicariousness the typical law of its peculiar authoritative structure, in such a way that authority passing through the people rises, degree by degree, from the base to the summit of the hierarchic structure of the community; and so that the exercise of power by men, in whom authority is brought periodically to reside through the designation of the people, attests the constancy of the passage of sovereignty through the multitude" Maritain, *Scholasticism and Politics*, trans. And ed. Mortimer J. Adler, (Indianapolis: Liberty Fund, 2012), 1364. The reference is to St. Thomas Aquinas, *Summa theol.*, I-II, 90, 3.

24. Robert A. Nisbet, *The Quest for Community: A Study in the Ethics of Order and Freedom* (Washington, DC: ISI Books, 2010), 4176. Nisbet writes later on: "As Jefferson shrewdly pointed out, the State with the power to do things for people has the power to do things to them. In plain fact the latter power increases almost geometrically in proportion to the former" (4310), and also: "For, despite the unquestioned moral rightness of the proposition that all legitimate political power must flow from the people, we are living in an age in which all forms of government, totalitarianism as well as liberal democracy, seek to root their authority in the soil of popular acquiescence" (4414).

25. Francis Fukuyama, *The Origins of Political Order: From Prehuman Times to The French Revolution* (New York: Farrar, Straus, and Giroux, 2011), 12–13.

26. Voegelin, *Science, Politics and Gnosticism*, 244.

27. Voegelin explains his understanding of Gnosticism, old and new, in his Introduction to *Science, Politics, and Gnosticism*, 189–274. In fact, Voegelin refers to Irenaeus' presentation of various gnostic currents in *Adversus Haereses* (180 AD) and refers to this work of Irenaeus as "a standard treatise on the subject that still will be consulted with profit by the student who wants to understand modern political ideas and movements." Eric Voegelin, *The New Science of Politics: An Introduction* (Chicago, IL: University of Chicago Press, 1987), 126.

28. Voegelin, *Science, Politics, and Gnosticism*, 75–89.

29. Hanna Arendt, *The Origins of Totalitarianism* (San Diego: Harcourt, Brace, Jovanovich, 1994), 462.

30. Arendt, *Origins of Totalitarianism*, 475.

31. John Milbank, "The Impossibility of Gay Marriage and the Threat of Biopolitical Control," *ABC Religion and Ethics*, April 23, 2013, https://www.abc.net.au /religion/the-impossibility-of-gay-marriage-and-the-threat-of-biopolitical/10099888 (accessed October 15, 2023).

32. George Orwell, "Review of Adolph Hitler's 'Mein Kampf,'" *New English Weekly*, March 21, 1940.

33. French political philosopher Yves R. Simon, *A General Theory of Authority* (Notre Dame, IN: University of Notre Dame Press, 1980), 157. It is not difficult see that when a real common good is absent from political aspirations, and in its place is put the anarchic freedom of separated individuals, any notion of authority is seen as inhibiting and oppressive. Hanna Arendt observes on this disappearance of authority that "The most significant symptom of the crisis, indicating its depth and seriousness, is that it has spread to such prepolitical areas as child-rearing and education, where authority in the widest sense has always been accepted as a natural necessity . . . so that the fact that even this prepolitical authority which ruled the relations between adults and children, teachers and pupils, is no longer secure signifies that all the old time-honored metaphors and models for authoritarian relations have lost their plausibility. Practically as well as theoretically, we are no longer in a position to know what authority really is" Arendt, "Authority," in *Between Past and Future: Eight Essays in Political Thought* (Harmondsworth, UK: Penguin Books, 2006), 1746.

34. Del Noce, *Crisis of Modernity*, 192.

35. Max Weber, *Economy and Society: An Outline of Interpretive Sociology*, ed. Guenther Roth and Clause Wittich (Berkeley: University of California Press, 1978), 212. Weber goes on to describe the three basic types of authority in this sense: traditional authority, rational-legal authority, and charismatic authority. Weber's reference in the text to the previously given definition of domination is to chapter 1, 16. For a description of these three types of authority, see Robert A. Nisbet, *The Sociological Tradition* (London: Routledge, 2017), 141–43. Nisbet also comments on the influence of the German sociologist F. Tönnies (1855–1936) on Max Weber's thought, particularly Tönnies' description of the progressive transformation of state power into a form of *Gesellschaft*, an institutional form of public power detached from the values and customs of local communities. Cf Nisbet, *Sociological Tradition*, 144.

36. Max Weber, *The Vocation Lectures: "Science as a Vocation" and "Politics as a Vocation,"* ed. David Owen and Tracy B. Strong, trans. Rodney Livingstone (Indianapolis: Hackett, 2004), 2097. As footnote 3 of the text explains, the reference to Trotsky is to the negotiation with Germany in 1918 for the withdrawal of Russia from World War I.

37. Del Noce, *Crisis of Modernity*, 193.

38. Del Noce, *Crisis of Modernity*, 197.

39. Arendt, *Between Past and Future*, 1737, 1881.

40. Arendt, *Between Past and Future*, 1794. Proteus was the sea god of Greek mythology who could change his form at will.

41. Arendt, *Between Past and Future*, 1940.

42. Maritain, *Scholasticism and Politics*, 1191.

43. Arendt, *Between Past and Future*, 2575.

44. Arendt, *Between Past and Future*, 2096. As Arendt explains, "good" in the Greek vocabulary always means "good for," or "fit." "The ideas become the unwavering, 'absolute' standards for political and moral behaviour and judgment in the same sense that the 'idea' of a bed in general is the standard for making and judging the fitness of all particular manufactured beds" (2043).

45. Plato, *Republic*, Book VII, 520c, in *Complete Works of Plato*, 34664.

46. Plato, *Republic*, 2143.

47. Aristotle, *Politics*, 1328b, in *Complete Works of Aristotle* (KTHTK, 2023), Kindle, 8664.

48. John Milbank, *Theology and Social Theory: Beyond Secular Reason*, 2nd ed. (Malden, MA: Blackwell, 2006), 16–17. This is the theme of the entire chapter, "Political Theology and the New Science of Politics," 9–25. Spiritual authority—the truth of spiritual realities—is "systematically deprived of independent public authority and relegated to the private sphere without power to command the temporal in anyway." Simpson, *Political Illiberalism*, 74.

49. Cf. Voegelin, *New Science of Politics*, chap. 4, "Gnosticism—The Nature of Modernity," which begins with what Voegelin recognizes as "a re-divinization of man and society" in secular terms (107–31). In the same line of thought, American theologian William T. Cavanaugh's *Migrations of the Holy: God, State, and the Political Meaning of the Church* (Grand Rapids, MI: Eerdmans, 2011), is an example of Cavanaugh's writings on the theme of the political state's assumption of religious categories and dimensions.

50. Michael Burleigh, *Earthly Powers: Religion and Politics in Europe from the Enlightenment to the Great War* (New York: Harper Perennial, 2005); and Burleigh, *Sacred Causes: Religion and Politics from the European Dictators to Al Qaeda* (New York: Harper Press, 2006).

51. Leo Strauss, *What Is Political Philosophy? And Other Studies* (Chicago: University of Chicago Press, 1988), 41–42. As Harvey C. Mansfield point out, there is a fundamental coherence, despite Machiavellian appearances, between Niccolò Machiavelli's *The Prince*, 2nd ed., trans. Harvey C. Mansfield (Chicago: University of Chicago Press, 1998), on the role of the unscrupulous ruler, and his *Discourses on Livy*, which expound the virtues of the republican political form. Republics are in continual need of being "reformed" or, in Machiavelli's term "refounded," by renewing the citizens' necessary fear as the condition of rule. Therefore, it is the absolute and unscrupulous prince or ruler who continually is needed to renew the republic: "The need for continual refounding involves republics in a continual dependence on princely or tyrannical men and princely or tyrannical means" Mansfield, Introduction to *Discourses on Livy*, by Niccolò Machiavelli, trans. Harvey C. Mansfield and Nathan Tarcov (Chicago: University of Chicago Press, 1996), xxvi.

52. Jean Bodin, *Six Books of the Commonwealth*, abridged and trans. M. J. Tooley (Oxford: Basil Blackwell, c. 1576), esp. book 1, chap. 8, "On Sovereignty." Milbank affirms that the political proposals of J. Bodin and T. Hobbes were based on theological principles that were to justify the myth of the political sovereign power or person. In was only in theological terms that the modern categories of "sovereign" political power could be justified. In this sense, theology was not excluded from political theory, but rather the new political models used theological categories to justify their new absolute political authority. Milbank notes that, in this theological justification of sovereign political power, spiritual authority was relegated into oblivion, and political power (with its theological justification) becomes dominant and self-referential, arbitrary. What we have is a new conception of sovereign political power that takes the place of all other powers and authorities, especially spiritual authority, and by doing

so redefines political power in terms that originally referred only to God. Theology is transmuted into modern politics. Milbank, *Theology and Social Theory*, 27.

53. "Rule, legitimated by the idea of rule, over all the human beings circumscribed by the territorial limits over which that rule can be effectively exercised, that is what the state is. It is what Immanuel Kant called 'the Idea of the unity of a people as such under a powerful supreme will'" Francis Slade, "Rule as Sovereignty: The Universal and Homogenous State," in *The Truthful and the Good: Essays in Honour of Robert Sokolowski*, ed. John J. Drummond and James G. Hart (Dordrecht: Springer, 2011), 160. The quotation from Kant is from *The Metaphysics of Morals, The Doctrine of Right.*

54. Slade, "Rule as Sovereignty," 163–64.

55. Slade, "Rule as Sovereignty," 175. The quotation at the end is from Alexis de Tocqueville's *Democracy in America.: The Complete and Unabridged Volumes I and II* (New York: Bantam Classics, 2000). Slade also cites from French philosopher Bertrand de Jouvenel's *On Power: The Natural History of its Growth*, trans. J. F. Huntington (Indianapolis: Liberty Fund, 1993), who observes the inherent homogenizing nature of state power, and who, in turn, cites De Tocqueville's *Democracy in America* who makes the same point: "Every central authority which follows its natural instincts likes and favours equality, for equality more than anything else facilitates the working of this sort of authority" in de Jouvenel, *On Power*, 174. American sociologist Nisbet comments in a similar vein on the historical loss of natural and diffused forms of authority and the rise of concentrated forms of political power in *The Sociological Tradition*, chap. 4 "Authority." Pierre Manent notices as the predominant characteristic of authority of the pre-democratic age that of filiation, of belonging to the authority of a family. Cf. Pierre Manent, "The Return of Political Philosophy," *First Things* 103 (May 2000): 15–22, https://www.firstthings.com/article/2000/05/the-return-of-political-philosophy.

56. Arendt, *Between Past and Future*, 1737.

57. See *Constitution of Ireland*, last updated January 2020, enacted July 1, 1937, https://www.irishstatutebook.ie/eli/cons/en/html (accessed October 12, 2023); and *The Constitution of Ireland*, independently published, September 21, 2021, https://www.irishstatutebook.ie/eli/cons/en/html.

58. For a representation of this political maneuver and its legal imposition, see Life Institute, "Ireland's Fall: The Abortion Deception," YouTube, September 21, 2018, https://www.youtube.com/watch?v=eCsOE7HHe9Y. Irrespective of one's views on the issue of abortion, was the political campaign a fair process without undue influence?

59. Slade, "Rule as Sovereignty," 160. Slade is commenting on Michael Oakeshott's *On Human Conduct* (Oxford: Oxford University Press, 1975). Slade also refers to Thomas Hobbes' *Elements of Law, Natural and Politi* (1640), ed. Ferdinand Tonnies, 2nd ed. (Cambridge: Frank Cass / Cambridge University Press, 1969).

60. Arendt, "Authority," in *Between Past and Future*, 2575.

Chapter 7

Forms of Political Government

In this chapter we examine the forms of government. One of the curious things about modern politics is the fact that while ancient political philosophies considered the relative merits of different forms of government, today we generally consider there to be only one acceptable form of political government—democracy. A closer look at what democracy really is shows that often it is explained only in negative terms of what it opposes.

We also notice that democracy is used in two different senses, as an ideal of political government and as a particular form of government. It is unclear whether particular forms of democratic government, even when they exist in reality, actually reflect the democratic ideal of government.

Historically, the word democracy has had a generally negative meaning, even at its origin in Ancient Greece. British professor of Political Theory John Dunn mentions that only in the seventeenth century does the term democracy begin to be used as a positive ideal of government, and then takes on two different forms in France and in the United States.

The fact that the word democracy resonates within us implies that the word contains a political truth that we can spontaneously experience. What that truth is, is something harder to identify. I suggest that ideas such as "power to the people" and "equality for all" are insufficient as a moral justification of democracy as an ideal.

To try to elucidate the real moral sense of democracy, two fundamental considerations are important: the nature of personal and social inequalities, and the true purposes of political government. First, I suggest that society is naturally unequal and only in the recognition of these inequalities can the real harmony of purposes be achieved. At the same time, unjust inequalities need to be overcome. Second, good government, what we would call the democratic ideal, necessarily includes some form of common truthful purpose. In other words, it is the purposes, and not a particular way of government, that primarily determine the validity of the various possible forms of government.

When we look at what we today call democracy, there are two basic distortions of our form of democratic government. On the one hand, there is the concentration of civil power in the modern political state that presumes to express the vision of "the people." It is this impersonal structure of power, not purpose, that claims to procure the equal good of equal individuals, according to the primary criterion of the equality of justice. Structure, not persons, are supposed to provide the ethos of social communion, and equality is supposed to produce what social flourishing requires.

On the other hand, our democratic form of government reduces persons to equal individual numbers and the fundamental decisions as to the true good of society are made to depend on numerical majorities, however contrived or minimal these majorities may be. Alexis de Tocqueville and others recognize the forms of manipulation and tyranny that this form of democracy can easily produce.

Is the contemporary democratic form of government good government? Robert A. Nisbet notices that ironically the recognition of the individual's rights and freedoms was paid for by an ever-increasing dependence on the modern state. He writes that "the most powerful resources of democracy lie in the cultural allegiances of citizens" that are nurtured "in the smaller, internal areas of family, local community, and associations."[1]

We also notice that the modern form of democracy pre-empts a truthful purpose that reflects the common striving for a greater collective vision. In conclusion, the word democracy seems to conceal more than it discloses. We seem to be trapped in a form of government and a way of thinking that does not allow communities of purpose to flourish.

NEXUS

We have seen that the theme of political authority is a difficult one today. On the one hand, the human person is structurally drawn into purposeful communion with others and the Other toward a transcendent destiny. The required human response must always be free because it is the consciously perceived vision of truthful communion and the free response to that truthful perception that make that response entirely human, that is, worthy of what human persons are capable of, and what constitutes human communion. On the other hand, even though the political dimension of human society is only a part of human society, this political dimension in its historically modern form of the sovereign state presupposes a very distinct vision of the human person's social existence. The abstract form of the political state seems to project power, not authority, as the justification for government. Authority as a term is often used, but its meaning is derived ultimately from the form of power of the state. For this reason, political philosophers Hanna Arendt and Augusto Del Noce declare that the real question of political authority has disappeared from modern political thought and practice, and that we really speak and think only in terms of state power, legitimated by the procedural formalities of the use of sovereign power.

We have also seen that the modern form of the political state imposes an artificial uniformity on all individuals in the state, to the degree that the spontaneous and real manifestations of the authority of truth are replaced by the criterion of numerical equality and the authority of numerical advantage. What ultimately justifies the pervasive uses of state power is numerical majority, a seemingly unquestionable criterion.

What is important to recognize here is that the real issue of the legitimacy of political power is mutated into a sum of numbers. The fundamental questions of the proper vision of human personal society disappeared, and the apparently indisputable numerical advantage of equal individuals gives winners' rights to abstract and sovereign state power. This prevailing situation provides a curious context for the discussion of the forms of political government.

FORMS OF GOVERNMENT

Students frequently ask what the best form of government is. One can imagine so many diverse cultural forms of human society and so many diverse situations that require distinct forms of government, that the answer should be that there is not any one preferred form of government, that the form is relative to the context. This, however, is not what we think. Surprisingly, we spontaneously assume that democracy is the ideal and only legitimate form of political government.

In *Metamorphoses of the City*, Pierre Manent points out that in ancient political philosophy the classification of the forms of government was all-important, as is seen primarily in Plato and Aristotle. In their analysis what was important was the classification according to number, whether by one (monarchy or tyranny), by the few (aristocracy or oligarchy), or by the many (polity or pejoratively, democracy), with the consequent changes in the form of government according to these numbers. In modern political thought, however, the relative number of rulers seems not to be an important or relevant issue. Instead, a new category of "the people" (a collective of everyone) takes precedence and is in fact the only criterion of legitimacy of political action, that an action was taken in the name of all, by the collective of everyone. Manent concludes that this is so because in modern political thought there is only one legitimate form of government—democracy, government by all.

This also requires that everyone has the equal right to participate in this government by all, this democracy.[2]

Indian economist Amarya Sen sees democracy as a universal value and its almost universal recognition, at least conceptually, as a political achievement of the twentieth century:

> While democracy is not yet universally practiced, nor indeed uniformly accepted, in the general climate of world opinion, democratic governance has now achieved the status of being taken to be generally right. The ball is very much in the court of those who want to rubbish democracy to provide justification for that rejection. . . . This recognition of democracy as a universally relevant system, which moves in the direction of its acceptance as a universal value, is a major revolution in thinking, and one of the main contributions of the twentieth century. It is in this context that we have to examine the question of democracy as a universal value.[3]

It seems that there is a certain ambiguity in the current use of the term "democracy" which, in broad strokes, can be clarified by distinguishing between democracy as an ideal and democracy as a form of government. Democracy as an ideal is much more evident in what it opposes: oppressive forms of political government, the invidious discrimination, exclusion, and persecution of certain groups or nations, the denial of personal freedoms, the freedom of association, and so on. What is behind these undeniable claims, although so often only in the negative expression of what is being denied, is the genuine claim and responsibility of social participation in authentic human society. Today, the expression of the democratic ideal is almost always in terms of what is being denied, and not in what is required of each person in political society. While these claims to freedom, expression, and representation are indeed authentic aspects of interpersonal communion, of which politics is a part, democracy as the ideal tends to be stratified in these terms of freedom from the many forms of political oppression. It is this democratic ideal as a series of freedoms from oppression that is at the center of former American Secretary of State Dr. Condoleezza Rice's experience and promotion of the democratic ideal:

> If democracy is broadly understood to mean the right to speak your mind, to be free from the arbitrary power of the state, and to insist that those who would govern you must ask for your consent, then democracy—the only form of government that guarantees these freedoms—has never been more widely accepted as right.[4]

This last century in particular has witnessed advances over oppressive or discriminatory use of political power: the principle of the self-determination of peoples and nations, the promotion of human rights, government account-ability, freedom of elections, etc. These are all manifestations of an ideal of truly human and personal participation in social communion that we have called "democracy." Even in this use, the meaning of the word democracy is strained, which seems to suggest that this word does not precisely cor-respond to the ideal of social communion in its political dimension. Even its etymological meaning of "people" and "power" does not really indicate the substance of social political communion. The British political philosopher John Dunn remarks on the peculiar historical fortune of this misnomer:

> Why should be it be the case that, for the first time in the history of our still conspicuously multi-lingual species, there is for the present a single world-wide name for the legitimate basis of political authority? . . . What is very strange indeed (in fact, quite bizarre) is the fact that this single term, endlessly transliter-ated or translated across all modern languages, should turn out to be the ancient Greek noun δημοκρατία (demokratia), which originally meant not a basis for legitimacy, or a regime defined by its good intentions or its noble mission, but simply one particular form of government, and that a form, for almost two thousand years of its history as a word, which, it was overwhelmingly judged by most who used the term, had proved grossly illegitimate in theory and every bit as disastrous in practice.[5]

To try to clarify the political ideals, practices, and realities to which this ambiguous use of the word democracy refers, and the inherent moral justi-fications that the word democracy invokes, we need to distinguish between the true elements of political government, on the one hand, and, on the other hand, the variable ways or forms those elements may be achieved and expressed.

To speak of true elements of political government is to identify the essen-tial characteristics of interpersonal social communion in public, civil mat-ters. This requires the acknowledgment of the human person as a free and responsible agent of truth, structurally drawn to communion with others and the Other, oriented toward a transcendent social destiny. Among the multiple forms of association as expressions of the social dimension of personal being, there is also the positive, public, and yet limited role of political association, that also reflects the truth of personal being, on which political authority is based, and which is the justification of political power.

Basic and obvious principles of right political government flow from this understanding of interpersonal social communion; active participation and representation in matters of common political good, which themselves derive from free personal responsibility, a truthful sense of the social good to be pursued, on which social communion and cohesion are based, the recognition of the primacy of social association over political exigency, the discriminate support of naturally unequal personal and social circumstances, and so on.

It is not at all evident that "democracy" is the term that best describes this ideal of the political dimension of social communion.[6]

To speak of the *forms* of government, in the sense of the diverse ways by which the ideal of the political dimension of social communion may be achieved, it is also easy to identify ideal elements of any form of government: knowing and taking into account the needs of all groups and persons, periodic accountability of the use of public authority, established laws and procedures, informed public debates and discussions according to the terms of a prior social vision, the competent and just use of political authority and its means, etc. What becomes evident here is that the reality of power residing in and being exercised by "the people" is largely a fiction. All the forms of political government require the use of authority and its legitimate means and powers in the hands of one or a few people, certainly not the majority or the totality of the people. There may well be a residual power of the people of election of those who govern (a power which may be more or less meaningful and effective), but political government itself is by the one or the few, not the many, and certainly not "the people," as a unanimous identity. We should, therefore, also call into question the epithet "democratic" in reference to the modern form of political government. The fact that a numerical majority elect those few who govern is one small indication of a form of government that may use or abuse its political authority; it would seem to be extending much too far the meaning and legitimacy of the term "democratic" to a form of government that is characterized only by elected agents of government.

In *Quest for Community*, Nisbet points out that even though it is undoubtedly true that the justification of political power comes derivatively from the people as the proximate source of authority, today all governments of whatever political persuasion want to justify their existence and actions by claiming that they act in the name of the people. Nisbet ironically observes that one of the most important political discoveries of the nineteenth century was the realization that State power could be more easily increased and justified by invoking the participation of and reference to the people, however nominally represented.[7]

The moral implications of the content of democracy, both as an ideal of political communion and as one particular modern form or method of political authority, are clear. What is much less clear is whether the modern form of democracy corresponds in fact to democracy's moral implications. It seems, rather, that the word democracy, as it is used in its modern sense, is used to foreclose all discussions on any real sense of common social good and any real public participation in political society.[8]

My primary focus in this chapter is on the democratic form of nation-state government because I think that what the democratic form is understood to be is more clearly seen in its greater operation. Political parties, electoral processes, local forms of government, caucuses, town meetings, etc. are all shaped, I suggest, by what democracy is taken to mean in its greater operation, in the context of the state.

ANCIENT AND MODERN DEMOCRACY

What is curious about the term democracy is the pejorative sense that it has had until modern times. Athenian democracy[9] was a short-lived period of political history that formally began with the constitutional reforms of Cleisthenes (508 BC), an Athenian lawgiver who increased the Athenian citizens' powers over the nobility and established a series of public institutions such as the Assembly. Open to all citizens for debate and law-making, the Assembly included the Council of 500, officials for public administration who prepared the agenda for the Assembly, and chosen territorial areas, and law courts of the people's representatives, 6,000 representatives per year, chosen by lot.[10] While the number of full citizens of Athens was about 30,000 of a total population of about 300,000 (comprising of citizens of partial rights, resident foreigners, and a large slave population), these full citizens of equal standing had equal rights of political participation. In spite of two oligarchic revolutions, this form of Athenian democracy continued until suppressed by the Macedonians in 322 BC.

While the democratic nature of the political institutions of this period of Athenian government changed and developed, there was a real sense of influence by the free citizens of Athens in public decisions, seen in the dependence on the Assembly by the political leaders, the public accountability of its magistrates, the public trials, and the elections of the various public officials. British historian Arnold H. M. Jones asked the question how Athenian democracy worked:

Alcibiades once described the Athenian democracy as "acknowledged folly," and *prima facie* this would seem to be fair enough comment on a political system which entrusted most of the administration of the State to magistrates annually chosen by lot, and all political decisions to mass meetings which any citizen might—or might not—attend. Yet the fact remains that Athens was, by ancient standards, a remarkably efficient State, and that her foreign and domestic policy was directed as well as, if not better than, that of contemporary cities with what might seem to be more sensible constitutions.[11]

At the same time, this assertion of the free and participating citizen came at a price. While there was the gradual breakup of older nations into smaller *poleis*, there was also, as historian Alfred Eckhard Zimmern points out, "What we have now to watch is the gradual snapping of the lesser loyalties which form the intermediate links between the State and the individual, till the citizen stands, free and independent, face to face with the city."[12]

Nisbet goes on to write in *Quest for Community*:

> To Thucydides, in the late fifth century B.C., individualism could appear increasingly symptomatic of a fatal disease, stasis, internal fragmentation and disruption. To him and others it constituted a threat both to the stability of society and to the integrity of the individual. Above all, to Plato at the very end of the fifth century B.C. the conflict of allegiances in Athens and the increasing alienation of individuals from morality seemed intolerable. What Plato saw in the society about him was disorganization and conflict, alienation and frustration. The bases of the old society were gone; internal strife and political misrule had replaced the religious and communal supports of the old order in Athens. The individual was left ever more precariously exposed to moral uncertainty and conflict of allegiances.[13]

It would not be difficult to extract from this historical example of direct Athenian citizens' participation in these public political institutions a type of model of citizen power based on the fundamental equality of each citizen and the supposed ideal of the equality of all, in all respects. What this would imply is political movement toward uniform equality as the determining condition of the justice of politics. It is also not difficult to see how this simplification of Athenian democracy could be seen, alternatively, as the justification of mob rule over all possible forms of social and political authority. Historically, it seems that it was this negative sense of demagogic dominance that the word democracy was associated with.

In Dunn's *Democracy: A History*, the author notes that the word democracy was not used in Roman times, not because in Roman political institutions there was no reference to the *populus* (the people), but because there did not exist the political idea of the people (*populus*) ruling itself and free to determine and review its own form of government. Dunn notes that the structure of political organization in Rome included the Senate and the People of Rome (*Senatus Populusque Romanus, SPQR*), with the Senate having priority of authority and influence. The term *populus* was thus always used in conjunction with and in subservience to other structures of government, and never in the modern sense of democracy, the overriding authority and power of the people.[14]

The word democracy entered European thought through the translations of Aristotle's *Politics* and maintained its negative sense; it was, according to Dunn, not until the seventeenth century that the term democracy begins to shed its negative meaning and to be used to legitimize and promote new political arrangements that based their authority on the rightful demands and on the power of the *demos*, the people.[15]

Dunn recognizes the American and French political crises and revolutions as the harbingers of the new sense of the political term democracy. On the one hand, the reflective analysis of Tocqueville described the new American experiment of democracy. Tocqueville bases his study of American government and social life on the social condition of equality that he found to be at the center of social life in America, and that he perceived to be inexorably advancing in Europe as well:

> Amongst the novel objects that attracted my attention during my stay in the United States, nothing struck me more forcibly than the general equality of conditions. . . . The more I advanced in the study of American society, the more I perceived that the equality of conditions is the fundamental fact from which all others seem to be derived, and the central point at which all my observations constantly terminated. I then turned my thought to our own hemisphere, where I imagined that I discerned something analogous to the spectacle which the New World presented to me. I observed that the equality of conditions is daily progressing toward those extreme limits which it seems to have reached in the United States, and that the democracy which governs the American communities appears to be rapidly rising into power in Europe.[16]

What follows in Tocqueville's *Democracy in America* is a careful analysis of this new social fact of equality of conditions and the identification of the necessary elements of political government, given this social fact of equality.

On the other hand, in Europe, Dunn identifies the change in meaning of politics brought about by the turmoil of the French Revolution as the context within which "democracy forced itself, slowly but inexorably, upon one community after another."[17] Dunn further states that with "Maximilian Robespierre, for the first time in modern history, democracy at last appears not merely as a passing expression of political taste but as an organizing conception of an entire vision of politics."[18]

In the words of Robespierre:

> All citizens, no matter who they are, have the right to aspire to every degree of representation. Anything less would be out of keeping with your declaration of rights, to which every privilege, every distinction and every exception must yield. The constitution has established that sovereignty resides in the People, in every member of the populace. Each individual therefore has the right to a say in the laws by which he is governed and in the choice of the administration which belongs to him. Otherwise it is not true to say that all men are equal in

rights, that all men are citizens. . . . Democracy is a state in which the sovereign people, guided by laws which are its own work, does by itself all it can do well, and by delegates all that it could not do. It is therefore in the principle of democratic government that you must look for the rules of your political conduct. To found and consolidate democracy amongst us, to reach the peaceful reign of constitutional laws, we must end the war of liberty against tyranny and pass happily through the storms of the Revolution. . . . The fundamental principle of democratic or popular government, the essential resort which sustains it and makes it move, is virtue, the public virtue which worked such miracles in Greece and Rome and which would produce even more startling ones in republican France—the love of country and its laws. Since the essence of the Republic or democracy is equality, the love of country necessarily embraces the love of equality. It therefore presupposes or produces all virtues.[19]

From these two very different origins of democracy as the form of government that necessarily flows from "the equality of conditions," Dunn observes two radically different political intentions in the democratic form of government: democracy understood as the guarantor of individual rights and freedoms (what Dunn calls "the order of egoism"), and democracy as a driving force for achieving real equality of conditions ("the order of equals").[20] In Dunn's view, and in spite of notable gains in political rights and freedoms, it is the order of egoism that has generally usurped the democratic ideal of the order of equals.[21]

The fact that the term democracy finds such universal appeal today implies that the term, admittedly ambiguous, does refer to something in politics that we consider to be universally true and good. The word expresses, at least in part, an ideal by which we critique our politics, although the ambiguity of the word derives from the varying ways the democratic ideal is or may be expressed. In some cases, it seems that that the word is used to give moral approval to a form of government that may in fact hardly reflect at all the democratic ideal.

Therefore, to find out why the term democracy resonates within us we need to ask ourselves what good government is and what forms such good government may take. The truth contained in Greek democracy is that all (all who were full Athenian citizens) could take part equally, voice their opinions, and participate in collective processes of the various political and legal aspects of the government of their city, presumedly as a way to promote their individual and collective interests. It is in this sense that Dunn understands democracy, when he writes:

What the term means (even now, when that so clearly is not how matters are in the outside world) is that the people (we) hold power and exercise rue. That was what it meant at Athens, where the claim bore some relation to the truth.

That is what it means today, when it very much appears a thumping falsehood: a barefaced lie.[22]

Is that really all that democracy means, all of what resonates within us when we refer to the democratic ideal? As we have seen in the judgment of Thucydides and Plato, the results in Athens were of mixed quality. It seems that the mere fact of popular and equal participation and representation is, of itself, no necessary or sufficient guarantee of good government or the good of each one. Something more is needed.[23]

TWO FUNDAMENTAL CONSIDERATIONS FOR GOOD GOVERNMENT: THE UNDERSTANDING OF INEQUALITIES AND THE PURPOSES OF GOVERNMENT

It seems that there are two basic issues that need to be clarified before we can speak of the proper forms of political government. In the first place, some inequalities are natural and not therefore inevitable signs of perpetrated injustice. While the respect for and attention to each person as a person is inviolable, persons are different in qualities, talents, and capacities, and in their particular circumstances. These differences are given facts and not of themselves signs of injustice to another, though they may at times be used in that way. To consider the differences (inequalities) between people as something inherently unjust is to succumb to an unreal illusion that denies to persons the freedom to be and to develop themselves according to their particular and unequal possibilities. To base a political program on the need to crush all such differences (inequalities) for the sake of some vast uniformity is indeed to destroy the unique and therefore unequal givenness of each person.[24]

C. S. Lewis noticed this abuse of the term equality, smuggled in within the high-sounding term democracy:

> When equality is treated not as a medicine or a safety-gadget but as an ideal we begin to breed that stunted and envious sort of mind which hates all superiority. That mind is the special disease of democracy, as cruelty and servility are the special diseases of privileged societies. It will kill us all if it grows unchecked.[25]

Also, in the *Screwtape Letters*, Lewis explains the deception caused by this term democracy as a cover for equality understood as the factual sameness of all persons:

You are to use the word purely as an incantation; if you like, purely for its selling power. It is a name they venerate. And of course it is connected with the political ideal that men should be equally treated. You then make a stealthy transition in their minds from this political ideal to a factual belief that all men are equal. Especially the man you are working on. As a result you can use the word Democracy to sanction in his thought the most degrading (and also the least enjoyable) of all human feelings. You can get him to practise, not only without shame but with a positive glow of self-approval, conduct which, if undefended by the magic word, would be universally derided.[26]

The rejection of an order of equals does not necessarily imply the equality of an order of egoism; that would perhaps mean coming to a premature conclusion about the expression and development of inequality, as if inequality of itself were morally reprehensible. To recognize and to affirm individual inequality simply expresses the reality of inherent inequalities of persons of equal worth, and the consequent inherent social inequalities that are the precondition of political government. There is nothing undemocratic in this recognition.[27]

Aristotle recognized this naturally given inequality of human society, as Robert Sokolowski explains:

> In the Politics, Aristotle describes political society as the culmination of human communities. In cities, he says, there are two irreducible parts, the wealthy and the poor, and the shape that political life takes on results from the perennial struggle between these two groups to rule over the whole. The tension between the richer and the poorer parts of a society makes up the perpetuum mobile for politics. When the wealthy rule for their own benefit, the city is an oligarchy; when the poor rule for their own benefit, the city is literally a democracy, a rule by the people or the many, since there normally are more poorer than wealthier members of society. Aristotle says that the best outcome for most people in most places at most times, the practically best form of the city generally, is the republic, the *politeia*, which is intermediate between oligarchy and democracy. In a republic, a large middle class—middle in both an economic and an ethical sense—is established between the rich and the poor, and the laws and not men rule, and they do so for the benefit of the whole city, not for any particular part.[28]

The background for Aristotle's understanding of political communion (κοινωνία, koinonia) is the acceptance and reconciliation of individual and social inequalities as the *perpetuum mobile* of any given political situation. In other words, a true political government should represent all the different social inequalities present in a political context. This aim of inclusive representation of inequalities is much different to the homogenizing aim of a particular group and justified by use of the term democracy.

For this reason, "in Aristotle's view, the best kind of political community will be made up of elements from all the good regimes: there will be monarchic, aristocratic, and popular elements in the various parts of the government. This variety will provide a kind of tensile strength for the city."[29]

The type or form of political government will depend on the *de facto* distinctions and weight of social groups in each particular society, and what combination oligarchic or democratic forms corresponds to each given social situation.[30]

The second consideration relevant to proper forms of government is as to the ultimate purposes of political government. The modern sense of democracy seems to avoid this consideration because democracy or the democratic process seems to be self-justifying; the fact that "the people" (which usually really means, not the people, but a particular group that has achieved numerical majority) has participated and decided is, *ipso facto*, the justification for any and all measures decided in this way.

For Aristotle, political government is above all an ideal of the practical possibilities of human communion, which is above political institutions and processes. In *Political Illiberalism*, Peter L. P. Simpson writes that in Aristotle's *Politics*, the emphasis in forming the best government is on education and not on processes, law, or structures. For Aristotle, the best form of government depends primarily not on the system or division of power, but rather on the virtuous living of the citizens. If the government is just, it will be because its citizens are just and will determine the just use of the form of government. Simpson recalls that for Aristotle, the best form of government is in fact a community of virtuous friends living the virtues of the political life and Simpson compares this vision of political life to the experience of the medieval Knights Templar rather than to anything resembling the modern State.[31]

Transmuting this political ideal into terms of personalist philosophy, we can say that political government, of whatever form, is part of and should contribute to the person's social living that has discoverable truthful forms of human existence and purpose. Political structure, therefore, is not only about the form or process, but about common and right purposes.

Aristotle observes that a city may be governed by one person, by a few, or by the many. Even so, as Simpson points out, the division according to number that Aristotle makes of the forms of government, whether by one or few or many, is not for Aristotle the determining factor. While each of the three numerical forms has its good and its corrupt form, thus making six categories of government, what is paramount is the virtuous or vicious actions of the one or the few or the many. It is not number that produces justice or good, but persons. Monarchy represents the virtuous form of government by one, tyranny the corrupt form of government by one. Correspondingly, aristocracy is the virtuous form of government by the few, oligarchy the corrupt form.

Polity is the virtuous form of government by the many, democracy its corrupt form. As Simpson emphasizes, it is the moral determinations of people that determine the moral worth of the varying numerical forms of government.[32]

What this implies is that the mere form of political government is an insufficient description of its true worth to human society. Two points are relevant here. First, the free and positive contribution to interpersonal society is essential to the formation of society, which includes political society. Second, processes and institutions have their necessary politically formative and practical function when they can presuppose this free and positive personal response to society. The processes and institutions can also serve when the personal response is less than adequate and, in this way, make up for, in part, what is freely required for social communion.

This vital distinction in politics between the primary moral strength of the people and the secondary use of institutions and structures is made clear in a further comment in *Political Illiberalism* by Simpson, on Aristotle's *Politics*. Simpson observes that when Aristotle in the *Politics* writes of the imperfect and the corrupt forms of government, he writes on institutions, the different types of offices, and their limits. When Aristotle writes about the best form of government, the government of virtue, he writes on the role and purpose of education. What is clear is that the greater the shared practice of virtue, the less need there is for structures and for law to enforce what is not found freely. In other words, at the heart of good government is the living of the political virtues and this depends on the education and formation in virtue of its citizens and rulers. Structures, offices, and laws are thus only secondary measures in achieving good government.[33]

Aristotle bases his analysis of the *polis* of human society on the anthropological fact that people only achieve their plenitude in human society, that it is the virtue of friendship that forms and maintains the fundamental social bonds, that the laws and institutions make up for what may be lacking in the political virtue of friendship and are thus oriented toward forming good citizens. At the basis of a good political society are good citizens. Conversely, a good life requires living in political communion:

> The truest form of friendship is friendship in virtue, and it is one of the properties of such friendship that friends care for and promote virtue in each other, since this is indeed what they love in each other (NE: 1166a1-33; 1165b13-36; 1170a11-13). Moreover Aristotle also notes that the city is more held together by friendship than justice, and that legislators concern themselves more with friendship than justice (NE: 1155a22-28). . . . But how does one become a lawgiver? . . . The Politics, which studies all these things, is meant to provide this kind of knowledge and this kind of training in lawgiving. The Politics is therefore the natural and inevitable sequel of the Ethics and one has not completed

one's studies of ethics, or of the philosophy concerning the human things (1181b15), until one has gone on to the study of politics.[34]

TWO FUNDAMENTAL CONSIDERATIONS OF THE CONTEMPORARY FORM OF DEMOCRATIC GOVERNMENT: THE STRUCTURE OF POWER AND PERSONS AS NUMBERS

A cursory glance at our contemporary political situation reveals a very different set of suppositions as to what constitutes political life, its purposes, and the role of political laws and institutions.

In *Metamorphoses of the City*, Manent recognize something of a subterfuge in the democratic process and its claim to represent all "the people." He remarks that in practical terms it is not all the people who decide but rather always a majority of greater or lesser number. This means that it is no longer all the people who legitimate the governmental form, but only a majority. Manent asks how this change of legitimacy, deriving from all the people to a majority of the people, is to be justified in theory, and why theoretically the legitimacy of that majority has precedence over the minority.[35]

Where does the legitimacy of the "all" come from? What distinguishes modern political theory and practice from the premodern forms of political analysis is the modern political state that supposedly legitimizes a numerical majority, as small as a majority of one vote, to act and to determine public issues in the name of all the people:

> But in the modern European nations, unlike what took place in the Greek cities, the confrontation between the many and the few was decisively mediated by the one, that is, by the State, which was at first royal and later Republican, but always "monarchical" . . . The modern State signifies, by imposing it, this plane of equality on which we have been living for two or three centuries—the plane of equal human rights, the plane of the equal or similar human condition. Henceforth, the few as few no longer have any admissible claim. Any political or moral argument, and human argument, is acceptable only if it can be generalised or universalised. Henceforth democracy is the only legitimate political regime.[36]

What this means is that politics, the means and purposes of public human society, in our modern form, is conceptually predetermined by a notional arrangement of power that is abstract, universal, and homogenous. What legitimately inspires us by the *ideal* of democracy—truths such as the responsible participation and representation in society, fairness and opportunity for all, a common striving for good society, the recognition, protection, and promotion of each person, the freedom and support for human forms of association, and the recognition of the true aspirations of human existence—all come to us filtered by one particular *form* of political arrangement that interprets the ideals of democracy in a particular way that tends artificially to reshape the human person and human society. The task is to distinguish the legitimate ideals from these artificial forms and to imagine the corrective measures that would make politics a true reflection and promotion of interpersonal society.

Two fundamental criticisms may be leveled at the model of the modern state: its claim to abstract and universal power, its sovereignty in claiming to represent each one and all of "the people," and its homogenizing imposition on real people, far beyond the legitimate recognition of certain social equalities, to reduce each person to an anonymous and identical individuality whose differences can only be recognized by numerical distinction. This imposition of equality also negates the possibility of any form of authority other than the weight of numbers of equal individuals.

The idea of political sovereignty was evident in the ideas of Niccolò Machiavelli, Jean Bodin, and Thomas Hobbes; the common theme was power, absolute power to rule and to maintain rule by power. In the greater historical context:

> With Machiavelli we begin to see the transition to a more abstract sense of the State as an independent political entity, but only in the works of sixteenth-century French and English humanists does there emerge the modern idea of the state as "a form of public power separate from both ruler and the ruled, and constituting the supreme political authority within a certain defined territory." . . . The Lutheran doctrine of the two kingdoms signifies, therefore, the defeat of the medieval metaphor of the two swords . . . The policy of *cuius regio, eius religio* was more than just a sensible compromise to prevent bloodshed among the people, now divided by commitment to different faiths. It was in fact a recognition of the dominance of secular rulers over the Church, to the extent that the faith of a people was controlled by and large by the desires of the prince.[37]

The subsumption of all forms of social authority by the new abstract and universal model of the political state was a new theory of political government, very different from the 3 general premodern forms of the *de regimine principum* [On the Government of Rulers, the qualities of a good ruler], the *de republica* [On the Republic, that is the forms of government], and the *de amiticia* [On Friendship]. As American philosopher Francis Slade indicates:

> None of these forms has a place, even a significant place, in modern political philosophy for which 1(a) rule must be understood apart from the human beings who exercise it and 1(b) rule is a self-sufficient exercise of the mind, one not dependent on, and therefore not subordinate to, wisdom in any sense beyond

the exercise of rule itself (2) rule is the same in every form of government and (3) the state is not a community of men. Modern political philosophy effects the separation of rule from the human beings who are rulers and the human beings who are ruled. The state, which is the product of modern political philosophy, is the disembodiment of rule.[38]

This distinctively modern model of political authority and power is the framework for what we call democracy and is supposed to be the universal foundation for political society. It presupposes that there is nothing of a pre-given structure of human persons and their relation to society, and subjects the institution of the state to nothing more than an equality of fairness among individuals and in relation to the institution of the state. Simpson recognizes John Rawls as a primordial expression of this type of state institution:

> Rawls begins with justice, which he calls the first virtue of social institutions. How is an institution just? It is just by how it fashions itself in view of the equal good of equal individuals. What are individuals? They are different combinations of desires and interests, which combinations individuals may and perhaps should put into some hierarchy or order but which have no hierarchy or order by nature. The institution is the state, and the state is an impersonal structure to enable individuals to satisfy their desires in peace, or without coming into conflict with each other in their different interests.[39]

This perspective eliminates the possibility of a pregiven truth of the person and subjects any and all notions of rights and liberties to the dictamen of the state, which in practice means a particular group with universal powers of imposition. This perspective also implies that the good of society, however it may be conceived, is left to impersonal institutions to produce and to guarantee. The role of the impersonal state is (theoretically) to preserve individual freedoms and equalities by its laws and institutions of power. These are supposed to produce and to maintain human society.

Jospeh Ratzinger, in an essay titled *Eschatology and Utopia*, commenting on Tocqueville's *Democracy in America*, points out that, as Tocqueville showed, what is paramount for the maintenance of democracy are the shared beliefs and convictions of a people rather than the structures and institutions of government. When these shared values do not exist, the institutions have no common foundation, and the only resort is to force as the only means to a cohesive society. In this regard, shared fundamental values and beliefs are essential for the shared exercise of freedom of a people. Ratzinger goes to say that when idealistic plans for society propose only social mechanisms and structures, a fundamental truth has been lost from sight. It is the strength of spirit of a people that shapes and forms society much more than economic plans and policies. To plan for a society requires attention to the cultivation of the resources of the spirit of a people, as well as the particular forms and processes of government. If the common cultivation of the strength of the spirit of a people is made a priority, fewer structures and processes will be required.[40]

The suppositions of the present political framework for democracy reduce the construction of human society to the impartial functioning of anonymous institutional procedures that preclude personal responsibility for any more substantive notion of human society other than fairness and equality.

This is not to say that particular political institutions and procedures are of little consequence for public matters. They are ways of establishing the use of public authority, of distributing and dividing such public authority, to provide ways that can ensure public debate, and so on. New Zealand professor of law Jeremy Waldron has drawn attention to the importance of the "structural, constitutional, and institutional issues in politics":

> In legal systems and in nation-building (whether we are overhauling our own constitution or trying to establish a new one in Iraq or Afghanistan), it matters what processes we set up. Institutions make a difference, not just to the political game but, through the inclusiveness of the order they establish, to the security, prosperity, and openness of the societies in which they are established.[41]

Even so, there is a tendency to trust structures, institutions, and processes alone to produce social harmony and to offer solutions to social problems. This misplaced, exaggerated trust in structures is something that Ratzinger sees as a common error of Marxist and Western political thought:

> The ethos does not support the structures, but rather the structures support the ethos, precisely because the ethos is the fragile thing, while the structures are considered firm and reliable. I see in this reversal, which is at the root of the myth of the better world, the real essence of materialism, which does not just consist of the denial of one sphere of reality but is at bottom an anthropological program that is necessarily connected with a certain idea about the interrelations among the individual spheres of reality. The claim that mind or spirit is not the origin of matter but only a product of material developments corresponds to the notion that morality is produced by the economy (instead of the economy being shaped, ultimately, by fundamental human decisions).[42]

The other misshaping of the modern political model of the state is in the notion of the relations of human society, that are recast in terms of equal numerical individuals within a structure of anonymous and universal power. Against a given background of personal and social inequalities, the state presupposes an imagined numerical identity of persons, each person considered as an equal numerical "one":

For the State what is paramount are the "rights" it confers upon its subjects, not the protection and promotion of virtue or of vice in human beings. In becoming a citizen, everyone exchanges whatever diverse social identities they had possessed for the identity conferred by the common status of State membership. The civil law emancipates individuals from all forms of social definition and dependence. "Civil liberties" mean "that each citizen should be perfectly independent from all his fellow citizens." As a citizen each is an autonomous individual over against society and its institutions. To society the individual may say "Do not ask me who I am, and do not ask me to remain the same." But for the State, whose power alone makes the individual, because it makes everyone free vis-à-vis social institutions, all citizens are homogenous. The content of citizenship is universal, egalitarian "human rights." So far as the State is concerned citizens might be interchangeable, "the particular features of each individual lost in the common physiognomy."[43]

Tocqueville also noted the dangers of this form of undifferentiated equality, especially in its relation to despotic public power:

Equality places men side by side, unconnected by any common tie; despotism raises barriers to keep them asunder; the former predisposes them not to consider their fellow-creatures, the latter makes general indifference a sort of public virtue. Despotism then, which is at all times dangerous, is more particularly to be feared in democratic ages.[44]

The point here is that beneath the imagined superficial numerical equality lie profound and important inequalities and differences, found in unequal proportion and measure. These include natural personal qualities such as forms of intelligence, levels of education, moral and religious capabilities and responses, social and economic circumstances, and so on. To deny these inequalities, found in proportionally unequal numbers, is to impose a fictitious uniformity that can only recognize a numerical majority, whether real or contrived. There is no real representation of real inequalities and differences and no criteria of what may be true, or better, or more just, or more representative, only the power of a greater number.

Lewis writes of this publicly and ubiquitously imposed equality:

Equality (outside mathematics) is a purely social conception. It applies to man as a political and economic animal. It has no place in the world of the mind. Beauty is not democratic; she reveals herself more to the few than to the many, more to the persistent and disciplined seekers than to the careless. Virtue is not democratic; she is achieved by those who pursue her more hotly than most men. Truth is not democratic; she demands special talents and special industry in those to whom she gives her favours. Political democracy is doomed if it tries to extend its demand for equality into these higher spheres. Ethical, intellectual, or aesthetic democracy is death.[45]

It is clear that there are also particular inequalities that are not natural or pregiven, but that are the result of injustice, oppression, and exploitation. These are, of course, to be recognized and overcome; but this is not to say that all inequalities are necessarily unjust and the result of forms of injustice. Neither is it the case that all differences are to be equally recognized and promoted, just because each person has an equal right to freedom.

Tocqueville, in his acute observation of equality and democracy in America, recognized the potential for equality to lead to political forms of tyranny, whether in the form of one ruler over all, or of the many rulers over the few, or, as a novel form of tyranny, of the rule of all over all. Noticing that the fiction of universal equality drives men to assume that all things are attainable by everyone, Tocqueville recognizes the ironic consequence that men will be led to hand over their freedom in order to preserve the illusion of equality. This may happen by the election (or otherwise) of a tyrant, and, as Jesuit philosopher James V. Schall notes, our contemporary tyrants have justified their imposition of power by reference to some overriding, noble purpose, often in the name of future equality, "The modern tyrant, however, has demanded our thoughts and our souls, demanded that his ideas be put into reality, not just for his good but for the good of all humanity. No other kind of good, divine or human, existed but that of the tyrant's mind."[46]

Tyranny in democracy may also arise by the role of the anonymous and all-powerful state:

> Democratic men will abandon their freedom to these mighty authorities in exchange for a "soft" despotism, one which "provides for their security, foresees and supplies their necessities, facilitates their pleasures, manages their principal concerns, directs their industry," and, ultimately, "spares them all the care of thinking and all the trouble of living. . . . Democracy originates a new form of despotism, society tyrannizing over itself."[47]

Tocqueville also recognizes another form of democratic tyranny, the tyranny of the majority over the minority.[48] With the justification of numerical superiority, the numerical majority imposes the weight of numbers over all the other considerations thus leading to the situation where:

> The majority not only demand conduct that conforms but strive also to make it impossible for individuals to conceive of nonconformity. To hold an opinion on an important matter contrary to that of the majority is not merely imprudent or unavailing but even dehumanizing. "The power of the majority is so absolute and irresistible that one must give up one's rights as a citizen and almost abjure

one's qualities as a man if one intends to stray from the track which it pre-scribes." The tyranny of the majority over the minds of those who are its intel-lectual superiors absolutizes the disposition of democracy toward mediocrity.[49]

It seems that the illusion of numbers combined with the fiction of universal equality and an induced sense of being separated individuals has a bind on our sense of political judgment. It seems that we are told that we decide for ourselves (only), while the state ("the people," in reality a particular numeri-cal majority) decides for everyone. It is assumed that all participate and that the interests of all are represented, equally of course. Who represents the unborn and are they given an equal right to life?

At the heart of the difficulty with what is called democracy is the recog-nition of pregiven inequalities that require a much greater recognition, rep-resentation, and, when necessary, protection, than the illusion of numerical equality. Without this discernment of inequalities, the democracy of numbers quickly slides into totalitarianism, soft or hard, by one, the few, or the many, in the name of the people but in fact by the use of sovereign state power.

In John Paul II's *Centesimus Annus*, written in 1991, the Pope from Poland stated that:

> Authentic democracy is possible only in a State ruled by law, and on the basis of a correct conception of the human person. It requires that the necessary condi-tions be present for the advancement both of the individual through education and formation in true ideals, and of the "subjectivity" of society through the creation of structures of participation and shared responsibility. Nowadays there is a tendency to claim that agnosticism and sceptical relativism are the philoso-phy and the basic attitude which correspond to democratic forms of political life. Those who are convinced that they know the truth and firmly adhere to it are considered unreliable from a democratic point of view, since they do not accept that truth is determined by the majority, or that it is subject to variation according to different political trends. It must be observed in this regard that if there is no ultimate truth to guide and direct political activity, then ideas and convictions can easily be manipulated for reasons of power. As history demon-strates, a democracy without values easily turns into open or thinly disguised totalitarianism.[50]

If the only or overriding objective of the democratic form of government is equality of persons and conditions, then, as Tocqueville noted, this equality can be found in tyrannical as well as free forms of government.[51]

IS THE CONTEMPORARY DEMOCRATIC FORM
OF GOVERNMENT GOOD GOVERNMENT?

It is common to think of the democracy process as a major step forward in the political liberation of all peoples, manifested in their individual and collective power to choose their government, propose their ideas to their political representatives, and hold the government to account for its actions. While these are indeed important elements of the democratic ideal, the historical context of the present democratic process tells a different story. It is ironic that with the modern gains of mass education, an increasing popular power of franchise, Constitutional guarantees of individual liberties and rights, and so on, that, along with the nominal rights and freedoms of all individuals, ever greater forms of governmental power have concomitantly arisen.

In *Quest for Community*, Nisbet notices a strange paradox in the totalitarian forms of political power of the twentieth century that followed the apparently individualistic tendencies in economics and morality of the nineteenth centuries. Why was this so? Nisbet proposes that the explanation lies in the close dependence of the individual on State power throughout the nineteenth century. This reinforcement of the dependence of the individual on the State caused the general disassociation of the individual from other social bonds that were independent of State control.[52]

What Nisbet is pointing out is that the progressive democratic processes and institutions that were to affirm the individual's rights and freedoms were achieved at the cost of a greater dependence on the political state. This was done by defining the human person in terms of a political individual, and the subjection of all other forms of human society to this one central political authority. The consequences of this modern state usurpation of total power have taken time to reveal themselves. A brief consideration of the pervasive domination of state power in matters of family bonds, home schooling, sexual identity, the termination of human life, Church practice, forms of electronic surveillance, national economic debt (spending of citizens' income), and so on, shows how predominant and potentially ubiquitous is state power. All such forms of state control are done in the name of and with the presumed consent of the people. We seem to see ever greater concentrations of political power and ever greater intrusiveness in the lives of individuals, that is, persons stripped of all other forms of social identity other than belonging to the state.

In this political context, the democratic process is seen in a much more skeptical way. It is not that the language of promises, rights, and consent is absent; it is just that the framework of the democratic process is predetermined to produce a very particular type of political society, at the dictates of the powerful, while the illusion of participation and consent are maintained.

In *Quest for Community*, Nisbet thus claims that the surreptitious slide from democracy to state dominance will happen in an undramatic and innocuous way. In fact, Nisbet claims that the change will hardly be noticed at all, except by those who will be labeled as extremists and radicals.[53]

What Nisbet points out is that human society is more complex than the enforced political model of individuals and the state. Nisbet claims that the real political and social dichotomy is not between state and the individual. The state cultivates its status and dominance by cultivating the dependence of the individual by what it gives and promises to the individual. At the same time, what the state is increasingly giving to the individual it is taking from the other social bonds, such as the family, communities, church, and so on.[54]

While these groups and association are often referred to as intermediary, in the sense of being between the individual and the state, this term may not be exactly right. Some of these associations, such as the family, some forms of local communities, and church groups are intimately related to the needs and purposes of human society far more than the political state. As sources of human growth in profound dimensions of human social existence, these associations surpass in profundity and in value all aspects of political forms of government. In this sense, theses associations are not intermediary, but demonstrate the greater extension and depth of social existence than any form of the political state. They relativize political government and, when properly exercised, provide the social bond on which politics and the political form of democracy depend.

Nisbet notes that, although legislative efforts and diplomatic agreements can be made to strengthen democracies throughout the world, the real source of strength of truly democratic government is in the cultural and social bonds of the people, which are more effectively perceived in the closer and more intimate relations of the family and local communities and groups.[55]

The difficulty with our ubiquitous democratic form of political government is that it is presented within the framework of the modern political state that recognizes itself as the ultimate public power and reduces the social bond to individuals within this anonymous collective power.

According to Nisbet, the crux of the challenge to real democratic government is to be found in the predominant power of politics over the other forms of social authority. Nisbet sees the need to strengthen the independence of these other forms of social authority and to safeguard these social bonds from the potentially overbearing interference of state control.[56]

Tocqueville notices in his *Democracy in America* a connection between despotism and equality. Tocqueville affirms that the evils that despotism promotes are the same as those equality produces:

These two things mutually and perniciously complete and assist each other. Equality places men side by side, unconnected by any common tie; despotism raises barriers to keep them asunder; the former predisposes them not to consider their fellow-creatures, the latter makes general indifference a sort of public virtue. Despotism then, which is at all times dangerous, is more particularly to be feared in democratic ages.[57]

For Tocqueville, the phenomenon of association, to which the Americans seemed particularly adept, operates to counter the separating tendency that equality fosters and that predisposes democratic society to forms of despotism. Multiple forms, especially of local association, spontaneously promote a sense of participation in the public good.

Tocqueville explains that it is difficult to motivate the citizen to see beyond his particular and local interests precisely because the citizen does not see clearly what impact the state will have on the citizen's own particular interests. Tocqueville suggests, however, that if there is a proposal to build a road at the end of his property, he will immediately appreciate the relevance of this minor public affair to his own private interests, and he will thus discover, in this case, the clear nexus between his private interests and the public concern.[58]

Tocqueville's perception of the divisive nature of equality is profound. The imposition of sameness as the goal of political government produces a major shift in the nature of human society. If, in terms of interpersonal relations, the goal of human flourishing is precisely the communion of life in common, the proposed aim of equality of life favors above all the sense of the assertion of individuals and what pertains, or should pertain, to each one. It is not surprising that the common good is described almost exclusively in terms of individual rights and benefits and the distributive justice required to produce equality. It is not difficult to trace the causes of this radical change in the purposes of human society; a contractual theory of political power and association, freedom understood only in terms of individual assertion, the rise of empirical positivism as the criterion of truth, the expression of the modern state's justification in terms of the assertion of individual rights of and so on. It is surprising how ingrained has become the idea of social good in terms of individual advantage, in the terms of the British utilitarian Jeremy Bentham:

> The interest of the community is one of the most general expressions that can occur in the phraseology of morals: no wonder that the meaning of it is often lost. When it has a meaning, it is this. The community is a fictitious body, composed of the individual persons who are considered as constituting as it were its members. The interest of the community then is, what?—the sum of the interests of the several members who compose it.[59]

The regulation of a political society that proposes only the separated cohabitation of individual freedoms, and subject to ever more pervasive forms of uniform equality, can hardly constitute the common good of social communion, or even contribute to it any substantive way. Italian political philosopher Vittorio Possenti writes that: "A group of individuals who reciprocally adopt criteria of distributive justice and freedom, and otherwise do not cooperate or ignore each other, does not constitute a true and proper political society."[60]

While we may be accustomed to think of the common good merely in terms of individual freedoms and benefits, usually of a material sort, this is not the extent of the genuine aspiration of interpersonal society. On an experiential level, the human desire for real communion, for belonging to something greater than oneself (without losing one's own identity), and for permanence and completeness of communion beyond this existence, are also present in human experience. Manifestations of solidarity, the pursuit of transcending excellence, engrossing experiences of ecstasy, can be identified in the voluntary actions of ordinary persons, as well as in social events such as national and international sports events, World Youth Day, rock concerts, even fashion. The more we think about it, the less apparent is the political aim of "the sum of the interests of the several members who compose it."

In *Metamorphoses of the City*, Manent identifies the root of this impoverishment of political aspiration in a shift of perspective in the currents of modernity. Manent recalls Descartes' hope that the new science of modernity could be used to help us to dominate and to exploit nature, and this became one of the principal objectives, if not the primary goal, of modernity and its understanding and use of science. Manent observes that there is another objective of modernity that Francis Bacon expressed that also became characteristic of the modern approach, and that is expressed in Bacon's well-known phrase "the relief of man's estate," that is, a certain betterment of the human condition, nothing more. It is this all too modest goal that permeates modern political thought and circumscribes what Descartes proposed as the domination of nature. Bacon's maxim expresses the immanence of modern thought and its reduction of horizons of thought and ambition to this human existence, with its problems and concerns.[61]

In contrast to the ancient ambition of immortality through glory, Bacon's formula domesticates human ambition and, ultimately, suppresses the desire to defy and defeat the mortality of human existence.

At the heart of modern political arrangements there is, therefore, a deep-rooted pessimism toward human nature and social ambition, and one that does not conform to the aspirations of the human person, even though we have become accustomed to this immanent and minimalist approach. The difficulty with this repression of our political aspiration is that it exposes us to the moral claims of ideologies that, on the one hand, reveal the inadequacies of mundane political practice, while, on the other hand, purport to justify their political agenda by appeal to inherent and legitimate human aspirations to transcendence.

Our current *form* of democratic process thus pre-empts the necessary search for a greater collective vision, something that would be implicit in the democratic *ideal* of society.

In *Political Illiberalism*, Simpson makes clear that the search for the truth of reality is something innate and natural to personal existence and it is this truth that shows us the purpose of our freedom. This is also true of the communion of persons, that needs to be based on the same truth of personal existence. Authentic communities, including the political community, are and should be authentic reflections of the common grasp of the purpose and meaning of human existence. Communities that do not have this basic authentic vision of the person will necessarily frustrate and distort the true expression of social communion. Simpson claims that Liberalism, which relegates questions of common truth and good to the realm of private option, is thus a distorted form of social communion and frustrates the attaining of the real common good.[62]

A personalist enrichment of political categories of thought would enhance political institutions and practices by rediscovering the great moral and religious sources of human integration, what Ratzinger refers to as the "pre-political foundations" of the free state: "Ultimately, the essential values and norms that are in some way known or sensed by all men will take on a new brightness in such a process, so that that which holds the world together can once again become an effective force in mankind."[63]

Something of the renewal of interpersonal communion is required if the stifled image of human persons and their aspirations are to be experienced again and a true sense of common interpersonal good to be established. In the 2010 re-publication of Nisbet's *The Quest for Community*, American writer David Bosworth summarizes the relevance of Nisbet's thought by writing that:

> It remains as true now as it was in 1953 that "the prime psychological problems of the age . . . are those not of release but of reintegration." Rather than simply medicate our anxieties or depressions, treating them as discrete and biochemically based diseases of the social atom, we need to reconsider the size, shape, pace, and quality of our interrelationships, the ethos and the telos of our most common associations. In the place of Nisbet's reintegration, I prefer to use re affiliation, whose Latin root—to adopt a son—better evokes the sorts of long-term devotion, freely chosen, that have been gradually expunged from American life. But that edit is a refinement on what remains a profound

observation about the course of Western history: a necessary reversal of emphasis in the well-established democracies from emancipation to association, from the assertion of individual rights to the nurture of sociability within communities of purpose.[64]

CONCLUSION

Human society is formed by communities of interpersonal relations which, to differing degrees and extension, promote the truth of the human person in authentic and reciprocal bonds of communion and that will be structured to reflect the capabilities and needs of the unequal conditions of each person. The flourishing of each person and the collective benefit of the community are distinct and yet complementary dimensions of communion.

Political society is an expression of necessary public authority over such communities, which have both personal and common purposes. As such, political society needs to reflect this complex of communities of persons of unequal conditions and, to the extent necessary and possible, favor the flourishing of such communities and their harmonic interaction.

Seen in this light as the given truth of social existence, the historically modern hypothesis of contract between individuals and a central political power is clearly a distortion of the naturally given social condition of the person and of communion, in several ways. Social purpose is reduced to the protection of each individual's own interests, society is reduced to a collective of individuals with no recognition of communities, and the fiction of uniform equality as the goal of society is imposed on all individuals. The complexities of communities of persons of unequal conditions are reduced to individuals who are considered only as numbers, differentiated only by the weight of numbers.

Along with this, the modern forms of the political state tend toward ever greater centralized power, as the continuous affirmation of sovereignty requires an ever-greater assertion over all other sources of power. This centrifugal force is restrained only by the separated individuals of its political society and thus makes vast numbers of people vulnerable to those few who wield such universal power in the name of the people. Social agendas can and are imposed on the people by "the people" almost overnight.

From this perspective, what we call democracy takes on a less appealing aspect. We have distinguished between democracy as an *ideal*, compatible with a society of communities; the representation of each person of unequal condition, the collective search for the authentic good of both the person and the community, institutions and processes that assure both goodness and fairness for each and for all, and so on.

The democratic *form* we are accustomed to today does not as such correspond to the ideal because it presupposes a vision of man as I have described above, not one of communities but of contract, within a theory of the political state that recognizes only separated individuals.

It is indeed difficult even remotely to imagine the political state in terms of an interpersonal community and therefore as an expression or reflection, however faint, of authentic human social flourishing. Simpson proposes a different association of Aristotle's virtuous city with the modern state. He envisages the Aristotelean *polis*, with its emphasis on virtue and education as a community *within* the state; the modern state or states would serve the purpose of protection and the conditions required by all communities (*poleis*) to cooperate in these external matters, leaving each the real freedom to flourish as a true human community.[65]

As possible as this may be, the real source of political renewal, of its purposes and its processes, the *instituta et mores* [structures and morals], is in these communities of purpose and their contribution to authentic interpersonal life. Right now, the form of democracy as we know it seems to work in exactly the opposite direction.

What appears evident is that our modern use of the word democracy seems to obscure and restrain more than it reveals and achieves.

NOTES

1. Robert A. Nisbet, *The Quest for Community: A Study in the Ethics of Order and Freedom* (Washington, DC: ISI Books, 2010), Kindle 4277.

2. Pierre Manent, *Metamorphoses of the City: On the Western Dynamic*, trans. Marck LePain (Cambridge, MA: Harvard University Press 2013), 64–65. Manent, writing on Russian born Alexandre Kojève's exchange with Leo Strauss, comments that Kojève: "does draw our attention to the disturbing fact that modern democracy shares with totalitarianism the claim to have solved the human problem. Modern democracy understands itself not as a regime among others, not even as the best regime, but as the only legitimate regime: it embodies the final, because rational, state of humanity" Manent, "The Return of Political Philosophy," *First Things* 103 (May 2000): 8, https://www.firstthings.com/article/2000/05/the-return-of-political -philosophy.

3. Amarya Sen, "Democracy as a Universal Value," *Journal of Democracy* 10, no.3 (1999): 2, https://www.journalofdemocracy.org/articles/democracy-as-a-universal -value/. The article was written in response to what a leading Japanese newspaper asked Sen, a Nobel Prize Winner in Economics, what he considered to be the most important thing that had happened in the twentieth century. Sen had no difficulty in according "primacy to the emergence of democracy as the pre-eminently acceptable form of governance" (1).

4. Condoleezza Rice, *Democracy: Stories from the Long Road to Freedom* (New York: Hachette Book Group, 2017), 12. The title is reminiscent of Nelson Mandela's *Long Walk to Freedom* (South Africa: Little, Brown, 1994), cited on page 6.

5. John Dunn, *Democracy: A History* (New York: Atlantic Monthly Press, 2005), 15. According to Italian philosopher Giovanni Sartori: "Herodotus is often held to have been the first to say 'democracy'" (qtd. in Dunn, *Democracy*, 80–83). Actually, the term does not appear in his text but in its translations. But we do find in Herodotus a demos-commanded or many-commanded polity neatly contrasted to monarchy and oligarchy. It is also the case that Herodotus associates the rule of the demos to *isonomia* (ἰσονομία), equal law; an association that does remain preponderant, throughout the Greek experience, with respect to that between *demokratia* (δημοκρατία) and *eleutheria* (ἐλευθερία, freedom)." Sartori, *The Theory of Democracy Revisited: Part Two: The Classical Issues* (Chatham, NJ: Chatham House, 1987), 292.

6. This was the point of the Austrian political economist Joseph Schumpeter's 's critique of democracy, which he described as "a political method, that is to say, a certain type of institutional arrangement for arriving at political—legislative and administrative—decisions and hence incapable of being an end in itself, irrespective of what decisions it will produce under given historical conditions. And this must be the starting point of any attempt at defining it" Schumpeter, *Capitalism, Socialism, and Democracy* (Summit, NJ: Start Publishing, 2012), 4841. The difficulty here is that "democracy" as the term is commonly used, does imply something that should be an end in itself, and not just one possible political method. My attempt in this chapter is to clarify and distinguish democracy as a legitimate ideal, or end, and democracy understood as a method of government.

7. Nisbet, *Quest for Community*, 4411.

8. For a presentation of the different understandings and justifications of the modern forms of democratic government see Vittorio Possenti, *Le società liberali al bivio: Lineamenti di filosofia della società* (Casale Monferrato, Italy: Marietti, 1991), 281–314. "Giustificazioni della democrazia."

9. Athens and the surrounding Attica region were not the only or indeed the first Greek city-state to develop a form of democratic rule. Cf. Eric W. Robinson, *Early Popular Government Outside Athens* (Stuttgart: Franz Steiner Verlag, 1997).

10. Such institutions, characterized by the sense of equality of political rights and in the application of laws, were termed *isonomic* by the historians Herodotus and Thucydides, and reintroduced by F. A. [Fredrich A.] Hayek in his *The Constitution of Liberty* (1960): "The history of the concept in ancient Greece provides an interesting lesson, because it probably represents the first instance of a cycle that civilizations seem to repeat. When it first appeared, it described a state which Solon had earlier established in Athens when he gave the people 'equal laws for the noble and the base' and thereby gave them 'not so much the control of public policy, as the certainty of being governed legally in accordance with known rules'" Hayek, *The Constitution of Liberty: The Definitive Edition*, ed. Ronald Hamowy (Chicago: University of Chicago Press, 2011), 239–40. In his democratic reforms, Cleisthenes was preceded by the reforms of Solon (630–560 BC) and followed by the reforms of Ephialtes (–461 BC).

11. Arnold Hugh Marin Jones, *Athenian Democracy* (Oxford: Basil Blackwell, 1969), 99. The reference to Alcibiades is from *Thucydides* VI. 89. 6. The last chapter of Jones' text is dedicated to answering this question. "The success of Athens is a testimony to the basic sense of the ordinary Athenian citizen . . . moreover, the people demanded high standards of its leaders. Legally the proposer of a decree was responsible to the people; he could be—and frequently was—indicted if his proposal was illegal or even if his policy was inexpedient . . . . In practice the people did not suffer fools gladly. Socrates remarks that in discussing any technical problem the people would listen only to experts, and booed and shouted down a clever speaker who wasted its time by ill-informed rhetoric . . . . It was informed advice, and not mere eloquence, that people expected from rising politician, and they saw to it that they got it" (132–33).

12. Alfred Eckhard Zimmern, *The Greek Commonwealth: Politics and Economics in Fifth-Century Athens* (Oxford: Clarendon Press, 1911), 76, as cited in Nisbet, *Quest for Community*, 2133.

13. Nisbet, *Quest for Community*, 2163.

14. Dunn, *Democracy*, 54. Dunn observes that the Greek historian Polybius did write of the democratic element in Roman government, but always held in check by the aristocratic and monarchical powers of government (Cf. 55–57).

15. Dunn, *Democracy*, 59.

16. Alexis de Tocqueville, *Democracy in America.: The Complete and Unabridged Volumes I and II* (New York: Bantam Classics, 2000), 690.

17. Dunn, *Democracy*, 92.

18. Dunn, *Democracy*, 114.

19. Quoted from Malcom Crook, *Elections in the French Revolution*; and Maximilian Robespierre, *Discours et rapports à la Convention*, both cited in Dunn, *Democracy*, 115–17.

20. The Conspiracy of Equals was a failed attempt in 1796 by François-Noël Babeuf, to overthrow the French Directory of France's First Republic and establish a more egalitarian government on Jacobin lines. One of the conspirators, Buonarroti, wrote *Conspiracy of Equals,* which was published in 1828 and influenced Karl Marx, Friedrich Engels, and Antonio Gramsci. Cf. Philippe Buonarroti, *Buonarroti's History of Babeuf's Conspiracy of Equals* (1828) (London: Andesite Press, 2015).

21. For a profound political analysis of these two revolutions, their different historical settings and their different outcomes, see Hanna Arendt, *On Revolution* (New York: Penguin Books, 2006).

22. Dunn, *Democracy*, 51.

23. As Leo Strauss points out: "the classics rejected democracy because they thought that the aim of human life, and hence of social life, is not freedom but virtue. Freedom as a goal is ambiguous, because it is freedom for evil as well as for good. Virtue emerges normally only through education, that is to say, through the formation of character, through habituation, and this requires leisure on the part of both parents and children" Strauss, *What Is Political Philosophy? And Other Studies* (Chicago: University of Chicago Press, 1988), 36–37.

24. Italian philosopher Antonio Rosmini recognized: "This abstract principle, which presupposes that all human beings are equal (that is, possess human essence, but nothing more), does in fact assign to each an equal share of freedom . . . . But it is precisely this arithmetically equal quantity of free action which is never verified in reality. People are naturally unequal as a result of their inborn talents, powers, and so on, and as a consequence of their varying age, etc. It is completely impossible, therefore, for them all to exercise the same share of activity." American political philosopher Robert P. Kraynak draws the conclusion from Rosmini's observation that: "The implication is that social justice as a shared ideal must be concerned with people in their concrete social roles as well as their abstract humanity—and it is their concrete existence in society that determines the true, real 'rights that bind people together.'" Both quotations are from Kraynak, "The Origins of 'Social Justice' in the Natural Law Philosophy of Antonio Rosmini" Review of Politics 80, no. 1 (2018): 9, 10, https://doi.org/10.1017%2FS0034670517000754. The quotation from Rosmini is from his *The Essence of Right*.

25. C. S. [Clive Staples] Lewis commented on this notion of equality: *Present Concerns: Journalistic Essays* (New York: HarperCollins, 2017), 158–60.

26. C. S. Lewis, *The Screwtape Letters* (New York: HarperCollins, 2002), 197–98.

27. For example, The *Catechism of the Catholic Church* recognizes *two* fundamental causes of inequality. Nos. 1936 and 1937 state that: "On coming into the world, man is not equipped with everything he needs for developing his bodily and spiritual life. He needs others. Differences appear tied to age, physical abilities, intellectual or moral aptitudes, the benefits derived from social commerce, and the distribution of wealth. The 'talents' are not distributed equally. These differences belong to God's plan, who wills that each receive what he needs from others, and that those endowed with particular 'talents' share the benefits with those who need them. These differences encourage and often oblige persons to practice generosity, kindness, and sharing of goods; they foster the mutual enrichment of cultures." In the next number the Catechism states: "There exist also sinful inequalities that affect millions of men and women. These are in open contradiction of the Gospel: 'Their equal dignity as persons demands that we strive for fairer and more humane conditions. Excessive economic and social disparity between individuals and peoples of the one human race is a source of scandal and militates against social justice, equity, human dignity, as well as social and international peace (Second Vatican Council, *Gaudium et spes*, sec. 29.3).'"

28. Robert Sokolowski, "The Human Person and Political Life," in *Christian Faith and Human Understanding. Studies on the Eucharist, Trinity, and the Human Person* (Washington, DC: Catholic University of America Press, 2006), 184.

29. Sokolowski, "Human Person," 186. As Sokolowski points out, here "Aristotle does not claim that the republic as such promotes virtue or nobility; he presents it rather as a resolution of the parallelogram of political forces, in which the interests of both the poor and the rich are best reconciled. The two groups are blended into a middle class that will rule through the laws for the advantage of the whole" (186, footnote 12).

30. Sokolowski also points out that "Aristotle also discusses monarchy and aristocracy, in which one man or a few virtuous men rule for the good of the whole, and these two forms serve as a kind of norm for what all cities can be. Because they admit only a few people to rule, however, they may not be possible once societies become very large (Aristotle admits this limitation), but they must be kept in mind as part of how we design and live our politics: when the laws are made to govern, they should rule as virtuous agents would rule." Sokolowski, "Human Person," 185. Sokolowski refers to Aristotle *Politics*, book III, 14–17 and book VII.

31. Peter L. P. Simpson, *Political Illiberalism: A Defence of Freedom* (London: Routledge, 2015), 136. Simpson's reference is to Aristotle's *Politics* 4(7).15.1334a11–34.

32. Simpson, *Political Illiberalism*, 134–35. Simpson's reference is to Aristotle's *Politics* 3.8.1279b20–80a6.

33. Simpson, *Political Illiberalism*, 138. Simpson's references to Aristotle's *Politics* are to books 6(4)–8(6) and books 4(7)–5(8).

34. Peter Simpson, "Making the Citizens Good: Aristotle's City and Its Contemporary Relevance," *Philosophical Forum* 22, no. 2 (1990): 157–58. In this article, Simpson makes an argument for a creative application of Aristotle's political thought to contemporary political phenomena and, *inter alia*, two kinds of political philosophy: "the type that examines the nature of the democratic state insofar as it is an alliance for mutual protection and defence, and what rules should govern it (which would be the sort of thing that Rawls and other theorists of the modem democratic state are engaged in); and the type that examines the nature of the communities united in the alliance and what rules should govern them (and this is the sort of thing that Aristotle and most premodern political theorists would be engaged in). But the latter will in some sense give the measure to the former, for the alliance must be such that it allows and encourages the flourishing of the allied communities. The alliance is for the sake of the allies and not vice versa. Hence there will be a feedback from the latter to the former" (165–66, footnote 21).

35. Manent, *Metamorphoses of the City*, 65. Manent goes on to explain how majorities and minorities are not representative numbers of groups, but only relative numbers, that depend on counting: "Neither the majority nor the minority exist as real, effective, active numbers as long as they are not in effect counted, and then what effectively exists is their difference, which can be reduced to one unit of counting" (65).

36. Manent, *Metamorphoses of the City*, 98.

37. William T. Cavanaugh "'A Fire Strong Enough to Consume the House': The Wars of Religion and the Rise of the State," *Modern Theology* 11, no. 4 (1995): 398, 399, 400. The quotation in the text is from the British historian Quentin Skinner's *The Foundations of Modern Political Thought*. Cavanaugh argues that it is anachronistic to refer to "the Wars of Religion"; in fact, according to Cavanaugh, "what was at issue in these wars was the very creation of religion as a set of privately held beliefs without direct political relevance. The creation of religion was necessitated by the new State's need to secure absolute sovereignty over its subjects." Cavanaugh, "Fire Strong Enough," 398. This is also a theme in John Milbank's *Theology and Social Theory: Beyond Secular Reason* (Oxford: Blackwell Publishing, 2006), esp. part 1,

chap. 2 "Political Theology and the New Science of Politics," 9–25. American sociologist Nisbet also points out the conflictive origins of the modern state in *Quest for Community*, chap. 5 "The State as Revolution."

38. Francis Slade, "Rule as Sovereignty: The Universal and Homogenous State," in *The Truthful and the Good: Essays in Honor of R. Sokolowski*, ed. John J. Drummond and James G. Hart (Dordrecht, NL: Springer, 1996), 167. As Slade observes, Hegel concisely marked the difference in the modern structure of authority and power: "The division of constitutions into democracy, aristocracy, and monarchy, is still the most definitive statement of their difference in relation to sovereignty" (163).

39. Simpson, *Political Illiberalism*, 131–32. The references are to John Rawls' original edition of *A Theory of Justice* (Cambridge, MA: Belknap Press, 1971), 15n1 and 85nn1–6.

40. Joseph Ratzinger, "Eschatology and Utopia," in *Church, Ecumenism and Politics: New Endeavours in Ecclesiology* (San Francisco: Ignatius Press, 2008), 237. In a comment on the Jewish journalist Franz Oppenheimer's statement that democracies arose in the Jewish-Christian world of the West, Ratzinger says: "I can only underscore what Oppenheimer has said. We know today that the democratic model developed out of the monastic constitutions, which provided such models with their chapters and the voting that took place there" Ratzinger, *Salt of the Earth: The Church at the End of the Millennium. An Interview with Peter Seewald* (San Francisco: Ignatius Pres, 1997), 225. What goes without saying is that each monastic community shared common religious *mores* that sustained the processes and institutions of each monastic community.

41. Jeremy Waldron, *Political Political Theory: Essays on Institutions* (Cambridge, MA: Harvard University Press, 2016), ix, 7. This is what Waldron means by political political theory, "theory addressing itself to politics and to the way our political institutions house and frame our disagreements about social ideals and orchestrate what is done about whatever aims we can settle on" (6). Waldron refers, as an example of what he suggests, to the 2012 publication of Daron Acemoglu and James A. Robinson, *Why Nations Fail: The Origins of Power, Prosperity, and Poverty* (New York: Crown Currency, 2012).

42. Ratzinger, "A Christian Orientation in a Pluralistic Democracy," in *Church, Ecumenism and Politics*, 3023. Aleksandr Solzhenitsyn wrote that "In relation to the true ends of human beings have on earth . . . the state structure is of secondary significance" Solzhenitsyn, *From Under the Rubble* (New York: Bantam Books, 1976), 37. See T.S. Eliot for a familiar quotation that comes to mind: "They constantly try to escape from the darkness outside and within by dreaming of systems so perfect that no one will need to be good" Eliot, "The Rock," in *The Complete Poems and Plays of T. S. Eliot* (London: Faber and Faber, 2004), 159.

43. Slade, "Rule as Sovereignty," 175. The first quotation is from Michel Foucault (footnote 66), and the second from Tocqueville's *Democracy in America*, footnote 67.

44. Tocqueville, *Democracy in America*, 10375. Joseph Ratzinger also comments on the difficulties of an undifferentiated notion of universal equality in *The Meaning of Christian Brotherhood* (San Francisco: Ignatius Press, 1993), 5–19.

45. Lewis, *Present Concerns*, 349. He finishes this essay with the quip: "Democracy demands that little men should not take big ones too seriously; it dies when it is full of little men who think they are big themselves" (377). A similar theme is dealt with in the second essay of this volume, "Equality."

46. James V. Schall, "A Reflection on the Classical Tractate on Tyranny: The Problem of Democratic Tyranny," *American Journal of Jurisprudence* 41, no.1 (1996): 11. Hanna Arendt describes totalitarianism as a radically new form of government: "Instead of saying that totalitarian government is unprecedented, we could also say that it has exploded the very alternative on which all definitions of the essence of governments have been based in political philosophy, that is the alternative between lawful and lawless government, between arbitrary and legitimate power" Arendt, *The Origins of Totalitarianism* (New York: Mariner Books, 1976), 461. Interestingly, Arendt notes the tactics of isolation and subjugation toward a controlled and dominated people. Cf. chap. 13 "Ideology and Terror: A Novel Form of Government," 460–79. Leo Strauss also recognized the novel forms of tyranny, those who: "fancied themselves to be philosophers, inventive thinkers capable of conjuring up a new and more dangerous form of tyranny in the name of mankind's wellbeing" qtd. in Schall, "A Reflection on the Classical Tractate on Tyranny," 7.

47. Marvin Zetterbaum, "Alexis de Tocqueville," in *History of Political Philosophy*, 3rd ed., ed. Leo Strauss and Joseph Cropsey (Chicago: University of Chicago Press, 1987), 15368. The quotations are from Tocqueville's *Democracy in America*.

48. Alexander Hamilton, James Madison, and John Jay, *The Federalist Papers*, ed. Lawrence Goldman (Oxford: Oxford University Press, 2008), Hamilton, Jay, and Madison also feared this type of tyrannical abuse of power: "It is of great importance in a republic not only to guard the society against the oppression of its rulers, but to guard one part of the society against the injustice of the other part. Different interests necessarily exist in different classes of citizens. If a majority be united by a common interest, the rights of the minority will be insecure" (5912; 259n51).

49. Zetterbaum, "Alexis de Tocqueville," 15387. The quotation in the text is from Tocqueville's *Democracy in America*. Ratzinger has observed a similar phenomenon: "The danger of a dictatorship of opinion is growing, and anyone who doesn't share the prevailing opinion is excluded, so that even good people no longer dare to stand by such nonconformists. Any future anti-Christian dictatorship would probably be much more subtle than anything we have known until now. It will appear to be friendly to religion, but on the condition that its own models of behaviour and thinking not be called into question" Ratzinger, *Salt of the Earth*, 153. Ratzinger makes similar comments in *Europe: Today and Tomorrow* (San Francisco: Ignatius Press, 2007), 63.

50. John Paul II, *Centesimus Annus. Acta Apostolicae Sedis (AAS)* 83 (1991): 46. John Paul II makes similar reflections in *Evangelium Vitae* [The Gospel of Life]. *Acta Apostolicae Sedis (AAS)* 87 (1995): 68–74.

51. As Zetterbaum, "Alexis de Tocqueville," explains in his commentary on Tocqueville's *Democracy in America*: "The fundamental paradox of democracy, as Tocqueville understands it, is that equality of conditions is compatible with tyranny as well as with freedom. A species of equality, at least, can coexist with the greatest

inequality. Left to its own devices, democracy is actually prone to the establishment of tyranny, whether of one over all, of the many over the few, or even of all over all" (15343).

52. Nisbet, *Quest for Community*, 2796.

53. Nisbet, *Quest for Community*, 4400.

54. Nisbet, *Quest for Community*, 4292.

55. Nisbet, *Quest for Community*, 4276. These smaller, internal areas also do far more than nourish psychologically the cultural allegiances of citizens; they are at the core of the experience and formation of personal development. Ratzinger also recognizes the importance of these associations. He recognizes the family as a first sphere of freedom from state interference and control. This is why, according to Ratzinger, totalitarian forms of government always try to break up this area of freedom that is the family and that is beyond the state's control. Ratzinger also points to liturgical and Church communities as likewise areas of freedom from the state. The fact that these communities have a strong sense of the own identity demands of the state respect and freedom. There are also other areas of freedom in society. Ratzinger notes that even the state itself that recognizes its own inherent limitations and whose legal system is based on an independent moral foundation can itself become an area of freedom for all. Cf. Ratzinger, *Church, Ecumenism, and Politics*, 3782–90.

56. Nisbet, *Quest for Community*, 4411. To this list should be added "big media." He refers to what he terms the "stifling effects" of the concentration of power not only in political government but also in the private industrial sector. Nisbet sees that both political power and private industrial power have developed together and helped to foster each other's control of society. Nisbet also notes that syndicated labor had also, in his time, become a centralized source of power. He notices that in these areas, as in the areas of university education, charity foundations, and other groups, the pattern of power has been modeled on forms of power of the seventeenth and eighteenth centuries (4577).

57. Tocqueville, *Democracy in America*, vol. 2, sec. 2, chap. 4 "That The Americans Combat The Effects Of Individualism By Free Institutions" (Toronto: Bantam Classics, 2000), 10375.

58. Tocqueville, *Democracy in America*, 10397–404.

59. Jeremy Bentham, *An Introduction to the Principles of Morals and Legislation*, repr. of new ed., corrected by author 1823 (Oxford: Oxford Clarendon Press, 1907), chap. 1 "On the Principle of Utility," 180.

60. Possenti, *Le società liberali al bivio*, 90; my translation.

61. Manent, *Metamorphoses of the City*, 262–63.

62. Simpson, *Political Illiberalism*, 95. Simpson goes on to write that there is a fundamental contrast between the classification of the government of communities, such as Aristotle makes, and which are directed in their varying forms toward an ideal of the common and collective good, and, on the other hand, our concern with the modern form of political states with their rival interests and political compromises. Simpson explains that the ancient philosophers addressed their political concerns to the greater notions of human meaning and purpose in order to shape their political communities accordingly. For the classical philosophers the really important and practical

questions were to do with the greater purposes of human existence rather than the
political clashes and conflicts that seem to dominate our political imagination (148).

John Milbank and Adrian Pabst propose ideas for "The Post-liberal Alternative" in
chapter 2 of *The Politics of Virtue: Post-Liberalism and the Human Future* (Lanham,
MD: Rowman & Littlefield, 2016), 69–90.

63. Ratzinger, "That Which Holds the World Together: The Pre-Political Moral
Foundations of a Free State," in *Europe: Today and Tomorrow*, 82. A. Solzhenitsyn
intimated a similar thought when he wrote that: "In relation to the true ends of human
beings here on earth . . . the state structure is of secondary significance" Solzhenitsyn,
From Under the Rubble, 22.

64. David Bosworth, "Modernity's New World Dangers," in Nisbet, *Quest for
Community*, 4985. As Nisbet wrote: "Belonging, not escape, is the imperative moral
value" (794).

65. Simpson, "Making the Citizens Good," 149–66. Simpson identifies a passage
in Aristotle's *Politics* (1296a32-b2) that "hints" at the role of Philip of Macedonia and
the Macedonian Empire as the type of external empire that would correspond to the
external role of the modern state, leaving the Greek *poleis* free to pursue more essential social purposes (Cf. 165–66, footnote 20). Simpson also refers to the required
change in thinking in terms of the devolution of power, greater emphasis on community rights (not just individual rights) and two kinds of political philosophy, one for
the external role of the "state," the other for the nature of the communities within this
external alliance, with the latter determining the former.

Chapter 8

Law and Society

Government by public authority is expressed and accomplished by Law. As an overview, in this chapter we look at what Law and laws mean, what they actually represent to us today, and their real content, how they should rightly be understood and applied.

There is today a residual respect for Law, which expresses something more than just the sum total of laws or the legal system. In some way, we consider Law as having a certain aura of importance and requiring due respect. At the same time, there is also a growing opposition, even hostility, to laws as unwanted restrictions on human freedom. Ironically, this opposition occurs at a time when governments regulate more and more our personal and social activity.

The first question that arises is to what Law is, what it tries to express. The International Theological Commission proposes that primarily Law responds to a people's "vision of the world as well as their thoughtful perception of the place that man holds in society and the cosmos."[1] I take the Jewish Biblical understanding of Law as an example of what Law means as a positive expression of the social, moral, and religious purposes of a society. This notion of Law contrasts sharply with our contemporary notion as an instrument of public power. It is clear, therefore, that what we consider Law to be depends on the greater notion of what human society is, the nature of interpersonal relations, society's collective purposes, and its vision of what is good and holy.

This leads us, then, to the question of the role of Law in constituting and maintaining society. It seems clear that mere laws and regulations are insufficient to form human society. Society needs more than the measure of justice, and the increasing legal regulation of our society is a sign of the increasing breakdown of social communion. Law only functions properly within a context of friendship, something that was at the origin of Western political thought, as seen, for example in Aristotle's *Nicomachean Ethics*, as a moral preparation for political society.[2] Today we would speak of friendship in personalist terms that would include social communion and participation. This is the essential prerequisite for Law in society.

Laws have both a functional role, and a referential role, in reference to a common vision of society and its purposes and authentic values. Many theoretical explanations of the nature of Law point only to its functional role, while other explanations may include reference to social values as customs or conventions, but not as truth. I propose here that these formal descriptions of Law contradict our spontaneous and intuitive demand that Law reflect truth, goodness, and justice. To consider Law only in its functional role, as an instrument of public power, with no necessary reference to what we know Law should achieve for our social communion, is to distort the nature of Law.

This modern distortion of Law has its particular historical setting. The development of an integrated and systematic body of laws in Western Europe occurs in the eleventh and twelfth centuries with the legal reform of the Church in the context of the struggle for independence from the encroach-ment of civil powers. The Church canonists developed a system of law that was integrated into a theological and philosophical context, where the *lex positiva* [positive law] was an expression of the *ius naturale* [natural law]; humanly made laws were to be an expression of mankind's place in society and in the universe. With the breakup of unity of ecclesiastical and civil authority, and the accompanying separation of theology from philosophy and jurisprudence, Law (*lex*) become much more the authoritative instrument of dominant civil power, rather than the expression of *ius*, the right order of a moral and religious universe. It is this notion of *lex* that prevails today.

These distinctions have serious and practical consequence. Our prevalent notion of Law today leaves us vulnerable to the arbitrary use of public power being vested in legality, and not in truth. Furthermore, our current definition of law only as a functional tool prohibits the real use and role of Law. We have outlawed the moral and religious purposes and content of Law, as an expression of *ius* (what is right) and pre-empted our capacity to express in legal terms the vision of what truly constitutes and protects our society.

LAW AS WE SEE IT TODAY

Law is the means by which the power of public authority is exercised. As such, Law is distinguished from mere rules or procedures that may be applied to any activity or organization. Intuitively, there is a sense of some-thing solemn in this notion of Law. The Law represents the expression of legitimate public authority and is thus vested with an importance because of its binding application to all. This sense of the Law's importance is seen in the formalities of its particular processes, in the specific technical language of laws, in the traditions of the legal and juridical professions, and in the obligatory consequences for the inobservance of laws. Although it is hard to discern today, there remains this residual respect for the Law, distinct from, but implicit, in individual laws, that refers to something more than the sum of all laws and their formalities. Even linguistically, students study Law, and not just laws, and in other languages Law is translated as *"diritto," "derecho." "droit," "Recht,"* implying something more than the collection of distinct laws. To speak of the majesty of the Law today may sound archaic, but only just so. Law refers to something real and compelling for human society.

> Nor can it be denied that—at least in Western societies, although I suspect the phenomenon is more universal—people distinguish between particular laws and that which they call "the law." It is the latter that partakes of a numinous, even a divine character that, like religion, is binding. In everyday language a person who protests what he thinks to be the unfairness or silliness of a particular rule is told, "But that's the law." He may with Mr. Bumble respond that "the law is an ass, an idiot." But it is with respect to "the law" that a particular law or system of laws is declared deficient. While particular rules may be deemed silly or unfair, it is acknowledged that they have an authority that, however wrong in particular application, is derived from "the law."[3]

While all of this may be true, the popular conception of law today is somewhat less majestic. We tend to think of law only as state law, the only real type of law. We also tend to think of law as something primarily restrictive and therefore a curb on our freedom, something like an obstacle we need to find a way around, or through, if the penalties of the law are to be avoided. Law is the price for living in society and should be kept as low as possible. We assume that law has its ultimate origin and legitimacy in the governmental processes of legislation and promulgation, that provide a clear and conclusive standard of legality. On a broader basis, there is a spontaneous attitude of the rejection of law as an imposition on the freedom of expression of the human spirit and a growing justification of the reduction and elimination of laws in reference to the vindication of individual freedom.

Joseph Ratzinger, in an essay titled *"Freedom and Constraint in the Church,"* notices a strange reversal of perspective regarding the role of law in government and society. Previously, law as an instrument of coercion was perceived as something necessary and positive for society; laws had the purpose of protecting personal freedom and society in general by penalizing those who would go against the proper purposes of society. Laws thus protected the personal and common good of all. Today, this perception has changed radically. It seems that laws today are seen as unwanted impositions and an unacceptable burden on freedom. The use of the force of law is therefore seen as an oppressive measure of government, while the use of force against the state becomes justified as a struggle for freedom from oppression.[4]

The freedom to choose becomes the right to choose, an expression of the right to uninhibited human freedom. All law is therefore seen as an unwelcome encroachment on what should be the free and unfettered expression of the human spirit.

A GREATER NOTION OF WHAT LAW IS

Although this perspective on law may well prevail today, it is only one particular perspective of what law is. There is greater context for understanding what public law is. Philosophical reflection shows that there is an order (structure) and purpose to reality, the truth and goodness of which persons are capable, to an extent, of identifying and to which they need to respond adequately and freely if they are to fulfil the aspirations of their social destiny. That part of the order of reality that the human person discovers, experiences, and responds to (adequately or inadequately), is the order of truth on which life in society depends. People's efforts to express that order in human society, their human ordering according to the order of reality is what human law is, the posited—humanly made—attempts to grasp and conform social life according to the shared vision of reality. Here the words "order" and "law" are interchangeable; the primary element of law is an expression of the order or structure of reality, something different and prior to what we today consider law to be. The International Theological Commission (ITC) expresses this interpretation of reality in this way:

> In diverse cultures, people have progressively elaborated and developed traditions of wisdom in which they express and transmit their vision of the world as well as their thoughtful perception of the place that man holds in society and the cosmos. Before all conceptual theorizing, these wisdom traditions, which are often of a religious nature, convey an experience that identifies what favours and what hinders the full blossoming of personal life and the smooth running of social life. They constitute a type of "cultural capital" available in the search for a common wisdom necessary for responding to contemporary ethical challenges.[5]

If this is true, then we have here the original sources of law, Law as order, Law and laws as a reflection of discovered and received personal and social meaning, value, and purpose. This gives us a much broader and more positive understanding of law as an expression of the truth of social and political activity. One such tradition that shows this role of law as an expression of a society's understanding of themselves and of their place in the universe is the Jewish religion. Their term for law, "*halakhah*" came from the root "*halkhah*" meaning "to go," giving to law the sense of a path to fulfilment and prosperity. Over time, *halakhah* referred not just to a particular law or legal decision, but to the entirety of the Jewish content and procedure of Law. Their *halakhah* applied to every aspect of life, personal, social, and national, and in the dealings with other nations, in the religious context of the collective response to God.[6]

As Biblical exegete Jean Louise Ska points out:

> What, then, is the function of the collections of laws attributed to Moses in the Pentateuch? A first text taken from the book of Proverbs provides an answer to this question (Pro 6:23): "For the bidding is a lamp, and the teaching (the Torah) a light, and a way to life are the reproofs of discipline." According to this text, the first task of the precepts is to point out the "way to life." The task is pedagogic, educational. We are in the world of wisdom more than a reference to the juridical world. The "law" (Torah in Hebrew) is a light. Let us not forget that the Hebrew word "Torah" can be translated by "teaching," by "instruction."[7]

What is interesting here is not only the understanding of Law as a way or path to fulfilment, but also the context of Law as applying to all aspects of one's life, giving both personal and social living an integrated expression of meaning. While there is an area of law that applies to what we would call civil and political issues, this area was viewed within the greater context of the moral and religious purpose of life. It goes without saying that not only did moral and religious considerations give meaning to the legal prescriptions, but also personal and collective moral and religious actions were also to be expressed and channeled according to the light of the Law.

Also, Law was something originally given, not made; rabbinic traditions and applications were always in reference to the given source of Law. Law was fundamentally sacred because it had its origin in God.

> The Bible avoids representing the king as legislator. The one lawgiver is God. That idea was an unparalleled novelty in the ancient Middle East, where only the king made law. The Torah has no real parallel in those ancient civilizations. The God of Israel replaces the oriental king in the role of lawgiver. Hence the predicates attributed to the pharaoh in Egypt are reserved for God alone in Israel. In Israel the Torah replaces the king. It replaces the word endowed with authority of the Oriental king, the king whose word has force of law. To repeat a felicitous expression of Aleida Assmann, we see here an "excarnation" of the law.[8]

This also meant that the human role in reference to the given law was one of interpretation and application, not invention. This could and did lead to differences, as in the case of the tradition of the Pharisees, who seem to have wanted to apply the priestly legal provisions of Leviticus to all Jews, and thus make priests of all Israelites (Exodus 19:6, RSV) and every meal a ritual Temple meal, and the Pharisees were therefore open to the criticism of exaggerating ritual observance at the cost of the greater precepts of the Law.[9] It seems also that the Pharisees appealed not only to the Scriptures but also to the authority of their forefathers[10] (presumably as venerated interpreters of God's Law), which led to the charge of substituting God's Law for man-made traditions.[11] Even so, the Lord God, his creation and his Law, was the intentional source of this religious law that applied to all areas of Israelite life.[12]

One can also see in the detailed prescriptions of the Law that applied also to such mundane matters as eating and dress, the human religious need to give practical expression to the Jewish vision of the meaning and purpose of the world and their place and response within it.

All of this clearly demonstrates the fundamental differences of meaning contained in the word "Law" and the clear difference between Law as an expression of the meaning of the world and the human person's place and purpose in it, according to various historical and cultural forms, and, in contrast, "law" as we assume it to be today, as an exercise of political power legitimated by procedural rules of recognition. The ambit of law is also much different. It seems that today law may legitimately be applied only to very circumscribed aspects of social relations. What also seems to dominate today is the notion of constraint in law, a primarily negative and minimal understanding of the role of law to what is not legally permitted, outside of which there is no valid application of law. Central to the modern notion of law is the idea of the sovereign lawgiver, that it is the state, through its procedural mechanisms, that has, at least in principle, absolute lawgiving power:

> So also State-Power, so soon as it became conscious of its own existence, began to strive for a similar emancipation from the fetters of the Law. . . . Almost unanimously medieval Publicists are agreed that the State is based on no foundation of mere Law, but upon moral and natural necessity: that the realization of Law is but one of the appropriate means to this end: and that the State's relation to Law is not merely subservient and receptive, but is creative and dominant.[13]

While this notion of the absolute state's dominance over law was subsequently modified in its forms by the development of parliaments, doctrines of the division of government powers expressed in Constitutions, and so on, the fundamental dominance of public power over law remains. The law's domain and justification are an expression of, and determined by, the sovereign political power.

It was this political dominance expressed through legislation that caused the Italian political philosopher Bruno Leoni to fear for individual freedom in the face of this ubiquitous political power of legislation:

> Legislation appears today to be a quick, rational, and far-reaching remedy against every kind of evil or inconvenience, as compared with, say, judicial decisions, the settlement of disputes by private arbiters, conventions, customs, and similar kinds of spontaneous adjustments on the part of individuals. A fact that almost always goes unnoticed is that a remedy by way of legislation may be too quick to be efficacious, too unpredictably far-reaching to be wholly beneficial, and too directly connected with the contingent views and interests of a handful of people (the legislators), whoever they may be, to be, in fact, a remedy for all concerned.[14]

In summary, what is important to realize is that this modern notion of law contains a series of presumed notions about man, human society, moral and religious truth. Our contemporary public and political context are contingent on these current notions of people and society, and necessarily include a reductive and distorted notion of what Law is. What this means is that the framing of so many of our public issues to do with Law, such as law and morality, Church and State, human rights, the very notion of what law is, and the role of the lawgiver, needs to be reconfigured, to avoid merely staying within and assuming an impoverished modern notion of law.

Harvard Law Professor Harold J. Berman, in *Faith and Order: The Reconciliation of Law and Religion*, recognized this impoverished contemporary notion of law and audaciously associated what he saw to be a crisis of identity of law with a crisis of confidence in religion. Berman claims that the present-day skepticism toward institutional religion and toward the formality of law and its institutions are a sign of a deeper cultural malaise, that is, the loss of the transcendent meaning and purpose of our existence, and the loss of an adequate response to such a greater purpose. Consequently, we trust less, and are less committed to, institutions and structures that promote social cohesion and harmony. Berman observes that this skepticism towards the moral and religious realities that were the foundation of our cultural existence leaves us exposed to the meaningless of death as the endpoint of our existence.[15]

So, what is Law? It seems here, given the historical changes of the concept of Law and the premises these very different concepts presuppose, that contemporary language can express better both what is valid in our current notions and what is missing. The contemporary writer Richard John Neuhaus offers this description:

> The law is more than a body of rules; it is the historical, living process of people legislating, adjudicating, administering, and negotiating the allocation of rights and duties. Its purpose is to prevent harm, resolve conflicts, and create means of cooperation. Its premises, from which it derives its perceived legitimacy and therefore its authority, is that it strives to anticipate and give expression to what a people believes to be its collective destiny or ultimate meaning within a moral universe.[16]

The first lines of Neuhaus's description point to the practical functions of law in society, the particular utility role that laws fulfill in human society. The last lines of this description express the necessary source of law from which the ultimate authority of and respect for law is derived, the various wisdom traditions of cultures that contain a moral and religious vision of collective meaning and purpose. Both dimensions of law are vital. On the one hand, the proper system of legal procedure—what is called "the rule of law"—with its necessary institutions and processes, is a prerequisite for social stability, economic growth, and the functioning of society. New Zealand professor of law and philosophy Jeremy Waldron has emphasized this procedural dimension of politics and law, what he calls *political* political theory, "theory addressing itself to politics and to the way our political institutions house and frame our disagreements about our social ideals and orchestrate what is done about whatever aims we can settle on."[17] On the other hand, law is not to be reduced to its legal procedures, but is to contain and be guided by a necessary vision of the real collective vision and purpose of society. In fact, the type of institutions and processes will depend ultimately on this collective vision and purpose—or its absence.

Given both this function and this purpose of law, we now ask how Law should contribute to the formation of human society.

THE ROLE OF LAW IN SOCIETY

In our contemporary view of law and freedom as opposing forces, with the rising affirmation of individual freedom and the consequent opposition to law as an unwanted restriction on the self-affirmation of freedom, a necessary consequence follows. The more freedom from societal restraint is asserted, the more law is required to guarantee the requirements of social living. The difficulty with this is that while laws serve a necessary purpose in society to "prevent harm, resolve conflicts and create means of cooperation," laws are only very blunt instruments of the social bond. They are a necessary but not sufficient condition of social and political life. The growing legalism in our social relations is a sign of the growing break-down of the spontaneous and vital social bonds that then have to be substituted by legal obligations that can never adequately replace necessary social communion.

Irish writer John Waters noticed the contrast between the human response of care in a hospital and the substitute legal form of regulations and paperwork:

> Once you prohibit the person at the cutting edge of the ministering activity (in this case, nursing in a hospital) from being totally and uninhibitedly herself, you create conditions where authentic human contact ceases, and you're a short step from patients getting beaten up by their "carers." Regulation is necessary, yes, but the current obsession with developing perfect systems and protocols invites a creeping dehumanisation because it removes the possibility of a true encounter.[18]

Waters goes on to state that because excessive regulations do not permit the helper to be fully himself or herself, this enforced lack of personal encounter will probably produce much worse abuses, arising from a totally dehumanized social and medical service. Systems of excessive regulation cause both the helper and the person dependent on personal care to suffer a loss of their humanity. Anyone who has been in hospital knows the personal need for much more than just charts, analyses, and protocols. The impersonal following of regulations leaves the patient in anonymity, precisely when he or she needs to experience the presence and reassurance of another person.

For whatever justifications—and, of course, a minimum of regulation is often necessary—whether to provide perfect systems of safety, or to substitute for the break-down or lack of spontaneous social relations such as in the family, or in community friendships, laws reduce human relations to the obligation of fulfilling legal requirements and expose persons to the risk of legal responsibility for anything above and beyond what is legally stipulated.

In his well-known *Harvard Commencement Address*, Aleksandr Solzhenitsyn pointed to this defect in Western society:

> I have spent all my life under a Communist regime, and I will tell you that a society without any objective legal scale is a terrible one indeed. But a society with no other scale than the legal one is not quite worthy of man either. A society which is based on the letter of the law and never reaches any higher is taking very scarce advantage of the high level of human possibilities. The letter of the law is too cold and formal to have a beneficial influence on society. Whenever the tissue of life is woven of legalistic relations, there is an atmosphere of moral mediocrity, paralyzing man's noblest impulses. And it will be simply impossible

to stand through the trials of this threatening century with only the support of a legalistic structure.[19]

What Solzhenitsyn is criticizing here is not the role of law itself, but the substitution of the personal response for a set of legal regulations and the accompanying mentality that considers that one's responsibilities have ended in the fulfilment of such regulations.[20]

The fundamental point here is not precisely the limit of law as an instrument of social cohesion and unity, but its radical dependence on an adequate personal response to others for law to function at all. In other words, as David Walsh writes, Law, and laws, require the context and motivation of "the free response to transcendent goodness, undertaken in the full awareness of the direction and validity pursued, (which) could be counted as the properly human mode of fulfilment."[21]

What this means for law is that:

> Law is, despite all the appearances of self-containment, not a realm apart from the whole of existence. It is rather a moment within the dynamic that contains the whole life of a human being and cannot be properly understood without that gift of self as the infinite possibility of the person.[22]

What is at the basis of political society, therefore, is not the type or structure of the laws we have, but the nature and quality of the interpersonal relation on which Law depends and to which the fulfilment of laws should draw us. What constitutes and sustains human society is the communion of friendship among people. While this may sound naïve or impractical today, the notion of friendship has been at the heart of classical and medieval political philosophy. Professor of Political Science Horst Hutter has written that:

> Western political speculation finds its origin in a system of thought in which the idea of friendship is the major principle in terms of which political theory and practice are described, explained, and analysed.[23]

We may suppose today that the central notions of political society are justice and equality, and while these moral realities are fundamental to social cohesion, they are not sufficient. More is required of persons to live humanly in society, more is needed by persons than the mere standard of justice, and both natural and intentional human inequalities necessarily require unequal provision. Neither can the political authority respond to all the needs and requirements of a vast number of people, even if only on a material basis. The social communion of unequal persons who have fundamental needs that go beyond what are the strict obligations of others to give, necessarily require a much greater personal response than justice and equality, if a human society is to be formed and sustained. As Josef Pieper comments:

> Communal life will necessarily become inhuman if man's dues to man are determined by pure calculation. That the just man gives to another what is not due to him is particularly important since injustice is the prevailing condition in our world. Because men must do without things that are due to them (since others are withholding them unjustly); since human need and want persist even though no specific person fails to fulfil his obligation, and even though no binding obligation can be construed for anyone; for these very reasons it is not "just and right" for the just man to restrict himself to rendering only what is strictly due. For it is true, as Thomas (Aquinas) says, that "mercy without justice is the mother of dissolution"; but, also, that "justice without mercy is cruelty."[24]

In contemporary personalist terms, the communion of persons based on a metaphysics of love is the only adequate foundation of human society.

The modern notions of a contractual relation between the individual and the state, the expression of individual rights, the handing over of social responsibility to representative government, and the consequent dependence on a government that is to produce welfare for all, all these considerations tend to obscure the real conditions of persons in society and the adequate personal response to the needs and requirements of others that correspond to each person *in love* even though not *in justice*.[25]

> Justice and law are indispensable requisites, but they do not suffice. Society cannot exist without the perpetual gift and the perpetual surplus which derive from persons, without the wellsprings of generosity hidden in the very depths of the life and liberty of persons, and which love causes to flow forth.[26]

This may clarify the essential role of friendship in politics, not as something utopian but as the only adequate social response. In personalist philosophy one speaks in terms of inter-personal communion, participation, affirmation, relation, and authentic intersubjectivity. Martin Buber summarized this social condition and demand of human existence: "It is from one man to another that the heavenly bread of self-being is passed."[27] This is also politically true and politically necessary, and it is what needs to imbue the authentic spirit of the Law, without which all laws are dead letters.

Aristotle, in his *Nicomachean Ethics*, as an introduction to *Politics*, outlines the type of person on whom the *polis* depends, the virtues of the political person, something we seem to have lost sight of (our universal suffrage supposes the automatic qualification of all people of a minimum age to an equal political opinion and action).[28] Robert Sokolowski notices in

Aristotle's *Nicomachean Ethics* a threefold development of the politically virtuous person:

> Aristotle's description of the moral virtues in the Nicomachean Ethics is developed in a logical progression. His analysis, as it moves along, reaches three successive summits or crests, each higher than the previous one. (1) The first crest is the treatment of the virtue of pride or magnanimity, megalopsychia, in book 4, chapter 3. Magnanimity is the completion of what we could call our "internal" or "individual" virtues, such as courage, temperance, and generosity . . . (2) The second high point in Aristotle's treatment of moral virtue is found in the discussion of justice in book 5. Justice goes beyond the virtues treated in the earlier books because it deals with our relationships with other people and not just the control we have over ourselves and our impulses . . . (3) We might think that the treatment of justice is the culmination of Aristotle's discussion of moral excellence. . . . But there is still another crest to be reached beyond justice in the study of moral virtue. It is reached in books 8 and 9 of the Nicomachean Ethics, which discusses friendship. Friendship should not be taken as a mere appendix to ethics; it completes justice and the other moral virtues.[29]

Sokolowski quotes Aristotle on the political importance of friendship:

> Friendship seems to hold cities together, and lawgivers seem to care for it more than for justice; for concord is like friendship, and this they aim at most of all . . . and when men are friends, they have no need of justice, while when they are just they need friendship as well.[30]

Again, in contemporary personalist terms, friendship is translated in terms of interpersonal communion based on a profound experience of "the other" (and "the Other") that elicits from me the response of affirmation of the other as the only adequate response, and which is also the path of my own fulfillment, the person I am called to be.

Talk of friendship or interpersonal communion may sound far-fetched in politics today. The model of some type of social contract dominates the political framework of discussion of political relations and the consequent social measures of justice, equality, and fairness. It may sound quaint to speak of friendship in political terms—it certainly implies a different understanding of the human person and human relations than the assumed individualism of contract theory. And yet the attempt to found a political state on a society based merely on equality and justice has been seen to be fundamentally inadequate. Authors John Von Heyking and Richard Avramenko note in contemporary Muslim literature the theme of loneliness and the isolation of Muslims living in liberal societies. The authors also quote from Marc Sageman's *Understanding Terrorist Networks* as to the profound motivations of recruitment to jihadist groups: "Relative deprivation, religious predisposition, and ideological appeal are necessary but not sufficient to account for the decision to become a mujahed. Social bonds are the critical element in this process and precede ideological commitment."[31]

This essential social basis of interpersonal communion founded on a common vision of meaning and purpose is not just a favorable addition to the rule of Law but is an essential requirement for the role and functioning of Law itself.[32] Even for the minimum requirements of social justice and equality, laws presuppose a general context of cooperation, loyalty, civic observance, tolerance, and reconciliation, all of which cannot be expressed or demanded by laws but are essential for laws to function. The contemporary demand that laws and lawsuits resolve all our needs and conflicts, even among family members, is a clear sign that the social bond is eroding and that the law is being required to oblige and regulate what can only come from spontaneous social communion—an impossible task.

THE CHARACTER OF LAW

One of the principal difficulties in realizing what Law and laws are today is that we have already assumed a certain understanding of Law and interpret the various schools of jurisprudential meaning according to our already accepted premises of thought. Law is something we make, posited by us; we are the lawgivers, and we decide the terms of the laws according to our common (or majoritarian) agreement. This perspective of Law is encased in a political framework of social contract, individual human freedom, and a minimum requirement of social responsibility founded on the handing over of social responsibility through representation, and, additionally, the accepted impossibility of finding common purposes and meanings above a necessary minimum.

Seen in this light, law takes on a series of familiar possible descriptions; the original formula of Thomas Hobbes, *auctoritas* (understood as political power), *non veritas facit legem*[33], taken up by Jeremy Bentham and his disciple John Austin. What was fundamentally characteristic of law, for Austin, was its commanding nature: "Every law or rule (taken with the largest signification which can be given to the term properly) is a command. Or rather, laws and rules, properly so called are a species of commands."[34] In this sense the obligatory characteristic of law by the legitimate political authority is what defines law.

Other descriptive analyses of what law is are based on the identification of the procedural structure of law as a system. The Austrian legal philosopher

Hans Kelsen's attempt to describe "pure" law was in order to free descriptions of law from what he considered to be elements of other sciences or political ideologies:

> It is called "pure" because it seeks to preclude from the cognition of positive law all elements foreign thereto. The limits of this subject and its cognition must be clearly fixed in two directions: the specific science of law, the discipline usually called jurisprudence, must be distinguished from the philosophy of justice, on the one hand, and from sociology, or cognition of social reality, on the other.[35]

What Kelsen searches for is the formal description of systems of laws, the specific nature of the external form and hierarchical structure of positive laws, the formal validity of laws as ultimately depending on a foundational basic norm.[36]

Another positivist approach, with important differences, is the linguistic analysis of the Oxford professor of jurisprudence H. L. A. Hart, summarized in his *The Concept of Law* (1961). Using the analysis of the use of words in given contexts, in this case legal discourse, an approach brought to Oxford and Cambridge by Ludwig Wittgenstein, Hart describes the conventional understanding of law in terms of primary and secondary rules, with the difference between them as follows:

> Under rules of the one type, which may well be considered the basic or primary type, human beings are required to do or abstain from certain actions, whether they wish to or not. Rules of the other type are in a sense parasitic upon or secondary to the first; for they provide that human beings may by doing or saying certain things introduce new rules of the primary type, extinguish or modify old ones, or in various ways determine their incidence or control their operations. Rules of the first type impose duties; rules of the second type confer powers, public or private. Rules of the first type concern actions involving physical movement or changes; rules of the second type provide for operations which lead not merely to physical movement or change, but the creation or variation of duties or obligations.[37]

For Hart, the ultimate justification of these secondary rules is social construction, how a concept of law is constructed from social life. Hart himself described his work as "an essay in descriptive sociology."[38]

> Law is a social construction. It is an historically contingent feature of certain societies, one whose emergence is signalled by the rise of a systematic form of social control administered by institutions. . . . In one way law supersedes custom, in another it rests on it, for law is a system of primary rules that direct and appraise conduct together with secondary rules about how to identify, enforce, and change the primary rules. . . . There can be no "pure" theory of

law: jurisprudence built only using concepts drawn from the law itself is inadequate to understand law's nature; it needs the help of resources from social theory and philosophic inquiry . . . (Jurisprudence) is but one part of a more general political theory.[39]

While Hart thus recognizes the influence of a given social morality on the foundation and development of a system of law, he is unwilling to accept that, among the various social and moral customs there is a moral or religious vision that must sustain any given set of social customs that are the foundation of a legal system. While he acknowledges the real influence on law of conventional morality and individual advocates of morality that are above the conventional standard of morality:

> It is possible to take this truth illicitly, as a warrant for a different proposition: namely that a legal system must exhibit some specific conformity with morality or justice, or must rest on a widely diffused conviction that there is a moral obligation to obey it. Again, though this proposition may, in some sense, be true, it does not follow from it that the criteria of legal validity of particular laws used in a legal system must include, tacitly if not explicitly, a reference to morality or justice.[40]

In *Faith and Order*, Berman observes that this conventional approach to values in a legal system—laws as having their origin as expressions of relative social customs and conventions and yet not expressive of any real social truths—is strongly influenced by Max Weber's sociological approach, which distinguishes between facts and values. According to Weber, facts do not have moral meaning, purpose, or moral content; the moral values that are ascribed to them have their origin in those who observe and describe these facts, and such moral values are dependent on nothing more than the arbitrary choice of those who choose to impute moral values into mere facts.[41]

As for legal theory, Berman states that, given Weber's sociological separation of facts and values, the study of law should be something value-free, without attributing normative value to the expression of such laws. Therefore, the study of jurisprudence should abstain from the consideration of the moral content of such laws, because such moral content is not factual, not part of law's content, but merely the particular views of those who make or apply laws. As these views have no basis in fact, according to Weber, they are not part of the factual description of law.[42]

A more pragmatic approach to law is to be found in legal "realism," the belief that, as the American Supreme Court Justice O. W. Holmes said, "The life of the law has not been logic, it has been experience."[43] At the basis of this view is that much of law is contingent on its historical context; when that context changes, law takes on the meaning and purpose of the new context.

What counts is the practice of law, what actually happens. In an extreme view, this pragmatic view of law "is not a philosophy, but a technology. . . . What realism was, and is, is a method nothing more."[44]

What is generally common to the different methods and philosophies of law today is the assumption that law is always and only made ("posited") and justified, whether by the recognition of formal procedures of validation, or by reflecting the social practice at any given time. Laws are human constructions of public authority and relative to the particular rules of recognition and/or the social acceptance of time and place. They are, therefore, always malleable, depending on the prevailing opinions of the lawgivers. Almost always, it is the particular formal or procedural aspect of law that justifies the authority of law.

This understanding of the justification of law as always and only posited, and the assumption that law can, in the last analysis, only be justified by external rules of recognition, leaves law on very fragile foundations. Even appeal to "equality" and "respect," such as the American legal philosopher Ronald Dworkin introduces, are understood in terms of the formal respect for self-interest and personal freedom, with little other content.[45]

It is not surprising, therefore, that notions such as truth, moral goodness, substantive justice find no place in most contemporary philosophies of law and are alien to our assumed understanding of what law is, at least in theory. In practice, that is, in our spontaneous experience of life, such pared down notions of law do not correspond to reality. Consider the case of the Hillsborough tragedy, at a football ground in Sheffield in the north of England in 1989. As it was eventually shown, the incompetence and lack of preparation by the police officer in command led to many supporters being sent into the same small area of one of the stands. The result was that a total of ninety-seven people were crushed to death and 766 injured. To avoid blame, the police said that many of the spectators were drunk and therefore responsible for their own deaths. The coroner's initial report said that the supporters' death was accidental. The families of the deceased never accepted this verdict and after many legal struggles, twenty-seven years later, in 2016, the second coroner's report concluded that the police authorities had been grossly negligent in their responsibility and that this was the reason for the unlawful deaths and injuries. The families, finally vindicated, put a huge banner on the front of the city hall in Liverpool that had two words: "Truth" and "Justice."[46]

What this tragic example shows is the spontaneous association of law and legal process with innate standards of truth and justice. We know spontaneously that an unjust law is no law, just as an unjust legal process is no real legal process at all. What this implies is that truth, moral goodness and justice are in some way bound up with what laws are supposed to be and to achieve and protect. It is hard to maintain theories of law that rely only on formality or only on social construction in the face of such spontaneous real experience to the contrary. In this case, it is precisely the external formality of law and the legal process that is shown to be vastly inadequate to the working of justice that is rightly presupposed in law and its processes.[47]

It would also be almost offensive to dismiss such moral experience as only conventional, of a particular group of persons of a given time and place, and that supposedly could be the opposite, in another time and place.

So, what has happened? Why do our definitions of law, as clear and logical as they are expressed, seem to omit, or even contradict, the spontaneous experience of justice and truth as essential characteristics of what law should necessarily express? It appears that the notion of law assumed by the various schools of philosophy is of one particular type, man-made positive law, with its distinctive procedures, rules of recognition, and formalities. While conventional morality is seen as an origin of positive law it is not constitutive of law. There is a separation of law and morality; law contains consensus, formality, authority and establishes fairness, the stability of due process and regulation, and the notion of equality before the law. These are all important and necessary benefits of a legal system for society, and yet, in the face of the experience of some substantive social values, this description of law seems to fall short. Instead of delimiting our experience of moral value to a description of law that is essentially morally valueless (although, as a social construction, it often contains given moral values), we should perhaps reverse the thought process, and allow our moral and religious experience to determine what and how our posited laws should be, both as to content and form.

What I am suggesting is that the necessary greater context of posited law has been lost from contemporary view. Man-made law is not fundamentally best explained and described by what we propose in our legislatures, but is, in the last analysis, a response to a given moral and religious universe, that is the given context for our spontaneous judgments of truth and justice. Claims of truth and justice are not just claims of things we want to be, or even that we have decided are to be a certain way, but recognitions of relations that *should* be, irrespective of how such relations are, or how some or even many would want them to be. This, I suggest, is at the back of our minds when we appeal to the truth and justice of laws. This means that we do not arrive to our legislatures to make laws as if they were open contractual agreements made for all interested and represented parties; there is already in our minds an experience of reality to which our posited laws need to conform if they are to be true expressions of what social relations are and should be.

This is not to say, of course, that the human experience of moral truth is something facile and obvious. It certainly can be, as it was for the families of the Hillsborough tragedy, but there are also at times personal and social obstacles to the recognition of fundamental truths vital for the welfare of society. This curious condition of moral blindness makes moral truth harder to discern.

We have here two meanings of law; the current notion of law as a formal and functional instrument of authority, and a more profound notion of law as a response to the given order or structure of reality as we experience it.

LAW AS AN APPROXIMATE REFLECTION
OF TRUTH AND GOODNESS

Berman considers our current notion of law to be insufficient for the purposes we require of law; "for as it now presents itself, shorn of its mystique and its authority and its role in the grand design of the universe, is too weak a reed to support the demands we place upon it."[48]

In classical philosophical thought the consciousness that law was more than what someone (be that an emperor, a democratic majority, as in the case with Socrates, or a representative legislative assembly) decided it would be. At the origin of all cultures the traditions, customs and laws of the people were of divine origin.[49] What is distinctive of the Greek enlightenment is the recognition of *logos*, a divine order of reason partly accessible to human minds, within the religious context. Heraclitus wrote that "They who would speak with intelligence must hold fast to the (wisdom that is) common to all, as a city holds fast to its law, and even more strongly. For all human laws are fed by one divine law."[50]

While the development of this *logos* is at the foundation of the thought of Plato and Aristotle, it is in its Stoic development that this divine reason accessible to human reason—what was termed *ius naturale*—flourished and was given juridical effect in Rome:

> For Gaius, Paulus, and Marcian, the *ius naturae* is a norm which from the very beginning lies forever imbedded in the nature of things; since it also reveals itself in things, it can be discovered in them. The Stoic idea of an eternal law of the order of the universe was present to their minds. This law emanates from the logos, which in turn is itself the law of things. The logos, moreover, expresses itself conceptually in the nature of things, and it destines them for harmony with the universe.[51]

What is clear from this long tradition of law is the discovery of a perceptible, given moral order or structure which the laws and customs of society reflect. While the historical cultural context of this meaning of law is predominantly religious, the perception of order or structure is a shared human capability through the light of the intellect. This is what is at the basis of the instinctual experience of notions of justice, dignity, truth, and moral value. This insight developed historically within a greater religious context while, at the same time, this insight was humanly recognizable through what is humanly knowable.

The radically different notion of what we understand law to be today in our Western legal systems is indicative of a radical historical change in the understanding of the origin and notion of law. Identifying this change helps elucidate the emaciated notion of what we consider law to be today. From a political and legal perspective, the modern transformation of the nature of what law is extends from before the eleventh century, to what Berman calls the Papal Revolution, with the codification of Church Canon Law, and from there to the so-called wars of religion with the rise of modern sovereign states, and to the development of Enlightenment philosophies.

As Berman explains in *Faith and Order*, and with particular reference to Germanic Europe, before the Papal Revolution of the eleventh and twelfth centuries, the law was not as we tend to think and find it today, that is, a distinct and codified corpus of laws and rules, which a specific technical language and with skilled professional practitioners of this legal science. Instead, law was considered an integral part of the culture and customs of the peoples of Europe, so much so that laws and legal decisions formed part of the whole cultural vision of the people and their sense of the value and meaning of life and of reality. This was the vital cultural context from which laws, legal decisions, and institutions originated and of which they formed an integral part.[52]

Christianity and the Church initially lived within these multiple feudal and tribal customary laws and ways of living. The legal reform of the Church began with the monastic orders and their regulated ways of life, and came to a dramatic climax with the Investiture controversy of 1075–1122, starting with Pope Gregory VII and ending officially with the agreement of the Concordat of Worms of 1122.

As Berman explains, this Papal Revolution had the effect of making clergy independent of the other various jurisdictional authorities of empires, kingdoms, and feudal lords, and thus constructing in Western Europe an independent and solid papal monarchy. This development spurred the renewed interest in Roman Law and the discovery of the Justinian Code, as also the study of the science of law, as witnessed by the first European university, at Bologna, to do so. The Papal Revolution also necessarily created separate civil and ecclesiastical jurisdictions and institutions. In Berman's view, the Church was thus the first model of the modern state, which depended on this new legal system to organize its internal affairs and its relations with the newly forming secular powers. Theses secular powers also needed similar legal systems for the management of their secular affairs.[53]

Chief among these new integrated systems of law was the *Decretum Gratiani*, "the first comprehensive legal treatise, the first systematic analysis of an entire body of law, ever written."[54] This systematic development of law occurred within the particular intellectual climate of Scholasticism that integrated into an organic whole the major academic sciences:

> It was the remarkable achievement of the European schoolmen of the late eleventh and twelfth centuries to have combined, for the first time, these three diverse and even mutually antagonistic outlooks—the Hebrew, the Greek, and the Roman—and to have founded on that combination the modern Western disciplines of theology, philosophy, jurisprudence, and political science. Only in the seventeenth century did the latter three disciplines break off from theology, and only in the nineteenth and twentieth centuries did they break off from each other.[55]

In jurisprudence, the importance of Gratian's code, with the work of many other canonists, is that not only does it draw on the philosophical insights of Greece and Rome, but that this vision of a greater given context of reality is given expression in terms of law as a practical instrument of social formation. The pre-existing basis of local custom were now to be subject to legal conditions of reasonableness and conscience. This was, as Berman comments, one of the greatest achievements of the canonists.[56]

Gratian brought together in an ordered and relational way the different types and categories of law. As Berman notes:

> Gratian was the first to explore systematically the legal implications of these distinctions and to arrange the various sources of law in a hierarchical order. He started by interposing the concept of natural law between the concepts of divine law and human law. Divine law is the will of God reflected in revelation, especially the revelation of Holy Scripture. Natural law also reflects God's will; however, it is found both in divine revelation and in human reason and conscience. From this Gratian could conclude that "the laws (leges) of princes (that is, of the secular authorities) ought not to prevail over natural law (ius naturale)." Likewise, ecclesiastical "laws" may not contravene natural "law."[57]

Significantly, Gratian distinguishes between *ius* and *lex*, and refers to the *ius naturale* as the source and maximum expression of what individual *leges* should convey. "Ius is the genus, lex is a species of it."[58] While this terminological distinction between *ius* and *lex* was used less in theological writings, the canonists' distinction between the two terms clarifies well the necessary greater context of *ius*, to which all laws need to correspond; *lex* is not something sufficient of itself.[59]

This context and relation between *ius naturale* and *lex positiva* were to change dramatically in the centuries that followed. The appropriation by civil authorities of sovereign power over positive law (*ius civile*) brought a radical change to the notion of *lex civile*:

> This doctrine . . . taught that the *Ius Civile* was the freely created product of the Power of a Community, an instrument mutable in accordance with estimates of utility, a set of rules that had no force of their own. It followed that in every Community the wielder of Sovereignty stood above the positive law that prevailed therein, Nay, always more decisively, men found the distinguishing note of Sovereignty, ecclesiastical or temporal, in the fact that the Sovereign was not bound by any human law.[60]

Another radical change was the break-up of the religious unity of Europe and the need to find sources of social unity other than religious ones. Both the Lutheran Reformation of the sixteenth century in Germany and the Calvinist inspired English Puritans of the seventeenth century brought with their distinct theological doctrines profound consequences for the understanding of law, secular authority, the shift from the doctrine of two swords of authority within a single jurisdiction to two kingdoms of jurisdiction with the consequent separation of civil and religious powers, mostly at the expense of religious and ecclesiastical authority. Most profoundly there is the rupture of the relation between law (*lex*) as an expression of order (*ius*). Law becomes much more the authoritative instrument of dominant secular power, rather than an expression of *ius*, right order as a part of a moral and religious universe.[61]

Subsequent doctrines of epistemological empiricism and materialism, rationalist restrictions on the scope and capacity of the human intellect, and mental subjectivism as an expression of man's incapacity to perceive reality, have all influenced the role and content of law (*lex*) cut off from its source (*ius*), to be described and defined in positivist terms of its own external form or social conventions and constructions.

It is also understandable that to speak of *ius naturale* as an essential content of a particular law (*lex*) is tantamount to putting new wine into old wineskins; our understanding of law has become too limited to allow for law's greater context within a moral and religious reality. There is, of course, a recognizable functionality of our legal systems that resolves practical and procedural issues, but what we are confronted with is a generally diffused notion of law that is inadequate for its social purpose, a notion of *lex* that is distorted and disfigured because it is cut off from its source (*ius*) in reality. Ratzinger recognizes our difficulty in recognizing the reality of *lex (ius) naturalis*:

The capacity to see the laws of material being makes us incapable of seeing the ethical message contained in being, a message that tradition calls *lex naturalis*, natural moral law. This word for many today is almost incomprehensible due to a concept of nature that is no longer metaphysical, but only empirical. The fact that nature, being itself, is no longer a transparent moral message creates a sense of disorientation that renders the choices of daily life precarious and uncertain.[62]

Our laws are equally precarious and uncertain.

In summary, Berman proposes that "the primary cause of the crisis of the Western legal tradition is the disintegration of its religious foundations."[63] He distinguishes between the *structure* of the Western legal tradition and the *foundation* of that structure:

> The structure of the Western legal tradition, during its formative era, was its division between secular and spiritual authorities, the one chiefly responsible for order and justice, the other chiefly responsible for faith and morals, and the consequent proliferation of diverse autonomous bodies of law as a means of maintaining the jurisdiction of each and the equilibrium between the two. The foundation of that structure was an entirely different concept and an entirely different experience, namely the integration of law and religion, of order and justice with faith and morals, in an integrated community which transcended both.[64]

This is not just a theoretical problem. Law and laws have a limited but vital social and political role; how one understands law and legal process determines how society will be shaped by laws, what justification is offered for law, and, most importantly, what its content should be. One of the classic expositors of the real depth and context of law was the practicing German lawyer Heinrich A. Rommen (1897–1967), also a prisoner in Nazi Germany. Rommen saw with what ease Hitler exploited legal institutions to sweep to power. Rommen observed that "Our modern dictators are masters of legality."[65]

This serves as a warning and as a recommendation to look beyond the formal legality of our laws to the necessary moral and religious vision that should sustain and be embodied by laws.

CONCLUSION

We see therefore that law can be spoken about in very different ways, depending on the premises of thought one starts from. It is not surprising today to see the growing disrespect for legal institutions, processes, and for laws themselves, when, in reality, they express and are used only as instruments of the political power of the day, and not as an approximate expression of the shared truth of human society that can be recognized, appreciated, and reflected in public laws that have the vital role of sustaining and protecting the collective vision of society. It was this vital role of law in society that was so important to Thomas More, the first lay Lord Chancellor of England. American judge Robert H. Bork emphasizes that, for Thomas More, obedience to the Law was vital:

> Law and its institutions were, of course, major forces of cohesion in More's age, and are perhaps the primary symbols in ours of stability and continuity as well as justice. When moral consensus fades, as it did in More's time and does in ours, we turn to law; when law falters, as it must when morality is no longer widely shared, society and culture teeter on the brink of chaos.[66]

Law and laws express the collective vision of human society, of what forms and sustains social and political life, and it is this necessary purpose that is at the heart of the veneration for Law as a function of society. The artificial abstraction of the form of law from its collective social origin and purpose is to distort the meaning of law into some empty shell to be abused by forms of public power. Bork continues:

> That is another way of saying that law cannot be divorced from morality—and, there is reason to think, morality, at least in the long run, cannot be divorced from religion. Law and religion are alike, therefore, as reinforcements of social order. It is a subject for speculation at least, whether either can long remain healthy and self-confident without the other. Each imposes obligations, but each is subject to the therapeutic heresy, softening those obligations to accommodate individual desires. It is a sign of our distemper that Thomas More is today so often regarded as a hero of civil disobedience, a man who refused to obey law with which he was in profound moral disagreement. That is a considerable distortion of the truth, and it was not More's understanding of his motives. For him, in a very real sense, law was morality. It is equally true that for More morality was superior to law and was the standard by which law must be judged.[67]

The new danger we face, when Law no longer reflects the truth of social living, is that the institution of Law and laws become the instruments of political power in the hands of those who will manipulate society according to particular ideological interests. This happened with forms of Marxism, where the classless society became the justifying principle for any and all means to achieve it. Today, we are exposed to similar manipulations of society justified by some unreal vision of human technological transformation.

Ratzinger notes that this Marxist vision began with the belief that the present world is to be done away with, a world full of various forms of oppression and slavery. In its place is to be put a new and better world based on human planning and to be achieved by human work:

> In this case, the real and ultimate source of law becomes the idea of the new society: which is moral, of juridical importance and useful to the advent of the future world. Based on this criterion, terrorism was articulated as a totally moral plan: killings and violence appeared like moral actions, because they were at the service of the great revolution, of the destruction of the present evil world and of the great ideal of the new society. Even here, the end of metaphysics is a given, whose place is taken in this case not by the consensus of contemporaries, but by the ideal model of the future world. There is even a crypto-theological origin for this negation of law. Because of this, it can be understood why vast currents of theology—especially the various forms of liberation theology—were subject to these temptations.[68]

The recovery of the spirit of Law depends on the renewal of a shared truthful vision of society.

NOTES

1. International Theological Commission (ITC), *In Search of a Universal Ethic: A New Look at the Natural Law 2009* (Città del Vaticano: Libreria Editrice Vaticana, 2009), n12. https://www.vatican.va/roman_curia/congregations/cfaith/cti_documents /rc_con_cfaith_doc_20090520_legge-naturale_en.html (accessed October 14, 2023).

2. See Aristotle, *Nicomachean Ethics*, ed. Harris Rackham (Cambridge, MA: Harvard University Press, 1934).

3. Richard John Neuhaus, *The Naked Public Square: Religion and Democracy in America*, 2nd ed. (Grand Rapids, MI: Eerdmans, 1997), 253. American political philosopher Harvey C. Mansfield in the Wiley Vaughan Lecture at Harvard University titled his paper *On the Majesty of the Law* to emphasise the necessary aura of respect and importance that the law of political authority has and needs. In his opening lines he refers to the United States Supreme Court Justice Sandra Day O'Connor's autobiography *The Majesty of the Law: Reflections of a Supreme Court Justice* (New York: Random House, 2004), in Harvey C. Mansfield, "The Majesty of the Law," *Wiley Vaughn Lecture*, Harvard Law School, April 4, 2012, https://scholar.harvard .edu/harveymansfield/publications/majesty-law.

4. Joseph Ratzinger [Pope Benedict XVI], *Church, Ecumenism, and Politics: New Endeavours in Ecclesiology* (San Francisco: Ignatius Press, 2008), 242. At the same time, Ratzinger notes that ironically this "hitherto unimaginable 'freedom of movement' is counterbalanced by an increasing 'area of compulsion' of the technological civilization with its increasing regulations and ordinances, justified 'to safeguard the citizens' rights to freedom" Cf. Ratzinger, "Freedom and Constraint in the Church,"

in *Church, Ecumenism and Politics New Endeavours in Ecclesiology*, trans. Michael J. Miller et al. (San Francisco: Ignatius Press, 2008), 175.

5. ITC, *In Search of a Universal Ethic*, n12.

6. The *halakhah* is thus the entire body of Jewish law and legal traditions of the Torah, the Mishnah ("Oral Torah") and the Talmud and rabbinic law.

7. Jean Louis Ska, "Law, Freedom and Responsibility According to the Old Testament," in *Fundamental Rights and Conflicts among Rights*, ed. Mary Ann Glendon and Pierluca Azzaro (Steubenville, OH: Franciscan University Press, 2020), 51. Ska also notes that many laws of the Bible are in the second person, "a trait typical of the teachings of wisdom . . . . The effect of this characteristic is to involve the addressees of the laws more directly, appealing to their freedom of decision." Ska also observes that "the first text of law in the history of Israel—the history as it is presented in the Pentateuch—is the Decalogue . . . . We rightly identify the Decalogue with the Ten Commandments but we forget one essential thing, namely that the first sentence of the decalogue is not in the imperative but in the indicative. Before the requirements, the duties of the people towards its God, the Decalogue speaks about how much God has done for his people" (52, 53).

8. Rémi Brague, *The Law of God: The Philosophical History of an Idea*, trans. Lydia G. Cochrane (Chicago: University of Chicago Press, 2007), 49–50.

9. This is the view of Judaic scholar Jacob Neusner in *The Rabbinical Traditions about the Pharisees Before 70* (Eugene, OR: Wipf and Stock, 2005), in 3 vols., as cited in Oskar Skarsaune, *In the Shadow of the Temple: Jewish Influences on Early Christianity* (Downers Grove, IL: InterVarsity Press, 2002), 118, to which I refer, esp. 117–22.

10. Skarsaune, *In the Shadow of the Temple*, 119.

11. As in Mark 7:8, RSV: "You leave the commandment of God, and hold fast the tradition of men. And he [Jesus] said to them, 'You have a fine way of rejecting the commandment of God, in order to keep your own tradition.'"

12. Interestingly, Rabbi David Novak reinterprets the contemporary debate on rights and duties in the greater context of God's creation and God's covenant with the Jewish people. In critiquing politically liberal notions of individual rights and duties, Novak writes: "So . . . only when God's authority is presented in the covenant do the lesser authority of society and the lesser authority of the individual person find their rightful places respectively and their rightful correlation with one another" D. Novak, *Covenantal Rights: A Study in Jewish Political Theory* (Princeton, NJ: Princeton University Press, 2000), 205. On this theme there is also Eckart Otto, "Human Rights: The Influence of the Hebrew Bible," *Journal of Northwest Semitic Language* 25, no1 (1999): 1–20.

13. Otto [von] Gierke, *Political Theories of the Middle Ages*, trans. Frederic William Maitland (Eastford, CT: Martino Fine Books, 2014), 73–74. Gierke (1841–1921), German legal scholar and historian, describes this historical transformation of the understanding of Law from the time (up to the late 1400s) "when men supposed . . . that before the State existed the Lex Naturalis already prevailed as an obligatory statute, and that immediately or mediately from this flowed those rules of right to which the State owed even the possibility of its own rightful origin," to the

time when "the opinion which would free the sovereign (whenever he is acting in the interest of the public weal) from the bonds of the Moral Law in general, and therefore from the bonds of the Law of Nature. Therefore when Machiavelli based his lesson for Princes upon this freedom from restraint, this seemed to the men of his time an unheard of innovation and also a monstrous crime. Thus was laid the foundation for a purely 'political' theory of the State, and thenceforward this theory appeared as a rival of the 'nature-rightly' doctrine." As Gierke notes: "The Sovereignty of the State and the Sovereignty of the Individual were steadily on their way towards becoming the two central axioms from which all theories of social structure would proceed, and whose relationship to each other would be the focus of all theoretical controversy" (75, 86, 87).

14. Bruno Leoni, *Freedom and the Law* (Los Angeles: Nash Publishing, 1972), 15.

15. Harold J. Berman, *Faith and Order: The Reconciliation of Law and Religion* (Atlanta: Scholars Press, 1993), 3. The strength of Berman's argument is in his historical analysis in various chapters of this book of the various systems of law and their origin in custom and religion. Richard J. Neuhaus arrives to a similar conclusion: "This is the cultural crisis—and therefore the political and legal crisis—of our society: the popularly accessible and vibrant belief systems and world views of our society are largely excluded from the public arena in which the decisions are made about how the society should be ordered . . . . The result, quite literally, is the outlawing of the basis of law" Neuhaus, *Naked Public*, 258–59.

16. Neuhaus, *Naked Public Square,* 253.

17. Jeremy Waldron, *Political Political Theory: Essays on Institutions* (Cambridge, MA: Harvard University Press, 2016), 6.

18. John Waters, "Fixation with Regulations and eliminating human contact is what leads to Bungalow 3," *Irish Independent*, December 16, 2014. This article is complemented by Waters' experience of the discreet yet vital attention of a nurse the night after a cancer operation in Waters, "When I Met Christ," *First Things* (February 21, 2018), https://www.firstthings.com/web-exclusives/2018/02/when-i-met-christ.

19. Aleksandr Solzhenitsyn, "A World Split: Commencement Address at Harvard University June 8, 1978," in *Solzhenitsyn at Harvard: The Addresses, Twelve Early Responses and Six Later Reflections*, ed. Ronald Berman (Washington, DC: Ethics and Public Policy Center, 1980), 8.

20. Berman, *Faith and Order*, qualifies Solzhenitsyn's critique of the law by noting the Russian Orthodox view of law in general as "hard, cold, impersonal, formal, intellectual," contrasted with the Russian cultural tradition which emphasises "informal, spontaneous relations within the group, on togetherness, or what in Russian Christianity is called 'sobornost' (conciliatory, community spirit)" Berman notes that: "When Solzhenitsyn speaks of law, he speaks only of the letter of the law, which kills, never of the spirit of the law, which gives life." Berman agrees with Solzhenitsyn as to the abuse of law, not as to its proper social function (388).

21. David Walsh, *Politics of the Person as the Politics of Being* (Notre Dame, IN: University of Notre Dame Press, 2016), 1162.

22. Walsh, *Politics of the Person*, 1174.

23. Horst Hutter, *Politics as Friendship: The Origins of Classical Notions of Politics in the Theory and Practice of Friendship* (Waterloo, ON: Wilfred Laurier University Press, 1978), 2, as cited in *Friendship and Politics: Essays in Political Thought*, ed. John Von Heyking and Richard Avramenko (Notre Dame, IN: University of Notre Dame Press, 2008), 1. The editors of *Friendship and Politics* note that: "In the case of premodern thinkers considered in this volume, including Plato, Aristotle, Cicero, Augustine, and Aquinas, the connection between friendship and politics is close; for many modern thinkers, including Montaigne, Martin Luther, John Calvin, Thomas Hobbes John Locke, the American Founders, Tocqueville, Nietzsche, and various social scientists inquiring into 'trust,' the connection between personal friendships and politics can become tenuous, though never completely lost" (5).

24. Josef Pieper explains Thomas Aquinas' thought on the limits and insufficiency of justice in his chapter "The Limits of Justice," in *The Four Cardinal Virtues* (Notre Dame, IN: Notre Dame University Press, 1966), 104–13. The quotation is from 112.

25. The difference between contractual bonds and bonds of communion is described in Mary F. Rousseau's *Community: The Tie That Binds* (Lanham, MD: University Press of America, 1991), esp. chap. 3 "Communities and Contracts," 49–64.

26. Jaques Maritain, *Christianity and Democracy and The Rights of Man and The Natural Law*, trans. Doris C. Anson (San Francisco: Ignatius Press, 2012), 1535.

27. Martin Buber, *The Knowledge of Man*, 71, as cited in John F. Crosby, *The Selfhood of the Human Person* (Washington, DC: Catholic University of America Press, 1996), 120.

28. As Walsh observes, at the centre of Aristotle's political treatise is not a set of laws or a system of government, but "the evocation of a concrete type as the only norm and measure of right action. This is the mature man, or *spoudaios,*" Walsh, *Politics of the Person*, 1162. The first reference in Aristotle to the *spoudaios*, the mature man of practical reasonableness, is in chap. 7 of Book 1 of the *Nicomachean Ethics*. For a reflection on Aristotle's precise meaning, see Mathew Lu, "Getting Serious about Seriousness: On the Meaning of Spoudaios in Aristotle's Ethics," *Proceedings of the American Catholic Philosophical Association* 87 (2013): 285–293, https://doi.org/10.5840/acpaproc201441412.

29. Robert Sokolowski, "Phenomenology of Friendship," *Review of Metaphysics* 55, no. 3 (2002): 451–52, https://www.jstor.org/stable/20131748.

30. Aristotle, *Nicomachean Ethics*, 8.1.1155^{a}22–7, qtd. in Sokolowski, *Phenomenology of Friendship*, 453.

31. Marc Sageman, *Understanding Terrorist Networks* (Philadelphia: University of Pennsylvania Press, 2004), 134, qtd. in von Heyking and Avramenko, eds., *Friendship and Politics*, 16. The Muslim novels referred to that describe the loneliness and isolation of liberal societies are Orhan Pamuk, *Snow* (New York: Knopf, 2004); and Nahid Rachlin, *Foreigner: A Novel of an Iranian Woman Caught Between Two Cultures* (New York: W. W. Norton, 1999). Robert A. Nisbet in chap. 10 of *Quest for Community: A Study in the Ethics of Order and Freedom* (Washington, DC: ISI Books, 2010), comments on the modern and contemporary development of individualism. Hanna Arendt also comments on the political use of individual isolation and

Chapter 8

loneliness in the control and manipulation of people. Arendt, *The Origins of Totalitarianism* (San Diego: Harcourt Brace, 1994), 474–79.

32. Berman provides an historical account of the development of the Western legal tradition that was firmly rooted in the customs and values of the community: "As in many non-Western cultures, the European folk law was not a body of rules imposed from on high but was an integral part of the common consciousness of the community. The people themselves, in their public assemblies, legislated and judged; and when kings asserted their authority over the law it was chiefly to guide the custom and the legal consciousness of their people, not remake it" Berman, "Individualistic and Communitarian Theories of justice: An Historical Approach," in *Faith and Order*, 265.

33. "That which I have written in this treatise, concerning the moral virtues, and of their necessity, for the procuring, and maintaining peace, though it be evident truth, is not therefore presently law; but because in all commonwealths in the world, it is part of the civil law. For though it be naturally reasonable; yet it is by the sovereign power that it is law: otherwise, it were a great error, to call the laws of nature unwritten law." Thomas Hobbes, *Leviathan*, ed. J. C. A. Gaskin, (Oxford: Oxford University Press, 1998), book 2, chap. 26, 4402–4413.

34. John Austin, *The Province of Jurisprudence Determined* (1832), as cited in J. W. [James William] Harris, *Legal Philosophies* (London: Butterworths, 1997), 30.

35. Hans Kelsen, *What Is Justice? Justice, Law and Politics in the Mirror of Science* (Clark, NJ: Lawbook Exchange, 2013), 4695.

36. The major outlines of Kelsen's thought on law are to be found in the revised and extended second edition of the first edition of *Pure Theory of Law*, trans. Max Knight (Berkeley: University of California Press, 1967); and *General Theory of Law and State*, trans. Anders Wedberg (New York: Russell & Russell, 1961).

37. H. L. A. [Herbert Lionel Adolphus] Hart, *The Concept of Law*, 3rd ed. (Oxford: Oxford University Press, 2012), 2128.

38. Hart, *Concept of Law*, 54.

39. Leslie Green, Introduction to *The Concept of Law*, by Herbert L. A. Hart, 3rd ed. (Oxford: Oxford University Press, 2012) 172. In this sense, the role that Hart gives to custom is similar to the historical school of jurisprudence, such as that of German jurists Friedrich Carl von Savigny (1779–1861), and Friedrich Julius Stahl (1802–1861), who recognised the customs of particular historical societies as the source of laws and rights, but whose validity depended only on the particular and transient customs of each society. For a note on this school of jurisprudence, see Joseph de Finance, *An Ethical Inquiry* (Rome: Editrice Pontificia Università Gregoriana, 1991), 370–72.

40. Hart, *Concept of Law*, 3847. In a 1958 essay, Hart expresses his view of social purpose as "the humble aim of survival in close proximity to our fellows . . . it seems to me that above this minimum the purposes men have for living in society are too conflicting and varying to make possible much extension of the argument that some fuller overlap of legal rules and moral standards is 'necessary' in this sense." Herbert L. A. Hart, "Separation of Laws and Morals," in *The Philosophy of Law*, by Ronald Myles Dworkin (Oxford: Oxford University Press, 1982), 36. This volume of essays

also presents the different views of Dworkin, Lord Patrick Baron Devlin, John Rawls, J.J. [Sir Joseph John] Thomson, John Finnis, and Thomas Scanlon.

41. Berman, "Some False Premises of Max Weber's Sociology of Law," in *Faith and Order*, 241. Berman's conclusion on Weber's sociology of law is that it has had a generally detrimental effect on legal philosophy because this approach tends to promote the view that jurisprudence and the various systems of law have no greater purpose than for those in power, those who have "a monopoly of the legitimate use of force within a given territory," to gain and maintain control of the people within their jurisdiction. Berman also notes that Weber's sociology of law also reduces the scholarly analysis of different systems and expressions of jurisprudence merely to ideological forms of political power, serving no greater sense of purpose or truth.

42. Berman, "Some False Premises," in *Faith and Order*, 241–42.

43. Cited in Harris, *Legal Philosophies*, 99.

44. Karl Llewellyn (1893–1962), an American jurisprudential scholar, cited in Harris, *Legal Philosophies*, 103.

45. American professor David S. Crawford finds little real difference between Hart's justification of law as a social construction and Dworkin's formal categories of justice as equality and respect for individual freedom. Both views seem to be empty of any real content of the value of the human person. Cf. Crawford, "Public Reason and the Anthropology of Orientation: How the Debate over 'Gay Marriage' has been shaped by some Ubiquitous but Unexamined Presumptions," *Communio* 43, no. 2 (2016): particularly 259–63, https://www.communio-icr.com/files/43.2_Crawford .pdf.

46. David Conn, "Hillsborough Verdict: Victims' Families' 27-Year Struggle for Truth Vindicated," *Guardian*, April 27, 2016, https://www.theguardian.com/football /2016/apr/26/hillsborough-families-27-year-struggle-for-truth-vindicated (accessed October 12, 2023).

47. The same spontaneous rejection of the notion of law that is devoid of justice and moral good, can be seen in Adolf Eichmann's final plea while on trial in Jerusalem in 1961 for war crimes. Obeying orders, fulfilling duties, not being given other opportunities of work, as any other considerations, are all insufficient justifications in the personal involvement in moral iniquity: "I did try to leave my position, to leave for the front, for honest battle. But I was held fast in those dark duties. Once again I would stress that I am guilty of having been obedient, having subordinated myself to my official duties and the obligations of war service and my oath of allegiance and my oath of office, and in addition, once the war started, there was also martial law. This obedience was not easy. And again, anyone who has to give orders and has to obey orders knows what one can demand of people. I did not persecute Jews with avidity and passion. That is what the government did. Nor could the persecution be carried out other than by a government. But I never . . . I accuse the leaders of abusing my obedience. At that time obedience was demanded, just as in the future it will also be demanded of the subordinate. Obedience is commended as a virtue. May I therefore ask that consideration be given to the fact that I obeyed, and not whom I obeyed." Eichmann, "Adolf Eichmann's Final Plea," *Remmber.org* (Israel; 1961), https:// remember.org/eichmann/ownwords (accessed October 12, 2023).

48. Berman, *Faith and Order*, 15.

49. Heinrich A. Rommen, *The Natural Law: A Study in Legal and Social History and Philosophy*, trans. Thomas R. Hanley (Indianapolis: Liberty Fund, 1998), 3.

50. Heraclitus, *Fragments* 112–114, as cited in Rommen, *Natural Law*, 6

51. Rommen, *Natural Law*, 24.

52. Berman, *Faith and Order*, 46, 49.

53. Berman, *Faith and Order*, 26. Berman notes the particular influence of the Benedictine monastery of Cluny, founded in France in 910, which, within a hundred years, had 1450 similar foundations. Berman claims that it was the Benedictine monastery of Cluny, with its reform and renewal of monastic life and practice, that marked the course that the Papal Revolution would take. It was the Cluniac reform that was used by Pope Gregory VII to renew the Western Roman Church, its institutions, and its practices (52).

54. Berman, *Faith and Order*, 27. Gratian was a religious monk and canonist from Bologna, Italy, of the 12th century. From the 11th century Bologna was a centre of study of Canon and Roman law. The impact of this canonical reform is also described in Larry Siedentop, *Inventing the Individual: The Origins of Western Liberalism* (Cambridge, MA: Belknap Press, 2014), chap. 16 "Natural Law and Natural Rights," 242–57.

55. Siedentop, *Inventing the Individual*, 258.

56. Harold J. Berman, *Law and Revolution Volume I: The Formation of the Western Legal Tradition* (Cambridge, MA: Harvard University Press, 1983), 145.

57. Berman, *Law and Revolution*, vol. 1, 145.

58. Gratian, *Decretum, Distintiones* 1, c.2, qtd. in Berman, *Law and Revolution*, vol. 1, 145.

59. For an historical account of this divergence of terminology, see Kenneth Pennington, "Lex Naturalis and Jus Naturale," in *Crossing Boundaries at Medieval Universities*, ed. Spencer E. Young (Leiden: Brill, 2010), 227–53.

60. Gierke, *Political Theories*, 77. An overview of this historical development is given in chap. 19 ("Steps towards the Creation of Nation States") of L. Siedentop's *Inventing the Individual*, 291–305. Siedentop relies on Berman's *Law and Revolution*, as well as Brian Tierney's *The Crisis of Church and State, 1050–1300* (Toronto: University of Toronto Press, 1988); and, *inter alia*, Joseph R. Strayer, *On the Medieval Origins of the Modern State* (Princeton, NJ: Princeton University Press, 1970).

61. Harold J. Berman's *On Law and Revolution Volume II: The Impact of the Protestant Reformations on the Western Legal Tradition* (Cambridge, MA: Harvard University Press, 2006), recounts the impact on the understanding of law and the legal system of the Lutheran Reformation (1517–1555) and the Calvinist inspired English Reformation and revolution (1640–1689).

62. Benedict XVI, *Address to the Participants of the International Congress on Natural Moral Law*, February 12, 2007, https://www.vatican.va/content/benedict-xvi/en/speeches/2007/february/documents/hf_ben-xvi_spe_20070212_pul.html (accessed October 12, 2023).

63. Berman, *Faith and Order*, 45.

64. Berman, *Faith and Order*, 46.

65. Cited in Russell Hittinger's introduction to Rommen, *Natural Law*, xi.

66. Robert H. Bork, "Thomas More for Our Season," *First Things* 94 (June/July 1999): 17, https://www.firstthings.com/article/1999/06/thomas-more-for-our-season intolerance (accessed October 12, 2023).

67. Bork, "Thomas More," 17. I suggest that law and religion are not only reinforcements of social order, but that morality and religion are the fundamental content of human society, which laws reflect as well as reinforce. In his article, Bork refers to Peter Ackroyd's *The Life of Thomas More* (New York: Anchor Books, 1999), and esp. chap. 6 "Duty is the Love of Law," which describes the value given to law in Thomas More's era and its perceived relation to morality and religion.

68. Joseph Ratzinger, *Crisis of Law*, Address at LUMSA Faculty of Jurisprudence, Rome. November 10, 1999, https://www.ewtn.com/catholicism/library/crises-of-law -10080.

Chapter 9

Human Rights

This overview of the chapter starts with the discussion of one legal notion that today seems to stand out in contrast to the prevailing positive origin of Law, the notion of human rights. While the established parliamentary and administrative processes are considered sufficient in themselves for the validity and application of laws, the notion of human rights seems intuitively to represent values that we all should agree on, recognize, and vindicate, when in practice they are ignored or denied. In other words, we recognize the truth of human rights independently of legal processes of recognition. This recognition of the truth of human rights has been given legal effect in state Constitutions and at the level of public international law, especially in this last century.

At the same time, beneath the popularity of human rights in political and legal discourse, profound questions arise as to what human rights are, their extension, types, their legal recognition, the problem of conflicting human rights, and their justification. It is evident that the term "human rights" can have different meanings and contexts of interpretation.

To clarify the real truth of legal human rights it is necessary to identify the historical origin of rights, which is to be found not in the political philosophers of the sixteenth or seventeenth centuries, but in an earlier period particularly associated with the Church Canonists of the eleventh and twelfth centuries who gave legal expression to the term *ius*, as one of its meanings, as a personal right.

At the same time, the use of *ius* in reference to the right of the individual presupposed a Christian notion of the person that was also fundamentally relational, with "ties of justice and charity that bound individuals to one another."[1] This relational mode of personal substance was subsequently transmuted into an isolated and individual notion of substance, no longer structurally relational. The notion of person consequently assumed the characteristics of this impoverished notion of substance.

The history of the notion of *ius* from the Canonists' use in the twelfth century follows this shift from the relational to the separated notion of substance, and the meaning of *ius* (right) changes from a reflection of the moral and religious order of reality, to an individual power of freedom to be asserted for oneself as against others, either as individuals or as a political society (the state). It is this latter context of meaning that has prevailed in the political recognition of rights today.

In order to rectify the one-sided understanding of rights as individual powers of freedom, I propose three dimensions of human personal existence that place rights as individual powers within a greater and more sufficient anthropological context.

There is thus a present-day ambiguity of meaning to human rights, based on this one-sided affirmation of individual freedom. This prevalent notion of rights has the political effect of denying a priori any possible common understanding of what is truly good and conducive of human flourishing. The mere public acknowledgment of individual freedoms imposes on political society a nihilistic context of public debate, which is destructive of any common vision of human society.

The multiple problems produced by this notion of human rights are pointed out by the Italian philosopher and senator Marcello Pera, who refers to the Pandora's Box of ever more numerous rights and the ultimate irony of the invention by the State—that is, humanly made—human rights, whose strength supposedly lies in not depending on variable positive law for their validity and justification.

All of this is not to deride the notion of human rights, as some contemporary writers do, but to recognize the vital kernel of truth that human rights possess, when seen and interpreted in their right anthropological context.

NEXUS

I have tried to show that the idea of law that we generally assume today is in fact an emaciated form of a much fuller notion that has at times been evident in history. The twelfth-century canonist Gratian, in his assembly and codification of a unitary and coherent ecclesiastical legal system, declared that *"ius* is the genus, *lex* is a species of it."[2] By this we clarify that laws necessarily find their context in a given order or structure of moral and religious reality, and such laws are human attempts to reflect what is perceived of that background order. While in most theoretical explanations of laws and legal systems today positive law is taken as the genus, I have suggested that spontaneous human experience shows that these concepts, either as formal descriptions of the external characteristics of law or as only conventional social constructions, do not adequately correspond to our experience of what laws *should* be, what they *should* conform to. Without this basic conformity to our sense of the moral and religious structure of reality, laws become increasingly of arbitrary value, external forms of obligation and control that are as changeable as the political wind.

THE CONTEMPORARY ACKNOWLEDGMENT OF HUMAN RIGHTS

One legal notion that is an exception to this arbitrary form of law is that of human rights. Curiously, this is a term that resonates with our contemporary way of thinking and perceiving society and politics. Contained within this notion is the affirmation of the human person as an innate subject of freedom and value, without further need of justification or qualification. Also inherent in the notion is what is due to the person, the necessary conditions for the free development of one's life, irrespective of any consideration other than being a person. While the history of the emergence of the individual human person as a subject of rights is much longer than the modern usage of the term "rights," the second part of the twentieth century has witnessed the rapid growth of a legal doctrine of human rights:

> The outrages committed in the 1930s and 1940s in the name of the state against elementary human rights reached such a paroxysm that, as soon as the war was over, significant movements took place towards strengthening the institutional safeguards against abuse of authority. The idea of objective individual rights and an objective principle such as the rule of law remained incompatible with the theory and practice of . . . Marxist-ruled states, but in the democratic West these values now received both doctrinal acceptance and practical application in an unprecedented degree.[3]

What is distinctive about the contemporary notion of human rights is that they were found to be legally actionable. High sounding Constitutional declarations and aspirations were used as the bases for legal claims in the law courts and given legal vindication as against the state or other institutions or legal persons. This gave the courts a vibrant new area of interpretation in both civil and political issues as well as economic and social areas. Some Supreme Courts also found unspecified or implied individual rights not expressly stated in the Constitution or laws. In the context of the vast cultural and moral changes of the last sixty years, the courts were also asked to give new meanings to social forms, and the combined effects of these developments was to give the courts the possibility of an active role in legislating social change, not without controversy.

The power of the human rights doctrine was both in its universality and in its legal enforcement. The value of the human person was brought into sharp legal relief in oppressive governments, a value that was not dependent on a particular belief or situation, but on the human person *simplicitur*, a value that could be used against any ideology or unjust system; apartheid, discrimination based on race, sex, religion, economic injustice, and so on. Also, the notion of a legal right was also potentially much more powerful than the mere recognition of *licitude*, the giving of legal permission to do or not to do something. Rights were potentially to be affirmed, made practically possible, and to be recognized by all.

Also, to be noted is the substantive content of human rights, that recognize and affirm not just formal freedoms, but also a specific content of what is worthy of the human person. The recognition of human rights affirms and vindicates truths about human life and the necessary expressions of what makes life truly human.

The international effort to give cognizance to human rights was made in the *Universal Declaration of Human Rights* of 1948 by the United Nations organization, "as a common standard of achievement for all peoples and all nations."[4] While not itself a legally binding document on the member states, it has influenced the Constitutions of a number of states and may well have become part of international law.[5] The *Declaration* has been followed by binding *Covenants on Civil and Political Rights* (1966), Economic and *Social Covenants of Civil and Political Rights* (1966) and *Economic and Social Rights* (1966), and conventions on genocide (1948), racial discrimination (1969), measures to protect the rights of minorities, indigenous peoples, with particular committees to oversee specific areas such as the elimination of discrimination against women, the prohibition of torture, the rights of the child, migrant workers, and so on, and juridical structures to support the implementation of these areas of public international law. Regional conventions, such as the treaty of the *European Convention on Human Rights* (1953) promote human rights among signatory states in Europe.[6]

Analogously, the growing international recognition of the right of all peoples to self-determination, not included in the League of Nations Covenant, but expressed in general terms in the *United Nations Charter*,[7] provided an incipient legal basis in international law for the freedom of former colonial peoples and minorities within states. The *Declaration on the Granting of Independence to Colonial Countries and Peoples* (1960) stated that "all peoples have the right to self-determination; by virtue of that right they freely determine their political status and freely pursue their economic, social and cultural development."[8]

Similar United Nations declarations relate explicitly to minorities within political states (*Declaration on the Rights of Persons Belonging to National or Ethnic, Religious and Linguistic Minorities,* 1992) and to indigenous peoples (*Declaration on the Rights of Indigenous Peoples,* 2007).

John Paul II, himself an advocate of human rights from his years of struggle with communism in his native Poland, declared that the *Universal Declaration on Human Rights* "remains one of the highest expressions of human conscience in our times."[9]

The real value and strength of the contemporary recognition of human rights is its instinctive and emotive appeal to the truth about the human person. It is an area of law that manifests the moral and religious reality of the person that has wide acceptance today, even if the particular lists of enumerated rights can vary.[10] What is necessary is to elucidate this evident intuition of the value of each human person that sustains this doctrine of rights:

> Experience shows that legality often prevails over justice when the insistence upon rights makes them appear as the exclusive result of legislative enactments or normative decisions taken by the various agencies of those in power. When presented purely in terms of legality, rights risk becoming weak propositions divorced from the ethical and rational dimension which is their foundation and their goal. The Universal Declaration, rather, has reinforced the conviction that respect for human rights is principally rooted in unchanging justice, on which the binding force of international proclamations is also based . . . Human rights, then, must be respected as an expression of justice, and not merely because they are enforceable through the will of the legislators.[11]

And for this reason, "there is a sound core to the idea of rights, and so it continues to be a guide to the truth and a protective barrier against positivism. There is something that is right in itself, and this constitutes the true bond among men, because it stems from our common nature."[12]

The appeal of and for human rights is based, therefore, not on the consensus of declarations and covenants, but on the experience of the truth of the person, each individual person without distinction, that has become particularly evident in our times, given the abuses of persons, and categories of persons, in the last century:

> The evil of our times consists in the first place in a kind of degradation, indeed in a pulverization, of the fundamental uniqueness of each human person. This evil is even much more of the metaphysical order than of the moral order. To this disintegration, planned at times by atheistic ideologies, we must oppose, rather than sterile polemics, a kind of "recapitulation" of the inviolable mystery of the person. I firmly believe that the truths attacked compel with more urgency the recognition of those who are often the involuntary victims of it.[13]

It is vital that we value this fundamental insight, vision, of the human person that has become especially apparent in our times. In *Politics of the Person as the Politics of Being (2016),* David Walsh indicates that the present-day acknowledgment of human rights has a particular significance that goes beyond a general recognition of a common humanity and the establishment of a universal moral standard. Walsh affirms that the recognition of a human right gives a direct glimpse of what it means to be a person and he suggests that this is a momentous philosophical insight of our time, because human rights do not simply point out that we share a common humanity, but they manifest the personal nature of that humanity. It is not just that we human persons are someone, as contrasted with something, but our insight into rights discloses descriptive aspects of this personal being, who a person is. This is the profound importance of human rights; they are direct experiences of personal being and they reveal not only what we are, but also who we are. [14]

The luminosity of the person that is evident to us provides the fundamental experience of personal being that we express spontaneously in doctrines of human rights. We are stirred by the conviction that human rights are not honors or privileges, but are recognitions due to the human person, to each human person. It is here, in our time, that we can experience the pre-existing background that our laws try to express, give legal effect to, and without which a law is hollow and void.

THE ORIGIN OF HUMAN RIGHTS

While the self-evident clarity of human rights is something characteristic of our recent times, and as vital a perception of moral and religious reality as human rights offers, the doctrine should not and indeed cannot be taken as the sum total of social and political life. Human rights are, as Walsh has stated, a direct experience of the transcendent worth of each human person, above all other considerations, and the various descriptions of particular rights give an insight into fundamental expressions of the quality of human life (freedom, association, marriage, work, conscience, and religion). At the same time, the doctrine of human rights does not answer other vital considerations of social and political life. The question whether human persons are required to respond to human duties as well as having rights is not explicit. This raises the further question as to how human persons relate to each other in society; human rights emphasize what is owed to each person, or to a group, but says nothing about the interaction of these rights among people. At times, in state constitutions there are phrases such as "subject to public order and morality," but these qualifications of certain human rights are legal minimums and not sufficient criteria for the positive interaction of rights.

A related issue here is how rights are to be vindicated and by whom. Some rights are defended by laws that protect the human freedom to exercise rights such as the right to public expression, public worship, the right of association, etc. Other rights require more than the protection of freedom; for example, the right to sustenance, to health, and to education, require support and financial contributions.[15] Who is responsible, to what degree, and on what basis is the distinction between public, private, and individual responsibility made?

Another question that remains unanswered about human rights is about the essential content of such right. While declarations can enumerate specific rights, there is the question whether enumerated rights are real goods of the human person or only examples of the exercise of human freedom. In this case, human rights become human freedom, which is to be respected to the maximum degree possible, without enquiring whether rights exercised in freedom have a specifically human content that can and should be recognized and promoted as right.

Different answers can and have been given to these and other questions that the phrase "human rights" evokes. It seems, therefore, that the sound core of truth that we recognize in human rights can be understood in different contexts and made to yield different results. Given the legal effectiveness of human rights it is important to try to understand how we have arrived at such an important social and political insight and the proper context within which human rights can influence the structures and content of politics.

Although the pre-eminence of the individual human person in the legal concept of human rights is something that is spontaneously assumed in political thought today, this insight is not the result of spontaneous social or political history.

Ancient and medieval societies emphasized the collective form of social living (family, tribe, groups of tribes, cities), and the fundamental religious bond of such societies. Laws had their origin in community custom and practice. Cultures were wholistic, in the sense of containing all aspects of life within the family or tribe. As historian Christopher Dawson writes:

> The unity of a culture rests not only on a community of place—the common environment, a community of work—the common function, and a community of blood—the common race, it springs also, and above all, from a community of thought . . . a common conception of reality, a view of life, which even in the most primitive societies expresses itself through magical practices and religious belief, and which in the higher cultures appears in a fuller and more conscious form in religion, science and philosophy.[16]

What is paramount in these societies is the sense of belonging to the social group, of whatever form, but most particularly of the family. These social groups, and particularly the family were also and primarily religious:

> The whole life of society had a religious orientation, and religion was the vital centre of the social organism. This is not because primitive man is essentially more religious than modern man, or less interested in the material side of life. It is because the material and spiritual aspects of his culture are inextricably intermingled with one another, as that the religious factor intervenes at every moment of his existence.[17]

This was also and especially true of ancient Greek society. In his still widely respected study of Greek and Roman civilization, French historian Fustel de Coulanges explained the central and religious role of the family: "The ancient Greek language has a very significant word to designate a family. It is ἐπίστιον, a word which signifies, literally, that which is near a hearth. A family was a group of persons whom religion permitted to invoke the same sacred fire, and to offer the funeral repast to the same ancestors."[18]

The basic pattern of these societies was also hierarchical and structural, social stratification based on traditions and beliefs. If this is the general pattern of historical social life, where does the counter-cultural pre-eminence of the individual person come?

British political philosopher Larry Siedentop argues that the origin of what we term human rights is usually misplaced. Writing of the origin of natural rights he says that:

> Historians of social and political thought have usually located such a moment in the sixteenth and seventeenth centuries. This "early modern period" is the period when it is conventional to say that the doctrines of liberalism and secularism first raised their heads, not least because of the needs of nation-states struggling with bitter confessional conflicts arising from the Reformation. The conventional interpretation also relates the emergence of liberalism and secularism bred by the interest in and sympathy with antiquity . . . Taken together, these trends suggested that (the inspiration for) the emergent secularism or proto-liberalism should be located in antiquity and paganism.[19]

Siedentop tells a different story. Basing his account particularly on the historical research of historians such as Fustel de Coulanges (1830–1889), Francois Guizot (1787–1874), Brian Tierney (1922–2019), Harold Berman (1918–2007), and Peter Brown (1935–), Siedentop traces the path of Christianity, as the new religion seeps into cultures and civilizations, and finds its expression through Greek and Roman philosophy (while transforming the meanings of these philosophical expressions), its political freedom and subsequent monastic civilization, the clash of Papal and civil authorities in what Berman has called the Papal Revolution of the eleventh and twelfth centuries, the rise of nation states, the Renaissance and the Reformation, at which time, according to Siedentop "the roots of liberalism . . . firmly established in the arguments of philosophers and canon lawyers by the fourteenth and early fifteenth centuries . . . combined to create a coherent programme or theory for reform of the sovereign state into what we have come to call 'secularism.'"[20]

In this historical account, the common theme of Siedentop's work is the revolutionary content of Christianity in its relation to the prevailing social and political structures and their underlying beliefs. Christianity's concern for the individual person before God, the salvation of each soul, the emphasis on individual conscience and responsibility, the freedom from the detailed prescriptions of Jewish Law, the universality of its message to all peoples, the supremacy of and the distinction between religious and secular authority, all implicitly contained a radically new evaluation of social structures and categories. The importance, freedom, and consequent equality of each person before God was a direct challenge to the societies of innate hierarchy, structure, collective identity, and monolithic culture. From an historical perspective, Siedentop proposes that the modern notions of our political cultures—the primacy of the individual person expressed in human rights, equality before the law, and many civilizing and rational political and legal forms—have their origin in the radical, counter-cultural content of Christianity. Siedentop concentrates on the theme of the Christian exaltation of the individual person and its progressive historical influence in the social, legal, and political structures of Europe. Austrian theologian Christoph Schönborn describes the same Christian effect:

> With this definition of personhood, there is initiated a transition that becomes understandable only against the background of the Christian conception of man: the particular individual, and the unique reality of this singular human being, moves to the centre of interest. No longer is the generality of the essence deemed the higher reality, but rather the individual personality. The uniqueness of the individual no longer is seen so much as a restriction, always inadequate because limited, of a necessarily general essence—a basic tendency of Greek philosophy—but rather as the more important and significant reality. This gradual growth in emphasis centred on the individual person is a profound process of transformation involving all cultural areas, changing the conception of the arts as well as of history. What triggered and motivated this process was without doubt the awareness, gained within the context of Judeo-Christian revelation, that each man is unique.[21]

The explicit use of the term "right" in our modern sense of an action-able personal affirmation or power seems to come from the twelfth- and thirteen-century canonists who were codifying and shaping a unitary system of law for the Christian Church and the Papacy. Among the canonists' uses of the term *ius*, there was also the meaning of an inherent subjective exercise of power. This was a new meaning of *ius*. Speaking of the Stoic doctrine of *ius naturale*, Tierney writes:

> A decisive shift of meaning and emphasis occurred in the twelfth century. For some of the stoics and for Cicero there was a force in man through which he could discern *ius naturale*, the objective natural law that pervaded the whole universe; but for the canonists *ius naturale* itself could be defined as a subjective force or faculty or power or ability inherent in human persons. Although such definitions do not in themselves express a doctrine of natural rights, once the term *ius naturale* was clearly defined in this subjective sense the argument could easily move in either direction, to specify natural laws that had to be obeyed or natural rights that could be licitly exercised; and canonistic argument soon did move in both directions. Stoic authors when they wrote of *ius naturale*, were thinking in terms of cosmic determinism; the canonists were thinking more in terms of human free choice. When the concept of *ius naturale* was associated in the canonists' glosses with the words like "power," "faculty," "free will," it was moving in a different semantic field of force so to speak, and took on new meanings. Stoic refection on *ius naturale* never led to a doctrine of natural rights; canonistic reflection did so, and quickly.[22]

What Siedentop concludes from this is the influence of the Christian notion of person—the importance, equality, freedom, and responsibility of the individual person that came to be expressed in the legal term *ius* that would gradually promote the individual persons, their basic rights and purposes, and their consent to and participation in the authority of government.

> The sequence began with insistence on equality of status, moved on to the assertion of a range of basic human rights, and concluded with the case of self-government. Thus, from Hobbes's insistence on basic human equality, in preparation for defining sovereignty of "equal subjection," through Locke's defence of human freedom by identifying a range of natural rights, to Rousseau's making the case for the sovereignty of the people and self-government.[23]

What is important to remember is that the canonists who first explicitly identified the use of the term *ius* as right or power did not do so indepen-dently of the traditional use of *ius* as right order, as the objective right or truth of reality. It was freedom for and within truth. As Tierney states "The first natural law rights theories . . . derived from a view of individual human persons as free, endowed with reason, capable of moral discernment, and from a consideration of the ties of justice and charity that bound individuals to one another."[24]

This is important because the political development of *ius* as individual power or faculty seems to have been one-sided; while rightly affirming individual persons as the source and summit of political government and affirming and respecting the fundamental individual expressions of their freedom for truth, there has been an emphasis only on the individuality of personal rights. The reason the canonists developed their incipient natural rights theories "from a consideration of the ties of justice and charity that bound individuals to one another" is because the Christian faith not only revealed a new universality of *individuals* but also a new community of *persons*.

THE HUMAN RIGHTS OF THE PERSON

What Christianity brought to light was the relational mode of personal being. The discovery of relation as "an equally primordial mode of being" was originally in reference to Trinitarian Christian theology and applied afterward, analogously, to human beings. Its import is that human persons are not only an individual "substance" but also "relational," in the sense of finding and developing their own being in relation with others and with the Other. Persons do not lose their identity in developing relations with others, but only progressively find their being and identity in, from, and for others. Christianity not only emphasized the individuality of persons and their transcendence over imposed forms of government, but also marked the relational nature of each person and a common social and transcendent destiny.

The Christian term for this essential relatedness is person, a term taken from Greek culture and given a new meaning in Christian theology as being-in-relation, modeled on the Trinitarian personal relations; being in its maximum expression is being-in-relation. The Scholastic description of the human person included the notion of substance, which meant much more than the individuality or the independence of the person:

> The medievals, especially St. Thomas, restored in principle the complementarity between substance and relation by their doctrine of real being as intrinsically ordered toward action and self-communication; for all action necessarily generates a web of relations between agents and recipients. . . . The notion of the human being as by nature social, hence as embedded in a web of relations to others in the social and political community, also clearly implied the key role of relations. This aspect is quite explicit in Aristotle too.[25]

Again, this insight into the essentially relational nature of the human person (and in relation to God) was of Christian origin and was also behind the universality of the Christian religion. Christianity's purpose was not only to affirm the transcendent dignity and importance of each person, with the gradual social and political consequences that Siedentop traces, but also to bring humanity into a living social and transcendent communion. Persons are a dynamic substance-in-relation that can only flourish and come to fulfillment from, in, and for others. These structural relations were the "ties of justice and charity that bound individuals to one another."[26]

To speak of the Christian context for the origin of natural rights and the incipient use of the term *ius* as a power or force is to speak of this metaphysical context of the human person's relational being oriented toward social and transcendent fulfilment. The progressive recognition of human rights based on the fundamental freedom of moral conscience and self-determination was understood within the social context of communion and a metaphysics of love.

This essentially relational and communicative context of personal being that was contained in the Medieval term substance, full of Christian import, began to slip from view. New meanings of substance changed and obscured this relational context. For Descartes, substance was "that which exists by itself, that which needs nothing else (save God) to exist."[27] Here we find the understanding of man as independent individuality in no essential relation to anyone except God. For John Locke, substance is "the inert, unknowable substratum of accidents, which are alone known to us. These accidental properties need substance as an ontological support . . . (but) which is itself inert, static, without dynamic, self-communicative relationship with them and through them to the outside world."[28]

David Hume would go further to deny the existence of "the notion of an abiding, self-identical substance, as an invention of the metaphysicians with no grounding in reality."[29]

It is important, in identifying the origin of the notion of natural, human rights to recognize not only the assertion of the individual person, the person's rightful freedom and responsibility based on moral conscience, the capacity to discern what is good, but also to complement this Christian vision of human persons with the relational context of their personal being, within which persons freely exercises their self-determination, from, with, and for others. It was in this context that *ius* as power or strength was born.

The notion of the self, the person, as primordially an isolated, atomic individual, only accidentally related to others, came in much later, with Descartes and Locke. It is as alien to the classical and medieval Christian tradition, both theological and philosophical, as their notions of substance are to the classical and medieval one of substance as active relation-generating centre. The human person, in fact, comes into existence enveloped in a web of relations of dependence on others even before it can begin to generate its own relations actively: dependence on God as the ultimate source of its being, on its parents for the gift of its nature, on the surrounding environment for the necessary conditions for its survival and growth (air, temperature, food, etc.). And its whole development will consist in relating itself appropriately, both actively and responsively, to the world around it and especially to other persons, both human and divine.[30]

TWO NOTIONS OF *IUS* (RIGHT)

Emerging from Medieval thought, both from the Canonists and from the theologians, we have two distinct understandings of *ius* with respect to natural rights. Both notions refer to an individual power of action, but in different ways. In St. Thomas, for example, we find the suggestion of the meaning of *ius* as an individual moral claim, but always in the context of and based on what is called "the moral order" of justice and duty. For St. Thomas, "right is the object of justice"[31] and the emphasis here is more on the duty owed to someone else in justice (what is right), rather than an individual power of freedom.[32]

Contrastingly, in the canonists, in incipient form, is the meaning of individual *ius* as an independent and free use of a power. A clear use of this subjective sense of *ius* is found in the writings of Jean Gerson (1363–1429) a Conciliarist theologian. Tierney finds in Gerson's writings "a clearly subjective definition of *ius*, and also presented a distinction between lex and *ius* that we more commonly associate with seventeenth-century natural rights theorists. For Gerson lex was objective law; *ius* was a subjective power or right inhering in individual persons."[33]

While, as Tierney points out, it is wrong to label Gerson as a one-sided subjective rights advocate, his explicit use of *ius* as an individual free power significantly moved forward this subjective understanding of rights.[34] Gerson's thought was taken up at the universities of Tubingen and Paris in the fifteenth and sixteenth centuries. Gerson's followers "had converted the claim-right theory of the twelfth century completely into an active right theory, in which to have any kind of right was to be a *dominus*, to have sovereignty over that bit of one's world—such that even a child had sovereignty over its parents when it came to questions of its welfare."[35]

The obvious contrast in views is that now *ius* finds its justification not in a moral order but in the sovereign freedom of the individual. As intricate as the historical path was for the political assumption of this new, subjective meaning of *ius*, it is on flagrant display in Thomas Hobbes' *Leviathan*:

The right of nature, which writers commonly call *jus naturale*, is the liberty each man hath, to use his own power, as he will himself, for the preservation of his own nature; that is to say, of his own life; and consequently, of doing any thing, which in his own judgment, and reason, he shall conceive to be the aptest means thereunto.

For though they that speak of this subject, use to confound *jus*, and *lex*, right and law; yet they ought to be distinguished; because RIGHT, consisteth in liberty to do, or to forbear: whereas LAW, determineth, and bindeth to one of them: so that law, and right, differ as much, as obligation, and liberty; which in one and the same matter are inconsistent.[36]

It is this sense of right as subjective freedom that Locke describes his foundational right of property:

Though the earth and all inferior creatures be common to all men, yet every man has a property in his own body. This nobody has any right to but himself. The labour of his body, and the work of his hands, we may say, are properly his. . . . For this labour being the unquestionable property of the labourer, no man but he can have a right to what that is once joined to, at least where there is enough, and as good left in common for others.[37]

The supreme power cannot take from any man any part of his property without his own consent. For the preservation of property being the end of government, and that for which men enter into society . . . Men therefore, in society having property, they have such a right to the goods, which by the law of the community are theirs, that nobody hath a right to take them, or any part of them, from them without their own consent.[38]

Freedom becomes for Jean Jacques Rousseau the goal of the social contract of free individuals "To find a form of association which shall defend and protect with the public force the person and property of each associate, and by means of which, uniting with all, shall obey however only himself, and remain as free as before."[39]

For Rousseau the fundamental motivation for the individual is self-love, from which can flow compassion and the search for the good, and virtues (or vices), but all from the original love of self. Justice itself is based on this self-love:

Our first duties are to ourselves; our primary sentiments are centred on ourselves; all our natural movements relate in the first instance to our preservation and our well-being. Thus, the first sentiment of justice does not come to us from the justice we owe but from that which is owed us; and it is again one of the mistakes of ordinary educations that, speaking at first to children of their duties, never of their rights, one begins by telling them the opposite of what is necessary, what they cannot understand, and what cannot interest them.[40]

Rousseau's setting of human rights in terms of the heart and of love gave the doctrine of human rights an emotional appeal and, as Irish jurist J. M. Kelly writes, "gave what might be called the plain chant of natural rights, as Locke had intoned them, a polyphonic charm."[41]

The contemporary notion of human rights is therefore based on an idea of an individualized person, an idea that has become ingrained in our way of thinking but that is really incongruent with the social reality of the human person:

> The individual is that being who, because he is human, is naturally entitled to "rights" that can be enumerated, rights that are attributed to him independently of his function or place in society, and that make him the equal of any other man. As familiar as this idea may seem, it really ought to strike us as strange. How can rights be attributed to the individual as individual if rights govern relationships between several individuals, if the very idea of a right presupposes an already instituted community or society. How can political legitimacy be founded on the right of the individual, if he never exists as such, if he is always necessarily linked to other individuals, to a family, class, profession, or nation? . . . Nor is there any doubt that this individual, so obviously "imaginary," has tended more and more to become reality. The inhabitants of Western democracies have become ever more autonomous, ever more equal, and have felt themselves progressively less defined by the family or social class to which they belong.[42]

PERSONAL HUMAN RIGHTS

We have three basic elements that need to be held together in the necessary recognition of human rights, elements that have not coincided historically. In the first place, and what seems to be at the source of the contemporary appreciation of human rights is the perceived *dignity* of each person, which is not just a special price or value, but also the experience of each person as inviolable, as to be affirmed unconditionally, to be loved and respected as an end in oneself (to use Immanuel Kant's phrase[43]) and thus never to be subjected to demeaning abstractions such as numbers, ideologies, categories of description or discrimination, stages of physical development, etc. There is an evident worth of being a human person that *commands* a response of affirmation, not just respect or neutral indifference. The experience of the person goes beyond categories of mere justice and equality to the imperative of affirmation. As we have seen, this is due to not only to common human nature, but also to the uniquely personal way of being human of each one.[44] It is hardly coincidental that this luminosity of personal being, the imperative that emanates from each personal being to command affirmation, has come to light as an aftermath of the political trampling of so many human persons in this last century. It is precisely in its abuse that the inherent inviolability of each human person becomes more dramatically evident. The danger is that we can lose again, almost without realizing it, the appreciation of what we once experienced.

The second essential element of modern human rights is the recognition of the power of moral freedom. The theme of Siedentop's account of the political and social impact of Christianity on Western Europe and beyond is precisely in its emphasis on the individual as a moral agent, personal responsibility for one's actions and salvation, the individual as answerable to God and the consequent relativization, and at times repudiation, of social and political forms that subjugated individuals to collective forms and purposes of public authority. This truth is also vital for the person and for society. Freedom is a condition of genuinely human actions; the subjective perception of what is good can only be achieved within the experience of freedom, not compulsion. Self-determination is each person's free responsibility. This sense of *ius* as a power of free determination is, I suggest, an essential element of human rights, as can be seen by the inevitable failure of governments and regimes that impose on their people restrictions on basic freedoms of expression. Jospeh Ratzinger, speaking of the events of 1989, writes:

> The ideological wall that divided not only Europe but in an invisible manner the whole world everywhere no longer stands as once it did. And it was not thrown down by the power of weapons. Certainly, it was not thrown down simply by means of prayers but through an eruption of the spirit, through processions for freedom that were ultimately de facto stronger than barbed wire and cement.[45]

The third essential element of human rights is the inherent relational nature of human life. We do not start our existence as isolated, independent, self-seeking individuals, but we come into personal existence from, with, and for others and the Other.[46] These real relations exist before our consciousness of them; we grow in gradual awareness of them, and their recognition and affirmation is our path to personal fulfilment. The progressive discovery of others and the Other enlightens the necessary existing bonds of our coexisting humanity and draw us to their fulfilment. They are the source of our ethical and religious values, which are not abstract or impersonal values, but whose origin is located in the inchoate perception of the other and to which we are freely drawn in the affirmative love of their being. This fundamental relational mode of personal being was inherent in the Medieval notion of substance but subsequently lost from sight by the adoption of methods of perception from the physical sciences. Personalist philosophy today is uniting findings from sciences such as biology, neurology, and psychology to a relational mode of personal being.[47]

> The human experience to the relation to the Other, to God, is vital and is the foundational setting for all rights and duties:
> Freedom from profit and emancipation from the aims of power find their deepest guarantee only in the absolute rights of the One who is not subordinate to any human power: in the freedom vis-à-vis the world which God both has and is.
> In the long run, it is impossible to maintain the unique identity of the truth, in other words, its dignity (which, in turn is the basis of the dignity both of man and of the world), without learning to perceive in it the unique identity and dignity of the living God. Ultimately, therefore, reverence for the truth is inseparable from that disposition of veneration which we call adoration.[48]

In a real sense, all human rights and duties are relative to the creative order of personal reality, which means the communion of persons in dependent communion with God. It is only the discovery of the Other that permits the real communion with others, expressed in rights, and duties of love.[49] On an experiential level, the experienced relation with the Other is the source of the proper response of affirmation of others and the recognition of what is owed to each one.[50]

THE AMBIGUITY OF HUMAN RIGHTS DOCTRINES

As French philosopher Joseph de Finance points out there have been political and social thinkers who have rejected the notion of natural human rights, such as Hobbes, who considered all laws and rights as humanly made, or those who attribute the origin of human rights to particular social conventions or customs that change and are transformed in time, with no underlying reality, a form of social positivism.[51] Karl Marx considered such language as human rights as part of an ideological structure that perpetuates a particular capitalist economic structure with an isolated individual as its necessary component. Recently, Scottish philosopher Alasdair MacIntyre has rejected the notion of human rights, rights that adhere to the human person as person, for the reason that "every attempt to give good reasons for believing that there are such rights has failed."[52] MacIntyre argues that the term "right" only appears in the 1400s and has no equivalent in Hebrew, Greek, Latin, or Arabic. He also argues that justifications such as the self-evidence of such rights or the moral intuition of such rights are evasive of reason, and the *United Nations Declaration on Human Rights* (1948), for example, enunciates a list of human rights but gives no reasoned justification for them. MacIntyre's view is radical and seems to cancel out something of common agreement and, with it, a hope for true human collective development. MacIntyre, also, may well have a valid point: the particular interpretation given to human rights may presume a context of individualism that is contrary to human nature and human existence. Ratzinger's expression of human rights is more circumspect and points to a more authentic context for such rights: "there is a sound core to the idea of rights, and so it continues to be a guide to the truth and a protective barrier against positivism. There is something that is right in itself, and this constitutes the true bond among men, because it stems from our common nature."[53]

Here, in the terms and philosophical context in which human rights have been described, there is an important truth about man that is being affirmed and that is popularly perceived in our time. Even so, the whole contextual truth of human rights needs to be appreciated. To isolate and propagate one feature or element of human rights leads to ambiguous results that, due to the emotional and legal impact of the invocation of the polyphonic charm of human rights, can lead to aberrations in the name of such rights.

One such misuse of human rights is the isolation of free will and its propagation as the exclusive source and content of human rights. Freedom is an essential component of human action, and it is the necessary condition with which we choose what we perceive as good. As we have seen, the human person cannot live socially or politically without freedom and will sooner or later break free of imposed authoritarianism. At the same time, freedom facilitates the choosing, but is not constitutive, of what is good. What this means is that we experience, perceive, and respond—in freedom—to all that surrounds us, and to ourselves. Freedom allows us to perceive and to respond personally to reality and thus make profoundly human choices and decisions that we identify with, as my owned decision. What we are not free to do is to reverse the process, and impose on reality what I want it, or the other, or the Other, to be.[54] When human rights become merely the legally protected and vindicated expression of arbitrary and individual (or collective) free will, they are torn from their relational pregiven context and become a source of imposed anarchy on society. The first consequence of this aberration of the meaning of human rights is the legal justification of just about anything on the grounds of being an identified expression of someone's freedom.

What we can recognize here is a very particular understanding of the common good of society and the nature of man's freedom, which American political philosopher Michael Sandel recognizes as the core ethical posture of political liberalism:

Society, being composed of a plurality of persons, each with his own aims, interests, and conceptions of the good, is best arranged when it is governed by principles that do not themselves presuppose any particular conception of the good; what justifies these regulative principles above all is not that they maximize the social welfare or otherwise promote the good, but rather that they conform to the concept of right, a moral category given prior to the good and independent of it.[55]

The full import of this exaltation of the concept of right, and the understanding of human freedom on which it is based, becomes clear; justice, equality, respect become the predominant categories of social union. These formal categories pre-empt any possibility of shared common good:

> On the full deontological view, the primacy of justice describes not only a moral priority but also a privileged form of justification; the right is prior to the good not only in that its claims take precedence, but also in that its principles are independently derived. This means that, unlike other practical injunctions, principles of justice are justified in a way that does not depend on any particular vision of the good. To the contrary: given its independent status, the right constrains the good and sets its bounds. "The concept of good and evil is not defined prior to the moral law, to which, it would seem, the former would have to serve as foundation; rather the concept of good and evil must be defined after and by means of the law" (Kant 1788: 65).[56]

It is this notion of human rights only in terms of human freedom that seems to have taken hold of the liberal political vision. Again, the assertion of the uniqueness and individuality of each person is a tremendous good to be affirmed and legally vindicated in society. When this vital freedom is taken out of the context of the person's constitutive and structural relations with others and the Other, and when the political and legal measures serve only to protect freedoms and deny or ignore the insight into the given context of human freedom, then such human rights have the effect of imposing on society the explicit denial of any greater social union or vision beyond the protection of individual spheres of freedom.

But is this really the case? Is it not true that the liberal political vision of "neutrality" toward any substantive vision of the person and society precisely avoids imposing any particular viewpoint, but allows all views equal tolerance? David L. Schindler, in his analysis of Locke's doctrine of rights, coms to a different conclusion. Having explained the content of Locke's three basic rights of life, liberty, and property in the context of a social contract with the state, Schindler makes explicit what is implicitly contained in Locke's vision of man and his relation to others:

> Liberalism's intended strictly juridical order, in the name of avoiding a metaphysics, advances a definite metaphysics centred in freedom of indifference,

whose central burden is to displace the person's natural community with God and others, and with truth and goodness, by an extrinsic and so far voluntaristic community—what is commonly termed a contractual community—made up of formal-independent, logically self-centered individuals.

The hallmark claim of liberalism—that its juridical order remains ex officio empty of any one metaphysical truth, in order that individuals and groups in civil society may be left free to seek and defend the truth on its own terms—thus harbors within itself a subtle, but truly massive, deception.[57]

Precisely because human rights are considered universal—that is, definitive claims to what and who the human person is—they necessarily contain a vision of what and who that human person is:

> Any defence of rights that would be conceived with consistency as universal must indeed be—because it cannot not be—tethered to some definite claim of truth regarding the nature of the human being, of the relations between self and others, of the self in relation to a transcendent order of being and truth and goodness and hence to God. Liberalism does not avoid such a claim; on the contrary, it merely hides its claim to truth even as it implicitly frames this claim in reductive and deeply fragmented terms.[58]

As we have seen before, this imposed skepticism predetermines the conditions of public debate. Anything that may impose itself on individual freedom, that is, claim to be an authentic, true expression of the human condition or the human good, is *a priori* excluded from public consideration as an invasion of, and offence to, individual freedom. We are deemed to be incapable of common understanding and growth in agreement. These are the terms of public reason.[59]

This supposedly neutral, impartial, liberalism that is to promote respect and tolerance for human differences in fact obliterates the public possibility of recognizing and favoring actions and relations that can be shown to be necessary and of benefit to the human person and to society. The vast amount of biological, neurological, psychological, social, and economic facts that sustain the vital importance of the man-woman relationship of marriage and family is irrelevant from the liberal perspective. What is to be upheld is the freedom to enter into, and have the same recognition, for any and all social unions. To favor or promote one form of social union is considered necessarily to discriminate and treat unequally all other forms of union. This approach necessarily implies that all social forms of union are publicly equal and that sexual identity and stable forms of man-woman relations are basically irrelevant to the common good of society.[60] The tyranny of this view dictates that in all public fora the essential equality of all forms of social union must be preached; to make distinctions is to discriminate.

There are also many other difficulties regarding the current usage of the notion of human rights, though most, if not all, of the difficulties center on a notion of rights abstracted from their anthropological context. Given the one-sided insistence on the power of individual self-determination of freedom, how can one reasonably, and with the same emotional appeal, speak of responsibilities? It seems that duties and obligations do not belong in the discourse of human rights, though duties are the necessary inverse of rights.

> The criterion of real right—right entitled to call itself true right which accords with freedom—can therefore only be the good of the whole, the good itself. . . . On the basis of this insight, Hans Jonas has defined responsibility as the central concept of ethics. This means that in order to understand freedom properly we must always think of it in tandem with responsibility. Accordingly, the history of liberation can never occur except as a history of growth in responsibility. Increase of freedom can no longer simply lie in giving more and more latitude to individual rights—which leads to absurdity and to the destruction of those very individual freedoms themselves. Increase in freedom must be an increase in responsibility, which includes acceptance of the ever greater bonds required both by the claims of humanity's shared existence and by conformity to man's essence.[61]

Italian philosopher and senator M. Pera sees the worrying proliferation of rights as a "uncontrollable phenomenon," what he calls a Pandora's Box of unlimited rights, especially at the hands of judicial power, irrespective of the views of a majority or minority of the people.[62] He sees that ever-expanding rights will end by consuming themselves. His example is abortion: "the right to life leads by implication to the right to suppress life; in general, the right to the dignity of the person leads ultimately to the right to the destruction of the person."[63]

"What limit do rights have, if indeed they have one, and how may it be imposed?"[64] Pera is also aware of the doctrinal import of the current use of human rights and wonders if, for example, Christianity's leaders are aware of the profound change in anthropology contained in the present use of the term. He states that "the contemporary religion of human rights is a religion without God, and a religion without God is an ideology, however disguised and embellished."[65] Pera asks if the doctrine of human rights shines with the same luminosity when their proliferation causes "forms of new oppression of individuals and peoples."[66] He asks how ever-increasing, conflicting rights can at all be considered "universal, inherent, non-negotiable."[67]

Pera also underlines the difficulties in the distinction made between active rights, rights to be and to do, and passive rights, rights to receive or from which to benefit.[68] Liberal thinkers would consider the first group of rights universal, absolute and clearly definable, the second group as pertaining to

Chapter 9

some rights, but not all, dependent on the practical possibilities of providing these rights and therefore not absolute rights, and not clearly definable. Pera argues that this distinction is not really as coherent as it may seem.[69] Pera concludes his critique of human rights doctrines recognizing certain advantages of this doctrine, while recognizing the enforced secularization of the public forum, the ever increasing role of the state as provider of rights, and the current phenomenon of the creation of rights by the law courts, provoking, *inter alia*, the irony of turning human rights into rights of positivist origin and, instead of being a protection against state power, the doctrine of human rights becomes an ideological weapon of state power, control and imposition. Pera recognizes a *"dictatorship"* of human rights ideology.[70]

CONCLUSION

There is no doubt that the invocation of human rights has become an ambiguous moral and religious claim. The legal implications of the recognition and vindication of rights are enormous, precisely because of the inherent claim of human rights to be universal, inherent, and imperative—therefore, unquestionable. Human rights *are* all these things, because the human person communicates an experience of being that compels unconditional affirmation, as something inherent in the common structure of the human person and the uniqueness of the way of being human of each person. The tragic and cruel history of this last century teaches us, if only by the horror of negation, this *a priori* truth of each person, irrespective of condition or development. It is the possibility of this experience of personhood, both universal and particular, that is the source of social and political renewal. This experience is not one of abstract categories, or numbers or notions, but of the singular, affirmative, and unconditional value of each distinct human person as person.

The evocative power of human rights can also, and has been, politically misused and distorted, and such misuses and distortions have been imposed by the law. This happens when human rights are taken out of their context of the full truth of the human person and become volatile weapons of social destruction. The underlying mentality, when human rights are understood and presented only as powers of individual freedom, is the imposed negation of what we can know as true and good.[71] This political imposition circulates with the aura of freedom and tolerance, while in reality denying people the right to challenge power with truth.

Politics and law, if they are to serve the social integration and authentic social aspirations of man, need the full truth of the human person:

We can in the end secure the freedom and rights that are the hallmark intention of liberalism's juridical order only by tying them to a human nature understood to bear an intrinsic order of transcendent relations (to the true and the good, to others, and finally to God). Liberalism's universalist intention of securing equality of rights for all, in other words, can actually be realized only via a metaphysics rooted in the natural truth regarding the person.[72]

NOTES

1. Brian Tierney, *The Idea of Natural Rights* (Grand Rapids, MI: Eerdmans, 2001), 77.

2. Gratian, *Decretum, Distintiones* 1, c.2, in Harol J. Berman, *Law and Revolution Volume I: The Formation of the Western Legal Tradition* (Cambridge, MA: Harvard University Press, 1983), 145.

3. J. M. [John Maurice] Kelly, *A Short History of Western Legal Theory* (Oxford: Oxford University Press, 1992), 353.

4. United Nations Organization, *Universal Declaration of Human Rights*, December 10, 1948), https://www.un.org/en/about-us/universal-declaration-of-human-rights (accessed October 15, 2023). Preamble. For an historical account of the impact of this Declaration, see Mary Ann Glendon's essay "The Universal Declaration of Human Rights at 70," in *Fundamental Rights and Conflicts among Rights*, ed. Mary Ann Glendon and Pierluca Azzaro (Steubenville, OH: Franciscan University Press, 2020), 227–43. For its origins, and Eleanor Roosevelt's role, see Mary A. Glendon, *A World Made New: Eleanor Roosevelt and the Universal Declaration of Human Rights* (New York: Random House, 2002).

5. "Although clearly not a legally enforceable instrument as such, the question arises as to whether the Declaration has subsequently become binding either by way of custom or general principles of law, or indeed by virtue of interpretation of the UN Charter itself by subsequent practices." Cf. Malcom N. Shaw, *International Law*, 7th ed. (Cambridge: Cambridge University Press, 2014), 204.

6. A summary of the international protection of human rights is provided in Shaw, *International Law*, chap. 6.

7. United Nations Organisation, *Charter of the United Nations*, October 24, 1945, 1 UNTS XVI, Article 1(2) and article 55. https://www.un.org/en/about-us/un-charter (accessed October 15, 2023).

8. United Nations Organization, *Declaration on the Granting of Independence to Colonial Countries and Peoples*, December 14, 1960, A/RES/1514(XV), article 2, https://www.ohchr.org/en/instruments-mechanisms/instruments/declaration-granting-independence-colonial-countries-and-peoples (accessed October 15, 2023).

9. John Paul II, Address to the General Assembly of the United Nations," *L'Osservatore Romano* (Weekly edition in English), October 5, 1995, https://www.vatican.va/content/john-paul-ii/en/speeches/1995/october/documents/hf_jp-ii_spe_05101995_address-to-uno.html (accessed October 14, 2023). for the celebration of the 50th anniversary of its founding.

10. For example, the *Cairo Declaration on Human Rights in Islam* (1990) refers to some of the United Nations Declaration's human rights, but does not include all, notably, for example, the omission of the right to freedom of religion or the non-prohibition of discrimination against women. Cf. Organization of Islamic Cooperation (OIC), *The Cairo Declaration of the Organization of Islamic Cooperation on Human Rights,* 2021, https://www.oic-oci.org/upload/pages/conventions/en/CDHRI _2021_ENG.pdf (November 7, 2023).

11. Benedict XVI [Joseph Ratzinger], *Meeting with Members of the General Assembly of the United Nations,* April 18, 2008, https://www.vatican.va/content/ benedict-xvi/en/speeches/2008/april/documents/hf_ben-xvi_spe_20080418_un-visit .html (accessed October 12, 2023), on the 60th anniversary of the UN's Universal Declaration on Human Rights.

12. Joseph Ratzinger, *A Turning Point for Europe? The Church in the Modern World: Assessment and Forecast* (San Francisco: Ignatius Press, 1994), 513.

13. Karol Wojtyla [Pope John Paul II], in a letter written to the French theologian Henri de Lubac in February 1968, published in De Lubac, *At the Service of the Church: Henri de Lubac Reflects on the Circumstances That Occasioned His Writings* (San Francisco: Ignatius Press, 1993), 171–72. Wojtyla, as archbishop of Cracovia, Poland, in the 1960s and 1970s, faced the oppressive communist imposition of its materialist ideology. In particular, Wojtyla fought with the people of a newly built city, Nova Huta, to build a church there, something not contemplated by the communist authorities. Stanislaw Dziwisz, Wojtyla's personal secretary for almost forty years, remarked that Wojtyla's battle "on behalf of the dignity of the human person began right there at Nova Huta" Dziwisz, *A Life with Karol: My Forty-Year Friendship with the Man Who Became Pope* (New York: Image, 2008), qtd. in George Weigel, *The End and the Beginning: Pope John Paul II—The Victory of Freedom, the Last Years, the Legacy* (New York: Doubleday, 2010), 86.

14. David Walsh, *Politics of the Person as the Politics of Being* (Notre Dame, IN: University of Notre Dame Press, 2016), section "Rights as an Epiphany of the Person," 4517 and following.

15. For example, Mary Ann Glendon, speaking at the Beijing Conference on Women in 1995 and in reference to the Universal Declaration on Human Rights' phrase to provide "special care and assistance" to motherhood, said: "Surely this international gathering could have done more for women and girls than to leave them alone with their rights! Surely we must do more for the girl child in poor nations than give lip service to providing access to education, health and social services while carefully avoiding any concrete commitment of new and additional resources to that end" Glendon, "Holy See's Final Statement at Women's Conference in Beijing United Nations 1995," Beijing, September 15, 1995, in Mary A. Glendon, *Traditions in Turmoil,* Sapientia Press, Washington D.C. 2006, 300.

16. Christopher Dawson, *Progress and Religion: An Historical Inquiry* (Washington, DC: Catholic University of America Press, 2001), 66–67.

17. Dawson, *Progress and Religion,* 82.

18. Fustel de Coulanges, *The Ancient City,* qtd. in Larry Siedentop, *Inventing the Individual: The Origins of Western Liberalism* (Cambridge, MA: Harvard University

Press, 2017), 15. De Coulanges dedicates the second book of *The Ancient City* to all customs and rites pertaining to the family.

19. Siedentop, *Inventing the Individual*, 386.

20. Siedentop, *Inventing the Individual*, 381.

21. Christoph Schönborn, *God's Human Face: The Christ-Icon* (San Francisco: Ignatius Press, 1994), 412. Ratzinger also notices, in a comment on the text of the prophet Ezekiel, this "clear and decisive personalism." "This text (Ezekiel 18:21–28) signifies completely overcoming any kind of primitive collectivism, by which individuals inevitably form part of their clan, their social group, and can have no personal destiny distinct from that of the clan. Here we can see the emancipation, the liberation, of the person, with the person's unique and singular destiny. This liberation, this discovery of the uniqueness of the person, is at the heart of any freedom" Ratzinger, *Journey to Easter: Spiritual Reflections for the Lenten Season* (New York: Crossroad, 1987), 53.

22. Tierney, *Idea of Natural Rights*, 65–66.

23. Siedentop, *Inventing the Individual*, 386.

24. Tierney, *Idea of Natural Rights*, 77.

25. W. Norris Clarke, *Explorations in Metaphysics: Being-God-Person* (Notre Dame, IN: University of Notre Dame Press, 1994), 103.

26. Tierney, *Idea of Natural Rights*, 77.

27. Descartes, qtd. In Elizabeth Haldane and George R. T. Ross, *Philosophical Works of Descartes*, II, 101, qtd. in Clarke, *Explorations in Metaphysics*, 109.

28. John Locke, qtd. in Clarke, *Explorations in Metaphysics*, 111.

29. David Hume, qtd. in Clarke, *Explorations in Metaphysics*, 112.

30. Clarke, *Explorations in Metaphysics*, 118.

31. Thomas Aquinas, *Summa Theologica*, 2ª, 2ae, q.57, article 1, qtd. in Bernard V. Brady, "An Analysis of the Use of Rights Language in Pre-Modern Thought," *Thomist* 57, no. 1 (1993): 98, https://doi.org/10.1353/tho.1993.0052. This article by Brady relates the historical shift in the meaning of *ius* ("right") in Catholic theologians and philosophers from St. Thomas Aquinas to Francisco Suárez.

32. This understanding of *ius* as corresponding to the moral order, as contrasted in meaning with *ius* as a power of freedom, is found later in the writings of Spanish theologian and jurist Francisco de Vitoria (1483–1546) in his affirmation of the American Indians, as also, although more arguably, in the writings of the Spanish philosopher of lawyer, Francisco Suárez (1548–1617).

33. Tierney, *Idea of Natural Rights*, 211. Jean Gerson's definition of the subjective sense of *ius*, "a proximate faculty or power which belongs to some subject as prescribed by primary justice," is taken from his *On Church Power and the Origin of Law and Right*, as quoted in Oliver O'Donovan and Joan Lockwood O'Donovan, eds. *From Irenaeus to Grotius: A Sourcebook in Christian Political Thought* (Grand Rapids, MI: Eerdmans, 1999), 527. What is evident is that Gerson himself still considered the subjective *ius* within the objective context of "primary justice."

34. Tierney's analysis of J. Gerson is in chap. 9 "Gerson, Conciliarism, Corporatism, and Individualism" of *Idea of Natural Rights*, 207–35.

35. Richard Tuck, *Natural Rights Theories* (Cambridge: Cambridge University Press, 1979), 28.

36. Thomas Hobbes, *Leviathan*, ed. J. C. A. Gaskin (Oxford: Oxford University Press, 1998), part 1 "Of Man," chap. 14 "Of the First and Second Natural Laws, and of Contract," 2523.

37. John Locke, *Second Treatise on Civil Government*, ed. C. B. Macpherson (Indianapolis: Hackett, 1980), 19.

38. Locke, *Second Treatise on Civil Government*, 72–73.

39. Jean Jacques Rousseau, *On the Social Contract*, 2nd ed., trans. Donald A. Cress (Indianapolis: Hackett, 2019), book 1, chap. 6, 11.

40. Jean Jacques Rousseau, *Emile, or On Education*, trans. Allan Bloom (New York: Basic Books, 1979), book 2, 97.

41. Kelly, *Short History of Western Legal Theory*, 269.

42. Pierre Manent, *An Intellectual History of Liberalism* (Princeton, NJ: Princeton University Press, 1995), xvi.

43. "The principle, so act with reference to every rational being (yourself and others) that in your maxim it holds at the same time as an end in itself, is thus at bottom the same as the basic principle, act on a maxim that at the same time contains in itself its own universal validity for every rational being" Immanuel Kant, *Groundwork of the Metaphysics of Morals* (1797), trans. and ed. Mary Gregor (Cambridge: Cambridge University Press, 1997), 4:438, 45.

44. John F. Crosby emphasizes this point: "One of the best-known utterances of the Roman jurists about the person connects bring a person with being incommunicable: *persona est sui iuris et alteri incommunicabilis*. It is precisely as person that I am myself (*sui iuris*) and no other (*alteri incommunicabilis*). St. Thomas clearly teaches that being a person is not a common nature like human nature that can be shared in by many; being a person is rather a matter of being an incommunicable individual within some common rational nature" Cf. Crosby, *Personalist Papers* (Washington, DC: Catholic University of America Press, 2004), 8. The reference to St. Thomas is *Summa Theologiae* I, q. 30, a. 4, esp. the second objection and the response to it.

45. Ratzinger, *Turning Point for Europe*, 1368.

46. W. Norris Clarke recognizes the validity of a comment by American philosopher D.L. Schindler who, in Clarke's summation, has emphasized the "primordial relation of receptivity constitutive of its very being before it can pour over into action at all: namely, that it has received its very act of existence from another, ultimately from God, the Source of all existence. Thus we should describe every created being as possessing its own existence from another, in itself, and oriented toward others—a triadic rather than just a dyadic structure" Cf. Clarke, *Explorations in Metaphysics*, 119. Clarke's summation of Schindler's thought on this point is drawn from the review of Clarke's paper by David L. Schindler, "Norris Clarke on Person, Being, and St. Thomas," *Communio* 20, no. 3 (1993): 580–92.

47. Cf. Paul C. Vitz and Susan M. Felch, eds., *The Self: Beyond the Postmodern Crisis* (Wilmington, DE: ISI Books, 2006).

48. Joseph Ratzinger, *The Nature and Mission of Theology: Approaches to Understanding Its Role in the Light of Present Controversy* (San Francisco: Ignatius Press, 2010), 41, 40.

49. On this theme of the religious origin of human rights, there is the reflection by David Novak, *Covenantal Rights: A Study in Jewish Political Theory* (Princeton, NJ: Princeton University Press, 2000). Novak states: "This book is my attempt to show that Judaism provides a broader meaning of rights than the one provided by liberalism and a deeper meaning of rights than the one denied by conservatism. I even attempt the more ambitious task of showing Judaism itself to be constituted by rights at all levels from top to bottom" (x). What is of great interest in this study is the theological foundation of *covenantal* rights.

50. "Only if man, every man, stands before the face of God and is answerable to him, can man be secure in his dignity as a human being" Joseph Ratzinger, *The Feast of Faith: Approaches to a Theology of the Liturgy* (San Francisco: Ignatius Press, 1986), 8.

51. Joseph de Finance, *An Ethical Inquiry* (Rome: Editrice Pontificia Università Gregoriana, 1991), 370–72. In Jeremy Waldron's *Nonsense upon Stilts: Bentham, Burke, and Marx on the Rights of Man* (New York: Methuen, 1987), the editor takes texts from these three authors that show their critique of human rights. As Waldron notes, each was opposing the same particular historical form of human rights, the Declaration of the Rights of Man and the Citizen, by the French National Assembly of 1789.

52. Alasdair MacIntyre, *After Virtue: A Study in Moral Theory*, 3rd ed. (Notre Dame, IN: University of Notre Dame Press, 2007), 69. Italian philosopher Marcello Pera lists other authors who are critical of the notion of human rights, in his *Diritti umani e cristianesimo: La Chiesa alla prova della modernità* [Human Rights and Christianity: The Church Put to the Test of Modernity] (Venezia: Marsilio, 2015), 1062, footnote 14. Pera himself is highly doubtful of the validity of the notion of human rights as it used today and of its compatibility with the Christian faith. Cf. Pera, *Diritti umani*, 126. For another critical view of the possible distortion of human rights, see James V. Schall, "Human Rights as an Ideological Project," *American Journal of Jurisprudence* 32, no. 1 (1987): 47–61, https://doi.org/10.1093/ajj/32.1.47.

53. Ratzinger, *Turning Point for Europe*, 513.

54. American philosopher David C. Schindler explains this conditional rather than constitutive role of the free will, basing his arguments on Augustine and British philosopher I. Murdoch, in "Freedom Beyond Our Choosing: Augustine on the Will and Its Objects," *Communio* 29, no. 4 (2002): 618–53.

55. Michael Sandel, *Liberalism and the Limits of Justice* (Cambridge: Cambridge University Press, 1998), 4.

56. Sandel, *Liberalism and the Limits of Justice*, 2. The quotation is from Immanuel Kant's *Critique of Practical Reason* (1788) *and Other Writings in Moral Philosophy*, trans. Lewis White Beck (Chicago: University of Chicago Press, 1949), 65. Both Sandel and Pera are critical of the sufficiency of this ethical vision. Pera, in particular, shows how contrary this view is to the Christian metaphysical and teleological vision of the human person, naturally inclined to flourishing and fulfilment, in communion

with God and others. Pera notes how this formal Kantian ethics has been adopted into Catholic Church teaching, contrary to Tradition, by the acceptance of the Kantian version of human rights and human dignity. Cf. Pera, *Diritti umani e cristianesimo*. For a general historical overview of the differing ethical visions of man, and the difference each makes, see Robert Kraynak, *Christian Faith and Modern Democracy: God and Politics in the Fallen World* (Notre Dame, IN: University of Notre Dame Press, 2001).

57. David L. Schindler, "The Repressive Logic of Liberal Rights: Religious Freedom, Contraceptives, and the 'Phony' Argument of the *New York Times*," *Communio* 38, no. 4 (2011): 533.

58. Schindler, "Repressive Logic of Liberal Rights," 542. Sandel makes a similar point: "In short, the ideal of a society governed by neutral principles is liberalism's false promise. It affirms individualistic values while pretending to a neutrality which can never be achieved" Sandel, *Liberalism and the Limits of Justice*, 11.

59. For an explanation of this political precondition of participation in politics, see Peter L. P. Simpson, *Political Illiberalism: A Defence of Freedom* (London: Routledge, 2015), 124–28.

60. On this theme there is David S. Crawford's "Recognising the Roots of Society in the Family, Foundation of Justice," *Communio* 34, no. 2 (2016): 247–73. https://www.communio-icr.com/files/43.2_Crawford.pdf.

61. Joseph Ratzinger, "Truth and Freedom," *Communio* 23, no. 1 (1996): 30. The reference is to Hans Jonas, *The Imperative of Responsibility: In Search of an Ethics for the Technological Age* (Chicago: University of Chicago Press, 1994).

62. Pera, *Diritti umani*, 634.

63. Pera, *Diritti umani*, 927.

64. Pera, *Diritti umani*, 152.

65. Pera, *Diritti umani*, 177.

66. Pera, *Diritti umani*, 682.

67. Pera, *Diritti umani*, 694.

68. Pera, *Diritti umani*, 705.

69. Pera, *Diritti umani*, 783.

70. Pera, *Diritti umani*, 936.

71. Explaining this phenomenon of imposed negation of what we can and do know as true and good, Ratzinger explains that we seem to have been convinced that the various moral and religious ideas in the world are necessarily in conflict with each other, a conflict based on profound and irreconcilable contradictions. These conflicts are taken as evidence of their arbitrary human origins, not based on reality, and which need to be overcome by human scientific and rational knowledge. However, Ratzinger writes that: "this diagnosis is extremely superficial. It clings to a series of details that are lined up alongside each other in no particular order and thus arrives at its banal know-it-all attitude. In reality, the fundamental intuition about the moral character of Being itself and about the necessary harmony between the human being and the message of nature is common to all the great cultures, and therefore the great moral imperatives are likewise held in common" Ratzinger, *Turning Point for Europe*, 290. In the same essay, Ratzinger also states that: "the conviction that man's Being contains an imperative; the conviction that he does not himself invent morality on the

basis of calculations of expediency but rather finds it already present in the essence of things" (275).

72. Schindler, "Repressive Logic of Liberal Rights," 542. For a fuller treatment of the theme of rights, see David C. Schindler, *The Politics of the Real: The Church Between Liberalism and Integralism* (Steubenville, OH: New Polity Press, 2021), 120–46, chap. 4 "Unnatural Rights: The Dangers of a Disembedded Theory."

Chapter 10

The Unity of the Nations

The mention of international politics as a theme most often makes us think of the relations between political states and all the institutions and persons that represent these states. In this chapter, I would like to question these normal assumptions as to the relations and context of international politics and to propose a more profound international context, expressed in the phrase "unity of the nations."

The chapter starts with a summary of the real conditions a human society requires to orient social actions toward communion, conditions that go beyond the actual political realities of the modern state, democracy, the rule of law, and so on. The actual reality that these terms represent does not contain the necessary or sufficient conditions for real political communion. Something similar occurs with "international politics"; the actual reality that this phrase describes does not correspond to the necessary political conditions to aspire legitimately to the unity of the nations.

To make this evident, I start with two fundamental notions: (1) the modern nation-state as the fusion of state and society; and (2) the principle of the self-determination of peoples. Two legal cases from international law highlight the difficulty of reconciling the legally defined notion of the modern state with the expression of a people's cultural identity. This mismatch becomes acutely relevant today, as cultural identities, more than geographical borders, are becoming the real fault-lines of international society.

Two questions then arise: In what sense can or should we aspire to social and cultural unity, in a world of evident cultural diversity and conflict? How does one avoid simplified notions of one humankind, or, alternatively, the pragmatic acceptance of the de facto clash of civilizations? In answer to the complex human aspiration for the unity of the nations, I propose the Judeo-Christian understanding of original unity, actual rupture, and transcendent unity of the nations, as an explanation that best corresponds to our human condition and aspirations.

I then suggest that it is culture—the expression of meaning that we give to our lives and to reality—that is the real potential source of unity among peoples. I take the example of the European Union as a project that was intended to create not just economic, but deep cultural bonds between the peoples of Europe, but seems to have fallen short of that greater purpose.

The chapter finishes with a reflection on the political idea of a universal humanity and the different ways this notion has been understood. There is no one simplified reality; the real challenge is to live an authentic cultural identity and to be drawn into a beneficial conflict of cultures that can inspire and purify particular ways of living, and thus develop into a greater unity.

The conclusion ventures to understand the contemporary change from poles of state power to diffused networks of economic interest, and what this change will require of us, if we are to live with deep and authentic bonds of social identity.

In this way, we can at least frame the many themes of international politics in their real and proper context, and to search for a greater unity of the nations where it may truly be found.

NEXUS

We have seen that human society is necessarily oriented toward a flourishing that is only achieved in the communion of persons and entails both personal and collective achievement. This interpersonal relation is the necessary context for personal flourishing and is based on a metaphysics of love, that is, reciprocal relations that respond to the worth of each human person as persons and to the unique way of being of each person.

The society of persons requires an authority of order to orient social actions toward communion. This is true also of the political dimension of human society. Anarchic notions of spontaneous harmony are impractical, as also the notion that society can be manufactured or produced solely by structures or economic conditions.

While the forms of political authority can vary, the conditions for the authentic use of political authority are clear; the participation and representation of all persons, a basic agreed content of authentic social values and aspirations, the respect for personal freedom and responsibility, and, at the same time, the active promotion of persons of unequal circumstances. These conditions we have called the democratic ideal. Distinct from this ideal is the modern democratic form of government that has its origins in a particular historical setting of the modern political state, the assumption of state sovereignty (ultimate social power), the political theory of social contract between equal individuals, and the subsequent institutions and processes that enshrine and enact this particular form of political government. The historical result has been the justification and almost universal acceptance of one particular form of government as the only legitimate expression of the democratic ideal. I have tried to point out the limitations, at times leading to the misrepresentation, of the democratic ideal by this particular historic form of democratic government. So much so that present democracies often flatter to deceive, give the appearance of the democratic ideal while in fact exposing people to ideological manipulation and subservience. Pierre Manent quotes the Russian-born French philosopher Alexander Kojève in writing that Kojève:

> Draw(s) our attention to the disturbing fact that modern democracy shares with totalitarianism the claim to have solved the human problem. Modern democracy understands itself not as a regime among others, not even as the best regime, but as the only legitimate regime: it embodies the final, because rational, state of humanity.[1]

Manent himself draws attention to the misleading terms of universality such as "the state," "citizen," and "democracy." He writes that "The modern nation-state is unquestionably more 'general' or more 'universal' than the ancient city; it is not evident that its 'self-government' is better, more complete, more accomplished, more in keeping with what the word 'democracy' necessarily leads one to understand."[2]

The political challenge is to identify, beyond the particular historical mold of the democratic form of the modern state, both the real given circumstances of human existence and the real and ideal aspirations of social communion. In a similar way, the understanding of international politics requires a recasting of current political categories, in order to discern both the real fault lines of society and the real sources of social union. In this sense, the programs of international politics are seen in the greater and deeper context of the unity of the nations.

INTERNATIONAL POLITICS

International politics is primarily considered to be the role of political states, a particular model of political organization that emerged first in Europe and that were recognized in the aftermath of internal European wars by the Peace of Augsburg (1555) and the later Treaty of Westphalia (1648). Contrary to their name, these wars were fundamentally political, not theological, and the principal underlying issue was the assertion of the several civil powers of Europe over all other forms of authority:

What was at stake was rather the aggrandisement of the centralizing territorial state over the remnants of the transnational ecclesial order and the remnants of local privilege and custom. The rise of the state was not necessitated by the "Wars of religion"; rather, these were the birth pangs of the state, in which the overlapping jurisdictions, allegiances, and customs of the medieval order were flattened and circumscribed into a new creation of the sovereign state (not always yet nation-state), a centralising power with a monopoly on violence within a defined territory.[3]

The nineteenth century saw the development of the state into the nation state:

> When the vertical relationship of state and individual is opened to include a horizontal relationship among individuals, an increasingly cohesive mass relationship. . . . In other words, when state becomes nation-state, it represents the fusion of state and society. The state precedes the idea of the nation and creates it, promoting the imagination of a unitary space and a common history. But in contrast to the absolutist state, the nation-state does not merely enforce its will through coercion. In order fully to realize the doctrine of territorial sovereignty and extend governance to every individual within its borders, the nation-state finds the participation of the many in a unitive project to be essential. Nationalism becomes a popular movement founded on consent.[4]

In their respective reflections on international relations both Immanuel Kant and G. W. F. Hegel assume the modern political state as the given form of national government and the prospect of international concord in terms of relations between these political states. Kant envisages these relations between states as naturally one of strife, just as Thomas Hobbes considered the natural social life of individuals as one of conflict. For this reason, Kant maintains that inter-state concord, on which the peace of individual states depends, must and can only be formally established, given the insufficient actual moral condition of mankind, by a formal civil constitution and not left to the spontaneous actions of individual states. At the same time, Kant does not advocate a universal state (an international state that stands to individual states as individual states stand to their citizens), but rather a "republic of republics" and warns that:

> The idea of international right presupposes the separation of several independent, neighbouring states from one another. And although such a state of affairs in itself is already a state of war (if a federative union of these states does not prevent the outbreak of hostilities), even this state of war is, according to the idea of reason, better than the blending of these states into a power that overgrows the existing ones and ultimately turns into a universal monarchy. This is so because laws increasingly lose their force as the borders of a government are

extended, and a soulless despotism, after having eliminated the seeds of good, ultimately declines into anarchy.[5]

For Hegel, "world history is essentially the dialectic of national spirits, of States, which are the determinate shape which Spirit assumes in history."[6] Hegel, too, rejected the notion of some universal sovereign federation of states, "but since the sovereignty of a state is the principle of its relations to others, states are to that extent in a state of nature in relation to each other. Their rights are actualized only in their particular wills and not in a universal will constituted as a power over them."[7]

Hegel also viewed the relations between states as a natural and necessary condition of conflict, but viewed the positive effects of this dialectic of national spirits, and not in terms of the pacific association of states that would progress toward perpetual peace:

> War has the higher significance that by its agency, as I have remarked elsewhere, the ethical health of peoples is preserved in their indifference towards the stabilization of finite determinacies; just as the blowing of the winds preserves the sea from the stagnation which would be the result of a prolonged calm, so also stagnation in peoples would be the product of prolonged, let alone perpetual, peace.[8]

For Hegel, therefore, it is the good of each state that is each state's supreme law. As Romanian French philosopher Pierre Hassner explains "the conflict between morality and politics is resolved by the concrete existence of the state and not by the abstract demands of a universal justice. But to the extent to which the good of the state is the supreme law, war remains the supreme recourse by which this law is necessarily expressed."[9]

Ingrained in both these distinct views is the dominant political model of the modern state as the prevailing pattern for international law and relations, a model that perdures today, although in a much more pragmatic form than with pretensions for perpetual peace or the manifestation which the Spirit assumes in history.

In the nineteenth and early twentieth centuries the rise of nationalist movements within the empires of Europe, Asia and Africa was followed by the successive break-up of the European empires and their hold on colonial territories in the world. American President Woodrow Wilson's *Fourteen Points* (1918) for world peace made reference to the right of self-determination: "a strict observance of the principle that in determining all such questions of sovereignty the interests of the populations concerned must have equal weight with the equitable government whose title is to be determined" and that the forming of "a general association of nations" (what was to become the League of Nations), "must be formed under specific covenants for the purpose of affording mutual guarantees of political independence and territorial integrity to great and small states alike."[10]

This principle of self-determination of peoples was not included in the 1919 Treaty of Versailles and was much more complicated to apply given the difference between political state boundaries and cultural, linguistic, and religious groups of peoples and the vested interest of colonial powers.

The United Nations Organisation *Charter* made specific reference to the aim of developing "friendly relations among nations based on respect for the principle of equal rights and self-determination of peoples, and to take other appropriate measures to strengthen universal peace."[11]

Subsequent interpretation of the *Charter* and practice has determined the legal status of the principle, as seen in Resolution 1514 (XV), the *Declaration on the Granting of Independence to Colonial Countries and Peoples*, which states that "All peoples have the right to self-determination; by virtue of that right they freely determine their political status and freely pursue their economic, social and cultural development."[12]

This acceptance of the self-determination of peoples was reiterated in the 1970 *Declaration on Principles of International Law*, which clarified the *Charter* articles and was unanimously adopted by the General Assembly. There have been a few judicial cases in the International Court that recognize the principle.[13]

At the same time, there has been, and there continues to be, a real tension between the traditional subject of international, the political state, and this recognized principle of the self-determination of peoples. Even though individuals and groups have acquired a certain legal status in international law, as British jurist Malcom N. Shaw states, "states retain their attraction as the primary focus for the social activity of humankind and thus for international law."[14]

Statehood, in traditional terms of international law, is described in Article 1 of the *Montevideo Convention on Rights and Duties of States* of 1933: "(a) a permanent population; (b) a defined territory; (c) government; and (d) capacity to enter into relations with other states."[15] While these criteria have been subsequently subject to qualification in new situations, such as the disintegration of the Soviet Union and Yugoslavia, for example, the criteria remain substantially intact.[16]

The difference between the characteristics of the political and legal state, on the one hand, and the principle of the self-determination of peoples "to freely pursue their economic, social and cultural development" on the other hand, are substantial. Two recent legal cases demonstrate the conflict.[17] In 1998, the Supreme Court of Canada decided that neither under Canadian nor international law was it legitimate for the province of Quebec unilaterally to secede from Canada and establish political independence, with the purpose of expressing the province's distinctive history, culture, and language. On the question of the self-determination of Quebecers, the Canadian Supreme Court stated:

> The recognized sources of international law establish that the right to self-determination of a people is normally fulfilled through internal self-determination—a people's pursuit of its political, economic, social and cultural development within the framework of an existing state. A right to external self-determination (which in this case potentially takes the form of the assertion of a right to unilateral secession) arises in only the most extreme of cases and, even then, under carefully defined circumstances.[18]

In an advisory opinion by the International Court of Justice on the unilateral declaration of independence by Kosovo from the state of Serbia in 2008, the Court found that while the evolution of the principle of self-determination had been "one of major developments of international law during the second half of the twentieth century":

> Whether, outside the context of non-self-governing territories and peoples subject to alien subjugation, domination and exploitation, the international law of self-determination confers upon part of the population of an existing State a right to separate from that State is, however, a subject on which radically different views were expressed by those taking part in the proceedings and expressing a position on the question. Similar differences existed regarding whether international law provides for a right of "remedial secession" and, if so, in what circumstances. There was also a sharp difference of views as to whether the circumstances which some participants maintained would give rise to a right of "remedial secession" were actually present in Kosovo.[19]

What both these cases show, both in domestic state law and in public international law is the predominance of the political state as the primary unit of international relations. The economic cultural, social, and religious identities of peoples are to be identified and protected within the context of political states as described by international law, in terms of territory, stable population, and control. Individual persons have acquired a certain international legal standing, especially in the area of human rights, and individuals can be criminally responsible for war crimes, as, for example, established by the International Criminal Tribunal for the former Yugoslavia and for Rwanda. The same time, international organizations may acquire international legal personality, although in most cases these organizations are *de facto* subject to the political power and interests of member states.

These cases manifest the difficulty of associating the complex cultural, linguistic, social, and religious unity of peoples with a definition of a legal state that is described in terms of geographical boundaries, a controlling government and a fixed population, and then to think that "international relations" may be fully addressed by working out the relations between these state entities. The recent centenary of the 1916 Sykes-Picot Agreement between Britain and France, with the consent of the Russian Empire and the Kingdom of Italy, to draw straight line boundaries in the Middle East (the *Levant*) and which divided the region into spheres of influence and control, did not correspond to the real social, religious, or ethnic and tribal differences in the area and was one of the continuing causes of Middle East conflict.[20]

Karl Popper was critical of this identification of cultural or ethnic groups with the legal framework of the state and the supposition that legal states represented such cultural, ethnic, and religious identities, or that such groups could practically claim to be legal states, which seemed to be implicit in the promise of the self-determination of peoples:

> The principle amounts to the demand that each state should be a nation-state: that it should be confined within a natural border, and that this border should coincide with the location of an ethnic group; so that it should be the ethnic group, the "nation," which should determine and protect the natural limits of the state. But nation-states of this kind do not exist. . . . Nation-states do not exist, simply because the so-called "nations" or "peoples" of which the nationalists dream do not exist. There are no, or hardly any, homogenous ethnic groups long settled in countries with natural borders. . . . There are ethnic minorities everywhere. The proper aim cannot be to "liberate" all of them; rather, it must be to protect all of them.[21]

The fundamental problem here is the identification of the predominant framework of the legal state with the deeper distinctions of culture, ethnicity, and religion, as if states were adequate summaries of these profound and varied manifestations of the human spirit and, concomitantly, that the only adequate public expression of these cultural manifestations is in terms of absolute political state power.

> Liberalism has supported an artificial state system wherein membership is defined exclusively in terms of central sovereign power without any reference to the national character of the societies in question. When in 1918 Woodrow Wilson elevated the "self-determination of people" into an absolute principle (which still governs the inter-state system to this day), he did not so much defend popular sovereignty or the consent of the governed for all the nations. Rather, he encouraged the process of empire-building and state-building that inaugurated liberal hegemony and led to new wars.[22]

The point here is that the legal description of the state is in terms of territory, power, and a stable population, with no reference to the real identities and distinction of peoples, as varied and complex as they are within the same geographical territory. This leaves international relations in terms of concentrated and artificial centres of power with no real sources of unity other than the advantage of one state over another. Christopher Dawson identifies this problem as at the root of international conflicts:

> Thus the greatest single cause of the breakdown of internationalism both in theory and practice has been the failure to recognise the artificial and unstable character of the political unit on which all our schemes for international organisation rest. The word State simply signifies an independent political organisation, and does not tell us anything about the nature of the society that is organised.[23]

Dawson sees two primordial dangers that are already present:

> The fact is that the modern world is being driven along at the same time in two opposite directions. On the one hand the nations are being brought into closer contact by the advance of scientific and technical achievements; the limits of space and time that held them asunder are being contracted or abolished, and the world has become physically one as never before. On the other hand, the nations are being separated from one another by a process of intensive organization which weakens the spiritual links that bound men together irrespective of political frontiers and concentrates the whole energy of society on the attainment of a collective purpose, so as inevitably to cause a collision with the collective will of other sources. What makes the danger of war so great today is not that men are more warlike than in the past, but that they are more highly organised. War is no longer the pastime of kings and the trade of professional armies, it is the death-grapple of huge impersonal mass Powers which have ground out the whole life of the whole population in the wheels of their social mechanism.[24]

Something of the real concerns and themes of international politics is suggested by the American political scientist Samuel Huntington in an article titled "The Clash of Civilizations?" in which the author suggests the new real source of conflicts in our time. Written in 1993, when Huntington observed a new phase of world politics, the article proposes what will be at the heart of present and future conflicts:

> It is my hypothesis that the fundamental source of conflict in this new world will not be primarily ideological or primarily economic. The great divisions among humankind and the dominating source of conflict will be cultural. Nation states will remain the most powerful actors in world affairs, but the principal conflicts of global politics will occur between nations and groups of different

civilizations. The clash of civilizations will dominate global politics. The fault lines between civilizations will be the battle lines of the future.[25]

Huntington offers several reasons for this conjecture; apart from obvious reasons such as the world becoming more interconnected, and the loosening of the identity of the nation state and economic regionalism, the author remarks that the cultural identities of peoples, their core beliefs and practices about the most fundamental questions of existence, are "more basic" and therefore "far more fundamental than differences among political ideologies and political systems."[26] Huntington also notes that cultural identity and characteristics are "less mutable and less easily compromised and resolved than political and economic ones."[27]

What Huntington refers to as the fault lines of civilizations may indicate the real context of international politics, beyond and beneath the straight lines of geographical borders. The phenomenon of profound collective and varied expressions of human existence raises the deeper issues of what human cultures express and why they differ. The question also arises as to why cultures or civilizations can be in conflict with each other. Along with the cultural conflicts goes a desire for unity in diversity and the attempts through associations and sports, for example, to refer to collective humanity, a universal fraternity, a unity of the nations. How can these diverse expressions be brought into unity—this would seem to be the core question of which international politics is but an outer layer.

THE UNITY OF THE NATIONS

In trying to understand the phenomenon of the clash of civilizations, not just as a given phenomenon, but its origin, dynamics, and possible resolution, a hypothesis is necessary. The signs we find in the clash of civilizations require understanding and require to be put in a greater context, whatever that context may be. Not to search for that greater context is to accept the permanence of conflict and violence, and the ultimate meaninglessness of our human condition, which contravenes the demands of human hope as an inbuilt condition of our human existence. The Hobbesian premise of individuals at war with each other may represent what often happens in our world; it is not what we hope for and aspire to as a human society. We cannot not hope, and the desire of the unity of the nations is a fundamental human aspiration. We are therefore required to propose a hypothesis for that political hope, a justification for that legitimate aspiration, in spite of the historical and actual evidence to the contrary.

The belief in inexorable progress, a classless society, universal and perpetual peace, all presuppose a sense of completion and perfection that goes beyond the actual evidence for such beliefs. The supposition of a greater context and the fulfilment of our collective hopes and aspirations is a human and political necessity. In proposing the Judeo-Christian explanation of the origin and destiny of man, I make a philosophical appeal for such a necessary explanation that, I propose, most adequately corresponds to, and respects, the complex phenomena of the human existential condition, as we experience it.

The Judeo-Christian explanation of this greater context is one of the original unity of humankind, humankind's actual rupture, and its destined achievement of unity. The actual ruptured condition of humanity retains the marks of an original natural unity of humanity. This original structural unity of humankind was fractured by human agency, and the effects of this rupture were not just within each person, as we can easily identify; there was also the effect of the division and clash between and among peoples:

> Instead of trying, as we do almost entirely nowadays, to find within each individual nature what is the hidden blemish and, so to speak, of looking for the mechanical source of the trouble which is the cause of the faulty running of the engine—some exaggerating the trouble, others inclined to minimise it—these Fathers preferred to envisage the very constitution of the individuals considered as so many cores of natural opposition. This was not taken as the first or only cause of sin, of course, but at least as a secondary result, "equal to the first," and the inner disruption went hand in hand with the social disruption.[28]

This explanation of the phenomenon of the clash of cultures highlights the exaggerated notion of individualism that we often take as the sole description of man. The hypothesis presented here suggests that this polarized individualism of humankind was not the original condition or state of humankind, but the consequence of an original rupture of a multiplicity of one human nature which "was shattered into a thousand pieces and humanity which ought to constitute a harmonious whole, in which 'mine' and 'thine' would be no contradiction, is turned into a multitude of individuals, as numerous as the sands of the seashore, all of whom show violently discordant inclinations."[29]

What is of vital importance here is the vision, based not only on Judeo-Christian Scripture but also on the complex phenomenon of the human person's actual experience of unity and rupture, of an original unity of the nations, the fact that the meaning of existence of peoples is to be found as pertaining to an original whole, of which the shattering division and conflict is only a later development. The fundamental participation in a greater whole or unity—or body, as we are referring to a living organism—is the natural and original condition of peoples, and thus at the origin of the desire and aspiration for the unity of the nations that we experience. This explanation thus suggests an order of participation in unity that pre-exists humankind's actual condition of division and separation. What this means is that societies of peoples are fundamentally structured toward unity in diversity, both anterior to and beyond the merely contractual relations of treaties and agreements. At their most profound and real level, international relations are founded on the discovery and development of pre-existing bonds of unity, and not merely the contractual agreements of separated interests, as presupposed by the political form of the modern state. Therefore, at this profound level of relations between societies of peoples, one must go beyond the inherent limitations of modern state theory:

> The state mythos is based on a "theological" anthropology that precludes any truly social process. The recognition of our participation in one another through creation in the image of God is replaced by the recognition of the other as the bearer of individual rights, which may or may not be given by God, but which serve only to separate what is mine from what is thine. Participation in God and in one another is a threat to the formal mechanism of contract, which assumes that we are essentially individuals who enter into relationship with one another only when it is to one's individual advantage to do so. The mechanism of contract is purely "formal" in the sense that it has no intrinsic relationship to ends—the providential purpose of God—but is definable only as a means. The state can never truly integrate the individual and the group because there is nothing transcending the two-dimensional calculus of individual/aggregate through which individual and group are related.[30]

Discerning a pre-existing ordering of the nations toward unity liberates the political mind from the narrow context of relations between political states, and self-interest and self-determination as the only goals of international communion. Geographical borders and control of territory are important issues in the practical determination of particular interests and procedures, but they are not the real purposes of international politics. There are deeper sources of participation and unity that need to be searched for and recognized if the relations between peoples are truly to aspire to, and in some way reflect, the unity of the nations.

Equally, achieving the unity of the nations is not the result of some international political status quo. If the sources of unity of the nations are to be found in the participating and purifying syntheses of cultural, social, and religious visions of peoples according to a pre-existing order of being and purpose, then the unity of the nations is something greater than any imagined political effort. Again, the Judeo-Christian vision enlightens this phenomenon:

In Greco-Roman culture the unity of the world had its source in pantheism; the divine was itself a part of the world, and the world had divine status. Hence the unity of humanity could be converted directly into political reality. There was unity in the world itself, and so this unity could be realized within the world and from out of the world's own resources. The Roman emperor saw himself as the one who would bring this divine world power into being and therefore as a channel connecting the divine and the world of human beings. In the Bible, on the other hand, God stands free vis-à-vis the world. The story of the Tower of Babel in Gn.11:1–10, which follows right after the list of the peoples that points to the unity of all human beings, informs the reader that God punishes humanity, which had grown sinful, by breaking it up into a multiplicity of different and mutually incomprehensible languages. The division of humanity is, to be sure, the fault of men, but it is also their punishment and hence not merely something that one day, when they wanted to, they could get themselves out of . . . [the unity of the nations is seen] not as a mission that can be carried out in a directly political fashion but rather as an eschatological hope whose accomplishment is, in the last resort, God's doing.[31]

What this means for political endeavour is that the aspiration for united nations of peoples is both necessary and ultimately beyond the power of any political program to achieve. This means that the genuine political aspiration of universal peace and unity points to a political endeavour beyond any human capacity to achieve and that, therefore, no political program can claim to be the source of final unity. This does not imply a sense of political failure, but a necessary modification of political ambition, something that is ultimately positive in recognizing the limits of political endeavour. We are obliged to recognize that public meaning and purposes are not fundamentally the creation of our own minds and imaginations and that the resolution of our existential situation is not to be found in the fabrication of our ideas, but something that depends on a power that is not our own. This fundamental philosophical truth is also a Judeo-Christian one:

The Christian believes that the final achievement of linguistic and political unification is a matter of eschatology; he finds something sacrilegious in every imperialistic or syncretizing program of standardization or Gleichschaltung: but this does not require him to adopt an attitude of passive resignation towards the hermetic sealing-off of communication between the people of the earth, each isolated in its private world . . . his creed, on the contrary, includes belief in one fellowship of man; but not in an external uniformity that would abolish distinctions ordained by Providence.

The events of the present generation are symptomatic of the fundamental condition of fallen man, which is a state of dispersal. We have tried to regain the benefits of a homeland in the rigid mould of nation-states—the fractures appearing in the mould remind us that we are all really stateless persons, sojourners: we rediscover no less than the basic truth about our life on earth, through the crimes of contemporary society.[32]

What all this tells us about international politics is that the real sources of unity of the nations are to be found in the various collective and authentic cultural, social, and religious expressions of the human spirit. These are not merely fault lines of division and conflict, but diverse manifestations of a unity that we find shattered and broken, but not without traces of original unity. The movement toward the unity of the nations is a fundamental human aspiration and needs to be developed through what is most basic and immutable in cultural identities, and not just based on political plans or economic welfare. At the same time, political unity is not a human fabrication, not something that can be compressed into a program of political building and spending. The ultimate sources of unity lie in a power beyond human capacity and requires a political disposition of active adaptation to a greater dynamic reality that is always beyond the conditions of this human existence. This does not mean that political structures and political activity are ultimately meaningless, but rather that their meaning and purpose is contingent and circumscribed by a greater source of social unity from which political activity draws its authentic purposes.[33] "Human progress" is a phrase with a certain ambiguity. While it has a clear meaning in all that improves and enhances human life and the conditions of life, including ecological life, it is at times hard to evaluate what is truly human progress without reference to a greater context of truth. As we have seen, human activity is not necessarily and inexorably on a path of progress, and therefore human activity does not *per se* justify all increases in technical, economic, industrial, and social powers and forms. Without a reference to a framework of authentic human flourishing, correct decisions on what really constitutes progress are very difficult.[34]

THE SOURCES OF THE UNITY OF THE NATIONS

Breaking out intellectually from the rigid mold of nation-states requires the recognition that cultural, social, and religious bonds are the real sources of unity, and not only conflict, among the nations. This was recognized by the Irish politician Edmund Burke:

> In the intercourse between nations, we are apt to rely too much on the instrumental part. We lay too much weight upon the formality of treaties and compacts. We do not act much more wisely when we trust to the interests of men as guarantees of their engagements. The interests frequently tear to pieces the engagements; and the passions trample upon both. Entirely to trust to either, is

to disregard our own safety, or not to know mankind. Men are not tied to one another by papers and seals. They are led to associate by resemblances, by conformities, by sympathies. It is with nations as with individuals.

Nothing is so strong a tie of amity between nation and nation as correspondence in laws, customs, manners, and habits of life. They have more than the force of treaties in themselves. They are obligations written in the heart. They approximate men to men, without their knowledge, and sometimes against their intentions. The secret, unseen, but irrefragable bond of habitual intercourse, holds them together, even when their perverse and litigious nature sets them to equivocate, scuffle, and fight about the terms of their written obligations.[35]

For this reason, the truth that peoples can only establish lasting communion on the basis of a communion of authentic, if differing, cultural expressions of the human spirit, it is imperative that international relations move beyond the mold of political states to areas of cultural communion that can create lasting bonds of unity in cultural diversity. On the breakup of the political structure of the Soviet Union, the underlying cultural identities of the peoples within the political borders of the Soviet Union became apparent, identities that the Soviet Union had tried to eliminate and homogenize into a Communist mold.

John Paul II, himself a member of a Slavic and Polish cultural identity, appreciated the vital importance of cultural identity in an international context. While recognizing the contemporary mobility of peoples and what is generically called "globalization," John Paul II asserted another tendency of far more importance. In his *Address to the General Assembly of the United Nations Organisation* (1995), John Paul II recognized that while contemporary global trends caused by vast migrations of peoples, by ubiquitous media communications and a globally connected economy tend toward creating a homogenous world horizon, at the same time there has arisen, as a type of counterweight, a new consciousness of ethnic and national identities. These local identities seem to surge from the need for local and distinct identities as opposed to the forces of uniform global trends. John Paul II draws attention to this cultural phenomenon and underlines its importance. Such particular identities are not merely residues of the past but are expressions of real cultural needs and should be understood and appreciated in their anthropological dimension as well as in the ethical and legal consequences of these cultural expressions.[36]

What John Paul II is emphasizing is that there is no simplified generic category of humanity; humanity only exists in complex and varied cultural expressions that should not be glossed (or trampled) over in a facile vision of international politics. The realities of local and particular cultures are the vital context for human existence. To speak of humanity is, therefore, to refer to two existential contexts that are complex but not contradictory:

This tension between the particular and the universal can be considered immanent in human beings. By virtue of sharing in the same human nature, people
automatically feel that they are members of one great family, as is in fact the
case. But as a result of the concrete historical conditioning of this same nature,
they are necessarily bound in a more intense way to particular human groups,
beginning with the family and going on to the various groups to which they
belong and up to the whole of their ethnic and cultural group, which is called,
not by accident, a "nation," from the Latin word "nasci": "to be born." This
term, enriched with another one, "patria" (fatherland/motherland), evokes the
reality of the family. The human condition thus finds itself between these two
poles—universality and particularity—with a vital tension between them; an
inevitable tension, but singularly fruitful if they are lived in a calm and balanced way.[37]

John Paul II goes on to explain what is owed publicly to these cultural
nations, in which the human spirit finds its collective, local expression. What
is of note in his thought is the distinction between these cultural nations and
the mold of the political state, and the right to cultural existence, whether or
not this may be reflected in political statehood:

A presupposition of a nation's rights is certainly its right to exist: therefore no
one—neither a State nor another nation, nor an international organization—is
ever justified in asserting that an individual nation is not worthy of existence.
This fundamental right to existence does not necessarily call for sovereignty as
a state, since various forms of juridical aggregation between different nations
are possible, as for example occurs in Federal States, in Confederations or in
States characterized by broad regional autonomies. There can be historical circumstances in which aggregations different from single state sovereignty can
even prove advisable, but only on condition that this takes place in a climate of
true freedom, guaranteed by the exercise of the self-determination of the peoples
concerned. Its right to exist naturally implies that every nation also enjoys the
right to its own language and culture, through which a people expresses and
promotes that which I would call its fundamental spiritual "sovereignty."[38]

John Paul II goes on to recall the experience of his own country, Poland, to
show that it is the sense of a people's culture that permits a nation to continue
to exist even when its political and economic independence is compromised.
He concludes that every nation should have the right to determine the shape
of its collective existence according to its cherished values and customs,
provided of course that human rights are always respected and that cultural
or religious minorities have the freedom to coexist. In this sense, John Paul
claims that every nation should be free to determine its own cultural existence
and to offer a corresponding education to its young people.[39]

It is clear, therefore, that the cultural settings of peoples are the foundations of human society and are what should inform political considerations, most especially the political relations between peoples. The extent to which international politics has reversed this order and subjugated the cultural lives of peoples in terms of the geographical boundaries of statehood and prevailing forms of political power has exacerbated the tensions of international relations. At the same time, the requirements of citizenship of a state become paper-thin as the political state dominates and suppresses real cultural identities.[40]

A clear example of the contrast between the identity of peoples based on their cultural expressions and identity based on political power can be seen in the phases of development of the European Union, which began as a project of a common European economic market and that, by means of the *Single European Act of 1987* and the *Maastricht Treaty of 1992*, has established the framework for a single European state. The actual fabrication of this single European state has been problematic. At first, it was thought that economic integration would of itself generate bonds of European unity. As British political anthropologist Cris Shore writes:

> The neofunctionalist theory (as developed by Haas, Lindberg and others) held that political union would evolve gradually from a steady, cumulative process of economic integration: that is, the progressive enmeshing of economic institutions and harmonisation of laws would inevitably spill over into the hitherto sacrosanct social, cultural and political spheres. Political union was seen as a rational and mechanical process; a "functional" by-product of economic and technical measures. Neofunctionalist theory assumed that once federal political institutions were established, the transfer of loyalties from the nation states to the federation would follow automatically. A small number of successful international institutions would thus generate a process that would progressively wean people away from their attachment to the nation-state and re-focus those loyalties upon themselves. This unflinching confidence in the inevitability of the "spill over" effect—the famous "Monnet Method"—explains why European Union elites felt little need to involve the peoples of Europe in their project of political engineering; their "passive consent" was deemed sufficient.[41]

This failure led to a new approach, one that required investment in cultural symbols that were to catch the European imagination and becomes sources of European identity. In 1984, the European Council established a committee to promote European cultural identity. Apart from an emblem and flag:

> Other symbolic vehicles for communicating the "Europe idea" included proposals for European postage stamps bearing portraits of EC pioneers (like Schuman and Monnet); a standardised European passport and driving license;

car number-plates bearing the EU emblem; and a European anthem, taken from the fourth movement of Beethoven's Ninth symphony—the "Ode to Joy"—which the Committee recommended be played at all suitable ceremonies and events. The "high profile initiatives to boost the Community's image" also included new EC-sponsored sporting competitions and awards, the formation of an "EC Youth Orchestra," a series of projects to conserve Europe's architectural heritage (the largest of which was the restoration of the Parthenon in Athens), and the invention of a "European Woman of the Year Award." In addition, the Commission has financed over one thousand "Jean Monnet Awards" to create new university Chairs and lectureships in European integration studies with the aim of "Europeanising" university teaching (CEC 1996a).[42]

Even so, these efforts to create cultural identity have had only a sporadic impact and have been recognized as being used as a tool of political integration rather than the discovery and development of authentic European cultures:

> The various "cultural initiatives" described above were intended not simply to promote consciousness of Europe but to create a new kind of "European consciousness," one capable of mobilising Europe's 370 million citizens towards a new conception of themselves as "Europeans" rather than simply nationals. Just as the rise of nationalism had turned "peasants into Frenchmen" (Weber 1979), so "Europeanism" would transform Frenchmen, Greeks, Danes and Germans into "Europeans." During the 1980s, therefore, "culture" became an increasingly politicised domain as its importance to the integration process was recognised (hence the repeated references in EC discourse to Monnet's supposed statement "if we had to begin all over again, we would start with culture").[43]

What this meant for those who wanted to integrate the peoples of Europe was a new emphasis on the importance of "European culture" as the key to bring about a popular European identity that would be as meaningful as, or even replace, national loyalties.

Clearly, European culture means much more than the political and economic integration of governments and budgets, and the attempts to achieve that integration by symbolic means. Certainly, political and economic arrangements can facilitate and dispose peoples to integrate, but, fundamentally, the structures need to reflect the real cultural integration of peoples and cannot substitute for the real sources of unity in diversity.[44]

At the same time, the cultural integration of Europe faces a distinct challenge. If the point of the argument is that political, economic, and administrative structures are dependent on deeper interpersonal cultural bonds, the crisis of European integration is dependent on a crisis of what European culture is considered to be. Joseph Ratzinger has noticed an unease with reference to the historical contributions to European culture, its distinctive assimilation of faith and reason that enlightened the cultural expressions of education, literature, science, law, politics that are the undeniable historical basis for European society.

Ratzinger, in a chapter of *Without Roots: The West, Relativism, Christianity, Islam,* in reference to the use of freedom of speech to denigrate expressions of the sacred, points out that there is in the West a strange self-loathing that has become extreme. Ratzinger recognizes the importance of the West's openness to other cultures and values and its attempts to understand and appreciate these cultures and values. At the same time, Western Europe needs to relearn an appreciation for its own identity and heritage. It seems that the general Western view of Europe's cultural heritage and history is entirely nega-tive and destructive, and that we are longer capable of recognizing its great achievements and cultural value. Ratzinger sees that a positive and balanced re-evaluation of Europe's identity and heritage is essential for its survival.[45]

The successful political integration of the nations of Europe depends on the integration of the profound cultural expressions of European culture. Ratzinger notices that the popular term multiculturalism can be an ambigu-ous term because it can mean the rejection and abandonment of one's own culture, and the denial of its values. Ratzinger suggests that an authentic multiculturalism can only be pursued from a position of real self-identity and the recognition of one's own real values. He also suggests that culture as such depends on an explicit reference to and respect for the sacred.[46]

The present war on Ukrainian soil has had, and will continue to have, profound ramifications for the European Union. At the same time, whether the war will awaken the profound roots of European identity and lead to a recognition of a common social and cultural identity, remains to be seen. At present, it seems that the war precludes any such deeper discussions.

The real and lasting context of international political relations is not to be found in the lines of geographical borders or in the exclusive control of stable and identifiable populations, but in the shared depth of varied cultural expres-sions of original unity.

THE POLITICAL IDEA OF UNIVERSAL BROTHERHOOD

There is a simplistic notion of a universal humanity that can and has been used as a political instrument for the imposition of uniformity. While there is an important social and political truth in the idea of universal humanity, the real relation of peoples to each other is more complex than the supposition that we are all brothers and sisters and therefore we all are, or can become, equal and the same, and that all differences and inequalities are necessarily the result of some form of injustice.

The difficulty with the social and political notion of a universal humanity lies in the fact that establishing a category of humanity always implies
establishing a common particular identity and therefore necessarily a separation from others who do not have this identity and are therefore not brothers
or sisters.

Historically, in ancient Greece there were two discernible tendencies. On
the one hand, there was the understanding of metaphorical common identity
for co-citizens and for members of the same nation, with ties of consanguinity
or friendship.[47] When the system of the poleis ("city-states") broke up, new
groups of religious brotherhood developed, at times developing into secret
societies with initiation ceremonies and mystery cults. As Ratzinger notices
in these cases:

> Brotherhood implies a frontier. In Plato, if the community of the state bestows
> brotherhood, then the foreigner, the barbarous, is regarded as a nonbrother.
> Xenophon's brotherhood of friends not only unites friends, but also divided off
> those who are not friends. All unions involve the separating of those who are
> united together from others. Although neither Plato nor Xenophon specifically
> refer to it, the basic problem of every brotherhood ethos arises here. If, for
> example, the people united in one polis form a brotherhood, the ethos within
> that polis will necessarily differ from the attitude toward those outside it, who
> are not brothers: ethical responsibility is different within the "extended family"
> than outside it. In other words, this broadened concept of brotherhood inevitably
> creates two different kinds of ethos.[48]

What one recognizes here is the human need and tendency to form closer
bonds, based either on relations of blood or notions of friendship and close-
ness, which necessarily push all others into the background. This implies a
human need for a certain particularity and exclusivity of relations, making
difficult a notion of a universal humanity.

On the other hand, the philosophical currents of Stoicism, as, for example,
in Seneca, Epictetus, and Marcus Aurelius, all emphasized the relationship
that exists among all human beings, a cosmopolitanism, and the love of
humanity.[49] As Ratzinger explains that "Behind the difference of cultural
forms Stoicism had discovered the unity of the being 'man,' the unvarying
humanity of man, which exists throughout all times and places. It had discovered that the entire cosmos was nothing other than Zeus's immense body, and
that all of humankind was a single body."[50]

Here the other, and seemingly opposite, dimension of the notion of a universal humanity is displayed, the recognition of a universal similitude and
bond that requires an ethical and religious response.

It is not surprising that these two apparently contrasting notions cause a
social political dilemma that is played out in doctrines of state nationalism,

the emphasis on affirming one's own political state identity, as opposed to varieties of internationalism, which at times can take the guise of universal equality and uniformity, with many practical consequences.[51]

It was in the French Revolution that the modern political version of universal humanity found renewed vitality:

> The French Revolution proclaimed liberté, egalité, fraternité, and made the brotherhood of men with equal rights a political, revolutionary program. The origin of this brotherhood in the common paternity of God now moved very much into the background. It has too remote, too hypothetical a ring when Schiller sings in his "Ode to Joy": "Brothers, above the starry sky there must dwell a loving father"; the brotherhood of man seems independent of this idea. It is conceived as coming from this world, from the similar heredity and nature of all men. It involves going behind history to the nature of man that is anterior to it.[52]

The revolutionary claim to the notion of a universal mankind was taken up and found a new expression in Marxism. While the goal of a classless society and universal comradeship was proposed, the path to this ideal future society was by the establishment of a workers' fraternity that would take on and oppose the oppressive superstructure of the capitalists. In this division, Marxism reverts to the notion of humanity as implying separation, even if, theoretically, only maintained until the class society won through.

In *The Meaning of Christian Brotherhood*, Ratzinger points out that Marxism as a militant ideology represents in this sense a rejection of the Enlightenment idea of universal fraternity and a return to the notion of two ethical categories of humanity. Instead of the Enlightenment claim to a notion of a universal humanity, Marxism promoted a radical division of humanity into two opposing classes, that of the proletariat and of the capitalists. The conflict between these classes was the fault line of history and all people found themselves necessarily in one of the classes or the other; to be of one class meant of necessity to be against and in conflict with the other class. Within this ideological premise, some people are brothers and sisters; others are enemies.[53]

In international relations we have proposed that culture, in its entire extension of the manifestation of the human spirit, is the real foundation of the unity of the nations, as admittedly also, the real source of conflict between peoples. The question we now face is how to resolve seemingly opposing human needs and tendencies and to unite in closer bonds of relation while, at the same time, to retain the universal dimension of humanity.

> The naiveté of Schiller's "Be embraced ye millions" has often been remarked on in this connection. In fact, a brotherliness which embraces everyone equally

cannot expect to be taken seriously by anyone. This insight rather deepens the problem we have set for ourselves, for it raises these questions: Must an ethos, to be realizable, perhaps contain some form of duality? Does it inevitably require a closed "inner ring" to be fully workable? We should remember here that the program of the enlightenment did not emerge very well as realized through the French Revolution which differentiated drastically and bloodily between the inner fraternal circle of the revolutionaries and the outer circle of the nonrevolutionaries. We must also remember that liberalism, the heir of the Enlightenment ideology, also created in freemasonry its own highly differentiated inner fraternal group.[54]

It seems ingenuous, an unwarranted simplification, to speak in political terms of an undistinguished and homogenous humanity. As Manent writes in *Metamorphoses of the City*, this category of humanity is very difficult to determine and qualify, and this makes the category very useful for those who would wish to make humanity according to their own criteria and for their own objectives. Such ideologues can then determine who belongs and who is to be rejected from their particular description of humanity. It is precisely the noble vagueness of the term that makes it susceptible to this type of ideological exploitation.[55]

The point here is not to deny a common humanity but to recognize that such a vast category does not represent the complexity of the whole reality, even if this homogenous term seems to prevail in contemporary international politics. More descriptive of the complex actual condition of humanity, its original unity, its actual brokenness, and its desire for wholeness, is, I suggest, the biblical phrase "unity of the nations." As Ratzinger notes:

> All men, Israelites and Gentiles, ultimately constituted a single humanity because of their single human source and the single creative act of God . . . the duality comes from the elective exclusiveness of God toward Israel and the exclusive descent from the fathers of the covenant, Abraham, Isaac, and Jacob. In practical terms, this meant that direct brotherhood applied only to those who shared one's country and faith.[56]

This meant, as Ratzinger explains, that the obligations of the Israelites among themselves were thus different and greater than those owed to the Gentiles. Even so:

> This evident and undeniable duality could never degenerate into dualism, however, as was possible in the Greek world and in the religions of the countries surrounding Israel; rather it was held together through unity of God and the unity of humanity, so that human responsibility went beyond the framework of the brotherly community, as is shown concretely by the Old Testament's

laws concerning strangers (*Ex* 22:20, 23:9; *Dt* 14:29, and elsewhere; *Lv* 19:33f; 19:10; 23:22; Nb9:14; 15:14ff; 35:15).[57]

What this implies about the underlying condition of humanity is the real difference of the nations, of what truly constitutes a people—its cultural vision, its relation to transcendent purpose and meaning, the significance of its personal, family, and social bonds, with the many manifestations of this cultural spirit—and implies a double movement toward unity. On the one hand, the growth in the community's distinctive collective identity, and, on the other hand, the search for greater fulfilment in the active openness to the other authentic manifestations of human culture, which entails positive conflict and avoids the superficial settlement of some lowest common denominator. It is this, ultimately, what distinguishes short-visioned international politics based on the mold of the modern state from the real search for the unity of the nations based on the integration of authentic elements of diverse cultural spirits. This movement, with its polarity oriented toward unity is reflected (not exclusively) in the Christian faith:

> In contrast to the Stoics and the Enlightenment, Christianity affirms the existence of two different zones and calls only fellow believers "brothers." On the other hand, however, Christianity, unlike the mystery cults, is wholly free from a desire to form some self-sufficient esoteric group. Rather the separating off of some has its ultimate significance only in the service it fulfils for the others who are, at bottom, the "other brother" and whose fate is in the hands of the first brother.[58]

While expressed in a Judeo-Christian context, I suggest that this description of human society and their cultures provides the most accurate paradigm of unity and diversity that is also of political relevance. Unwarranted simplifications of one universal humanity of one homogenous equality are avoided, and cultures are called to reflect what is truly and completely human in social life—they express real and significant bonds of particular unity and identity. In this sense, cultural conflict has its positive dimension as a representation of authentic human existence that challenges (and are challenged) by other authentic cultural manifestations that both express legitimate variations and challenge inauthentic ways of social living. In other words, there is a healthy conflict of cultures that is lost in notions of protected zones of isolated indifference. At the same time, the search for a greater unity of diverse cultures reflects both the original unity of mankind and the real aspiration toward this greater unity.

This understanding of the unity of the nations is a far deeper expression of the complex reality of human society, something that reflects much better the difficult and necessary global need of unity than the artificial notion of a political state and the attempt to frame and resolve international political problems and their solutions in terms of inter-state relations.

CONCLUSION

The theme of this chapter has centered on the real terms of international relations beyond, and to an extent, opposed to the prevailing model of the political state. Huntington pointed to this reality when he wrote that although "nation states will remain the most powerful actors in world affairs" he considered that "the great divisions among humankind and the dominating source of conflict will be cultural."[59] Others are less certain about the survival of the modern political nation state. Jean-Marie Guéhenno, professor at the *Institut d'Études Politiques* in Paris and former French ambassador to the European Union, recognizes that the model of the modern political state no longer corresponds to the reality of networks of economic modernity:

> The "territorial given" is outmoded, and no utilitarian, functional vision of the state can replace it. . . . Everything changed when human activity liberates itself from space; when the mobility of the population and the economy makes nonsense of geographical demarcations. The spatial solidarity of territorial communities is disappearing, to be replaced by temporary interest groups. Now, the nation-state, in its pretension to combine in a unique framework the political, cultural, economic, and military dimensions of power, is prisoner to a spatial conception of power, even as it tries to redistribute its competences according to a federal principle. Space has ceased to be the pertinent criterion. Will politics survive a similar revolution? From the beginning, since the Greek city (polis), politics has been the art of governing a collectivity of people defined by their rootedness in a location, city, or nation. If solidity can no longer be locked into geography, if there is no longer a city, if there is no longer a nation, can there still be politics?[60]

What Guéhenno envisages are multiple, vast, interconnected, impersonal, and diffused networks of power, primarily economic, a blanket of conformity to formal procedures and rules, the reign of interests rather than principles. And what of the individual person in this new de-politicized society?

> Without any links to a territory, "nomadic," and nevertheless imprisoned in a function, without an overarching perspective to give a meaning to a given task, modern man, a social nodule infinitely reproduced and nevertheless always single, solitary, is condemned to find difference in a search for origins—a

difference that he needs in order to share with others, as different as he is, a feeling of common heritage.[61]

This is an entirely functional society of networks, which will "not claim either to elevate itself to the heavens or to appropriate the heavens for its earthly purposes." To react against this bland oppression, Guéhenno recognizes that:

The revolution to be accomplished is of a spiritual order. The debates of the future will focus on the relationship of man with the world: they will be ethical debates, and through them, perhaps, politics may one day be born again, in a process that will start from the bottom, from local democracy and the account that a community will give of itself, and proceed upward.[62]

It is of course notoriously hard to predict the dominant future forms of social and public power. What does seem increasingly evident is that the form of the modern political state represents less and less the real contours of social identity. International politics is still generally framed in the context of independent and sovereign states and in terms of central power and geographical borders. The reality is that the deeper and more authentic bonds of social identity overrun these political parameters. However, the future forms of international politics may be expressed, any real steps toward a unity of the nations will need to rely on these deeper and more authentic bonds of social identity.

NOTES

1. Pierre Manent, "The Return of Political Philosophy," *First Things* 103 (May 2000): 15, https://www.firstthings.com/article/2000/05/the-return-of-political -philosophy intolerance (accessed October 12, 2023). Manent begins this article with the phrase: "It could be said that the twentieth century has witnessed the disappearance, or withering away, of political philosophy." I suggest that the present form of "democracy," as we call it, has its part in dissolving the real challenges of political philosophy into misleading simplifications of the democratic form.

2. Pierre Manent, *Metamorphoses of the City: On the Western Dynamic*, trans. Marc LePain (Cambridge, MA: Harvard University Press, 2013), 297.

3. William Cavanaugh, "The City: Beyond Secular Parodies," in *Radical Orthodoxy: A New Theology*, ed. John Milbank, Catherine Pickstock, and Graham Ward (London: Routledge, 1999), 191. Both Milbank and Cavanaugh comment on the use of religion in cultivating allegiance to these new sovereign powers. Cf. John Milbank, *Theology and Social Theory;Beyond Secular Reason*, 2nd ed. (Malden, MA: Blackwell, 2006), 9–25, chap. 1 "Political Theology and the New Science of Politics"; and

William Cavanaugh, *Migrations of the Holy: God, State, and the Political Meaning of the Church* (Grand Rapids, MI: Eerdsmans, 2011).

4. Cavanaugh, *Migrations of the Holy*, 374–83. In this quotation Cavanaugh refers to Robert A. Nisbet's *Quest for Community*, where Nisbet points out acutely that the modern or contemporary state is not the mere natural and formal expression of the nation; in fact, Nisbet claims that the national identity is something that has been exploited by the state. The nationalistic development of the state in the nineteenth and twentieth centuries was not the spontaneous outgrowth of more basic cultural forms of social identity. What is true, Nisbet states, is that these real emotional and affective cultural expressions of people have been purposefully grafted onto the form of the modern state, giving to and making the state a symbolic national identity, but this national identity does not belong naturally to the state. In fact, the grafting process of cultural forms onto the form of the modern state necessarily implied a severance of earlier bonds of cultural allegiance and belief and their artificial transferral to the new form of the state. Cf. Nisbet, *The Quest for Community: A Study in the Ethics of Order and Freedom* (Washington, DC: ISI Books, 2010), 2900–2915.

5. Immanuel Kant, *Toward Perpetual Peace and Other Writings on Politics, Peace, and History* (1795), ed. Pauline Kleingeld, trans. David L. Colclasure (New Haven, CT: Yale University Press, 2006), 91. The Romanian French philosopher Pierre Hassner notes that "Kant firmly decides in favour of the difficult reconciliation of the multiplicity of states and a lawful order, although it is true that, in *Religion within the Limits of Reason Alone*, he refers to the 'premature and therefore fatal fusion of states (if it occurs before men have become morally better)' thus leaving open the possibility of the universal state as the culmination of a historical progress that has moral progress as its prerequisite condition." Cf. Leo Strauss and Joseph Cropsey, eds. *History of Political Philosophy*, 3rd ed. (Chicago: University of Chicago Press, 1987), 12170.

6. Frederic Copleston, *A History of Philosophy* (New York: Doubleday, 1985), vol. 7, 225.

7. Georg W. F. Hegel, *Outlines of the Philosophy of Right*, rev. ed., trans. T. M. Knox, notes by Stephen Holgate (Oxford: Oxford University Press, 2008), 312. Hassner comments on Hegel's thought: "During history, wars and revolutions are the instruments of the universal spirit. The rise of the people which bears the Idea and the diffusion of the principle in which the universal Spirit is incarnated are effectuated by wars" Strauss and Cropsey, eds., *History of Political Philosophy*, 15084.

8. Hegel, *Outlines of the Philosophy of Right*, 306–7. Kant also envisaged the natural necessity of war: "All wars are therefore only so many attempts (not, to be sure, in the aims of human beings, but yet in the aim of nature) to bring about new relationships between states, and through destruction or at least dismemberment of all of them . . . until finally, partly through the best possible arrangement of their civil constitution internally, partly through a common agreement and legislation externally, a condition is set up which, resembling a civil commonwealth, can preserve itself like an automaton." Cf. Immanuel Kant, "Idea for a Universal History," in *Anthropology, History, and Education*, ed. and trans. Günter Zöller and Robert B. Louden (Cambridge: Cambridge University Press, 2007), 114–15.

9. Pierre Hassner, qtd. in Strauss and Cropsey, *History of Political Philosophy*, 15071.

10. Woodrow Wilson, *Fourteen Points*, January 8, 1918, Goldman Law Library, 2008, points 5 and 14, https://avalon.law.yale.edu/20th_century/wilson14.asp. For a concise conceptual and historical study of the modern development of the right of self-determination, see Jörg Fisch, *The Right of Self-Determination of Peoples: The Domestication of an Illusion*, trans. Anita Mage(Cambridge: Cambridge University Press, 2015).

11. United Nation Organisation, *Charter of the United Nations*, October 24, 1945, 1 UNTS XVI. https://www.un.org/en/about-us/un-charter (accessed October 15, 2023). Charter 1(2). This reference to self-determination is reiterated in article 55, with reference to international economic and social cooperation.

12. United Nation Organisation, *Declaration on the Granting of Independence to Colonial Countries and Peoples*, December 14, 1960, A/RES/1514(XV), n2, https://www.ohchr.org/en/instruments-mechanisms/instruments/declaration-granting -independence-colonial-countries-and-peoples (accessed October 15, 2023).

13. United Nations Organisation, *Declaration on Principles of International Law concerning Friendly Relations and Cooperation among States in accordance with the Charter of the United Nations*, October 24, 1970, A/RES/2625(XXV), https:// digitallibrary.un.org/record/202170?ln=en (accessed October 15, 2023). In Malcom N. Shaw's *International Law*, 7th ed. (Cambridge: Cambridge University Press, 2014), the author refers to cases referring to Namibia, the Western Sahara, East Timor, and Kosovo (Cf. 185–87).

14. Shaw, *International Law*, 143.

15. As cited in Shaw, *International Law*, 144. This description of the political state is similar to Max Weber's description of a state as an entity holding a monopoly on the legitimate use of force within a certain geographical area. Cf. Weber, *The Theory of Social and Economic Organization*, trans. Talcott Parsons and A. M. Henderson (New York: Free Press, 1964), 154–56.

16. As Shaw observes, the unilateral declaration of independence of Lithuania from the Soviet Union in 1990 went internationally unrecognized until 1991. On the other hand, the international recognition of Croatia and Bosnia-Herzegovina and their admittance to the United Nations occurred while much of their territory was under the control of non-governmental forces (Cf. Shaw, *International Law*, 143–48).

17. Both cases are analysed in Shaw's *International Law*; Reference Re Secession of Quebec (1998) (186–88), and the Kosovo advisory opinion (2010) (171–72).

18. Reference Supreme Court of Canada. *Re Secession of Quebec*, 1998, 2 SCR 217, CanLII 793 (1998), Docket No. 25506, 2 SCR 217, n126. The Court did recognize, however, that "the continued existence and operation of the Canadian constitutional order could not be indifferent to a clear expression of a clear majority of Quebecers that they no longer wish to remain in Canada. The other provinces and the federal government would have no basis to deny the right of the government of Quebec to pursue secession, should a clear majority of the people of Quebec choose that goal, so long as in doing so, Quebec respects the rights of others" (n151).

19. International Court of Justice, Reports of Judgments, Advisory Opinions and Orders, *Accordance with International Law of the Unilateral Declaration of Independence in Respect of Kosovo*, Advisory Opinion of July 22, 2010, n82, https://www.icj -cij.org/case/141 (accessed October 14, 2023). *Accordance with International Law of the Unilateral Declaration of Independence in Respect of Kosovo*, Advisory Opinion of July 22, 2010, n.82. The Court's comment on the evolution of the principle of self-determination is from n79 of the Advisory Opinion. This was Kosovo's second declaration of independence, the first being in September 1990. Today Kosovo is recognized by 93 of the 193 political states of the United Nations member states.

20. Cf. Tarek Osman, "Why Border Lines Drawn with a Ruler in WW1 Still Rock the Middle East," *BBC News*, December 14, 2013, https://www.bbc.com/news/world -middle-east-25299553 (accessed October 15, 2023).

21. Karl Popper, *Conjectures and Refutations: The Growth of Scientific Knowledge*, 2nd ed. (London: Routledge Classics, 2002), 9825–26.

22. John Milbank and Adrian Pabst, *The Politics of Virtue: Post-Liberalism and the Human Future* (Lanham, MD: Rowman & Littlefield, 2016), 318.

23. Christopher Dawson, *The Judgment of the Nations*, ed. John J. Mulloy (Washington, DC: Catholic University of America Press, 2011), 53. *The Judgment of the Nations* was published in 1942 during World War II, barely twenty years after World War I.

24. Dawson, *Judgment of the Nations*, 52, cited in Milbank and Pabst, *Politics of Virtue*, 318–19.

25. Samuel Huntington, "The Clash of Civilizations?" *Foreign Affairs* 72, no. 3 (1993): 22. This article was extended into *The Clash of Civilizations and the Remaking of World Order* (New York: Simon and Schuster, 2011). Benedict XVI, in his Christmas message to the Roman Curia in 2006, referred to "the general danger of a clash between cultures and religions—a danger that hangs threateningly over our time in history." Benedict XVI, *Address of His Holiness Benedict XVI to the Members of the Roman Curia at the Traditional Exchange of Christmas Greetings*, December 22, 2006, https://www.vatican.va/content/benedict-xvi/en/speeches/2006/december /documents/hf_ben_xvi_spe_20061222_curia-romana.html (accessed October 12, 2023).

26. Huntington, "Clash of Civilizations?" 25.

27. Huntington, "Clash of Civilizations?" 27.

28. Henri de Lubac, *Catholicism: Christ and the Common Destiny of Man*, trans. Lancelot Sheppard (San Francisco: Ignatius Press, 1988), 34–35. The reference to the "Fathers" is to the early theologians and intellectuals of the Christian Church, in the Western tradition of the first five centuries of the Christian faith. In the East, the category is open-ended, up to the present day.

29. De Lubac, *Catholicism*, 34. He refers also to Augustine's use of a symbolic image: "After establishing a connection between the four letters of Adam's name and the Greek names for the four points of the compass, he adds: 'Adam himself is therefore now spread out over the whole face of the earth. Originally one, he has fallen, and, breaking up as it were, he has filled the whole world with the pieces'" (34). The reference to Augustine is from *In Psalm*, 95n15 (PL 37, 1236).

30. William T. Cavanaugh, *Theopolitical Imagination: Discovering the Liturgy as a Political Act in an Age of Global Consumerism* (London: Bloomsbury, 2013), 44.

31. Joseph Ratzinger, *The Unity of the Nations: A Vision of the Church Fathers* (Washington, DC: Catholic University of America Press, 2013), 11–13. It is a curious detail that the building of the European Union at Strasburg bears a striking similarity to the sixteenth-century Dutch Renaissance painter Pieter Bruegel the Elder's Tower of Babel painting. Apparently, the architects of the building, Architecture Studio, did not have this intention.

32. Jean Daniélou, *The Lord of History: Reflections on the Inner Meaning of History* (New York: Meridian Books, 1968), 58, 59–60.

33. This was Augustine's thought which, while rejecting Roman political theology, allows for a temporary and positive role of political authority: "God, who created the world, also remained its Lord; the Creator God was also the God of history. From this realiation sprang the leitmotif of Augustine's political theology: *ipse dat regna terrena*. It is God himself who distributes earthly kingdoms. The political world, with its manifold and opposing states, had no special divinities but rather was subordinate to the one God, whose works were creation and history" Ratzinger, *Unity of the Nations*, 85.

34. The question of true human progress arose in the context of the Second Vatican Council in relation to the Catholic Church and "the world," and the degree to which the signs of the times of the world could be identified with the Christian truth about man and society. Cf. Joseph Ratzinger, *Principles of Catholic Theology: Building Stones for a Fundamental Theology* (San Francisco: Ignatius Press, 1987), 378–93.

35. Edmund Burke, "The First Letter on a Regicide Peace," in *Revolutionary Writings*, ed. Iain Hampsher-Monk (Cambridge: Cambridge University Press, 2014), 316, cited in Milbank and Pabst, *Politics of Virtue*, 357–58. As Charles J. Chaput points out in a chapter commentary on "The Song of Roland": "Our loves and loyalties desire public and durable forms. We seek to celebrate the bonds that unite us. These bonds precede formal expressions of official ties. The impulse to recognize preexisting bonds is the key impulse of civic life. We have nation-states because we have nations, not the other way round" Chaput, *Things Worth Dying For: Thoughts on a Life Worth Living* (New York: Henry Holt, 2021), 96.

36. John Paul II, "Address to the General Assembly of the United Nations," *L'Osservatore Romano* (Weekly edition in English), October 5, 1995, n7. https://www.vatican.va/content/john-paul-ii/en/speeches/1995/october/documents/hf_jp-ii_spe_05101995_address-to-uno.html (accessed October 14, 2023).

37. John Paul II, "Address to the General Assembly of the United Nations," n7. There is a direct analogy here with the nature of the human persons who, as persons, both share in a rational nature, and, at the same time, are themselves and no other. "One of the best-known utterances of the Roman jurists about the person connects being a person with being incommunicable: persona est *sui iuris et alteri incommunicabilis*. It is precisely as person that I am myself (*sui iuris*) and no other (*alteri incommunicabilis*). St. Thomas Aquinas clearly teaches that being a person is not a common nature like human nature that can be shared in by many; being a person is rather a matter of being an incommunicable individual within some rational

nature" John F. Crosby, *Personalist Papers* (Washington, DC: Catholic University of America Press, 2004), 8.

38. John Paul II, "Address to the General Assembly of the United Nations," n8. John Paul II refers to his own experience in occupied Poland during the World War II. Karol Wojtyla, with others, enacted clandestine theatrical performances of Polish historical literature in an effort "'to save our culture from the Occupation' and to help restore the nation's soul, which was a precondition to its political resurrection" George Weigel, *Witness to Hope: The Biography of Pope John Paul II* (New York: HarperCollins, 1999), 65. The quotation is from Danuta Michalowska, a fellow actress with Wojtyla. On John Paul II's view of nation and patria, see his *Memory and Identity: Conversations at the Dawn of a Millennium* (New York: Rizzoli, 2005), esp. 57–87.

39. John Paul II, "Address to the General Assembly of the United Nations," n8.

40. How arbitrary and superficial state identity has become can be seen in the case of millions of young people who entered the United States and countries of Europe as undocumented minors, have lived in these countries for years, and yet are subject to deportation "because they lack the right piece of paper": "Millions of young people across Europe have, like Thomas, been born on the wrong side of little-known laws—in her case a 1981 restriction on automatic citizenship at birth. They grew up feeling British or French or Italian or European, but are now trapped in a state of limbo. The threat of deportation hangs over them because, like the US Dreamers, they lack the right piece of paper" Charlotte Alfred, "'We Want to Build a Life': Europe's Paperless Young People Speak Out," *Guardian*, August 3, 2020, https://www.theguardian.com/world/2020/aug/03/europe-paperless-young-people-speak-out-undocumented-dreamers (accessed October 12, 2023).

41. Cris Shore, *European Union and the Politics of Culture*. Bruges Group (pamphlet), March 2001, https://www.brugesgroup.com/media-centre/papers/8-papers/900-european-union-and-the-politics-of-culture (accessed October 15, 2023). Shore's argument is developed in *Building Europe: The Cultural Politics of European Integration* (London: Routledge, 2013). The author refers to Ernst B. Haas, *The Uniting of Europe: Political, Social, and Economic Forces* (Stanford, CA: Stanford University Press, 1958); Leon N. Lindberg, *The Political Dynamics of European Economic Integration* (Stanford, CA: Stanford University Press, 1963); Paul Taylor, *The Limits of European Integration* (London: Croom Helm, 1983); and Michael O'Neill, *The Politics of European Integration* (London: Routledge, 1996). For past and present models of European integration see Ben Rosamond, *Theories of European Integration* (New York: Red Globe Press, 2000). The reference is to Jean Monnet (1888–1979), the first leader of a European executive body (the High Authority of the European Coal and Steel Community), and one of the chief architects of the project of European unity.

42. Shore, "European Union and the Politics of Culture."

43. Cris Shore, "European Union and the Politics of Culture."

44. This greater spiritual and cultural union of the European peoples was at the heart of the intentions of the founding statemen of the European Union; Robert Schuman, Konrad Adenauer, Alcide De Gasperi, and Jean Monnet. Speaking at the signing of the new statutes of the Council of Europe on May 5, 1949, Schuman spoke

of the binding rule of law, which "created the foundations of a spiritual and political cooperation, from which the European spirit will be born, the principle of a vast and enduring supranational union." Schuman, 1949, cited in Jonathan Chaplin and Gary Wilton, eds., *God and the EU:: Faith and the European Project* (London: Routledge, 2015), 32. On Schuman's own religious and political ideals, see Alan Paul Fimister, *Robert Schuman: Neo-Scholastic Humanism and the Reunification of Europe* (Brussels: Peter Lang, 2008).

45. Joseph Ratzinger, "The Spiritual Roots of Europe," in *Without Roots: The West, Relativism, Christianity, Islam*, by Joseph Ratzinger and Marcello Pera (New York: Basic Books, 2006), 78–79. On Ratzinger's view of Europe, its history, cultural identity and present challenges, see, *inter alia*, Joseph Ratzinger, *Europe: Today and Tomorrow* (San Francisco: Ignatius Press, 2007), and also the essays "Europe—Hopes and Dangers," and "A Turning Point for Europe?" in *A Turning Point for Europe? The Church in the Modern World: Assessment and Forecast* (San Francisco: Ignatius Press, 1994), 1046–1340, 1355–1640.

46. Ratzinger, "Spiritual Roots of Europe," in *Without Roots*, 79.

47. "In Plato we find the description of one's fellow citizen as a brother (Menexenos, 239a): 'We and our fellow citizens are all brothers born of one another.' Xenophon calls a friend a 'brother' (Anabasis, II,2,25;38)" Ratzinger, *The Meaning of Christian Brotherhood* (San Francisco: Ignatius Press, 1993), 5.

48. Ratzinger, *Meaning of Christian Brotherhood*, 5–6.

49. "Nature bids me to be of use to men whether they are slave or free, freedmen or free born. Wherever there is a human being there is room for benevolence" (Seneca, De Vita Beata); "Will you not remember who you are and whom you rule? That they are kinsmen, that they are brethren by nature, that they are offspring of Zeus?" (Epictetus, Discourses); "Love mankind, follow God" (Marcus Aurelius, Meditations), cited in Copleston, *History of Philosophy*, vol. 1, 428–37.

50. Ratzinger, *Unity of the Nations*, 4.

51. Eric Voegelin writes that one of the characteristic symbols of modern political immanent ideologies is "that of the brotherhood of autonomous persons. The third age of Joachim, by virtue of its new descent of the spirit, will transform men into members of the new realm without sacramental mediation of grace . . . in its secularised form it has become a formidable component in the contemporary democratic creed; and it is the dynamic core in the Marxian mysticism of the realm of freedom and the withering-away of the state" Voegelin, *The New Science of Politics: An Introduction* (Chicago: University of Chicago Press, 1987), 112.

52. Ratzinger, *Meaning of Christian Brotherhood*, 15.

53. Ratzinger, *Meaning of Christian Brotherhood*, 17.

54. Ratzinger, *Meaning of Christian Brotherhood*, 16.

55. Manent, *Metamorphoses of the City*, 298.

56. Ratzinger, *Meaning of Christian Brotherhood*, 9, 10.

57. Ratzinger, *Meaning of Christian Brotherhood*, 11. Present in Old Testament prophecies is the extended salvation to "the nations," as, for example, in Isaiah 66:18–19: "For I know their works and their thoughts, and I am coming to gather all nations and tongues; and they shall come and shall see my glory, and I will set a sign

among them. And from them I will send survivors to the nations, to Tar'shish, Put,g and Lud, who draw the bow, to Tu'bal and Ja'van, to the islands afar off, that have not heard my fame or seen my glory; and they shall declare my glory among the nations." As Dead Sea Scroll scholar John Bergsman points out, the word in both Hebrew and Greek for "nation" and "Gentile" is the same. Cf. Bergsma, *Jesus and the Dead Sea Scrolls: Revealing the Jewish Roots of Christianity* (New York: Image, 2019), 40.

58. Ratzinger, *Meaning of Christian Brotherhood*, 80–81. Manent notes a similar pattern in Greek philosophy as well as the Judeo-Christian vision: "The formation of the Jewish people, like the elaboration of philosophy, both mark a decisive qualitative progress of the 'self-awareness' of humanity. This progress in both cases comes at the price of a separation or rupture within humanity: the separation or rupture between the people of God and the 'nations' and the separation or rupture between the philosopher or wise man and the 'vulgar' . . . In the perspective drawn by Augustine, one can say that Christianity preserves or confirms the advances achieved by these two ruptures while it overcomes them by restoring human unity on a higher plane through the mediation of the God-man." Manent, *Metamorphoses of the City,* 293–94. Manent further comments that: "The modern political movement—including in this term political philosophy and the transformation of public spirit and of the political and social affects it arouses or accompanies—can be understood as an effort to overcome the Christian separation, to bring about a universality that is at last truly and effectively universal" (297–98).

59. Huntington, "Clash of Civilizations?" 22.

60. Jean-Marie Guéhenno, *The End of The Nation State*, trans. Victoria Elliott (Minneapolis: University of Minnesota Press, 2000), 16–17.

61. Guéhenno, *End of The Nation State*, 45.

62. Guéhenno, *End of The Nation State*, 127.

Chapter 11

Political Ideologies and Their Justifications

The usual approach to political ideologies is to present an historical and contemporary overview of the major currents of political thought such as liberalism, socialism, and conservatism, with their hybrid and extreme forms, as well as their new developments, all on an approximate scale of left-and right-wing colocation. The limitation of this valid approach is that the great ideological failures of this last century have quashed the notion of a greater vision of society and, by doing so, reduced ideological differences to matters of real but much lesser importance. The major currents of political thought all seem to share similar basic suppositions about individual and social existence.

In this chapter, as an overview, I try to understand the present universal aversion to a greater political ideological vision and to show both the real use and role, as well as the limitations and abuse, of the tainted word "ideology" in politics. At the core of human and political ideological aspiration is the apparent conflict between human existence and its essential dynamism toward fulfilment, on the one hand, and, on the other hand, human history that seems to destine all things to decay and death. To overcome this frustration, the modern approach has been to imbue history with a sense of inevitable progress based on what man can envisage and fabricate. While history has failed us again, the basic view of man and society as products of political endeavour remains present today as the prevailing and tacitly accepted crypto ideology.

The real political challenge is to reacquire our experience of reality, the real terms and aspirations of our human existence, and to strive to build our human and political society—as imperfect and incomplete as it will always be—on the greatness and the givenness of man. This is what is required to reassert an authentic ideological political vision; all else is secondary.

NEXUS

We have spoken before of the contemporary disillusionment with politics and for reasons that are more profound than actual political malpractice. In *Metamorphoses of the City*, Pierre Manent has observed how the modern construction of the State curbs and denies the fundamental human aspiration to participate in political endeavour—in the modern State this can only be done by the representation of others.[1]

Manent thus refers to the structural terms in which political activity is expressed today as a cause of our disillusionment and skepticism toward politics, even as we are naturally drawn to a "passionate interest in the common thing." We have seen elements of these structural terms in an assumed individualistic conception of the human person, social bonds understood in a merely contractual way, a model of state power that views human society according to uniform individuals in relation to a remote and anonymous center of power, the common good seen just in terms of freedoms and equalities, and so on. Relations among societies of peoples are reduced to the artificial rapport between political states that concentrate on power and economy. It is the presently prevailing structure of political activity, with its embedded premises and assumptions, that stultifies and frustrates the passionate interest in real political communion.

The other related cause of disenchantment with politics is the historical epoch within which we find ourselves. Not for the first time in human history have we experienced the disillusionment of shattered expectations: human capabilities, the ingenuity of the industrial revolutions, scientific and technological reason at work, have not brought universal and perpetual peace and prosperity. The post-ideological condition in which we find ourselves reveals more than the false promises and ideals of former totalitarian projections of power; the failure of these projects has also manifested the poverty of their alternatives. Political liberalism had a meaning and purpose in opposition to the imposed social projects of the various forms of totalitarian power. The disintegration of these enforced communal programs also exposed the superficiality of political liberalism. This was evident to Aleksandr Solzhenitsyn, who recognized the hollowness of Western life even as he exposed the persecution of the Soviet system.[2]

In *After Ideology*, David Walsh recognizes this double-faceted aspect to what he calls "the spiritual crisis of the modern world."[3] He explains that the modern age began in the context of the breakup of an encompassing world view that found expression in the integration of a rational philosophy with Judeo-Christian Revelation. Hence the need for a substitute rational explanation of the new modern world that would take the place of the synthesis of philosophy and Christianity. Walsh observes that liberalism attempted to resolve this vacuum by attending to more practical issues in politics and refraining from greater theories and explanations. Others who did propose ideological visions assumed the human person's capacity to reinvent and fabricate the meaning and purpose of the world. In either case, the end result is now the same. We find ourselves without fundamental meaning and purpose, either because liberalism has by now shown its shortcomings, or because political ideologies have manifested their disastrous errors. What is missing in both these political currents is a real and profound understanding of the depths and dimensions of the human person.[4]

We therefore find the root causes of political pessimism and skepticism in the prevailing liberal terms and structures that are inadequate to respond to the noble and necessary aspirations of human society. They both promise and demand too little of the human person and perpetuate social existence in an infantile relation of consumer dependence on state power, along the lines envisaged by Alexis de Tocqueville in his description of democratic despotism that purports to spare people "all the care of thinking and all the trouble of living."[5] It is not difficult to see that in this arrangement, human society has no future and exposes people to those who will seek to dominate and to subjugate.

At the same time, the ideological failures seem to communicate the futility of rising above this mundane mediocrity. The very search for an ideal is tainted with failure and we continue to suffer the effects of this political disillusionment. The only adequate response seems to be the abandonment of the search for anything greater than political liberalism's poor and lowest common denominator. The question, and the challenge, therefore, is how to reconfigure the political project in terms that reflect the true and authentic social aspirations of human persons in ways that genuinely correspond to the actual human condition and the real terms of one's political vocation.

THE REAL ASPIRATIONS OF
HUMAN SOCIAL EXISTENCE

Underlying its apparent neutrality toward a social or political vision, the predominant form of liberal democracy, in its variant manifestations, is a very specific notion of people and society. Implicit are the ideas that persons, as individuals, are and should be free choose their own ends and purposes, that all human relations with others are optional, and that there is no overarching greater social collective purpose. These convictions, in turn, have their origin in a view that defers to subjective value as the justification of choice, to the fundamental separateness of persons, and to the rejection of common and final purpose, and subject to the power of technical malleability of all of what surrounds us, people included.

This notion of human society contains important truths; one's authentically human acts require that they be exercised in freedom, that each person is distinctly and uniquely different, and that the denial of the human person for the sake of some collective purpose is an unwarranted abuse of what is most important in society, human persons. Even so, historically we have been shaped politically to think that these liberal convictions constitute the complete social context and that all political theories need to confine themselves within these parameters of thought. In this sense, these truths become exclusive and absolute, and thus pre-empt any attempt to widen their application. The political discussion remains within these premises of liberal thought.

In these essays, I have tried to show that the true approach to politics is, in reality, much broader. Our subjective experience has its origin, in fact, as a response to a pregiven reality which determines the context of our free and adequate responses. Human freedom is therefore a necessary condition, but not the final purpose, of our response to reality, and we are required to grow in the assimilation of the various modes of our experience to shape our adequate personal response to the reality of our context.

I have pointed out that the human person is more than personal individual uniqueness, that we discover ourselves in structural relation with others and that the development and flourishing of our own personhood depends fundamentally on our affirmative response to the personhood of others, what, in his reference to interpersonal relations, W. Norris Clarke called "the metaphysics of love."[6] This is not some poetical description but a necessary condition of human flourishing.

The human experience of the constitutive social nature of the human person reveals also traces of original unity, actual rupture, and the desire for future wholeness. While the brokenness of our actual condition is most apparent, it is not the full description of our complex social experience. We experience the actual condition of rupture not just as a given fact of our existence, but as something that should not be, in other words, that there is an order of harmony that has been broken, both within each human person and among human persons. We also experience, often after violent expressions of this social rupture, the need, the desire, and the possibility of transcendent social harmony, even unity.

It is also true that the human person does not exist as a neutral bystander but is structured, and therefore experiences a dynamism toward a plenitude of fulfilment. This dynamism is a pregiven orientation of our being that moves us daily in search of this plenitude. This existential phenomenon of our existence contains two aspects; the spontaneous movement toward fulfilment, and the experience of not yet attaining what we strive for. We do not choose this dynamism; we only respond to this inner drive of our being: "It would be difficult to conceive of another statement that penetrates as deeply into the innermost core of creaturely existence as does the statement that man finds himself, even until the moment of death, in the *status viatoris*, in the state of being con the way."[7]

The complexity of this experience of dynamic orientation toward future plenitude lies in the fact that the experience leads us beyond this existence, beyond the apparent finality of death. What we strive for, which we also trust ourselves to find, is beyond the confines of this human existence. As Josef Pieper mentions, "The 'way' of man leads to death as its end but not as its meaning."[8]

What this implies, as in fact it corresponds to our existential experience, is that the expectation of fulfilment reaches beyond the death of this actual existence, beyond our experience of time. Our experience of expectation, that structural dynamism of our being toward future fulfilment is in fact an experience of the expectation of fulfilment beyond time. To limit the fulfilment of our hope within temporal limits is to distort our experience of hope:

> To the extent that this existential philosophy conceives of man's existence as essentially and "in the foundation of its being temporal" (Heidegger), it too fails to comprehend the true nature of its subject. Anyone, in other words, who seeks to understand temporality without restriction as the necessary mark of human existence will find hidden from him not only the "life beyond" time, but also the very meaning of life in time . . . existentialism fails to recognise the true nature of human existence because it denies the "pilgrimage" character of the status viatoris, its orientation toward fulfilment beyond time, and hence, in principle, the status viatoris itself.[9]

THE NEED OF A POLITICAL VISION OF TRANSCENDENT FULFILMENT

Given these realities of our social existence that in one way or another are present in our human experience, it seems apparent that there is a need for a collective orientation or vision, however inchoate or incomplete that vision may be. We need to approach social order because we experience its structure within and among ourselves. We know that we can only live and flourish in an order of social harmony and unity that favors each one's own flourishing within a greater social reality that transcends but at the same time includes the temporal structures of our public and social existence, our political communion.

Our antipathy toward the search for and acceptance of a political vision is derived from our historical circumstances of disillusionment with "the horror, vacuity, and mediocrity of the twentieth century."[10] To this description we could add other elements; the culture of death, the dictatorship of relativism, a throwaway culture, economic anarchy. Even so, it is precisely in the depths of these phenomena that one can experience again a new and greater vision of human society. The greater the rejection of the experience of personal and social reality, the greater is the possibility of recognising the emergence of truth by way of the failure and cost of its denial. The pessimism and frustration of the political vocation can lead to a renewed vision of what truly binds us together in unity.

In *After Ideology*, Walsh proposes an alternative path to the frustration and skepticism of our times. Faced with the failure of the experience of human reason to fashion a world according to its own idea of progress, there is a movement, an opening of minds, to a transcendent truth of reality. The events of recent political and social history have obliged us to look beyond ourselves to a source of reality that is not of our making. Walsh observes that the right response to this modern failure reveals the possibility of a rediscovery of a pregiven structure and nature of reality in which we find ourselves and to which we belong. The conceit of the brave new world has faded and there are signs that we are rediscovering our place and purpose within an order of transcendent origin, that gives our own existence its coherence and real purpose. This prompting of our minds and hearts arises precisely from the recognition of our present failure that turns us from error and points us in the direction of the truth of reality.[11]

To refer, therefore, to our present times as post-ideological can distort the challenge we face. We have seen that neither the false illusions of some future idyllic political state, nor the permissive, ultimately nihilistic political state of individual freedom is sufficient basis for authentic human society. The abandonment of insufficient or abusive political plans does not avoid the need for what can, in reality, sustain a true vision of political society. It is from the depths of the present failures that new, real foundations of human society can and need to emerge.

In this sense, the pragmatic answer to politics is manifestly insufficient. To avoid the challenge of a vision for politics is not to answer the need for such a vision. "Non-ideological pragmatists" assume the impossibility or the impracticality of a greater vision of political society. This is demeaning of the human person and leaves unanswered, behind a veil of supposed ignorance, the real foundations of what can in reality make everything else work.

The real and unavoidable political question is, therefore, not whether a vision of society is possible, nor merely the description of the current diverse opinions of what politics is for, but the vital search for the truth of what can bind people in a human society of real and adequate purposes.

POLITICAL IDEOLOGY

The usual context in which reference is made to political ideologies is a negative one, though this tendency obscures two distinct elements in ideology. An ideology refers to any set of related beliefs and values, as an identifiable sociological phenomenon. The related but distinct philosophical question is whether, and to what degree, a particular ideology conforms to the reality of persons and society. The British professor of political theory Michael Freeden describes ideologies as "complex combinations and clusters of political concepts in sustainable patterns."[12] In a political context, Freeden describes ideologies as having the following characteristics:

> A political ideology is a set of ideas, beliefs, opinions, and values that (1) exhibit a recurring pattern; (2) are held by significant groups; (3) compete over providing and controlling plans for public policy; and (4) do so with the aim of justifying, contesting or changing the social and political arrangements and processes of a political community.[13]

Ideologies therefore present an internally consistent and coherent system of beliefs and values that interpret political phenomena in the way determined by the chosen priorities and language of a particular ideology. At the same time, ideologies are fluid structures of thought and can evolve into other similar or quite distinct sets of thought patterns, though their core set of ideas will not usually change. It is also the case that the same political terms can have disparate meanings, according to their ideological context of meaning.[14]

Ideological systems can overlap and penetrate each other. Freeden proposes that ideologies are practical political tools that are used to convey to and to convince groups of a set of ideas.[15] For this reason, ideologies are usually presented in a clear and appealing form, as their purpose is to communicate a political vision to a wide audience. This is the concern for what Freeden calls "the best order of magnification."[16] According to Freeden, this need for an ideology to convince people can lead to the deliberate use of "vagueness and elusiveness" to reconcile inconsistencies within an ideological cluster of political ideas.[17]

The Positive Need that Ideologies Express

Given this descriptive account of political ideology, we can recognize the possibilities such a description contains. The need and the effort to bring together "complex combinations and clusters of political concepts in sustainable patterns" is at the center of philosophical endeavour, something that the human mind both requires and attempts to do.

We have seen this previously in Clarke's *Explorations in Metaphysics*. It seems that our intellect is structured not only to receive the presence and significance of specific things and persons but is also structured to attempt to bring all of what we experience into some form of integrated vision, however partial or inchoate our cumulation of experience may be. In other words, we naturally strive for an overarching explanation of our many experiences, one that conforms to the evidence of each experience and that also integrates each experience in a broader sense of meaning and purpose. This is precisely the philosophical instinct that motivates our search for significance and that motivates our adequate response to what we perceive as greater purpose or vision.[18]

We are intellectually structured not only to the analysis of component parts, divisions, and distinctions, but also to attempt to bring together into a unity our experiences of distinct and yet related reality. Our existential being requires intellectual foreclosure of meaning, of the integrated meaning of reality, and especially of our own existence in the greater context of reality. This experience of the need for overarching meaning is particularly acute in times of crisis or suffering, precisely because of the experienced lack of meaning or goodness. Skepticism and pragmatism are unsustainable human conditions.

This is precisely the disposition that needs to remain alive in what is termed our post-ideological era. The rupture of false hopes inevitably induces what Pieper called "a retaliatory pessimism," which prepares for "a catastrophic end . . . which is supposed, if that were possible, to possess the character of annihilation."[19]

The rejection of an ideological framework of meaning, as described above, often includes the explicit or implicit rejection of any greater context of meaning. As British professor of political theory Andrew Vincent explains, describing the modern disparagement of political ideologies:

> It was held that in industrialized democratic societies [political ideologies] no longer served anything more than a decorative role. Consensus on basic aims was agreed. Most of the major parties in industrialized societies had achieved, in the welfare, mixed economy structure, the majority of their reformist aims. The Left had accepted the dangers of excessive state power and the Right had accepted the necessity of the welfare state and the rights of working people. Consensus and convergence of political aims were seen in many industrialized countries. . . . Basic agreement on political values had been achieved. Politics was about more peripheral pragmatic adjustment, gross national products, prices, wages, the public-sector borrowing requirement, and the like. All else was froth.[20]

Vincent also alludes to the mid-twentieth century popularity of sociology and its claim to be an ideologically free science. Sociology was a descriptive, not a normative science, and therefore simply presented empirical facts to be discovered rather than purposes and standards:

> The development of empirical social science demanded a value-free rigour, scepticism and empirical verification, unsullied by the emotional appeals of ideological and normative political philosophy. A neo-positivism rigidly sepa-rating facts and values lurked behind these judgments. In this context it was argued that ideology had literally ended in advanced industrialized democratic societies. Ideology was contrasted with empirically based social science. The latter was the path to political knowledge; the former connoted illusion. As Edward Shils commented: "Science is not and never has been part of an ideo-logical culture. Indeed the spirit in which science works is alien to ideology."[21]

On a more profound level, much of the pragmatic and relativist approaches not only to politics but also to many areas of human knowledge, ethics, and religion may be understood as forms of "retaliatory pessimism" that are, at root, reactionary to perceived false claims to "an 'optimistic' simplification of the philosophy of progress."[22] In other words, many of the arguments that would deny or reduce the vision of politics are reactions to the overreach of past historical ideological explanations and determinations. In Karl Popper's introduction to *The Open Society and Its Enemies,* the Austrian-British phi-losopher explains that his text:

> Attempts to show that this civilization has not yet fully recovered from the shock of its birth—the transition from that tribal or "closed society," with its submission to magical forces, to an "open society" which sets free the critical powers of man. It attempts to show that the shock of this transition is one of the factors that have made possible the rise of those reactionary movements which have tried, and still try, to overthrow and to return to tribalism. And it suggests that what we call nowadays totalitarianism belongs to a tradition which is just as old or just as young as our civilization itself. It tries thereby to contribute to our understanding of totalitarianism, and of the significance of the perennial fight against it. It further tries to examine the application of the critical and rational methods of science to the problems of the open society. It analyses the principles of democratic social reconstruction, the principles of what I may term "piecemeal social engineering" in opposition to "Utopian social engineering."[23]

The question we ask here is whether Popper's view of "piecemeal social engineering" does full justice to the desire and capacity of the human person to know and to express the *logos* of Being in the social and political context. There is much wisdom in Popper's reaction to the overreaching visions of

"Utopian social engineering," and he is right in emphasizing the responsibility of human persons for the type of society we wish to shape:

> Only we the human individuals, can do it; we can do it by defending and strengthening those democratic institutions upon which freedom, and with it progress, depends. And we shall do it much better as we become more fully aware of the fact that progress rests with us, with our watchfulness, with our efforts, with the clarity of our conception of our ends, and with the realism of their choice.[24]

At the same time, while Popper underlines the necessity of the approach of "piecemeal social engineering," which strikes an important chord of reasonableness and prudential wisdom, his description of "the piecemeal engineer's" vision of society seems unduly and unreasonably modest: "The piecemeal engineer will, accordingly, adopt the method of searching for, and fighting against, the greatest and most urgent evils of society, rather than searching for, and fighting for, its greatest ultimate good. The difference is far from being merely verbal. In fact, it is the most important."[25]

It seems that Popper sacrifices too much to safeguard societies from unwarranted ideological visions and the inevitable sufferings they inflict on populations. Popper's reaction to the various forms of Utopian social engineering seems at its core to be influenced by a "retaliatory pessimism" that does not express the positive need for greater political vision. Václav Havel intimates this in his introduction to the 2011 edition of Popper's work:

> My relatively brief sojourn in the realm of so-called high politics convinces me time and again of the need to take this very approach: most of the threats hanging over the world now, as well as many of the problems confronting it, could be handled much more effectively if we were able to see past the needs of our noses and take into consideration, to some extent at least, the broader interconnections that go beyond the scope of our immediate or group interests.[26]

More explicitly and more profoundly, Joseph Ratzinger points to the practical need to reaffirm the vision of the ideal precisely to guide the "piecemeal social engineering" that Popper advocates. In this sense, Ratzinger integrates the Platonic ideal into a "piecemeal" approach to politics. In his essay *Eschatology and Utopia*, Ratzinger sees a connection between the Christian notion of eschatology and the Platonic "utopian" vision of the ideal. Ratzinger notes that an ideal just order of being is necessary as the model from which both the individual person and society can judge themselves and draw their criteria and standards. Ratzinger claims that we can only know how to live and act justly and responsibly if these ideals are real; they are a necessary presupposition of our moral judgments that show us how we should be and live, however imperfectly, in this existence. Ratzinger sees in Plato's representation of the ideal Republic and his doctrine of ideal forms an essential component of political philosophy, even if not intended to be actually achieved. Plato's ideals serve as the criteria by which we attempt to organize our actual societies, as contingent and imperfect as they are and always will be.[27]

Ideological visions of society, "complex combinations and clusters of political concepts in sustainable patterns," can, and indeed must, contain a positive vision of the ideal, of the *logos* of Being, which the human person both can and needs to experience, to the degree that is humanly possible. The present negation of that possibility is generally the consequence of a retaliatory pessimism to false ideal visions of society and the belief of their facile implementation; this spontaneous negation of false ideals should not obscure the need for the knowledge of the ideal as the guide for authentically human society.

Where Ideologies Fail

While the capacity and need for a vision of the ideal is real, we also need to know how political ideologies can mislead and manipulate with false promises and illusions, rather than with real ideals. If the clusters of ideas in sustainable patterns can lack the light and purpose of the truth of the ideal, ideologies can also deceive and manipulate, precisely because we live dependent on ideals and the possibility of their ultimate attainment. This condition leaves us susceptible to promises and interpretations of phenomena that purport to provide complete explanations and value systems that are, and have historically been shown to be, false and misleading.

In the first place, the limits of human knowledge impede a greater perception of we need to know. The experience of intimations of the truth of reality, physical, moral, religious, are only really outlines of so much more that we know can and or must exist, but that in fact we do not know. This is an incommoding experience but describes accurately our existential condition. We experience what is real, and we also experience, either by intuition or by inductive or deductive reason, what must also be, but of which we have no or insufficient experience. We also experience what does not fit into humanly known categories of what is real, and we find ourselves in the existential condition of what the French philosopher Maurice Blondel has described as reality that is "beyond the power of man to discover for himself and yet imposed on his thought and on his will."[28]

What all of this means is that the experience of human knowledge is real and yet incomplete, deficient, and sporadic. It is easy to simplify this complex situation of our comprehension of reality, to reduce reality to clear and distinct ideas, or the skepticism of refusing to admit what we do not fully know and experience, or to banish the standard of reality by reverting to the subjective origin of experience, or as is often the case with ideological visions, to claim to interpret all of reality through the prism of selected categories of experience. The tendency to do this arises from the human desire and the need for fulfilment, for completion, for totality, and it is this that makes us gullible to believe what we want to believe because we need to believe.

The philosophizing approach seeks to maintain the complexity of human experience and understanding, and to distil what we can of the *logos* of Being, without simplifying and thus distorting the vision of reality that we can attain and that we need, as partial and incomplete as it is, "And yet this is the task specific to philosophy: to preserve man's openness to this incomprehensible 'complete fact'; to sow distrust for any claim to have discovered the universal cosmic formula, to resist any attempt to suppress or otherwise obscure a single element of the unvarnished truth, say, in the interests of a premature systematization or harmonization."[29]

This is why Pieper sees in Georg W. F. Hegel's *Phenomenology of Spirit* (1807) the overextension of Hegel's philosophical intention, that seems to identify the desire for complete knowing with the capacity to do so. Hegel states that:

> The true shape in which truth exists can only be the scientific system of that truth. To participate in the collaborative effort at bringing philosophy nearer to the form of science—to bring it nearer to the goal where it can lay aside the title of love of knowing and be actual knowing—is the task I have set for myself. The inner necessity that knowing should be science lies in the nature of knowing, and the satisfactory explanation for this inner necessity is solely the exposition of philosophy itself.[30]

The risk of political ideologies is thus to presume too much and thus to explain too little. The most trenchant criticism of the over-extension of ideologies is, ironically, found in Karl Marx and Friederich Engels' *A Critique of The German Ideology* (1846), written two years before *The Communist Manifesto* and not published until 1932. Influenced (and critical) of Ludwig Feuerbach's explanation of religion in the projections of human consciousness, Marx goes further to dismiss all philosophical and religious visions as bogus distortions of reality:

> The production of ideas, of conceptions, of consciousness, is at first directly interwoven with the material activity and the material intercourse of men, the language of real life. Conceiving, thinking, the mental intercourse of men, appear at this stage as the direct efflux of their material behaviour. The same applies to mental production as expressed in the language of politics, laws,

morality, religion, metaphysics, etc. of a people. Men are the producers of their conceptions, ideas, etc.—real, active men, as they are conditioned by a definite development of their productive forces and of the intercourse corresponding to these, up to its furthest forms. Consciousness can never be anything else than conscious existence, and the existence of men is their actual life-process. If in all ideology men and their circumstances appear upside-down as in a camera obscura, this phenomenon arises just as much from their historical life-process as the inversion of objects on the retina does from their physical life-process.[31]

For Marx, therefore, all that is not derived from the development of material being is as illusionary as the effects of opium:

The phantoms formed in the human brain are also, necessarily, sublimates of their material life-process, which is empirically verifiable and bound to material premises. Morality, religion, metaphysics, all the rest of ideology and their corresponding forms of consciousness, thus no longer retain the semblance of independence. They have no history, no development; but men, developing their material production and their material intercourse, alter, along with this their real existence, their thinking and the products of their thinking. Life is not determined by consciousness, but consciousness by life.[32]

The historical irony of Marx's critique of ideology was that his own explanation of the historical determinism of matter was itself an ideological all-embracing explanation of reality as much as all the other interpretations of human and social meaning and purpose. Even the term "ideology" became accepted in communist teaching, as Vladimir Lenin, in *What Is to be Done?* (1902) writes: "Hence, to belittle the socialist ideology in any way, to turn aside from it in the slightest degree means to strengthen bourgeois ideology."[33]

The negative possibilities of ideological systems of thought and explanation are therefore evident. Political ideologies can easily become what Marx describes as theoretical panaceas for maintaining the convenient *status quo*, for resisting necessary change and for inducing passivity in those who suffer unjustly. Ideologies can also be used to stoke the fires of social revolution and the false hope of a proximate paradise, induced by all means that the revolution may require.

The question therefore arises as to how to propose a real vision of society that corresponds to the authentic aspirations of man while, at the same time, avoiding the illusions of simplified solutions. To what can people commit themselves wholeheartedly socially and politically without suffering the deceptions of false hopes?

NATURE AND HISTORY

All ideologies respond, either by affirming or denying, to a pregiven existential structure of human person that is complex. On the one hand, persons as dynamic beings, are structured to fulfilment beyond the confines of this existence and beyond the confines of their own actual condition. This presupposes acknowledging both *being* and *becoming* at the same time. We are grounded in the reality of our own being, we possess the reality of our own personal being, which contains an inbuilt orientation toward a fulfilment of reality that we do not yet possess and yet aspire to attain. Our only real and free choice here is *how* we may respond of necessity to these pregiven conditions.

On the other hand, we find ourselves in an historical context, both personally and collectively, that seems circular and enclosed, and therefore at odds with the fundamental linear advance of our dynamic being. How do we reconcile the essential movement of our being toward fulfilment with our experience of history that seems to be locked into a determined cycle of progress and regress, growth, and decay.[34] While the phrase is theological, the unavoidable challenge of "salvation history" is a philosophical one, an unavoidable enigma of our human existence, what Eric Voegelin refers to as "the problem of an *eidos* of history."[35]

Political ideologies, in one way or another, purport to answer in the social context the enigma of the apparent conflict of being and history. This conflict is seen especially in times, like now, when history seems not to usher in the greater fulfilment of mankind but rather makes evident the frustration and failure of human progress:

> History always becomes problematical for us when a crisis occurs in a particular historical configuration. When that happens, we become conscious of the distance—or, indeed, the contradiction—between history and being, between our historical and our ontological nature; we must search again for the union between our being and history, either by invalidating history as it has been up to the present or by conceiving it anew from its roots. . . . The suspicion arises that history does not lead to being but confuses it; that it is not healing but opium; not the way to what is essential but a form of alienation. When historical consciousness is affected to this extent, then the human individual, who exists in history, also undergoes a crisis; he must seek and struggle to construct for himself a new way.[36]

Therefore, the experienced aspirations of persons demand the transformation of the world and of themselves, and therefore search to find in human history signs of this real advancement and progress, either in some identifiable pattern of historical change, or our fabrication of our own and society's transformation in time, or by a combination of both. The claim to have found the key to human history thus sustains the efforts and justifies the means to be used in fulfilling human historical transformation. This identification of human transformation and some ideal social condition that was determined to come about within historical time was seen in certain *chiliastic* Biblical interpretations of divine prophecies.[37]

In *Eschatology and Utopia*, as Ratzinger explains, this chiliastic interpretation of God's promises through the prophets does indeed accept the eschatological belief of a new heaven and a new earth through God's action but proposes that this ultimate perfection is to be realized within this existence and within historical time, at some definite future moment of time, supposing that what will happen beyond time will also happen within time. Ratzinger sees in this interpretation the confusion of time with eternity. The chiliastic interpreters of Christian eschatological fulfilment await in the proximate future what is to happen beyond time and this expectation of immanent perfection leads them to search for the signs in history of a condition that is in reality beyond history.[38]

This perennial tendency to identify the definitive transformation of human society in present and proximate historical events surfaced again in what the twelfth-century monk Joachim da Fiore (1130–1202) recognized as the new incipient kingdom of the Holy Spirit, as the third stage of human history, after the kingdom of the Father and of the Son. While da Fiore claimed to recognize within human history this third phase of Trinitarian revelation, specifically the kingdom of the Holy Spirit, a new interpretation of the worldly fulfilment of history was developing.

In *The New Science of Politics*, Voegelin detects that the belief in an intra-historical fulfilment of perfection was something that developed gradually and that it was only with the eighteenth-century Enlightenment that this entirely secular belief in the immanent transformation of people and society prevailed. By this time the transcendent and supernatural dimension of this transformation had largely and practically disappeared from view.[39]

As Voegelin points out, this justification of human history, the problem of an *eidos* of history, was new and found three basic forms. The first form that tries to validate the pattern of history is one that believes in the purposeful course of history but is unclear about its final outcome. This is what Voegelin refers to as the progressive interpretation of historical purpose. The second form purports to have a clear image of the ideal condition of perfection but is not clear on how that ideal is to be achieved. This is what Voegelin refers to as utopianism and may take various forms or ideal conditions such as everlasting peace and a weapons free world, definitive release from suffering and want, universal equality, and so on. The third form is the most radical and Voegelin sees its origins in the secular appropriation of Christian theology.

The ideal condition is immanent, to be achieved by people within time and includes a metamorphosis through revolutionary means, as, for example, in Marxist ideology.[40]

The justification of the *eidos* of human history in terms of Christian eschatology finds its expression in the rationalizing of history of Hegel. Hegel undertook the task of attempting to reconcile the understanding of nature in scientific terms and nature in the Christian sense of moral values and religion.[41] In his introduction to the *Lectures on the Philosophy of History*, Hegel rejects the superficial view of history merely as cyclical change or the eternal recurrence of life and death cycles, a "spectacle of confusion and wreckage" and recognizes that, even from such a "peddler's view of providence," "as we look upon history as an altar on which the happiness of nations, the wisdom of states, and the virtue of individuals are slaughtered, our thoughts inevitably impel us to ask: to whom, or to what ultimate end have these monstrous sacrifices been made?"[42]

Hegel's ambition was therefore, to interpret human history as the manifestation of the Absolute World Spirit (of God) in time:

> History is the unfolding of God's nature in a particular, determinate element, so that only a determinate form of knowledge is possible and appropriate to it. The time has now surely come for us to comprehend even so rich a product of creative reason as world history. The aim of human cognition is to understand that the intentions of eternal wisdom are accomplished not only in the natural world, but also in the realm of the (spirit) which is actively present in the world. From this point of view, our investigation can be seen as a theodicy, a justification of the ways of God (such as Leibniz attempted in his own metaphysical manner, but using categories which were as yet abstract and indeterminate). It should enable us to comprehend all the ills of the world, including the existence of evil, so that the thinking spirit may be reconciled with the negative aspects of existence; and it is in world history that we encounter the sum total of concrete evil.[43]

The inexorable manifestation of the World Spirit in and through the events and forms of human history absorbs the evils caused by the freedom of persons and makes them serve "the cunning of Reason":

> The particular interests of passion cannot therefore be separated from the realisation of the universal; for the universal arises out of the particular and determinate and its negation. The particular has its own interests in world history; it is of a finite nature, and as such, it must perish. Particular interests contend with one another, and some are destroyed in the process. But it is from this very conflict and destruction of particular things that the universal emerges, and it remains unscathed itself. For it is not the universal Idea which enters into opposition,

conflict, and danger; it keeps itself in the background, untouched and unharmed, and sends forth the particular interests of passion to fight and wear themselves out in its stead. It is what we may call the cunning of reason that it sets the passions to work in its service, so that the agents by which it gives itself existence must pay the penalty and suffer the loss.[44]

As German philosopher Karl Löwith comments on this Hegelian understanding of the particular intention and the universal purpose as evidenced in history:

The universal purpose and the particular intention meet in this dialectic of passionate action; for that which world-historical individuals are unconsciously driving at is not what they are consciously planning but what they must will, out of an urge which seems to be blind and yet has a wider perspective than personal interests. Hence men achieve, with an instinctive comprehension, that which is intended with them. They act historically by being acted upon by the power and cunning of reason, which is to Hegel a rational expression for divine providence: thus the motives, passions, and interests in history are indeed what they appeared to be at first glance, namely, the human stuff of it, but within the framework of a transcending purpose, promoting an end which was no part of conscious intentions.[45]

One can appreciate in Hegel the search for the overarching meaning in history and the attempt to explain what can often appear as the slaughter bench of history. At the same time, the radical identification of the omnipotent providential design of the Christian God's purposes with the unfolding of the events of human history is not only unwarranted but also particularly dangerous. The supposition of finding a determinism in historical events leads to the inevitability of what is to happen and necessarily reduces or abolishes human freedom, and with it, human responsibility. Contingent historical forms, such as the modern state, become invested with a sense of perfection, at least in reference to past forms, and there is contained in this sense of history the determinism of an ever-better world.

The logical consequence of Hegel's rationalized theological notion of providence is the transformation of the kingdom of God into the dimensions of a foreseeable and practicable kingdom of human perfection. Whatever human reason identifies as human and social perfection becomes the key with which history can be interpreted and its course identified. This key of interpretation is also in human hands and becomes the instrument by which people will fabricate perfection. What is important to realize is that God and nature, as established order, have dropped out of the picture, even if nominally they are still mentioned. What in fact prevails is an idea of the person and the world that can be constructed. Humanly made history determines and can perfect nature.

In an entry in his edition of Leo Strauss' *History of Political Philosophy*,[46] American political philosopher Joseph Cropsey claims that, in general terms, Marx's radical rendering of Jean Jacques Rousseau's political philosophy can be summarized by the dominance of the philosophy of history over the philosophy of nature. This meant that the meaning and purpose of existence was to be found in the descriptive analysis of changing and evolving historical processes and structures rather than in nature. History's path is an evolving one and the social contradictions and clashes were not random or contradictory phenomena, but rather the dialectic manifestation of historical reason and therefore manifestations of the struggle toward history's evolving purpose. In this view of history, contradictions are positive manifestations of determined progress and people are to be helped and guided to accept and participate in this struggle of progress, confident in the historical determinism that is bringing this struggle to a greater completion and fulfilment, in Marxist terms of a future classless society and a struggleless existence.[47]

Cropsey recognizes that it is this dominance of history over nature that displaced both political thought and religion, and proposed in their place explanations of a social and economic kind. Cropsey notes that both philosophy and religion shared a common basis in nature, and both recognized the inherent limitations of nature in this present existence. Reason's rejection of religion occurred when the sense of historical purpose claimed the ascendence over the philosophical and religious explanations of nature. In Cropsey's view, it was this turn to history as the manifestation of meaning and purpose that led to the explanation of social realities in terms of structures, processes, and economics, which is what Marxism came to promulgate and impose.[48]

What is important here is the radically new approach to reality that is assumed and that must therefore reinterpret reality—and people—in a new way:

> [Karl Marx] was the one who said that humankind should no longer inquire into its origins and that do so would be to act foolishly. . . . Inasmuch as the question of creation can ultimately not be answered apart from a creating Intelligence, the question is seen as foolish from the very start. Creation is of no consequence, it is humanity that must produce the real creation, and it is that which will count for something. This is the source of the change in humanity's fundamental directive vis-à-vis the world; it was at this point that progress became the real truth and matter became the material out of which human beings would create the world that was worth being lived in.[49]

Ratzinger further describes Marx's version of the new interpretation of worldly salvation and the revolution it required:

Karl Marx took up the rallying call and applied his incisive language and intellect to the task of launching this major new and, as he thought, definitive step in history towards salvation—towards what Kant had described as the "Kingdom of God." Once the truth of the hereafter had been rejected, it would then be a question of establishing the truth of the here and now. The critique of Heaven is transformed into the critique of earth, the critique of theology into the critique of politics. Progress towards the better, towards the definitively good world, no longer comes simply from science but from politics—from a scientifically conceived politics that recognizes the structure of history and society and thus points out the road towards revolution, towards all-encompassing change.[50]

Hungarian philosopher Auriel Kolnai (1900–1973) described what he termed "the utopian mind" in this way of belief in a future perfectible society, "the perfectionist illusion," with the negation the actual order and structure of nature. American philosopher Daniel J. Mahoney summarizes Kolnai's thought in this way:

Utopians are convinced that a world in which moral choice exists, a world where conscience navigates and prudently attempts practical convergences among antinomic goods, is one where the objectification and alienation of human beings reign. Hence the utopians' endless preoccupation with the necessity of a planned world—a planning that is inevitably supported and buttressed by the illusion of historical necessity. The link between the perfectionist illusion characterized by the forced negation of ineliminable tensions and the parallel negations of conscience and practice is necessarily the work of a revolutionary project. This revolutionary project is by no means an overheated expression of idealism or an inordinate and unbalanced love of concrete human goods or values as is usually said. Instead, its aims are "atheistic" and "providential"—it desires nothing less than the movement of humanity (or pre-humanity) from an alienated world of disharmonious values to one where a fundamentally other, new, and transformed reality reigns. The utopian mind cannot be incarnate in the world unless it becomes "providential"—unless, that is, it gives birth to a utopian will.[51]

As we have noted, many of these ideological visions "buttressed by the illusion of historical necessity" and implemented by "a utopian will" have resulted in suffering and failure, as evidenced by recognizable rise and fall of totalitarian forms of power in this last century. Even so, something still remains: the conception of the human person that created these political illusions. The shift from a philosophy of nature to the human person's interpretation of historical process brought with this shift of perspective a profound change in the understanding of persons themselves and their relation to reality. We are still living under the illusion of historical determinism and the belief that reality is what we will it to be.

THE SUPPOSITIONS OF THE PRESENT TIMES

We recall that the human person's existential being is drawn to a transcendent social destiny. This condition is not primordially something that we choose, but the condition to which we are compelled to respond. It is in this existential experience that we perceive in ourselves both nature and history; nature, in the sense of a givenness of our being drawn toward fulfilment and history, in the sense of our need to progress in that personal and social fulfilment.

What has failed in modernity is the identifiable progress of history. The identification of the Christian notion of the kingdom of God with the coming kingdom of reason in the thought of Immanuel Kant was developed into a dynamic and identifiable philosophy of history in Hegel, that then became the assumed force of the inevitable development of matter in Marx and the political ideologies of this last century with their pseudo-religious promises of heaven on earth at some near point in the future. What has made these ideologies palatable was the supposed historical determinism of their fulfilment. Their cluster of ideas was supposed to be the key to the prediction or the production of human fulfilment in history, and thereby the moral justification for all means, actions, and purposes that would accelerate the inevitable course of historical development.

What has failed in ideologies is the breakup of history, the non-fulfilment of their predictions of the inevitable and immanent future, and the problematic and unreliable succession of events that is called history. In this breakup there is truth revealed, the incommoding truth of our ignorance of the logic of history from our rational perspective. C. S. Lewis distinguishes two forms of interpreting history. While acknowledging the modest and legitimate task of the historian, Lewis distinguished the presumptuous and illegitimate role of the historicist:

> The mark of the Historicist, on the other hand, is that he tries to get from historical premises conclusions which are more than historical; conclusions metaphysical or theological or (to coin a word) atheo-logical. The historian and the Historicist may both say that something "must have" happened. But must in the mouth of a genuine historian will refer only to a *ratio cognoscendi*: since A happened B "must have" preceded it; if William the Bastard arrived in England he "must have" crossed the sea. But "must" in the mouth of a Historicist can have quite a different meaning. It may mean that events fell out as they did because of some ultimate, transcendent necessity in the ground of things.[52]

Lewis explains the ludicrously hypothetical conditions for which this historicism could be valid:

If, by one miracle, the total content of time were spread out before me, and if, by another, I were able to hold all that infinity of events in my mind and if, by a third, God were pleased to comment on it so that I could understand it, then, to be sure, I could do what the Historicist says he is doing. I could read the meaning, discern the pattern. Yes; and if the sky fell we should all catch larks.[53]

Even as gullible as we are, the real past facts of history of this last century have disillusioned the historicist premise that sustained political programs until their own failure, and the consequent suffering of millions of people, revealed the intellectual emptiness and evil of their promises. History has failed us again, and yet the intellectual premises of these ideologies that were propped up by historicism seem to remain in place.

What are these intellectual premises? The common elements of this perduring crypto ideology include the exclusive concern with this existence as the only extension of personal possibilities of fulfilment, the assertion of personal free will as the source of meaning and purpose of all of reality, including personal being, and the belief that people's own fulfilment is and will be the product of their own work. This cluster of ideas, admittedly without the glamour of historicist prophecies, remains largely intact in our political vision, as much in Western political ideology as formerly in Marxist and Communist ideology. These premises are so ingrained that they operate in an undisclosed way like a crypto currency that records the transactions but leaves all other information anonymous.

It is important to lay bare what we assume before we even start to think politically and to recognize this radically different model of the human person that is firmly and *a priori* in place in our political institutions, processes, and programs. Voegelin discerns in these premises a revolt against the order of being, that is, the rejection of the given structure of reality and of persons that in fact we do know and experience to be the case. He detects a common mentality that is based on a knowing rejection of truth and the imposition of power. Voegelin uses Martin Heidegger's secular interpretation of the Christian term *parousia* to mean "the mentality that expects deliverance from the evils of the time through the advent, the coming in all its fullness, of being, construed as immanent."[54] Gnosticism, for Voegelin, is a collective term for systems of thought that are characterized by the human person's own imposition of power and construction of meaning for one's own purposes and programs.[55]

In *Science, Politics, and Gnosticism*,[56] Voegelin affirms that what *parousiastic Gnosticism* intends to accomplish is to fashion a new and perfect order which presupposes the destruction of the present given order of reality, with its imperfections and injustices. However, the given structure of reality is theoretically explained—as dependent on some remote and transcendent cosmic power or as the creative thought of the Judeo-Christian God, or as ancient Greek philosophy's understanding of Being—this given order or structure of reality is presupposed as something beyond the human power to dominate. Therefore, the first task of this Gnostic mentality, which proposes to fabricate a new and better world, is the need to overcome the sense of the givenness of reality and to show that reality is in fact within human power to dominate. This means that the theoretical explanations that presume the givenness of reality must also be overcome. If God is not dead, he must be killed.[57]

What Voegelin refers to here is not, of course, merely the loss of a religious sense, but rather the radical rejection of the order of being, of what we know nature to be and to become. The rejection of what is, of what is meant to be, and of what should be, is something deliberate and logically necessary. Givenness, of whatever aspect of reality, is a limitation on the human person's creative power and, therefore, something to be removed or eliminated. What this requires is the rejection of one's own nature and the reformulation of that nature in terms of its own transformation—and the transformation of his society—by human agency.

> The phenomenon that has dominated the history of the mind during the last few centuries seems both more profound and more arbitrary. It is not the intelligence alone that is involved. The problem posed was a human problem—it was *the* human problem—and the solution that is being given to it is one that claims to be positive. Man is getting rid of God in order to regain possession of the human greatness that, it seems to him, is being unwarrantably withheld by another. In God he is overthrowing an obstacle in order to gain his freedom.[58]

What began with the attempt to dominate physical nature developed logically to the attempt not just to liberate persons from their religious chains to an order of being, but to undertake the transformation of personal being, in accordance with prevailing human aspirations:

> But, since man, too, had become an object of science like all the rest, why would what was true for the external world be any the less true for man himself? The dream of technology and its first major achievements coincided, moreover, with a sudden awareness of social unity and with a powerful surge of social aspirations which were also something new in humanity. To the transformation of nature, they thought, must thus be added the transformation of society. Social science gave the rise to "social engineers." And, since it was the whole man, too, who was henceforth going to be manipulated and worked like an object. One after the other, an applied biology, an applied psychology, an applied sociology were founded. . . . Through science, man was going to make himself "master and possessor of the human forces." A whole technology of man developed.[59]

It may be that we have not yet realized the mistaken project we are in and the denial of reality that the project presupposes. This modern project justifies our political notions of freedom as acknowledged lack of restraint, religion as irrelevant and a source of social enmity, progress in terms of increased technological power, moral value considered only in terms of preference, and economic welfare as the measure of social and political health.

It seems that the cluster of ideas of the ideology of the modern project live on within us, while the sheen of their historical fulfilment has long since worn off. There may be a similarity between this residual social and political mentality and the situation Havel describes as *post-totalitarian* dominance, an imposed system of thought and practice that requires pervasive, low-level conformity.

In *Power of the Powerless*, Havel recognizes that in our present post-modern condition an ideology of post-totalitarian dominance can have a certain appeal. The skepticism toward a greater context of truth and the progressive sense of personal alienation from a collective sense of meaning and purpose can make the passive acceptance of post-totalitarian dominance an easy option. One can quietly dispense with the concern for greater meaning and personal coherence, and one can again recover a sense of belonging to something, being a part of something. At the same time, as Havel points out, this facile acceptance of political dominance demands the sacrifice of one's own judgment and conscience, handing ourselves and our more important decisions and determinations over to someone else. The power of the political post-totalitarian dominance substitutes for the personal search for and acceptance of truth and goodness.[60]

So much of social and political debate is surreptitiously framed in the cluster of ideas of a "modern" mentality that is, deep down, a revolt against the order of being that can be, and is, experienced, and then rejected. The political words we use are reassuring—democracy, law, human rights, freedom—but they are all set against a background of a protest against reality, a protest that has settled into a passive conformity of post-totalitarian imposition. We are also, and have been conditioned to be, creatures of conformity, of what Nietzsche and others have termed a "herd mentality."[61]

To turn from untruth to truth, to refuse to live the lie, not to conform to the convention of remaining post-ideological dictate is not an easy thing to do. At the same time, the truth of reality requires no propaganda; the experience of truth is its own universal power, and, as Havel pointed out, becomes a power to influence and awaken the dormant experience of truth in others. In *The Power of the Powerless*, Havel recognizes that within each person there is the openness to the truth, to the real meaning and purposes of human existence, to personal conscience and to the desire for authentic living in the truth. This openness may often remain dormant within people, but the action of someone living in the truth causes a spark to ignite within people to arouse their sense of truth and reality. It is this universal sense of truth, even if as yet unconscious, that is the power of the powerless and gives single valiant acts of truth their effective power of communication.[62]

What is at stake here is the capacity to reacquire our experience of reality and the real terms of our human existence, and to respond adequately, both personally and socially, to who we are and who we are to become. This is not a restoration of tradition, in the sense of the good old days, but a renewed apprehension of reality and, in consequence, a truly human social and political communion. We can only do this by overcoming the residual cluster of ideas that had at their origin a rejection of the real terms of our existence and our fulfilment.

Political philosopher Walsh recognizes that the ideological categories of liberalism and socialism, with their own developments and hybrid clusters of ideas, do not mark the most fundamental issues in our politics, especially if we do not dismiss the horrific events of this last century simply as normal factual occurrences.

In *After Ideology*, Walsh maintains that we need to see beyond immediate phenomena if we are to try to understand and overcome the post-ideological skepticism that is the result of the horrors and atrocities of the twentieth century. Walsh sees a fundamental similarity between totalitarian and liberal ideologies; they are similar expressions of our inherited civilization. The modern world has unravelled, and the conceits of inevitable progress have turned into a postmodern disillusionment. To understand our present times, all we have to do is to follow the course of recent history and its manifestations. The tragic evidence of the obliteration of the human person in the twentieth century is only the logical unfolding of the errors and illusions that had their beginnings in the modern age since the Renaissance. Walsh also claims that this tragic character of these postmodern times can produce a type of catharsis, a purification through suffering, that can evoke a renewed beginning based on the truth of the person and of God.[63]

The point here is that humanity's experience of profound failure, evidenced in "the horrors that have taken place," induce in us both an acknowledgment of willful error and, among the rubble, the glimpse, once again, of what is real and our capacity to know and to love the order of reality and the innate imperative to fulfil our lives within the order of Being. This experience of humiliating failure, therefore, both reminds us of the real limits of our existence and, at the same time, offers us the possibility of responding to the real path of fulfilment. Quoting Voegelin's opening sentence of *Order and History*, "The order of history emerges from the history of order," Walsh explains:

There is no order or meaning to history apart from the direction illuminated through the human struggle to realize order in existence. We are participants and cannot apprehend what lies outside of this partial perspective. We cannot grasp the meaning of reality as a whole because we do not stand outside of it; we do not possess the capacity to view the total process as a unity from beginning to end. For this reason our existence is always surrounded by mystery. . . . Our part is only to follow the pull of divine truth that reveals itself in the Between state of existence.[64]

Our present and prevailing post-ideological condition is therefore grossly inadequate for real political society. The condition may well be a retaliatory pessimism toward the abusive totalitarianisms of our recent times. What is required of us is to rediscover the ideal of social and political living within the order of being of this existence, while recognizing its ultimate fulfilment beyond this present existence.[65] This is no philosophical luxury, but the necessary condition for politics here and now.

NOTES

1. Pierre Manent, *Metamorphoses of the City: On the Western Dynamic*, trans. Marc LePain (Cambridge, MA: Harvard University Press, 2013), 217.

2. This was the theme of Aleksandr Solzhenitsyn's 1978 Harvard University commencement address: "A decline in courage may be the most striking feature which an outside observer notices in the West in our days. The Western world has lost its civil courage, both as a whole and separately, in each country, each government, each political party, and, of course, in the United Nations. Such a decline in courage is particularly noticeable among the ruling groups and the intellectual elite, causing an impression of loss of courage by the entire society. Of course, there are many courageous individuals, but they have no determining influence on public life. Political and intellectual bureaucrats show depression, passivity, and perplexity in their actions and in their statements, and even more so in theoretical reflections to explain how realistic, reasonable, as well as intellectually and even morally worn it is to base state policies on weakness and cowardice" Solzhenitsyn, "A World Split Apart: Commencement Address at Harvard University June 8, 1978," in *Solzhenitsyn at Harvard: The Addresses, Twelve Early Responses and Six Later Reflections*, ed. Ronald Berman (Washington, DC: Ethics and Public Policy Center, 1980), 5–6.

3. David Walsh, *After Ideology: Recovering the Spiritual Foundations of Freedom* (San Francisco: HarperCollins, 1990), 257.

4. Walsh, *After Ideology*, 258. In his subsequent writings, and even intimated in *After Ideology*, Professor Walsh identifies political liberal thought with the recognition of rights, limits, and the rule of law, and not as an all-encompassing ideology.

5. Alexis de Tocqueville, *Democracy in America.: The Complete and Unabridged Volumes I and II* (New York: Bantam Classics, 2000), 336, as cited in Marvin

Zetterbaum, "Alexis de Tocqueville," in *History of Political Philosophy*, 3rd ed., ed. Leo Strauss and Joseph Cropsey (Chicago: University of Chicago Press, 1987), 15375. Tocqueville describes a new possible form of democratic despotism in *Democracy in America*, vol. 2, book 4, chap 6 "What Sort of Despotism Democratic Nations Have to Fear," trans. Henry Reeve (Kindle Edition). Tocqueville describes this form of benign despotism that could take hold in a democracy, a despotism that would debase people but without violence. People's lives would not be ruined but conformed to passivity, quietly and surreptitiously plied into a form of servitude that stultifies human existence and removes the ambition for greater aspirations. Tocqueville considers that this form of induced passive conformity of the people could easily be marketed under a public banner of personal freedom, making people think that this passive conformity is in fact personal realization, even to the extent of calling this conforming servitude a prerogative of the sovereignty of the people, an exercise of the people's political power.

6. W. Norris Clarke, *Person and Being. The Aquinas Lecture 1993* (Milwaukee, WI: Marquette University Press, 1993), 72.

7. Josef Pieper, *Faith, Hope, Love* (San Francisco: Ignatius Press, 1997), 92.

8. Pieper, *Faith, Hope, Love*, 94.

9. Pieper, *Faith, Hope, Love*, 95.

10. Walsh, *After Ideology*, 9.

11. Walsh, *After Ideology*, 1. In *After Ideology*, American political philosopher Walsh describes the cathartic experience of Fyodor Dostoevsky, Aleksandr Solzhenitsyn, Albert Camus, and Eric Voegelin, who, each in his own way, has experienced the despair of the present times and, in and through that experience, a catharsis of purification that has permitted each one to rediscover in an experiential way "the order of this transcendent source of existence."

12. Michael Freeden, *Ideology: A Very Short Introduction* (Oxford: Oxford University Press, 2003), 890. Freeden has written extensively on the nature and characteristics of political ideologies as social forms, particularly in *Ideologies and Political Theories* (Oxford: Clarendon Press, 1996); *Liberal Languages: Ideological Imaginations and Twentieth-Century Progressive Thought* (Princeton, NJ: Princeton University Press, 2005); and, as editor, *Reassessing Political Ideologies: The Durability of Dissent* (London: Routledge, 2001). Freeden's approach is in the vein of American cultural anthropologist Clifford Geertz, who writes, for example, on ideology as a cultural system in *The Interpretation of Cultures* (New York: Basic Books, 1973), chap. 8 "Ideology as a Cultural System" 193–233.

13. Freeden, *Ideology*, 615.

14. Freeden, *Ideology*, 900.

15. These characteristics are drawn from Freeden, *Ideology*, chap. 5 "Thinking about Politics: the new boys on the block."

16. Freeden, *Ideology*, 1070.

17. Freeden, *Ideology*, 966.

18. W. Norris Clarke, *Explorations in Metaphysics: Being-God-Person* (Notre Dame, IN: University of Notre Dame Press, 1994), 54. Pieper describes this philosophizing disposition as "someone who is concerned with keeping a certain question

alive, that is, the question of the ultimate meaning of the totality of what is—a question to which doubtless a series of provisional answers may certainly be found, but never the answer . . . . And yet this is the task specific to philosophy: to preserve man's openness to this incomprehensible 'complete fact,' to sow distrust for any claim to have discovered the universal cosmic formula, to resist any attempt to suppress or otherwise obscure a single element of the unvarnished truth, say, in the interests of a premature systematization or harmonization" Pieper, *For the Love of Wisdom: Essays on the Nature of Philosophy* (San Francisco: Ignatius Press, 2006), 312.

19. Josef Pieper, *The End of Time: A Meditation on the Philosophy of History*, rev. ed. (San Francisco: Ignatius Press, 1999), 91–92.

20. Andrew Vincent, *Modern Political Ideologies*, 3rd ed. (Oxford: Wiley-Blackwell, 2010), 10. As Vincent comments, quoting Alasdair MacIntyre, the "end of ideology theorists 'failed to entertain one critical alternative possibility: namely, that the end-of-ideology, far from marking the end-of-ideology, was itself a key expression of the ideology of the time and place where it arose.' . . . The 'end of ideology' was an ideological position committed to a form of pragmatic liberalism" Vincent, *Modern Political Ideologies*, 11. The quotation is from MacIntyre's *Against the Self-Images of the Age: Essays on Ideology and Philosophy* (Notre Dame, IN: University of Notre Dame Press, 1971).

21. Vincent, *Modern Political Ideologies*, 10. The reference is to Edward Shils, "The Concept and Function of Ideology," in *International Encyclopaedia of the Social Sciences*, vol. 7. In this sense, therefore, a "normative science" is a contradiction in terms. For an historical and critical appraisal of this understanding of sociology, see John Milbank, *Theology and Social Theory: Beyond Secular Reason*. 2nd ed. (Malden, MA: Blackwell, 2006), part 2 "Theology and Positivism," 49–144.

22. Pieper, *End of Time*, 88.

23. Karl Popper, *The Open Society and Its Enemies* (London: Routledge Classics, 2011), 513.

24. Popper, *Open Society*, 483. Popper describes what he means by "realism" in a footnote: "By the 'realism' of the choice of our ends I mean that we should choose ends which can be realized within a reasonable span of time, and that we should avoid distant and vague Utopian ideals, unless they determine more immediate aims which are worthy in themselves" (733).

25. Popper, *Open Society*, 148. Popper's "piecemeal social engineering" approach is explained in chapter 9 of *The Open Society and its Enemies*, "Aestheticism, Perfectionism, Utopianism" (147–56).

26. Popper, *Open Society*, 148. Václav Havel, "Karl Popper's 'The Open Society and Its Enemies' in the Contemporary Global World," preface to *Open Society*, by Popper, 150. Havel also cautions against the exaggeration of what we can know of "the broader interconnections that go beyond the scope of our immediate or group interests": "This awareness, of course, should never become an arrogant utopian conviction that alone possess the whole truth about these interconnections. On the contrary, it should emanate from a deep and humble respect for them and for their mysterious order" (150).

27. Joseph Ratzinger [Pope Benedict XVI], *Church, Ecumenism, and Politics: New Endeavours in Ecclesiology* (San Francisco: Ignatius Press, 2008), 230. It is clear that Popper does not find a use for Platonic ideals in Popper's own piecemeal approach to politics: "Yet I do not wish to end this long discussion without reaffirming my conviction of Plato's overwhelming intellectual achievement. My opinion that he was the greatest of all philosophers has not changed. Even his moral and political philosophy is, as an intellectual achievement, without parallel, though I find it morally repulsive, and indeed horrifying" Popper, *Open Society*, 211.

28. Maurice Blondel, *Letter on Apologetics & History and Dogma*, ed. and trans. Alexander Dru and Illtyd Trethowan (Grand Rapids, MI: Eerdmans, 1994), 152.

29. Pieper, *For the Love of Wisdom*, 312.

30. G. W. F. [Georg Wilhelm Friedrich] Hegel, *The Phenomenology of Spirit*, ed. and trans. Terry Pinkard and Michael Baur (Cambridge: Cambridge University Press, 2018), 939. Pieper responds to Hegel's claim to convert philosophy into a "scientific system" in this way: "This gives expression to a claim that fundamentally transcends what human means allow—a claim that led Goethe to speak of Hegel and philosophers of his ilk in an ironically dismissive tone as 'these men who believe themselves capable of mastering God, the soul, and the world (and whatever other names might exist for what no one comprehends).'" Pieper, *For the Love of Wisdom*, 66.

31. Karl Marx and Friederich Engels, *A Critique of The German Ideology* (Moscow: Progress Publishers, 1968), 11, https://www.marxists.org/archive/marx/works/download/Marx_The_German_Ideology.pdf (accessed October 15, 2023).

32. Marx and Engels, *Critique*, 11. In this context, Marx makes his criticism of the delusional nature of religion: "Religious suffering is, at one and the same time, the expression of real suffering and a protest against real suffering. Religion is the sigh of the oppressed creature, the heart of a heartless world, and the soul of soulless conditions. It is the opium of the people. The abolition of religion as the illusory happiness of the people is the demand for their real happiness. To call on them to give up their illusions about their condition is to call on them to give up a condition that requires illusions. The criticism of religion is, therefore, in embryo, the criticism of that vale of tears of which religion is the halo." Karl Marx, introduction to *A Contribution to a Critique of Hegel's Philosophy of Right* (1844), https://www.marxists.org/archive/marx/works/1843/critique-hpr/intro.htm (accessed October 15, 2023). Lenin made his own comment on Marx's image: "Religion is opium for the people. Religion is a sort of spiritual booze, in which the slaves of capital drown their human image, their demand for a life more or less worthy of man" Cf. Vladimir Lenin, *Socialism and Religion*, in *Lenin Collected Works* (Moscow: Progress Publishers, 1965), vol. 10, 83.

33. Vladimir Lenin, *What Is to Be Done? Burning Questions of our Movement*, Lenin Internet Archive, 1999. https://www.marxists.org/archive/lenin/works/1901/witbd/ (accessed October 14, 2023), chap. 2 "The Spontaneity of the Masses and the Consciousness of the Social-Democrats," 7.

34. Generally speaking, the ancient (pre-Christian) world believed in an eternal cosmos and a cyclical notion of time, and, as Russell Hittinger notes, in variable forms of palingenesis, "the notion of the generic, if not the individual, recurrence of phenomena," Hittinger, *The Virtue of Hope* (World and I Online, 2014. Kindle

edition), 112. History marked this repetition of cycles of phenomena (as, for example, in Plato and in historians Polybius and Sallust) and therefore did not have a linear direction of purpose. Ratzinger observes that in Rome, in its imperial epoch, "The cyclical scheme is replaced by the linear, which no longer contains any decline: it constructs history as progress that has attained its goal in Rome." Ratzinger, *Turning Point for Europe?*, 1253. Ratzinger notes that Augustine, precisely at the moment of the sack of Rome in 410, "blended the Platonic and Roman tradition on the basis of the new elements of the Christian faith. By uniting cyclical and linear, ascending and descending considerations of history, he corrected their one-sidedness and thus created the intellectual foundations on which Europe could be built" (1253). As Eric Voegelin notes, the Christian dimension of transcendent transformation opens the mundane experience of cyclical time with its growth and decay and proposes a real transformation and fulfilment of man by the Christian God beyond this temporal existence. Cf. Voegelin, *The New Science of Politics* (Chicago: University of Chicago Press, 1987), 119.

35. Voegelin, *New Science of Politics*, 119.

36. Ratzinger, *Principles of Catholic Theology*, 153–154.

37. The Greek term *chiliasm* originates in the Book of Revelation 20:1–6, that refers to a thousand-year reign of Christ before the end times: "Also I saw the souls of those who had been beheaded for their testimony to Jesus and for the word of God, and who had not worshiped the beast or its image and had not received its mark on their foreheads or their hands. They came to life and reigned with Christ a thousand years." Book of Revelation 20:4, RSV.

38. Ratzinger, *Church, Ecumenism, and Politics*, 3496.

39. Voegelin, *New Science of Politics*, 118. Voegelin explains how Joachim's vision of human history contrasted with that of Augustine. According to Voegelin, it was with Augustine that the Christian conception of history was discerned and distinguished with clarity. Augustine affirmed the transcendent, eschatological fulfilment of creation and, to do so, distinguished between the profane and the sacred dimensions of history. What we see of the rise and fall of empires and kingdoms, examples of the *civitas mundi*, is recognized as contingent and transitory, with a relative but not transcendent purpose. Within and beyond this profane dimension is the *civitas Dei*, with its sacred history, which includes its earthly pilgrimage, and that is definitively oriented toward transcendent eschatological fulfilment. This is the sacred dimension of history of the *civitas Dei*, directed toward transcendent fulfilment. The *civitas mundi*, the coming and going of temporal powers, does not share in this transcendent purpose or fulfilment. While kingdoms can and do serve good temporal purposes, they have no transcendent purpose or fulfilment. They are destined to fade away.

40. Voegelin, *New Science of Politics*, 119, 120–21. Voegelin points out that: "From the Joachitic immanentization a theoretical problem arises which occurs neither in classic antiquity nor in orthodox Christianity, that is, the problem of an eidos of history. In Hellenic speculation, to be sure, we also have a problem of essence in politics; the polis has an eidos both for Plato and for Aristotle. But the actualization of this essence is governed by the rhythm of growth and decay, and the rhythmical embodiment and disembodiment of essence in political reality is the mystery of existence; it

is not an additional eidos . . . . The problem of an eidos in history, hence, arises only when Christian transcendental fulfilment becomes immanentized" (119).

41. As the American political historians George H. Sabine and Thomas L. Thorson mention: "The philosophy of Hegel aimed at nothing less than a complete reconstruction of modern thought. Political issues and ideas were an important but still only a secondary factor in it as compared with religion and metaphysics. In a broad sense Hegel's problem was one that had grown steadily more acute with the progress of modern science, viz., the opposition between the order of nature as it must be conceived for scientific purposes and the conception of it implicit in the ethical and religious tradition of Christianity" Sabine and Thorson, *A History of Political Theory*, 4th ed. (New York: Holt, Rinehart, and Winston, 1973), 570. David Hume, Jean Jacques Rousseau, and Immanuel Kant had all emphasized the separation of these two orders.

42. G. W. F. Hegel, *Lectures on the Philosophy of History*, trans. H. B. Nisbet (Cambridge: Cambridge University Press, 1989), 69.

43. Hegel, *Lectures*, 42–43.

44. Hegel, *Lectures*, 89.

45. Karl Löwith, *Meaning in History* (Chicago: University of Chicago Press, 1949), 55–56. Löwith comments that the "the most impressive description of the List der Vernunft ('the cunning of reason') is contained in a letter of July 5, 1816, on Napoleon" (230). The sense of Hegel's philosophy of history is depicted well in his comment to a friend, Friedrich Niethammer, on October 13, 1806, the day Napoleon entered Jena: "I saw the Emperor—this soul of the world—go out from the city to survey his reign; it is a truly wonderful sensation to see such an individual, who, concentrating on one point while seated on a horse, stretches over the world and dominates it." Hegel wrote this just as he was finishing *Phenomenology of Mind* and a few years before his *Lectures on the Philosophy of History*. For a complete presentation of Hegel's view on Napoleon see Nicolas Broussard, "Napoleon, Hegelian Hero," *Revue de Souvenir napoléonien* 400 (1995), http://www.napoleon.org/en/reading_room/articles/files/napoleon_hegelian_hero.asp. The citation from Hegel's correspondence is from the Broussard article.

46. Strauss and Cropsey, *History of Political Philosophy*.

47. Cropsey, "Karl Marx," in *History of Political Philosophy*, 16450.

48. Cropsey, "Karl Marx," in *History of Political Philosophy*, 16498.

49. Ratzinger, *"In The Beginning . . . ": A Catholic Understanding of Creation and the Fall* (Grand Rapids, MI: Eerdmans, 1995), 35–36.

50. Benedict XVI, *Spe salvi* (Città del Vaticano: Libreria Editrice Vaticana, 2007), n20.

51. Auriel Kolnai, *Privilege and Liberty and Other Essays in Political Philosophy*, ed. Daniel J. Mahoney (Lanham, MD: Lexington Books, 1999), 23. Mahoney's summary is drawn from Auriel Kolnai's essay "The Utopian Mentality," in *The Utopian Mind and Other Papers: A Critical Study in Moral and Political Philosophy* (London: Athlone Press, 1995), 155–76, and esp. 160–61.

52. C. S. Lewis, *Christian Reflections*, ed. Walter Hooper (London: HarperCollins Publications, 2017), 125. Lewis observes that those who become historicists are "usually theologians, philosophers and politicians" (125).

53. Lewis, *Christian Reflections*, 129. Lewis also points out how Christian Scripture rejects the simplistic historicist interpretation of events and warns against being lured "into the vulgarest of all vulgar errors, that of idolizing as the goddess History what manlier ages belaboured as the strumpet Fortune" (126). And so: "When Carlyle spoke of history as a 'book of revelations' he was a historicist. When Novalis called history 'an evangel' he was a Historicist. When Hegel saw in history the progressive self-manifestation of absolute spirit he was a Historicist. When a village woman says that her wicked father-in-law's paralytic stroke is 'a judgement on him' she is a Historicist. Evolutionism, when it ceases to be simply a theorem in biology and becomes a principle for interpreting the total historical process, is a form of historicism. Keats' Hyperion is the epic of historicism, and the words of Oceanus, 'tis the eternal law That first in beauty should be first in might,' are as fine a specimen of historicism as you could wish to find" (125). As Lewis adds: "(Historicism) encourages a Mussolini to say that 'History took him by the throat' when what really took him by the throat was desire" (136).

54. Eric Voegelin, *Science, Politics and Gnosticism: Two Essays*, ed. Ellis Sandoz (Washington, DC: Gateway Editions, 1997), 625.

55. Voegelin terms as gnosticism the various attempts "at immanentizing the meaning of existence . . . an attempt at bringing our knowledge of transcendence into a firmer grip than the *cognitio fidei*, the cognition of faith, will afford; and Gnostic experiences offer this firmer grip in so far as they are an expression of the soul to the point where God is drawn into the existence of man" Cf. Voegelin, *New Science of Politics*, 123. Other thinkers, such as Hans Jonas and Thomas Altizer, have also used the Gnostic tradition as a key of interpretation of modern times, and the Gnostic interpretation of reality has influenced psychology (Carl Jung, for example), literary analysis (Harold Bloom) and literary fiction (Walker Percy, Flannery O'Connor).

56. Voegelin, *Science, Politics, and Gnosticism*.

57. Voegelin, *Science, Politics, and Gnosticism*, 639.

58. Henri de Lubac, *The Drama of Atheist Humanism*, trans. Mark Sebanc (San Francisco: Ignatius Press, 1995), 24–25.

59. De Lubac, *Drama of Atheist Humanism*, 406–7.

60. Václav Havel et al., *The Power of the Powerless: Citizens Against the State in Central-Eastern Europe*, ed. John Keane (London: Routledge Classics, 1985), 24–25. Havel notes that acceptance of this ideological dominance is not even required, just the acquiescence of living within the system. Havel reminds us that it is not necessary to be convinced of the system of political dominance; it is enough to want to conform outwardly to the falsehood that the system demands. In this sense, the dull compliance with what is required is enough for the system of falsehood to continue to dominate. It is enough not to ask questions, not to oppose what is demanded, not to think and judge for oneself. This is what the system requires, and it is the type of citizen that the system fosters (30).

61. Friedrich Nietzsche, *The Will to Power*, trans. Walter Kaufmann and R. J. Hollingdale, ed. Walter Kaufmann (New York: Vintage Books, 1968), 156, book 2 "The Herd." Interestingly, the dominating value and norm of the herd is equality: "The instinct of the herd considers the middle and the mean as the highest and most

valuable: the place where the majority finds itself; the mode and manner in which it finds itself . . . . Fear ceases in the middle: here one is never alone; here there is little room for misunderstanding; here there is equality; here one's own form of being is not felt as a reproach but as the right form of being; here contentment rules. Mistrust is felt toward the exceptions; to be an exception is experienced as guilt" (159n280).

62. Havel et al., *Power of the Powerless*, 41.

63. Walsh, *After Ideology*, 245. In this volume, Walsh takes guidance from four thinkers (Dostoevsky, Camus, Solzhenitsyn, and Voegelin) who have penetrated the "churning sea of experience within the human soul" and confronted "the question of the modern revolt against the divine ground" and have thus become "authoritative guides toward a postmodern order'" (36).

64. Walsh, *After Ideology*, 234–35. The reference is to Voegelin's 5 volume series *Order and History* (Columbia: University of Missouri, 2000). Walsh develops the personal sense of living in the truth, especially in times that require great sacrifice, as what gives meaning to history, as shown in Solzhenitsyn's *The Red Wheel* and that explains better the significance of history than Leo Tolstoy's historical determinism: "They are the points at which we see plainly that history does not occur in time, our everyday impression to the contrary notwithstanding, but within the irrefutable light of moral truth" David Walsh, *The Priority of the Person: Political, Philosophical, and Historical Discoveries* (Notre Dame, IN: University of Notre Dame Press, 2016), 247. What Walsh is suggesting is that living moments of moral truth ("the human struggle to realize order in existence") are the real moments of history, or the primacy of being over any impersonal sense of becoming.

65. As D. C. Schindler points out: "This transcendence of the end is what keeps a proper political community from becoming 'totalitarian'" Cf. Schindler, *The Politics of the Real: The Church Between Liberalism and Integralism* (Steubenville, OH: New Polity Press, 2021), 228.

Chapter 12

Politics and Religion

The major difficulty in dealing with the theme of politics and religion is that we have become accustomed (or conditioned) to think of religion in modern secular terms. Public debate on religion is predetermined according to slogans that seem right and undeniable; religion cannot be publicly imposed, the freedom of conscience, the complete separation of church and state, the danger to society of religious fanaticism, the necessary public neutrality towards religious diversity, the respect for those who do not believe, and the common, non-religious, context of human society.

In order to rediscover the real relation of politics and religion, it is necessary to recover the real significance of the human person as a religious being and the real content of religious experience as the vital source of fulfilment of personal and social (and hence, political) being. Not to do so is to remain within a context that has already predetermined in its own favour the terms of the debate.

As an overview, this chapter starts with a description of the contemporary view of religion in the political context. A recent judicial decision of the Court of Justice of the European Union gives an indication of how public religious manifestation is to be regarded according to the prevalent modern secular approach.

The term "secular" can be construed in different ways. I point out its original meaning and its appreciation of the secular dimension of reality within a greater religious context. I also indicate the very different modern meaning of secular with particular reference to the development of the modern political state.

I then try to show why the experience of religious truth, in its two basic forms of manifestation, the inner path of personal experience and the outer path of the structure of reality, is necessarily part of public reason.

We are faced, then, with two opposing approaches to religious truth, based on the original meaning of secular (historically Christian, but not exclusive to Christianity), and the modern meaning of secular. I try to elucidate what each approach entails and their mutual antithesis as a project of power (modern secularism) and as a response to order (the original meaning of secular). In particular, I point out the essential contribution of religious experience to the human person's being and flourishing in society.

The chapter concludes with a comment on the vital religious context of social life and society's dependence on the Source of the experience of religious truth. Modern secularism is essentially a rejection of man's real existential condition and an impediment to the possibilities of personal and social flourishing, to be found in the recognition and response to the Personal Source of being as its foundation and fulfilment.

There are, of course, many practical issues of politics and religion to be resolved. At the same time, unless the fundamental terms of the debate, as I have tried to present them here, are recognized and asserted, the religious question in politics will always be marginal and confined in freedom's ever decreasing places of refuge.

NEXUS

The last theme on political ideologies ended with a description by Eric Voegelin of the obliteration of the transcendent order of being by means of the modern "decapitation of being—the murder of God."[1] Today this dramatic phrase seems to have lost much of its importance because religion as such is considered as something of a spent force. There are various and interrelated reasons for this.

In the first place, by religion is meant something that is entirely of subjective origin, like a personal taste, that is only the expression of a random personal disposition. As such, religion has as much importance as personal tastes—relevant for the individual concerned but not something essentially communicable, and therefore of no real and universal significance. Religion is commonly regarded as something that originates from within the person and that colors what is outside. It can be a sentiment, an emotion, a disposition; it is not knowledge of what is real. Religion's content and categories of experience are not considered valid sources of knowledge and therefore relegated to what is sub-rational and unreal.

Publicly, religion and religious beliefs and practices, are officially viewed as tolerable as long as religion is practiced in private and in non-confrontational ways. There is the view that the public expression of religion can provoke hostility and social discord, as evidenced by the many wars of religion, and therefore is a potential threat to social communion. To hold the belief that the tenets of a particular religion are true for all, that is, universal, is considered something dangerous, an imposition on others and on public reason, and therefore incompatible with democratic pluralism. A religion can claim to be a private association of persons with private beliefs; it may not make the public claim that all should follow the same beliefs.

Politically, religion is viewed as largely irrelevant to society's problems and needs and therefore to be ignored or removed from political activities and processes, and this is expressed institutionally as "the separation of church and state."[2] Publicly, all religions are viewed and treated in this same way, and any public expressions of a particular religion are seen as discriminatory and unfair to other religions, as well as provocative to society in general. There is also a growing concern that the beliefs and values of religions are in contradiction to some contemporary basic human rights and so should not be expressed in public or even held in private, as such beliefs are seen as hateful and victimizing of minorities, who need to be protected and vindicated.

Much of the above evaluation of religion can be seen in the 2021 decision of the Court of Justice of the European Union in the case of two German Muslim women, one a carer and the other a sales assistant, who had been required by their employers to remove their Islamic headscarves (deemed "a conspicuous, large-sized religious sign") at their places of work, under threat of being suspended from their work. The highest court of European jurisdiction found that "A prohibition on wearing any visible form of expression of political, philosophical or religious beliefs in the workplace may be justified by the employer's need to present a neutral image towards customers or to prevent social disputes."[3]

The Court found that: "an employer's desire to display, in relations with customers, a policy of political, philosophical or religious neutrality may be regarded as a legitimate aim" provided that there is "a genuine need," such as "inter alia, the rights and legitimate wishes of customers or users and, more specifically, as regards education, parents' wish to have their children supervised by persons who do not manifest their religion or belief when they are in contact with the children."[4]

What this means, according to the Court, is that "Such a policy can be effectively pursued only if no visible manifestation of political, philosophical or religious beliefs is allowed when workers are in contact with customers or with other workers, since the wearing of any sign, even a small-sized one, undermines the ability of that measure to achieve the aim allegedly pursued."[5]

The Court also found that "neutrality" in the application of this right was necessary, that is, the prohibition of all religious dress signs in the workplace:

> In the present case, the rule at issue appears to have been applied in a general and undifferentiated way, since the employer concerned also required an employee wearing a religious cross to remove that sign. The Court concludes that, in those circumstances, a rule such as that at issue in the main proceedings

does not constitute, with regard to workers who observe certain clothing rules based on religious precepts, direct discrimination on the grounds of religion or belief.[6]

It takes little imagination to recognize the social import for public religious practice, when even a gesture as apparently socially innocuous as wearing a religious headscarf or a Christian cross can be legally banned even for commercial purposes. Is there indeed any limit to the conceivable extension of this decision? One can also ask whether this universal ban on the wearing of religious symbols is in fact a "neutral" stance to religious expression, or is, in fact, a blatantly hostile disposition to any and all religious signs of dress and other forms of religious expression. Another issue is what is referred to as "the rights and legitimate wishes of customers and users"; what exactly are those "rights and legitimate wishes"? Does the phrase mean that some people have the right and legitimate wish to impose on others a non-religious appearance, non-religious language, non-religious beliefs? Why should that imposition be a right and legitimate wish, and why are the rights and legitimate wishes of certain (hypothetical) customers and users to be preferred to the rights and legitimate wishes of sales assistants and carers?[7]

THE MANIFESTATION OF THE RELIGIOUS
DIMENSION IN HUMAN REASON

Clearly, what underlies this decision is a view of religions as we have described above, as something that is potentially and in fact nocuous for society that should be removed in the public interest. Nor can this decision be viewed in terms of civil tolerance, as the case is sometimes made that as religions claim to represent what is universally true, they are, therefore, intolerant of and hostile to different or opposing views. Here the decision is not merely to allow and protect non-religious views, but not to tolerate an expression of a religious view. Again, what do religions represent that make their public expression something that should reasonably be publicly suppressed or even prohibited?

This judgment of the European Court of Justice would perhaps claim to represent a fair and balanced view of European society, one that is called secular, that is, a society that bases itself on an assumed common agreement of reason and freedom, in which religions are a non-essential and divisive element. This secular view thus eliminates radical and irrational religious views and appeals to what is universally reasonable and free of religious interpretations that have only imposed irrational and divisive beliefs and, by so doing, denied or twisted reason to their own purposes. This is the positive appeal of secularism.

There are, no doubt, examples of this manipulating and dominating use of religion, what Joseph Ratzinger has called "pathologies of religion."[8] Sajda Mughal, a young Muslim woman who survived the London Underground bombings in the summer of 2005, described her reaction when she learned later that day who the perpetrators had been: "The fact that it was carried out by Muslim men was incomprehensible to me. My first feeling was: 'Why would you do that? This is not what Islam teaches us.' There was a level of anger there."[9]

The appeal of secularism as described above implies a vision of life and society unfettered by religion's distortion of reason and by unnecessary and divisive expressions of religious belief. This secularism suggests that the world and society can be understood and formed only when all ultimately irrelevant religious ornaments have been removed.[10]

In its Christian origin, secular did not mean "non-religious" or "exclusively human," as it is used today, but referred to the Biblical time interval between the fall from man's original state, and the end of time, the *eschaton*, the restoration of all things in Christ.[11] Biblical creational accounts demonstrate the religious origin and end of all creation and the religious rationality of the divine Creator. Human science presupposes, and in its discoveries reflects, such religious rationality. What we refer to when we use the word "secular" is the rationality of created reality in this present time, always within the religious creational context. Secular and religious are not, therefore, exclusionary opposites, as contemporary secularism presupposes. The real distinction is between the Sacred (God) and created reality (Creation), with the latter's implicit rational and religious structure and orientation both from and toward its Creator. Understood in this way, the religious dimension of reality is the ultimate meaning and purpose of all reality, and therefore the ultimate rational context of all being. Writing on the distinction between the sacred and the profane, Josef Pieper makes this point: "we necessarily miss the point of the distinction between 'sacred' and 'profane' unless we understand that this distinction exists within the framework of a large communality which embraces both terms."[12]

Pieper considers as contrary to the Christian vision of reality the contemporary secular view of a completely autonomous, non-religious, public space. Such a view implies that "the world lying 'before' the gate of the temple (in Latin 'fanum') cannot be regarded as 'good' and in some sense 'holy' by virtue of its created state; [then] the absurd oversimplification is true that the existence of a 'sacred' space implies that 'outside' this space ('pro-fanum') one is permitted to 'do or fail to do whatever one chooses.'"[13]

What this means is that the rational manifestation of reality presupposes a religious context, and therefore the religious dimension of reality is a necessary part of our experience and understanding of reality. The *a priori* denial or intentional elimination of the religious dimension of reality would be a violation of human reason.

Here I do not mean to impose and oblige a Christian perspective, but simply to point out that the so-called religiously "neutral" approach to reality, which requires the elimination of all religious meanings and manifestations, is not, in fact, our universal and spontaneous default position, one that we can all agree on, whether or not we recognize and respond to the Sacred in our lives. The manifestation of the religious dimension and context of human existence is a widespread and diffused experience among human cultures; to eliminate *a priori* this manifestation, or to exclude *a priori* the supernatural reality such manifestation indicates, is a distortion of human experience.[14]

To recognize the real manifestation of religious experience and its real significance does not, of course, deny the humanly rational understanding of our experience of reality as is shown in the different sciences of the various dimensions of reality, each dependent on the differing modes of manifestation of reality. In fact, the apprehension of what is humanly rational within the religious and revelational context, was one of the primary concerns of scholastic philosophy, to show:

> That reason has its own domain, its own sphere of operation, and that it is not absorbed by faith. Saint Anselm and the scholastics "made room" for reason within faith. . . . Among the great achievements of scholasticism were the distinctions between faith and reason and between grace and nature. Medieval thinkers, and saint Thomas Aquinas in particular, taught that natural evidences have their own integrity, and that reason can achieve truth through its own powers.[15]

WHAT DOES MODERN POLITICAL SECULARISM MEAN?

This Scholastic understanding of what is "secular" refers to the nature, pattern, structure, causality, and finality of what we can perceive of reality, and which also necessarily indicates (and presupposes, in the case of a religious believer) a greater religious context of action, structure, meaning, and purpose of reality.

This meaning of secular is much different from the contemporary use of "secular," which today often means forms of instrumental reason by autonomous agents of power. The progressive process of eliminating the religious meaning of reality, with occasional courtesies to the Deity, was not simply the removal of religious symbols and references, but a reinterpretation of the world in an entirely different way. Hugo Grotius' phrase *"etsi Deus non daretur"* (as if God did not exist) was not simply the proposal of an absentee landlord who had left everything in place to be administered as usual by responsible tenants, but came to mean something much more radical:

> With the writings of Grotius, Hobbes and Spinoza, political theory achieved a certain highly ambiguous "autonomy" with regard to theology. However, autonomization was not achieved in the sphere of knowledge alone; it was only possible because the new science of politics both assumed and constructed for itself a new autonomous object—the political—defined as a field of pure power. Secular "scientific" understanding of society was, from the outset, only the self-knowledge of the self-construction of the secular as power. . . . This autonomous object was, first of all, "natural." According to Grotius, the natural laws governing property and sovereignty could be known etsi Deus non daretur. . . . But now, for modernity, natural law transcribes the sealed-off totality of nature, where eternal justice consists in the most invariable rules. These are not (as for Aquinas) from the inner tendencies of the Aristotelian practical reason towards the *telos* of the good, but rather from purely theoretical reflections on the necessity for every creature to ensure its own self-preservation. Because nature, since the renaissance, was regarded as an "open book" which might be exhaustively read, Grotius, Hobbes and Spinoza can be confident that the self-preserving *conatus* provides the universal hermeneutic key for both nature and society. And the *etsi* is entirely a ruse, because the finite totality presupposes that nature is a legally governed domain, obeying completely regular laws of the operation of power and passion, which yet are wilfully laid down by the retired deity.[16]

Milbank finishes this point by stating that: "the new autonomous object of political science was not, therefore, simply 'uncovered.' The space of the secular had to be invented as the space of 'pure power.'"[17]

The *etsi Deus non daretur* formula, in fact, implies something much more than filling in for God; in God's absence, the modern secular mind and will rewrite the structure of reality. American historian Glenn Olsen points this out:

> In secularising the world, it was not just God who was isolated. Mother nature, who had formerly been *mater*, became matter, unendingly to be manipulated by reason because severed from God and God's designs. The severing of the created order from God typically involved the notion that there is no truth of creation, no plan of God for life, not even an organic structure proper to each creature that must be respected. Though those caught in modernity—say, the scientists who "create life in a dish"—continue to inhabit the space created by

severing nature from God, others have become very nervous about this, some ecologists going so far as to say that only piety will save the environment.[18]

Olsen conjectures that the development of the physical sciences in modernity could have been different:

> The discovery of the laws of nature, as Newton himself had hoped, could have encouraged piety and led to seeing all existence as theophanous. Man's task could have been seen as a "metaphysics of wholeness," the integration of the old and the new, the placement of man as spirit within a natural order that was relinquishing its secrets. Instead, man's spiritual nature was increasingly denuded, reduced to being merely another instance of matter in motion.[19]

There is nothing compelling, or indeed obvious, about the modern meaning of secular. In fact, it is the less obvious option, and harder to justify as a philosophical perspective, precisely because the secular perspective is committed to denying the spontaneous evidence of religious Being as expressed in so many ways in its sacred and secular manifestations.[20]

It is not difficult to see how this modern meaning of "secular" finds itself necessarily in opposition to the religious sense of "secular" and sees in the religious sense an obstacle to the expression of its own secular projects for human society. At the same time, one can see that the modern democratic form of government and society fits in very well with this secular projection of power. What is really at stake in a decision to prohibit religious headscarves and Christian crosses is not some neutral, tolerant society, but the anger of revolt against a worldview that purports to find meaning and purpose that is evident, reasonable, and indicative of a greater source and finality of being.

There is another aspect to the secular, in the modern sense. It is not just that the secular approach to reality ignores and forgets the greater religious context of reality and human existence; the modern secular approach attempts to substitute for the religious context, to make the human person's secular projects the sum total of reality and to absorb the religious sense of the sacred and the absolute within the secular self. The secular mentality is not merely our vision, interpretation, and construction of reality without God; it is to do all those things as if we were God.[21]

This omnipotent sense of the secular may be seen in the historical process of the formation of the modern political state. American political philosopher William T. Cavanaugh comments on the so-called "Wars of Religion":

> The wars in question, then, were not fought as between members of two different "religions." What was at stake was rather the aggrandizement of the centralizing territorial state over the remnants of the transnational ecclesial order and the remnants of local privilege and custom. The rise of the state was not

necessitated by the "Wars of Religion"; rather, these wars were the birthpangs of the state, in which the overlapping jurisdictions, allegiances, and customs of the medieval order were flattened and circumscribed into the new creation of the sovereign state (not always yet nation-state), a centralizing power with a monopoly on violence within a defined territory.[22]

Cavanaugh points out, quoting sociologist Robert A. Nisbet:

The view that the state is a natural outgrowth of family and community is false. As Robert Nisbet points out, the modern state arose from opposition to kinship and other local social groups: "(t)he history of the Western State has been characterized by the gradual absorption of powers and responsibilities formerly resident in other associations and by an increasing directness of relation between the sovereign authority of the State and the individual citizen."[23]

What Cavanaugh recognizes in this creation of the modern state is a type of alternative, secular soteriology, a substitute explanation for the origin, the condition, and purpose of the human person in terms of relation and subservience, not to the sovereign God, but to the sovereign state. Separated individuals, an absolute civil power, and contractual relations as circumscribed by the state, constitute the pervasive secular political context, which is the new corporate body. The reality of fundamental personal dependence on, and participation with others in God disappears, and this new secular composition takes its place. With this change, the meaning of religion is changed into a private belief and practice within the new political body. Belief in God remained, but Christian theology had to be reinterpreted in the light of this new political and social phenomenon of the secular state.[24]

Cavanaugh draws a radical historical conclusion:

The story of the death of the sovereign God and his rebirth in the sovereign state is not a story of the progressive stripping of the sacred from some secular remainder. It is instead the transfer of care for the holy from church to state. We not only expect the state to provide technical solutions to market imbalances. In a deeper sense, we want the state to absorb the risk involved in living a mortal human life. We want the state to defer the consequences of our actions to some undefined future. In other words, we want the state to help us cheat death.[25]

All of this explains the distorted context today when the relation of "religion" or "the Church" and the state are discussed. We live in political times in which God is obliged to apply for citizenship, and his public presence is at the pleasure (or displeasure) of the state.[26]

THE PERSON IN POLITICS AS A RELIGIOUS BEING

It seems, then, that the development of the modern form of political power has created a picture of the human person according to its own image and likeness, rather than the reality of the person determining the nature and scope of the political form. This is particularly the case with the religious context of man's being, ignored and stifled under the misused term "secular," so that all reference to the religious dimension of reality, and the Sacred, is dismissed *a priori* as "subjective" (meaning that there is no real religious object), private (meaning that its only relevance is for own's own thoughts), and publicly nocuous (offensive, harmful, and dangerous to society). Whatever the vestigial remains there are of God are to be interpreted in this "secular" sense; public society is to be protected from religion by the suppression of religious truth and its manifestation, a suppression that is shrouded in terms of tolerance, neutrality, and respect for those who may be exposed to the effects of religion's radiation.

Clearly, this mythos of the secular does not correspond to the truth of the human person as a religious being, or the truth of God, as the Absolute may be experienced and known. If it is accepted that there is within the person a longing for definitive meaning and purpose, as well as the inchoate but real sense of the Sacred Presence, if this is what we identify as religious experience—and there are vast historical cultural manifestations of these longings in all times and places—then religious experience is not just some private, esoteric taste, but a commonly (if inchoately) experienced need of daily existence:

In *The Growth of the Liberal Soul*, Walsh observes that as a people we cannot really live within the precincts of a finite and secularised world. We experience the dynamism toward what transcends our ordinary mundane lives. We depend on the existential hope of fulfilment and plenitude which we recognize is beyond this finitude of our actual existence. We could not really live if what we have and who we are now are everything that will ever be. Perhaps because this transcendent pull and expectation are so much a part of our experience of existence that we do not recognize or appreciate what pulls us forward in fundamental hope, notwithstanding all disappointments and failures. This is the real and yet unseen transcendent context of our experience of the finitude of everything in this existence. It is only this transcendent context that sustains our experience of finitude.[27]

We can go further in our descriptive analysis of human religious experience. We have become accustomed to certain empirical, positive modes of experience and interpretation that, while valid in themselves, do not—cannot—identify and explain other equally valid modes of experience, such as the ethical and religious experience of reality. The sense of the absolute, the spirit of worship of the transcendent God, the cultural manifestations of historical religions of human history, the experience of conversion, shared (indeed, massive) cultic expression of adoration and supplication, human actions that manifest supernatural power and wisdom cannot all be dismissed merely as subjective delusion. It is certainly true that these experiences conceal more than they reveal, that the acute human limitations of cognition and action are exposed, and yet it is impossible, with intellectual integrity, to deny the reality—the real Object—of these practices and experiences, even if these experiences are not our own. The prejudicial refusal to interpret these real experiences is no longer warranted, whether the religious experience be *personal* (an experience of the Absolute as Personal Being), or *cosmological* (an experience of the manifestation of the Absolute in the being of reality).

W. Norris Clarke gives philosophical credit to both these types of experience. In reference to the experience of our own intellectual consciousness, our experience of both knowing and willing, the Inner Way to God, Clarke explains:

> If I accept and listen to this radical innate pull of my nature as intellectual being, if I accept this nature gratefully and humbly as a gift, I will affirm with conviction the existence of the ultimate Fullness and Centre of all being, the lodestar that draws my intelligence ever onward, even though this ultimate goal remains for me at present only obscurely discerned, seen through a mirror darkly, pointed to beyond all conceptual grasp as the mystery of inexhaustible Light, a Light that with my present, body-obscured vision I cannot directly penetrate or master with my own powers, but that renders all else intelligible.[28]

Likewise, in our experience and reflection on the world outside of us, our cosmological experience, we need to broaden our minds and hearts to the greater source of Being that this universe reveals:

> And there is no good reason for us, 200 years later, to remain within the artificial prison (Kant) erected for himself by denying with no good evidence that most fundamental insight of all ancient and medieval metaphysicians as well as everyday practical wisdom—namely, that all action is of its nature revelatory of the nature of its agent-source, even if the latter lies beyond the range of our direct experience. Causal explanation, grounded on the principle that all action is the self-revelation of being (also its partial concealment, of course) is but another expression for the mind's radical openness from the narrow circle of its own inner experience to the vast world of the not-yet-experienced—perhaps never experienceable—surrounding environment of being, insofar as the latter manifests itself as the necessary support and ground of all experience.[29]

To experience the evidence, whether it be personal or cosmological, for the manifestation of God we need to reopen our minds and hearts to reality as we can experience it. This requires dismantling an artificial edifice that does not allow us to experience truth and goodness, and the Source from which they emanate. It is this truncated vision that produces and is produced by the modern secular mind. Ratzinger criticised a mentality that counts as reasonable only that which can be verified or falsified and thus:

> Ethics and religion must be assigned to the subjective field, and they remain extraneous to the realm of reason in the strict sense of the word. Where positivist reason dominates the field to the exclusion of all else—and that is broadly the case in our public mindset—then the classical sources of knowledge for ethics and law are excluded. This is a dramatic situation which affects everyone, and on which a public debate is necessary.[30]

Using a highly evocative image to German politicians in the Bundestag in Berlin, Ratzinger recognizes the danger of the fabrication of a humanly made world based on this narrow-minded vision of reality:

> I say this with Europe specifically in mind, where there are concerted efforts to recognize only positivism as a common culture and a common basis for law-making, reducing all the other insights and values of our culture to the level of subculture, with the result that Europe vis-à-vis other world cultures is left in a state of culturelessness and at the same time extremist and radical movements emerge to fill the vacuum. In its self-proclaimed exclusivity, the positivist reason which recognizes nothing beyond mere functionality resembles a concrete bunker with no windows, in which we ourselves provide lighting and atmospheric conditions, being no longer willing to obtain either from God's wide world. And yet we cannot hide from ourselves the fact that even in this artificial world, we are still covertly drawing upon God's raw materials, which we refashion into our own products. The windows must be flung open again, we must see the wide world, the sky and the earth once more and learn to make proper use of all this.[31]

Ratzinger refers to this contemporary blindness as a "pathology of reason":

> There are also pathologies of reason, although mankind in general is not as conscious of this fact today. There is a hubris of reason that is no less dangerous. Indeed, bearing in mind its potential effects, it poses an even greater threat—it suffices here to think of the atomic bomb or of man as a "product." This is why reason, too, must be warned to keep within its proper limits, and it must learn a willingness to listen to the great religious traditions of mankind. If it cuts itself completely adrift and rejects this willingness to learn, this relatedness, reason becomes destructive.[32]

ALTERNATIVE RESPONSES TO THE
RELIGIOUS DIMENSION OF EXISTENCE

Something of vital importance, not only for human fulfilment, but for the possibility of human existence, is at stake here.[33] It seems that we are fundamentally faced with two opposing perspectives on reality and two opposing religious visions of the human person, one based on power and one on order. The religious question, "the natural desire for truth about the ultimate meaning and end of human existence," is not an optional one; however we may answer it, by power or by order, we are committed to answer. Not to answer is in fact to answer in a specific way.

In *The Growth of the Liberal Soul*, as Walsh notes, it is only the hope of transcendent finality that gives the relative meaning and value to our necessary decisions in this actual existence. Therefore, the acceptance of the person's transcendent destiny is a necessity if we are to make sense of our actual and temporary condition. We either accept the validity of the hope of transcendence or we abandon our existence to the absurdity of a life without meaning. This openness to transcendence is not some esoteric optional but a demand that our hope of existence requires.[34]

The natural desire and need for truth about the ultimate meaning and end of human existence is thus our natural condition, and this desire and need are experienced not merely in some detached speculative way, but also as an immediate and pressing experience that percolates through the daily hopes and struggles or our lives.

The Secular Response

The secular response is to assume personal and collective sovereignty over all things and to attempt to fashion a life and a world in the image and likeness of our needs, desires, and wants, as transcendent as they are of everything we know and can do. This requires reverting the religious dimension back on ourselves and on this actual existence. While the developing strands of modernity generally maintained a religious gloss, the nature of the Christian God was becoming more and more nominal and otiose. It was the nineteenth-century German Ludwig Feuerbach (1804–1872) who made explicit the humanistic replacement of God by man:

> The absolute to man is his own nature. The power of the object over him is therefore the power of his own nature. Thus the power of the object of feeling is the power of feeling itself; the power of the object of the intellect is the power of the intellect itself; the power of the object of the will is the power of the will itself.[35]

It is interesting to note the emphasis on power; not the object of real experience, but the power of persons to will, to extend themselves, to dominate. The religious dimension thus becomes interpreted as the call and the task of persons to complete themselves by their own power:

> Religion, at least the Christian, is the relation of man to himself, or more correctly to his own nature (i.e., his subjective nature); but a relation to it, viewed as a nature apart from his own. The divine being is nothing else than the human being, or, rather, the human nature purified, freed from the limits of the individual man, made objective—i.e., contemplated and revered as another, a distinct being. All the attributes of the divine nature are, therefore, attributes of the human nature.[36]

Feuerbach later extended this individual appropriation of power to fulfil oneself to a social and political context:

> The essential differences within philosophy are the essential differences within mankind. The place of belief has been taken by unbelief and that of the Bible by reason. Similarly, religion and the Church have been replaced by politics, the heaven by the earth, prayer by work, hell by material need, and the Christian by man. . . . If man has now taken over the place of the Christian in practice, then in theory, too, the human essence must take over the place of the divine. . . . Only thus can we free ourselves from the contradiction that is at present poisoning our innermost being—the contradiction between our life and thought on the one hand, and a religion that is fundamentally opposed to them on the other. For religious we must once again become if politics is to be our religion. But this can be achieved only if we possess the highest point of reference within ourselves as the condition for making politics our religion.[37]

At the heart of the secular mentality, therefore, is the autonomous mind and will of persons that experience the transcendent demands of nature and the presence of the Sacred Absolute but revert this experience and these demands on themselves and their power to construct and fabricate a world that will answer their thirst for the absolute and the eternal. What is essential is the expropriation of power and the radical denial of all conceived limits to that power. What we find here, in this reversion of the religious context and experience, is the root justification of anarchic freedom, of the exploitation of nature, of the refabrication of personal being, and the illusion of a future world free of imperfection and suffering—all within human grasp and power.

Here we can recognize the most profound source of secular antagonism toward order, toward the given structure and purpose of reality. To respond to the human person's fundamental transcendental aspirations, people need to be all-powerful and to be able to dominate all things so as to refabricate them for their own purposes and solutions. All of what appears as already given, structured, oriented toward fulfilment is therefore an affront and challenge to the individual's capacity for power and therefore needs to be deconstructed. Voegelin describes in dramatic terms the secular project, which is fundamentally the task of destroying the sense of the givenness of reality and convincing people that all is within one's personal power to change and to transform. Reality does not have a nature or a given structure but is malleable according to each one's mind and hands. The world is not to be understood but to be technically fabricated and made amenable to our purposes and our projection of what the world and we ourselves want to be:

> In order, therefore, that the attempt to create a new world may seem to make sense, the givenness of the order of being must be obliterated; the order of being must be interpreted, rather, as essentially under man's control. And taking control of being further requires that the transcendent origin of being be obliterated: it requires the decapitation of being—the murder of God.[38]

This includes the human person's own condition of freedom, which cannot be permitted by those of power precisely because it is a limit of that power. It is not surprising, therefore, that we find today so many increasing means of surveillance, regulations, control, the intentional breakup of interpersonal relations, and the pre-empting of human choice. More and more, we have the sense of a political trade-off, the benefits of bread at the price of someone's dominating power over us, the demanded negation of spiritual freedom for benefits of this mundane existence. The Russian writer Fyodor Dostoyevsky represents this in *The Legend of the Grand Inquisitor*, in his novel *The Brothers Karamazov*, the necessity of the dominance of power, the promise of bread, and the control of conscience:

> Receiving bread from us, they will see clearly that we take the bread made by their hands from them, to give it to them, without any miracle. They will see that we do not change the stones to bread, but in truth they will be more thankful for taking it from our hands than for the bread itself! For they will remember only too well that in old days, without our help, even the bread they made turned to stones in their hands, while since they have come back to us, the very stones have turned to bread in their hands. Too, too well will they know the value of complete submission! And until men know that, they will be unhappy. . . . But the flock will come together again and will submit once more, and then it will be once for all. Then we shall give them the quiet humble happiness of weak creatures such as they are by nature. . . . Oh, we shall persuade them at last not to be proud, for Thou didst lift them up and thereby taught them to be proud. We shall show them that they are weak, that they are only pitiful children, but that childlike happiness is the sweetest of all.[39]

There is a religious tone to this project of power because the secular project necessarily assumes the religious context of personal and social aspirations and submits them to the human project of power. The secular mentality is, therefore, in its ultimate expression, a project of power and immanence of religious proportions and, as we have seen, invasive of human freedom and conscience. As Ratzinger observed:

> The real opposition that characterizes today's world is not that between various religious cultures, but that between the radical emancipation of man from God, from the roots of life, on one hand, and from the great religious cultures on the other. If there were to be a clash of cultures, it would not be because of a clash of the great religions which have always struggled against one another, but which, in the end, have also always known how to live with one another but it will be because of the clash between this radical emancipation of man and the great historical cultures. Thus, even the rejection of the reference to God, is not the expression of a tolerance that desires to protect the non-theistic religions and the dignity of atheists and agnostics, but rather the expression of a conscience that would like to see God cancelled definitively from the public life of humanity, and relegated to the subjective realm of residual cultures of the past.[40]

The Religious Response

If this project of power is fundamentally a reaction against the experience of what is, of what can be experienced as real and to which we are called to respond adequately, then we need to ask what the totality of our experience means, what our real circumstances are, and what the real sources of our hopes and aspirations are. The secular political project assumes a certain model of man which is fundamentally a rejection of order (reality) and an imposition of power. It is this model of the person that prevails in public discourse today and frames *a priori* all discussions of religion. We now need to unmask this distortion and to rediscover the reality of the human person, so that politics can adequately reflect the essential religious being of persons in society.

To rediscover the religious being of the human person what is first of all required is a public respect for religious experience and the sacred reality that it discloses. While pathologies of religion exist, irrational and emotional actions that are attributed to a religious experience for their justification, these do not disqualify real religious experience, just as pathologies of reason do not nullify the proper expression of the light of reason. The philosophical approach, that is, what reason favors, is one that ponders "the ontological implications of the givenness of things as originally experienced" and that recognizes that "experience itself, in other words, bears an ontology in its distinctness as subjective."[41] This requires the recognition of different modes of human experience and the unprejudicial openness of the person's perceptive capacities, "the determination not to allow any element of the totality of truth to escape us, and consequently to accept a less exact method of verifying results rather than risk losing contact with some portion of reality."[42]

Authentic religious experience, as varied and oblique as it is, is an expression of the personal perception of the Sacred,[43] and is, therefore, a source of truth that reason needs to include and comprehend for the reality it manifests, and therefore cannot reasonably be reduced to something else, even less to some subjective state of feeling:

> This is therefore the first sure truth of all religious phenomenology: on whatever level of his religious development he may be, the human being is invariably looking into a realm of being and value which is in basis and origin utterly different from the whole remaining empirical world; it is not inferred from that other world, neither won from it by idealization, and access to it is possible solely in the religious act. . . . This is the proposition of the originality and non-derivation of religious experience.[44]

We have become so used to the imposed sense of public reason that we are slow to admit that religious experience, and the ontology it discloses, is part of our experience of reason, part of the social domain of public reason. If this is so, then the rejection of religious experience becomes unreasonable, and, as a basis for social communion, our public reason is insufficient and unstable.

Ratzinger, in his essay *A Christian Orientation in a Pluralistic Democracy*,[45] claims that mere ethical standards are not enough because they cannot provide their own necessary foundation. He mentions that the ethics of the Enlightenment, which are still generally the moral substratum of our political states, depend on the vital source of Christianity for their existence and which gives this moral substratum its sense of being reasonable and coherent. Ratzinger affirms that if this Christian context is lost or removed, then this moral substratum too will disintegrate. This is so because, as Ratzinger points out, isolated reason, reason that has no greater context or foundation than its own functioning and calculations, ends up becoming unreasonable. Human reason only functions properly within a greater context of a reality that lies beyond reason, that is, a context that is known to reason only by revelation. Ratzinger maintains that the state depends on this greater Christian context even for its own survival as a state that wishes to be open to varying traditions and beliefs.[46]

The social recognition of the truth manifested in religious experience is a requirement of reason for social and political cohesion. Seen in this light, the wearing of a Muslim headscarf and of a Christian cross are manifestations of public reason rather than acts of public aggression.

The religious sense, undeniably part of the experience of human reason, communicates and sustains in us the experience of what is, of the structure and purpose of reality, and in this sense, of the order of being, what in religious terms, is called the creational character of all of reality, the fundamental experience of being, drawn obliquely from the experience of Being. While in prison, Václav Havel describes this oblique but real sense of what sustains all phenomena:

> The answer, of course, cannot logically be sought "inside" the entities whose meaning we seek, that is, in the world of those relative and ephemeral contexts, but only inside "life itself": in the context of the absolute, against the absolute horizon. Which of course ultimately means that all those partial "signifying circumstances" are themselves given meaning by this "deepest of anchorings," which through them provides a basis for the identity of all things. The hidden backbone and the deepest source of everything that has meaning is always—whether we realize it or not—this "anchoredness in the absolute."[47]

This sense of being anchored in the Absolute applies also to one's own existence:

> A search for the meaning of life, then, is in fact a search for the absolute horizon. It is as though we were constantly striving for something beyond us and above us, something firm, something we wish to grasp and hold on to and which we in fact—or so it seems to us—do grasp and hold on to. . . . We do not know the meaning of life—just as we do not know the mystery of Being—and yet in some way we "possess" it—as our own, immediate version of that "anchoredness" or as our own way of longing for it were we in some way not to "possess" it, search for it or at least feel its lack, we couldn't begin to live as what we are, that is, as creators of the "order of the spirit," as "re-creators" of the world, as dignified beings, capable of stepping beyond ourselves, that is, beyond the shadow of our animal foundations.[48]

What real religious experience includes, therefore, is an oblique but real sense of what sustains all things as they are, the source to which all things mutely refer, which is the guarantee and confirmation of their existence, in other words, the truth of their being. This means that the recognition, implicit or explicit, of religious experience is the source of our recognition of the truth of Being (though often, the process is from the truth of beings to the truth of Being); the experience of truth is a religious experience:

> To think through the essence of truth is to arrive at the notion of God. In the long run, it is impossible to maintain the unique identity of the truth, in other

words, its dignity (which, in turn is the basis of the dignity both of man and of the world), without learning to perceive in it the unique identity and dignity of the living God. Ultimately, therefore, reverence for the truth is inseparable from that disposition of veneration which we call adoration.[49]

This religious sense of being anchored in the absolute (which can often be experienced, but not recognized, as a religious experience), which is the source of our experience of truth, applies also to personal being, as Havel describes above. It is the sense of having been given our being with its dynamic nature toward transcendent fulfilment. The experience of being anchored in the absolute frees us from the experience of absurdity, the experience of which is also described by Havel.[50] This freedom allows us to recognize our own fragile, contingent being precisely because we experience our pre-existing dependence or reliance on the Absolute. This experience of dependence is not a stifling of our being, but the vital recognition of its source and destiny. In personalist terms, it is the recognition of the Source of the fatherhood of our being, rather than the oppressive presence of the jailor of our existence.[51]

What all of this implies is the human capacity to recognize the pre-existing reality of all things, and especially their own being, in the light and by the strength of the experience of the anchoredness of being. Pragmatism can be seen for what it really is—a blindness to what is and the reckless disregard for the truth of reality and has its root in the rejection of the religious experience of one's reason. More perniciously, the ignorance or rejection of the anchoredness of one's being in God leads inevitably to the appropriation by the human person of the absolute, antagonism toward the real structure of being, and the madness of a world fabricated by human power alone.

Authentic religious experience thus allows us to see and to respond to things and to persons as they are, as we progressively discover them to be, and thus to respond by our adequate action. In a democratically inspired political society, this is precisely the promise implicit in democracy; that all contributions to the common truth and the common good are valued and brought into synthesis. The primordial condition for this democratic consensus, therefore, is the recognition of religious experience as the foundation of our experience of truth. It is no coincidence that the present exclusion and prohibition of religious experience and its public manifestations runs parallel with the dictatorship of relativism; with the denial of the recognition of all being's relation to the Absolute, everything, persons included, stands alone in a void of insecure isolation as contingent, non-necessary, and arbitrary beings.

To exclude religious experience from public reason and to prohibit its public manifestations is also, and unreasonably, to withhold the means of ultimate personal and social fulfilment. Despite the prevailing political belief that the good of society will be achieved through new structures, processes, the level of economic benefit, imposed equality, etc., it is not difficult to recognize that it is the human person that is at the origin of social and political transformation. People cannot be made good, cannot be compelled to want and to do what is right personally and socially, and yet human society depends on the goodness of persons to flourish. Aleksandr Solzhenitsyn recognized through his own experience of suffering and conversion in the Soviet gulags that the real measure of humanity is the personal response to the order of good that we unavoidably experience:

> If only it were all so simple! If only there were evil people somewhere insidiously committing evil deeds, and it were necessary only to separate them from the rest of us and destroy them. But the line dividing good and evil cuts through the heart of every human being. And who is willing to destroy a piece of his own heart? During the life of any heart this line keeps changing place; sometimes it is squeezed one way by exuberant evil and sometimes it shifts to allow enough space for good to flourish. One and the same human being is, at various ages, under various circumstances, a totally different human being. At times he is close to being a devil, at times to sainthood. But his name doesn't change, and to that name we ascribe the whole lot, good and evil. Socrates taught us: Know thyself![52]

It is strange how in contemporary political thought this dramatic personal and social condition of man seems to be ignored or forgotten. The determinisms of ideologies still seem to dominate our minds and cause us to think that what is external to us can transform us. The security that the religious experience gives us of being anchored in the Absolute enables us to recognize the real existential condition in which we find ourselves and what we truly require to be transformed into who we aspire to be.

In personalist terms, we are called to fulfil ourselves through love, that is, the realization of our being through the progressive personal response to the experience of personal being. At the same time, we also experience our own need for radical love, for the radical affirmation of our own being, as a precondition of our capacity to love.

J. Pieper observes this need of radical love in his analysis of the human necessity of being loved. In his *About Love*,[53] Pieper observes that human love in a real way contributes to and continues the creative act of love of the Deity. So much so that persons who receive the love of another experience a fulfilment of this need of self-existence and recognize that the other person gives them what they need to flourish in existence. This experience of the need of human love does not, of course, exempt persons from their own responsibility, but it does highlight one's real dependence on the love of others as a condition of the flourishing of our existence. Importantly, our very capacity to love, which is the most fundamental action of human flourishing, depends on our prior real experience of having received love, of having been loved.[54]

Here we are affirming a truth of human nature and human existence; the human person as a person requires to be loved in order to be able to love, which is one's way to flourishing and fulfilment. The individual, independent, self-interested person is also the indigent person who is incapable of loving because the individual has not experienced the liberating experience of being loved. The assumption in politics and economics of free and unencumbered individuals who manage their own lives and interests in a utilitarian and rational way is grossly and dangerously inadequate. The need for the experience of unconditioned love for the possibility of human development is a psychologically evidenced fact of human existence. To deny or to restrict the possibility of this experience is a basic abuse of the person, even when material needs are provided for.[55]

Religious experience claims to be of this essential, affirming nature. Speaking of the religious origin of the human person in God, Pieper states that it becomes vitally important to one's being-in-the-world to know oneself as radically and absolutely affirmed, and one's existence as an expression of that radical affirmation of personhood. Here Pieper invokes precisely the deepest significance of the theological term *creatura*, the world and the person as affirmation of God's creative love. Our radical existential need of personal affirmation reveals the radical and creative affirmation of the Being who is our Source.[56]

What is evident here is not only the person's dependence on the love of others for one's own personal development and fulfilment, but the even more radical dependence on an even more radical affirmation of his being for its origin and continuing existence. At the core of personal being and existence is a radical dependence on the creative affirmation of one's being by the Creating Absolute Being. Without the progressive appropriation of this religious experience of radical affirmation, persons suffer a stunted development that inhibits their capacity to love and thus to fulfil the experienced requirements of their own being.

Pieper finds in the psychoanalysis of Sigmund Freud evidence of this radical contingent dependence of the human condition:

Here, at any rate, is the point to remind ourselves of those thought-provoking phrases of Sigmund Freud, who speaks of the "part played by love in the genesis of conscience" and defines "evil" as that "for which we are threatened with loss of love." In all "guilt feelings," he argues, "fear of the loss of love" is at work, the fear "that we will no longer be loved by this supreme power."[57]

Pieper asks what this "supreme power" is and does not, unlike Freud, try to cancel out such profound existential phenomena:

> What if our existence itself really depended upon being wanted and being loved, not by an imaginary prehistoric father figure, but by an extremely real, absolute Someone, by the Creator himself? And what if at bottom being guilty ("sin") were really lack of being, resistance—to the extent that it is up to us—to that creative want and love of another in which, as we have already said, our existence literally consists? That, to be sure, is a totally different matter; and yet does not everything that Freud, with the penetration of genius, has to say about the part that love, including our own love, plays in the genesis of conscience and in the fear of losing love suddenly acquire a remarkable pertinacity within this framework?[58]

THE VITAL RELIGIOUS CONTEXT OF SOCIAL LIFE

The real (conscious or unconscious) acceptance or rejection of this experience of radical and continuing affirmation by the Creative Absolute Being—and this is at the core of religious experience—also suddenly acquires a vital personal and social importance. If this is the fundamental condition of personal existence, then the access to, the availability, and the communication of this religious experience is essential for personal and social development and fulfilment. In this very clear sense, religious experience is a vital public good without which human society cannot be achieved. Christopher Dawson, as an historian of world cultures, came to this conclusion:

> The central conviction which has dominated my mind ever since I began to write is the conviction that the society or culture which has lost its spiritual roots is a dying culture, however prosperous it may appear externally. Consequently the problem of social survival is not only a political or economic one; it is above all things religious, since it is in religion that the ultimate spiritual roots both of society and the individual are to be found. When the prophets are silent and society no longer possesses any channel of communication with the divine world, the way to the lower depths is still open and man's frustrated spiritual powers will find their outlet in the unlimited will to power and destruction.[59]

Therefore, the openness to and recognition of the religious experience, which is vital to personal and social existence, is of primordial public interest.[60] At the same time, there is a strange actual resistance to this experience, which, as Pieper suggests, may well be the resistance to recognizing our own fundamental need, and the illusion of "modern man's claim to equality with

God."[61] At the root of this resistance is the fear of finding in this relation to the Absolute a form of limitation or even humiliation, rather than fulfilment:

> The atheistic humanist, however, raises humiliation to transcendental import. He alleges that if there were a creator *ex nihilo*, then the human condition would be one of abject and total dependence; so that the only worthy response on man's part would be to abolish the very structure itself through the free production of meaning out of himself. (Hence, Marx's "man alone," and the secular atheisms of Nietzsche and Sartre). Moreover, the atheist refuses to avoid the problem by relativizing the creator, as though it could become a more or less equal party in interaction with man. In any event such a relativism abandons the issues by abandoning the conception of a creator *ex nihilo*. The atheist, on the other hand, does not ignore the conception; he seeks to deny its validity. He doesn't want compromise; he wants refutation.[62]

It seems here that the capacity to recognize religious experience, that is, the real presence of God, however varied, inchoate, and obscure that experience may be, is the fundamental condition of the perception of reality, of truth. Also, the capacity to recognize the truth in and of all things is the path that inevitably leads to the Truth that sustains all things.[63]

The argument here is philosophic and goes beyond the strictures of modern rationality. The experience of the Absolute and the existential indigence of the person are real facts, and the radical dependence of our being on the experience of the Absolute for both our origin and our fulfilment are the given parameters of personal existential experience. It is only in coming to terms with the religious experience of these realities that persons respond adequately to this existential condition and to the dynamism of their being. On this depends the development and fulfilment of our relational being and therefore the possibility of human society. This is the existential drama of our human condition; for those given to recognize the further significance of this drama:

> In the confrontation between the "man-god" and the "God-man," the former has melted away. The figmentary character of humanity's grandiose posturing as its own messiah stands exposed for what it is. Such delusions are no more than the vain overheated evaporations of a fevered soul. The reality of God's love present in Christ offering himself up for us is so patently the redemptive victory over evil, that all other schemes fade away into unreality. Our efforts at autonomous self-transformation cannot stand comparison with the reality of divine love infused into our soul. The movement of human nature toward God could not take place unless God had previously inclined toward us. Even the stirring that urges us to seek God would not be there unless God had first moved us. The divinization of human nature is entirely the work of God, for the

transcendent divine reality is unutterably beyond the reach of our power or the paltry determination of our will.[64]

What Walsh emphasises here is that this existential drama of our time is not only played out in intellectual discourse but also is primarily what the experience of this post-modern and post-ideological age offers us, if we are prepared and disposed to encounter this experience of reality.

In whatever way the experience of the human drama, both personal and social, may be recognized intellectually, and however each one necessarily responds in freedom to the experience of this drama, these real parameters of human existence do not change. *The divinization of human nature, unutterably beyond the reach of our power, by the transcendent divine reality that is God*—this is the ultimate real religious context of our personal and social existence.

It is, of course, true that those who speak and present the religious dimension and experience of human existence do not always do so according to the real dimensions and the authentic content of religious experience. The modern secular mentality has become so pervasive that inevitably religion and the religious experience of God are reduced to convenient caricatures of reality, a domesticated religion that conforms to the limits of our own reason and purposes:

> The deist's God, the God of several modern "theodicies" which weigh and measure him rather than defend him, the God who can hardly say "I am" any longer, the God who tends to be no more than "the universal harmony of things," who rules over a beyond where "everything is the same as here," the God imprisoned "within the limits of reason," who no longer intervenes in the world, who is really nothing but the projection of natural man, who is distant yet without mystery, a God made to our measure and defined according to our rules, a God merged in the "moral order of the universe" as man understands it, a God who is not adored and whom one can only serve by the cult of morality, a God who is "only accessible in pure knowledge" and who is "nothing but that knowledge itself," a God in fact whose thoughts are our thoughts and whose ways are our ways: such a God has proved very useless in practice and has become the object of a justified ressentiment. And when at last man decided to get rid of him altogether in order to enter into his own inheritance, he was only a shade, "reduced to the narrow limits of human thought."[65]

One of the greatest challenges of theology today is to break loose from a type of religion that has been secularly shaped and to rediscover the real Source of being and, in that light, the renewed meaning and purpose of reality.

CONCLUSION

There are many practical issues to be resolved in the relation of politics and religion, just as there are many emotive and intellectual prejudices that pre-empt the real colocation of politics within the religious context of man's existence. Today, any insistence on public religious truth immediately sounds the alarm bells of religious imposition, the spectre of a church-controlled state, the denial of the freedom of conscience, intolerance, religious fanaticism, followed by the mantras of the complete separation of church and state, the privatization of religion, and the promotion of the neutral secular mindset. At the heart of all these slogans is the obfuscation of the real religious condition of personal existence and the radical dependence on the Absolute Personal God—however God may be experienced and known—to sustain human society and to make it ever more authentically human.

"Reason is the faculty man possesses to seek God."[66]

It should also be clear that there is much more at stake when we speak of politics and religion than the civil recognition of the right to the public manifestation of religious belief, as important and necessary as that recognition is today. The knowledge of the Object of religious experience is what ultimately gives the certainly and the security of all of what we know, as well as the foundation of our capacity to know reality itself. All things manifest, in different ways and degrees—and always only partially—the Source of their being, their origin, and their destiny. All knowledge and science manifest this Source in cognitive ways that we can grasp and experience, however incompletely. The rejection, ignorance, or the indifference to the experience of the Source of all being, in all being, distorts all of what we know. To deny this manifestation of the Source makes everything appear only as contingent, random, and unrelated—no longer real, ultimately meaningless.

This applies also to human society and to the political forms of human society. Our social relations are not fundamentally arbitrary or merely contractual, but constitutive of our human being. Religious knowledge is the experience of the personal constitutive relation to God and, in God, to others. It is only the experience of the person, and the communion of persons in God, that permits persons to treat persons as persons, and to aspire to build a truly human society, that is the communion of persons in God.

NOTES

1. Eric Voegelin, *Science, Politics, and Gnosticism: Two Essays*, ed. Ellis Sandoz (Washington, DC: Gateway Editions, 2012), 639.

2. As American professor Andrew Willard Jones writes, "such spiritual things, now called religious things, are put into a box called private, where they are held captive and steadily starved out of existence" Jones, "The End of Sovereignty: An Essay in Christian Postliberalism," *Communio* 45, no. 3–4 (2018): 454–55.

3. Court of Justice of the European Union, *Press Release* No 128/21, Luxembourg, July 15, 2021, https://curia.europa.eu/jcms/upload/docs/application/pdf/2021-07/cp210128en.pdf (accessed October 12, 2023).

4. Court of Justice of the European Union, *Press Release*, No 128/21, 2.

5. Court of Justice of the European Union, *Press Release*, No 128/21, 3.

6. Court of Justice of the European Union, *Press Release*, No 128/21, 2. The European Court did allow for a certain discretionary derogation of power to member states: "However, that justification must correspond to a genuine need on the part of the employer and, in reconciling the rights and interests at issue, the national courts may take into account the specific context of their Member State and, in particular, more favourable national provisions on the protection of freedom of religion" Court of Justice of the European Union, *Press Release*, No 128/21, 1. Even so, the legal and political influence of this decision is, obviously, enormous. On the theme of the invidious discrimination of Christians in European politics, see Martin Kugler and Gudrun Kugler, eds., *Exiting a Dead-End Road: A GPS for Christians in Public Discourse* (Wien: Kairos Publications, 2010), "a collection of publications on discrimination against Christians in Europe. This problem is deliberately hushed up in the 'free continent.' For many this affirmation may seem strange, untrue, exaggerated and even artificial. However, the book cites numerous concrete facts pointing to discrimination against Christians, violations of their rights to freedom of expression and conscience and ultimately to the free expression of their faith (Russian Metropolitan Hilarion Alfeev of Volokolamsk, 3)." American writer Mary Eberstadt writes of "the slow-motion marginalizing and penalizing of believers on the very door-steps of churches of North America, Europe, and elsewhere, in societies that are the very historical strongholds of political and religious liberty" Eberstadt, "The New Intolerance," *First Things* (March 1, 2015): 34, https://www.firstthings.com/article/2015/03/the-new-intolerance (accessed October 12, 2023).

7. For a sample of other European cases that prejudice religious freedom, see the Alliance Defending Freedom legal advocacy's publication, Robert Clarke, ed., *The 'Conscience of Europe': Navigating Shifting Tides at the European Court of Human Rights* (Wien: Kairos Publications, 2017). On the perceived religious duty to profess and publicly to make known one's religious beliefs, see, for example, Libreria Editrice Vaticana, *The Catechism of the Catholic Church* (Vatican City: Veritas Publications, 1994), n2105: "The duty of offering God genuine worship concerns man both individually and socially . . . . The social duty of Christians is to respect and awaken in each man the love of the true and the good. It requires them to make known the worship of the one true religion which subsists in the Catholic and apostolic Church."

8. Joseph Ratzinger, "That Which Holds the World Together: The Pre-political Moral Foundations of a Free State," in *Europe: Today and Tomorrow* (San Francisco: Ignatius Press, 2007), 80: "We have seen that there exist pathologies in religion that are extremely dangerous and that make it necessary to see the divine light of

reason as a 'controlling organ.' Religion must continually allow itself to be purified and structured by reason; and this was the view of the Church Fathers, too."

9. Arifa Akbar, "Sajda Mughal: The Woman Who Survived 7/7 – Quit Her Job and Fights for a Better World" *Guardian*, July 28, 2021, https://www.theguardian.com/society/2021/jul/28/sajda-mughal-the-woman-who-survived-77-and-began-fighting-extremism (accessed October 12, 2023). As a consequence of having survived the London bombings, Mughal left her job in recruitment for the City in London and dedicates her life to fighting extremism.

10. Christopher Dawson remarks that this world-wide secularism, the "separation and dislocation between religion and culture" is a new social phenomenon. Cf. Dawson, *The Judgment of the Nations*, ed. John J. Mulloy (Washington, DC: Catholic University of America Press, 2011), 65. D. C. Schindler observes that: "the oldest human cultures, religion is an essential dimension of 'natural' human existence even considered entirely within the limits of the age; the temporal is not in the least opposed to the spiritual but is itself fully spiritual; the sacred does not stand in relative opposition to the human but is precisely what distinguishes the human as human, what makes it human in the proper sense" Schindler, *The Politics of the Real: The Church Between Liberalism and Integralism* (Steubenville, OH: New Polity Press, 2021), 255.

11. "Once, there was no 'secular.' And the secular was not latent, waiting to fill more space with the steam of the 'purely human,' when the pressure of the sacred was relaxed. Instead there was the single community of Christendom, with its dual aspects of sacerdotium and regnum. The saeculum, in the medieval era, was not a space, a domain, but a time—the interval between fall and eschaton where coercive justice, private property and impaired natural reason must make shift to cope with the unredeemed effects of sinful humanity" John Milbank, *Theology and Social Theory: Beyond Secular Reason*, 2nd ed. (Malden, MA: Blackwell, 2006), 9.

12. Josef Pieper, *Problems of Modern Faith: Essays and Addresses*, trans. Jan van Heurck (Chicago: Franciscan Herald Press, 1985), 20–21.

13. Pieper, *Problems of Modern Faith*, 21. I have included the Latin word *fanum* (temple). Linguistically the term *pro-fanum* necessarily refers to the Sacred source of all that is not Sacred. Interestingly, Christian Biblical theology sees all of reality (creation) *within* God's Temple, as imaged in the Jewish temple of Jerusalem: "The land and the seas to be subdued by Adam outside the Garden were roughly equivalent to the outer court of Israel's subsequent Temple. Thus, one may be able to perceive an increasing gradation in holiness from outside the garden proceeding inward: the region outside the Garden is related to God and is 'very good' (Genesis 1:31) in that it is God's creation (i.e., the outer court)." Cf. Gregory K. Beale, *The Temple and the Church's Mission: A Biblical Theology of the Dwelling Place of God* (Leicester, UK: InterVarsity Press, 2004), 75, as cited in Steven C. Smith, *The House of the Lord: A Catholic Biblical Theology of God's Temple Presence in the Old and New Testaments* (Steubenville, OH: Franciscan University Press, 2017), 46.

14. For an historical and panoramic view of the cultural manifestation of religious experience, see, for example, Mircea Eliade, *A History of Religious Ideas*, trans. Willard R. Trask (Chicago: University of Chicago Press, 1981), in 3 volumes.

15. Robert Sokolowski, *Introduction to Phenomenology* (Cambridge: Cambridge University Press, 2000), 207. Sokolowski recognizes, however, that our starting point today requires a different, if complementary, approach, as culturally we do not start, as the Scholastics did, within a context of Biblical faith. Sokolowski proposes the phenomenological approach, what he calls a philosophy (and theology) of disclosure: "Phenomenology does not try to derive philosophy from within religious faith. Rather, it takes philosophy simply as a natural human excellence, one that completes the prephilosophical exercises of reason. Phenomenology thus begins philosophy in a manner different from the way Thomism begins it, but in a way that complements and does not contradict the Thomistic approach" (207).

16. Milbank, *Theology and Social Theory*, 10. Milbank refers to Grotius' *The Law of War and Peace,* Prolegomena, XI: "And indeed, all we have now said would take place, though we should even grant, what without the greatest Wickedness cannot be granted, that there is no God, or that he takes no Care of human Affairs" Hugo Grotius, *The Rights of War and Peace*, ed. Jean Barbeyrac (Indianapolis: Liberty Fund, 2005), 89.

17. Milbank, *Theology and Social Theory*, 13. Interestingly, two new studies have traced the political use and interpretation of the Bible in justifying the modern project of the political state; Scott W. Hahn and Benjamin Wiker, *Politicizing the Bible: The Roots of Historical Criticism and the Secularization of Scripture, 1300–1700* (New York: Herder & Herder, 2013); and Scott W. Hahn and Jeffrey L. Morrow, *Modern Biblical Criticism as a Tool of Statecraft (1700–1900)* (Steubenville, OH: Emmaus Academic, 2020).

18. Glenn Olsen, *Beginning at Jerusalem: Five Reflections on the History of the Church* (San Francisco: Ignatius Press, 2004), 176.

19. Olsen, *Beginning at Jerusalem*, 176.

20. The Romanian historian and philosopher of religion Mircea Eliade comments that the sense of the reality of the sacred and of nature as revealing "cosmic sacrality" was part of the experience of all human societies until the present modern one, and that "the wholly desacralized cosmos, is a recent discovery in the history of the human spirit . . . modem man has desacralized his world and assumed a profane existence." Mircea Eliade, *The Sacred and the Profane: The Nature of Religion*, trans. Willard R. Trask (New York: Harcourt Brace & World, 1959), 12, 13, cited in David Walsh, *After Ideology: Recovering the Spiritual Foundations of Freedom* (San Francisco: HarperCollins, 1990), 199.

21. John Henry Newman commented that when, in education, secular education is separated from religion, the secular sciences themselves become perverted: "And now I have said enough to explain the inconvenience which I conceive necessarily to result from a refusal to recognize theological truth in a course of Universal Knowledge;—it is not only the loss of Theology, it is the perversion of other sciences. What it unjustly forfeits, others unjustly seize. They have their own department, and, in going out of it, attempt to do what they really cannot do; and that the more mischievously, because they do teach what in its place is true, though when out of its place, perverted or carried to excess, it is not true. And, as every man has not the capacity of separating truth from falsehood, they persuade the world of what is false by urging upon it what

is true" Newman, *The Idea of a University Education*, Discourse 4 "Bearing of Other Branches of Knowledge on Theology" (The National Institute for Newman Studies online edition, 2007), n78, https://www.newmanreader.org/works/idea/discourse4 .html; D. C. Schindler notes that, in the practical absence of God, what predominates "is a nothingness that hiddenly governs as first principle" Schindler, *Politics of the Real*, 37.

22. William T. Cavanaugh, "The City: Beyond Secular Parodies," in *Radical Orthodoxy: A New Theology*, ed. John Milbank, Catherine Pickstock, and Graham Ward (London: Routledge, 1999), 191.

23. Cavanaugh, "City," 191–92. The reference is to Robert A. Nisbet's *The Quest for Community: A Study in the Ethics of Order and Freedom* (Washington, DC: ISI Books, 2010). Cavanaugh's research and further explanation of the secular mythos can be found, for example, in "'A Fire Strong Enough to Consume the House': The Wars of Religion and the Rise of the State," *Modern Theology* 11, no. 4 (1995): 397–420, https://doi.org/10.1111/j.1468-0025.1995.tb00073.x; and in his *Migrations of the Holy: God, State, and the Political Meaning of the Church* (Grand Rapids, MI: Eerdmans, 2011). In his historical research, Cavanaugh draws *inter alia* on Joseph R. Strayer, *On the Medieval Origins of the Modern State* (Princeton, NJ: Princeton University Press, 2016), Charles Tilly, ed., *The Formation of National States in Western Europe* (Princeton, NJ: Princeton University Press, 1975); and Thomas Ertman, *Birth of the Leviathan: Building States and Regimes in Medieval and Early Modern Europe* (Cambridge: Cambridge University Press, 1997).

24. John Milbank describes how this new secular vision of society was "theologically promoted" by reinterpreting Judeo-Christian theology in terms that would justify the secular state. Cf. Milbank, *Theology and Social Theory*, chap. 1 "Political Theology and the New Science of Politics," 11–25.

25. Cavanaugh, *Migrations of the Holy*, 30.

26. D. C. Schindler's *Politics of the Real* is a profound study of the liberal replacement of God in modernity. As A.W. Jones comments on Schindler's work: "Schindler shows that liberalism is wrong, not because it has simply 'relegated God to the private,' but because it has inverted the world: giving us power without authority, in what becomes a closed, necessarily totalitarian, horizon. Here, nothing else can be done with the transcendent God but to find a quiet little place to keep him, harmless and out of the way." Andrew Willard Jones, foreword to *Politics of the Real*, 7.

27. David Walsh, *The Growth of the Liberal Soul* (Columbia: University of Missouri, 1997), 242.

28. W. Norris Clarke, *The Philosophical Approach to God: A New Thomistic Perspective* (New York: Fordham University Press, 2007), 21. While here Clarke refers explicitly to the dynamism of the intellect (12–21), he makes a similar argument from the description of the dynamism of the will "The Ascent through the Dynamism of the Will" (22–36), both manifestations of the Inner Way to God.

29. Clarke, *Philosophical Approach to God*, 68.

30. Benedict XVI, *The Listening Heart: Reflections on the Foundations of Law* in *Address of His Holiness Benedict XVI*, Reichstag Building, Berlin, September 22, 2011, 4, https://www.vatican.va/content/benedict-xvi/en/speeches/2011/september/

documents/hf_ben-xvi_spe_20110922_reichstag-berlin.html (accessed October 18, 2023).

31. Benedict XVI, *Listening Heart*, 4.

32. Joseph Ratzinger, *Europe: Today and Tomorrow* (San Francisco: Ignatius Press, 2007), 80. Ratzinger indicates that this merely functional, technological reason is the mentality behind much of Western aid to poorer countries: "But this already brings us to the dubious point of the Western form of aid: namely, the belief that one could prescind altogether from ethical problems and bring about in a purely mechanical fashion the construction of modern economies while bypassing the existing ethical and social systems. Even the churches, who really ought to have known better, often succumbed to this materialistic illusion. Many of their emissaries were of the opinion that one must first spread the blessing of prosperity, and then one could also go on to speak of God. But this is a fundamentally false application of the axiom '*primum vivere, deinde philosophari*' ('first let us live, then let us philosophize'). For the core of faith in God and of its ethical force is not a philosophy that lies within the reach only of those who have enough for their life: rather, it is the precondition of life, it is life. The young African intellectuals who studied at European universities acquired for the most part only an academic knowledge completely devoid of the ethical and the religious. All that remained to them was the choice between positivism and Marxism, but neither of these two philosophies is capable of building up a society in which freedom and justice are connected in a meaningful way. Here lie the deepest roots of the anger that is spreading in the Third World today against Europe and America in particular," *Turning Point for Europe* (1508–23).

33. On the necessity of the experience of the Sacred for human living, see Roger Scruton, *The Soul of the World* (Princeton, NJ: Princeton University Press, 2016).

34. Walsh, *Growth of the Liberal Soul*, 270.

35. Ludwig Feuerbach, *The Essence of Christianity*, trans. George Eliot (London: e-artnow, 2021), 17, Kindle. On this theme of the atheism of human autonomy in Feuerbach, there is an illustrative section in Walter Kasper, *The God of Jesus Christ* (New York: Crossroad, 1984), 26–46, which also includes a similar analysis of Sigmund Freud, Karl Marx, and Friedrich Nietzsche. On the general historical development of the modern forms of atheism see Michael J. Buckley, *At the Origins of Modern Atheism* (New Haven, CT: Yale University Press, 1987); and Buckley, *Denying and Disclosing God: The Ambiguous Progress of Modern Atheism* (New Haven, CT: Yale University Press, 2004). Buckley includes reference to some religiously minded thinkers whose attempts to found God's existence or action on arguments of modern science or psychology that only contributed to the growth of real atheism.

36. Feuerbach, *Essence of Christianity*, 24.

37. Ludwig Feuerbach, *The Fiery Brook: Selected Writings*, trans. Zawar Hanfi (London: Verso, 2013), 148–49.

38. Voegelin, *Science, Politics, and Gnosticism*, 639.

39. Fyodor Dostoevsky, *The Brothers Karamazov*, trans. Constance Garnett (Mineola, NY: Dover Thrift Editions, 1998), 302. The story is told by Ivan Karamazov to his brother Alyosha, who is a novice monk, and tells of the return of Christ to Sevilla during the time of the Inquisition. Christ performs some miracles and is arrested and

sentenced to death by the Inquisition officials. The Grand Inquisitor visits Christ in his cell that night to tell him that he, Christ, is no longer needed on earth. David Walsh draws inspiration from the writings of Dostoyevsky in both Walsh, *After Ideology*; and Walsh, *Growth of the Liberal Soul*. Walsh comments on this Legend of the Grand Inquisitor in *Growth of the Liberal Soul*, 227–33.

40. Joseph Ratzinger, "Europe in the Crisis of Cultures." *Communio* 32, no. 2 (2005): 345–56.

41. David L. Schindler, *Ordering Love: Liberal Societies and the Memory of God* (Grand Rapids, MI: Eerdmans, 2011), 3695.

42. Pieper, *Problems of Modern Faith*, 4.

43. Adequate investigations and interpretations of the inner experience and meaning of forms of religion were undertaken in the late nineteenth century and early twentieth century by, among others, Wilhelm Schmidt, Franz Joseph Dölger, Gerard van der Leeuw, Joachim Wach, and Mircea Eliade. Their various findings produced a more circumspect understanding of the phenomenon of religion than certain positivist interpretations like Émile Durkheim's, that seem to impose preconceived categories on the religious facts. In Catholic theology Karl Adam and Romano Guardini developed this phenomenological approach to faith.

44. Max Scheler, *On the Eternal in Man* (London: Routledge, 2017), 173. August Brunner sums up Scheler's characteristics of religion: "It is a particular essence, which cannot be reduced to anything else. It is a sphere that belongs essentially to man; without it he would not be man. If genuine fulfilment is denied it, substitutes come into being. This religious sphere is the most essential, the decisive one. It determines man's basic attitude toward reality and thus in a sense the colour, extent and position of all the other human domains in life. It forms the basis for all sorts of views about life and thought." Brunner, in his foreword to Scheler's *On the Eternal in Man*, 8. On the natural roots of religious experience as well as the philosophical limitations of diverse religious experience, see W. Norris Clarke, "Spiritual Experience and Metaphysical Interpretation," in *Man and Nature*, ed. George F. McLean (Oxford: Oxford University Press, 1978), 188–97; and Clarke's "The Natural Roots of Religious Experience," *Religious Studies* 17, no. 4 (1981): 511–23, https://doi.org/10.1017/S0034412500013275.

45. Joseph Ratzinger, "A Christian Orientation in a Pluralistic Democracy," in *Church, Ecumenism, and Politics: New Endeavours in Ecclesiology* (San Francisco: Ignatius Press, 2008), 2966.

46. Ratzinger, "A Christian Orientation in a Pluralistic Democracy," in *Church, Ecumenism, and Politics*, 3175.

47. Václav Havel, *Letters to Olga* (New York: Henry Holt, 1989), 243. This quotation is mentioned in Walsh, *Growth of the Liberal Soul*, 351.

48. Havel, *Letters to Olga*, 243.

49. Joseph Ratzinger, *The Nature and Mission of Theology: Approaches to Understanding Its Role in the Light of Present Controversy* (San Francisco: Ignatius Press, 2010), 40.

50. Havel, *Letters to Olga*, 242.

51. Kenneth L. Schmitz describes the nineteenth century atheism as: "based upon the primacy of man, the will to reject such a religious structure expressed itself in a positive demand for unbelief as the condition of human well-being (Comte, Marx, Nietzsche). It was urged, on general grounds and on the basis of criteria external to the religious structure, that religion is really man's concession to his own impotency and that it is merely a fearful and ineffectual hope for security, an illusion in need of therapy, perhaps also a social and political strategy of priestcraft" Schmitz, *The Gift: Creation* (Milwaukee, WI: Marquette University Press, 1982), 64.

52. Aleksandr Solzhenitsyn, *The Gulag Archipelago, 1918–1956: An Experiment in Literary Investigation*, trans. Thomas P. Whitney (New York: Harper & Row, 1974), vol. 1, 168.

53. Josef Pieper, *Faith, Hope, Love* (San Francisco: Ignatius Press, 1997).

54. Pieper, *Faith, Hope, Love*, 176. Pieper mentions that the exact phrase "being confirmed" was used by Karl Marx in his early writings.

55. Pieper refers to the psychoanalytic studies of R. Spitz that observe the difference, after the Second World War, between infants raised in well-furnished and hygienic homes for orphans, and infants born in prison who had their mother's care. The children born in prison were less susceptible to illness, to mortality and to neuroses. Pieper, *Faith, Hope, Love*, 175. The need for the experience of love in the family as the key to forming mature persons in society is the theme of Jennifer Roback Morse's *Love and Economics: It Takes a Family to Raise a Village* (Lake Charles, LA: Ruth Institute Books), 2008.

56. Pieper, *Faith, Hope, Love*, 177.

57. Pieper, *Faith, Hope, Love*, 184.

58. Pieper, *Faith, Hope, Love*, 185.

59. Christopher Dawson, *The Dynamics of World History* (*'Enquiries'* 1933 and *'Religion and Culture'* 1948) (Wilmington, DE: Intercollegiate Studies Institute, 2002), xxxi, xxxvi.

60. "When faith is weakened, the foundations of life also risk being weakened, as the poet T. S. Eliot warned: 'Do you need to be told that even those modest attainments / As you can boast in the way of polite society / Will hardly survive the Faith to which they owe their significance?' If we remove faith in God from our cities, mutual trust would be weakened, we would remain united only by fear and our stability would be threatened" Pope Francis, "Lumen Fidei," *Acta Apostolicae Sedis (AAS)* 105 (2013): 591–92, n55. https://www.vatican.va/content/francesco/en/encyclicals/documents/papa-francesco_20130629_enciclica-lumen-fidei.html (accessed October 13, 2023). The reference is to T. S. Eliot, "Choruses from the Rock," in *The Complete Poems and Plays of T. S. Eliot* (London: Faber and Faber, 2004), 159.

61. Pieper, *Faith, Hope, Love*, 184.

62. Schmitz, *Gift*, 70–71. I distinguish here between nominal atheists, who notionally reject the existence of God, and real atheists who reject religious experience. While both types may coincide, this is not always the case. Jaques Maritain reminds us: "Under many names, names which are not that of God, in ways only known to God, the interior act of a soul's thought can be directed towards a reality which in fact truly may be God" Maritain, *True Humanism*, trans. Margot Adamson (New

York: C. Scribner, 1938), 56. For believers, there is the cautionary reminder that *actus credentis non terminatur ad enuntiabile, sed ad rem* [meaning that the act of faith finds its completion not in concepts, but in God].Cf. Jean Mouroux, *I Believe: The Personal Structure of Faith* (New York: Sheed and Ward, 1959), 74.

63. Robert Sokolowski notes, for example, that in relation to the work of Edmund Husserl, "It has been observed that several followers of Husserl converted to Catholicism or Protestantism; this occurred not because Husserl encouraged such a move (indeed, he seemed somewhat embarrassed by it), but because his work restored respectability to various domains of experience and thus allowed people to cultivate their own religious development without hindrance" Sokolowski, *Introduction to Phenomenology*, 215. As students of Husserl and converts to Christianity, one thinks of Adolf Reinach (1883–1917) and Edith Stein (1891–1942).

64. Walsh, *After Ideology*, 181.

65. Henry De Lubac, *The Discovery of God*, trans. Alexander Dru (Grand Rapids, MI: Eerdmans, 1996), 178. Referring to one such God, De Lubac writes: "Whenever it abandons a system of thought, humanity imagines it has lost God. The God of 'classical ontology' is dead, you say? It may be so; but it does not worry me overmuch" (177).

66. Robert Spaemann, "Rationality and Faith in God," *Communio* 32, no. 4 (2005): 629. The entire article presents a similar theme to that expressed in this chapter.

Bibliography

Acemoglu, Daron, and James A. Robinson. *Why Nations Fail: The Origins of Power, Prosperity, and Poverty*. New York: Crown Currency, 2012.

Ackroyd, Peter. *The Life of Thomas More* (New York: Anchor Books, 1999.

Akbar, Arifa. "Sajda Mughal: The Woman Who Survived 7/7 – Quit Her Job and Fights for a Better World." *Guardian*. July 28, 2021. https://www.theguardian .com/society/2021/jul/28/sajda-mughal-the-woman-who-survived-77-and-began -fighting-extremism (accessed October 12, 2023).

Alfred, Charlotte. "'We Want to Build a Life': Europe's Paperless Young People Speak Out." *Guardian*. August 3, 2020. https://www.theguardian.com/world /2020/aug/03/europe-paperless-young-people-speak-out-undocumented-dreamers (accessed October 12, 2023).

Andersen, Hans Christian. *The Emperor's New Clothes* (1837). New York: Random House, 1975.

Arendt, Hanna. *Between Past and Future: Eight Essays in Political Thought*. Harmondsworth, UK: Penguin Books, 2006.

. *The Human Condition*. Chicago: University of Chicago Press, 1998.

. *On Revolution*. New York: Penguin Books, 2006.

. *The Origins of Totalitarianism*. New York: Mariner Books, 1976; San Diego: Harcourt, Brace, Jovanovich, 1994.

Aristotle. *Nicomachean Ethics*. Translated by David Ross. In *Aristotle: The Complete Works (English Edition)*. KTHTK 2023. Kindle.

. *Nicomachean Ethics*. Edited by Harris Rackham. Cambridge, MA: Harvard University Press, 1934.

. *Politics*. Translated by Benjamin Jowett. In *Aristotle: The Complete Works (English Edition)*. KTHTK 2023. Kindle.

Bacon, Francis. *The Advancement of Learning (English Edition)*. (Classics, Literature, Politics & Social Sciences). Annotated ed. KTHTK 2021. Kindle.

Baghramian, Maria, and Annalisa Coliva. *Relativism*. London: Routledge, 2004.

Bauman, Zygmunt. *Liquid Modernity*. Cambridge: Polity Press, 2000.

Beale, Gregory K. *The Temple and the Church's Mission: A Biblical Theology of the Dwelling Place of God*. Leicester, UK: InterVarsity Press, 2004.

Becker, Carl Lotus. *The Heavenly City of the Eighteenth-Century Philosophers*. New Haven, CT: Yale University Press, 1932.

Bibliography

Benedict XVI [Pope; Joseph Ratzinger]. *Address of His Holiness Benedict XVI,* Reichstag Building, Berlin. September 22, 2011. https://www.vatican.va/content /benedict-xvi/en/speeches/2011/september/documents/hf_ben-xvi_spe_20110922 _reichstag-berlin.html (accessed October 18, 2023).

. *Address of His Holiness Benedict XVI to the Members of the Roman Curia at the Traditional Exchange of Christmas Greetings.* December 22, 2006. https://www .vatican.va/content/benedict-xvi/en/speeches/2006/december/documents/hf_ben _xvi_spe_20061222_curia-romana.html (accessed October 12, 2023).

———. *Address to the Participants of the International Congress on Natural Moral Law.* February 12, 2007. https://www.vatican.va/content/benedict-xvi/en/speeches /2007/february/documents/hf_ben-xvi_spe_20070212_pul.html (accessed October 12, 2023).

———. *Church Fathers: From Clement of Rome to Augustine.* San Francisco: Ignatius Press, 2017.

———. *Meeting with Members of the General Assembly of the United Nations.* April 18, 2008. https://www.vatican.va/content/benedict-xvi/en/speeches/2008/april/ documents/hf_ben-xvi_spe_20080418_un-visit.html (accessed October 12, 2023).

———. *Saint Paul.* San Francisco: Ignatius Press, 2009.

———. *Spe Salvi.* Città del Vaticano: Libreria Editrice Vaticana, 2007.

Bentham, Jeremy. *An Introduction to the Principles of Morals and Legislation.* Reprint of New Edition, corrected by author 1823. Oxford: Oxford Clarendon Press, 1907.

Bergsma, John. *Jesus and the Dead Sea Scrolls: Revealing the Jewish Roots of Christianity.* New York: Image, 2019.

Berman, Harold J. *Faith and Order: The Reconciliation of Law and Religion.* Atlanta: Scholars Press, 1993.

———. *Law and Revolution Volume I: The Formation of the Western Legal Tradition.* Cambridge, MA: Harvard University Press, 1983.

———. *Law and Revolution Volume II: The Impact of the Protestant Reformations on the Western Legal Tradition.* Cambridge, MA: Harvard University Press, 2006.

Blondel, Maurice. *Action (1893): Essay on a Critique of Life and a Science of Practice.* 2nd ed., Translated by Oliva Blanchette. Notre Dame, IN: University of Notre Dame Press, 1984.

———. *Letter on Apologetics & History and Dogma.* Edited and translated by Alexander Dru and Illtyd Trethowan. Grand Rapids, MI: Eerdmans, 1994.

Bodin, Jean. *Six Books of the Commonwealth.* Abridged and translated by M. J. Tooley. Oxford: Basil Blackwell, c. 1576.

Bork, Robert H. "Thomas More for Our Season." *First Things* 94 (June/July 1999): 17–21. https://www.firstthings.com/article/1999/06/thomas-more-for-our -season intolerance (accessed October 12, 2023).

Brady, Bernard V. "An Analysis of the Use of Rights Language in Pre-Modern Thought." *Thomist* 57, no. 1 (1993): 97–121. https://doi.org/10.1353/tho.1993 .0052.

Brague, Rémi. *The Law of God: The Philosophical History of an Idea.* Translated by Lydia G. Cochrane. Chicago: University of Chicago Press, 2007.

Brenner, Marie. "Marie Colvin's Private War." *Vanity Fair*. July 18, 2012. https: //www.vanityfair.com/news/politics/2012/08/marie-colvin-private-war (accessed October 12, 2023).

Broussard, Nicolas. "Napoleon, Hegelian Hero." *Revue de Souvenir Napoléonien* 400 (1995). http://www.napoleon.org/en/reading_room/articles/files/napoleon _hegelian_hero.asp.

Brugger, E. Christian. "Interview with Paul C. Vitz: A Catholic Looks at the Past, Present and Future of Christian Psychology." *Edification: Journal of the Society for Christian Psychology* 3, no. 1 (2009): 5–19.

Buckley, Michael J. *At the Origins of Modern Atheism*. New Haven, CT: Yale University Press, 1987.

———. *Denying and Disclosing God: The Ambiguous Progress of Modern Atheism*. New Haven, CT: Yale University Press, 2004.

Buonarroti, Philippe. *Buonarroti's History of Babeuf's Conspiracy for Equality* (1828). London: Andesite Press, 2015.

Burke, Edmund. *Revolutionary Writings*. Edited by Iain Hampsher-Monk. Cambridge: Cambridge University Press, 2014.

Burleigh, Michael. *Earthly Powers: Religion and Politics in Europe from the Enlightenment to the Great War*. New York: Harper Perennial, 2005.

———. *Sacred Causes: Religion and Politics from the European Dictators to Al Queda*. New York: Harper Press, 2006.

Cassirer, Ernst. *The Philosophy of the Enlightenment*. Princeton, NJ: Princeton University Press, 1951.

Cavanaugh, William T. "The City: Beyond Secular Parodies." In *Radical Orthodoxy: A New Theology*, edited by John Milbank, Catherine Pickstock, and Graham Ward, 182–200. London: Routledge, 1999.

———. "'A Fire Strong Enough to Consume the House': The Wars of Religion and the Rise of the State." *Modern Theology* 11, no.4 (1995): 397–420. https://doi.org /10.1111/j.1468-0025.1995.tb00073.x.

———. *Migrations of the Holy: God, State, and the Political Meaning of the Church*. Grand Rapids, MI: Eerdmans, 2011.

———. *Theopolitical Imagination: Discovering the Liturgy as a Political Act in an Age of Global Consumerism*. London: Bloomsbury, 2013.

Chandler, Walter M. *The Trial of Jesus from a Lawyer's Standpoint*. New York: Empire Publishing, 1908.

Chaplin, Jonathan, and Gary Wilton, eds. *God and the EU: Faith and the European Project*. London: Routledge, 2015.

Chaput, Charles J. *Things Worth Dying For: Thoughts on a Life Worth Living*. New York: Henry Holt, 2021.

Clarke, Robert, ed. *The 'Conscience of Europe?': Navigating Shifting Tides at the European Court of Human Rights*. Vienna: Kairos Publications, 2017.

Clarke, W. Norris. *Explorations in Metaphysics: Being-God-Person*. Notre Dame, IN: University of Notre Dame Press, 1994.

———. "Interpersonal Dialogue: Key to Realism." In *Person and Community: A Philosophical Exploration*, edited by Robert J. Roth, 141–53. Fordham University Press, 1975.

———. "The Natural Roots of Religious Experience." *Religious Studies* 17, no. 4 (1981): 511–23. https://doi.org/10.1017/S0034412500013275.

———. *The One and the Many: A Contemporary Thomistic Metaphysics*. Notre Dame, IN: University of Notre Dame Press, 2001.

———. *Person and Being: The Aquinas Lecture 1993*. Milwaukee, WI: Marquette University Press, 1993.

———. "Person, Being, and St. Thomas." *Communio* 19, no. 4 (1992): 601–18.

———. *The Philosophical Approach to God: A New Thomistic Perspective*. 2nd ed. New York: Fordham University Press, 2007.

———. "Spiritual Experience and Metaphysical Interpretation." In *Man and Nature*, edited by G. F. McLean, 188–97. Oxford: Oxford University Press, 1978.

Conn, David. "Hillsborough Verdict: Victims' Families' 27-Year Struggle for Truth Vindicated." *Guardian*. April 27, 2016. https://www.theguardian.com/football/2016/apr/26/hillsborough-families-27-year-struggle-for-truth-vindicated (accessed October 12, 2023).

Constitution of Ireland. Last updated January 2020. Enacted July 1, 1937. https://www.irishstatutebook.ie/eli/cons/en/html (accessed October 12, 2023).

The Constitution of Ireland. Independently published. September 21, 2021. https://www.irishstatutebook.ie/eli/cons/en/html.

Cooper, Barry. *New Political Religions, or An Analysis of Modern Terrorism*. Columbia: University of Missouri Press, 2004.

Copleston, Frederic. *A History of Philosophy*, 11 vols. New York: Doubleday, 1985.

Corby, Paschal. *The Hope and Despair of Human Bioenchantment: A Virtual Dialogue between the Oxford Transhumanists and Joseph Ratzinger*. Eugene, OR: Pickwick Publications, 2019.

Court of Justice of the European Union. *Press Release* No 128/21. Luxembourg. July 15, 2021. https://curia.europa.eu/jcms/upload/docs/application/pdf/2021-07/cp210128en.pdf (accessed October 12, 2023).

Crawford, David S. "Public Reason and the Anthropology of Orientation: How the Debate over 'Gay Marriage' has been shaped by some Ubiquitous but Unexamined Presumptions." *Communio* 43, no. 2 (2016): 247–73. https://www.communio-icr.com/files/43.2_Crawford.pdf.

———. "Recognising the Roots of Society in the Family, Foundation of Justice." *Communio* 34, no. 3 (2007): 379–412. https://www.communio-icr.com/files/crawford34-3.pdf.

Crawford, James. *Brownlie's Principles of Public International Law*, 9th ed. Oxford: Oxford University Press, 2019.

Crosby, John F. *Personalist Papers*. Washington, DC: Catholic University of America Press, 2004.

———. *The Selfhood of the Human Person*. Washington, DC: Catholic University of America Press, 1996.

Cullmann, Oscar. *The Christology of the New Testament*. 2nd ed. Translated by Shirley C. Guthrie and Charles A. M. Hall. London: SCM Press, 1963.

Daniélou, Jean. *The Lord of History: Reflections on the Inner Meaning of History*. New York: Meridian Books, 1968.

Dawson, Christopher. *The Dynamics of World History ('Enquiries'* 1933 and *'Religion and Culture'* 1948). Wilmington, DE: Intercollegiate Studies Institute, 2002.

———. *The Judgment of the Nations*. Edited by John J. Mulloy. Washington, DC: Catholic University of America Press, 2011.

———. *Progress and Religion: An Historical Inquiry*. Washington, DC: Catholic University of America Press, 2001.

Del Noce, Augusto. *The Crisis of Modernity*. Edited and translated by Carlo Lancellotti. Montreal: McGill Queens University Press, 2015.

De Lubac, Henri. *At the Service of the Church: Henri de Lubac Reflects on the Circumstances That Occasioned His Writings*. San Francisco: Ignatius Press, 1993

———. *Catholicism: Christ and the Common Destiny of Man*. Translated by Lancelot Sheppard. San Francisco: Ignatius Press, 1988.

———. *The Discovery of God*. Translated by Alexander Dru. Grand Rapids, MI: Eerdmans, 1996.

———. *The Drama of Atheist Humanism*. Translated by Mark Sebanc. San Francisco: Ignatius Press, 1998.

Dostoyevsky, Fyodor. *The Brothers Karamazov*. Translated by Constance Garnett. Mineola, NY: Dover Thrift Editions, 1998.

Dunn, John. *Democracy: A History*. New York: Atlantic Monthly Press, 2005.

Dupré, Louis. *A Dubious Heritage*. New York: Paulist Press, 1977.

———. *Passage to Modernity: An Essay in the Hermeneutics of Nature and Culture*. New Haven, CT: Yale university Press, 1993.

———. *Religion and the Rise of Modern Culture*. Notre Dame, IN: University of Notre Dame Press, 2008.

Dworkin, Ronald Myles. *The Philosophy of Law*. Oxford: Oxford University Press, 1982.

Dziwisz, Stanislaw. *A Life with Karol: My Forty-Year Friendship with the Man Who Became Pope*. New York: Image, 2008.

Eberstadt, Mary. "The New Intolerance." *First Things* (March 1, 2015): 33–39. https://www.firstthings.com/article/2015/03/the-new-intolerance (accessed October 12, 2023).

Eco, Umberto. *The Name of the Rose*. Translated by William Weaver. New York: Random House, 2006.

Eichmann, Adolf. "Eichmann's Final Plea, 'In His Own Words.'" *Remember.org*. Israel, 1961. https://remember.org/eichmann/ownwords (accessed October 12, 2023).

Eliade, Mircea. *A History of Religious Ideas*. Translated by Willard R. Trask. 3 vols. Chicago: University of Chicago Press, 1981.

———. *The Sacred and the Profane: The Nature of Religion*. Translated by Willard R. Trask. New York: Harcourt, Brace & World, 1959.

Eliot, T. S. [Thomas Stears]. *The Complete Poems and Plays of T. S. Eliot.* London: Faber and Faber, 2004.

———. *The Idea of a Christian Society.* New York: Harcourt Brace, 1940; Boston, MA: Houghton Mifflin Harcourt, 2014.

———. *Murder in the Cathedral.* London: Faber and Faber, 1968.

Engels, Friedrich. *Ludwig Feuerbach and the Outcome of Classical German Philosophy.* New York: International, 1941.

Ertman, Thomas. *Birth of the Leviathan: Building States and Regimes in Medieval and Early Modern Europe.* Cambridge: Cambridge University Press, 1997.

Feuerbach, Ludwig. *The Essence of Christianity.* Translation by George Eliot, London: e-artnow 2021. Kindle.

———. *The Fiery Brook: Selected Writings.* Translated by Zawar Hanfi. London: Verso, 2013.

Fideler, David. *Restoring the Soul of the World: Our Living Bond with Nature's Intelligence.* Rochester, VT: Inner Traditions, 2014.

Fimister, Alan Paul. *Robert Schuman: Neo-Scholastic Humanism and the Reunification of Europe.* Brussels: Peter Lang, 2008.

Finance, Joseph de. *An Ethical Inquiry.* Roma: Editrice Pontificia Università Gregoriana, 1991.

Fisch, Jörg. *The Right of Self-Determination of Peoples: The Domestication of an Illusion.* Translated by Anita Mage. Cambridge: Cambridge University Press, 2015.

Foucault, Michel. *"Discourse and Truth" and "Parrēsia."* Edited by Henri-Paul Fruchaud and Daniele Lorenzini. Chicago: University of Chicago Press, 2019.

Francis (Pope). "Evangelii Gaudium," *Acta Apostolicae Sedis (AAS)* 105 (2013): 1–224. https://www.vatican.va/content/francesco/en/apost_exhortations/documents/papa-francesco_esortazione-ap_20131124_evangelii-gaudium.html (accessed October 16, 2023).

———. *Fratelli tutti.* Vatican City: Libreria Editrice Vaticana, 2020.

———. "Laudato sì," *Acta Apostolicae Sedis (AAS)* 107 (2015), 937–38. https://www.vatican.va/content/francesco/en/encyclicals/documents/papa-francesco_20150524_enciclica-laudato-si.html (accessed October 16, 2023).

———. "Lumen Fidei." *Acta Apostolicae Sedis (AAS)* 105 (2013): 591–92. https://www.vatican.va/content/francesco/en/encyclicals/documents/papa-francesco_20130629_enciclica-lumen-fidei.html (accessed October 13, 2023).

Frankl, Viktor E. *Man's Search for Meaning.* Boston: Beacon Press, 2006.

Freeden, Michael. *Ideologies and Political Theories.* Oxford: Oxford Clarendon Press, 1996.

———. *Ideology: A Very Short Introduction.* Oxford: Oxford University Press, 2003.

———. *Liberal Languages: Ideological Imaginations and Twentieth-Century Progressive Thought.* Princeton, NJ: Princeton University Press, 2005.

———, ed. *Reassessing Political Ideologies: The Durability of Dissent.* London: Routledge, 2001.

Fukuyama, Francis. "The End of History?" *National Interest*, no. 16 (1989): 3–18. https://www.jstor.org/stable/24027184.

———. *The End of History and the Last Man.* New York: Free Press, 2006.

————. *The Origins of Political Order: From Prehuman Times to the French Revolution*. New York: Farrar, Straus, and Giroux, 2011.

————. *Political Order and Political Decay: From the Industrial Revolution to the Globalization of Democracy*. New York: Farrar, Straus, and Giroux, 2015.

Fuller, Timothy, and John P. Hittinger, eds. *Reassessing the Liberal State: Reading Maritain's Man and the State*. Washington, DC: Catholic University of America Press, 2001.

Gandhi, Mahatma. "The Doctrine of Satyagraha as set forth by M. K. Gandhi," In *The Collected Works of Jacques Maritain, Vol. 2: Theonas, Antimodern, Three Reformers, The Dream of Descartes*, edited by John Hittinger and Richard Lemp. Notre Dame, IN: University of Notre Dame Press 1996.

Geertz, Clifford. *The Interpretation of Cultures*. New York: Basic Books, 1973.

Germino, Dante. "Eric Voegelin's Contribution to Contemporary Political Philosophy." *Review of Politics* 26, no. 3 (1964): 378–402. https://doi.org/10.1017/S003467050000509X.

Gierke, Otto [von]. *Political Theories of the Middle Ages*. Translated by Frederic William Maitland. Eastford, CT: Martino Fine Books, 2014.

Gilbert, Martin. *The Righteous: The Unsung Heroes of the Holocaust*. New York: Henry Holt, 2003.

Glendon, Mary Ann. *The Forum and the Tower: How Scholars and Politicians Have Imagined the World, from Plato to Eleanor Roosevelt*. New York: Oxford University Press, 2011.

————. "Holy See's Final Statement at Women's Conference in Beijing United Nations 1995." Beijing. September 15, 1995. https://campus.udayton.edu/mary/resources/12holysee.html (last retrieved April 20, 2014).

————. *Traditions in Turmoil*. Ann Arbor, MI: Sapientia Press Ave Maria University, 2006.

————. *A World Made New: Eleanor Roosevelt and the Universal Declaration of Human Rights*. New York: Random House, 2002.

Glendon, Mary Ann, and Pierluca Azzaro, eds. *Fundamental Rights and Conflicts among Rights*. Steubenville, OH: Franciscan University Press, 2020.

Goodwin, Doris Kearns. *Teams of Rivals: The Political Genius of Abraham Lincoln*. New York: Simon & Schuster, 2006.

Grabowski, John S. "Person: Substance and Relation." *Communio* 22, no. 1 (1995): 139–63.

Green, Leslie. "Introduction." In *The Concept of Law*, by H. L. A. Hart, 3rd ed. Oxford: Oxford University Press, 2012.

Greene, Graham. *The Power and the Glory*. New York: Viking Press, 1968.

Grotius, Hugo. *The Rights of War and Peace*. Jean Barbeyrac ed. 3 vols. Indianapolis: Liberty Fund, 2005.

Guardini, Romano. *The Death of Socrates: An Interpretation of the Platonic Dialogues. Euthyphro, Apology, Crito, and Phaedo.* Translated by Basil Wrighton. New York: Sheed and Ward, 1948.

Guéhenno, Jean-Marie. *The End of the Nation-State*. Translated by Victoria Elliott. Minneapolis: University of Minnesota Press, 2000.

Gunderman, Richard. "The Cries of the Children." *Law & Liberty*. April 14, 2022. https://lawliberty.org/the-cries-of-the-children/ (accessed October 17, 2023).

Haas, Ernst B. *The Uniting of Europe: Political, Social, and Economic Forces*. Stanford, CA: Stanford University Press, 1958.

Hahn, Scott W., and Jeffrey Morrow. *Modern Biblical Criticism as a Tool of Statecraft (1700–1900)*. Steubenville, OH: Emmaus Academic, 2020.

Hahn, Scott W., and Benjamin Wiker. *Politicizing the Bible: The Roots of Historical Criticism and the Secularization of Scripture, 1300–1700*. New York: Herder & Herder, 2013.

Hamilton, Alexander, James Madison, and John Jay. *The Federalist Papers*. Edited by Lawrence Goldman. Oxford: Oxford University Press, 2008.

Harris, J. W. [James William]. *Legal Philosophies*. London: Butterworths, 1997; 2nd ed. Oxford: Oxford University Press, 2005.

Hart, H. L. A. [Herbert Lionel Adolphus]. *The Concept of Law*. 3rd ed. Oxford: Oxford University Press, 2012.

———. "Separation of Laws and Morals." In *The Philosophy of Law*, by Ronald M. Dworkin. Oxford: Oxford University Press, 1982.

Havel, Václav. *Letters to Olga*. Translated by Paul Wilson. New York: Henry Holt, 1989.

———. "On This Day, in 1990: John Paul II Became the First Pope to Visit Prague." *Kafkadesk*. April 21, 2021. https://kafkadesk.org/2021/04/21/on-this-day-in-1990 -john-paul-ii-became-the-first-pope-to-visit prague/#:~:text=Greeting%20John%2 0Paul%20II%20as,am%20the%20witness%20of%20one%E2%80%9D.

Havel, Václav, et al. *The Power of the Powerless: Citizens Against the State in Central-Eastern Europe*. Edited by John Keane. London: Routledge Classics, 1985.

Hayek, F. A. [Friedrich A.]. *The Constitution of Liberty: The Definitive Edition*. Edited by Ronald Hamowy. Chicago: University of Chicago Press, 2011.

Hegel, G. W. F. [Georg Wilhelm Friedrich]. *Lectures on the Philosophy of History*. Translated by H. B. Nisbet. Cambridge: Cambridge University Press, 1989.

———. *Outlines of the Philosophy of Right*. Revised ed. Translation by T. M. Knox. Notes by Stephen Holgate. Oxford: Oxford University Press, 2008.

———. *The Phenomenology of Spirit*. Edited and translated by Terry Pinkard and Michael Baur. Cambridge: Cambridge University Press, 2018.

Henrici, Peter. "Modernity and Christianity." *Communio* 17, no. 2 (1990): 141–51.

———. "The Philosophers and Original Sin." *Communio* 18, no. 4 (1991): 489–501.

———. "Sophistry and Philosophy." *Communio* 15, no. 3 (1988): 384–94.

———. "The Spiritual Dimension and Its Form of Reason." *Communio* 20, no. 4 (1993): 638–51.

Hittinger, Russell. *The Virtue of Hope*. World and I Online, 2014. Kindle edition.

Hobbes, Thomas. *Elements of Law, Natural and Politi* (1640). 2nd ed. Edited by Ferdinand Tonnies. Cambridge: Frank Cass / Cambridge University Press, 1969.

———. *Leviathan*. Edited by J. C. A. Gaskin. Oxford: Oxford University Press, 1998.

Huffman, Richard. 'The Limits of Violence,' *Satya*, March 2004. http://www .satyamag.com.

Huntington, Samuel P. "The Clash of Civilizations?" *Foreign Affairs* 72, no. 3 (1993): 22–49. https://doi.org/10.2307/20045621.

———. *The Clash of Civilizations and the Remaking of World Order*. New York: Simon and Schuster, 2011.

Hutter, Horst. *Politics as Friendship: The Origins of Classical Notions of Politics in the Theory and Practice of Friendship*. Waterloo, ON: Wilfred Laurier University Press, 1978.

International Court of Justice. Reports of Judgments. Advisory Opinions and Orders. *Accordance with International Law of the Unilateral Declaration of Independence in Respect of Kosovo*. Advisory Opinion of July 22, 2010. https://www.icj-cij.org/case/141 (accessed October 14, 2023).

International Theological Commission (ITC). *In Search of a Universal Ethic: A New Look at the Natural Law*. Città del Vaticano: Libreria Editrice Vaticana, 2009. https://www.vatican.va/roman_curia/congregations/cfaith/cti_documents/rc_con_cfaith_doc_20090520_legge-naturale_en.html (accessed October 14, 2023).

Jaeger, Werner. *Aristotle: Fundamentals of the History of His Development*. 2nd ed. Translated by Richard Robinson. Oxford: Oxford University Press, 1968.

Jägerstätter, Franz. *Letters and Writings from Prison*. Edited by Erna Putz. Maryknoll, NY: Orbis, 2009.

Jankunas, Gediminas T. *The Dictatorship of Relativism: Pope Benedict XVI's Response*. New York: Alba House, 2011.

John Paul II. "Address to the General Assembly of the United Nations." *L'Osservatore Romano* (Weekly edition in English). October 5, 1995. https://www.vatican.va/content/john-paul-ii/en/speeches/1995/october/documents/hf_jp-ii_spe_05101995_address-to-uno.html (accessed October 14, 2023).

———. *Centesimus Annus*. *Acta Apostolicae Sedis (AAS)* 83 (1991): 793–867.

———. *Evangelium Vitae*. *Acta Apostolicae Sedis (AAS)* 87 (1995): 401–522.

———. *Fides et Ratio*. Saint Peters, Rome. September 14, 1998. https://www.vatican.va/content/john-paul-ii/en/encyclicals/documents/hf_jp-ii_enc_14091998_fides-et-ratio.html (accessed October 19, 2023).

———. *Memory and Identity: Conversations at the Dawn of a Millennium*. Milano: Rizzoli, 2005.

———. *Veritatis Splendor*. *Acta Apostolicae Sedis (AAS)* 85 (1993): 1225–28.

Johnson, Paul. *Modern Times: The World from the Twenties to the Nineties*. New York: Harper Perennial, 1992.

Jonas, Hans. *The Imperative of Responsibility: In Search of an Ethics for the Technological Age*. Chicago: University of Chicago Press, 1994.

Jones, Andrew Willard. "The End of Sovereignty: An Essay in Christian Postliberalism." *Communio* 45, no. 3-4 (2018): 408–56.

Jones, Arnold Hugh Martin. *Athenian Democracy*. Oxford: Basil Blackwell, 1969.

Jouvenel, Bertrand de. *On Power: The Natural History of its Growth* (1952). Translated by J. F. Huntington. Indianapolis: Liberty Fund, 1993.

Kant, Immanuel. *Anthropology, History, and Education* (1764-1803). Edited and translated by Günter Zöller and Robert B. Louden. Cambridge: Cambridge University Press, 2007.

———. *Critique of Practical Reason* (1788) *and Other Writings in Moral Philosophy*. Translated by Lewis White Beck. Chicago: University of Chicago Press, 1949.

———. *Groundwork of the Metaphysics of Morals* (1797). Translated and edited by Mary Gregor. Cambridge: Cambridge University Press, 1997.

———. *Toward Perpetual Peace and Other Writings on Politics, Peace, and History* (1795). Edited by Pauline Kleingeld. Translated by David L. Colclasure. New Haven, CT: Yale University Press, 2006.

Kasper, Walter. *The God of Jesus Christ*. New York: Crossroad, 1984.

Kaufmann, Walter, ed. *Existentialism from Dostoevsky to Sartre*. Revised and expanded ed. Harmondsworth, UK: Penguin Books, 1975.

Kelly, J. M. [John Maurice]. *A Short History of Western Legal Theory*. Oxford: Oxford University Press, 1992.

Kelsen, Hans. *General Theory of Law and State*. Translated by Anders Wedberg New York: Russell & Russell, 1961.

———. *Pure Theory of Law*. Translated by Max Knight. Berkeley, CA: University of California Press, 1967.

———. *What Is Justice? Justice, Law, and Politics in the Mirror of Science*. Clark, NJ: Lawbook Exchange, 2013.

Kolnai, Aurel. *Privilege and Liberty and Other Essays in Political Philosophy*. Edited by Daniel J. Mahoney. Lanham, MD: Lexington Books, 1999.

———. *The Utopian Mind and Other Papers: A Critical Study in Moral and Political Philosophy*. Edited by Francis Dunlop. London: Athlone, 1995.

Koritansky, Peter Karl. "Thomas Aquinas: Political Philosophy." *Internet Encyclopaedia of Philosophy*, 2007. https://iep.utm.edu/thomas-aquinas-political -philosophy/ (accessed October 14, 2023).

Krastev, Ivan, and Stephen Holmes. *The Light that Failed: A Reckoning*. London: Allen Lane, 2019.

Kraynak, Robert P. *Christian Faith and Modern Democracy: God and Politics in the Fallen World*. Notre Dame, IN: University of Notre Dame Press, 2001.

———. "The Origins of 'Social Justice' in the Natural Law Philosophy of Antonio Rosmini." *Review of Politics* 80, no. 1 (2018): 3–29. https://doi.org/10.1017/S0034670517000754.

Kugler, Martin, and Gudrun Kugler, eds. *Exiting a Dead-End Road: A GPS for Christians in Public Discourse*. Wien: Kairos Publications, 2010.

Kuhn, Thomas. *The Structure of Scientific Revolutions*. 4th ed. Chicago: University of Chicago Press, 2012.

Lenin, Vladimir. *Lenin Collected Works*. 54 vols. in 45 translated English vols. Moscow: Progress Publishers, 1965.

———. *What is to be Done? Burning Questions of our Movement* (1902). Lenin Internet Archive, 1999. https://www.marxists.org/archive/lenin/works/1901/witbd/ (accessed October 14, 2023).

Leoni, Bruno. *Freedom and the Law*. Los Angeles: Nash Publishing, 1972.

Lewis, C. S. [Clive Staples]. *Christian Reflections*. Edited by Walter Hooper. London: HarperCollins, 2017.

———. *A Grief Observed*. New York: HarperCollins, 2001.

———. *Present Concerns: Journalistic Essays*. London: HarperCollins, 2017.

———. *The Screwtape Letters*. New York: HarperCollins, 2002.

Libreria Editrice Vaticana. *Catechism of the Catholic Church*. Dublin: Veritas Publications, 1994.

Life Institute. "Ireland's Fall: The Abortion Deception." YouTube. September 21, 2018. https://www.youtube.com/watch?v=eCsOE7HHe9Y.

Lindberg, Leon N. *The Political Dynamics of European Economic Integration*. Stanford, CA: Stanford University Press, 1963.

Locke, John. *Second Treatise of Government*. Edited by C. B. Macpherson. Indianapolis: Hackett, 1980.

Louth, Andrew. *The Origins of the Christian Mystical Tradition: From Plato to Denys*. 2nd ed. Oxford: Oxford University Press, 2007.

Löwith, Karl. *Meaning in History*. Chicago: University of Chicago Press, 1949.

Lu, Mathew. "Getting Serious about Seriousness: On the Meaning of Spoudaios in Aristotle's Ethics." *Proceedings of the American Catholic Philosophical Association* 87 (2013): 285–93. https://doi.org/10.5840/acpaproc201441412.

Machiavelli, Niccolò. *Discourses on Livy*. Translated by Harvey C. Mansfield and Nathan Tarcov. Chicago: University of Chicago Press, 1996.

———. *The Prince*. 2nd ed. Translated by Harvey C. Mansfield. Chicago: University of Chicago Press, 1998.

MacIntyre, Alasdair. *After Virtue: A Study in Moral Theory*. 3rd ed. Notre Dame, IN: University of Notre Dame Press, 2007.

———. *Against the Self-Images of the Age: Essays on Ideology and Philosophy*. Notre Dame, IN: University of Notre Dame Press, 1971.

Magida, Arthur J. *Code Name Madaleine: A Sufi Spy in Nazi-Occupied Paris*. New York: W. W. Norton, 2020.

Mandela, Nelson. *Long Walk to Freedom*. South Africa: Little, Brown, 1994.

Manent, Pierre. *An Intellectual History of Liberalism*. Translated by Rebecca Balinski. Princeton, NJ: Princeton University Press, 1996.

———. *Metamorphoses of the City: On the Western Dynamic*. Translated by Marc LePain. Cambridge, MA: Harvard University Press, 2013.

———. "The Return of Political Philosophy." *First Things* 103 (May 2000): 15–22. https://www.firstthings.com/article/2000/05/the-return-of-political-philosophy intolerance (accessed October 12, 2023).

Mansfield, Harvey C. Introduction to *Discourses on Livy*, by Niccolò Machiavelli. Chicago: University of Chicago Press, 1996.

———. "The Majesty of the Law." *Wiley Vaughan Lecture*. Harvard Law School. April 4, 2012. https://scholar.harvard.edu/harveymansfield/publications/majesty -law.

———. *A Student's Guide to Political Philosophy*. Wilmington, DE: ISI Books, 2014.

Manuel, Frank E., and Fritzie P. Manuel. *Utopian Thought on the Western World*. Oxford: Blackwell, 1979.

Maritain, Jacques. *Christianity and Democracy and The Rights of Man and The Natural Law*. Translated by Doris C. Anson. San Francisco: Ignatius Press, 2012.

———. *The Collected Works of Jacques Maritain.* 20 vols. Notre Dame, IN: University of Notre Dame Press 1996.

———. *The Person and the Common Good.* Notre Dame, IN: University of Notre Dame Press, 1966.

———. *True Humanism.* Translated by Margot Adamson. New York: C. Scribner, 1938.

———. *Scholasticism and Politics.* Translated and edited by Mortimer J. Adler. Indianapolis: Liberty Fund, 2012.

Marx, Karl. *A Contribution to a Critique of Hegel's Philosophy of Right* (1844). https://www.marxists.org/archive/marx/works/1843/critique-hpr/intro.htm (accessed October 15, 2023).

———. *Critique of the Gotha Programme.* In *Marx/Engels Selected Works*, vol. 3, 13–30. Moscow: Progress Publishers, 1970. https://www.marxists.org/archive/marx/works/1875/gotha/index.htm (accessed October 15, 2023).

———. *The Victory of the Counter-Revolution in Vienna.* Translated by Marx-Engels Institute. https://www.marxists.org/archive/marx/works/1848/11/06.htm (accessed October 15, 2023).

Marx, Karl, and Friedrich Engels. *Basic Writings in Politics and Philosophy.* Edited by Lewis S. Feuer. New York: Doubleday, 1989.

———. *A Critique of The German Ideology.* Moscow: Progress Publishers 1968. https://www.marxists.org/archive/marx/works/download/Marx_The_German_Ideology.pdf (accessed October 15, 2023).

McAleer, Graham. "Not the End of Politics." *Law and Liberty.* May 31, 2022. https://lawliberty.org/forum/not-the-end-of-politics (accessed October 16, 2023).

McCoy, Charles N. R., ed. *The Structure of Political Thought: A Study in the History of Ideas.* London: Routledge, 2017.

Milbank, John. "The Impossibility of Gay Marriage and the Threat of Biopolitical Control." *ABC Religion and Ethics,* April 23, 2013. https://www.abc.net.au/religion/the-impossibility-of-gay-marriage-and-the-threat-of-biopolitical/10099888 (accessed October 15, 2023).

———. *Theology and Social Theory: Beyond Secular Reason.* 2nd ed. Malden, MA: Blackwell, 2006.

Milbank, John, and Adrian Pabst. *The Politics of Virtue: Post-Liberalism and the Human Future.* Lanham, MD: Rowman & Littlefield, 2016.

Milbank, John, Catherine Pickstock, and Graham Ward, eds. *Radical Orthodoxy: A New Theology.* London: Routledge, 1999.

Morse, Jennifer Roback. *Love and Economics: It Takes a Family to Raise a Village.* Lake Charles, LA: Ruth Institute Books, 2008.

Mouroux, Jean. *I Believe: The Personal Structure of Faith.* New York: Sheed and Ward, 1959.

Nussbaum, Martha C. *Fragility of Goodness: Luck and Ethics in Greek Tragedy and Philosophy.* 2nd ed. Cambridge: Cambridge University Press, 2001.

Neuhaus, Richard John. "The Idea of Moral Progress." *First Things* (August 1999). https://www.firstthings.com/article/1999/08/the-idea-of-moral-progress (accessed October 16, 2023).

————. *The Naked Public Square: Religion and Democracy in America.* 2nd ed. Grand Rapids, MI: Eerdmans, 1997.

Neusner, Jacob. *The Rabbinical Tradition about the Pharisees Before 70.* 3 vols. Eugene, OR: Wipf and Stock, 2005.

Newman, John Henry. *An Essay in Aid of a Grammar of Ascent.* Edited by Ian Ker. Oxford: Oxford University Press, 1985.

————. *The Idea of a University.* New York: Longmans, Green, 1917. National Institute for Newman Studies. Online ed., 2007. https://digitalcollections .newmanstudies.org/.

Nietzsche, Friedrich. *Beyond Good and Evil: Prelude to a Philosophy of the Future.* Translated by Walter Kaufmann. New York: Vintage Books, 1989.

————. *The Portable Nietzsche.* Edited and translated by Walter Kaufmann. Harmondsworth, UK: Penguin Books 1977.

————. *The Will to Power.* Translated by Walter Kaufmann and R. J. Hollingdale. Edited by Walter Kaufmann. New York: Vintage Books, 1968.

Nisbet, Robert A. *The Quest for Community: A Study in the Ethics of Order and Freedom.* Washington, DC: ISI Books, 2010.

————. *The Sociological Tradition.* London: Routledge, 2017.

————. *Twilight of Authority.* Indianapolis: Liberty Fund, 2000.

Novak, David. *Covenantal Rights: A Study in Jewish Political Theory.* Princeton, NJ: Princeton University Press, 2000.

Novak, Michael. *The Spirit of Democratic Capitalism.* Lanham, MD: Madison Books, 1992.

Oakeshott, Michael. *On Human Conduct.* Oxford: Oxford University Press, 1975.

————. *The Politics of Faith and the Politics of Perfection.* Edited by Timothy Fuller. New Haven, CT: Yale University Press, 1996.

————. *Rationalism in Politics and Other Essays.* New and expanded ed. Indianapolis: Liberty Fund, 1991.

O'Connor, Sandra Day. *The Majesty of the Law: Reflections of a Supreme Court Justice.* New York: Random House, 2004.

O'Donovan, Oliver, and Joan Lockwood O'Donovan, eds. *From Irenaeus to Grotius: A Sourcebook in Christian Political Thought.* Grand Rapids, MI: Eerdmans, 1999.

Olsen, Glenn W. *Beginning at Jerusalem: Five Reflections on the History of the Church.* San Francisco: Ignatius Press, 2004.

————. *The Turn to Transcendence: The Role of Religion in the Twenty-First Century.* Washington DC: Catholic University of America Press, 2010.

O'Neill, Michael, ed. *The Politics of European Integration.* London: Routledge, 1996.

Organization of Islamic Cooperation (OIC). *The Cairo Declaration of the Organization of Islamic Cooperation on Human Rights.* 2021. https://www.oic-oci.org/upload/ pages/conventions/en/CDHRI_2021_ENG.pdf (November 7, 2023).

Orwell, George. "Review of A. Hitler's Mein Kampf." *New English Weekly.* March 21, 1940.

Osman, Tarek. "Why Border Lines Drawn with a Ruler in WW1 Still Rock the Middle East." *BBC News,* December 14, 2013. https://www.bbc.com/news/world -middle-east-25299553 (accessed October 15, 2023).

Otto, Eckart. "Human Rights: The Influence of the Hebrew Bible." *Journal of Northwest Semitic Language* 25, no1 (1999): 1–20.

Paldiel, Mordecai. "Is Goodness a Mystery?" *Jerusalem Morning Post*. October 8, 1989.

Pamuk, Orhan. *Snow*. New York: Knopf, 2004.

Pennington, Kenneth. "Lex Naturalis and Ius Naturale." In *Crossing Boundaries at Medieval Universities*, edited by Spencer E. Young, 227–53. Leiden: Brill, 2010.

Pera, Marcello. *Diritti umani e cristianesimo: La Chiesa alla prova della modernità*. Venezia: Marsilio, 2015.

Pieper, Josef. *The End of Time: A Meditation on the Philosophy of History*. Revised ed. San Francisco: Ignatius Press, 1999.

———. *Faith, Hope, Love*. San Francisco: Ignatius Press, 1977.

———. *For the Love of Wisdom: Essays on the Nature of Philosophy*. San Francisco: Ignatius Press, 2007.

———. *The Four Cardinal Virtues*. Notre Dame, IN: University of Notre Dame, Press 1966.

———. *Happiness and Contemplation*. South Bend, IN: St. Augustine's Press, 1998.

———. *Hope and History*. San Francisco: Ignatius Press, 1994.

———. *In Tune with the World: A Theory of Festivity*. South Bend, IN: St. Augustine's Press, 1999.

———. *Leisure: The Basis of Culture*. South Bend, IN: St. Augustine's Press, 1998.

———. *Living the Truth: Reality and the Good* and *The Truth of All Things*. San Francisco: Ignatius Press, 1989.

———. *Only the Lover Sings: Art and Contemplation*. San Francisco: Ignatius Press, 1990.

———. *Problems of Modern Faith: Essays and Addresses*. Translated by Jan van Heurck. Chicago: Franciscan Herald Press, 1985.

———. *The Silence of St. Thomas*. South Bend, IN: St. Augustine's Press, 1999.

Plato. *The Republic*. In *The Complete Works of Plato*. Translated by Benjamin Jowett. Kirkland, WA: Latus e-Publishing, 2012. Kindle.

Popper, Karl. *Conjectures and Refutations: The Growth of Scientific Knowledge*. 2nd ed. London: Routledge Classics, 2002.

———. *The Open Society and Its Enemies*. London: Routledge Classics, 2011.

Possenti, Vittorio. *Le società liberali al bivio: Lineamenti di filosofia della società*. Città Castello, Italy: Marietti, 1992.

Pritzl, Kurt. "Truth in Fides et Ratio." *Communio* 29, no. 1 (2002): 89–106.

Rachlin, Nahid. *Foreigner: A Novel of an Iranian Woman Caught Between Two Cultures*. New York: W. W. Norton, 1999.

Ratzinger, Joseph [Pope Benedict XVI]. *Church, Ecumenism, and Politics: New Endeavours in Ecclesiology*. San Francisco: Ignatius Press, 2008.

———. *Crisis of Law*. Address at LUMSA Faculty of Jurisprudence, Rome. November 10, 1999. https://www.ewtn.com/catholicism/library/crises-of-law-10080.

———. *Dogma and Preaching: Applying Christian Doctrine to Daily Life*. San Francisco: Ignatius Press, 2011.

———. "Europe in the Crisis of Cultures." *Communio* 32, no. 2 (2005): 345–56.

———. *Europe: Today and Tomorrow*. San Francisco: Ignatius Press, 2007.

———. *The Feast of Faith: Approaches to a Theology of the Liturgy*. San Francisco: Ignatius Press, 1986.

———. "Freedom and Constraint in the Church." In *Church, Ecumenism, and Politics: New Endeavours in Ecclesiology*, translated by Michael J. Miller et al., 175–92. San Francisco: Ignatius Press, 2008.

———. *"In the Beginning ...": A Catholic Understanding to the Story of Creation and the Fall*. Grand Rapids, MI: Eerdmans, 1995.

———. *Introduction to Christianity*. San Francisco: Ignatius Press, 2004.

———. *Journey to Easter: Spiritual Reflections for the Lenten Season*. New York: Crossroad, 1987.

———. *The Meaning of Christian Brotherhood*. San Francisco: Ignatius Press, 1993.

———. *The Nature and Mission of Theology: Approaches to Understanding Its Role in the Light of Present Controversy*. San Francisco: Ignatius Press, 2010.

———. *A New Song for the Lord*. New York: Crossroad, 1996.

———. *Preaching and Dogma: Applying Christian Dogma to Daily Life*. San Francisco: Ignatius Press, 2011.

———. *Principles of Catholic Theology: Building Stones for a Fundamental Theology*. San Francisco: Ignatius Press, 1987.

———. *Salt of the Earth: The Church at the End of the Millennium, An Interview with Peter Seewald*. San Francisco: Ignatius Press, 1997.

———. "Truth and Freedom." *Communio* 23, no. 1 (1996): 16–35.

———. *A Turning Point for Europe? The Church in the Modern World: Assessment and Forecast*. San Francisco: Ignatius Press, 1994; 2010.

———. *The Unity of the Nations: A Vision of the Church Fathers*. Washington, DC: Catholic University of America Press, 2013.

———. *Values in a Time of Upheaval*. New York: Crossroad, 2006.

Ratzinger, Joseph, and Marcello Pera. *Without Roots: The West, Relativism, Christianity, Islam*. Translated by Michael F. Moore. New York: Basic Books, 2006.

Rawls, John. *Political Liberalism*. New York: Columbia University Press, 2005.

———. *A Theory of Justice*. Cambridge, MA: Belknap Press, 1971.

Rhonheimer, Martin. *The Common Good of Constitutional Democracy*. Translated by William F. Murphy Jr. Washington, DC: Catholic University of America Press, 2013.

Rice, Condoleezza. *Democracy: Stories from the Long Road to Freedom*. New York: Hachette Book Group, 2017.

Robinson, Eric W. *The First Democracies: Early Popular Government Outside Athens*. Stuttgart: Franz Steiner Verlag, 1997.

Rommen, Heinrich A. *The Natural Law: A Study in Legal and Social History and Philosophy*. Translated by Thomas R. Hanley. Indianapolis: Liberty Fund, 1998.

Rosamond, Ben. *Theories of European Integration*. New York: Red Globe Press, 2000.

Rosenthal, Debra. *At the Heart of the Bomb: The Dangerous Allure of Weapons Work*. Boston: Addison-Wesley, 1990.

Rorty, Richard. "The Priority of Democracy to Philosophy." In *The Pragmatism Reader: From Peirce through the Present*, edited by Robert B. Talisse and Scott F. Aikin, 281–402. Princeton, NJ: Princeton University Press, 2011.

———. "The Priority of Democracy to Philosophy." In *Prospects for a Common Morality*, edited by Gene Outka and John P. Reeder, 254–78. Princeton, NJ: Princeton University Press, 1993.

Rousseau, Jean Jacques. *Emile, or On Education*. Translated by Allan Bloom. New York: Basic Books, 1979.

———. *On the Social Contract*. 2nd ed. Translated by Donald A. Cress. Indianapolis: Hackett, 2019.

Rousseau, Mary F. *Community: The Tie That Binds*. Lanham, MD: University Press of America, 1991.

Russell, Bertrand. *Authority and the Individual*. London: Routledge Classics, 2010.

Sabine, George H., and Thomas L. Thorson. *A History of Political Theory*. 4th ed. New York: Holt, Rinehart, and Winston, 1973.

Sageman, Marc. *Understanding Terror Networks*. Philadelphia: University of Pennsylvania Press, 2004.

Sandel, Michael J. *Democracy's Discontent: America in Search of a Public Philosophy*. Cambridge, MA: Harvard University Press, 1998.

———. *Liberalism and the Limits of Justice*. Cambridge: Cambridge University Press, 1998.

Sartori, Giovanni. *The Theory of Democracy Revisited: Part Two: The Classical Issues*. Chatham, NJ: Chatham House, 1987.

Schall, James V. "Human Rights as an Ideological Project." *American Journal of Jurisprudence* 32, no. 1 (1987): 47–61. https://doi.org/10.1093/ajj/32.1.47.

———. *The Mind that is Catholic: Philosophical and Political Essays*. Washington, DC: Catholic University of America Press, 2008.

———. "A Reflection on the Classical Tractate on Tyranny: The Problem of Democratic Tyranny." *American Journal of Jurisprudence* 41, no. 1 (1996): 1–19. https://doi.org/10.1093/ajj/41.1.1.

Scheler, Max. *On the Eternal in Man*. London: Routledge, 2017.

Schindler, D. C. [David C.], "Freedom beyond Our Choosing: Augustine on the Will and Its Objects." *Communio* 29, no. 4 (2002): 618–53.

———. *The Politics of the Real: The Church Between Liberalism and Integralism*. Steubenville, OH: New Polity Press, 2021.

Schindler, David L. "Norris Clarke on Person, Being, and St. Thomas." *Communio* 20, no. 3 (1993): 580–92.

———. *Ordering Love: Liberal Societies and the Memory of God*. Grand Rapids, MI: Eerdmans, 2011.

———. "The Repressive Logic of Liberal Rights: Religious Freedom, Contraceptives, and the 'Phony' Argument of the *New York Times*." *Communio* 38, no. 4 (2011): 523–47.

———. "Sanctity and the Intellectual Life." *Communio* 20, no. 4 (1993): 652–72.

Schmitz, Kenneth L. "Community: The Elusive Unity." *Review of Metaphysics* 37, no. 2 (1983): 245–64. https://www.jstor.org/stable/20128006.

———. *The Gift: Creation*. Milwaukee, WI: Marquette University Press, 1982.

———. "Post-Modernity or Modern-Plus?" *Communio* 17, no. 2 (1990): 152–66.

———. *The Texture of Being: Essays in First Philosophy*. Edited by Paul O'Herron. Washington, DC: Catholic University of America Press, 2007.

Schneider, Reinhold. *Imperial Mission*. Translated by Walter Oden. New York: Gresham Press, 1948.

Schönborn, Christoph. *God's Human Face: The Christ-Icon*. San Francisco: Ignatius Press, 1994.

Schumpeter, Joseph. *Capitalism, Socialism, and Democracy*. Summit, NJ: Start Publishing, 2012.

Scruton, Roger. *The Soul of the World*. Princeton, NJ: Princeton University Press, 2016.

———. *The Uses of Pessimism: And the Dangers of False Hope*. London: Atlantic Books, 2010.

Sen, Amarya. "Democracy as a Universal Value." *Journal of Democracy* 10, no. 3 (1999): 1–17. https://www.journalofdemocracy.org/articles/democracy-as-a-universal-value/.

Shaw, Malcolm N. *International Law*. 7th ed. Cambridge: Cambridge University Press, 2014.

Shils, Edward Albert. *The Concept and Function of Ideology*. New York: Crowell Collier and Macmillan, 1968.

Shore, Cris. *Building Europe: The Cultural Politics of European Integration*. London: Routledge, 2013.

———. *European Union and the Politics of Culture*. Bruges Group (pamphlet). March 2001. https://www.brugesgroup.com/media-centre/papers/8-papers/900-european-union-and-the-politics-of-culture (accessed October 15, 2023).

Siedentop, Larry. *Democracy in Europe*. London: Penguin Books, 2011.

———. *Inventing the Individual: The Origins of Western Liberalism*. Cambridge, MA: Harvard University Press, 2014.

Simon, Yves R. *A General Theory of Authority*. Notre Dame, IN: University of Notre Dame Press, 1980.

Simpson, Peter L. P. "Making the Citizens Good: Aristotle's City and Its Contemporary Relevance." *Philosophical Forum* 22, no. 2 (1990): 149–66.

———. *A Philosophical Commentary on the Politics of Aristotle*. Chapel Hill: University of North Carolina Press, 1998,

———. *Political Illiberalism: A Defence of Freedom*. London: Routledge, 2015.

———. "What's It Like To Be a Christian." *First Things*. June 1, 2004. 23–28. https://www.firstthings.com/article/2004/06/what-its-like-to-be-a-christian (accessed October 15, 2023).

Ska, Jean Louis. "Law, Freedom and Responsibility According to the Old Testament." In *Fundamental Rights and Conflicts among Rights*, edited by Mary Ann Glendon and Pierluca Azzaro, 47-64. Steubenville, OH: Franciscan University Press, 2020.

Skarsaune, Oskar. *In the Shadow of the Temple: Jewish Influences on Early Christianity*. Downers Grove, IL: InterVarsity, 2002.

Slade, Francis. "Rule as Sovereignty: The Universal and the Homogenous State." in *The Truthful and the Good: Essays in Honour of Robert Sokolowski*, edited by John J. Drummond and James G. Hart, 159–80. Dordrecht, IL: Springer, 2011.

―――. "Two Versions of Political Philosophy: Teleology and the Conceptual Genesis of the Modern State." In *Natural Moral Law in Contemporary Society*, edited by Holger Zaborowski, 235–63. Washington, DC: Catholic University of America Press, 2010.

Smith, John E. *Experience and God*. New York: Fordham University Press, 1995.

Smith, Steven C. *The House of the Lord: A Catholic Biblical Theology of God's Temple Presence in the Old and New Testaments*. Steubenville, OH: Franciscan University Press, 2017.

Sokolowski, Robert. *Christian Faith and Human Understanding: Studies on the Eucharist, Trinity, and the Human Person*. Washington, DC: Catholic University Press, 2006.

―――. *Eucharistic Presence: A Study in the Theology of Disclosure*. Washington, DC: Catholic University Press, 1993.

―――. "The Human Person and Political Life." In *Christian Faith and Human Understanding: Studies on the Eucharist, Trinity, and the Human Person*, 188–89. Washington DC: Catholic University of America Press, 2006.

―――. *Introduction to Phenomenology*. Cambridge: Cambridge University Press, 2000.

―――. "Phenomenology of Friendship." *Review of Metaphysics* 55, no. 3: 451–70. https://www.jstor.org/stable/20131748.

―――. *Phenomenology of the Human Person*. Cambridge: Cambridge University Press, 2008.

Solzhenitsyn, Aleksandr. *From Under the Rubble*. New York: Bantam Books, 1976.

―――. *The Gulag Archipelago, 1918-1956: An Experiment in Literary Investigation*. Translated by Thomas P. Whitney. New York: Harper & Row 1974.

―――. "A World Split Apart: Commencement Address at Harvard University June 8, 1978." In *Solzhenitsyn at Harvard: The Addresses, Twelve Early Responses and Six Later Reflections*, edited by Ronald Berman, 3–21. Washington, DC: Ethics and Public Policy Center, 1980.

Spaemann, Robert. *Persons: The Difference Between "Someone" and "Something."* Oxford: Oxford University Press, 2017.

―――. "Rationality and Faith in God." *Communio* 32, no. 4 (2005): 619–36.

Strauss, Leo. *What Is Political Philosophy? And Other Studies*. Chicago: University of Chicago Press, 1988.

Strauss, Leo, and Joseph Cropsey, eds. *History of Political Philosophy*. 3rd ed. Chicago: University of Chicago Press, 1987.

Strayer, Joseph R, *On the Medieval Origins of the Modern State*. Princeton, NJ: Princeton University Press, 1970.

Supreme Court of Canada. *Re Secession of Quebec*. 1998. 2 SCR 217. CanLII 793 (1998). Docket No. 25506.

Talisse, Robert B. *Pluralism and Liberal Politics*. London: Routledge, 2012.

Talisse, Robert B., and Scott F. Aikin, eds. *The Pragmatism Reader: From Peirce through the Present*. Princeton, NJ: Princeton University Press, 2011.

Tallon, Andrew. *Head and Heart: Affection, Cognition, Volition as Triune Consciousness*. New York: Fordham University Press, 1997.

Taylor, Charles. *A Secular Age*. Cambridge, MA: Harvard University Press, 2007.

Taylor, Paul. *The Limits of European Integration*. London: Croom Helm, 1983.

Tierney, Brian. *The Crisis of Church and State, 1050-1300*. Toronto: University of Toronto Press 1988.

———. *The Idea of Natural Rights*. Grand Rapids, MI: Eerdmans, 2001.

Tilly, Charles, ed. *The Formation of National States in Western Europe*. Princeton, NJ: Princeton University Press, 1975.

Tocqueville, Alexis de. *Democracy in America.: The Complete and Unabridged Volumes I and II*. New York: Bantam Classics, 2000.

Tuck, Richard. *Natural Rights Theories*. Cambridge: Cambridge University Press 1979.

United Nations Organisation. *Charter of the United Nations*. October 24, 1945. 1 UNTS XVI. https://www.un.org/en/about-us/un-charter (accessed October 15, 2023).

———. *Declaration on Principles of International Law concerning Friendly Relations and Cooperation among States in accordance with the Charter of the United Nations*. October 24, 1970. A/RES/2625(XXV). https://digitallibrary.un.org/record/202170?ln=en (accessed October 15, 2023).

———. *Declaration on the Granting of Independence to Colonial Countries and Peoples*. December 14, 1960. A/RES/1514(XV). https://www.ohchr.org/en/instruments-mechanisms/instruments/declaration-granting-independence-colonial-countries-and-peoples (accessed October 15, 2023).

———. *Universal Declaration of Human Rights*. December 10, 1948. https://www.un.org/en/about-us/universal-declaration-of-human-rights (accessed October 15, 2023).

Usborne, Simon. "I Don't Intend to Let My Son Down Twice." *Guardian*. August 11, 2021. https://www.theguardian.com/society/2021/aug/11/i-dont-intend-to-let-my-son-down-twice-the-bereaved-father-trying-to-end-suicide (accessed October 15, 2023).

Vincent, Andrew. *Modern Political Ideologies*. 3rd ed. Oxford: Wiley-Blackwell, 2010.

Vitz, Paul C., and Susan M. Felch, eds. *The Self: Beyond the Postmodern Crisis*. Wilmington, DE: ISI Books, 2006.

Voegelin, Eric. *From Enlightenment to Revolution*. Edited by John H. Hallowell. Durham, NC: Duke University Press, 1975.

———. *The Glory of the Lord: A Theological Aesthetics. Volume 1, Seeing the Form*. San Francisco: Ignatius Press, 1989.

———. *Hitler and the Germans*. In *Collected Works of Eric Voegelin*. Vol. 1. Translated and edited by Detlev Clemens and Brendan Purcell. Columbia, MI: University of Missouri Press, 1999.

———. *The New Science of Politics: An Introduction*. Chicago: University of Chicago Press, 1987.

————. *Order and History.* 5 vols. Columbia: University of Missouri, 2000.

————. *Science, Politics and Gnosticism: Two Essays.* Edited by Ellis Sandoz. Washington, DC: Gateway Editions, 1997; 2012.

————. "Why Philosophize? To Recapture Reality!" *Communio* 28, no. 4 (2001): 875–83.

Von Balthasar, Hans Urs. "Eternal Life and the Human Condition." *Communio* 18, no. 1 (1991): 4–23.

————. "Truth and Sanctity." In *Explorations in Theology*, 181–209. San Francisco: Ignatius Press, 1989.

Von Heyking, John. "David Walsh's Anamnesis of Modernity: A Preface to a Preface." *Political Science Reviewer* 39 (Spring 2010): 140–69.

Von Heyking, John, and Richard Avramenko, eds. *Friendship and Politics: Essays in Political Thought.* Notre Dame, IN: University of Notre Dame Press, 2008.

Waldron, Jeremy. *Nonsense upon Stilts: Bentham, Burke, and Marx on the Rights of Man.* New York: Methuen, 1987.

————. *Political Political Theory: Essays on Institutions.* Cambridge, MA: Harvard University Press, 2016.

Walsh, David. *After Ideology: Recovering the Spiritual Foundations of Freedom.* San Francisco: HarperCollins, 1990.

————. *The Growth of the Liberal Soul.* Columbia: University of Missouri, 1997.

————. *The Modern Philosophical Revolution: The Luminosity of Existence.* Cambridge: Cambridge University Press, 2008.

————. *Politics of the Person as the Politics of Being.* Notre Dame, IN: University of Notre Dame Press, 2016.

————. *The Priority of the Person: Political, Philosophical, and Historical Discoveries.* Notre Dame, IN: University of Notre Dame Press, 2020.

Waters, John. "Fixation with Regulations and eliminating human contact is what leads to Bungalow 3." *Irish Independent.* December 16, 2014.

————. "When I Met Christ." *First Things* (February 21, 2018). https://www.firstthings.com/web-exclusives/2018/02/when-i-met-christ (accessed October 26, 2023).

Weber, Max. *Economy and Society: An Outline of Interpretive Sociology.* Edited by Guenther Roth and Clause Wittich. Berkeley: University of California Press, 1978.

————. *The Theory of Social and Economic Organization.* Translated by Talcott Parsons and A. M. Henderson. New York: Free Press, 1964.

————. *The Vocation Lectures: "Science as a Vocation" and "Politics as a Vocation."* Edited by David Owen and Tracy B. Strong. Translated by Rodney Livingstone. Indianapolis: Hackett, 2004.

Weigel, George. *The End and the Beginning: Pope John Paul II—The Victory of Freedom, the Last Years, the Legacy.* New York: Doubleday, 2010.

————. *Witness to Hope: The Biography of Pope John Paul II.* New York: HarperCollins, 1999.

Whitehead, Alfred North. *Essays in Science and Philosophy.* New York: Philosophical Library, 1947.

Wilson, Woodrow. *Fourteen Points*. January 8, 1918. Goldman Law Library. 2008. https://avalon.law.yale.edu/20th_century/wilson14.asp.

Wolin, Sheldon S. *Fugitive Democracy: And Other Essays*. Princeton, NJ: Princeton University Press, 2018.

———. *Politics and Vision: Continuity and Innovation in Western Political Thought*. Expanded ed. Princeton, NJ: Princeton University Press, 2016.

Worsnip, Alex. "Against Pragmatism: The Vapid Philosophy of Modern Politics." *Prospect Magazine*. December 29, 2012. https://www.prospectmagazine.co.uk/politics/50637/against-pragmatism (accessed October 15, 2023).

Zaborowski, Holger, ed. *Natural Moral Law in Contemporary Society*. Washington, DC: Catholic University Press, 2010.

Zetterbaum, Marvin. "Alexis de Tocqueville." In *History of Political Philosophy*, 3rd ed., edited by Leo Strauss and Joseph Cropsey, 761–83. Chicago: University of Chicago Press, 1987.

Zimmern, Alfred Eckhard. *The Greek Commonwealth: Politics and Economics in Fifth-Century Athens*. Oxford: Clarendon Press, 1911.

Index

abortion, 80, 90, 189–90

absolutism: philosophical, 70–71; political, 70; power and, 71

abstraction, 104–5

action: being and, 31n34; freedom and, 284; knowledge and, 101; living in the truth and, 104–7; of truth, 87; truth expressed through, 106

actual rupture, 148–50

Address to the General Assembly of the United Nations Organization (John Paul II), 311–12

adults, development into, 169

After Ideology (Walsh), 11, 49, 160, 330, 334, 352

Age of Reason, 11

Alcibiades, 205, 228n11

American Civil War, 114

anarchic attitudes, 167; utopianism and, 172

Anderson, Hans Christian, 107

antagonism, 115

anti-clericalism, 62n39

apophansis, 29n21

Aquinas, Thomas (St.), xii, 97n70, 98n77, 130n33, 279; social living and, 55–56

Arendt, Hanna, 78, 178–79, 183, 201; on authority, 189, 195n33; on totalitarianism, 232n46

aristocracy, 211

Aristotle, 41, 82, 87, 155, 226, 235; on best government, 22, 211–12; democracy and, 159, 206; forms of government and, 201, 230n30; greatest good and, 135, 142; justification of power and, 187; *logos* and, 252; metaphysics and, 17–18; on *polis*, 6–7, 27n2; political authority and, 168, 185–86; on political community, 143; on political society, 210–11; reason and, 63n45; relation and, 50; social living and, 55–56; substitute intelligence and, 94n39; truth of predication and, 29n21; on virtues of political person, 245–46; on virtuous person, 22

association, 222, 233n55

atheism, 392n51, 392n62

atheistic humanism, 383

Athens, 108–9, 121; democracy in, 205–6

Augustine, 54, 90, 148, 154, 325n33, 357n39

Austin, John, 247

417

authority: as domination, 181–82; justification of, 183–84; law expressing, 235; political liberalism and, 184; political society and, 184, 225; power and, 181–82, 186–91, 200–201; prepolitical, 195n33; religious, 186; social, 41, 190; sovereignty and, 194n23; spiritual, 196n48; types of, 195n35
autonomy, 171
Avramenko, Richard, 246

Bacon, Francis, 72–73, 93n26, 139, 147, 223
Baghramian, Maria, 12
von Balthasar, Hans Urs, 98n77, 138
Baptism of Poland, x
basic rights, 285
Bauman, Zygmunt, xiii–xiv
Being: action and, 31n34; consciousness and reality of, 96n56; experience of, 15, 81, 378–79; logos of, 16, 337, 339–40; modes of truth of, 83–86; personal, 36, 66, 83, 90; personhood and, 48; truth and, 82; in truth of reality, 78–91
Being-as-Relation, 51
Benedict XVI (Pope), 73
Bentham, Jeremy, 222, 247
Berman, Harold J., 241, 249, 253–54, 274–75
Between Past and Future (Arendt), 189
biopolitical tyranny, 179
Bloch, Ernst, 164n49
Blondel, Maurice, 105, 339
Bodin, Jean, 7, 187, 214; rule and, 188
Bork, Robert H., 257
Bosworth, David, 224
The Brothers Karamazov (Dostoyevsky), 375
Brown, Peter, 274
Buber, Martin, 245
Burke, Edmund, 310–11
Burleigh, Michael, 187

Canada, 302–3, 323n18
Canonists, 267–68
care: friendship and, 212; regulation and, 243
Cassirer, Ernst, 149–50
Cavanaugh, William T., 42, 60n11, 196n49, 230n37, 321n3, 322n4, 368–69, 389n23
cave of shadows, 185
Centesimu Annus (John Paul II), 219
Christian Faith and Human Understanding (Sokolowski), 89
Christianity: brotherhood and, 317–18; civil society and, 52; culture development and, 274–75; legal reform and, 253; pagan glory and, 54, 161n11; personhood and, 276; political and social impacts of, 282; purpose of, 278
"A Christian Orientation in a Pluralistic Democracy?" (Ratzinger), 174, 377
Chrysostom, John, 52–53
Church Canon Law, 253, 267
citizens: in Athens, 205–6; in French Revolution, 207–8; person as, 43; understandings of, 43–44
citizenship, 188–89
civil courage, 353n2
civil law, 217
civil liberties, 188, 217
civil power, 200, 299–300
civil rule, 188
civil society, 42, 52
Civil War, American, 114
Clarke, W. Norris, 5, 14–17, 36, 50–51, 138, 332, 336; relation and, 54; on religious experience, 371; on self-consciousness, 81
"The Clash of Civilizations?" (Huntington), 305–6
clash of cultures, 307, 376
Cleisthenes, 205
closed society, 337
coercion, 13, 24
Coliva, Annalisa, 12

collective decisions: individual person in, 21; political decisions as, 111
collectivism, 48
Colvin, Marie, 36–37
common good, 71, 142, 195n33, 223; liberalism and, 170; political liberalism and, 284–85
communion: human, 200; interpersonal, 169–70; order and, 298; of persons, 298; political, 297; purposeful, 200; social, 169, 203–4, 223–24
Communism, 193n15
The Communist Manifesto (Marx and Engels), 340
Comte, Auguste, 146
concentration camps, 123
concentration of power, 233n56; international relations and, 305
The Concept of Law (Hart), 248
Concordat of Worms, 253
Condorcet, Nicolas de, 146
conflict, 116–17; international, 305; between moral and religious ideas, 294n71; as natural state, 300; shared truth and, 137
conformity, 106, 170
conscience, 375
consciousness, 30n32, 51; illusion of detachment and, 79; Marx on, 340–41; reality of Being and, 96n56; of self, 80–81
conservatism, 329
Conspiracy of Equals, 228n20
constitutional government, 39
consumer value system, 9–10
contemplation, 93n26
contemporary democracy: good government and, 200, 220–25; power structure and persons as numbers in, 213–19
contractualism, 63n53
Du Contrat Social [The Social Contract] (Rousseau), 150
Cosmic Liturgy, xi
cosmological experience, 371

cosmopolitanism, 316
Coulanges, Fustel de, 274
courage, 353n2
Covenants on Civil and Political Rights, 270
Crawford, David S., 72
creatura, 381
A Critique of The German Ideology (Marx and Engels), 340
Cropsey, Joseph, 346
Crosby, John F., 53
cultural initiatives, 314–15
culture: clash of, 307, 376; European, 314–15; political phenomena and, 23; politics as part of, 136; unity and, 273–74, 298
custom: civil powers and, 300; law and, 236, 248, 253, 262n32, 262n39; moral and social, 249
Czechoslovakia, 120; Prague Spring in, 35, 37–38

Dahrendorf, Ralf, x
Dante, 18
Dawson, Christopher, 305, 382; on unity of culture, 273–74
Decalogue, 259n7
Declaration on the Granting of Independence to Colonial Countries and Peoples, 270, 302
Declaration on the Principles of International Law, 302
Decretum Gratiani, 254
democracy, ix, xi–xii, 14, 24–25, 65, 199, 226n2; ancient and modern, 205–9; Aristotle and, 159; classics' rejection of, 228n23; conditions of, 8; descriptions of "the people" and, 176; despotism and, 354n5; disillusionment and, 8–11; ethical relativism and, 78; forms of government and, 201–3; good government and, 220–25; legitimacy in, 213; liberal, 8; morality and, 95n46; origins of term, 227n5,

231n40; as political method, 227n6; power structure and persons as numbers in contemporary, 213–19; relativism and, 70–71; religious experience and, 379; representative, 159; social communion and, 203–4; totalitarianism and, 299; tyranny in, 218–19

Democracy (Dunn), 206

Democracy in America (Tocqueville), 207, 215, 221

democratic despotism, 331

democratic government, distortions of, 200

democratic relativism, 71

democratic tyranny, 158

demos, x–xi, xiv

despotism, 158, 354n5; democratic, 331; equality and, 221–22

detachment, 98n76; illusion of, 79, 105; knowledge validity and, 105; perception and, 105

dictatorial power, 78

dictatorship of opinion, 232n49

dignity, of person, 281

disclosure: of experience, 50; of reality, 29n21; truth of, 49–50

Discourses on the First Ten Books of Titus Livius (Machiavelli), 112–13

discrimination, committees on elimination of, 270

disillusionment, 8–12; with politics, 330

Divine Comedy (Dante), 18

division of powers, 39

dominance attitudes, 167, 177–80

domination: authority as, 181–82; ideological, 359n60; of nature, 223, 350; political, 359n60; post-totalitarian, 351

Don Giussani, xii

Dostoyevsky, Fyodor, 126, 375

due process, 39

Dunn, John, 199, 203, 206–8

Dupré, Louis, 18, 28n14, 86

Dutschke, Rudi, 193n15

Dworkin, Ronald, 250

ebed Yahweh, 125

Eco, Umberto, 68

Economic and Social Covenants of Civil and Political Rights, 270

Economic and Social Rights, 270

economic modernity, 320

Economy and Society (Weber), 181

education: secular, 388n21; virtuous persons and, 22

effective power, 168

effectual truth, 113, 168, 187

egocentric predicament, 79

egoism, 208, 210

Eichmann, Adolf, 263n47

Eliot, T. S., 171

The Emperor's New Clothes (Anderson), 107

empiricism, 35, 105

The End of Time (Pieper), 12, 144, 147

Engels, Friedrich, 146, 173, 340; on utopians, 192n10

Enlightenment, 5, 11–12, 43, 52, 149, 317; hope and, 147

Epictetus, 316

Epicureanism, 155

epistemology, 18; morals and, 87

equality, 199, 209; dangers of undifferentiated, 217–18; despotism and, 221–22; freedom and, 229n24; imposed, 222; justice and, 142; modern and classical meanings of, 158–59; political abuse of term, 189; political society and, 244–45

eschatology, 132n60, 343; Ratzinger on, 166n62; unity and, 309

Eschatology and Utopia (Ratzinger), 215, 343

eschaton: immanentizing, 145–46, 163n30; secularism and, 365

eternal life, 154

ethical experience, 120

ethical relativism, 78

ethical standards, 377

ethics, 20; freedom and, 57; ontological conception of, 82
Ethics (Aristotle), 22, 142
etne, xi
European Constitution, xi
European Convention on Human Rights, 270
European Council, 313–14
European Court of Justice, 361, 363–64, 386n6
European culture, 314
European Union, 313, 320, 326n44, 363; Court of Justice of, 361
Evangelii Gaudium (Francis), xiv
evangelization, xiv
experience: of Absolute, 383; active response role in, 31n34; of Being, 15, 81, 378–79; conceptual abstraction of, 104–5; cosmological, 371; disclosure of, 50; ethical, 120; of hope, 135; interpersonal, 81, 97n65; originary, 82; personal, 371; personal, of truth, 103; of personal Being, 83, 88, 90; phenomenological description of, 49–50; of reality, 19, 84, 103; reason and, 84–85; religious, 85, 371, 377, 379, 381; social bonds and common, 104; subjectivity of, 67; theological, 50, 103–4; transcendence and, 370; unity and, 15
Explorations in Metaphysics (Clarke), 336

fairness, 68
faith: freedom and, xiii; politics of, 76, 94n40
Faith and Order (Berman), 241, 249, 253
falsehoods: conformity with, 106; resisting, 107
Fascism, 180
Feuerbach, Ludwig, 340, 373–74
Fides et Ratio [Faith and Reason] (John Paul II), 68

Finance, Joseph de, 120, 283
folk law, 262n32
foreign aid, 390n32
The Forum and the Tower (Glendon), 113
Foucault, Michel, on *parresia*, 110
Fourier, François Charles, 172, 174
Fourteen Points (Wilson), 301
Francis (Pope), xi–xii, xiv
Frankl, Viktor E., 123
Freeden, Michael, 335, 354n12
freedom, 38; action and, 284; contemporary views of, 67; equality and, 229n24; ethics and, 57; faith and, xiii; human society and, 170; individual, 46, 223; law and, 242; liberal democracy and, 331–32; liberalism and, 170; modern politics and, 67; moral, 282; of movement, 258n4; *parresia* and, 110; political, 60n16; political authority and, 14; power and, 41; Ratzinger on, 67–68, 91n6; religious, 386n7; rights and, 268, 273, 285; of speech, 110; truth and, 110–11, 170
Freedom and Constraint in the Church (Ratzinger), 237
Freedom House, 8
free will, 284
French Revolution, 172, 207, 317
French Utopians, 172
Freud, Sigmund, 381
friendship: brotherhood and, 316; law and, 235–36; personalism and, 246; politics and, 246
Fukuyama, Francis, 8, 167; on spontaneous society, 177
fulfilment, 154–57, 159–60, 165n58, 179, 332; need of political vision of transcendent, 333–34
fundamentalism, 47–48

Gandhi, Mahatma, 59n5, 102, 123–24, 131n58
general will (*volonté générale*), 150–51

genocide, conventions on, 270
Gerson, Jean, 279
Gilbert, Martin, 117–18
Glendon, Mary Ann, 113, 290n15
globalization, 311
glory, 54, 161n11
Gnosticism, 94n40, 163n30, 349–50, 359n55; modern political forms of, 178
God: law and, 239–40; origin of human person in, 381; as power, 125
Godwin, William, 172
goodness, law as reflection of, 252–56
Goodwin, Doris Kearns, 114
government: considerations for good, 209–13; democracy and good, 220–25; forms of, 199, 201–5, 211–12; power as justification for, 200; representative, 39
Gramsci, Antonio, 193n15
Gratian, 254, 268
Greek democracy, xii
Gregory VII (Pope), 253
Grotius, Hugo, 367
The Growth of the Liberal Soul (Walsh), 80, 87, 107, 116–17, 126, 370, 373
Guardian (newspaper), 143
Guardini, Romano, 108
Guéhenno, Jean-Marie, 320–21
Guizot, Francois, 274

halakhah, 239
Hart, H. L. A., 248–49
Harvard Commencement Address (Solzhenitsyn), 243–44, 353n2
Hassner, Pierre, 301
Havel, Václav, ix, xiv, 120, 127, 338; on consumer value system, 9–10; on experience of Being, 378–79; on ideological and political dominance, 359n60; on living publicly in the truth, 101, 106–8; on post-totalitarian dominance, 351; on Prague Spring, 35, 37–38; on renewal of politics, 21
heart, human person and, 89

Hegel, Georg Wilhelm Friedrich, 146, 152, 340, 348; goals of philosophy of, 358n41; on human history, 344–45, 358n45; on international relations, 300–301
Heidegger, Martin, 349
Herder, Johann Gottfried, 147
Herodotus, 227n5
Hillsborough tragedy, 250–51
historical determinism, 346
historical perspective, 138–40
historicism, 348–49, 359n53
history: *eidos* of, 342–44; hope and, 144–48; justification of, 343–44; nature and, 342–47; political language and, 5, 7; salvation, 342
History of Political Philosophy (Strauss), 346
Hitler, Adolf, 180; legal institutions exploited by, 256
Hittinger, Russell, 136, 155–56
Hobbes, Thomas, 40, 145, 187, 367; on conflict as natural, 300; human ambition and, 139; human equality and, 276; on *ius* and *lex*, 279–80; on laws as humanly made, 283; modern state and, 42–44; natural state of, 140–41, 147; political sovereignty and, 214; political structure of, 141–43; rule and, 188; social contract and, 135
Holmes, Oliver Wendall, 249
homosexual marriage, 179
honesty, 103
Hooker, Richard, 42
hope, 136; Enlightenment and, 147; as essential condition of political society, 154–56; existential experience of, 135; history and, 144–48; of transcendence, 373; transcendent fulfilment and, 150–53; types of, 144–45
"How Liberalism Became 'the God That Failed' in Eastern Europe" (Krastev and Holmes), 8

human agency, 307
human aspirations: modern state and, 9; politics of person and, 53–54, 56–58
human communion, 200
human development, 168–69
human existence, 24, 46, 140; historical perspective and, 138
human fulfilment, 154–56
humankind, unity of, 307
human person: conceptions of existence of, 148–49; heart and, 89; as individual, 35; interiority of, 53; origin in God of, 381; political liberalism and, 56; process of knowledge and, 105; relational structure of, 50–52; rights and, 269; Scholasticism and, 277; social nature of, 332; transmodern approach to, 47–53; unity, brokenness, and transcendent fulfilment of, 140–44
human rights, 25, 189, 267–68, 270–71; ambiguity of doctrines of, 283–88; contemporary acknowledgment of, 269–72; origin of, 272–77; of person, 277–79; personal, 281–83
human social existence, aspirations of, 331–33
human society: foundations of, 245; freedom and, 170; Platonic approach to, 21–22; social participation in, 202
Hume, David, 44, 278
Huntington, Samuel, 305–6
Hussein, Saddam, 37
Husserl, Edmund, 393n63
Hutter, Horst, 244

Ideal Forms, 185
Ideal of a Universal History Based on the Principle of World-Citizenship (Kant), 147
ideas: conflict between moral and religious, 294n71; implicit, of liberal democracy, 331–32; subjective, 79, 104; universal brotherhood as political, 294n71

ideological dominance, 359n60
ideology, 25–26, 76–77, 329; defining, 335; Marx critique of, 340–41; not asking questions and, 108; over-extension of, 340; social bonds and, 246–47; society visions of, 339
immunity to refutation, 151–52
Imperial Mission (Schneider), 122
Indian National Congress, 123
indigenous peoples, protecting rights of, 270
individual, ix; dependence on state of, 220; modern state and, 38–42; motivations of, 280; person and, 35, 62n43; as social role, 52
individual freedom, 46; common good and, 223; rights and, 268
individualism, 46, 48, 55, 153, 206, 246
individual rights, 141
industrial revolutions, 330
inequality: causes of, 229n27; good government and, 209–13; political society and, 210; of society, 199
An Inquiry Concerning Political Justice (Godwin), 172
institutions, 215; Communism and, 193n15
intellect, 89
intelligence, substitute, 75, 94n39
international conflicts, 305
International Court of Justice, 303
International Criminal Tribunal for Rwanda, 303
International Criminal Tribunal for the former Yugoslavia, 303
international law, 267, 270, 297, 302–3
international politics, 25, 297, 299–306; sources of unity and, 310
international relations, 300–301, 305, 308
International Theological Commission (ITC), 235, 238
interpersonal communion, 169–70
interpersonal experience, 97n65; origin of, 81

interpersonal love, metaphysics of, 169
Iraq, 37
Irish Constitution, 189–90
isolation, 246
ITC. *See* International Theological
    Commission
ius, 267–68, 276–78; notions of, 279–81
ius naturale, 252, 254–56, 276

Jaeger, Werner, 17
Jägerstätter, Franz, 120
Jefferson, Thomas, 194n24
Joachim of Fiore, 145–46, 163n29, 343,
    357n39
John Paul II (Pope), x, xii, xiv, 68, 78,
    219, 311–12; on human rights, 271
Johnson, Paul, 57
Jonas, Hans, 287
Jones, Arnold H. M., 205
justice: institutions and, 215; law and,
    250–51, 263n45, 263n47; political
    society and, 244–45; Rawls and, 142;
    self-love and, 280; social, 229n24
justified power, 181
Justinian Code, 253
just man, 116

Kant, Immanuel, 44, 69, 322n5, 347–48;
    action as information-bearing and,
    96n61; civil society and, 147; evil
    and, 152; on international relations,
    300–301; metaphysics and, 130n33;
    sovereignty and, 187; on war, 322n8
Kelly, J. M., 281
Kelsen, Hans, 70–71, 248
Khan, Noor Inayat, 124–25
King, Martin Luther, Jr., 119
knowledge, 17; action and, 101;
    detachment and validity of, 105;
    human persons in process of, 105;
    limits of human, 339; notional,
    30n33; objective, 96n61; philosophy
    and, 30n26; real, 30n26, 30n33; self,
    367; of truth, 86–87
Kojève, Alexandre, 226n2, 299

Kolnai, Aurel, 172, 347
Kosovo, 303

Laudato sì' (Francis), xii
law, 25; abstraction from social origin
    and purpose of, 257; character
    of, 247–52; civil, 217; classical
    philosophical thought and, 252;
    custom and, 262n39; defining, 235;
    exploitation of, 256; folk, 262n32;
    freedom and, 242; friendship
    and, 235–36; God and, 239–40;
    greater context for, 238–42; as
    human construction, 248–50, 283;
    international, 267, 270, 297, 302–3;
    justice and, 250–51, 263n45, 263n47;
    justification of, 250, 263n45;
    morality and, 249, 251, 257; natural,
    236, 367; order and, 238; political
    power and, 240; positive, 236, 251;
    positivism and, 248; pure, 248; as
    reflection of truth and goodness,
    252–56; role in society of, 242–47;
    roles of, 236; rule of, 25, 39, 242;
    Russian Orthodox view of, 260n20;
    as seen today, 236–38; sociology of,
    263n41; state and, 259n13; truth and,
    250–51
League of Nations Covenant, 270
Lectures on the Philosophy of History
    (Hegel), 344
legalism, 243
legal realism, 249
The Legend of the Grand Inquisitor
    (Dostoyevsky), 375
legislation, political power of, 241
Leibniz, Gottfried Wilhelm, 44
Lenin, Vladimir, 341
Leoni, Bruno, 241
Leviathan, 40, 43, 140–42
Leviathan (Hobbes), 279–80
Levinas, Emmanuel, x
Lewis, C. S., 66, 209, 217, 348, 359n53
lex, 254, 268, 279
lex civile, 255

lex naturalis, 255–56, 259n13
lex positiva, 255
liberal: origins of term, 60n19; political meaning of, 43
liberal democracy, 8; implicit ideas of, 331–32
liberalism, 8, 45, 56, 60n18, 72, 275, 329; artificial state system and, 304; metaphysics and, 285–86. *See also* political liberalism
liberal society, 14
libertarianism, 177
liberty, 43
Lincoln, Abraham, 101, 114, 129n30, 176
The Listening Heart (Ratzinger), 85
Lithuania, 323n16
living in the truth, 128n13, 352, 360n64; action and, 104–7; human development and, 169; public opinion and, 111
living publicly in the truth, 24, 101; context for, 115–17; cost of, 137; effectiveness of, 119–26; moral experience of, 117–19
Locke, John, 143, 145, 278; doctrine of rights of, 285; modern state and, 40, 42, 44; natural state and, 141; on right of property, 280; social contract and, 135; sovereignty and, 187; state of nature and, 147
logos, 252, 337
logos of Being, 16, 337, 339–40
loneliness, 246
Louth, Andrew, 32n49
love, xiii; human society and, 245; metaphysics of, 169–70, 332; radical, 380
Löwith, Karl, 345
de Lubac, Henri, 149
Lutheran Reformation, 255
lying, 103

Maastricht Treaty, 313

Machiavelli, Niccolò, 101, 112–13, 168, 186, 196n51, 214; justification of power and, 187; rule and, 188
MacIntyre, Alasdair, 283
Mahoney, Daniel J., 347
Mallen, Steve, 143
man, as person, 45–47
Mandela, Nelson, 119
Manent, Pierre, 9, 54, 139, 148, 299; on democratic process, 213; on forms of government, 201; on humanity, 318; on modernity, 223; on political participation, 330
Mansfield, Harvey C., 20
Marcus Aurelius, 316
Maritain, Jacques, 184, 194n23
marriage, 179
Marx, Karl, 146, 187, 348; anarchism and, 173; on consciousness, 340–41; on counterrevolution, 193n15; on human rights, 283; on ideology, 340–41; objective truth and, 73; on religion, 356n32; on revolutionary moment, 152–53, 156; salvation interpretation of, 346–47; study of history and, 346; on utopians, 192n10
Marxism, 78, 153, 174, 257, 317; materialism and, 54; Rousseau and, 346; trust in structures and, 216
materialism, 54, 63n46, 75, 216
Maximus the Confessor, xi, 149
McCoy, Charles N. R., 75
meaning: need for, 90; of political authority, 168
The Meaning of Christian Brotherhood (Ratzinger), 317
mechanics, 43
Mein Kampf (Hitler), 180
Metamorphoses of the City (Manent), 9, 54, 139, 148, 201, 213, 223, 318, 330
metaphysics, 17, 30n32; liberalism and, 285–86; of love, 169–70, 332; morals and, 87
Middle East, division of, 304

Milbank, John, 39, 179, 186,
    196n52, 367
Mill, John Stuart, 42
minorities, protecting rights of, 270
missionary disciple, xiv
modernity, 11–13; economic, 320;
    phases of emergence of, 28n14;
    transmodern approach and, 47
modern mentality, 351
modern state, ix, 27n2; architects of, 42;
    development of, 300–301; human
    aspirations and, 9; individual subject
    and, 38–42; *polis* difference from, 7;
    power and, 40–41; social relations
    and, 35; as *societas*, 76; subject of,
    42–45; violence and, 32n55
Montesquieu, Baron de, 42
*Montevideo Convention on Rights and
    Duties of States*, 302
moral freedom, 282
morality: law and, 249, 251, 257; self-
    contained, 160; social, 249
moral restraint, xiii
morals: democracy and, 95n46;
    epistemology and metaphysics and,
    87; perception and truths of, 88
moral standards, politics and, 22
moral truth, 98n75; decisions of, 111
More, Thomas, 257
Morse, Jennifer Roback, 98n76, 169
Mouroux, Jean, 88
Mughal, Sajda, 365
multiculturalism, 62n39

naked public square, 33n61, 163–64n35
nationalist movements, 301
national unity, 10
nations: sources of unity of, 310–15;
    state and, 322n4
nation-state, 297; development of, 300
natural condition, 140–41, 147, 158
natural inequalities, 209
natural law, 236, 367
natural rights, 274, 278, 283

nature, 73; asserting itself, 103;
    domination of, 223, 350; history and,
    342–47; substitute intelligence and,
    75, 94n39
Nazis, 120, 146, 180
neofunctionalism, 313
neo-positivism, 337
Neuhaus, Richard James, 33n61, 242
neutral stance, 79
The New Science of Politics
    (Voegelin), 343
Newton, Isaac, 172, 368
Nicomachean Ethics (Aristotle), 22, 82,
    235, 245–46
Nietzsche, Friedrich, 89, 102, 121–22,
    126, 146, 351
nihilism, 74–75, 84
Nisbet, Robert A., 28n11, 40–41,
    45–46, 55, 224; on Athens, 206; on
    concentration of power, 233n56;
    on democratic government, 176; on
    modern state, 369; on nation and
    state, 322n4; on political power, 204;
    on state and recognition of rights and
    freedoms, 200; on state dominance,
    220–21; on totalitarianism, 220
del Noce, Augusto, 73–75, 136, 153,
    167, 181–83, 201
non-violence, 124
notional knowledge, 30n33
nous, 22, 32n49
Novum Organum (Bacon), 72

Oakeshott, Michael, 65, 76, 190
obedience, 263n47
objective knowledge, 96n61
objectum, 30n32
O'Higgins, Eamonn, ix–xiv
Olsen, Glenn, 367–68
On Human Conduct (Oakeshott), 190
ontological conception of ethics, 82
ontology, 20
open society, 337
The Open Society and Its Enemies
    (Popper), 26, 337

order: communion and, 298; law and, 238; premises of political, 156–60; secular antagonism toward, 374–75; social contract and, 39; truth of, 102
Order and History (Voegelin), 352
Origen of Alexandria, 149
original sin, 149
original unity, 148–50; of human person, 140–44
originary experience, 82
Orwell, George, 180
Other, 282–83

Paldiel, Mordecai, 118
pantheism, 309
Papal Revolution, 253, 275
parousia, 349
parresia, 109–10, 117–20, 129n22
partisanship, 20
Pascal, Blaise, 148–50, 152
pathologies of religion, 365, 376, 386n8
Patocka, Jan, x
Peace of Augsburg, 299
Péguy, Charles, xii
Pera, Marcello, 268, 287–88
perception: detachment and, 105; moral truths and, 88; of religion, 361–63; of social reality, 105; of truth, contemporary, 105
perfectionist illusion, 347
person, ix, xii; as citizen and as subject, 43; collective decisions and individual, 21; communion of, 298; contemporary democracy and structure of numbers of, 213–19; development of, 168–69; dignity of, 281; human rights of, 277–79; individual and, 35, 62n43; interiority of, 53; man as, 45–47; political activity and, 20–23; political liberalism and, 56; political role of, 43; in politics, 36–38; in politics, as religious being, 370–72; politics of, 53–58; relational structure of, 50–52; righteous, 118–19; transmodern

approach to, 47–53; as unique self and relational being, 52–53; virtuous, 22
personal Being, 36, 66, 83, 88, 90
personal existence, 148–49
personal experience, 371; of truth, 103
personal human rights, 281–83
personalism, 48; friendship and, 246
personalist philosophy, 48, 245, 282–83
personal love, metaphysics of, 169
personal responsibility, anarchism and, 175–76
Person and Community (Wojtyla), 61n34
personhood, 35, 275–76
phenomenological method, xi; experience descriptions and, 49–50; reason and, 49–50
phenomenology, 29n21, 388n15
Phenomenology of Spirit (Hegel), 340
philosophical absolutism, 70–71
philosophical approach, 13–19; personalist, to politics, 23–26; to politics, 20–23
philosophical relativism, 70
philosophy: knowledge and, 30n26; personalist, 48, 245, 282–83; public, 94n34
piecemeal social engineering, 337–38
Pieper, Josef, 12–13, 17, 19, 89, 135; on death, 333; on existence, 382; on foundations of human society, 245; on Hegel's philosophical intention, 340; on history, 144; on hope, 144, 147; on need of radical love, 380; on origin of human person in God, 381; on powers of soul, 130n33; on prudence, 114–15; on retaliatory pessimism, 336; on secularism, 365; on social conflicts, 66
Plato, xii–xiii, 6, 113, 136, 168, 209; on Athenian society, 206; on brotherhood, 316; on city of pigs, 175; forms of government and, 201; human society and, 21–22;

ideal republic of, 55; justification of power and, 187; on just man, 116; on leadership, 111–12; *logos* and, 252; metaphysics and, 17–18; on *polis*, 41; political authority and, 185; Ratzinger on ideal Republic of, 338–39; reason and, 63n45; truth and, 69

Plato and Europe (seminar), x

Platonism, 155

plenitude, 332–33

pluralism, 39

pluralistic society, truth and, xi

Poland, x, 312

polis, 27n2, 41, 212; as *macro-anthropos*, 136; modern state difference from, 7; political persons and, 245

politeia, xiv, 7

political absolutism, 70

political activity, person and, 20–23

political anarchy, 167

political authority, 24, 200–201, 325n33; anarchic attitudes to, 167, 171–77; conditions for authentic use of, 298; definitions and misunderstandings of, 180–83; dominance attitudes to, 167, 177–80; freedom and, 14; justification of, 176, 184–85; meaning of, 168; real sense of, 183–86; roles of, 181

political communion, 297

political disenchantment, 8–11

political dominance, 167, 177–80, 359n60

political freedom, 60n16

political government: forms of, 24–25; law and, 25; social communion and, 203

political ideologies, 25–26, 329; defining, 335; eschaton and, 146; failures of, 339–41; nature and history and, 342–47; not asking questions and, 108; positive need expressed by, 335–39; religious

language and symbols used in, 186–87; totalitarian, 157

Political Illiberalism (Simpson), 22, 58, 71, 142, 211–12

political institutions, 215–16

political liberalism, 45, 60n18, 72, 330; authority and, 184; common good and, 170, 284–85; freedom and, 170; hope and, 155–56; human person and, 56; lack of shared principles and, 170–71

political order, premises of, 156–60

political phenomena, 24; culture and, 23

political philosophy: political science difference from, 20; types of, 230n34

political power: Jefferson on legitimacy of, 194n24; justification of, 204; law and, 240; of legislation, 241; Machiavelli on, 113; religion and, 186

political pragmatism, 73–75

political science, political philosophy difference from, 20

political secularism, defining, 366–69

political society, 211; authority and, 184, 225; hope as essential to, 154–56; inequality and, 210; justice and equality as central to, 244–45; regulation of, 223; truth and, 24

political sovereignty, 214

political structures, procedures and, 77

political unions, 313

political unity, 65

political visions: postmodern times and, 11–13; of transcendent fulfilment, 333–34

politics: of aspiration, 135–36, 150–153; as battlefield of truth, 80; causes of disillusionment with, 330; as civil war, 161n5; culture and, 136; disillusionment with, 8–12; of faith, 76, 94n40; freedom and modern, 67; friendship and, 246; historical contexts and language of, 5, 7; international, 25, 297, 299–306;

moral standards and, 22; of person, 53–58; personal existence and, 1–2; personalist philosophical approach to, 23–26; person in, 36–38; person in, as religious being, 370–72; philosophical approach to, 20–23; philosophy of, 5–6; pragmatism and, 334; religion and, 361; remoteness from life, 14; of restraint, 135; of skepticism, 76–77, 85; spontaneous implications of, 6–7; as tactical, 101; truth and, 65; universal brotherhood as idea of, 315–20; waning of, 28n11

Politics (Aristotle), 6, 22, 55–56, 211–12

Politics of the Person as the Politics of Being (Walsh), 271–72

Popper, Karl, xii, 26, 95n43, 304; on utopian social engineering, 337–38, 356n27

positive law, 236, 251

positivism, 85, 372; law and, 248; neo, 337; social, 283

Possenti, Vittorio, 223

post-modern epoch, 5; political vision and, 11–13

post-totalitarian dominance, 351

post-totalitarian society, ix

power: absolutism and, 71; authority and, 181–82, 186–91, 200–201; civil, 200; concentration of, 233n56, 305; contemporary democracy and structure of, 213–19; dictatorial, 78; effective, 168; freedom and, 41; God as, 125; as justification for government, 200; justification of, 187–88; justified, 181; of love, 126; Machiavelli on, 113; minimalist approaches to, 76; "the people" and, 204; political, 113, 186, 194n24, 204, 240–41; social contract and, 39; sovereignty and, 41, 187–90, 196n52; state monopoly of, ix, 40–41; truth and, 121–22

The Power of the Powerless (Havel), ix, 106–8, 351

pragmatism, 73–75, 77, 334, 336, 379

Prague Spring, 35, 37–38

prepolitical authority, 195n33

pride, reason and, 31n41

Principia Mathematica (Russell and Whitehead), 84

Pritzl, Kurt, 89

private property, 141

privatization, of religious truth, 174

procedure, social consensus and, 70–72

prophets, suffering and, 132n61

Protagoras of Abdera, xi

Proudhon, Pierre-Joseph, 172–73

prudence, 114–15

Psalm 127, ix

psychoanalysis, 381, 392n55

public opinion, living in the truth and, 111

public philosophy, 94n34

public reason, 71

public square, naked, 33n61, 163–64n35

pure law, 248

pursuit of glory, 54, 161n11

Quebec, 302–3, 323n18

The Quest for Community (Nisbet), 40, 45–46, 176, 204, 220–21, 224

racial discrimination, conventions on, 270

radical love, 380

rationality, 89, 97n67

Ratzinger, Joseph, 16, 18, 22–23; on antagonism, 115; on "area of compulsion," 258n4; on brotherhood, 317–18; on clash of cultures, 376; on conflict between moral and religious ideas, 294n71; on cyclical and linear conceptions of time, 357n34; on democracy, 215, 231n40; on eschatology, 166n62, 343; on eternal life, 154; on ethical standards, 377; on European culture, 314–15;

on events of 1989, 282; on foreign
aid, 390n32; on foundations of
free state, 224; on freedom, 67–68,
91n6, 110; on good society, 174;
on humanity, 318; on human rights,
284; on human spirit, 53–54; on just
man, 116; on law, 237–38, 257–58;
on *lex naturalis*, 255–56; on Marx
interpretation of salvation, 346–47;
on Marxism, 317; on materialism,
63n46, 75; on moral foundations of
state, 32n56; on need for meaning,
90; on *parresia*, 110; on pathologies
of religion, 365, 386n8; on Platonic
approach to human society, 22; on
Platonic ideals and politics, 338–39;
on positivism, 85, 372; on reason,
372, 377; on relation, 51, 62n37;
on Schneider, 122; on Stoicism,
316; on totalitarianism, 233n55; on
transcendence, 161n7, 165n58; on
trust in structures, 216; on truth,
164n49. *See also* Benedict XVI
Rawls, John, 68–69, 135, 142–43; state
institutions and, 215
realism, legal, 249
reality: Being in truth of, 78–91;
consciousness and, of Being, 96n56;
disclosure of, 29n21; experience
of, 19, 84, 103; listening to, 15;
reaction to, 105; search for truth of,
224; social, 105; social bonds and
common experience of, 104
real knowledge, 30n26, 30n33
reason, 15, 63n45, 372, 377; experience
and, 84–85; phenomenological
method and, 49–50; pride and,
31n41; public, 71; religious
dimension in, 364–66; Stoicism
and, 252
Reformation, 38, 255, 275
regulation, care and, 243
Reign of Terror, 172
relation, 69; Aristotle and, 50; human
life and, 282; international, 300–301,

305, 308; as primordial mode of
persons, 51; Ratzinger on, 51;
selfhood and, 54
relational structure of human person,
50–52
relativism, 5, 12, 84, 383; democracy
and, 70–71; ethical, 78;
philosophical, 70
religion, 26; brotherhood and, 316;
Marx on, 356n32; neutral stance to
expressions of, 363–64; pathologies
of, 365, 376, 386n8; political
power and, 186; politics and, 361;
public perceptions of, 361–63; real
manifestation of experience, 366;
reason and, 364–66; response to
religious dimension of existence of,
376–82; social life context and, 382–
84; state and, 186; unity of culture
and, 273–74; wars and creation of,
230n37; wars of, 368–69
religious authority, 186
religious experience, 85, 371, 377,
379, 381
religious freedom, 386n7
religious truth, privatization of, 174
Renaissance, 275
representative democracy, 159
representative government, 39
The Republic (Plato), 112, 175, 185
retaliatory pessimism, 336–38
revolution, 152–53
Rhonheimer, 63n53
Rice, Condoleezza, 202
Richteous Among the Nations, 118
Ricoeur, Paul, x
righteous persons, 118–19
rights: basic, 285; freedom and, 268,
273, 285; modern usage of term,
269; natural, 274, 278, 283; as
uncontrollable phenomenon, 287
Robespierre, Maximilian, 207
Roman Law, 253
Rome: political institutions of, 206;
reason and, 252

Romeo and Juliet (Shakespeare), xiii
Rommen, Heinrich A., 256
Rorty, Richard, 65, 68
Rosmini, Antonio, 229n24
Rousseau, Jean Jacques, 187; modern
state and, 40, 42–43; on "new man,"
170; politics of aspiration and, 150–
52; on self-love and human rights,
280–81; social contract of, 43, 280,
346; state of nature and, 147
rule, 188, 197n53
"Rule as Sovereignty" (Slade), 188
rule of law, 25, 39, 242
rupture, 135–36; actual, 148–50
Russell, Bertrand, 10, 84
Rwanda, 303

sacrifice, 119
Sageman, Marc, 246
Saint-Simon, Henri de, 172, 174
salvation history, 342
Sandel, Michael J., 56, 284
Satyagraha, 59n5, 102, 123–24, 131n58
Schall, James V., 87, 218
Scheler, Max, 391n44
Schindler, David C.: on free will,
293n54; on liberalism, 389n26;
on prudence, 115; on science in
abscence of God, 389n21; on
temporal and spiritual, 387n10; on
tragic nature of history, 132n65;
on transcendence and political
community, 360n65
Schindler, David L., 82, 285, 292n46
Schindler, Oskar, 117
Schmitz, Kenneth L., 44–45, 55; on
atheism, 392n51, 392n62
Schneider, Reinhold, 122
Scholasticism, 73, 101, 144, 254; human
person and, 277; secularism and, 366
Schönborn, Christoph, 255
Schumpeter, Joseph, 227n6
Science, Politics, and Gnosticism
(Voegelin), 349
Screwtape Letters (Lewis), 209

Scruton, Roger, 151, 164n47, 390n33
Second Vatican Council, 325n34
secular education, 388n21
secularism, 46, 362, 365, 387n10; order
and, 374–75; political, 366–69;
response to religious dimension of
existence of, 373–76
self-awareness, 328n58
self-consciousness, 80–81
self-determination, 24, 181, 282, 287,
297, 302–4, 308
self-government, 276
selfhood, relation and, 54
self-interest, 308, 381
self-justification, 148–49
self-knowledge, 367
self-love, justice and, 280
self-transcendence, 149
self-transformation, 383
Sen, Amarya, 202
Seneca, 316
Serbia, 303
Shakespeare, William, xiii
shared principles, lack of, 170–71
Shaw, Malcolm N., 302
Shils, Edward, 337
Shore, Chris, 313
Siedentop, Larry, 36, 52, 274–75,
278, 282
Simon, Yves R., 57
simpliciter, 18
Simpson, Peter L. P., 6, 15; on Aristotle
and best government, 211–12; on
comprehensive truth and political
thought, 58; on government forms,
211–12; on kings, 175; on modern
state, 27n2; on personal experience,
50; on *polis*, 226; on political
community, 143; on politics and
moral standards, 22; on public
reason, 71; on Rawls and state
institutions, 215; on representative
democracy, 159; on themes for forms
of government, 142–43; on types of
political philosophy, 230n34

Single European Act of 1987, 313

Ska, Jean Louise, 239, 259n7

skepticism, 65, 84, 104, 336; politics of, 76–77, 85; root causes of, 331

Slade, Francis, 77, 188, 190–91, 214

slavery, 114

Smith, John E., 84

social authority: state and, 41, 190, 214; suppression of, 190

social bonds, 137; common experience and, 104; ideological commitment and, 246–47; truthful agreement and, 102–3

social communion, 169, 203–4, 223–24

social conflicts, 66

social consensus: based on practical and material concerns, 72–75; procedure and, 70–72

social contract, 39, 43, 135, 150, 280

social engineering, 337–38, 356n27

social existence, aspirations of, 331–33

social groups, 42

socialism, 329

social justice, 229n24

social life, religious context of, 382–84

social living, 55–56, 273

social morality, 249

social participation, in human society, 202

social positivism, 283

social purpose, 225

social reality, 105

social relations, modern state and, 35

societas, 76

society: authentic vision of, 168; ideological visions of, 339; inequality of, 199; law role in, 242–47

sociology, 337; of law, 263n41

Socrates, 108–9, 117, 121; on city of pigs, 175

Sokolowski, Robert, xii, 7, 19, 29n21, 49, 89; on forms of government, 230n30; on illusion of detachment, 79; on nature asserting itself, 103;
on phenomenology, 388n15; on political person, 245–46; on political society, 210

solidarity, 223

Solidarity Union, 120

Solzhenitsyn, Aleksandr, 243–44, 260n20, 330, 353n2, 380

Somalia, 177

sovereign power, 196n52; centralization of, 41; referendums and, 189–90; Supreme Court decisions as, 190

sovereign state, modern conception of, 39

sovereignty, 7, 39, 59n7, 194n23; as equal subjection, 276; political, 214; power and, 187–88

Soviet Union, breakup of, 311, 323n16

space, state and, 320

Spaemann, Robert, 89

Sparta, 108

speech: freedom of, 110; truth in, 106

spirit, 15

spiritual authority, 196n48

spontaneous society, 177

Sri Lanka, 36–37

state: artificial system of, 304; del Noce defining, 182; development into nation-state, 300; dominance by, 220–21; individual dependence on, 220; legal descriptions of, 304–5; *lex naturalis* and, 259n13; monopoly of power of, ix, 40–41; moral foundations of, 32n56; mythos of, 308; nations and, 322n4; *polis* difference from, 7; recognition of rights and freedoms and, 200; religion and, 186; social authority and, 41, 190, 214; social life and, 42; space and, 320; violence and, 182, 300. *See also* modern state

state Constitutions, human rights and, 267, 269

statehood, 302

state identity, 326n40

state of nature, 140–41, 143, 147, 158

Stoicism, 155, 316; *ius naturale* and, 276; reason and, 252
Strauss, Leo, 226n2, 346
struggle, shared truth and, 137
subject: of modern state, 42–45; person as, 43
subjective ideas, 79, 104
subjectivism, 35
subjectivity, 61n34, 84; of experience, 67
substitute intelligence, 75, 94n39
suffering, prophets and, 132n61
Sufis, 124–25
suicide, 143
summum bonum, 135–36, 142–43
Supreme Court decisions, 190; rights and, 269
Sykes-Picot Agreement, 304
Syria, 36–37

Taylor, Charles, 138
Team of Rivals (Goodwin), 114
technology, 72–73
telos, 76
Ten Commandments, 259n7
theodicies, 384
theological experience, 50, 103–4
A Theory of Justice (Rawls), 68, 135, 142
Theses on Feuerbach (Marx), 73
The Social Contract [Du Contrat Social] (Rousseau), 150
Things as They Are (Godwin), 172
Third Kingdom, 145–46
Thirty Tyrants, 108
Thucydides, 206, 209
Tierney, Brian, 274, 276, 279
Tocqueville, Alexis de, 158, 200, 207, 215, 331, 354n5; on dangers of undifferentiated equality, 217–18; on democratic tyranny, 218–19; on despotism and equality, 221–22
tolerance, 286, 364
torture, prohibition of, 270
totalitarian dictatorship, 26

totalitarianism, 78, 157, 179, 226n2; defining, 232n46; democracy and, 299; democracy of numbers and, 219; gnosticism and, 163n30; Supreme Court decisions and, 190; Voegelin on, 178
totalitarian lawfulness, 178
transcendence, 135, 138, 161n7; experience and, 370; fulfilment in, 140–44; hope of, 373; politics of aspiration and, 150–53; self, 149
transcendent fulfilment, 159–60, 165n58; political vision of, 333–34
transmodern approach, 35, 47–53; personalist philosophy and, 48; person as unique self and relational being, 52–53; phenomenological description of experience and, 49–50; relational structure of human person and, 50–52
Treaty of Lisbon, xi
Treaty of Versailles, 302
Treaty of Westphalia, 299
tribal society, 337
Trinitarian revelation, 145
trust, 115; in structures, institutions, and processes, 216
truth, 1; abuses of term, 68; action of, 87; Being and, 82; claims to, 65; conflict and shared, 137; contemporary perceptions of, 67–69; of correctness, 49; of disclosure, 49–50; effectual, 113, 168, 187; expression in action, 106; freedom and, 110–11, 170; of knowledge, 17; knowledge of, 86–87; law and, 250–51; law as reflection of, 252–56; living publicly in, 24, 101, 115–26, 137; modes of, of Being, 83–86; moral, 98n75, 111; of order, 102; path to, 86–91; personal experience of, 103; pluralistic society and, xi; political forms denying, 69–75; political society and, 24; politics and, 65; politics as battlefield of, 80;

power and, 121–22; privatization of religious, 174; public struggle for recognition of, 107–15; of reality, Being in, 78–91; resistance to, 108; response to reality and, 105; search for, ix, x, xi, xiii, 224; in speech, 106

truthful agreement, social bonds and, 102–3

truth of disclosure, 29n21

truth of predication, 29n21

Twelve Angry Men (film), 86

tyranny, 80; biopolitical, 179; in democracy, 218–19; democratic, 158

Ukraine, 315; war in, 1

Understanding Terrorist Networks (Sageman), 246

United Nations, 270, 283

United Nations Charter, 270, 302

United Nations General Assembly, 302

unity, 10; culture and, 273–74, 298; eschatology and, 309; experience and, 15; of humankind, 307; of nations, 25, 297, 306–10; original, 148–50; original, of human person, 140–44; sources of, 307–10; sources of, of nations, 310–15

universal brotherhood, political idea of, 315–20

Universal Declaration of Human Rights (United Nations), 270–71, 283, 290n15

Unmoved Mover, 50

utopian anarchy, 172–74

utopian fallacy, 151–52

utopian mind, 347

utopian social engineering, 337–38, 356n27

utopian thought, 172, 192n8, 192n10, 347

Vico, Giambattista, 147

Vincent, Andrew, 336–37

violence: modern state and, 32n55; state and, 182, 300

virtuous persons, 22

Vitz, Paul C., 35, 47

Voegelin, Eric, 6–7, 15, 49, 78, 82, 172; on conceptions of history, 357n39; on consciousness, 96n56; on difference between Aristotle and Hobbes, 142; on *eidos* of history, 342; on Gnosticism, 163n30, 178, 349–50, 359n55; on immanent fulfilment, 145–46; on justification of history, 343–44; on Marx and revolution, 152–53; on not asking question, 108; on order and history, 352, 362; on *parousia*, 349; on Platonic approach to human society, 21–22; on political immanent ideologies, 327n51; on religious language and symbols in political ideology, 186–87; on secularism, 375; on totalitarianism, 178

volonté général (general will), 150–51

Von Heyking, John, 246

Waldron, Jeremy, 216, 242

Walesa, Lech, 120

Walsh, David, 18, 76; on conflict and strife, 116–17; on contemporary political context, 11–13; on encounter with truth, 49; on hope of transcendent finality, 373; on human rights, 272; on lack of shared principles, 170–71; on law, 244; on liberalism, 170; on living in the truth, 107, 128n13; on political community, 66; on political liberalism, 60n18; on political organization and structure, 58; on politics as battlefield of truth, 80; on power, 126; on Reformation impacts, 38; on right living, 87–88; on self-contained morality, 160; on similarities of liberal and totalitarian ideologies, 352; on spiritual crisis of modern world, 330–31; on transcendence, 370; transcendent

fulfilment and, 334; on truth and
order, 102
war crimes, 263n47
wars of religion, 368–69
Waters, John, 243
Weber, Max, 24, 181, 249, 263n41; on
types of authority, 195n35
What Is to be Done? (Lenin), 341
"What Sort of Despotism Democratic
Nations Have to Fear"
(Tocqueville), 158
Whitehead, Alfred North, 84
White Rose Movement, 117
Wilson, Woodrow, 301, 304

Without Roots (Ratzinger), 315
Wittgenstein, Ludwig, 248
Wojtyla, Karol, 50, 61n34. *See also*
John Paul II (Pope)
Wolin, Sheldon S., 69
World Spirit, 344
Worsnip, Alex, 74

Xenophon, 316

Yugoslavia, 303

Zimmern, Alfred Eckhard, 206

About the Author

Fr. Eamonn Gerard O'Higgins, L.C., is a full-time professor of philosophy at the Pontifical Athenaeum Regina Apostolorum in Rome, where he currently teaches moral and political philosophy as well as courses on contemporary political philosophers and the political thought of Joseph Ratzinger/ Pope Benedict XVI. He studied an honours degree in Law at Trinity College, Dublin (Ireland) and philosophy and theology at the Pontifical Gregorian University and at the Pontifical Athenaeum Regina Apostolorum in Rome. He was ordained priest in 1994 and is a member of the Congregation of the Legionaries of Christ.